Pro Vue.js 2

■ ■ ■

Adam Freeman

Apress®

Pro Vue.js 2

Adam Freeman
London, UK

ISBN-13 (pbk): 978-1-4842-3804-2   ISBN-13 (electronic): 978-1-4842-3805-9
https://doi.org/10.1007/978-1-4842-3805-9

Library of Congress Control Number: 2018956735

Managing Director, Apress Media LLC: Welmoed Spahr
Acquisitions Editor: Joan Murray
Development Editor: Laura Berendson
Coordinating Editor: Mark Powers

Cover designed by eStudioCalamar

Cover image designed by Freepik (www.freepik.com)

Distributed to the book trade worldwide by Springer Science+Business Media New York, 233 Spring Street, 6th Floor, New York, NY 10013. Phone 1-800-SPRINGER, fax (201) 348-4505, e-mail orders-ny@springer-sbm.com, or visit www.springeronline.com. Apress Media, LLC is a California LLC and the sole member (owner) is Springer Science + Business Media Finance Inc (SSBM Finance Inc). SSBM Finance Inc is a **Delaware** corporation.

For information on translations, please e-mail editorial@apress.com; for reprint, paperback, or audio rights, please email bookpermissions@springernature.com.

Apress titles may be purchased in bulk for academic, corporate, or promotional use. eBook versions and licenses are also available for most titles. For more information, reference our Print and eBook Bulk Sales web page at www.apress.com/bulk-sales.

Any source code or other supplementary material referenced by the author in this book is available to readers on GitHub via the book's product page, located at www.apress.com/9781484238042. For more detailed information, please visit www.apress.com/source-code.

Printed on acid-free paper

Dedicated to my lovely wife, Jacqui Griffyth.
(And also to Peanut.)

Table of Contents

About the Author xxi

About the Technical Reviewer xxiii

■Part I: Getting Started with Vue.js 1

■Chapter 1: Your First Vue.js Application 3

Preparing the Development Environment...3

    Installing Node.js 3

    Installing the @vue/cli Package 4

    Installing Git..5

    Installing an Editor..5

    Installing a Browser..6

Creating the Project...6

    Understanding the Project Structure 6

    Starting the Development Tools...8

Replacing the Placeholder Content 9

    Adding a CSS Framework..11

    Styling the HTML Elements...12

Adding Dynamic Content...13

    Displaying the List of Tasks 14

    Adding a Checkbox...16

    Filtering Completed Tasks 19

    Creating New Tasks 21

    Storing Data Persistently...23

    Adding the Finishing Touches...25

Summary..28

v

■**Chapter 2: Understanding Vue.js** **29**

Should I Use Vue.js? 29

Understanding Round-Trip Applications 30

Understanding Single-Page Applications 30

Understanding Application Complexity 31

What Do I Need to Know? 32

How Do I Set Up My Development Environment? 32

What Is the Structure of This Book? 32

Part 1: Getting Started with Vue.js 32

Part 2: Working with Vue.js 32

Part 3: Advanced Vue.js Features 33

Are There Lots of Examples? 33

Where Can You Get the Example Code? 35

Where Can You Get Corrections for This Book? 35

How Can You Contact Me? 35

Summary 36

■**Chapter 3: HTML and CSS Primer** **37**

Preparing for This Chapter 37

Understanding HTML Elements 40

Understanding Element Content 41

Understanding Attributes 42

Examining the Live HTML Document 44

Understanding Bootstrap 45

Applying Basic Bootstrap Classes 46

Using Bootstrap to Create Grids 47

Using Bootstrap to Style Tables 48

Using Bootstrap to Style Forms 50

Summary 51

■ **Chapter 4: Essential JavaScript Primer** **53**

Preparing for This Chapter 54

Using Statements 56

Defining and Using Functions 57

Defining Functions with Parameters 58

Defining Functions That Return Results 60

Using Functions as Arguments to Other Functions 61

Using Variables and Types 62

Using the Primitive Types 64

Using JavaScript Operators 66

Using Conditional Statements 67

The Equality Operator vs. the Identity Operator 68

Explicitly Converting Types 69

Working with Arrays 71

Using an Array Literal 71

Reading and Modifying the Contents of an Array 71

Enumerating the Contents of an Array 72

Using the Spread Operator 73

Using the Built-in Array Methods 74

Working with Objects 75

Using Object Literals 76

Using Functions as Methods 77

Copying Properties from One Object to Another 78

Understanding JavaScript Modules 78

Creating and Using a Simple JavaScript Module 79

Defining Multiple Features in a Module 81

Combining Multiple Files in a Module 83

Understanding JavaScript Promises 84

    Understanding the Asynchronous Operation Problem 84

    Using a JavaScript Promise 85

    Simplifying the Asynchronous Code 86

Summary 87

■Chapter 5: SportsStore: A Real Application 89

Creating the SportsStore Project 89

    Adding Additional Packages 90

    Preparing the RESTful Web Service 92

    Starting the Project Tools... 95

Creating the Data Store 96

Creating the Product Store 98

    Creating the Product List... 100

    Adding the Product List to the Application 101

    Filtering the Price Data... 103

    Adding Product Pagination 104

    Adding Category Selection 112

Using the RESTful Web Service 115

Summary 118

■Chapter 6: SportsStore: Checkout and Orders 119

Preparing for This Chapter 119

Creating the Shopping Cart Placeholder 120

Configuring URL Routing 121

    Displaying a Routed Component... 122

Implementing the Cart Features 123

    Adding a Module to the Data Store... 123

    Adding the Product Selection Feature 125

    Displaying the Cart Contents 127

    Creating a Global Filter 131

    Testing the Basic Cart Features... 132

Making the Cart Persistent 132

Adding the Cart Summary Widget 136

Adding the Checkout and Orders Features 138

Creating and Registering the Checkout Components 139

Adding Form Validation 143

Adding the Remaining Fields and Validation 147

Summary 150

■Chapter 7: SportsStore: Scaling and Administration 151

Preparing for This Chapter 151

Dealing with Larger Amounts of Data 153

Improving Page Navigation 153

Reducing the Amount of Data Requested by the Application 155

Adding Search Support 161

Starting the Administration Features 166

Implementing Authentication 166

Adding the Administration Component Structure 173

Implementing the Order Administration Feature 175

Summary 178

■Chapter 8: SportsStore: Administration and Deployment 179

Preparing for This Chapter 179

Adding the Product Administration Features 180

Presenting the Product List 182

Adding the Editor Placeholder and URL Routes 183

Implementing the Editor Feature 185

Deploying SportsStore 189

Preparing the Application for Deployment 189

Building the Application for Deployment 194

Testing the Deployment-Ready Application 195

Deploying the Application 197

Summary 200

■Part II: Vue.js in Detail 201

■Chapter 9: Understanding Vue.js 203

Preparing for This Chapter 203

Adding the Bootstrap CSS Framework 204

Running the Example Application 205

Creating an Application Using the DOM API 205

Understanding How the DOM API Application Works 207

Creating a Vue Object 208

Adding Data to the Vue Object 210

Adding an Event Handler 211

Correcting the Message 212

Understanding the Vue Object Structure 214

Introducing a Component 214

Registering and Applying the Component 216

Separating the Template from the JavaScript Code 218

Summary 220

■Chapter 10: Understanding Vue.js Projects and Tools 221

Creating a Vue.js Development Project 222

Configuring the Linter 225

Completing the Project Configuration 226

Understanding the Project Structure 227

Understanding the Source Code Folder 228

Understanding the Packages Folder 229

Using the Development Tools 233

Understanding the Compilation and Transformation Process 234

Understanding the Development HTTP Server 236

Understanding Hot Model Replacement 237

Understanding the Error Display 240

Using the Linter 242

Customizing the Linter Rules 245

Debugging the Application 247

    Exploring the Application State.. 247

    Using the Browser Debugger.. 248

Configuring the Development Tools.. 250

Building the Application for Deployment 250

    Installing and Using an HTTP Server 253

Summary.. 254

■Chapter 11: Understanding Data Bindings 255

Preparing for This Chapter 256

Understanding the Elements of a Component.. 258

    Understanding the Template Element... 259

    Understanding the Script Element... 259

    Understanding the Style Element 259

Resetting the Component in the Example Application 260

Displaying a Data Value... 261

    Using More Complex Expressions in a Data Binding 264

    Calculating Values with Computed Properties.. 267

    Calculating Data Values with a Method 270

    Formatting Data Values with Filters 273

Summary.. 279

■Chapter 12: Using the Basic Directives 281

Preparing for This Chapter 282

Setting an Element's Text Content... 284

Displaying Raw HTML.. 285

Selectively Displaying Elements.. 287

    Selectively Displaying Adjacent Peer Elements... 289

    Choosing Between Sections of Content.. 291

    Selectively Displaying Elements Using CSS 293

Setting an Element's Attributes and Properties... 296

    Using an Object to Configure Classes.. 298

Setting Individual Styles 301

Setting Other Attributes 302

Setting Multiple Attributes 303

Setting an HTMLElement Property 305

Summary 307

■Chapter 13: Using the Repeater Directive 309

Preparing for This Chapter 310

Enumerating an Array 311

Using the Alias 314

Identifying the Key 316

Getting the Item Index 319

Understanding Array Change Detection 322

Enumerating Object Properties 325

Understanding Object Property Ordering 327

Repeating HTML Elements Without a Data Source 329

Using Computed Properties with the v-for Directive 330

Paging Data 330

Filtering and Sorting Data 332

Summary 335

■Chapter 14: Handling Events 337

Preparing for This Chapter 338

Handling Events 339

Understanding Events and Event Objects 340

Using a Method to Handle Events 342

Combining Events, Methods, and Repeated Elements 345

Listening for Multiple Events from the Same Element 346

Using Event Handling Modifiers 350

Managing Event Propagation 350

Preventing Duplicate Events 357

Using Mouse Event Modifiers 358

Using Keyboard Event Modifiers 359

Summary 362

■Chapter 15: Working with Form Elements 363

Preparing for This Chapter 364

Creating Two-Way Model Bindings 366

Adding a Two-Way Binding 367

Adding Another Input Element 368

Simplifying Two-Way Bindings 370

Binding to Form Elements 372

Binding to Text Fields 372

Binding to Radio Buttons and Checkboxes 373

Binding to Select Elements 376

Using the v-model Modifiers 377

Formatting Values as Numbers 377

Delaying Updates 379

Removing Whitespace Characters 380

Binding to Different Data Types 381

Selecting an Array of Items 381

Using Custom Values for Form Elements 383

Validating Form Data 387

Defining the Validation Rules 389

Performing Validation 391

Responding to Live Changes 394

Summary 396

■Chapter 16: Using Components 397

Preparing for This Chapter 398

Understanding Components as Building Blocks 399

Understanding Child Component Names and Elements 402

Using Component Features in Child Components 404

Understanding Component Isolation 405

Using Component Props 407

Creating Custom Events 414

Using Component Slots 417

Summary 424

■Part III: Advanced Vue.js Features 425

■Chapter 17: Understanding the Component Lifecycle 427

Preparing for This Chapter 428

Understanding the Component Lifecycle 431

Understanding the Creation Phase 431

Understanding the Mounting Phase 433

Understanding Update Phase 436

Understanding the Destruction Phase 443

Handling Component Errors 446

Summary 449

■Chapter 18: Loosely Coupled Components 451

Preparing for This Chapter 452

Creating the Product Display Component 454

Creating the Product Editor Component 455

Displaying the Child Components 457

Understanding Dependency Injection 459

Defining a Service 459

Consuming a Service via Dependency Injection 460

Overriding Antecedent Services 461

Creating Reactive Services 463

Using Advanced Dependency Injection Features 466

Using an Event Bus 469

Sending Events Using an Event Bus 470

Receiving Events from the Event Bus 471

Creating Local Event Buses 474

Summary 477

■Chapter 19: Using RESTful Web Services 479

Preparing for This Chapter 480

Preparing the HTTP Server 480

Preparing the Example Application 481

Running the Example Application and HTTP Server 484

Understanding RESTful Web Services 486

Consuming a RESTful Web Service 488

Handling the Response Data 489

Making the HTTP Request 489

Receiving the Response 491

Processing the Data 492

Creating an HTTP Service 494

Consuming the HTTP Service 495

Adding Other HTTP Operations 496

Creating an Error Handling Service 499

Summary 504

■Chapter 20: Using a Data Store 505

Preparing for This Chapter 506

Creating and Using a Data Store 509

Understanding Separate State and Mutations 511

Providing Access to the Vuex Data Store 512

Using the Data Store 513

Inspecting Data Store Changes 516

Defining Computed Properties in the Data Store 518

Using a Getter in a Component 520

Providing Arguments to Getters 521

Performing Asynchronous Operations.. 522

Receiving Change Notifications... 525

Mapping Data Store Features into Components... 530

Using Data Store Modules.. 533

    Registering and Using a Data Store Module...534

    Using Module Namespaces...538

Summary... 540

■**Chapter 21: Dynamic Components** **541**

Preparing for This Chapter 542

Preparing Components for Dynamic Lifecycles... 543

    Getting the Application Data...543

    Managing Watch Events...545

Displaying Components Dynamically 546

    Presenting Different Components in an HTML Element...546

    Selecting Components Using a Data Binding 548

    Automatically Navigating Around the Application...552

Using Asynchronous Components 557

    Disabling Prefetch Hints 560

    Configuring Lazy Loading 561

Summary... 564

■**Chapter 22: URL Routing**... **565**

Preparing for This Chapter 566

Getting Started with URL Routing... 567

    Providing Access to the Routing Configuration...569

    Using the Routing System to Display Components...570

    Navigating to Different URLs 572

Understanding and Configuring URL Route Matching 577

    Understanding URL Matching and Formatting...578

    Using the HTML5 History API for Routing 578

    Using a Route Alias..582

Getting Routing Data in Components..583

Matching Routes Dynamically 587

Using Regular Expressions to Match URLs..591

Creating Named Routes..594

Dealing with Navigation Changes... 597

Summary.. 601

■Chapter 23: URL Routing Element Features... 603

Preparing for This Chapter 604

Working with Router-Link Elements... 606

Selecting the Element Type 608

Selecting the Navigation Event..610

Styling Router Link Elements 611

Creating Nested Routes.. 617

Planning the Application Layout 617

Adding Components to the Project..617

Defining the Routes 619

Creating the Navigation Elements 621

Testing the Nested Routes..622

Using Named Router-View Elements... 624

Summary.. 628

■Chapter 24: Advanced URL Routing... 629

Preparing for This Chapter 629

Using Separate Files for Related Routes... 630

Guarding Routes... 632

Defining Global Navigation Guards 632

Defining Route-Specific Guards...637

Defining Component Route Guards...640

Loading Components on Demand 648

Displaying a Component Loading Message..649

Creating Routing-Free Components 654

Summary 656

■ **Chapter 25: Transitions** **657**

Preparing for This Chapter 658

　Creating the Components 659

　Configuring URL Routing 662

　Creating the Navigation Elements 663

Getting Started with Transitions 665

　Understanding the Transition Classes and CSS Transition 668

　Understanding the Transition Sequence 670

Using an Animation Library 670

Switching Between Multiple Elements 672

　Applying a Transition to URL Routed Elements 675

　Applying a Transition for an Element's Appearance 676

Applying Transitions for Collection Changes 678

Using Transition Events 680

　Using the Enter and Leave Events 682

Drawing Attention to Other Changes 683

Summary 686

■ **Chapter 26: Extending Vue.js** **687**

Preparing for This Chapter 688

Creating Custom Directives 690

　Understanding How Directives Work 692

　Using Custom Directive Expressions 695

　Using Custom Directive Arguments 696

　Using Custom Directive Modifiers 698

　Communicating Between Hook Functions 700

　Defining Single Function Directives 701

Creating Component Mixins 702

Creating a Vue.js Plugin... 706

    Creating the Plugin 709

    Using a Plugin...711

Summary... 713

Index... 715

About the Author

Adam Freeman is an experienced IT professional who has held senior positions in a range of companies, most recently serving as chief technology officer and chief operating officer of a global bank. Now retired, he spends his time writing and long-distance running.

About the Technical Reviewer

Fabio Claudio Ferracchiati is a senior consultant and a senior analyst/developer using Microsoft technologies. He works for BluArancio (www.bluarancio.com). He is a Microsoft Certified Solution Developer for .NET, a Microsoft Certified Application Developer for .NET, a Microsoft Certified Professional, and a prolific author and technical reviewer. Over the past ten years, he's written articles for Italian and international magazines and coauthored more than ten books on a variety of computer topics.

PART I

■ ■ ■

Getting Started with Vue.js

CHAPTER 1

■ ■ ■

Your First Vue.js Application

The best way to get started with Vue.js is to dive in. In this chapter, I take you through a simple development process to create an application to keep track of to-do items. In Chapters 5–8, I show you how to create a more complex and realistic application, but for now, a simple example will be enough to demonstrate how Vue.js applications are created and how the basic features work. Don't worry if you don't understand everything in this chapter—the idea is to get an overall sense of how Vue.js works, and I explain everything in detail in later chapters.

■ **Note** If you want a conventional description of Vue.js features, then you can jump to Part 2 of this book, where I start the process of describing individual features in depth.

Preparing the Development Environment

There is some preparation required for Vue.js development. In the sections that follow, I explain how to get set up and ready to create your first project.

Installing Node.js

The tools used for Vue.js development rely on Node.js—also known as Node—which was created in 2009 as a simple and efficient runtime for server-side applications written in JavaScript. Node.js is based on the JavaScript engine used in the Chrome browser and provides an API for executing JavaScript code outside of the browser environment.

Node.js has enjoyed success as an application server, but for this book, it is interesting because it has provided the foundation for a new generation of cross-platform development and build tools. Some smart design decisions by the Node.js team and the cross-platform support provided by the Chrome JavaScript runtime have created an opportunity that has been seized upon by enthusiastic tool writers. In short, Node.js has become essential for web application development.

It is important that you download the same version of Node.js that I use throughout this book. Although Node.js is relatively stable, there are still breaking API changes from time to time that may stop the examples I include in the chapters from working.

The version I have used is 8.11.2, which is the current Long-Term Support release at the time of writing. There may be a later version available by the time you read this, but you should stick to the 8.11.2 release for the examples in this book. A complete set of 8.11.2 releases, with installers for Windows and macOS and binary packages for other platforms, is available at https://nodejs.org/dist/v8.11.2.

© Adam Freeman 2018
A. Freeman, *Pro Vue.js 2*, https://doi.org/10.1007/978-1-4842-3805-9_1

When you install Node.js, make sure you select the option to add the Node.js executables to the path. When the installation is complete, run command shown in Listing 1-1.

Listing 1-1. Checking the Node Version

```
node -v
```

If the installation has gone as it should, then you will see the following version number displayed:

```
v8.11.2
```

The Node.js installer includes the Node Package Manager (NPM), which is used to manage the packages in a project. Run the command shown in Listing 1-2 to ensure that NPM is working.

Listing 1-2. Checking That NPM Works

```
npm -v
```

If everything is working as it should, then you will see the following version number:

```
5.6.0
```

Installing the @vue/cli Package

The @vue/cli package is the standard way to create and manage Vue.js projects during development. You don't have to use this package, but it provides everything that is needed to get started with Vue.js, and I use it throughout this book.

■ **Note**   As I write this, the @vue/cli package has been released in beta. There may be small changes made before the final release, but the core features should remain the same. For details of any breaking changes, check the errata for this book, available at https://github.com/Apress/pro-vue-js-2.

To install @vue/cli, open a new command prompt and run the command shown in Listing 1-3. If you are using Linux or macOS, you may need to use sudo.

Listing 1-3. Installing the Vue Tools Package

```
npm install --global @vue/cli
```

Installing Git

The Git revision control tool is required to manage some of the packages required for Vue.js development. If you are using Windows or macOS, then download and run the installer from https://git-scm.com/downloads. (On macOS, you may have to change your security settings to open the installer, which has not been signed by the developers.)

Git is already included in most Linux distributions. If you want to install the latest version, then consult the installation instructions for your distribution at https://git-scm.com/download/linux. As an example, for Ubuntu, which is the Linux distribution I use, I used the command shown in Listing 1-4.

Listing 1-4. Installing Git

```
sudo apt-get install git
```

Once you have completed the installation, open a new command prompt and run the command shown in Listing 1-5 to check that Git is installed and available.

Listing 1-5. Checking Git

```
git --version
```

This command prints out the version of the Git package that has been installed. At the time of writing, the latest version of Git for Windows and Linux is 2.17, and the latest version of Git for macOS is 2.16.3.

Installing an Editor

Vue.js development can be done with any programmer's editor, from which there is an endless number to choose. Some editors have enhanced support for working with Vue.js, including highlighting keywords and expressions. If you don't already have a preferred editor for web application development, then Table 1-1 describes some popular options for you to consider. I don't rely on any specific editor for this book, and you should use whichever editor you are comfortable working with.

Table 1-1. *Popular Vue.js-Enabled Editors*

Name	Description
Sublime Text	Sublime Text is a commercial cross-platform editor that has packages to support most programming languages, frameworks, and platforms. See www.sublimetext.com for details.
Atom	Atom is a free, open source, cross-platform editor that has a particular emphasis on customization and extensibility. See atom.io for details.
Brackets	Brackets is a free open source editor developed by Adobe. See brackets.io for details.
Visual Studio Code	Visual Studio Code is a free, open source, cross-platform editor from Microsoft, with an emphasis on extensibility. See code.visualstudio.com for details.
Visual Studio	Visual Studio is Microsoft's flagship developer tool. There are free and commercial editions available, and it comes with a wide range of additional tools that integrate into the Microsoft ecosystem.

Installing a Browser

The final choice to make is the browser that you will use to check your work during development. All the current-generation browsers have good developer support and work well with Vue.js, but there is a useful extension for Chrome and Firefox called vue-devtools that provides insights into the state of a Vue.js application and that is especially useful in complex projects. See https://github.com/vuejs/vue-devtools for details of installing the extension, which I use in later chapters. I used Google Chrome throughout this book, and this is the browser I recommend you use to follow the examples.

Creating the Project

Projects are created and managed from the command line. Open a new command prompt, navigate to a convenient location, and run the command shown in Listing 1-6 to create the project for this chapter.

Listing 1-6. Creating the Project

```
vue create todo --default
```

The vue command was installed as part of the @vue/cli package in Listing 1-3, and the command in Listing 1-6 creates a new project called todo, which will be created in a folder of the same name. The project will be created, and all of the packages required for Vue.js development will be downloaded and installed, which can take a while because a large number of packages are required even for a simple project.

Understanding the Project Structure

Open the todo folder using your preferred editor, and you will see the project structure shown in Figure 1-1. The figure shows the layout in my preferred editor—Visual Studio—and you may see the project content presented slightly differently if you have chosen a different editor.

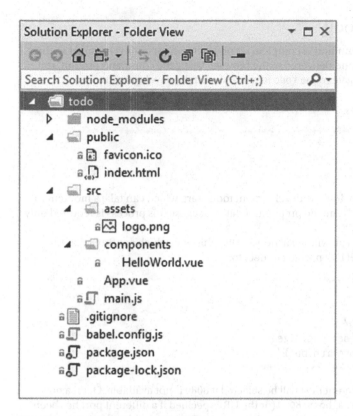

Figure 1-1. *The project structure*

The layout of the project can be daunting, but by the end of the book you will know what the different files and folders are for and how they are used. In Table 1-2, I have briefly described the files that are important in this chapter. I describe the structure of Vue.js projects in detail in Chapter 10.

Table 1-2. *The Important Files in the Project*

Name	Description
public/index.html	This is the HTML file that is loaded by the browser. It has an element in which the application is displayed and a script element that loads the application files.
src/main.js	This is the JavaScript file that is responsible for configuring the Vue.js application. It is also used to register any third-party packages that the application relies on, which you will see demonstrated in later chapters.
src/App.vue	This is the Vue.js component, which contains the HTML content that will be displayed to the user, the JavaScript code required by the HTML, and the CSS that styles the elements. Components are the main building blocks in a Vue.js application, and you will see them used throughout this book.
src/assets/logo.png	The assets folder is used to store static content, such as images. In a new project, it contains a file called logo.png, which is an image of the Vue.js logo.

Starting the Development Tools

When you create a project using the vue command, a complete set of development tools is installed so that the project can be compiled, packaged up, and delivered to the browser. Using the command prompt, run the commands shown in Listing 1-7 to navigate to the todo folder and start the development tools.

Listing 1-7. Starting the Development Tools

```
cd todo
npm run serve
```

There is an initial preparation process while the development tools start, which can take a moment to complete. Don't be put off by the amount of time the preparation takes because this process is required only when you start a development session.

When the startup process is complete, you will see a message like this one, which confirms that the application is running and tells you which HTTP port to connect to:

```
App running at:
- Local:   http://localhost:8080/
- Network: http://192.168.0.77:8080/
Note that the development build is not optimized.
To create a production build, run npm run build.
```

The default port is 8080 although a different port will be selected if 8080 is not available. Open a new browser window and navigate to http://localhost:8080 (or the URL specified if a different port has been selected), and you will see the placeholder content shown in Figure 1-2. (The placeholder content changes as new versions of the development tools are released, so don't worry if you don't see precisely the same content.)

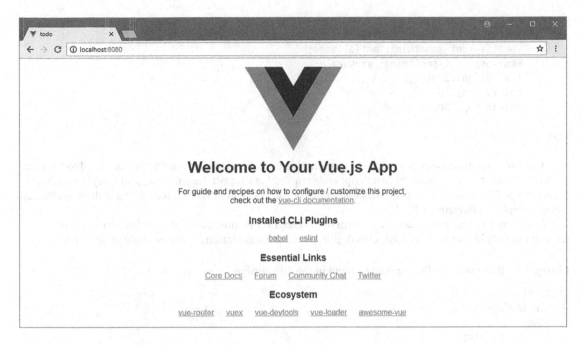

Figure 1-2. *Running the example application*

Replacing the Placeholder Content

The key building block in a Vue.js application is called a *component*, which is defined in files with the vue extension. Here is the content of the App component, which you will find in the App.vue file in the src folder:

```
<template>
    <div id="app">
        <img src="./assets/logo.png">
        <HelloWorld msg="Welcome to Your Vue.js App" />
    </div>
</template>
<script>
    import HelloWorld from './components/HelloWorld.vue'

    export default {
        name: 'app',
        components: {
            HelloWorld
        }
    }
</script>
<style>
```

```
    #app {
        font-family: 'Avenir', Helvetica, Arial, sans-serif;
        -webkit-font-smoothing: antialiased;
        -moz-osx-font-smoothing: grayscale;
        text-align: center;
        color: #2c3e50;
        margin-top: 60px;
    }
</style>
```

The component consists of a `template` element that contains HTML content to be presented to the user, a `script` element that contains the JavaScript code required to support the template, and a `style` element that contains CSS styles. Vue.js combines the `template`, `script`, and `style` element to create the placeholder content displayed in Figure 1-2.

In Listing 1-8, I have replaced the content in the `template` element, reset the `script` element, and removed the `style` element, all of which will give me a clean foundation for the example application.

Listing 1-8. Removing the Placeholder Content in the App.vue File in the src Folder

```
<template>
  <div id="app">
    <h4>
        To Do List
    </h4>
  </div>
</template>

<script>
  export default {
    name: 'app'
  }
</script>
```

When you save the changes, the application will be automatically recompiled, and the browser will be reloaded, producing the result shown in Figure 1-3.

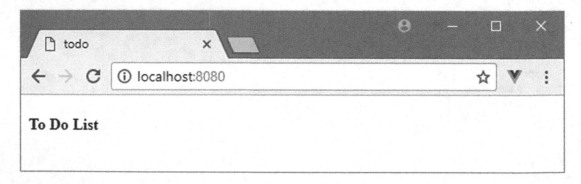

Figure 1-3. *Removing the placeholder content*

Adding a CSS Framework

The new content isn't going to appeal to many users. Although a component can contain CSS styles, I prefer to use a CSS framework that will allow me to style the HTML content in an application consistently. Throughout this book, I use the Bootstrap CSS framework. Stop the development tools using Control+C and run the command shown in Listing 1-9 in the todo folder to add Bootstrap to the project.

Listing 1-9. Adding Bootstrap to the Project

```
npm install bootstrap@4.0.0
```

You may see warnings about unmet peer dependencies, which can be ignored. To add the Bootstrap CSS file to the project, I added the statement shown in Listing 1-10 to the main.js file in the src folder.

Listing 1-10. Adding Bootstrap in the main.js File in the src Folder

```
import Vue from 'vue'
import App from './App.vue'

Vue.config.productionTip = false

import "bootstrap/dist/css/bootstrap.min.css";

new Vue({
    render: h => h(App)
}).$mount('#app')
```

The import statement ensures that the CSS stylesheet from the Bootstrap framework will be included in the application. (I explain how the import statement works in Chapter 4.) Don't worry if you are not familiar with Bootstrap because I describe the features I use in this book in Chapter 3.

CHOOSING A CSS FRAMEWORK FOR VUE.JS PROJECTS

Many of the most popular CSS frameworks—including Bootstrap—have JavaScript support for interactive components in addition to regular CSS styles. These JavaScript features often rely on packages like jQuery to access the elements in the HTML document, which conflicts with the way that Vue.js works. For this reason, it is important to either use only the CSS styles provided by a framework or to pick a framework that has been written specifically for Vue.js.

The first approach—using just the CSS styles—is the one that I have used throughout this book. Not only does this allow me to use a familiar framework, but it also helps keep the functionality provided by Vue.js separate from the content styling. This isn't possible with Vue.js-specific frameworks, which work by using the features that I describe in this book and which would complicate explaining many of the examples.

If you want to try a Vue.js-specific framework, then Veutify is a good place to start. (https://vuetifyjs.com/). There is also a project that adapts Bootstrap for use in Vue.js projects, called Bootstrap-Vue (https://bootstrap-vue.js.org).

Styling the HTML Elements

Now that Bootstrap is part of the application, I can style the content in the component's template element to improve the appearance, as shown in Listing 1-11.

Listing 1-11. Styling Content in the App.vue File in the src Folder

```
<template>
    <div id="app">
        <h4 class="bg-primary text-white text-center p-2">
            To Do List
        </h4>
    </div>
</template>

<script>
    export default {
        name: 'app'
    }
</script>
```

Run the command shown in Listing 1-12 in the todo folder to restart the application.

Listing 1-12. Restarting the Application

```
npm run serve
```

Use the browser window to navigate to http://localhost:8080 and you will see the content shown in Figure 1-4. If you see the text but it is not styled, then manually reload the browser window.

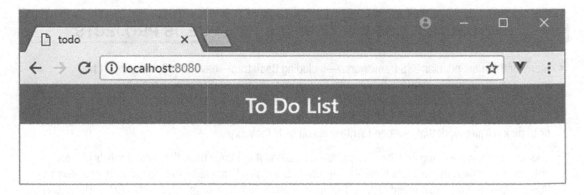

Figure 1-4. Styling the HTML content

Adding Dynamic Content

The next step is to add some data to the application and use it to display dynamic content to the user. In Listing 1-13, I have modified the App component so that it will display a data value.

Listing 1-13. Displaying Data in the App.vue File in the src Folder

```
<template>
    <div id="app">
        <h4 class="bg-primary text-white text-center p-2">
            {{name}}'s To Do List
        </h4>
    </div>
</template>

<script>
    export default {
        name: 'app',
        data() {
            return {
                name: "Adam"
            }
        }
    }
</script>
```

The addition to the `template` element is a data binding that tells Vue.js to insert a data value when it displays the HTML content. This type of data binding is called a *text interpolation binding* because it displays a data value as the text content of an HTML element. It is also known as a *mustache binding* because the double curly brackets (the {{ and }} characters) that denote the binding look like a handlebar mustache.

The data binding tells Vue.js to insert the `name` value into the `h4` element when the HTML is displayed. The `name` value used by the binding is provided by the change I made to the `script` element in Listing 1-13. The `data` property provides the template with `data` values, and when the data binding is processed, Vue.js checks the `data` property to look for a `name` value.

■ **Tip**   Don't worry about the odd syntax for the data function in Listing 1-13. It soon becomes a familiar pattern when working with Vue.js, and I explain how it works in Chapter 11.

When you save the `App.vue` file, the Vue.js development tools will detect the changes, update the application, and cause the browser window to reload automatically, which will display the content shown in Figure 1-5.

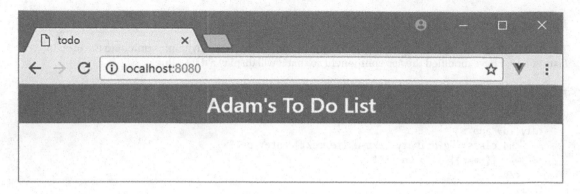

Figure 1-5. *Displaying a data value*

Notice that you don't have to manually reload the browser window when you make changes to the files in the project. The Vue.js development tools monitor the project for changes and trigger a browser reload automatically when a change is detected. I describe the development tools in more detail in Chapter 10.

Displaying the List of Tasks

Vue.js supports a range of data bindings that can be used to produce dynamic content in different ways, in addition to the text interpolation binding I used in the previous chapter. The next step for the example application is to define a collection of objects that represent the to-do tasks for the user and display them, as shown in Listing 1-14.

Listing 1-14. Displaying Tasks in the App.vue File in the src Folder

```
<template>
    <div id="app">
        <h4 class="bg-primary text-white text-center p-2">
            {{name}}'s To Do List
        </h4>
        <div class="container-fluid p-4">
            <div class="row">
                <div class="col font-weight-bold">Task</div>
                <div class="col-2 font-weight-bold">Done</div>
            </div>
            <div class="row" v-for="t in tasks" v-bind:key="t.action">
                <div class="col">{{t.action}}</div>
                <div class="col-2">{{t.done}}</div>
            </div>
        </div>
    </div>
</template>
```

```
<script>
    export default {
        name: 'app',
        data() {
            return {
                name: "Adam",
                tasks: [{ action: "Buy Flowers", done: false },
                        { action: "Get Shoes", done: false },
                        { action: "Collect Tickets", done: true },
                        { action: "Call Joe", done: false }]
            }
        }
    }
</script>
```

To display the list of tasks, I used the Vue.js feature that repeats a group of elements for each object in an array. Here is the element to which the feature has been applied, which can be difficult to spot in the other elements that are required to create the layout:

```
...
<div class="row" v-for="t in tasks" v-bind:key="t.action">
    <div class="col">{{t.action}}</div>
    <div class="col-2">{{t.done}}</div>
</div>
...
```

This is an example of a *directive*, which are special attributes whose names start with v- and that are applied to HTML elements to apply Vue.js functionality. This is the v-for directive, and it duplicates the element that it is applied to—and any contained elements—for each object in the array, assigning each object to a variable so that it can be accessed in data bindings.

The value assigned to the v-for directive specifies the source of the objects and the name of the variable that each one will be assigned to as they are processed. The expression in the example is t in tasks, which identifies a property called tasks as the source of the objects and t as the name of the variable that each one will be assigned to in turn as the objects are enumerated.

Within the elements contained by the v-for directive, the t variable can be used in data bindings to access the object that is currently being enumerated, like this:

```
...
<div class="row" v-for="t in tasks" v-bind:key="t.action">
    <div class="col">{{t.action}}</div>
    <div class="col-2">{{t.done}}</div>
</div>
...
```

There are two text interpolation bindings, which will set the contents of the div elements to the action and done properties of the object being processed. The v-bind element is another example of a directive, and its job in this example is to help the v-for directive keep track of the elements related to each object.

To provide the template with the source of the objects, I added a `tasks` property to the object returned by the data function, like this:

```
...
data() {
    return {
        name: "Adam",
        tasks: [{ action: "Buy Flowers", done: false },
                { action: "Get Shoes", done: false },
                { action: "Collect Tickets", done: true },
                { action: "Call Joe", done: false }]
    }
...
```

The result is that Vue.js will enumerate the objects that are contained in the `tasks` array and add a set of `div` element for each of them, with data bindings that display the values of the `action` and `done` properties.

When you save the changes to the `App.vue` file, the development tools will update the application and reload the browser to show the result in Figure 1-6. The additional `div` elements and the classes to which they are assigned create a grid layout for the content and are not part of the Vue.js features.

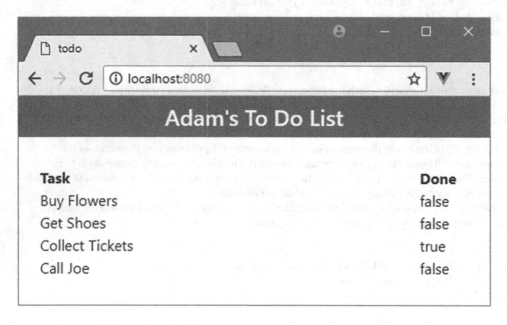

Figure 1-6. *Displaying a list of tasks*

Adding a Checkbox

The example application is starting to take shape, but using `true`/`false` values to indicate whether a task has been completed isn't what users expect. Vue.js includes directives that can be used to configure form elements using data values, and in Listing 1-15, I have added an `input` element that displays the value of the done property of each `tasks` object.

Listing 1-15. Adding a Form Element in the App.vue File in the src Folder

```
<template>
  <div id="app">
    <h4 class="bg-primary text-white text-center p-2">
      {{name}}'s To Do List
    </h4>
    <div class="container-fluid p-4">
      <div class="row">
        <div class="col font-weight-bold">Task</div>
        <div class="col-2 font-weight-bold">Done</div>
      </div>
      <div class="row" v-for="t in tasks" v-bind:key="t.action">
        <div class="col">{{t.action}}</div>
        <div class="col-2">
          <input type="checkbox" v-model="t.done" class="form-check-input" />
          {{t.done}}
        </div>
      </div>
    </div>
  </div>
</template>

<script>
  export default {
    name: 'app',
    data() {
      return {
        name: "Adam",
        tasks: [{ action: "Buy Flowers", done: false },
                { action: "Get Shoes", done: false },
                { action: "Collect Tickets", done: true },
                { action: "Call Joe", done: false }]
      }
    }
  }
</script>
```

The v-model directive configures an input element so that it displays the value specified by its expression. Vue.js adapts its behavior based on the type of the input element to which the v-model directive has been applied so that the value is displayed in a text input element, for example. When the type of an input element is checkbox, the v-model directive toggles the checkbox based on the value it is configured to display. When you save the change to the App.vue file, you will see how the checkboxes match the text values, as shown in Figure 1-7.

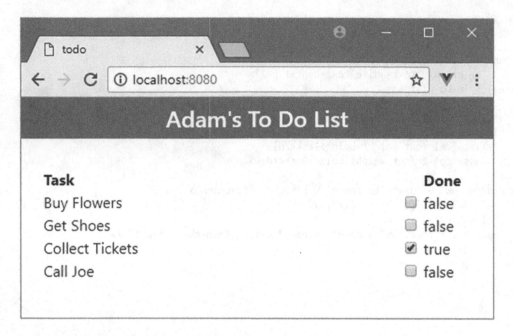

Figure 1-7. *Using a directive to display a checkbox*

This type of directive creates a *two-way data binding*, which means that when you change the input element, Vue.js will update the corresponding data value. You can see how this works by checking and unchecking one of the checkboxes. Each time you make a change, the text displayed by the adjacent text data binding also changes, as shown in Figure 1-8.

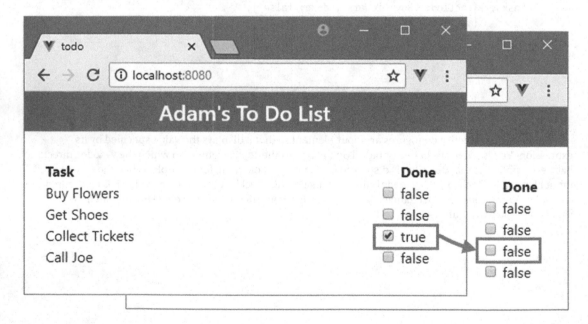

Figure 1-8. *The effect of a two-way data binding*

This demonstrates one of the most important aspects of Vue.js applications, which is that the application's data is "live," and when the data changes, all of the data bindings that use that data are updated to reflect the change. In this case, the two-way data binding I added to the input element updates the done property of the Collect Tickets to-do object. That change is reflected in the text data binding that displays the done property, illustrating how data bindings have an ongoing relationship with the data with which they are associated.

Filtering Completed Tasks

The live data model means you can easily add elements that allow the user to manage the presentation of the application's data. In the case of the example application, users care most about the tasks that remain incomplete, and in Listing 1-16, I added a feature that allows the user to filter out the tasks that are already done.

Listing 1-16. Filtering Tasks in the App.vue File in the src Folder

```
<template>
  <div id="app">
    <h4 class="bg-primary text-white text-center p-2">
      {{name}}'s To Do List
    </h4>
    <div class="container-fluid p-4">
      <div class="row">
        <div class="col font-weight-bold">Task</div>
        <div class="col-2 font-weight-bold">Done</div>
      </div>
      <div class="row" v-for="t in filteredTasks" v-bind:key="t.action">
        <div class="col">{{t.action}}</div>
        <div class="col-2 text-center">
          <input type="checkbox" v-model="t.done" class="form-check-input" />
        </div>
      </div>
      <div class="row bg-secondary py-2 mt-2 text-white">
        <div class="col text-center">
          <input type="checkbox" v-model="hideCompleted" class="form-check-input" />
          <label class="form-check-label font-weight-bold">
            Hide completed tasks
          </label>
        </div>
      </div>
    </div>
  </div>
</template>
```

```
<script>
  export default {
    name: 'app',
    data() {
      return {
        name: "Adam",
        tasks: [{ action: "Buy Flowers", done: false },
                { action: "Get Shoes", done: false },
                { action: "Collect Tickets", done: true },
                { action: "Call Joe", done: false }],
        hideCompleted: true
      }
    },
    computed: {
      filteredTasks() {
        return this.hideCompleted ?
          this.tasks.filter(t => !t.done) : this.tasks
      }
    }
  }
</script>
```

In the `script` element, I added a `computed` property using a function called `filteredTasks`. The `computed` property is used to define properties that operate on the application's data, and this allows Vue. js to detect changes to the application data efficiently, which is important in complex applications. The `filteredTask` property uses the value of the newly defined `hideCompleted` property in the `data` section to determine whether the user wants to see all of the tasks or just the ones that are incomplete.

To manage the value of the `hideCompleted` property, I added a checkbox to the `template` element and used the `v-model` directive, like this:

```
...
<input type="checkbox" v-model="hideCompleted" class="form-check-input" />
...
```

To ensure that the user sees the data they have selected, I changed the expression of the `v-for` directive so that it uses the `filteredTasks` property, like this:

```
...
<div class="row" v-for="t in filteredTasks" v-bind:key="t.action">
...
```

When the user toggles the checkbox, the `v-model` binding updates the `hideCompleted` property, which changes the result produced by the `filteredTasks` property and presents the user with the set of tasks they require. Save the changes and the browser will reload, producing the result shown in Figure 1-9.

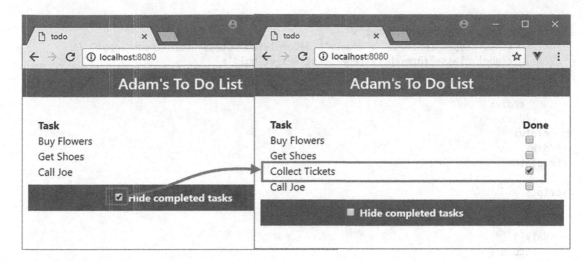

Figure 1-9. *Filtering tasks*

Creating New Tasks

A to-do application that doesn't allow the user to create new tasks isn't much use. In Listing 1-17, I have added new content to the template element that allows the user to enter details of a new to-do.

Listing 1-17. Creating New Tasks in the App.vue File in the src Folder

```
<template>
  <div id="app">
    <h4 class="bg-primary text-white text-center p-2">
      {{name}}'s To Do List
    </h4>
    <div class="container-fluid p-4">
      <div class="row">
        <div class="col font-weight-bold">Task</div>
        <div class="col-2 font-weight-bold">Done</div>
      </div>
      <div class="row" v-for="t in filteredTasks" v-bind:key="t.action">
        <div class="col">{{t.action}}</div>
        <div class="col-2 text-center">
          <input type="checkbox" v-model="t.done" class="form-check-input" />
        </div>
      </div>
      <div class="row py-2">
        <div class="col">
          <input v-model="newItemText" class="form-control" />
        </div>
        <div class="col-2">
          <button class="btn btn-primary" v-on:click="addNewTodo">Add</button>
        </div>
      </div>
```

```
        <div class="row bg-secondary py-2 mt-2 text-white">
          <div class="col text-center">
            <input type="checkbox" v-model="hideCompleted" class="form-check-input" />
            <label class="form-check-label font-weight-bold">
              Hide completed tasks
            </label>
          </div>
        </div>
      </div>
    </div>
</template>

<script>
  export default {
    name: 'app',
    data() {
      return {
        name: "Adam",
        tasks: [{ action: "Buy Flowers", done: false },
                { action: "Get Shoes", done: false },
                { action: "Collect Tickets", done: true },
                { action: "Call Joe", done: false }],
        hideCompleted: true,
        newItemText: ""
      }
    },
    computed: {
      filteredTasks() {
        return this.hideCompleted ?
          this.tasks.filter(t => !t.done) : this.tasks
      }
    },
    methods: {
      addNewTodo() {
        this.tasks.push({
          action: this.newItemText,
          done: false
        });
        this.newItemText = "";
      }
    }
  }
</script>
```

The input element uses the v-model directive to create a binding with a variable called newItemText, and when the user edits the contents element, Vue.js will update the value of the variable. To trigger the creation of the new data item, I applied the v-on directive to the button element, like this:

```
...
<button class="btn btn-primary" v-on:click="addNewTodo">
...
```

The v-on directive is used to respond to events, which are typically triggered when the user performs an action. In this case, I used the v-on directive to tell Vue.js to invoke a method called addNewTodo when the click event is triggered on the button element, which will happen when the user clicks the button.

To support the changes in the template element, I made corresponding changes to the JavaScript code in the script element. I added a methods property, which is where Vue.js looks for methods that are invoked by directive expressions. Within methods, I defined a method called addNewTodo that adds a new object to the tasks array using the value of the newItemText property as the action value. Once the new object has been added to the array, I reset the newItemText value. The v-model binding that updates the newItemText value when the content of the input element changes works in the other direction too, which means that setting the newItemText to the empty string will clear the contents of the input element.

Save the changes, and you will see the content shown in Figure 1-10 when the browser reloads. Enter a task description in the input element and click the Add button, and you will see a new to-do item appear in the list.

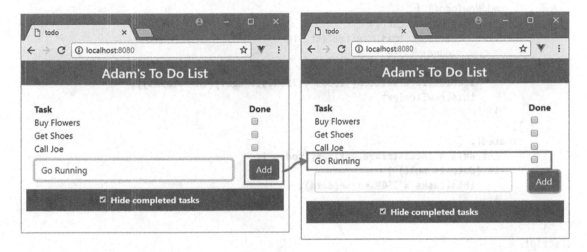

Figure 1-10. *Creating a new task*

Storing Data Persistently

There is no persistent data storage in the example application, which means that reloading the browser resets the to-do list and any changes made by the user are lost. I am going to use the local storage feature that is available in modern browsers so that I can store data without having to set up a server and also to demonstrate that you can work directly with the features provided by browsers in a Vue.js application. I show you how to work with servers in later chapters, but I am keeping things simple for this project. In Listing 1-18, I have added statements to the script element of the component to store and retrieve the to-do list data. (I have not shown the template element in the listing because it has not changed. I explain this convention in Chapter 2.)

Listing 1-18. Using Local Storage in the App.vue File in the src Folder

```
...
<script>

    export default {
        name: 'app',
        data() {
```

```
            return {
                name: "Adam",
                tasks: [],
                hideCompleted: true,
                newItemText: ""
            }
        },
        computed: {
            filteredTasks() {
                return this.hideCompleted ?
                    this.tasks.filter(t => !t.done) : this.tasks
            }
        },
        methods: {
            addNewTodo() {
                this.tasks.push({
                    action: this.newItemText,
                    done: false
                });
                localStorage.setItem("todos", JSON.stringify(this.tasks));
                this.newItemText = "";
            }
        },
        created() {
            let data = localStorage.getItem("todos");
            if (data != null) {
                this.tasks = JSON.parse(data);
            }
        }
    }
</script>
...
```

The local storage feature is provided through a global object called localStorage that defines getItem and setItem methods and that is provided by the browser.

■ **Tip**   The localStorage object isn't specific to Vue.js development. It is a standard JavaScript object that is available to all web applications, regardless of how they are written. See https://developer.mozilla.org/en-US/docs/Web/API/Window/localStorage for a good description of how local storage works.

The storeData method added to the component uses the setItem method to store the to-do items and is called when the user creates a new to-do or toggles an existing checkbox. The local storage feature is only able to store string values, which means that I have to serialize the data objects as JSON before they can be stored.

The created method that I added to the component in Listing 1-18 is called when Vue.js creates the component and it provides me with an opportunity to load the data from local storage before the application's content is presented to the user. The final change made in Listing 1-18 is to remove the placeholder to-do items, which are no longer required now that the user's data is persistently stored.

When you save the changes, the browser will reload, and the application will store any to-do items you create persistently, which means they will still be available when you reload the browser window or navigate away to a different URL, such as the Apress website, and then back to http://localhost:8080, as shown in Figure 1-11.

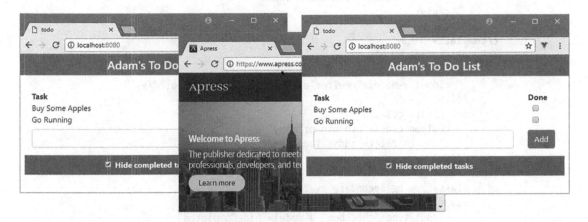

Figure 1-11. *Storing data*

Adding the Finishing Touches

I am going to add two features to complete the example application. The first feature is the ability to delete completed to-do tasks, which will be important now that they are stored persistently. The second feature is to display a message when there are no to-do items to display. I added both features to the App component, as shown in Listing 1-19.

Listing 1-19. Adding Finishing Touches in the App.vue File in the src Folder

```
<template>
    <div id="app">
        <h4 class="bg-primary text-white text-center p-2">
            {{name}}'s To Do List
        </h4>
        <div class="container-fluid p-4">
            <div class="row" v-if="filteredTasks.length == 0">
                <div class="col text-center">
                    <b>Nothing to do. Hurrah!</b>
                </div>
            </div>
            <template v-else>
                <div class="row">
                    <div class="col font-weight-bold">Task</div>
                    <div class="col-2 font-weight-bold">Done</div>
                </div>
```

```
            <div class="row" v-for="t in filteredTasks" v-bind:key="t.action">
                <div class="col">{{t.action}}</div>
                <div class="col-2 text-center">
                    <input type="checkbox" v-model="t.done"
                        class="form-check-input" />
                </div>
            </div>
        </template>
        <div class="row py-2">
            <div class="col">
                <input v-model="newItemText" class="form-control" />
            </div>
            <div class="col-2">
                <button class="btn btn-primary"
                    v-on:click="addNewTodo">Add</button>
            </div>
        </div>
        <div class="row bg-secondary py-2 mt-2 text-white">
            <div class="col text-center">
                <input type="checkbox" v-model="hideCompleted"
                    class="form-check-input" />
                <label class="form-check-label font-weight-bold">
                    Hide completed tasks
                </label>
            </div>
            <div class="col text-center">
                <button class="btn btn-sm btn-warning"
                        v-on:click="deleteCompleted">
                    Delete Completed
                </button>
            </div>
        </div>
        </div>
    </div>
</div>
</template>

<script>

    export default {
        name: 'app',
        data() {
            return {
                name: "Adam",
                tasks: [],
                hideCompleted: true,
                newItemText: ""
            }
        },
```

```
        computed: {
            filteredTasks() {
                return this.hideCompleted ?
                    this.tasks.filter(t => !t.done) : this.tasks
            }
        },
        methods: {
            addNewTodo() {
                this.tasks.push({
                    action: this.newItemText,
                    done: false
                });
                this.storeData();
                this.newItemText = "";
            },
            storeData() {
                localStorage.setItem("todos", JSON.stringify(this.tasks));
            },
            deleteCompleted() {
                this.tasks = this.tasks.filter(t => !t.done);
                this.storeData();
            }
        },
        created() {
            let data = localStorage.getItem("todos");
            if (data != null) {
                this.tasks = JSON.parse(data);
            }
        }
    }
</script>
```

The v-if and v-else directives are used to display elements conditionally, and I used them to display a message when there are no items in the tasks array and to otherwise display the list of tasks. I also added a button element and used the v-on directive to handle the click event by filtering out the completed to-do items and then storing the objects that remain. When you save the change to the App.vue file, the application will reload. If you check the Hide Completed Tasks checkbox and click the Delete Completed button, you will see the result shown in Figure 1-12.

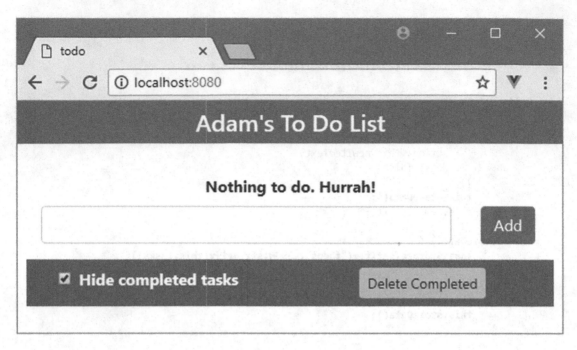

Figure 1-12. *Adding the finishing touches*

Summary

In this chapter, I created a simple example application to introduce you to Vue.js projects and the Vue.js development process. Although the example was simple, it allowed me to demonstrate some important Vue.js concepts.

You saw that Vue.js comes with all the tools you need for development, and when you create a project, everything that is required to prepare and package the application and deliver it to the browser for testing is included.

You learned that Vue.js applications are built around components, which combine HTML and JavaScript code. The JavaScript code is broken into sections, such as data and methods, and computed and accessed through directives and data bindings. Underneath all of these features is the idea of a reactive data model, which allows changes to be automatically reflected by the application.

There are many more Vue.js features available, as you can tell from the size of this book, but the basic application that I created in this chapter has shown you the most essential characteristics of Vue.js development and will provide a foundation for later chapters. In the next chapter, I put Vue.js in context and describe the structure and content of this book.

CHAPTER 2

■ ■ ■

Understanding Vue.js

Vue.js is a flexible and powerful open-source framework for developing client-side applications, taking design principles from the world of server-side development and applying them to HTML elements, creating a foundation that makes building rich web applications easier. In this book, I explain how Vue.js works and demonstrate the different features that it provides.

> ## THIS BOOK AND THE VUE.JS RELEASE SCHEDULE
>
> The Vue.js development team goes to a lot of effort to ensure that the Vue.js API changes as little as possible, which is a refreshing change from the constant stream of breaking updates that characterize other client-side frameworks. There are frequent updates to Vue.js, but you should find that they don't usually don't prevent existing applications from working, which is good news for your projects and the examples in this book.
>
> Even so, there is always the possibility that a Vue.js release will stop some of the examples from working as intended. It doesn't seem fair or reasonable to ask readers to buy a new edition of this book every time that happens, especially since the majority of Vue.js features are unlikely to change even in a major release. Instead, I am going to post updates following the major releases to the GitHub repository for this book, https://github.com/Apress/pro-vue-js-2.
>
> This is an ongoing experiment for me (and for Apress), and the form these updates may take is uncertain—not least because I don't know what the major releases of Vue.js will contain—but the goal is to extend the life of this book by updating the examples it contains.
>
> I am not making any promises about what the updates will be like, what form they will take, or how long I will produce them before folding them into a new edition of this book. Please keep an open mind and check the repository for this book when new Vue.js versions are released. If you have ideas about how the updates could be improved, then e-mail me at adam@adam-freeman.com and let me know.

Should I Use Vue.js?

Vue.js isn't the solution to every problem, and it is important to know when you should use Vue.js and when you should seek an alternative. Vue.js delivers the kind of functionality that used to be available only to native application developers and makes it available entirely in the browser. This puts a lot of demand on the browser, which has to run the Vue.js application, process the HTML elements, execute the JavaScript code, handle events, and perform all of the other tasks required to start a Vue.js application like the one you saw in Chapter 2.

© Adam Freeman 2018
A. Freeman, *Pro Vue.js 2*, https://doi.org/10.1007/978-1-4842-3805-9_2

This kind of work takes time to perform, and the amount of time depends on the complexity of the Vue.js application, the quality of the browser, and the processing capability of the device. You won't notice any delay when using the latest browsers on a capable desktop machine, but old browsers on underpowered smartphones can really slow down the initial setup of a Vue.js app.

The goal, therefore, is to perform this setup as infrequently as possible and deliver as much of the app as possible to the user when it is performed. This means giving careful thought to the kind of web application you build. In broad terms, there are two kinds of web application: *round-trip* and *single-page*.

Understanding Round-Trip Applications

For a long time, web apps were developed to follow a *round-trip* model. The browser requests an initial HTML document from the server. User interactions—such as clicking a link or submitting a form—led the browser to request and receive a completely new HTML document. In this kind of application, the browser is essentially a rendering engine for HTML content, and all of the application logic and data resides on the server. The browser makes a series of stateless HTTP requests that the server handles by generating HTML documents dynamically.

A lot of current web development is still for round-trip applications, especially for line-of-business projects, not least because they put few demands on the browser and have the widest possible client support. But there are some serious drawbacks to round-trip applications: they make the user wait while the next HTML document is requested and loaded, they require a large server-side infrastructure to process all the requests and manage all the application state, and they can require more bandwidth because each HTML document has to be self-contained, which can lead to the same content being included in each response from the server. Vue.js is not well-suited to round-trip applications because the browser has to perform the initial setup process for each new HTML document that is received from the server.

Understanding Single-Page Applications

Single-page applications (SPAs) take a different approach. An initial HTML document is sent to the browser, but user interactions lead to Ajax requests for small fragments of HTML or data inserted into the existing set of elements being displayed to the user. The initial HTML document is never reloaded or replaced, and the user can continue to interact with the existing HTML while the Ajax requests are being performed asynchronously, even if that just means seeing a "data loading" message.

Single-page applications are well-suited to Vue.js—and other client-side frameworks, including Angular and React—because the work that the browser has to perform to initialize the application has to be performed only once, after which the application runs in the browser, responding to user interaction and requesting the data or content that is required in the background.

COMPARING VUE.JS TO REACT AND ANGULAR

There are two main competitors to Vue.js: React and Vue.js. There are differences between them, but, for the most part, all of these frameworks are excellent, all of them work in similar ways, and all of them can be used to create rich and fluid client-side applications.

One key difference is that Vue.js focuses only on presenting HTML content to the user and doesn't directly include functionality for other features, such as asynchronous HTTP requests or URL routing. But this difference is largely academic since these features are provided through packages that are endorsed or even developed by the Vue.js development team, and most Vue.js projects use the same set of packages.

The real difference between these frameworks is the developer experience. Angular requires you to use TypeScript to be effective, for example, whereas it is just an option with Vue.js projects. Vue.js and React lean toward mixing HTML and JavaScript, which not everyone enjoys.

My advice is simple: pick the framework that you like the look of the most and switch to one of the others if you don't get on with it. That may seem like an unscientific approach, but there isn't a bad choice to make, and you will find that many of the core concepts carry over between frameworks even if you change the one you use.

If you want a careful comparison of features, then see `https://vuejs.org/v2/guide/comparison.html`, which has a comprehensive comparison between Vue.js and other frameworks, albeit one that is written by the Vue.js team. But don't get sucked into comparing low-level features because all of these frameworks are good; all of them can be used to write large and complex projects, and the best framework is always the one that suits your personal development style and in which you are most productive.

Understanding Server-Side Rendering

Server-side rendering (known as SSR) is another term that is related to SPAs and is intended to make web applications respond more quickly when the user first navigates to a URL and to allow search engines to better index web application content.

SSR uses Node.js as a server-side JavaScript runtime to execute the web application on the server to produce the content that is presented to the user. At this point, the application is a round-trip application, where each interaction results in a new HTTP request to the server, which continues to execute the application on the user's behalf and send the HTML that is produced back to the browser so that it can be displayed to the user. At the same time, the code and content required to execute the application is downloaded in the background and used to initialize the application, at which point it becomes a single-page application and user interaction is handled by the code running in the browser.

There are packages available that support SSR for Vue.js applications, but I do not describe them in this book. Server-side rendering is complex and is limited to servers that can execute JavaScript since they are responsible for running the application on behalf of users. Applications must take care not to rely on features or APIs that require a browser since those features are not available at the server. Seamlessly moving between server-side rendering and client-side rendering can also be difficult and confusing to the user, especially when there are problems. These difficulties and limitations mean that SSR is not suitable for most Vue.js projects and should be approached with caution. See `https://vuejs.org/v2/guide/ssr.html` for more details about the SSR support for Vue.js.

Understanding Application Complexity

The type of application isn't the only consideration when deciding whether Vue.js would be well-suited to a project. The complexity of a project is also important, and I often hear from readers who have embarked on a project using a client-side framework such as Vue.js, Angular, or React when something much simpler would have been sufficient. A framework such as Vue.js requires a substantial time commitment to master (as the size of this book illustrates), and this effort isn't justified if you just need to validate a form or populate a select element programmatically.

In the excitement that surrounds client-side frameworks, it is easy to forget that browsers provide a rich set of APIs that can be used directly and that these are the same APIs that Vue.js relies on for all of its features. If you have a problem that is simple and self-contained, then you should consider using the browser APIs directly, starting with the Document Object Model (DOM) API. You will see that some of the examples in this book use the browser APIs directly, but a good place to start if you are new to browser development is `https://developer.mozilla.org`, which contains good documentation for all of the APIs that browsers support.

The drawback of the browser APIs, especially the DOM API, is that they can be awkward to work with, and older browsers tend to implement features differently. A good alternative to working directly with the browser APIs, especially if you have to support older browsers, is jQuery (`https://jquery.org`). jQuery simplifies working with HTML elements and has excellent support for handling events, animations, and asynchronous HTTP requests.

Rich client-side frameworks like Vue.js require too much investment and too many resources for simple projects. They come into their own in complex projects, where there are complex workflows to implement, different types of user to deal with, and large amounts of data to be processed. In these situations, you can work directly with the browser APIs or with jQuery, but it becomes difficult to manage the code and hard to scale up the application. The features provided by Vue.js make it easier to build large and complex applications and to do so without getting bogged down in reams of unreadable code, which is often the fate of complex projects that don't adopt a framework.

What Do I Need to Know?

If you decide that Vue.js is the right choice for your project, then you should be familiar with the basics of web development, have an understanding of how HTML and CSS work, and, ideally, have a working knowledge of JavaScript. If you are a little hazy on some of these details, I provide primers for the HTML, CSS, and JavaScript features I use in this book in Chapters 3 and 4. You won't find a comprehensive reference for HTML elements and CSS properties, though. There just isn't the space in a book about Vue.js to cover all of HTML. If you want to brush up on the fundamentals of HTML, CSS, and JavaScript, then I recommend `https://developer.mozilla.org` as a good place to start.

How Do I Set Up My Development Environment?

The only development tools needed for Vue.js development are the ones you installed in Chapter 1 when you created your first application. Some later chapters require additional packages, but full instructions are provided. If you successfully built the application in Chapter 1, then you are set for Vue.js development and for the rest of the chapters in this book.

What Is the Structure of This Book?

This book is split into three parts, each of which covers a set of related topics.

Part 1: Getting Started with Vue.js

Part 1 of this book provides the information you need to get started with Vue.js development. It includes this chapter and primer/refresher chapters for the key technologies used in Vue.js development, including HTML, CSS, and JavaScript. I also show you how to build your first Vue.js application and take you through the process of building a more realistic application, called SportsStore.

Part 2: Working with Vue.js

Part 2 of this book takes you through the features that are required in most Vue.js projects. Vue.js includes a lot of built-in functionality, which I describe in depth, along with the way that custom code and content is added to a project to create bespoke features.

Part 3: Advanced Vue.js Features

Part 3 of this book explains how advanced Vue.js features can be used to create larger and more complex applications. I describe the lifecycle of a Vue.js application, show you how to create a common data store, and explain how to display parts of the application based on the user's actions. I also show you how to extend the built-in Vue.js features and how to perform unit testing in your projects.

Are There Lots of Examples?

There are *loads* of examples. The best way to learn Vue.js is by example, and I have packed as many of them into this book as I can, along with screenshots so you can see the effects of each feature. To maximize the number of examples in this book, I have adopted a simple convention to avoid listing the same code or content over and over. When I create a file, I will show its full contents, just as I have in Listing 2-1. I include the name of the file and its folder in the listing's header, and I show the changes that I have made in bold.

Listing 2-1. Getting Data in the App.vue File in the src Folder

```
<template>
    <div class="container-fluid">
        <div class="row">
            <div class="col"><error-display /></div>
        </div>
        <div class="row">
            <div class="col-8 m-3"><product-display /></div>
            <div class="col m-3"><product-editor /></div>
        </div>
    </div>
</template>

<script>
    import ProductDisplay from "./components/ProductDisplay";
    import ProductEditor from "./components/ProductEditor";
    import ErrorDisplay from "./components/ErrorDisplay";

    export default {
        name: 'App',
        components: { ProductDisplay, ProductEditor, ErrorDisplay },
        created() {
            this.$store.dispatch("getProductsAction");
        }
    }
</script>
```

This is a listing from Chapter 21, which shows the contents of a file called App.vue that can be found in the src folder. Don't worry about the content of the listing or the purpose of the file; just be aware that this type of listing contains the complete contents of a file and that the changes you need to make to follow the example are shown in bold.

Some files in a Vue.js application can be long, but the feature that I am describing requires only a small change. Rather than list the complete file, I use an ellipsis (three periods in series) to indicate a partial listing, which shows just part of the file, as shown in Listing 2-2.

Listing 2-2. Preparing for Dynamic Display in the ProductEditor.vue File in the src/components Folder

```
...
<script>

    let unwatcher;

    export default {
        data: function () {
            return {
                editing: false,
                product: {}
            }
        },
        methods: {
            save() {
                this.$store.dispatch("saveProductAction", this.product);
                this.product = {};
            },
            cancel() {
                this.$store.commit("selectProduct");
            },
            selectProduct(selectedProduct) {
                if (selectedProduct == null) {
                    this.editing = false;
                    this.product = {};
                } else {
                    this.editing = true;
                    this.product = {};
                    Object.assign(this.product, selectedProduct);
                }
            }
        },
        created() {
            unwatcher = this.$store.watch(state =>
                state.selectedProduct, this.selectProduct);
            this.selectProduct(this.$store.state.selectedProduct);
        },
        beforeDestroy() {
            unwatcher();
        }
    }
</script>
...
```

This is a later listing from Chapter 21, and it shows a set of changes that are applied to only one part of a much larger file. When you see a partial listing, you will know that the rest of the file does not have to change and that only the sections marked in bold are different.

In some cases, changes are required in different parts of a file, which makes it difficult to show as a partial listing. In this situation, I omit part of the file's contents, as shown in Listing 2-3.

Listing 2-3. Adding a Module in the index.js File in the src/store Folder

```
import Vue from "vue";
import Vuex from "vuex";
import Axios from "axios";

import PrefsModule from "./preferences";
import NavModule from "./navigation";

Vue.use(Vuex);

const baseUrl = "http://localhost:3500/products/";

export default new Vuex.Store({
    modules: {
        prefs: PrefsModule,
        nav: NavModule
    },
    state: {
        products: [],
        selectedProduct: null
    },

    // ...other data store features omitted for brevity...

})
```

The changes are still marked in bold, and the parts of the file that are omitted from the listing are not affected by this example.

Where Can You Get the Example Code?

You can download the example projects for all the chapters in this book from https://github.com/Apress/pro-vue-js-2. The download is available without charge and contains everything that you need to follow the examples without having to type in all of the code.

Where Can You Get Corrections for This Book?

You can find errata for this book at https://github.com/Apress/pro-vue-js-2.

How Can You Contact Me?

If you have problems making the examples in this chapter work or if you find a problem in the book, then you can e-mail me at adam@adam-freeman.com, and I will try my best to help. Please check the errata for this book to see whether it contains a solution to your problem before contacting me.

Summary

In this chapter, I explained when Vue.js is a good choice for projects and outlines the alternatives and competitors. I also outlined the content and structure of this book, explained where to get updates and how to contact me if you have problems with the examples in this book. In the next chapter, I provide a primer for the HTML and CSS features that I use in this book to demonstrate Vue.js development.

CHAPTER 3

HTML and CSS Primer

Developers come to the world of web app development via many paths and are not always grounded in the basic technologies that web apps rely on. In this chapter, I provide a brief primer for HTML and introduce the Bootstrap CSS library, which I use to style the examples in this book. In Chapter 4, I introduce the basics of JavaScript and give you the information you need to understand the examples in the rest of the book. If you are an experienced developer, you can skip these primer chapters and jump right to Chapter 5, where I use Vue.js to create a more complex and realistic application.

■ **Tip** You can download the example project for this chapter—and for all of the other chapters in this book—from https://github.com/Apress/pro-vue-js-2.

Preparing for This Chapter

For this chapter, I need a simple Vue.js project. I started by running the command shown in Listing 3-1 to create a project called htmlcssprimer.

Listing 3-1. Creating the Example Project

```
vue create htmlcssprimer --default
```

The process of creating the project can take a few moments because there is a large number of packages to be downloaded and installed.

■ **Note** At the time of writing, the @vue/cli package has been released in beta. There may be small changes made before the final release, but the core features should remain the same. For details of any breaking changes, check the errata for this book, available at https://github.com/Apress/pro-vue-js-2.

Once the project has been created, run the commands shown in Listing 3-2 to navigate to the project folder and install the Bootstrap CSS framework, which I use in this chapter (and throughout the book) to manage the appearance of the content in the Vue.js application.

A. Freeman, *Pro Vue.js 2*, https://doi.org/10.1007/978-1-4842-3805-9_3

Listing 3-2. Installing the Bootstrap Package

```
cd htmlcssprimer
npm install bootstrap@4.0.0
```

To include Bootstrap in the project, I added the statement shown in Listing 3-3 to the main.js file in the src folder. I explain how the import statement works in Chapter 4, but for now, it is enough to simply add the statement shown in the listing.

Listing 3-3. Adding a Statement in the main.js File in the src Folder

```
import Vue from 'vue'
import App from './App.vue'

Vue.config.productionTip = false

import "bootstrap/dist/css/bootstrap.min.css";

new Vue({
  render: h => h(App)
}).$mount('#app')
```

Next, I replaced the placeholder content in the App.vue file with the template and script element shown in Listing 3-4 and removed the style element entirely.

Listing 3-4. Replacing the Content of the App.vue File in the src Folder

```
<template>
    <div>
        <h4 class="bg-primary text-white text-center p-2">
            Adam's To Do List
        </h4>
        <div class="container-fluid p-4">
            <div class="row">
                <div class="col font-weight-bold">Task</div>
                <div class="col-2 font-weight-bold">Done</div>
            </div>
            <div class="row" v-for="t in tasks" v-bind:key="t.action">
                <div class="col">{{t.action}}</div>
                <div class="col-2">{{t.done}}</div>
            </div>
        </div>
    </div>
</template>

<script>
export default {
    data: function () {
        return {
            tasks: [{ action: "Buy Flowers", done: false },
```

```
                  { action: "Get Shoes", done: false },
                  { action: "Collect Tickets", done: true },
                  { action: "Call Joe", done: false }]
        }
    }
}
</script>
```

This is a simplified version of the to-do application from Chapter 1, with some basic dynamic content but without features such as completing or adding new items. Save all of the changes and run the command shown in Listing 3-5 in the `htmlcssprimer` folder to start the Vue.js development tools.

Listing 3-5. Starting the Vue.js Development Tools

```
npm run serve
```

The initial preparation of the project will take a moment, after which you will see a message telling you that the application is ready. Open a new browser window and navigate to `http://localhost:8080` to see the content shown in Figure 3-1.

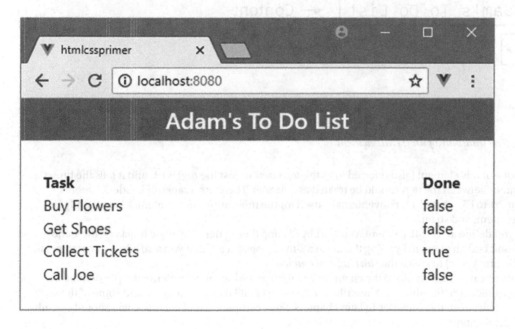

Figure 3-1. *Running the example application*

Understanding HTML Elements

At the heart of HTML is the *element*, which tells the browser what kind of content each part of an HTML document represents. Here is an element from the example HTML document:

```
...
<h4 class="bg-primary text-white text-center p-2">
    Adam's To Do List
</h4>
...
```

As illustrated in Figure 3-2, this element has several parts: the start tag, the end tag, attributes, and the content.

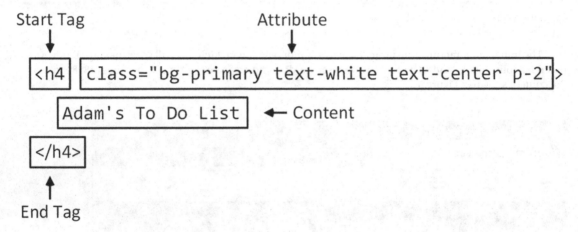

Figure 3-2. *The anatomy of an HTML element*

The *name* of this element (also referred to as the *tag name* or just the *tag*) is h4, and it tells the browser that the content between the tags should be treated as a header. There are a range of header elements, ranging from h1 to h6, where h1 is conventionally used for the most important content, h2 for slightly less important content, and so on.

When you define an HTML element, you start by placing the tag name in angle brackets (the < and > characters) and end an element by using the tag in a similar way, except that you also add a / character after the left-angle bracket (<) to create the *start tag* and *end tag*.

The tag indicates the purpose of the element, and there is a wide range of element types defined by the HTML specification. In Table 3-1, I describe the elements that I use in Listing 3-4 and some of the most common elements from the examples in later chapters. For a complete list of tag types, you should consult the HTML specification.

Table 3-1. *Common HTML Elements Used in the Examples*

Element	Description
a	Denotes a link (more formally known as an *anchor*), which the user clicks to navigate to a new URL or a new location within the current document.
button	Denotes a button; often used to submit a form to the server.
div	A generic element; often used to add structure to a document for presentation purposes.
h1-h6	Denotes a header.
input	Denotes a field used to gather a single data item from the user.
table	Denotes a table, used to organize content into rows and columns.
tbody	Denotes the body of the table (as opposed to the header or footer).
td	Denotes a content cell in a table row.
template	Denotes content that will be processed using JavaScript. Vue.js components use a template element to contain their HTML content, and the element is also used to apply Vue.js features to avoid creating invalid HTML documents.
th	Denotes a header cell in a table row.
thead	Denotes the header of a table.
tr	Denotes a row in a table.

Understanding Element Content

Whatever appears between the start and end tags is the element's content. An element can contain text (such as Adam's To Do List in this case) or other HTML elements. Here is an example of an element from Listing 3-4 that contains other HTML elements:

```
...
<div class="row">
    <div class="col font-weight-bold">Task</div>
    <div class="col-2 font-weight-bold">Done</div>
</div>
...
```

The outer element is known as the *parent*, while the elements it contains are known as *children*. Being able to create a hierarchy of elements is an essential HTML feature, which allows complex layouts to be created. The parent-child relationship is expanded in a large HTML document such that a single element can be an antecedent to many other elements, all of which are its descendants.

Understanding Element Content Restrictions

Some elements have restrictions on the types of elements that can be their children. The div elements shown in the previous section can contain any other element and are used to add structure, often so that content can be easily styled. Other elements have more specific roles that require specific types of elements to be used as children. For example, a tbody element, which you will see in later chapters and which represents the body of a table, can contain only one or more tr elements, each of which represents a table row.

■ **Tip**   Don't worry about learning all of the HTML elements and their relationships. You will pick up everything you need to know as you follow the examples in later chapters, and most code editors will display a warning if you try to create invalid HTML.

Understanding Void Elements

There are some elements that are not allowed to contain anything at all. These are called *void* or *self-closing* elements, and they are written without a separate end tag, like this:

```
...
<input />
...
```

A void element is defined in a single tag, and you add a / character before the last angle bracket (the > character). The element shown here is the most common example of a void element, and it is used to gather data from the user in HTML forms. You will see many examples of void elements in later chapters.

Understanding Attributes

You can provide additional information to the browser by adding *attributes* to your elements. Here is the attribute that was applied to the h4 element illustrated in Figure 3-2:

```
...
<h4 class="bg-primary text-white text-center p-2">
    Adam's To Do List
</h4>
...
```

Attributes are always defined as part of the start tag, and most attributes have a name and a value, separated by an equal sign, as illustrated in Figure 3-3.

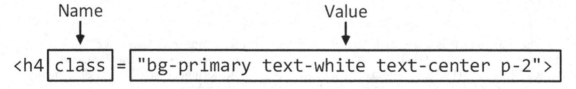

Figure 3-3. *The name and value of an attribute*

The name of this attribute is class, which is used to group related elements together, typically so that their appearance can be managed consistently. This is why the class attribute has been used in this example and the attribute value associates the h4 element with a number of classes that relate to styles provided by the Bootstrap CSS package, which I describe later in the chapter.

Quoting Literal Values in Attributes

Vue.js relies on HTML element attributes to apply a lot of its functionality. Most of the time, the values of attributes are evaluated as JavaScript expressions, such as with this element, taken from Listing 3-4:

```
...
<div class="row" v-for="t in tasks" v-bind:key="t.action">
...
```

The attribute values contain fragments of JavaScript. The value for the v-for attribute is an expression that will enumerate the objects in an array called tasks and assign each of them to a temporary variable called t. The tasks array is provided in the script element in Listing 3-4, but there will be occasions when you need to provide a specific value rather than have Vue.js read a value from the script element, and this requires additional quote characters to tell JavaScript that it is dealing with a literal value, like this:

```
...
<h3 v-on:click="name = 'Clicked'">{{ name }}</h3>
...
```

This element is from Chapter 14, and the value for the attribute is an expression that assigns the literal string Clicked to a property called name. To denote the literal value, Clicked is surrounded by single quotes (the ' character), which prevents Vue.js from looking for a Clicked value in the script element.

Applying Attributes Without Values

Not all attributes require a value; just defining them sends a signal to the browser that you want a certain kind of behavior associated with the element. Here is an example of an element with such an attribute, which you can find in Chapter 25:

```
...
<transition enter-active-class="animated fadeIn"
    leave-active-class=" animated fadeOut" mode="out-in"
    appear appear-active-class="animated zoomIn">
        <router-view />
</transition>
...
```

This is an element to which many attributes have been applied, but notice that the appear attribute doesn't have a value. It is the presence of the attribute that has an effect, and no value is required.

Examining the Live HTML Document

If you want to see the underlying HTML used by a web page, you may be used to right-clicking in the browser window and selecting View Page Source from the pop-up window (or a similarly named menu item if you are not using Google Chrome). But if you do that when the browser is displaying the example application, you won't see the HTML for the list of to-do items. Instead, you will see the following:

```html
<!DOCTYPE html>
<html>
  <head>
    <meta charset="utf-8">
    <meta http-equiv="X-UA-Compatible" content="IE=edge">
    <meta name="viewport" content="width=device-width,initial-scale=1.0">
    <link rel="icon" href="/favicon.ico">
    <title>htmlcssprimer</title>
    <link as="script" href="/app.js" rel="preload">
</head>
  <body>
    <noscript>
      <strong>
          We're sorry but htmlcssprimer doesn't work properly without
          JavaScript enabled. Please enable it to continue.
      </strong>
    </noscript>
    <div id="app"></div>
    <!-- built files will be auto injected -->
  <script type="text/javascript" src="/app.js"></script></body>
</html>
```

You need to use the browser's developer tools to see the HTML elements produced by a Vue.js application. When the application runs, its JavaScript code is executed, and that produces the content you see in the browser window.

Most browsers open their developer tools when the F12 key is pressed (which is why they are often called the F12 tools), but there is usually a menu option or an item on the pop-up menu that appears when you right-click in the browser window. For Google Chrome, this is the Inspect menu item, which opens the developer tools and focuses on the HTML element you clicked.

Figure 3-4 shows the developer tools display after I right-clicked the Collect Tickets text in the browser window and selected Inspect from the pop-up menu. It shows the HTML elements generated by the application, including their content, attributes, and details of the CSS styles that affect them.

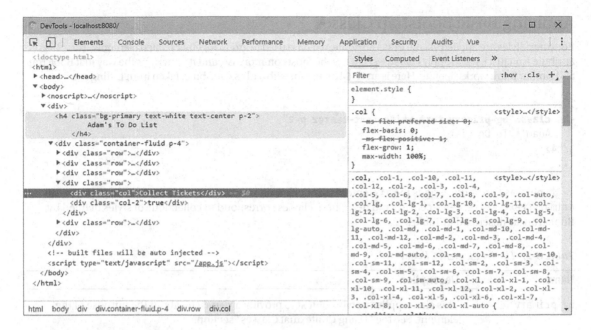

Figure 3-4. Inspecting an HTML element

The view presented by the F12 developer tools is live, meaning that changes to the content generated by the Vue.js application will be reflected in the elements you see. This is a good way of figuring out how your application behaves, especially when you don't get the results you expect.

Understanding Bootstrap

HTML elements tell the browser what kind of content they represent, but they don't provide any information about how that content should be displayed. The information about how to display elements is provided using *Cascading Style Sheets* (CSS). CSS consists of a comprehensive set of *properties*, which can be used to configure every aspect of an element's appearance, and a set of *selectors*, which allow those properties to be applied.

One of the main problems with CSS is that some browsers interpret properties slightly differently, which can lead to variations in the way that HTML content is displayed on different devices. It can be difficult to track down and correct these problems, and CSS frameworks have emerged to help web app developers style their HTML content in a simple and consistent way.

The most popular CSS framework is Bootstrap, which was originally developed at Twitter but has become a widely used open source project. Bootstrap consists of a set of CSS classes that can be applied to elements to style them consistently and some optional JavaScript code that performs additional enhancement (but which I do not use in this book). I use Bootstrap in my own projects; it works well across browsers, and it is simple to use. I use the Bootstrap CSS styles in this book because they let me style my examples without having to define and then list my own custom CSS in each chapter. Bootstrap provides a lot more features than the ones I use in this book; see http://getbootstrap.com for full details.

I don't want to get into too much detail about Bootstrap because it isn't the topic of this book, but I do want to give you enough information so you can tell which parts of an example are Vue.js features and which are related to Bootstrap.

Applying Basic Bootstrap Classes

Bootstrap styles are applied via the class attribute, which is used to group together related elements. The class attribute isn't just used to apply CSS styles, but it is the most common use, and it underpins the way that Bootstrap and similar frameworks operate. Here is an HTML element with a class attribute, taken from Listing 3-4:

```
...
<h4 class="bg-primary text-white text-center p-2">
    Adam's To Do List
</h4>
...
```

The class attribute assigns the h4 element to four classes, whose names are separated by spaces: bg-primary, text-white, text-center, and p-2. These classes correspond to collections of styles defined by Bootstrap, as described in Table 3-2.

Table 3-2. *The h4 Element Classes*

Name	Description
bg-primary	This class applies a style context to provide a visual cue about the purpose of the element. See the "Using Contextual Classes" section.
text-white	This class applies a style that sets the text color for the element's content to white.
text-center	This class applies a style that horizontally centers the element's content.
p-2	This class applies a style that adds spacing around the element's content, as described in the "Using Margin and Padding" section.

Using Contextual Classes

One of the main advantages of using a CSS framework like Bootstrap is to simplify the process of creating a consistent theme throughout an application. Bootstrap defines a set of *style contexts* that are used to style related elements consistently. These contexts, which are described in Table 3-3, are used in the names of the classes that apply Bootstrap styles to elements.

Table 3-3. *The Bootstrap Style Contexts*

Name	Description
primary	This context is used to indicate the main action or area of content.
secondary	This context is used to indicate the supporting areas of content.
success	This context is used to indicate a successful outcome.
info	This context is used to present additional information.
warning	This context is used to present warnings.
danger	This context is used to present serious warnings.
muted	This context is used to de-emphasize content.
dark	This context is used to increase contrast by using a dark color.
white	This context is used to increase contrast by using white.

Bootstrap provides classes that allow the style contexts to be applied to different types of elements. The h4 element with which I started this section has been added to the bg-primary class, which sets the background color of an element to indicate that it is related to the main purpose of the application. Other classes are specific to a certain set of elements, such as btn-primary, which is used to configure button and a elements so they appear as buttons whose colors are consistent with other elements in the primary context. Some of these context classes must be applied in conjunction with other classes that configure the basic style of an element, such as the btn class, which is combined with the btn-primary class.

Using Margin and Padding

Bootstrap includes a set of utility classes that are used to add *padding*, which is space between an element's edge and its content, and *margin*, which is space between an element's edge and the surrounding elements. The benefit of using these classes is that they apply a consistent amount of spacing throughout the application.

The names of these classes follow a well-defined pattern. Here is the h4 element from Listing 3-4:

```
...
<h4 class="bg-primary text-white text-center p-2">
    Adam's To Do List
</h4>
...
```

The classes that apply margin and padding to elements follow a well-defined naming schema: first, the letter m (for margin) or p (for padding), followed by an optional letter selecting specific edges (t for top, b for bottom, l for left, or r for right), then a hyphen, and, finally, a number indicating how much space should be applied (0 for no spacing, or 1, 2, 3, 4 or 5 for increasing amounts). If there is no letter to specify edges, then the margin or padding will be applied to all edges. To help put this schema in context, the p-2 class to which the h4 element has been added applies padding level 2 to all of the element's edges.

Using Bootstrap to Create Grids

Bootstrap provides style classes that can be used to create different kinds of grid layout, ranging from one to twelve columns and with support for responsive layouts, where the layout of the grid changes based on the width of the screen. I use the grid layout for many of the examples in this book, including the component in Listing 3-4, which presents its to-do items using this layout, like this:

```
...
<div class="container-fluid p-4">
    <div class="row">
        <div class="col font-weight-bold">Task</div>
        <div class="col-2 font-weight-bold">Done</div>
    </div>
<div class="row" v-for="t in tasks" v-bind:key="t.action">
    <div class="col">{{t.action}}</div>
        <div class="col-2">{{t.done}}</div>
    </div>
</div>
...
```

The Bootstrap grid layout system is simple to use. A top-level div element is assigned to the container class (or the container-fluid class if you want it to span the available space). You specify a column by applying the row class to a div element, which has the effect of setting up the grid layout for the content that the div element contains.

Each row defines 12 columns, and you specify how many columns each child element will occupy by assigning a class whose name is col- followed by the number of columns. For example, the class col-1 specifies that an element occupies one column, col-2 specifies two columns, and so on, right through to col-12, which specifies that an element fills the entire row. If you omit the number of columns and just assign an element to the col class, then Bootstrap will allocate an equal amount of the remaining columns.

Using Bootstrap to Style Tables

Bootstrap includes support for styling table elements and their contents, which is a feature I use in some of the examples in later chapters. Table 3-4 lists the key Bootstrap classes for working with tables.

Table 3-4. *The Bootstrap CSS Classes for Tables*

Name	Description
table	Applies general styling to a table element and its rows
table-striped	Applies alternate-row striping to the rows in the table body
table-bordered	Applies borders to all rows and columns
table-sm	Reduces the spacing in the table to create a more compact layout

All these classes are applied directly to the table element, as shown in Listing 3-6, where I have replaced the grid layout with a table.

Listing 3-6. Using a Table Layout in the App.vue File in the src Folder

```
<template>
    <div>
        <h4 class="bg-primary text-white text-center p-2">
            Adam's To Do List
        </h4>

        <table class="table table-striped table-bordered table-sm">
            <thead>
                <tr><th>Task</th><th>Done</th></tr>
            </thead>
            <tbody>
                <tr v-for="t in tasks" v-bind:key="t.action">
                    <td>{{t.action}}</td>
                    <td>{{t.done}}</td>
                </tr>
            </tbody>
        </table>
    </div>
</template>
```

```
<script>
    export default {
        data: function () {
            return {
                tasks: [{ action: "Buy Flowers", done: false },
                { action: "Get Shoes", done: false },
                { action: "Collect Tickets", done: true },
                { action: "Call Joe", done: false }]
            }
        }
    }
</script>
```

■ **Tip**   Notice that I have used the `thead` element when defining the tables in Listing 3-6. Browsers will automatically add any `tr` elements that are direct descendants of `table` elements to a `tbody` element if one has not been used. You will get odd results if you rely on this behavior when working with Bootstrap, and it is always a good idea to use the full set of elements when defining a table.

Figure 3-5 shows the result of using a table instead of a grid to display to-do items.

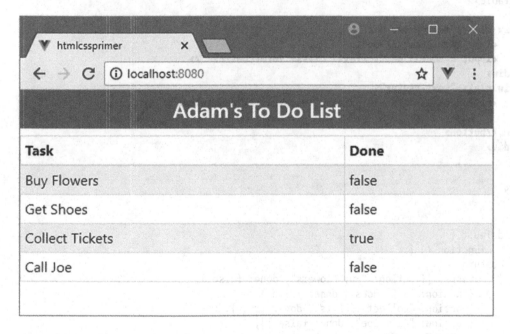

Figure 3-5. *Styling an HTML table*

Using Bootstrap to Style Forms

Bootstrap includes styling for form elements, allowing them to be styled consistently with other elements in the application. In Listing 3-7, I have added form elements to the example application.

Listing 3-7. Adding Form Elements in the App.vue File in the src Folder

```
<template>
    <div>
        <h4 class="bg-primary text-white text-center p-2">
            Adam's To Do List
        </h4>

        <table class="table table-striped table-bordered table-sm">
            <thead>
                <tr><th>Task</th><th>Done</th></tr>
            </thead>
            <tbody>
                <tr v-for="t in tasks" v-bind:key="t.action">
                    <td>{{t.action}}</td>
                    <td>{{t.done}}</td>
                </tr>
            </tbody>
        </table>

        <div class="form-group m-2">
            <label>New Item:</label>
            <input v-model="newItemText" class="form-control" />
        </div>
        <div class="text-center">
            <button class="btn btn-primary" v-on:click="addNewTodo">
                Add
            </button>
        </div>

    </div>
</template>

<script>
    export default {
        data: function () {
            return {
                tasks: [{ action: "Buy Flowers", done: false },
                { action: "Get Shoes", done: false },
                { action: "Collect Tickets", done: true },
                { action: "Call Joe", done: false }],
                newItemText: ""
            }
        },
```

```
        methods: {
            addNewTodo() {
                this.tasks.push({
                    action: this.newItemText,
                    done: false
                });
                this.newItemText = "";
            }
        }
    }
</script>
```

The basic styling for forms is achieved by applying the form-group class to a div element that contains a label and an input element, where the input element is assigned to the form-control class. Bootstrap styles the elements so that the label is shown above the input element and the input element occupies 100 percent of the available horizontal space, as shown in Figure 3-6.

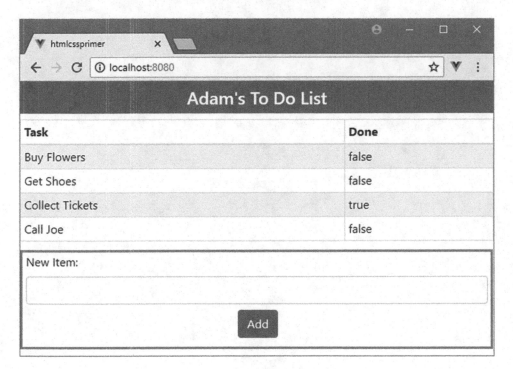

Figure 3-6. *Styling form elements*

Summary

In this chapter, I provided a brief overview of HTML and the Bootstrap CSS framework. You need to have a good grasp of HTML and CSS to be truly effective in web application development, but the best way to learn is by firsthand experience, and the descriptions and examples in this chapter will be enough to get you started and provide just enough background information for the examples ahead. In the next chapter, I continue the primer theme and introduce the most important JavaScript I use in this book.

CHAPTER 4

■ ■ ■

Essential JavaScript Primer

In this chapter, I provide a quick tour of the most important features of the JavaScript language as they apply to Vue.js development. I don't have the space to describe JavaScript completely, so I have focused on the essentials that you'll need to get up to speed and follow the examples in this book. Table 4-1 summarizes the chapter.

Table 4-1. *Chapter Summary*

Problem	Solution	Listing
Provide instructions that will be executed by the browser	Use JavaScript statements	5
Delay execution of statements until they are required	Use JavaScript functions	6–8, 11, 12
Define functions with variable numbers of parameters	Use default and rest parameters	9, 10
Express functions concisely	Use fat arrow functions	14
Define variables and constants	Use the let and const keywords	15, 16
Use the JavaScript primitive types	Use the string, number, or boolean keywords	17, 18, 20
Define strings that include other values	Use template strings	19
Execute statements conditionally	Use the if and else and switch keywords	21
Compare values and identities	Use the equality and identity operators	22, 23
Convert types	Use the type conversion keywords	24–26
Group related items	Define an array	27, 28
Read or change a value in an array	Use the index accessor notation	29, 30
Enumerate the contents of an array	Use a for loop or the forEach method	31
Expand the contents of an array	Use the spread operator	32, 33
Process the contents of an array	Use the built-in array method	34
Gather related values into a single unit	Define an object	35–37

(continued)

© Adam Freeman 2018
A. Freeman, *Pro Vue.js 2*, https://doi.org/10.1007/978-1-4842-3805-9_4

Table 4-1. (*continued*)

Problem	Solution	Listing
Define an operation that can be performed on the values of an object	Define a method	38, 39
Copy properties and value from one object to another	Use the `Object.assign` method	40
Group related features	Define a JavaScript module	41–49
Observe an asynchronous operation	Define a `Promise` and use the `async` and `await` keywords	50–54

Preparing for This Chapter

For this chapter, I need a simple Vue.js project. I started by running the command shown in Listing 4-1 to create a project called `jsprimer`.

■ **Tip**   You can download the example project for this chapter—and for all the other chapters in this book—from `https://github.com/Apress/pro-vue-js-2`.

Listing 4-1.   Creating the Example Project

```
vue create jsprimer --default
```

The project will be created, and the packages required for the application and the development tools will be downloaded and installed, which can take some time to complete.

■ **Note**   At the time of writing, the `@vue/cli` package has been released in beta. There may be small changes made before the final release, but the core features should remain the same. For details of any breaking changes, check the errata for this book, available at `https://github.com/Apress/pro-vue-js-2`.

Once the project has been created, use your preferred editor to replace the contents of the `main.js` file in the `src` folder with the single statement shown in Listing 4-2. For this chapter, the focus is on JavaScript rather than Vue.js, and the existing code is not required because it initializes a Vue.js application.

Listing 4-2.   Replacing the Content of the main.js File in the src Folder

```
console.log("Hello");
```

This project requires a configuration change to override the default settings for the project. Add the statements shown in Listing 4-3 to the `project.json` file, which is responsible for configuring the project and which I describe in Chapter 10.

Listing 4-3. Changing the Project Configuration in the package.json File in the jsprimer Folder

```
...
"eslintConfig": {
  "root": true,
  "env": {
    "node": true
  },
  "extends": [
    "plugin:vue/essential",
    "eslint:recommended"
  ],
  "rules": {
    "no-console": "off",
    "no-declare": "off",
    "no-unused-vars": "off"
  },
  "parserOptions": {
    "parser": "babel-eslint"
  }
},
"postcss": {
  "plugins": {
    "autoprefixer": {}
  }
},
...
```

These changes disable warnings about JavaScript features that I use in the examples in this chapter, produced by the JavaScript linter, which I describe in Chapter 10.

Save the changes to the main.js and package.json files; then open a new command prompt and run the commands shown in Listing 4-4 to navigate to the project folder and start the Vue.js development tools. Even though I am not using Vue.js features in this chapter, I am going to take advantage of the Vue.js toolchain, which simplifies the process of executing JavaScript code in the browser.

Listing 4-4. Starting the Vue.js Development Tools

```
cd jsprimer
npm run serve
```

The initial preparation of the project will take a moment, after which you will see a message telling you that the application is ready. Open a new browser window and navigate to http://localhost:8080, which will produce the empty window shown in Figure 4-1.

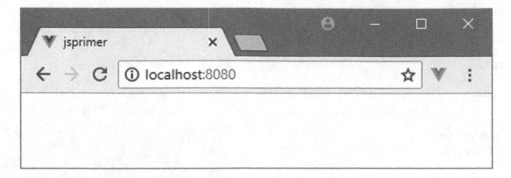

Figure 4-1. *Running the example application*

If you open the browser's F12 development tools and inspect the Console tab, you will see that the statement in Listing 4-2 has produced a simple result, as shown in Figure 4-2.

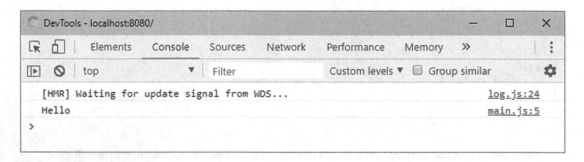

Figure 4-2. *A message in the browser's console*

All the examples in this chapter produce text output, so rather than show screenshots of the Console tab, I will use just the text, like this:

```
[HMR] Waiting for update signal from WDS...
Hello
```

The first line is a message from the development tool that automatically reloads the browser when a change in the src folder is detected. I won't include this in the output from subsequent examples.

Using Statements

The basic JavaScript building block is the *statement*. Each statement represents a single command, and statements are usually terminated by a semicolon (;). The semicolon is optional, but using them makes your code easier to read and allows for multiple statements on a single line. In Listing 4-5, I have added statements to the JavaScript file.

Listing 4-5. Adding JavaScript Statements in the main.js File in the src Folder

```
console.log("Hello");
console.log("Apples");
console.log("This is a statement");
console.log("This is also a statement");
```

The browser executes each statement in turn. In this example, all the statements simply write messages to the console. The results are as follows:

```
Hello
Apples
This is a statement
This is also a statement
```

Defining and Using Functions

When the browser receives JavaScript code, it executes the statements it contains in the order in which they are defined. This is what happened in the previous example. The statements in the main.js file were executed one by one, all of which wrote a message to the console, all in the order in which they were defined in the main.js. You can also package statements into a *function*, which won't be executed until the browser encounters a statement that *invokes* that function, as shown in Listing 4-6.

Listing 4-6. Defining a JavaScript Function in the main.js File in the src Folder

```
const myFunc = function () {
    console.log("This statement is inside the function");
};

console.log("This statement is outside the function");

myFunc();
```

Defining a function simple: use the `const` keyword followed by the name you want to give the function, followed by the equal sign (=) and the `function` keyword, followed by parentheses (the (and) characters). The statements you want the function to contain are enclosed between braces (the { and } characters).

In the listing, I used the name `myFunc`, and the function contains a single statement that writes a message to the JavaScript console. The statement in the function won't be executed until the browser reaches another statement that calls the `myFunc` function, like this:

```
...
myFunc();
...
```

When you save the changes to the main.js file, the updated JavaScript code will be sent to the browser, where it is executed and produces the following output:

```
This statement is outside the function
This statement is inside the function
```

You can see that the statement inside the function isn't executed immediately, but other than demonstrating how functions are defined, this example isn't especially useful because the function is invoked immediately after it has been defined. Functions are much more useful when they are invoked in response to some kind of change or event, such as user interaction.

You can also define functions so you don't have to explicitly create and assign a variable, as shown in Listing 4-7.

Listing 4-7. Defining a Function in the main.js File in the src Folder

```
function myFunc() {
    console.log("This statement is inside the function");
}

console.log("This statement is outside the function");

myFunc();
```

The code works in the same way as Listing 4-6 but is more familiar for most developers and is the way that I typically define functions in this book because it fits well into Vue.js development.

USING MODERN JAVASCRIPT FEATURES

JavaScript has been modernized in recent years with the addition of convenient language features and a substantial expansion of the utility functions available for common tasks such as array handling. Not all browsers support the latest features, so the Vue.js development tools include the Babel package, which is responsible for transforming JavaScript written using the latest features into code that can be relied on to work in most mainstream browsers. This means you are able to enjoy a modern development experience without needing to pay attention to dealing with the differences between browsers and keeping track of the features each supports. This translation is specific to the JavaScript language, and it doesn't extend to the broader set of APIs that you might want to use in your applications, such as the Local Storage feature I used in Chapter 1. For this type of feature, you will need to consider the browsers that your application must reach and whether the APIs you desire are available. A good place to start is caniuse.com, which will give you a good insight into the levels of support for an extensive set of APIs and related features.

Defining Functions with Parameters

JavaScript allows you to define parameters for functions, as shown in Listing 4-8.

Listing 4-8. Defining Functions with Parameters in the main.js File in the src Folder

```
function myFunc(name, weather) {
    console.log("Hello" + name + ".");
    console.log("It is" + weather + "today.");
}

myFunc("Adam", "sunny");
```

I added two parameters to the myFunc function, called name and weather. JavaScript is a dynamically typed language, which means you don't have to declare the data type of the parameters when you define the function. I'll come back to dynamic typing later in the chapter when I cover JavaScript variables. To invoke a function with parameters, you provide values as arguments when you invoke the function, like this:

```
...
myFunc("Adam", "sunny");
...
```

The results from this listing are as follows:

```
Hello Adam.
It is sunny today.
```

Using Default and Rest Parameters

The number of arguments you provide when you invoke a function doesn't need to match the number of parameters in the function. If you call the function with fewer arguments than it has parameters, then the value of any parameters you have not supplied values for is undefined, which is a special JavaScript value. If you call the function with more arguments than there are parameters, then the additional arguments are ignored.

The consequence of this is that you can't create two functions with the same name and different parameters and expect JavaScript to differentiate between them based on the arguments you provide when invoking the function. This is called *polymorphism*, and although it is supported in languages such as Java and C#, it isn't available in JavaScript. Instead, if you define two functions with the same name, then the second definition replaces the first.

There are two ways that you can modify a function to respond to a mismatch between the number of parameters it defines and the number of arguments used to invoke it. *Default parameters* deal with the situation where there are fewer arguments than parameters, and they allow you to provide a default value for the parameters for which there are no arguments, as shown in Listing 4-9.

Listing 4-9. Using a Default Parameter in the main.js File in the src Folder

```
function myFunc(name, weather = "raining") {
    console.log("Hello" + name + ".");
    console.log("It is" + weather + "today.");
}

myFunc("Adam");
```

The weather parameter in the function has been assigned a default value of raining, which will be used if the function is invoked with only one argument, producing the following results:

```
Hello Adam.
It is raining today.
```

Rest parameters are used to capture any additional arguments when a function is invoked with additional arguments, as shown in Listing 4-10.

Listing 4-10. Using a Rest Parameter in the main.js File in the src Folder

```
function myFunc(name, weather, ...extraArgs) {
    console.log("Hello" + name + ".");
    console.log("It is" + weather + "today.");
    for (let i = 0; i < extraArgs.length; i++) {
        console.log("Extra Arg:" + extraArgs[i]);
    }
}

myFunc("Adam", "sunny", "one", "two", "three");
```

The rest parameter must be the last parameter defined by the function, and its name is prefixed with an ellipsis (three periods, . . .). The rest parameter is an array to which any extra arguments will be assigned. In the listing, the function prints out each extra argument to the console, producing the following results:

```
Hello Adam.
It is sunny today.
Extra Arg: one
Extra Arg: two
Extra Arg: three
```

Defining Functions That Return Results

You can return results from functions using the return keyword. Listing 4-11 shows a function that returns a result.

Listing 4-11. Returning a Result from a Function in the main.js File in the src Folder

```
function myFunc(name) {
    return ("Hello" + name + ".");
}

console.log(myFunc("Adam"));
```

This function defines one parameter and uses it to produce a result. I invoke the function and pass the result as the argument to the console.log function, like this:

```
...
console.log(myFunc("Adam"));
...
```

Notice that you don't have to declare that the function will return a result or denote the data type of the result. The result from this listing is as follows:

```
Hello Adam.
```

Using Functions as Arguments to Other Functions

JavaScript functions can be treated as objects, which means you can use one function as the argument to another, as demonstrated in Listing 4-12.

Listing 4-12. Using a Function as an Arguments in the main.js File in the src Folder

```
function myFunc(nameFunction) {
    return ("Hello" + nameFunction() + ".");
}

console.log(myFunc(function () {
    return "Adam";
}));
```

The myFunc function defines a parameter called nameFunction that it invokes to get the value to insert into the string it returns. I pass a function that returns Adam as the argument to myFunc, which produces the following output:

```
Hello Adam.
```

Functions can be chained together, building up more complex functionality from small and easily tested pieces of code, as shown in Listing 4-13.

Listing 4-13. Chaining Functions Calls in the main.js File in the src Folder

```
function myFunc(nameFunction) {
    return ("Hello" + nameFunction() + ".");
}

function printName(nameFunction, printFunction) {
    printFunction(myFunc(nameFunction));
}

printName(function () { return "Adam" }, console.log);
```

This example produces the following output:

```
Hello Adam.
```

Using Arrow Functions

Arrow functions—also known as *fat arrow functions* or *lambda expressions*—are an alternative way of defining functions and are often used to define functions that are used only as arguments to other functions. Listing 4-14 replaces the functions from the previous example with arrow functions.

Listing 4-14. Using Arrow Functions in the main.js File in the src Folder

```
const myFunc = (nameFunction) => ("Hello" + nameFunction() + ".");

const printName = (nameFunction, printFunction) =>
    printFunction(myFunc(nameFunction));

printName(function () { return "Adam" }, console.log);
```

These functions perform the same work as the ones in Listing 4-13. There are three parts to an arrow function: the input parameters, then an equal sign and a greater-than sign (the "arrow"), and finally the function result. The return keyword and curly braces are required only if the arrow function needs to execute more than one statement. There are more examples of arrow functions later in this chapter, and you will see them used throughout the book.

■ **Caution**   Arrow functions cannot be used for all Vue.js features. Pay close attention to the examples in later chapters and use the type of function that is shown.

Using Variables and Types

The let keyword is used to declare variables and, optionally, assign a value to the variable in a single statement—as opposed to the const keyword I used in earlier examples, which creates a constant value that cannot be modified.

When you use let or const, the variable or constant that you create can be accessed only in the region of code in which they are defined, which is known as the variable or constant's *scope* and which is demonstrated in Listing 4-15.

Listing 4-15. Using let to Declare Variables in the main.js File in the src Folder

```
function messageFunction(name, weather) {
    let message = "Hello, Adam";
    if (weather == "sunny") {
        let message = "It is a nice day";
        console.log(message);
    } else {
        let message = "It is" + weather + "today";
        console.log(message);
    }
    console.log(message);
}

messageFunction("Adam", "raining");
```

In this example, there are three statements that use the let keyword to define a variable called message. The scope of each variable is limited to the region of code that it is defined in, producing the following results:

```
It is raining today
Hello, Adam
```

This may seem like an odd example, but there is another keyword that can be used to declare variables: var. The let and const keywords are relatively new additions to the JavaScript specification that is intended to address some oddities in the way var behaves. Listing 4-16 takes the example from Listing 4-15 and replaces let with var.

USING LET AND CONST

It is good practice to use the const keyword for any value that you don't expect to change so that you receive an error if any modifications are attempted. This is a practice that I rarely follow, however—in part because I am still struggling to adapt to not using the var keyword and in part because I write code in a range of languages and there are some features that I avoid because they trip me up when I switch from one to another. If you are new to JavaScript, then I recommend trying to use const and let correctly and avoiding following my poor behavior.

Listing 4-16. Using var to Declare Variables in the main.js File in the src Folder

```
function messageFunction(name, weather) {
    var message = "Hello, Adam";
    if (weather == "sunny") {
        var message = "It is a nice day";
        console.log(message);
    } else {
        var message = "It is" + weather + "today";
        console.log(message);
    }
    console.log(message);
}

messageFunction("Adam", "raining");
```

When you save the changes in the listing, you will see the following results:

```
It is raining today
It is raining today
```

The problem is that the var keyword creates variables whose scope is the containing function, which means that all the references to message are referring to the same variable. This can cause unexpected results for even experienced JavaScript developers and is the reason that the more conventional let keyword was introduced.

```
┌──────────────────────────────────────────────────────────────┐
│                  USING VARIABLE CLOSURE                        │
└──────────────────────────────────────────────────────────────┘
```

If you define a function inside another function—creating *inner* and *outer* functions—then the inner function is able to access the outer function's variables, using a feature called *closure*, like this:

```
function myFunc(name) {
    let myLocalVar = "sunny";
    let innerFunction = function () {
        return ("Hello" + name + ". Today is" + myLocalVar + ".");
    }
    return innerFunction();

}

console.log(myFunc("Adam"));
```

The inner function in this example is able to access the local variables of the outer function, including its parameter. This is a powerful feature that means you don't have to define parameters on inner functions to pass around data values, but caution is required because it is easy to get unexpected results when using common variable names like `counter` or `index`, where you may not realize that you are reusing a variable name from the outer function.

Using the Primitive Types

JavaScript defines a basic set of primitive types: `string`, `number`, `boolean`. This may seem like a short list, but JavaScript manages to fit a lot of flexibility into these types.

■ **Tip**   I am simplifying here. There are three other primitives that you may encounter. Variables that have been declared but not assigned a value are `undefined`, while the `null` value is used to indicate that a variable has no value, just as in other languages. The final primitive type is `Symbol`, which is an immutable value that represents a unique ID but which is not widely used at the time of writing.

Working with Booleans

The boolean type has two values: `true` and `false`. Listing 4-17 shows both values being used, but this type is most useful when used in conditional statements, such as an `if` statement. There is no console output from this listing.

Listing 4-17. Defining boolean Values in the main.js File in the src Folder

```
let firstBool = true;
let secondBool = false;
```

Working with Strings

You define `string` values using either the double quote or single quote characters, as shown in Listing 4-18.

Listing 4-18. Defining string Variables in the main.js File in the src Folder

```
let firstString = "This is a string";
let secondString = 'And so is this';
```

The quote characters you use must match. You can't start a string with a single quote and finish with a double quote, for example. There is no console output for this listing. JavaScript provides `string` objects with a basic set of properties and methods, the most useful of which are described in Table 4-2.

Table 4-2. Useful string Properties and Methods

Name	Description
length	This property returns the number of characters in the string.
charAt(index)	This method returns a string containing the character at the specified index.
concat(string)	This method returns a new string that concatenates together the string on which the method is called and the string provided as an argument.
indexOf(term, start)	This method returns the first index at which term appears in the string or -1 if there is no match. The optional start argument specifies the start index for the search.
replace(term, newTerm)	This method returns a new string in which all instances of term are replaced with newTerm.
slice(start, end)	This method returns a substring containing the characters between the start and end indices.
split(term)	This method splits up a string into an array of values that were separated by term.
toUpperCase() toLowerCase()	These methods return new strings in which all the characters are uppercase or lowercase.
trim()	This method returns a new string from which all the leading and trailing whitespace characters have been removed.

Using Template Strings

A common programming task is to combine static content with data values to produce a string that can be presented to the user. The traditional way to do this is through string concatenation, which is the approach I have been using in the examples so far in this chapter, as follows:

```
...
let message = "It is" + weather + "today";
...
```

JavaScript also supports *template strings*, which allow data values to be specified inline, which can help reduce errors and result in a more natural development experience. Listing 4-19 shows the use of a template string.

Listing 4-19. Using a Template String in the main.js File in the src Folder

```
function messageFunction(weather) {
    let message = `It is ${weather} today`;
    console.log(message);
}

messageFunction("raining");
```

Template strings begin and end with backticks (the ` character), and data values are denoted by curly braces preceded by a dollar sign. This string, for example, incorporates the value of the weather variable into the template string:

```
...
let message = `It is ${weather} today`;
...
```

This example produces the following output:

```
It is raining today
```

Working with Numbers

The number type is used to represent both *integer* and *floating-point* numbers (also known as *real numbers*). Listing 4-20 provides a demonstration.

Listing 4-20. Defining number Values in the main.js File in the src Folder

```
let daysInWeek = 7;
let pi = 3.14;
let hexValue = 0xFFFF;
```

You don't have to specify which kind of number you are using. You just express the value you require, and JavaScript will act accordingly. In the listing, I have defined an integer value, defined a floating-point value, and prefixed a value with 0x to denote a hexadecimal value.

Using JavaScript Operators

JavaScript defines a largely standard set of operators. I've summarized the most useful in Table 4-3.

Table 4-3. *Useful JavaScript Operators*

Operator	Description
++, --	Pre- or post-increment and decrement
+, -, *, /, %	Addition, subtraction, multiplication, division, remainder
<, <=, >, >=	Less than, less than or equal to, more than, more than or equal to
==, !=	Equality and inequality tests
===, !==	Identity and nonidentity tests
&&, ||	Logical AND and OR (|| is used to coalesce null values)
=	Assignment
+	String concatenation
?:	Three operand conditional statement

Using Conditional Statements

Many of the JavaScript operators are used in conjunction with conditional statements. In this book, I tend to use the if/else and switch statements. Listing 4-21 shows the use of both, which will be familiar to most developers.

Listing 4-21. Using Conditional Statements in the main.js File in the src Folder

```
let name = "Adam";

if (name == "Adam") {
    console.log("Name is Adam");
} else if (name == "Jacqui") {
    console.log("Name is Jacqui");
} else {
    console.log("Name is neither Adam or Jacqui");
}

switch (name) {
    case "Adam":
        console.log("Name is Adam");
        break;
    case "Jacqui":
        console.log("Name is Jacqui");
        break;
    default:
        console.log("Name is neither Adam or Jacqui");
        break;
}
```

This example produces the following results:

```
Name is Adam
Name is Adam
```

The Equality Operator vs. the Identity Operator

The equality and identity operators are of particular note. The equality operator will attempt to coerce (convert) operands to the same type to assess equality. This is a handy feature, as long as you are aware it is happening. Listing 4-22 shows the equality operator in action.

Listing 4-22. Using the Equality Operator in the main.js File in the src Folder

```
let firstVal = 5;
let secondVal = "5";

if (firstVal == secondVal) {
    console.log("They are the same");
} else {
    console.log("They are NOT the same");
}
```

The output from this example is as follows:

```
They are the same
```

JavaScript is converting the two operands into the same type and comparing them. In essence, the equality operator tests that values are the same irrespective of their type. If you want to test to ensure that the values *and* the types are the same, then you need to use the identity operator (===, three equal signs, rather than the two of the equality operator), as shown in Listing 4-23.

Listing 4-23. Using the Identity Operator in the main.js File in the src Folder

```
let firstVal = 5;
let secondVal = "5";

if (firstVal === secondVal) {
    console.log("They are the same");
} else {
    console.log("They are NOT the same");
}
```

In this example, the identity operator will consider the two variables to be different. This operator doesn't coerce types. The result is as follows:

```
They are NOT the same
```

Explicitly Converting Types

The string concatenation operator (+) has precedence over the addition operator (also +), which means that JavaScript will concatenate variables in preference to adding. This can cause confusion because JavaScript will also convert types freely to produce a result—and not always the result that is expected, as shown in Listing 4-24.

Listing 4-24. String Concatenation Operator Precedence in the main.js File in the src Folder

```
let myData1 = 5 + 5;
let myData2 = 5 + "5";

console.log("Result 1:" + myData1);
console.log("Result 2:" + myData2);
```

These statements produce the following result:

```
Result 1: 10
Result 2: 55
```

The second result is the kind that causes confusion. What might be intended to be an addition operation is interpreted as string concatenation through a combination of operator precedence and over-eager type conversion. To avoid this, you can explicitly convert the types of values to ensure you perform the right kind of operation, as described in the following sections.

Converting Numbers to Strings

If you are working with multiple number variables and want to concatenate them as strings, then you can convert the numbers to strings with the toString method, as shown in Listing 4-25.

Listing 4-25. Using the number.toString Method in the main.js File in the src Folder

```
let myData1 = (5).toString() + String(5);

console.log("Result:" + myData1);
```

Notice that I placed the numeric value in parentheses, and then I called the toString method. This is because you have to allow JavaScript to convert the literal value into a number before you can call the methods that the number type defines. I have also shown an alternative approach to achieve the same effect, which is to call the String function and pass in the numeric value as an argument. Both of these techniques have the same effect, which is to convert a number to a string, meaning that the + operator is used for string concatenation and not addition. The output from this script is as follows:

```
Result: 55
```

There are some other methods that allow you to exert more control over how a number is represented as a string. I briefly describe these methods in Table 4-4. All of the methods shown in the table are defined by the number type.

Table 4-4. *Useful Number-to-String Methods*

Method	Description
toString()	This method returns a string that represents a number in base 10.
toString(2) toString(8) toString(16)	This method returns a string that represents a number in binary, octal, or hexadecimal notation.
toFixed(n)	This method returns a string representing a real number with n digits after the decimal point.
toExponential(n)	This method returns a string that represents a number using exponential notation with one digit before the decimal point and n digits after.
toPrecision(n)	This method returns a string that represents a number with n significant digits, using exponential notation if required.

Converting Strings to Numbers

The complementary technique is to convert strings to numbers so that you can perform addition rather than concatenation. You can do this with the Number function, as shown in Listing 4-26.

Listing 4-26. Converting Strings to Numbers in the main.js File in the src Folder

```
let firstVal = "5";
let secondVal = "5";

let result = Number(firstVal) + Number(secondVal);
console.log("Result:" + result);
```

The output from this script is as follows:

```
Result: 10
```

The Number function is strict in the way that it parses string values, but there are two other functions you can use that are more flexible and will ignore trailing non-number characters. These functions are parseInt and parseFloat. I have described all three methods in Table 4-5.

Table 4-5. *Useful String to Number Methods*

Method	Description
Number(str)	This method parses the specified string to create an integer or real value.
parseInt(str)	This method parses the specified string to create an integer value.
parseFloat(str)	This method parses the specified string to create an integer or real value.

Working with Arrays

JavaScript arrays work like arrays in most other programming languages. Listing 4-27 shows how you can create and populate an array.

Listing 4-27. Creating and Populating an Array in the main.js File in the src Folder

```
let myArray = new Array();
myArray[0] = 100;
myArray[1] = "Adam";
myArray[2] = true;
```

I have created a new array by calling new Array(). This creates an empty array, which I assign to the variable myArray. In the subsequent statements, I assign values to various index positions in the array. (There is no output from this listing.)

There are a couple of things to note in this example. First, I didn't need to declare the number of items in the array when I created it. JavaScript arrays will resize themselves to hold any number of items. The second point is that I didn't have to declare the data types that the array will hold. Any JavaScript array can hold any mix of data types. In the example, I have assigned three items to the array: a number, a string, and a boolean.

Using an Array Literal

The array literal style lets you create and populate an array in a single statement, as shown in Listing 4-28.

Listing 4-28. Using the Array Literal Style in the main.js File in the src Folder

```
let myArray = [100, "Adam", true];
```

In this example, I specified that the myArray variable should be assigned a new array by specifying the items I wanted in the array between square brackets ([and]). (There is no console output from this listing.)

Reading and Modifying the Contents of an Array

You read the value at a given index using square braces ([and]), placing the index you require between the braces, as shown in Listing 4-29.

Listing 4-29. Reading the Data from an Array Index in the main.js File in the src Folder

```
let myArray = [100, "Adam", true];

console.log(`Index 0: ${myArray[0]}`);
```

You can modify the data held in any position in a JavaScript array simply by assigning a new value to the index. Just as with regular variables, you can switch the data type at an index without any problems. The output from the listing is as follows:

```
Index 0: 100
```

Listing 4-30 demonstrates modifying the contents of an array.

Listing 4-30. Modifying the Contents of an Array in the main.js File in the src Folder

```
let myArray = [100, "Adam", true];
myArray[0] = "Tuesday";

console.log(`Index 0: ${myArray[0]}`);
```

In this example, I have assigned a string to position 0 in the array, a position that was previously held by a number and produces this output:

```
Index 0: Tuesday
```

Enumerating the Contents of an Array

You enumerate the content of an array using a for loop or using the forEach method, which receives a function that is called to process each element in the array. Both approaches are shown in Listing 4-31.

Listing 4-31. Enumerating the Contents of an Array in the main.js File in the src Folder

```
let myArray = [100, "Adam", true];

for (let i = 0; i < myArray.length; i++) {
    console.log(`Index ${i}: ${myArray[i]}`);
}

console.log("---");

myArray.forEach((value, index) => console.log(`Index ${index}: ${value}`));
```

The JavaScript for loop works just the same way as loops in many other languages. You determine how many elements there are in the array by using the length property.

The function passed to the forEach method is given two arguments: the value of the current item to be processed and the position of that item in the array. In this listing, I have used an arrow function as the argument to the forEach method, and this is the kind of use for which they excel (and you will see used throughout this book). The output from the listing is as follows:

```
Index 0: 100
Index 1: Adam
Index 2: true
---
Index 0: 100
Index 1: Adam
Index 2: true
```

Using the Spread Operator

The spread operator is used to expand an array so that its contents can be used as function arguments. Listing 4-32 defines a function that accepts multiple arguments and invokes it using the values in an array with and without the spread operator.

Listing 4-32. Using the Spread Operator in the main.js File in the src Folder

```
function printItems(numValue, stringValue, boolValue) {
    console.log(`Number: ${numValue}`);
    console.log(`String: ${stringValue}`);
    console.log(`Boolean: ${boolValue}`);
}

let myArray = [100, "Adam", true];

printItems(myArray[0], myArray[1], myArray[2]);

printItems(...myArray);
```

The spread operator is an ellipsis (a sequence of three periods), and it causes the array to be unpacked and passed to the printItems function as individual arguments.

```
...
printItems(...myArray);
...
```

The spread operator also makes it easy to concatenate arrays together, as shown in Listing 4-33.

Listing 4-33. Concatenating Arrays in the main.js File in the src Folder

```
let myArray = [100, "Adam", true];
let myOtherArray = [200, "Bob", false, ...myArray];

myOtherArray.forEach((value, index) => console.log(`Index ${index}: ${value}`));
```

Using the spread operator, I am able to specify myArray as an item when I define myOtherArray, with the result that the contents of the first array will be unpacked and added as items to the second array. This example produces the following results:

```
Index 0: 200
Index 1: Bob
Index 2: false
Index 3: 100
Index 4: Adam
Index 5: true
```

Using the Built-in Array Methods

The JavaScript Array object defines a number of methods that you can use to work with arrays, the most useful of which are described in Table 4-6.

Table 4-6. *Useful Array Methods*

Method	Description
concat(otherArray)	This method returns a new array that concatenates the array on which it has been called with the array specified as the argument. Multiple arrays can be specified.
join(separator)	This method joins all the elements in the array to form a string. The argument specifies the character used to delimit the items.
pop()	This method removes and returns the last item in the array.
shift()	This method removes and returns the first element in the array.
push(item)	This method appends the specified item to the end of the array.
unshift(item)	This method inserts a new item at the start of the array.
reverse()	This method returns a new array that contains the items in reverse order.
slice(start,end)	This method returns a section of the array.
sort()	This method sorts the array. An optional comparison function can be used to perform custom comparisons.
splice(index, count)	This method removes count items from the array, starting at the specified index. The removed items are returned as the result of the method.
unshift(item)	This method inserts a new item at the start of the array.
every(test)	This method calls the test function for each item in the array and returns true if the function returns true for all of them and false otherwise.
some(test)	This method returns true if calling the test function for each item in the array returns true at least once.
filter(test)	This method returns a new array containing the items for which the test function returns true.
find(test)	This method returns the first item in the array for which the test function returns true.
findIndex(test)	This method returns the index of the first item in the array for which the test function returns true.
forEach(callback)	This method invokes the callback function for each item in the array, as described in the previous section.
includes(value)	This method returns true if the array contains the specified value.
map(callback)	This method returns a new array containing the result of invoking the callback function for every item in the array.
reduce(callback)	This method returns the accumulated value produced by invoking the callback function for every item in the array.

Since many of the methods in Table 4-6 return a new array, these methods can be chained together to process data, as shown in Listing 4-34.

Listing 4-34. Processing an Array in the main.js File in the src Folder

```
let products = [
    { name: "Hat", price: 24.5, stock: 10 },
    { name: "Kayak", price: 289.99, stock: 1 },
    { name: "Soccer Ball", price: 10, stock: 0 },
    { name: "Running Shoes", price: 116.50, stock: 20 }
];

let totalValue = products
    .filter(item => item.stock > 0)
    .reduce((prev, item) => prev + (item.price * item.stock), 0);

console.log(`Total value: $$${totalValue.toFixed(2)}`);
```

I use the `filter` method to select the items in the array whose `stock` value is greater than zero and use the reduce method to determine the total value of those items, producing the following output:

```
Total value: $2864.99
```

Working with Objects

There are several ways to create objects in JavaScript. Listing 4-35 gives a simple example to get started.

Listing 4-35. Creating an Object in the main.js File in the src Folder

```
let myData = new Object();
myData.name = "Adam";
myData.weather = "sunny";

console.log(`Hello ${myData.name}.`);
console.log(`Today is ${myData.weather}.`);
```

I create an object by calling `new Object()`, and I assign the result (the newly created object) to a variable called myData. Once the object is created, I can define properties on the object just by assigning values, like this:

```
...
myData.name = "Adam";
...
```

Prior to this statement, my object doesn't have a property called name. When the statement has executed, the property does exist, and it has been assigned the value Adam. You can read the value of a property by combining the variable name and the property name with a period, like this:

```
...
console.log(`Hello ${myData.name}.`);
...
```

The result from the listing is as follows:

```
Hello Adam.
Today is sunny.
```

Using Object Literals

You can define an object and its properties in a single step using the object literal format, as shown in Listing 4-36.

Listing 4-36. Using the Object Literal Format in the main.js File in the src Folder

```
let myData = {
    name: "Adam",
    weather: "sunny"
};

console.log(`Hello ${myData.name}.`);
console.log(`Today is ${myData.weather}.`);
```

Each property that you want to define is separated from its value using a colon (:), and properties are separated using a comma (,). The effect is the same as in the previous example, and the result from the listing is as follows:

```
Hello Adam.
Today is sunny.
```

Using Variables as Object Properties

If you use a variable as an object property, JavaScript will use the variable name as the property name and the variable value as the property value, as shown in Listing 4-37.

Listing 4-37. Using a Variable in an Object Literal in the main.js File in the src Folder

```
let name = "Adam"

let myData = {
  name,
  weather: "sunny"
};

console.log(`Hello ${myData.name}.`);
console.log(`Today is ${myData.weather}.`);
```

The name variable is used to add a property to the myData object; the property is called name, and its value is Adam. This is a useful technique when you want to combine a set of data values into an object, and you will see it used in examples in later chapters. The code in Listing 4-37 produces the following output:

```
Hello Adam.
Today is sunny.
```

Using Functions as Methods

One of the features that I like most about JavaScript is the way you can add functions to objects. A function defined on an object is called a *method*. Listing 4-38 shows how you can add methods in this manner.

Listing 4-38. Adding Methods to an Object in the main.js File in the src Folder

```
let myData = {
    name: "Adam",
    weather: "sunny",
    printMessages: function () {
        console.log(`Hello ${myData.name}.`);
        console.log(`Today is ${myData.weather}.`);
    }
};

myData.printMessages();
```

In this example, I have used a function to create a method called printMessages. Notice that to refer to the properties defined by the object, I have to use the this keyword. When a function is used as a method, the function is implicitly passed the object on which the method has been called as an argument through the special variable this. The output from the listing is as follows:

```
Hello Adam.
Today is sunny.
```

You can also define methods without using the function keyword, as shown in Listing 4-39.

Listing 4-39. Defining a Method in the main.js File in the src Folder

```
let myData = {
    name: "Adam",
    weather: "sunny",
    printMessages() {
        console.log(`Hello ${myData.name}.`);
        console.log(`Today is ${myData.weather}.`);
    }
};

myData.printMessages();
```

This is a more natural way to define methods, at least to my mind, and I have used this approach in many of the examples in this book. The output from this listing is as follows:

```
Hello Adam.
Today is sunny.
```

Copying Properties from One Object to Another

In the examples in later chapters, I need to copy all of the properties from one object to another to demonstrate different Vue.js features. JavaScript provides the Object.assign method for this purpose, as demonstrated in Listing 4-40.

Listing 4-40. Copying Object Properties in the main.js File in the src Folder

```
let myData = {
    name: "Adam",
    weather: "sunny",
    printMessages() {
        console.log(`Hello ${myData.name}.`);
        console.log(`Today is ${myData.weather}.`);
    }
};

let secondObject = {};

Object.assign(secondObject, myData);

secondObject.printMessages();
```

This example creates a new object that has no properties and uses the Object.assign method to copy the properties—and their values—from the myData object. This example produces the following output:

```
Hello Adam.
Today is sunny.
```

Understanding JavaScript Modules

The examples in the previous chapter were contained in a single JavaScript file. This is fine for simple examples, but a complex web application can contain a large amount of code and content, which is impossible to manage in one file.

To break up an application into more manageable chunks, JavaScript supports *modules*, which contain JavaScript code that other parts of the application depend on. In the sections that follow, I explain the different ways that modules can be defined and used.

Creating and Using a Simple JavaScript Module

Modules are typically defined in their own folders, so I created the src/maths folder and added to it a file called sum.js, with the content shown in Listing 4-41.

Listing 4-41. The Contents of the sum.js File in the src/maths Folder

```
export default function(values) {
    return values.reduce((total, val) => total + val, 0);
}
```

The sum.js file contains a function that accepts an array of values and uses the JavaScript array reduce method to sum them and return the result. What's important about this example is not what it does but the fact that the function is defined in its own file, which is the basic building block for a module.

There are two keywords used in Listing 4-41 that you will often encounter when defining modules. The export keyword is used to denote the features that will be available outside the module. By default, the contents of the JavaScript file are private and must be explicitly shared using the export keyword before they can be used in the rest of the application. The default keyword is used when the module contains a single feature, such as the function used in Listing 4-41. Together, the export and default keywords are used to specify that the only function in the sum.js file is available for use in the rest of the application.

Using a Simple JavaScript Module

Another keyword is required to use a module: the import keyword. In Listing 4-42, I used the import keyword to access the function defined in the previous section so that it can be used in the main.js file.

Listing 4-42. Using a Simple JavaScript Module in the main.js File in the src Folder

```
import additionFunction from "./maths/sum";

let values = [10, 20, 30, 40, 50];

let total = additionFunction(values);

console.log(`Total: ${total}`);
```

The import keyword is used to declare a dependency on the module. The import keyword can be used in a number of ways, but this is the format you will use most often when working with modules you have created yourself. Figure 4-3 illustrates the key parts.

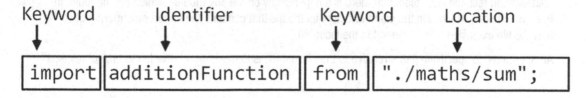

Figure 4-3. Declaring a dependency on a module

The import keyword is followed by an identifier, which is the name by which the function will be known by when it is used; the identifier in this example is additionFunction.

■ **Tip** Notice that it is the `import` statement in which the identifier is applied, which means that the code that consumes the function from the module chooses the name by which it will be known and that multiple `import` statements for the same module in different parts of the application can use different names to refer to the same function.

The `from` keyword follows the identifier, which is then followed by the location of the module. It is important to pay close attention to the location because different behaviors are created by different location formats, as described in the sidebar.

During the build process, the Vue.js tools will detect the `import` statement and include the function from the `sum.js` file in the JavaScript file that is sent to the browser so that it can execute the application. The identifier used in the `import` statement can be used to access the function in the module, in just the same way that locally defined functions are used.

```
...
let total = additionFunction(values);
...
```

If you examine the browser's JavaScript console, you will see that the code in Listing 4-42 uses the module's function to produce the following result:

```
Total: 150
```

UNDERSTANDING MODULE LOCATIONS

The location of a module changes the way that the build tools will look for the module when creating the JavaScript file that is sent to the browser. For modules you have defined yourself, the location is specified as a relative path, starting with one or two periods, indicating that the path is relative to the current file or to the current file's parent directory. In Listing 4-42, the location starts with a period.

```
...
import additionFunction from "./maths/sum";
...
```

This location tells the build tools that there is a dependency on the `sum` module, which can be found in the `maths` folder, which is in the same directory as the file that contains the import statement (notice that the file extension is not included in the location).

An alternative to specifying paths relative to the current file is to navigate relative to the project folder, like this:

```
...
import additionFunction from "@/maths/sum";
...
```

When a location is prefixed with the @ character, the module is located relative to the src folder.

If you omit the initial periods and the @ character, then the import statement declares a dependency on a module in the node_modules folder, which is where the packages installed during the project setup are installed. This kind of location is used to access features provided by third-party packages, including the Vue.js packages, which is why you will see statements like this in Vue.js projects:

```
...
import Vue from "vue";
...
```

The location for this import statement doesn't start with a period and will be interpreted as a dependency on the vue module in the project's node_modules folder, which is the package that provides the core Vue.js application features.

Defining Multiple Features in a Module

Modules can contain more than one function or value, which is useful for grouping related features. To demonstrate, I created a file called operations.js to the src/maths folder and added the code shown in Listing 4-43.

Listing 4-43. The Contents of the operations.js File in the src/maths Folder

```
export function multiply(values) {
    return values.reduce((total, val) => total * val, 1);
}

export function subtract(amount, values) {
    return values.reduce((total, val) => total - val, amount);
}

export function divide(first, second) {
    return first / second;
}
```

This module defines three functions to which the export keyword has been applied. Unlike the previous example, the default keyword is not used, and each function has its own name. A different approach is required when using a module that contains multiple functions, as shown in Listing 4-44.

Listing 4-44. Using a Module in the main.js File in the src Folder

```
import additionFunction from "./maths/sum";
import { multiply, subtract } from "./maths/operations";

let values = [10, 20, 30, 40, 50];

console.log(`Sum: ${additionFunction(values)}`);
console.log(`Multiply: ${multiply(values)}`);
console.log(`Subtract: ${subtract(1000, values)}`);
```

The braces that follow the import keyword surround the list of functions that I want to use, which is the multiply and subtract functions in this case, separated by commas. I only declare dependencies on the functions that I require, and there is no dependency on the divide function, which is defined in the module but not used in Listing 4-44. This example produces the following output:

```
Sum: 150
Multiply: 12000000
Subtract: 850
```

Changing Module Feature Names

One difference in this approach is that the names by which the functions are used are now defined by the module and not the code that uses the functions. If you don't want to use the names provided by the module, then you can specify a name using the as keyword, as shown in Listing 4-45.

Listing 4-45. Using a Module Alias in the main.js File in the src Folder

```
import additionFunction from "./maths/sum";
import { multiply, subtract as minus } from "./maths/operations";

let values = [10, 20, 30, 40, 50];

console.log(`Sum: ${additionFunction(values)}`);
console.log(`Multiply: ${multiply(values)}`);
console.log(`Subtract: ${minus(1000, values)}`);
```

I used the as keyword to specify that the subtract function should be given the name minus when imported into the main.js file. This listing produces the same output as Listing 4-44.

Importing an Entire Module

Listing the names of all the functions in a module gets out of hand for complex modules. A more elegant approach is to import all the features provided by a module and just use the features you require, as shown in Listing 4-46.

Listing 4-46. Importing an Entire Module in the main.js File in the src Folder

```
import additionFunction from "./maths/sum";
import * as ops from "./maths/operations";

let values = [10, 20, 30, 40, 50];

console.log(`Sum: ${additionFunction(values)}`);
console.log(`Multiply: ${ops.multiply(values)}`);
console.log(`Subtract: ${ops.subtract(1000, values)}`);
```

An asterisk is used to import everything in a module, followed by the as keyword and an identifier through which the module functions and values will be accessed. In this case, the identifier is ops, which means that the multiply, subtract, and divide functions can be accessed as ops.multiply, ops.subtract, and ops.divide. This listing produces the same output as Listing 4-44.

Combining Multiple Files in a Module

Modules can span multiple files and are combined by defining an index.js file that brings together the features that the module will provide to the rest of the application. I added an index.js file to the src/maths folder with the code shown in Listing 4-47.

Listing 4-47. The Contents of the index.js File in the src/maths Folder

```
import addition from "./sum";

export function mean(values) {
    return addition(values)/values.length;
}

export { addition };
export * from "./operations";
```

This file starts the same way as earlier examples with an import statement to declare a dependency on the function in the sum.js file, which is used in the exported function called mean.

The statement exports the function from the sum.js file so that it can be used outside of the module. I don't have to specify a location for this function since it has already been imported, and in this situation, the function is contained within braces.

The final statement exports all of the features defined in the operations.js file, without needing to import them first. This is useful when you want to make features available outside of the module but you don't need to use them directly in the index.js file.

Using an index.js file allows all the features to be imported in the main.js file in a single statement, as shown in Listing 4-48.

Listing 4-48. Importing an Entire Module in the main.js File in the src Folder

```
import * as math from "./maths";

let values = [10, 20, 30, 40, 50];

console.log(`Sum: ${math.addition(values)}`);
console.log(`Multiply: ${math.multiply(values)}`);
console.log(`Subtract: ${math.subtract(1000, values)}`);
console.log(`Mean: ${math.mean(values)}`);
```

The location for the import doesn't specify the file, which makes for a simplified statement. In this example, all the module features can be accessed through the math identifier without requiring any knowledge of which file in the module defines each feature. This example produces the following output:

```
Sum: 150
Multiply: 12000000
Subtract: 850
Mean: 30
```

Importing Individual Features from a Multifile Module

You don't have to import all the features from a module, even when it has been defined using several files. In Listing 4-49, I have changed the import statement so that only the functions that are used by the example are imported, and I have used the as keyword to demonstrate that functions can be renamed.

Listing 4-49. Importing Specific Features in the main.js File in the src Folder

```
import { addition as add, multiply, subtract, mean as average} from "./maths";

let values = [10, 20, 30, 40, 50];

console.log(`Add: ${add(values)}`);
console.log(`Multiply: ${multiply(values)}`);
console.log(`Subtract: ${subtract(1000, values)}`);
console.log(`Average : ${average(values)}`);
```

This example combines features from previous listings to import four functions from the module and rename two of them. This example produces the following output:

```
Add: 150
Multiply: 12000000
Subtract: 850
Average : 30
```

Understanding JavaScript Promises

A *promise* is a background activity that will be completed at some point in the future. The most common use for promises in this book is requesting data using an HTTP request, which is performed asynchronously and produces a result when a response is received from the web server.

Understanding the Asynchronous Operation Problem

The classic asynchronous operation for a web application is an HTTP request, which is typically used to get the data and content that a user requires. I'll get to the HTTP request shortly, but I need something simpler to get started, so I added a function to the index.js file in the maths module to perform a task asynchronously, as shown in Listing 4-50.

Listing 4-50. Adding a Function in the index.js File in the src/maths Folder

```
import addition from "./sum";

export function mean(values) {
    return addition(values)/values.length;
}

export { addition };
export * from "./operations";
```

```
export function asyncAdd(values) {
    setTimeout(() => {
        let total = addition(values);
        console.log(`Async Total: ${total}`);
        return total;
    }, 500);
}
```

The setTimeout function invokes a function asynchronously after a specified delay. In the listing, the asyncAdd function receives a parameter that is passed to the addition function after a delay of 500 milliseconds, creating a background operation that doesn't complete immediately for the examples in this chapter and representing more useful operations such as making an HTTP request. In Listing 4-51, I have updated the main.js file to use the asyncAdd function.

Listing 4-51. Performing Background Work in the main.js File in the src Folder

```
import { asyncAdd } from "./maths";

let values = [10, 20, 30, 40, 50];

let total = asyncAdd(values);

console.log(`Main Total: ${total}`);
```

The problem this example demonstrates is that the result from the asyncAdd function isn't produced until after the statements in the main.js file have been executed, which you can see in the output shown in the browser's JavaScript console:

```
Main Total: undefined
Async Total: 150
```

The browser executes the statements in the main.js file and invokes the asyncAdd function as instructed. The browser moves on to the next statement in the main.js file, which writes a message to the console using the result provided by asyncAdd—but this happens before the asynchronous task has been completed, which is why the output is undefined. The asynchronous task subsequently completes, but it is too late for the result to be used by the main.js file.

Using a JavaScript Promise

To solve the problem in the previous section, I need a mechanism that allows me to observe the asynchronous task so that I can wait for it to complete and then write out the result. This is the role of the JavaScript promise, which I have applied to the asyncAdd function in Listing 4-52.

Listing 4-52. Using a Promise in the index.js File in the src/maths Folder

```
import addition from "./sum";

export function mean(values) {
    return addition(values)/values.length;
}
```

```
export { addition };
export * from "./operations";

export function asyncAdd(values) {
    return new Promise((callback) => {
        setTimeout(() => {
            let total = addition(values);
            console.log(`Async Total: ${total}`);
            callback(total);
        }, 500);
    });
}
```

It can be difficult to unpack the functions in this example. The new keyword is used to create a Promise, which accepts the function that is to be observed. The observed function is provided with a callback that is invoked when the asynchronous task has completed and that accepts the result of the task as an argument. Invoking the callback function is known as *resolving* the promise.

The Promise object that has become the result of the asyncAdd function allows the asynchronous task to be observed so that follow-up work can be performed when the task completes, as shown in Listing 4-53.

Listing 4-53. Observing a Promise in the main.js File in the src Folder

```
import { asyncAdd } from "./maths";

let values = [10, 20, 30, 40, 50];

asyncAdd(values).then(total => console.log(`Main Total: ${total}`));
```

The then method accepts a function that will be invoked when the callback is used. The result passed to the callback is provided to the then function. In this case, that means the total isn't written to the browser's JavaScript console until the asynchronous task has completed and produces the following output:

```
Async Total: 150
Main Total: 150
```

Simplifying the Asynchronous Code

JavaScript provides two keywords—async and await—that support asynchronous operations without having to work directly with promises. In Listing 4-54, I have applied these keywords in the main.js file.

■ **Caution** It is important to understand that using async/await doesn't change the way that an application behaves. The operation is still performed asynchronously, and the result will not be available until the operation completes. These keywords are just a convenience to simplify working with asynchronous code so that you don't have to use the then method.

Listing 4-54. Using async and await in the main.js File in the src Folder

```
import { asyncAdd } from "./maths";

let values = [10, 20, 30, 40, 50];

async function doTask() {
    let total = await asyncAdd(values);
    console.log(`Main Total: ${total}`);
}

doTask();
```

These keywords can be applied only to functions, which is why I added the doTask function in this listing. The async keyword tells JavaScript that this function relies on functionality that requires a promise. The await keyword is used when calling a function that returns a promise and has the effect of assigning the result provided to the Promise object's callback and then executing the statements that follow, producing the following result:

```
Async Total: 150
Main Total: 150
```

Summary

In this chapter I provided a brief primer on JavaScript, focusing on the core functionality that will get you started for Vue.js development. In the next chapter, I start the process of building a more complex and realistic project, called SportsStore.

CHAPTER 5

■ ■ ■

SportsStore: A Real Application

Most of the chapters of this book contain small examples that are focused on a specific feature. This is a useful way to show you how different parts of Vue.js work, but there is sometimes a lack of context, and it can be hard to connect the features in one chapter with those in other chapters. To help overcome this problem, I am going to create a more complex application in this chapter and the chapters that follow.

My application, called SportsStore, will follow the classic approach taken by online stores everywhere. I will create an online product catalog that customers can browse by category and page, a shopping cart where users can add and remove products, and a checkout where customers can enter their shipping details and place their orders. I will also create an administration area that includes facilities for managing the catalog—and I will protect it so that only logged-in administrators can make changes. Finally, I show you how to prepare the application so that it can be deployed.

My goal in this chapter and those that follow is to give you a sense of what real Vue.js development is like by creating as realistic an example as possible. I want to focus on Vue.js, of course, and so I have simplified the integration with external systems, such as the back-end data server, and omitted others entirely, such as payment processing.

The SportsStore example is one that I use in a few of my books, not least because it demonstrates the ways in which different frameworks, languages, and development styles can be used to achieve the same result. You don't need to have read any of my other books to follow this chapter, but you will find the contrasts interesting if you already own my *Pro ASP.NET Core MVC 2 or Pro Angular* books, for example.

The Vue.js features that I use in the SportsStore application are covered in-depth in later chapters. Rather than duplicate everything here, I tell you just enough to make sense of the example application and refer you to other chapters for in-depth information. You can either read the SportsStore chapters end-to-end and get a sense of how Vue.js works or jump to and from the detail chapters to get into the depth.

■ **Caution** Don't expect to understand everything right away—Vue.js has a lot of moving parts, and the SportsStore application is intended to show you how they fit together without diving too deeply into the details that the rest of the book describes. If you get bogged down, then consider going to Part 2 of this book and starting to read about individual features and return to this chapter later.

Creating the SportsStore Project

The first step in any development effort is to create the project. Open a new command prompt, navigate to a convenient location, and run the command shown in Listing 5-1.

© Adam Freeman 2018
A. Freeman, *Pro Vue.js 2*, https://doi.org/10.1007/978-1-4842-3805-9_5

■ **Note**   At the time of writing, the `@vue/cli` package has been released in beta. There may be small changes made before the final release, but the core features should remain the same. For details of any breaking changes, check the errata for this book, available at `https://github.com/Apress/pro-vue-js-2`.

Listing 5-1. Creating the SportsStore Project

```
vue create sportsstore --default
```

The project will be created, and the packages required for the application and the development tools will be downloaded and installed, which can take some time to complete.

■ **Tip**   You can download the example project for this chapter—and for all of the other chapters in this book—from `https://github.com/Apress/pro-vue-js-2`.

Adding Additional Packages

Vue.js has a focus on core features that are supplemented by optional packages, some of which are developed by the main Vue.js team and others by interested third-parties. Most of the packages required for Vue.js development are added to the project automatically, but some additions are required for the SportsStore project. Run the commands shown in Listing 5-2 to navigate to the `sportsstore` folder and add the packages that are needed. (The npm tool can be used to add multiple packages in a single command, but I have separated out each package to make the names and versions easier to see.)

Listing 5-2. Adding Packages

```
cd sportsstore
npm install axios@0.18.0
npm install vue-router@3.0.1
npm install vuex@3.0.1
npm install vuelidate@0.7.4
npm install bootstrap@4.0.0
npm install font-awesome@4.7.0
npm install --save-dev json-server@0.12.1
npm install --save-dev jsonwebtoken@8.1.1
npm install --save-dev faker@4.1.0
```

It is important to use the version numbers shown in the listing. You may see warnings about unmet peer dependencies as you add the packages, but these can be ignored. The role that each package plays in the SportsStore application is described in Table 5-1. Some of the packages are installed using the `--save-dev` argument, which indicates they are used during development and will not be part of the SportsStore application.

Table 5-1. *The Additional Packages Required for the SportsStore Project*

Name	Description
axios	The Axios package is used to make HTTP requests to the web service that provides SportsStore with data and services. Axios is not specific to Vue.js, but it is a common choice for handling HTTP. I describe the use of Axios in Vue.js applications in Chapter 19.
vue-router	This package allows the application to display different content based on the browser's current URL. This process is known as URL routing, and I describe it in detail in Chapters 22–24.
vuex	This package is used to create a shared data store that simplifies managing data in a Vue.js project. I describe Vuex data stores in detail in Chapter 20.
veulidate	This package is used to validate the data that a user enters into form elements, as demonstrated in Chapter 6.
bootstrap	The Bootstrap package contains CSS styles that will be used to style the HTML content that the SportsStore application presented to the user.
font-awesome	The Font Awesome package contains a library of icons that SportsStore will use to denote important features to the user.
json-server	This package provides an easy-to-use RESTful web service for application development, and it is this package that will receive the HTTP requests made using Axios. This package is used in the JavaScript code added to the project in the "Preparing the RESTful Web Service" section of this chapter.
jsonwebtoken	This package is used to generate authorization tokens that will grant access to the SportsStore administration features, which are added to the project in Chapter 7.
faker	This package is used to generate test data, which I use in Chapter 7 to ensure that SportsStore can deal with large amounts of data.

■ **Note**   The vue-router and vuex packages can be installed automatically as part of the project template, but I have added them separately so that I can demonstrate how they are configured and applied to a Vue.js application. There is nothing wrong with using project tools to jump-start a project, but it is important that you understand how everything in a Vue.js project works so that you have a good idea of where to start looking when something goes wrong.

Incorporating the CSS Stylesheets into the Application

The Bootstrap and Font Awesome packages require `import` statements to be added to the `main.js` file, which is where the top-level configuration of the Vue.js application is performed. The `import` statements, shown in Listing 5-3, ensure that the content provided by these packages is incorporated into the application by the Vue.js development tools.

■ **Tip**   Don't worry about the rest of the statements in the `main.js` file at the moment. They are responsible for initializing the Vue.js application, which I explain in Chapter 9, but understanding how they function isn't essential to get started with Vue.js development.

Listing 5-3. Incorporating Packages in the main.js File in the src Folder

```
import Vue from 'vue'
import App from './App.vue'

Vue.config.productionTip = false

import "bootstrap/dist/css/bootstrap.min.css";
import "font-awesome/css/font-awesome.min.css"

new Vue({
    render: h => h(App)
}).$mount('#app')
```

These statements will let me use the CSS features that the packages provide throughout the application.

Preparing the RESTful Web Service

The SportsStore application will use asynchronous HTTP requests to get model data provided by a RESTful web service. As I describe in Chapter 19, REST is an approach to designing web services that use the HTTP method or verb to specify an operation and the URL to select the data objects that the operation applies to.

The `json-server` package that I added to the project in the previous section is an excellent tool for quickly generating web services from JSON data or JavaScript code. To ensure that there is a fixed state that the project can be reset to, I am going to take advantage of the feature that allows the RESTful web service to be provided with data using JavaScript code, which means that restarting the web service will reset the application data. I created a file called `data.js` in the `sportsstore` folder and added the code shown in Listing 5-4.

Listing 5-4. The Contents of the data.js File in the sportsstore Folder

```
var data = [{ id: 1, name: "Kayak", category: "Watersports",
        description: "A boat for one person", price: 275 },
    { id: 2, name: "Lifejacket", category: "Watersports",
        description: "Protective and fashionable", price: 48.95 },
    { id: 3, name: "Soccer Ball", category: "Soccer",
        description: "FIFA-approved size and weight", price: 19.50 },
    { id: 4, name: "Corner Flags", category: "Soccer",
        description: "Give your playing field a professional touch",
        price: 34.95 },
    { id: 5, name: "Stadium", category: "Soccer",
        description: "Flat-packed 35,000-seat stadium", price: 79500 },
    { id: 6, name: "Thinking Cap", category: "Chess",
        description: "Improve brain efficiency by 75%", price: 16 },
```

```
            { id: 7, name: "Unsteady Chair", category: "Chess",
                description: "Secretly give your opponent a disadvantage",
                price: 29.95 },
            { id: 8, name: "Human Chess Board", category: "Chess",
                description: "A fun game for the family", price: 75 },
            { id: 9, name: "Bling Bling King", category: "Chess",
                description: "Gold-plated, diamond-studded King", price: 1200 }]

module.exports = function () {
    return {
        products: data,
        categories: [...new Set(data.map(p => p.category))].sort(),
        orders: []
    }
}
```

This file is a JavaScript module that exports a default function, with two collections that will be presented by the RESTful web service. The products collection contains the products for sale to the customer, the categories collection contains the distinct category property values, and the orders collection contains the orders that customers have placed (but which is currently empty).

The data stored by the RESTful web service needs to be protected so that ordinary users can't modify the products or change the status of orders. The json-server package doesn't include any built-in authentication features, so I created a file called authMiddleware.js in the sportsstore folder and added the code shown in Listing 5-5.

Listing 5-5. The Contents of the authMiddleware.js File in the sportsstore Folder

```
const jwt = require("jsonwebtoken");

const APP_SECRET = "myappsecret";
const USERNAME = "admin";
const PASSWORD = "secret";

module.exports = function (req, res, next) {

    if ((req.url == "/api/login" || req.url == "/login")
            && req.method == "POST") {
        if (req.body != null && req.body.name == USERNAME
                && req.body.password == PASSWORD) {
            let token = jwt.sign({ data: USERNAME, expiresIn: "1h" }, APP_SECRET);
            res.json({ success: true, token: token });
        } else {
            res.json({ success: false });
        }
        res.end();
        return;
    } else if ((((req.url.startsWith("/api/products")
                || req.url.startsWith("/products"))
            || (req.url.startsWith("/api/categories")
                || req.url.startsWith("/categories"))) && req.method != "GET")
        || ((req.url.startsWith("/api/orders")
            || req.url.startsWith("/orders")) && req.method != "POST")) {
```

```
        let token = req.headers["authorization"];
        if (token != null && token.startsWith("Bearer<")) {
            token = token.substring(7, token.length - 1);
            try {
                jwt.verify(token, APP_SECRET);
                next();
                return;
            } catch (err) { }
        }
        res.statusCode = 401;
        res.end();
        return;
    }
    next();
}
```

This code inspects HTTP requests sent to the RESTful web service and implements some basic security features. This is server-side code that is not directly related to Vue.js development, so don't worry if its purpose isn't immediately obvious. I explain the authentication and authorization process in Chapter 7.

■ **Caution**   Don't use the code in Listing 5-5 other than for the SportsStore application. It contains weak passwords that are hardwired into the code. This is fine for the SportsStore project because the emphasis is on the development client side with Vue.js, but this is not suitable for real projects.

An addition is required to the package.json file so that the json-server package can be started from the command line, as shown in Listing 5-6.

Listing 5-6. Adding a Script to the package.json File in the SportsStore Folder

```
{
  "name": "sportsstore",
  "version": "0.1.0",
  "private": true,
  "scripts": {
    "serve": "vue-cli-service serve",
    "build": "vue-cli-service build",
    "lint": "vue-cli-service lint",
    "json": "json-server data.js -p 3500 -m authMiddleware.js"
  },
  "dependencies": {
    "axios": "^0.18.0",
    "bootstrap": "^4.0.0",
    "font-awesome": "^4.7.0",
    "vue": "^2.5.16",
    "vue-router": "^3.0.1",
    "vuex": "^3.0.1"
  },

  // ...other configuration settings omitted for brevity...

}
```

The package.json file is used to configure the project and its tools. The scripts section contains the commands that can be executed using the packages that have been added to the project.

Starting the Project Tools

All of the configuration for the project is complete, and it is time to start the tools that will be used for development and make sure everything works. Open a new command prompt, navigate to the sportsstore folder, and run the command shown in Listing 5-7 to start the web service.

Listing 5-7. Starting the SportsStore Web Service

```
npm run json
```

Open a new browser window and navigate to the URL http://localhost:3500/products/1 to test that the web service is working, which should produce the result shown in Figure 5-1.

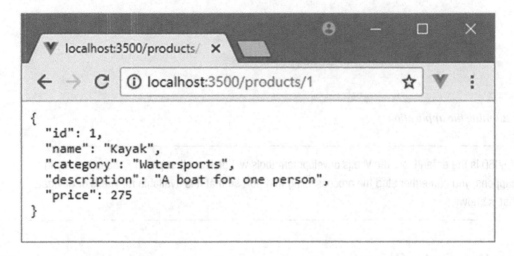

Figure 5-1. *Testing the web service*

Without stopping the web service, open a second command prompt, navigate to the sportsstore folder, and run the command shown in Listing 5-8 to start the Vue.js development tools.

Listing 5-8. Starting the Development Tools

```
npm run serve
```

The development HTTP server will be started, and the initial preparation process will be performed, after which you will see a message indicating that the application is running. Use the browser to navigate to http://localhost:8080, and you should see the content shown in Figure 5-2, which is a placeholder added when the project was created.

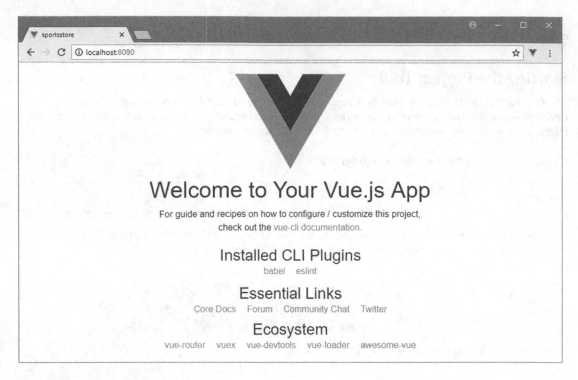

Figure 5-2. *Running the application*

■ **Tip** Port 8080 is the default, but the Vue.js development tools will pick another port if 8080 is already in use. If that happens, you can either stop the process using that port so that it is available for Vue.js or navigate to the URL that is shown.

Creating the Data Store

The best place to start with any new application is its data. In all but the simplest projects, the Vuex package is used to create a data store that is used to share data throughout the application, providing a common repository that ensures all parts of the application are using the same data values.

■ **Tip** Vuex isn't the only package that can be used to manage data in a Vue.js application, but it is developed by the core Vue.js team and is well-integrated into the rest of the Vue.js world. Unless you have a specific reason to do otherwise, you should use Vuex in your Vue.js projects.

Vuex data stores are generally defined as separate JavaScript modules, defined in their own directory. I created the src/store folder (which is the conventional name) and added to it a file called index.js with the content shown in Listing 5-9.

Listing 5-9. The Contents of the index.js File in the src/store Folder

```
import Vue from "vue";
import Vuex from "vuex";

Vue.use(Vuex);

const testData = [];

for (let i = 1; i <= 10; i++) {
    testData.push({
        id: i, name: `Product #${i}`, category: `Category ${i % 3}`,
        description: `This is Product #${i}`, price: i * 50
    })
}

export default new Vuex.Store({
    strict: true,
    state: {
        products: testData
    }
})
```

The import statements declare dependencies on the Vue.js and Vuex libraries. Vuex is distributed as a Vue.js plugin, which makes it easy to provide application-wide functionality in a project. I explain how plugins work in Chapter 26, but for the SportsStore application, it is enough to know that plugins must be enabled using the Vue.use method. If you forget to call the use method, then the data store features won't be available in the rest of the application.

A data store is created using the new keyword to create a Vuex.Store object, passing a configuration object. The purpose of the state property is used to define the data values contained in the store. To get the data store started, I have used a for loop to generate an array of test data that I have assigned to a state property named products. I'll replace this with data obtained from the web service in the "Using the RESTful Web Service" section, later in this chapter.

The purpose of the strict property is less obvious and relates to the unusual way that Vuex works. Data values are read-only and are modified only through mutations, which are just JavaScript methods that change the data. You'll see examples of mutations as I add features to the SportsStore application, and the strict mode is a useful feature that generates a warning if you forget to use a mutation and modify data values directly—something that happens often as you become used to the way that Vuex works.

To include the data store in the application, I added the statements shown in Listing 5-10 to the main.js file, which acts as the main point of configuration for the application.

Listing 5-10. Adding the Vuex Data Store in the main.js File in the src Folder

```
import Vue from 'vue'
import App from './App.vue'

Vue.config.productionTip = false

import "bootstrap/dist/css/bootstrap.min.css";
import "font-awesome/css/font-awesome.min.css"

import store from "./store";
```

```
new Vue({
    render: h => h(App),
    store
}).$mount('#app')
```

The import statement declares a dependency on the data store module and assigns it the store identifier. Adding the store property to the configuration property used to create the Vue object ensures that the data store features can be used throughout the application, as you will see as features are added to SportsStore.

■ **Caution** A common mistake is to add the import statement to the main.js file but forget to add the store property to the configuration object. This results in an error because the data store functionality won't be added to the application.

Creating the Product Store

The data store provides just enough of the application's infrastructure to allow me to start work on the most important user-facing feature: the product store. All online stores present the user with a selection of products to purchase, and SportsStore is no exception. The basic structure of the store will be a two-column layout, with category buttons that allow the list of products to be filtered and a table that contains the list of products, as illustrated by Figure 5-3.

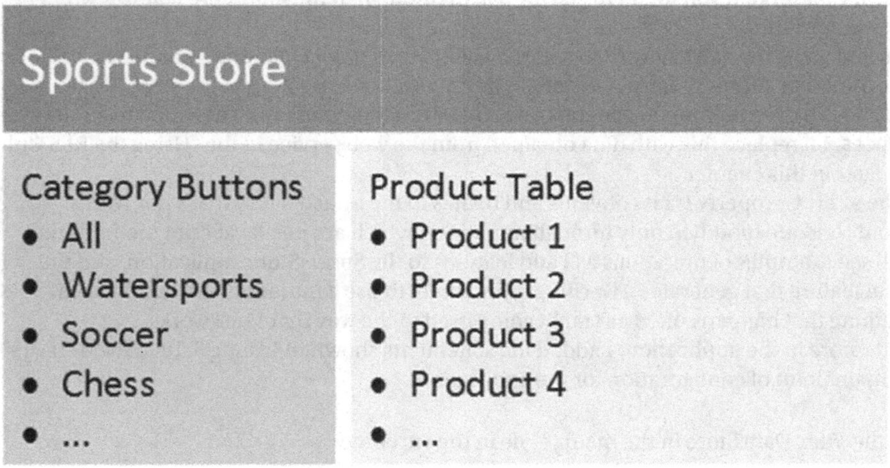

Figure 5-3. The basic structure of the store

The basic building block for Vue.js applications is the component. Components are defined in files with the .vue extension, and I started by creating a file called Store.vue in the src/components folder with the content shown in Listing 5-11.

Listing 5-11. The Contents of the Store.vue File in the src/components Folder

```
<template>
    <div class="container-fluid">
        <div class="row">
            <div class="col bg-dark text-white">
                <a class="navbar-brand">SPORTS STORE</a>
            </div>
        </div>
        <div class="row">
            <div class="col-3 bg-info p-2">
                <h4 class="text-white m-2">Categories</h4>
            </div>
            <div class="col-9 bg-success p-2">
                <h4 class="text-white m-2">Products</h4>
            </div>
        </div>
    </div>
</template>
```

This component contains only a `template` element at the moment, which I have used to define a basic layout using HTML elements styled with Bootstrap classes, which I described briefly in Chapter 3. There is nothing special about this content at the moment, but it corresponds to the structure shown in Figure 5-3 and provides me with a foundation as I build up the product store. In Listing 5-12, I have replaced the contents of the App.vue file, which allows me to replace the default content created when the project was set up with the Store component created in Listing 5-11.

Listing 5-12. Replacing the Contents of the App.vue File in the src Folder

```
<template>
    <store />
</template>

<script>
import Store from "./components/Store";

export default {
    name: 'app',
    components: { Store }
}
</script>
```

A Vue.js application usually contains a number of components, and in most projects, the App component, which is defined in the App.vue file, is responsible for deciding which of them should be displayed to the user. I demonstrate how this is done when I add the shopping cart and checkout features in Chapter 6, but the Store component is the only one I have defined so far, so this is the only one that can be shown to the user.

The `import` statement in the `script` element declares a dependency on the component from Listing 5-11 and assigns it the Store identifier, which is assigned to the components property, telling Vue.js that the App component uses the Store component.

When Vue.js processes the App component's template, it will replace the store element with the HTML in the template element in Listing 5-11, producing the result shown in Figure 5-4.

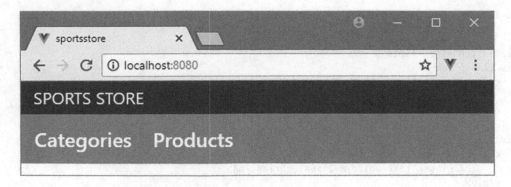

Figure 5-4. *Adding a custom component to the application*

Creating the Product List

The next step is to create a component that will display the list of products to the user. I added a file called ProductList.vue to the src/components folder with the content shown in Listing 5-13.

Listing 5-13. The Contents of the ProductList.vue File in the src/components Folder

```
<template>
    <div>
        <div v-for="p in products" v-bind:key="p.id" class="card m-1 p-1 bg-light">
            <h4>
                {{p.name}}
                <span class="badge badge-pill badge-primary float-right">
                    {{ p.price }}
                </span>
            </h4>
            <div class="card-text bg-white p-1">{{ p.description }}</div>
        </div>
    </div>
</template>

<script>

import { mapState } from "vuex";

export default {
    computed: {
        ...mapState(["products"])
    }
}
</script>
```

The script element imports the mapState function from the vuex package, which is used to provide access to the data in the store. There are different Vuex functions for different types of operation, and mapState is used to create a mapping between the component and state data in the data store. The mapState function is used with the spread operator because it can map multiple data store properties in a single operation, even though only the products state property is mapped in this example. Data store state properties are mapped as component computed properties, which I describe in detail in Chapter 11.

Vue.js uses a feature called *directives* to manipulate HTML elements. In the listing, I use the v-for directive, which duplicates an element and its contents for each item in an array.

```
...
<div v-for="p in products" v-bind:key="p.id" class="card m-1 p-1 bg-light">
...
```

The result of using the mapState function is that I can use the products property with the v-for directive to access the data in the data store, with the result that the same set of elements will be generated for each product. Each product is temporarily assigned to a variable named p, which I can use to customize the elements that are generated for each product, like this:

```
...
<div class="card-text bg-white p-1">{{ p.description }}</div>
...
```

The double braces (the {{ and }} characters) denote a data binding, which tells Vue.js to insert the specified data value into the HTML element when it is displayed to the user. I explain how data bindings work in Chapter 11, and I describe the v-for directive in detail in Chapter 13, but the result is that the value of the description property of the current product object will be inserted into the div element.

■ **Tip**   The v-for directive is applied alongside the v-bind directive, which is used to define an attribute whose value is produced through a data value or a fragment of JavaScript. In this case, the v-bind directive is used to create a key attribute, which the v-for directive uses to respond efficiently to changes in the application's data, as explained in Chapter 13.

Adding the Product List to the Application

Each component that you add to the project must be registered before it can be used to present content to the user. In Listing 5-14, I have registered the ProductList component in the Store component so that I can remove the placeholder content and replace it with the list of products.

Listing 5-14. Registering a Component in the Store.vue File in the src/components Folder

```
<template>
    <div class="container-fluid">
        <div class="row">
            <div class="col bg-dark text-white">
                <a class="navbar-brand">SPORTS STORE</a>
            </div>
        </div>
        <div class="row">
            <div class="col-3 bg-info p-2">
                <h4 class="text-white m-2">Categories</h4>
            </div>
```

```
            <div class="col-9 p-2 ">
                <product-list />
            </div>
        </div>
    </div>
</template>

<script>

import ProductList from "./ProductList";

export default {
    components: { ProductList }
}
</script>
```

When components are used together, they form a relationship. In this example, the Store component is the *parent* to the ProductList component, and, in return, the ProductList component is a child of the Store component. In the listing, I followed the same pattern to register the component as I did when added the Store component to the application: I imported the child component and added it to the parent component's components property, which allows me to use a custom HTML element to insert the child component's content into the parent component's template. In Listing 5-14, I inserted the contents of the ProductList component using a product-list element, which Vue.js understands as a common way to express multipart names (although I could also have used ProductList or productList for the HTML element tag instead).

The result is that the App component inserts the content from the Store component into its template, which contains the content from the ProductList component, producing the result shown in Figure 5-5.

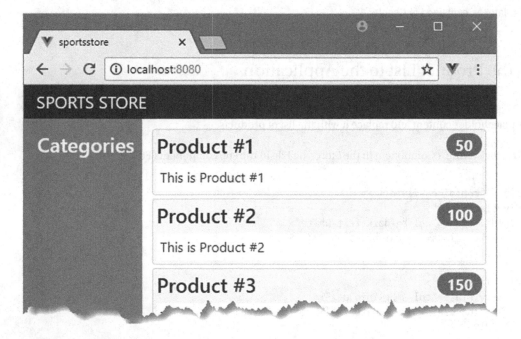

Figure 5-5. *Displaying a list of products*

Filtering the Price Data

Now that I have the basic list in place, I can start to add features. The first thing is to display the price property of each product as a currency amount, rather than just a number. Vue.js components can define *filters*, which are functions that are used to format data values. In Listing 5-15, I have added a filter to the ProductList component named currency that formats a data value into a dollar amount.

Listing 5-15. Defining a Filter in the ProductList.vue File in the src/components Folder

```
<template>
    <div>
        <div v-for="p in products" v-bind:key="p.id" class="card m-1 p-1 bg-light">
            <h4>
                {{p.name}}
                <span class="badge badge-pill badge-primary float-right">
                    {{ p.price | currency }}
                </span>
            </h4>
            <div class="card-text bg-white p-1">{{ p.description }}</div>
        </div>
    </div>
</template>

<script>

import { mapState } from "vuex";

export default {
    computed: {
        ...mapState(["products"])
    },
    filters: {
        currency(value) {
            return new Intl.NumberFormat("en-US",
                { style: "currency", currency: "USD" }).format(value);
        }
    }
}
</script>
```

Component features are grouped together using properties in the object defined in the script element. The ProductList component now defines two such properties: the computed property, which is providing access to the data in the data store, and the filters property, which is used to define filters. There is one filter in Listing 5-15, called currency, and it is defined as a function that accepts a value that uses the JavaScript localization features to format a numeric value as a U.S. dollar amount, expressed in the format used in the United States.

Filters are applied in the template by combining the name of a data value with the filter name, separated by a bar (the | character), like this:

```
...
<span class="badge badge-pill badge-primary float-right">
    {{ p.price | currency }}
</span>
...
```

When you save the changes to the ProductList.vue file, the browser will reload, and the prices will be formatted as shown in Figure 5-6.

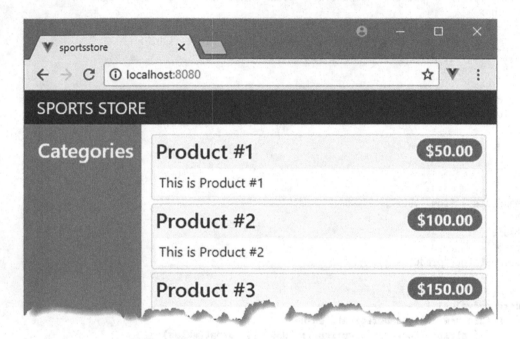

Figure 5-6. *Using a filter to format currency values*

Adding Product Pagination

The products are shown to the user in a continuous list, which will be overwhelming for the user as the number of products increases. To make the list of products more manageable, I am going to add support for pagination, where a specified number of products will be shown on a page and the user can move from one page to another to navigate through the products. The first step is to extend the data store so that details of the page size and the currently selected page are stored, which I have done in Listing 5-16.

Listing 5-16. Preparing for Pagination in the index.js File in the src/store Folder

```
import Vue from "vue";
import Vuex from "vuex";

Vue.use(Vuex);
```

```
const testData = [];
for (let i = 1; i <= 10; i++) {
    testData.push({
        id: i, name: `Product #${i}`, category: `Category ${i % 3}`,
        description: `This is Product #${i}`, price: i * 50
    })
}

export default new Vuex.Store({
    strict: true,
    state: {
        products: testData,
        productsTotal: testData.length,
        currentPage: 1,
        pageSize: 4
    },
    getters: {
        processedProducts: state => {
            let index = (state.currentPage -1) * state.pageSize;
            return state.products.slice(index, index + state.pageSize);
        },
        pageCount: state => Math.ceil(state.productsTotal / state.pageSize)
    },
    mutations: {
        setCurrentPage(state, page) {
            state.currentPage = page;
        },
        setPageSize(state, size) {
            state.pageSize = size;
            state.currentPage = 1;
        }
    }
})
```

The additions to the data store to support validation demonstrate some of the key features provided by the Vuex package. The first set of changes are new state properties, which define values for the number of products, the currently selected page, and the number of products to show on each page.

The getters section is for properties whose values are computed using state properties. In Listing 5-16, the getters section defines a processedProducts property, which returns only the products required for the current page, and a pageCount property, which works out how many pages are required to display the available product data.

The mutations section in Listing 5-16 is used to define methods that change the values of one or more state properties. There are two mutations in the listing: the setCurrentPage mutation changes the value of the currentPage property, and the setPageSize mutation sets the pageSize property.

The separation between standard data properties and computed properties is a theme that runs through Vue.js development because it allows for efficient change-detection. When a data property changes, Vue.js is able to determine the effect on the computed property and doesn't have to recalculate values when the underlying data has not changed. This is taken one step further by Vuex data stores, which require changes to data values to be performed through mutations, rather than by assigning a new value directly. This can feel awkward when you first start working with data stores, but it soon becomes second nature; in addition, following this pattern provides some useful features, such as the ability to track changes and undo/redo them using the Vue Devtools browser plugin, as described in Chapter 1.

■ **Tip** Notice that both the getters and the mutations in Listing 5-16 are defined as functions that receive a state object as their first parameter. This object is used to access the values defined in the state section of the data store, which cannot be accessed directly. See Chapter 20 for more details and examples.

Now that I have added the data and mutations to the data store, I can create a component that makes use of them. I added a file called PageControls.vue in the src/components folder with the content shown in Listing 5-17.

Listing 5-17. The Contents of the PageControls.vue File in the src/components Folder

```
<template>
    <div v-if="pageCount > 1" class="text-right">
        <div class="btn-group mx-2">
            <button v-for="i in pageNumbers" v-bind:key="i"
                    class="btn btn-secpmdary"
                    v-bind:class="{ 'btn-primary': i == currentPage }">
                {{ i }}
            </button>
        </div>
    </div>
</template>

<script>

    import { mapState, mapGetters } from "vuex";

    export default {
        computed: {
            ...mapState(["currentPage"]),
            ...mapGetters(["pageCount"]),
            pageNumbers() {
                return [...Array(this.pageCount + 1).keys()].slice(1);
            }
        }
    }
</script>
```

Not all of the pagination features are in place, but there is enough functionality here to get started. This component uses the mapState and mapGetters helper functions to provide access to the data store currentPage and pageCount properties. Not everything has to be defined in the data store, and the component defines a pageNumbers function that uses the pageCount property to generate a sequence of numbers that are used in the template to display buttons for the pages of products, which is done using the v-for directive, which is the same directive that I used in Listing 5-17 to generate a repeating set of elements in the product list.

■ **Tip** Data that is required by more than one part of the application should be placed in the data store, while data that is specific to a single component should be defined in its script element. I have put the pagination data in the store because I use it to request data from the web service in Chapter 7.

Earlier, I explained that the v-bind directive is used to define an attribute on an HTML element whose value is determined using a data value or a fragment of JavaScript code. In Listing 5-17, I used the v-bind directive to control the value of the class attribute, like this:

```
...
<button v-for="i in pageNumbers" v-bind:key="i" class="btn btn-secpmdary"
    v-bind:class="{ 'btn-primary': i == currentPage }">
...
```

Vue.js provides useful features for managing an element's class membership, which allows me to add the button element to the btn-primary class when it represents the current page of data, as I describe in detail in Chapter 12. The result is that the button that represents the active button has an obviously different appearance to the other page buttons, indicating to the user which page is being displayed.

To add the pagination component to the application, I used in import statement to declare a dependency and added it to the parent's component's property, as shown in Listing 5-18.

Listing 5-18. Applying Pagination in the ProductList.vue File in the src/components Folder

```
<template>
    <div>
        <div v-for="p in products" v-bind:key="p.id" class="card m-1 p-1 bg-light">
            <h4>
                {{p.name}}
                <span class="badge badge-pill badge-primary float-right">
                    {{ p.price | currency }}
                </span>
            </h4>
            <div class="card-text bg-white p-1">{{ p.description }}</div>
        </div>
        <page-controls />
    </div>
</template>

<script>

import { mapGetters} from "vuex";
import PageControls from "./PageControls";

export default {
    components: { PageControls },
    computed: {
        ...mapGetters({ products: "processedProducts" })
    },
    filters: {
        currency(value) {
            return new Intl.NumberFormat("en-US",
                { style: "currency", currency: "USD" }).format(value);
        }
    }
}
</script>
```

I also changed the source of the data that is displayed by the ProductList component, so that it comes from the data store's processedProducts getter, which means that only the products in the currently selected page will be displayed to the user. This use of the mapGetters helper function allows me to specify that the processedProducts getter will be mapped using the name products, which allows me to change the source of the data without having to make a corresponding change to the v-for expression in the template. When you save the changes, the browser will reload and display the pagination buttons shown in Figure 5-7.

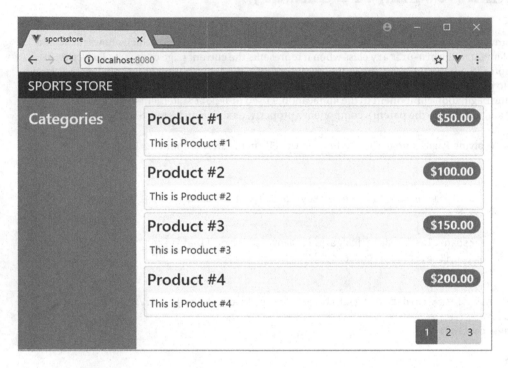

Figure 5-7. *Adding pagination buttons*

Changing the Product Page

To allow the user to change the page of products that the application displays, I need to respond when they click one of the page buttons. In Listing 5-19, I have used the v-on directive, which is used to respond to events, to respond when the click event is triggered by invoking the data store's setCurrentPage mutation.

Listing 5-19. Responding to Button Clicks in the PageControls.vue File in the src/components Folder

```
<template>
    <div class="text-right">
        <div class="btn-group mx-2">
            <button v-for="i in pageNumbers" v-bind:key="i"
                    class="btn btn-secpmdary"
                    v-bind:class="{ 'btn-primary': i == currentPage }"
                    v-on:click="setCurrentPage(i)">
                {{ i }}
            </button>
        </div>
```

```
    </div>
</template>

<script>

    import { mapState, mapGetters, mapMutations } from "vuex";

    export default {
        computed: {
            ...mapState(["currentPage"]),
            ...mapGetters(["pageCount"]),
            pageNumbers() {
                return [...Array(this.pageCount + 1).keys()].slice(1);
            }
        },
        methods: {
            ...mapMutations(["setCurrentPage"])
        }
    }
</script>
```

The mapMutations helper maps setCurrentPage to a component method, which is invoked by the v-on directive when the click event is received.

```
...
<button v-for="i in pageNumbers" v-bind:key="i" class="btn btn-secpmdary"
    v-bind:class="{ 'btn-primary': i == currentPage }"
    v-on:click="setCurrentPage(i)">
...
```

The type of event is specified as an argument to the directive, which is separated from the directive name using a colon. The expression for this directive tells Vue.js to invoke the setCurrentPage method and to use the temporary variable i, which indicates the page that the user wants to display. The setCurrentPage is mapped to the data store mutation of the same name, and the effect is that clicking one of the pagination buttons changes the selection of products, as shown in Figure 5-8.

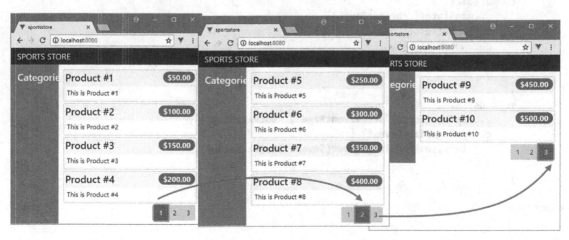

Figure 5-8. *Changing the product page*

Changing the Page Size

To complete the pagination feature, I want to allow the user to be able to select how many products are displayed on each page. In Listing 5-20, I added a select element to the component's template and wired it up so that it invokes the setPageSize mutation in the data store when the user picks a value.

Listing 5-20. Changing Page Size in the PageControls.vue File in the src/components Folder

```
<template>
    <div class="row mt-2">
        <div class="col form-group">
            <select class="form-control" v-on:change="changePageSize">
                <option value="4">4 per page</option>
                <option value="8">8 per page</option>
                <option value="12">12 per page</option>
            </select>
        </div>
        <div class="text-right col">
            <div class="btn-group mx-2">
                <button v-for="i in pageNumbers" v-bind:key="i"
                        class="btn btn-secpmdary"
                        v-bind:class="{ 'btn-primary': i == currentPage }"
                        v-on:click="setCurrentPage(i)">
                    {{ i }}
                </button>
            </div>
        </div>
    </div>
</template>

<script>

    import { mapState, mapGetters, mapMutations } from "vuex";

    export default {
        computed: {
            ...mapState(["currentPage"]),
            ...mapGetters(["pageCount"]),
            pageNumbers() {
                return [...Array(this.pageCount + 1).keys()].slice(1);
            }
        },
        methods: {
            ...mapMutations(["setCurrentPage", "setPageSize"]),
            changePageSize($event) {
                this.setPageSize(Number($event.target.value));
            }
        }
    }
</script>
```

The new HTML elements add structure to the component's template so that a `select` element is shown alongside the pagination buttons. The select element displays options for changing the page size, and the v-on directive listens for the change event, which is triggered when the user picks a value. If you just specify the name of a method when using the v-on directive, the methods will receive an event object, which can be used to access details of the element that triggered the event. I use this object to get the page size that the user has selected and pass it to the `setPageSize` mutation in the data store, which has been mapped to the component using the mapMutations helper. The result is that the page size can be changed by picking a new value from the select element's list, as shown in Figure 5-9.

■ **Tip** Notice that I only have to invoke the mutation to make a change to the application's state. Vuex and Vue.js then work through the impact of the update automatically so that the user sees the selected page or the number of products per page.

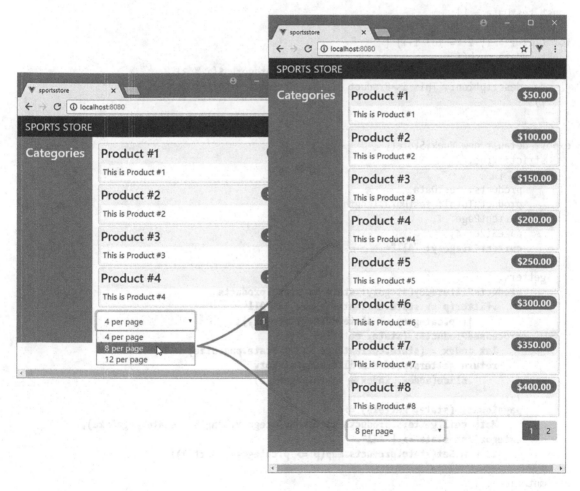

Figure 5-9. *Changing page size*

Adding Category Selection

The product list has started to shape up, and I am going to jump track and add support for narrowing the list of products by category. I am going to follow the same pattern to develop this feature: expand the data store, create a new component, and integrate the new component with the rest of the application. This is a pattern that you will become familiar with when you start a new Vue.js project and each component adds new content and features to the project. In Listing 5-21, I added a getter that returns a list of the categories that the user will be able to choose from.

Listing 5-21. Adding a Category List in the index.js File in the src/store Folder

```
import Vue from "vue";
import Vuex from "vuex";

Vue.use(Vuex);

const testData = [];

for (let i = 1; i <= 10; i++) {
    testData.push({
        id: i, name: `Product #${i}`, category: `Category ${i % 3}`,
        description: `This is Product #${i}`, price: i * 50
    })
}

export default new Vuex.Store({
    strict: true,
    state: {
        products: testData,
        productsTotal: testData.length,
        currentPage: 1,
        pageSize: 4,
        currentCategory: "All"
    },
    getters: {
        productsFilteredByCategory: state => state.products
            .filter(p => state.currentCategory == "All"
                || p.category == state.currentCategory),
        processedProducts: (state, getters) => {
            let index = (state.currentPage -1) * state.pageSize;
            return getters.productsFilteredByCategory
                .slice(index, index + state.pageSize);
        },
        pageCount: (state, getters) =>
            Math.ceil(getters.productsFilteredByCategory.length / state.pageSize),
        categories: state => ["All",
            ...new Set(state.products.map(p => p.category).sort())]
    },
    mutations: {
        setCurrentPage(state, page) {
            state.currentPage = page;
        },
```

```
        setPageSize(state, size) {
            state.pageSize = size;
            state.currentPage = 1;
        },
        setCurrentCategory(state, category) {
            state.currentCategory = category;
            state.currentPage = 1;
        }
    }
})
```

The currentCategory state property represents the category selected by the user, which defaults to All, which the application will use to display all products regardless of category.

Getters can access the results of other getters in the data store by defining a second argument. This allows me to define a productsFilteredByCategory getter and use it in the processedProducts and pageCount getters to reflect the category selection in their results.

I defined the categories getter so that I can present the user with a list of the categories that are available. The getter processes the products state array to select the values of the category properties and uses them to create a Set, which has the effect of removing any duplicates. The Set is spread into an array, which is sorted, resulting in an array of distinct categories, sorted by name.

The setCurrentCategory mutation changes the value of the currentCategory state property, which will be the means by which the user changes the selected category and also resets the selected page.

To manage the category selection, I added a file called CategoryControls.vue in the src/components folder, with the content shown in Listing 5-22.

Listing 5-22. The Contents of the CategoryControls.vue File in the src/components Folder

```
<template>
    <div class="container-fluid">
        <div class="row my-2" v-for="c in categories" v-bind:key="c">
            <button class="btn btn-block"
                    v-on:click="setCurrentCategory(c)"
                    v-bind:class="c == currentCategory
                        ? 'btn-primary' : 'btn-secondary'">
                {{ c }}
            </button>
        </div>
    </div>
</template>

<script>
    import { mapState, mapGetters, mapMutations} from "vuex";

    export default {
        computed: {
            ...mapState(["currentCategory"]),
            ...mapGetters(["categories"])
        },
        methods: {
            ...mapMutations(["setCurrentCategory"])
        }
    }
</script>
```

The component presents a list of button elements to the user, generated by the v-for directive based on the values provided by the categories property, which is mapped to the getter of the same name in the data store. The v-bind directive is used to manage the class membership of the button elements so that the button element that represents the selected category is added to the btn-primary class and all other button elements are added to the btn-secondary class, ensuring that the user can easily see which category has been chosen.

The v-on directive listens for the click event and invokes the setCurrentCategory mutation, which allows the user to navigate between categories. The live data model means the change will be immediately reflecting in the products shown to the user.

In Listing 5-23, I imported the new component and added to its parent's components property so that I can display the new features using the custom HTML element.

Listing 5-23. Adding the Category Selection in the Store.vue File in the src/components Folder

```
<template>
    <div class="container-fluid">
        <div class="row">
            <div class="col bg-dark text-white">
                <a class="navbar-brand">SPORTS STORE</a>
            </div>
        </div>
        <div class="row">
            <div class="col-3 bg-info p-2">
                <CategoryControls />
            </div>
            <div class="col-9 p-2">
                <ProductList />
            </div>
        </div>
    </div>
</template>

<script>

    import ProductList from "./ProductList";
    import CategoryControls from "./CategoryControls";

    export default {
        components: { ProductList, CategoryControls }
    }

</script>
```

The result is that the user is presented with a list of buttons that can be used to filter the products by category, as shown in Figure 5-10.

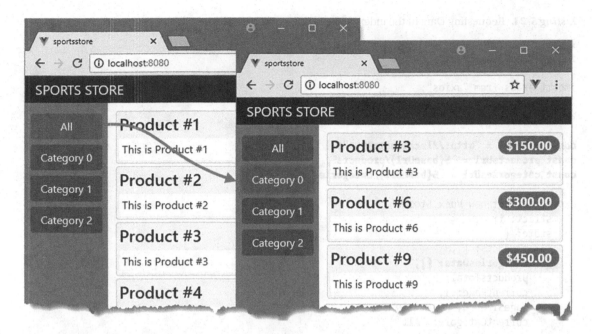

Figure 5-10. *Adding support for category filtering*

Using the RESTful Web Service

I like to start a project using test data because it lets me define the initial features without having to deal with network requests. But now that the basic structure is in place, it is time to replace the test data with the data provided by the RESTful web service. The `json-server` package that was installed and started at the beginning of the chapter will provide the data that the application requires using the URLs listed in Table 5-2.

Table 5-2. *The URLs to Get the Application Data*

URL	Description
http://localhost:3500/products	This URL will provide the list of products.
http://localhost:3500/categories	This URL will provide the list of categories.

Vue.js doesn't include built-in support for making HTTP requests. The most common choice of package to handle HTTP is Axios, which is not specific to Vue.js but fits nicely into the development model and is well-designed and easy to use.

HTTP requests are performed asynchronously. I want to perform my HTTP requests in the data store, and Vuex supports asynchronous tasks using a feature called *actions*. In Listing 5-24, I added an action to get the product and category data from the server and use it to set the state properties that the rest of the application relies on.

Listing 5-24. Requesting Data in the index.js File in the src/store Folder

```
import Vue from "vue";
import Vuex from "vuex";

import Axios from "axios";

Vue.use(Vuex);

const baseUrl = "http://localhost:3500";
const productsUrl = `${baseUrl}/products`;
const categoriesUrl = `${baseUrl}/categories`;

export default new Vuex.Store({
    strict: true,
    state: {
        products: [],
        categoriesData: [],
        productsTotal: 0,
        currentPage: 1,
        pageSize: 4,
        currentCategory: "All"
    },
    getters: {
        productsFilteredByCategory: state => state.products
            .filter(p => state.currentCategory == "All"
                || p.category == state.currentCategory),
        processedProducts: (state, getters) => {
            let index = (state.currentPage - 1) * state.pageSize;
            return getters.productsFilteredByCategory.slice(index,
                index + state.pageSize);
        },
        pageCount: (state, getters) =>
            Math.ceil(getters.productsFilteredByCategory.length / state.pageSize),
        categories: state => ["All", ...state.categoriesData]
    },
    mutations: {
        setCurrentPage(state, page) {
            state.currentPage = page;
        },
        setPageSize(state, size) {
            state.pageSize = size;
            state.currentPage = 1;
        },
        setCurrentCategory(state, category) {
            state.currentCategory = category;
            state.currentPage = 1;
        },
        setData(state, data) {
            state.products = data.pdata;
            state.productsTotal = data.pdata.length;
            state.categoriesData = data.cdata.sort();
```

```
        }
    },
    actions: {
        async getData(context) {
            let pdata = (await Axios.get(productsUrl)).data;
            let cdata = (await Axios.get(categoriesUrl)).data;
            context.commit("setData", { pdata, cdata} );
        }
    }
})
```

The Axios package provides a get method that is used to send HTTP get requests. I request the data from both URLs and use the async and await keywords to wait for the data. The get method returns an object whose data property returns a JavaScript object that has been parsed from the JSON response from the web service.

Vuex actions are functions that receive a context object that provides access to the data store features. The getData action uses the context to invoke the setData mutation. I can't use the mapMutation helper inside the data store, so I have to use the alternative mechanism, which is to call the commit method and specify the name of the mutation as an argument.

I need to invoke the action data store action when the application is initialized. Vue.js components have a well-defined lifecycle, which I describe in Chapter 17. For each part of the lifecycle, there are methods that a component can define that will be invoked. In Listing 5-25, I have implemented the created method, which is invoked when the component is created and which I use to trigger the getData action, which is mapped to a method using the mapActions helper.

Listing 5-25. Requesting Data in the App.vue File in the src Folder

```
<template>
    <store />
</template>

<script>
    import Store from "./components/Store";
    import { mapActions } from "vuex";

    export default {
        name: 'app',
        components: { Store },
        methods: {
            ...mapActions(["getData"])
        },
        created() {
            this.getData();
        }
    }
</script>
```

The result is that the test data has been replaced with the data obtained from the RESTful web service, as shown in Figure 5-11.

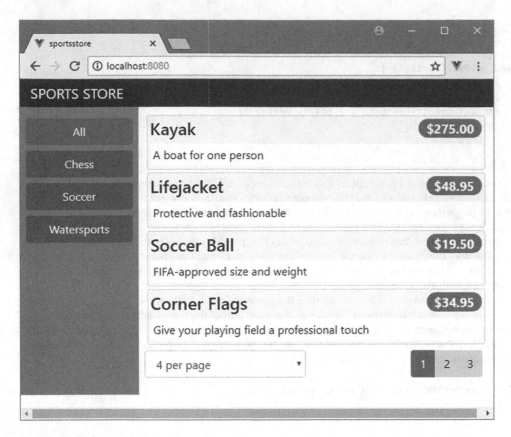

Figure 5-11. *Using data from the web service*

■ **Note** You may have to reload the browser to see the data from the web service. If you still don't see the new data, then stop and start the development tools using the command from Listing 5-25.

Summary

In this chapter, I started the development of the SportsStore project. I started by defining the data source, which provides access to shared data throughout the application. I also started work on the store, which presents products to the user, with support for pagination and filtering by category. I completed this chapter by using the Axios package to request data using HTTP from the RESTful web service, which allowed me to remove the test data. In the next chapter, I continue development of the SportsStore application by adding support for a shopping cart, checking out, and creating orders.

CHAPTER 6

SportsStore: Checkout and Orders

In this chapter, I continue adding features to the SportsStore application that I created in Chapter 5. I add support for a shopping cart and a checkout process that allows the user to submit orders to the web service.

■ **Tip** You can download the example project for this chapter—and for all of the other chapters in this book—from https://github.com/Apress/pro-vue-js-2.

Preparing for This Chapter

This chapter uses the SportsStore project from Chapter 5, and no changes are required in preparation for this chapter. To start the RESTful web service, open a command prompt and run the following command in the sportsstore folder:

```
npm run json
```

Open a second command prompt and run the following command in the sportsstore folder to start the development tools and HTTP server:

```
npm run serve
```

Once the initial build process is complete, open a new browser window and navigate to http://localhost:8080 to see the content shown in Figure 6-1.

© Adam Freeman 2018
A. Freeman, *Pro Vue.js 2*, https://doi.org/10.1007/978-1-4842-3805-9_6

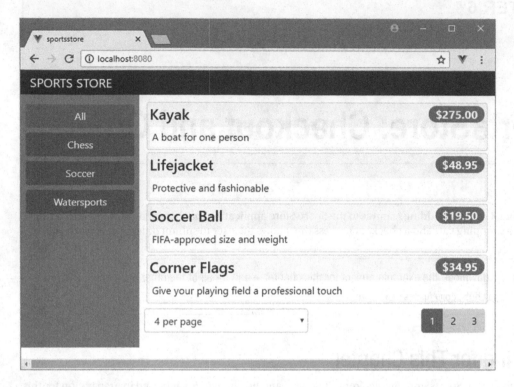

Figure 6-1. *Running the SportsStore application*

Creating the Shopping Cart Placeholder

The next feature for the SportsStore application is a shopping cart, which will allow the user to gather together the products they want to buy. I am going to create the shopping cart by adding a new component to the application with some placeholder content and then add support for displaying to the user. Once that is done, I'll go back and implement the cart. To begin, I created a file called ShoppingCart.vue in the src/ components folder with the content shown in Listing 6-1.

Listing 6-1. The Contents of the ShoppingCart.vue File in the src/components Folder

```
<template>
    <h4 class="bg-primary text-white text-center p-2">
        Placeholder for Cart
    </h4>
</template>
```

The new component doesn't provide any functionality currently, but it clearly indicates when the cart is being displayed.

Configuring URL Routing

Simple applications display the same content to the user all the time, but as you add more features, there comes a point where you need to display different components to the user. In the case of the example application, I want to allow the user to easily navigate between the list of products and the shopping cart. Vue.js supports a feature called *dynamic components*, which allows the application to change the content that the user sees. This feature is built-on the Vue Router package so that the URL is used to determine the content, which is known as *URL routing*. To set up the configuration required for the SportsStore application, I created the src/router folder and added to it a file called index.js with the content shown in Listing 6-2.

> ■ **Note** URL routing is described in detail in Chapters 23–25. The dynamic component feature is described in Chapter 21.

Listing 6-2. The Contents of the index.js File in the src/router Folder

```
import Vue from "vue";
import VueRouter  from "vue-router";

import Store from "../components/Store";
import ShoppingCart from "../components/ShoppingCart";

Vue.use(VueRouter);

export default new VueRouter({
    mode: "history",
    routes: [
        { path: "/", component: Store },
        { path: "/cart", component: ShoppingCart },
        { path: "*", redirect: "/"}
    ]
})
```

The Vue Router package must be registered with the Vue.use method in the same way as the Vuex package was in Chapter 5. The index.js file exports a new VueRouter object, which is passed a configuration object that sets up the mapping between URLs and the associated components.

> ■ **Note** In Listing 6-2, I have set the mode property to history, which tells Vue Router to use a recent browser API to handle the URLs. This produces a more usable result, but it isn't supported by older browsers, as I explain in Chapter 22.

The routes property contains a set of objects that maps URLs to components so that the default URL for the application will display the Store component, while the /cart URL will display the ShoppingCart component. The third object in the routes array is a catchall route, which redirects any other URL to /, which shows the Store as a useful fallback.

I added the statements shown in Listing 6-3 to the main.js file, which ensures that the routing features are initialized and will be available throughout the application.

Listing 6-3. Enabling URL Routing in the main.js File in the src Folder

```
import Vue from 'vue'
import App from './App.vue'

Vue.config.productionTip = false

import "bootstrap/dist/css/bootstrap.min.css";
import "font-awesome/css/font-awesome.min.css"

import store from "./store";
import router from "./router";

new Vue({
  render: h => h(App),
  store,
  router
}).$mount('#app')
```

The new statements import the module from Listing 6-3 and add it to the configuration object used to create the Vue object. Without this step, the routing features won't be enabled.

Displaying a Routed Component

Now that the routing configuration has been added to the application, I can ask it to manage the display of components in the SportsStore application. In Listing 6-4, I removed the custom HTML element that displayed the Store component and replaced it with one whose content will be determined by the current URL.

Listing 6-4. Adding a Routed View in the App.vue File in the src Folder

```
<template>
    <router-view />
</template>

<script>

  //import Store from "./components/Store";
  import { mapActions } from "vuex";

  export default {
      name: 'app',
      //components: { Store },
      methods: {
          ...mapActions(["getData"])
      },
      created() {
          this.getData();
      }
  }
</script>
```

The router-view element displays a component based on the configuration defined in Listing 6-4. I commented out the statements that add the Store component, which are no longer required because the routing system will be responsible for managing the content displayed by the App component.

If you navigate to http://localhost:8080, you will see the content displayed by the Store component, but if you navigate to http://localhost:8080/cart, you will see the placeholder content for the cart, as shown in Figure 6-2.

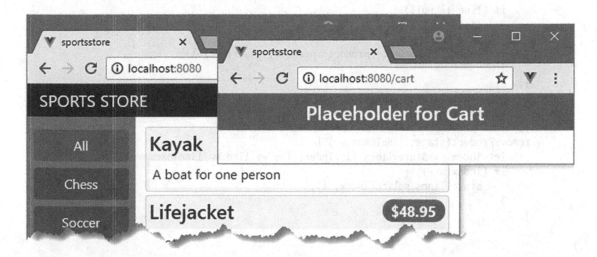

Figure 6-2. *Using URL routing*

Implementing the Cart Features

Now that the application can display the cart component, I can add the features that provide cart functionality. In the sections that follow, I expand the data store, add features to the Cart component to display the user's selection, and add navigation features so the user can select products and see a summary of those selections in the cart.

Adding a Module to the Data Store

I am going to start by expanding the data store, which I am going to do by defining a JavaScript module that is specific to the cart so that I can keep these additions separate from the existing data store features. I added a file called cart.js to the src/store folder with the content shown in Listing 6-5.

Listing 6-5. The Contents of the cart.js File in the src/store Folder

```
export default {
    namespaced: true,
    state: {
        lines: []
    },
    getters: {
        itemCount: state => state.lines.reduce((total, line) =>
            total + line.quantity, 0),
```

```
        totalPrice: state => state.lines.reduce((total, line) =>
              total + (line.quantity * line.product.price), 0),
    },
    mutations: {
        addProduct(state, product) {
            let line  = state.lines.find(line => line.product.id == product.id);
            if (line != null) {
                line.quantity++;
            } else {
                state.lines.push({ product: product, quantity:1 });
            }
        },
        changeQuantity(state, update) {
            update.line.quantity = update.quantity;
        },
        removeProduct(state, lineToRemove) {
            let index  = state.lines.findIndex(line => line == lineToRemove);
            if (index > -1) {
                state.lines.splice(index, 1);
            }
        }
    }
}
```

To extend the data store with a module, I created a default export that returns an object with state, getters, and mutations properties, following the same format I used in Chapter 5 when I added the data store to the project. I set the namespaced property to true to keep these features separate in the data store, which means they will be accessed with a prefix. Without this setting, the features defined in the cart.js file would be merged into the main data store, which can be confusing unless you ensure that the names used for properties and functions cannot be confused.

To incorporate the module into the data store, I added the statements shown in Listing 6-6 to the index.js file.

Listing 6-6. Adding a Module in the index.js File in the src/store Folder

```
import Vue from "vue";
import Vuex from "vuex";
import Axios from "axios";
import CartModule from "./cart";

Vue.use(Vuex);

const baseUrl = "http://localhost:3500";
const productsUrl = `${baseUrl}/products`;
const categoriesUrl = `${baseUrl}/categories`;

export default new Vuex.Store({
    strict: true,
    modules:  { cart: CartModule },
    state: {
        products: [],
```

```
            categoriesData: [],
            productsTotal: 0,
            currentPage: 1,
            pageSize: 4,
            currentCategory: "All"
        },

        // ...other data store features omitted for brevity...
})
```

I used an `import` statement to declare a dependency on the cart module and identified it as `CartModule`. To include the module in the data store, I added the `modules` property, which is assigned an object whose property name specifies the prefix that will be used to access the features in the module and whose value is the module object. In this listing, the features in the new data store module will be accessed using the prefix `cart`.

Adding the Product Selection Feature

The next step is to add the feature that will allow the user to add products to the cart. In Listing 6-7, I added a button to each product listing that updates the cart when it is clicked.

Listing 6-7. Adding Product Selection in the ProductList.vue File in the src/components Folder

```
<template>
    <div>
        <div v-for="p in products" v-bind:key="p.id" class="card m-1 p-1 bg-light">
            <h4>
                {{p.name}}
                <span class="badge badge-pill badge-primary float-right">
                    {{ p.price | currency }}
                </span>
            </h4>
            <div class="card-text bg-white p-1">
                {{ p.description }}
                <button class="btn btn-success btn-sm float-right"
                        v-on:click="handleProductAdd(p)">
                    Add To Cart
                </button>
            </div>
        </div>
        <page-controls />
    </div>
</template>

<script>

import { mapGetters, mapMutations } from "vuex";
import PageControls from "./PageControls";

export default {
    components: { PageControls },
    computed: {
```

```
            ...mapGetters({ products: "processedProducts" })
    },
    filters: {
        currency(value) {
            return new Intl.NumberFormat("en-US",
                { style: "currency", currency: "USD" }).format(value);
        }
    },
    methods: {
        ...mapMutations({ addProduct: "cart/addProduct" }),
        handleProductAdd(product) {
            this.addProduct(product);
            this.$router.push("/cart");
        }
    }
}
</script>
```

I added a button element to the template and used the v-on directive to respond to the click event by invoking the handleProductAdd method, which I added to the script element. This method invokes the cart/addProduct mutation on the data store, which is the way that the prefix I specified in Listing 6-7 allows me to access the features in the module when the namespaced property is true.

```
After the addProduct mutation has been invoked, the handleProductAdd method uses the routing
system to navigate to the /cart URL with this statement:...
this.$router.push("/cart");
...
```

The functionality provided by the Vue Router package is provided to components using the $router property (accessing all properties and methods in a component requires using the this keyword). The push method tells the router to change the browser's URL, which has the effect of displaying a different component. The result is that the cart component is displayed when you click one of the Add To Cart buttons, as shown in Figure 6-3.

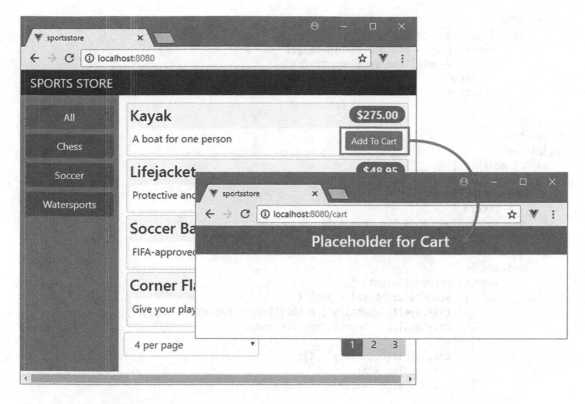

Figure 6-3. *Using URL navigation*

Displaying the Cart Contents

It is time to display the user's product selections instead of the placeholder content that is currently displayed. To make the content easier to manage, I am going to use a separate component that will be responsible for displaying a single product selection. I added a file called ShoppingCartLine.vue to the src/ components folder with the content shown in Listing 6-8.

Listing 6-8. The Contents of the ShoppingCartLine.vue File in the src/components Folder

```
<template>
    <tr>
        <td>
        <input type="number" class="form-control-sm"
                style="width:5em"
                v-bind:value="qvalue"
                v-on:input="sendChangeEvent"/>
        </td>
        <td>{{ line.product.name }}</td>
        <td class="text-right">
            {{ line.product.price | currency }}
        </td>
        <td class="text-right">
            {{ (line.quantity * line.product.price) | currency }}
```

```
            </td>
            <td class="text-center">
                <button class="btn btn-sm btn-danger"
                        v-on:click="sendRemoveEvent">
                    Remove
                </button>
            </td>
        </tr>
</template>
<script>
    export default {
        props: ["line"],
        data: function() {
            return {
                qvalue: this.line.quantity
            }
        },
        methods: {
            sendChangeEvent($event) {
                if ($event.target.value > 0) {
                    this.$emit("quantity", Number($event.target.value));
                    this.qvalue = $event.target.value;
                } else {
                    this.$emit("quantity", 1);
                    this.qvalue = 1;
                    $event.target.value = this.qvalue;
                }
            },
            sendRemoveEvent() {
                this.$emit("remove", this.line);
            }
        }
    }
</script>
```

This component uses the props feature, which allows the parent component to provide data objects to its children. In this case, the component in Listing 6-8 defines a prop called line, which its parent will use to provide the line from the shopping cart that it will display to the user. This component also sends custom event, which it uses to communicate with its parent. When the user changes the value of the input element that displays the quantity or clicks the Remove button, the component calls the this.$emit method to send an event to its parent component. These features are a useful way to connect components to create features that are local to one part of the application without using global features like the data store.

To display the contents of the cart to the user, I replaced the placeholder element in the ShoppingCart component and replaced it with the HTML and JavaScript code shown in Listing 6-9.

Listing 6-9. Displaying Products in the ShoppingCart.vue File in the src/components Folder

```
<template>
    <div class="container-fluid">
        <div class="row">
            <div class="col bg-dark text-white">
                <a class="navbar-brand">SPORTS STORE</a>
```

```
            </div>
        </div>
        <div class="row">
            <div class="col mt-2">
            <h2 class="text-center">Your Cart</h2>
            <table class="table table-bordered table-striped p-2">
                <thead>
                <tr>
                    <th>Quantity</th><th>Product</th>
                    <th class="text-right">Price</th>
                    <th class="text-right">Subtotal</th>
                </tr>
                </thead>
                <tbody>
                    <tr v-if="lines.length == 0">
                        <td colspan="4" class="text-center">
                            Your cart is empty
                        </td>
                    </tr>
                    <cart-line v-for="line in lines" v-bind:key="line.product.id"
                        v-bind:line="line"
                        v-on:quantity="handleQuantityChange(line, $event)"
                        v-on:remove="remove" />
                </tbody>
                <tfoot v-if="lines.length > 0">
                    <tr>
                        <td colspan="3" class="text-right">Total:</td>
                        <td class="text-right">
                            {{ totalPrice | currency }}
                        </td>
                    </tr>
                </tfoot>
            </table>
            </div>
        </div>
        <div class="row">
            <div class="col">
                <div class="text-center">
                  <router-link to="/" class="btn btn-secondary m-1">
                    Continue Shopping
                  </router-link>
                  <router-link to="/checkout" class="btn btn-primary m-1"
                        v-bind:disabled="lines.length == 0">
                    Checkout
                  </router-link>
                </div>
            </div>
        </div>
    </div>
</template>

<script>
```

```
import { mapState, mapMutations, mapGetters } from "vuex";
import CartLine from "./ShoppingCartLine";

export default {
    components: { CartLine },
    computed: {
        ...mapState({ lines: state => state.cart.lines }),
        ...mapGetters({  totalPrice : "cart/totalPrice"  })
    },
    methods: {
        ...mapMutations({
            change: "cart/changeQuantity",
            remove: "cart/removeProduct"
        }),
        handleQuantityChange(line, $event) {
            this.change({ line, quantity: $event});
        }
    }
}
</script>
```

Most of the content and code in this component uses features you have already seen, but there are a few points of note. The first is the way that this component configures its child ShoppingCartLine components, like this:...

```
<cart-line v-for="line in lines" v-bind:key="line.product.id"
    v-bind:line="line"
    v-on:quantity="handleQuantityChange(line, $event)"
    v-on:remove="remove" />
...
```

The cart-line element is used to apply the CartLine directive, and you can see the local connectivity features that component relies on from the other side of the parent-child relationship. The v-bind directive is used to set the value of the line prop, through which the CartLine directive receives the object it displays, and the v-on directive is used to receive the custom events emitted by the CartLine directive.

Some of the content in the template in Listing 6-9 is displayed only if there are products in the cart. Elements can be added or removed from the HTML document based on a JavaScript expression using the v-if directive, which I describe in Chapter 12.

The template in Listing 6-9 contains a new element that hasn't been seen before.

```
...
<router-link to="/" class="btn btn-primary m-1">Continue Shopping</router-link>
...
```

The router-link element is provided by the Vue Router package, and it is used to generate a navigation element. When the component's template is processed, the router-link element is replaced with an anchor element (an element whose tag is a) that will navigate to the URL specified by the to attribute. The router-link element is the counterpart to code-based navigation, and it can be configured to produce different elements and to apply classes to its element when its location matches the current URL, all of which I describe in Chapter 23. In Listing 6-9, I used the router-link element to allow the user to navigate back to the product list and to proceed to the /checkout URL, which I will add to the application later in the chapter to add support for the checkout process.

■ **Tip** The Bootstrap CSS framework can style a elements to look like buttons. The classes to which I added the `router-link` elements in Listing 6-9 are carried over to the a elements they produce and are presented to the user as Continue Shopping and Checkout buttons, which you can see in Figure 6-4.

The final feature of note in Listing 6-9 is the use of the data store state property that I defined in Listing 6-5. I chose to keep the features defined in the data store module separate from the rest of the data store, which means that a prefix must be used. When mapping getters, mutations, and actions, the prefix is included in the name, but a different approach is required for accessing state properties.

```
...
    ...mapState({ lines: state => state.cart.lines }),
...
```

State properties are mapped by defining a function that receives the state object and selects the property that is required. In this case, the selected property is `lines`, which is accessed using the `cart` prefix.

Creating a Global Filter

When I introduced the currency filter in Chapter 5, I defined it in a single component. Now that I have added features to the project, there are more values that I need to format as currency values, but rather than duplicate the same filter, I am going to register the filter globally so that it is available to all components, as shown in Listing 6-10.

Listing 6-10. Creating a Global Filter in the main.js File in the src Folder

```
import Vue from 'vue'
import App from './App.vue'

Vue.config.productionTip = false

import "bootstrap/dist/css/bootstrap.min.css";
import "font-awesome/css/font-awesome.min.css"

import store from "./store";
import router from "./router";

Vue.filter("currency", (value) => new Intl.NumberFormat("en-US",
    { style: "currency", currency: "USD" }).format(value));

new Vue({
  render: h => h(App),
  store,
  router
}).$mount('#app')
```

As you will learn in later chapters, many component features can be defined globally to avoid code duplication. Global filters are defined using the `Vue.filter` method, which must be called before the Vue object is created, as shown in Listing 6-10. See Chapter 11 for more details of using filters.

Testing the Basic Cart Features

To test the cart, navigate to http://localhost:8080 and click the Add To Cart button for the products you want to select. Each time you click the button, the data store will be updated, and the browser will navigate to the /cart URL, which will display a summary of your choices, as shown in Figure 6-4. You can increase and decrease the quantity of each product, remove the product, and click the Continue Shopping button to return to the store. (Clicking the Checkout button also returns you to the store at the moment because I have not yet set up a route for the /cart URL, and the catchall route I defined in Listing 6-10 is redirecting the browser to the default URL.)

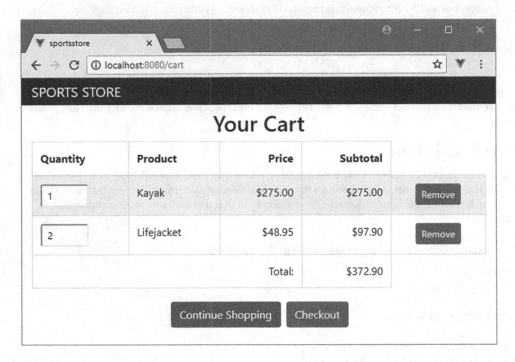

Figure 6-4. *The cart summary*

Making the Cart Persistent

If you reload the browser or try to navigate to http://localhost:8080/cart by entering the URL into the browser bar, you will lose any products that you have selected and will be presented with the empty cart shown in Figure 6-5.

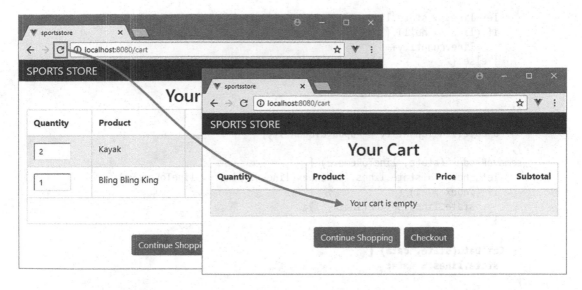

Figure 6-5. *The empty cart*

The URL changes performed using the routing system are handled differently from changes made by the user. When an application performs navigation, the change is interpreted as a request to move within that application, such as moving from the product list to the store. But when the user performs navigation, the change is interpreted as a request to change the page. The fact that the current application knows how to handle the new URL is irrelevant—the change terminates the current application and triggers fresh HTTP requests for the application's HTML document JavaScript, leading to a new instance of the application being created. Any state data is lost during this period, which is why you see an empty cart.

There is no way to change the behavior of the browser, which means the only way to deal with this problem is to make the cart persistent so that it is available to the newly created instance of the application after the navigation is complete. There are lots of different ways to persist cart data, and a common technique is to store the data on a server each time the user makes a change. I want to keep the focus on Vue. js development and not creating a back end to store the data, so I am going to use the same approach I used in Chapter 1 and store the data at the client using the local storage feature. In Listing 6-11, I have updated the data store so that the product selections are stored persistently when a change is made.

Listing 6-11. Storing Data Persistently in the cart.js File in the src/store Folder

```
export default {
    namespaced: true,
    state: {
        lines: []
    },
    getters: {
        itemCount: state => state.lines.reduce((total, line) =>
            total + line.quantity, 0),
        totalPrice: state => state.lines.reduce((total, line) =>
                total + (line.quantity * line.product.price), 0),

    },
    mutations: {
        addProduct(state, product) {
```

```
                let line  = state.lines.find(line => line.product.id == product.id);
                if (line != null) {
                    line.quantity++;
                } else {
                    state.lines.push({ product: product, quantity:1 });
                }
            },
            changeQuantity(state, update) {
                update.line.quantity =  update.quantity;
            },
            removeProduct(state, lineToRemove) {
                let index  = state.lines.findIndex(line => line == lineToRemove);
                if (index > -1) {
                    state.lines.splice(index, 1);
                }
            },
            setCartData(state, data) {
                state.lines = data;
            }
        },
        actions: {
            loadCartData(context) {
                let data = localStorage.getItem("cart");
                if (data != null) {
                    context.commit("setCartData", JSON.parse(data));
                }
            },
            storeCartData(context) {
                localStorage.setItem("cart", JSON.stringify(context.state.lines));
            },
            clearCartData(context) {
                context.commit("setCartData", []);
            },
            initializeCart(context, store) {
                context.dispatch("loadCartData");
                store.watch(state => state.cart.lines,
                    () => context.dispatch("storeCartData"), { deep: true});
            }
        }
    }
}
```

The actions I added to the data store module load, store, and clear the cart data using the local storage API. Actions are not allowed to modify state data directly in the data store, so I have also added a mutation that sets the lines property. The most important addition in Listing 6-11 is the initializeCart action, which is responsible for dealing with the cart when the application starts. When the action is invoked, the first statement calls the dispatch method, which is how actions are programmatically invoked. To observe the data store for changes to the lines state property, I used the watch method, like this:

```
...
store.watch(state => state.cart.lines,
   () => context.dispatch("storeCartData"), { deep: true});
...
```

The arguments to the watch method are a function that selects the state property and a function to invoke when a change is detected. This statement selects the lines property and uses the dispatch method to invoke the storeCartData action when there is a change. There is also a configuration object that sets the deep property to true, which tells Vuex that I want to receive notifications when there is a change to any of the properties in the lines array, which is not done by default. As I explain in Chapter 13, without this option, I would receive notifications only when the user adds or removes a line from the cart and not when the quantity of an existing product selection is changed.

Vuex doesn't provide a way to invoke any features when the data store is first initialized, so I added a statement to the App component that calls the initializeCart action, alongside the existing statement that requests the initial data from the RESTful web service, as shown in Listing 6-12.

Listing 6-12. Initializing the Cart in the App.vue File in the src Folder

```
<template>
    <router-view />
</template>

<script>
  import { mapActions } from "vuex";

  export default {
      name: 'app',
      methods: {
          ...mapActions({
              getData: "getData",
              initializeCart: "cart/initializeCart"
          })
      },
      created() {
          this.getData();
          this.initializeCart(this.$store);
      }
  }
</script>
```

The result of these changes is that the user's cart is stored locally and product selections are not lost when the user navigates directly to the /cart URL or when the browser is reloaded, as shown in Figure 6-6.

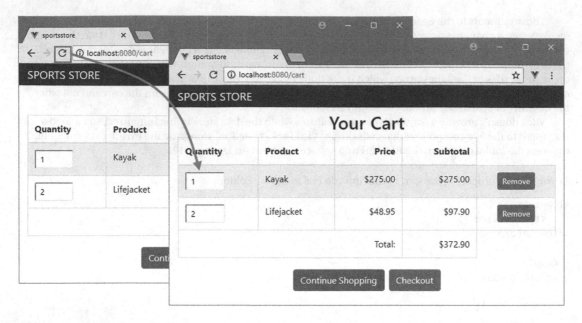

Figure 6-6. *Storing the cart data*

Adding the Cart Summary Widget

The final touch to complete the shopping cart is to create a summary that is shown at the top of the product list so that the user can see an overview of their selections and navigate directly to the /cart URL without having to add a product to the cart. I added a file called CartSummary.vue in the src/components folder and added the content shown in Listing 6-13 to create a new component.

Listing 6-13. The Contents of the CartSummary.vue File in the src/components Folder

```
<template>
    <div class="float-right">
        <small>
            Your cart:
            <span v-if="itemCount > 0">
                {{ itemCount }} item(s) {{ totalPrice | currency }}
            </span>
            <span v-else>
                (empty)
            </span>
        </small>
        <router-link to="/cart" class="btn btn-sm bg-dark text-white"
                v-bind:disabled="itemCount == 0">
            <i class="fa fa-shopping-cart"></i>
        </router-link>
    </div>
</template>
```

```
<script>
    import { mapGetters } from 'vuex';

    export default {
        computed: {
            ...mapGetters({
                itemCount: "cart/itemCount",
                totalPrice: "cart/totalPrice"
            })
        }
    }
</script>
```

This component uses the v-else directive, which is a useful companion to v-if and shows an element if the v-if expression is false, as described in Chapter 12. This allows me to display a summary of the cart if it contains items and show a placeholder message if not.

■ **Tip** The router-link element in Listing 6-13 contains an i element, which is styled using classes defined by Font Awesome, which I added to the project in Chapter 5. This open source package provides excellent support for icons in web applications, including the shopping cart I need for the SportsStore application. See http://fontawesome.io for details.

To incorporate the new component into the application, I updated the Store component, as shown in Listing 6-14.

Listing 6-14. Enabling the Component in the Store.vue File in the src/components Folder

```
<template>
    <div class="container-fluid">
        <div class="row">
            <div class="col bg-dark text-white">
                <a class="navbar-brand">SPORTS STORE</a>
                <cart-summary />
            </div>
        </div>
        <div class="row">
            <div class="col-3 bg-info p-2">
                <CategoryControls />
            </div>
            <div class="col-9 p-2">
                <ProductList />
            </div>
        </div>
    </div>
</template>

<script>

    import ProductList from "./ProductList";
```

```
import CategoryControls from "./CategoryControls";
import CartSummary from "./CartSummary";

export default {
    components: { ProductList, CategoryControls, CartSummary }
}
```

```
</script>
```

The effect is to present the user with a compact summary of the cart, as shown in Figure 6-7, and allow them to navigate directly to the cart summary by clicking the shopping cart icon.

Figure 6-7. *The cart summary widget*

Adding the Checkout and Orders Features

The next step after assembling a cart is to let the user check out and generate an order. To expand the data store to support orders, I added a file called orders.js to the src/store folder with the code shown in Listing 6-15.

Listing 6-15. The Contents of the orders.js File in the src/store Folder

```
import Axios from "axios";

const ORDERS_URL = "http://localhost:3500/orders";

export default {
    actions: {
        async storeOrder(context, order) {
            order.cartLines = context.rootState.cart.lines;
            return (await Axios.post(ORDERS_URL, order)).data.id;
        }
    }
}
```

The new data store module contains only an action to store an order, although I will add features when I implement some administration features. The storeOrder action uses the Axios package to send an HTTP POST request to the web service, which will store the order in the database.

To get data from another module, I use the rootState property of the action's context object, which lets me navigate to the cart module's lines property so that the products that the customer has selected is sent to the web service along with the details the user provided during the checkout process.

The json-server package that I have used as the RESTful web service for the SportsStore application responds to POST requests with a JSON representation of the object that includes an id property. The id property is assigned automatically and is used to uniquely identify the stored object in the database. In Listing 6-15, I use the async and await keywords to wait for the POST request to complete and then return the value of the id property that the server has provided.

For variety, I have not enabled the namespace feature, which means that this module's getters, mutations, and actions will be merged with those in the index.js file and will not be accessed using a prefix (although, as I explain in Chapter 20, the state properties are always prefixed, even when the namespace feature is not used and you can see an example of this in Chapter 7). In Listing 6-16, I imported the orders module into the main data store file and added it to the modules property, just as I did for the cart module earlier in the chapter.

Listing 6-16. Importing a Module in the index.js File in the src/store Folder

```
import Vue from "vue";
import Vuex from "vuex";
import Axios from "axios";
import CartModule from "./cart";
import OrdersModule from "./orders";

Vue.use(Vuex);

const baseUrl = "http://localhost:3500";
const productsUrl = `${baseUrl}/products`;
const categoriesUrl = `${baseUrl}/categories`;

export default new Vuex.Store({
    strict: true,
    modules: { cart: CartModule, orders: OrdersModule },

    // ...data store features omitted for brevity...

})
```

Creating and Registering the Checkout Components

To help the user complete the checkout process, I added a file called Checkout.vue in the src/components folder with the content shown in Listing 6-17.

Listing 6-17. The Contents of the Checkout.vue File in the src/components folder

```
<template>
    <div>
        <div class="container-fluid">
            <div class="row">
                <div class="col bg-dark text-white">
```

```
                        <a class="navbar-brand">SPORTS STORE</a>
                    </div>
                </div>
            </div>
            <div class="m-2">
                <div class="form-group m-2">
                    <label>Name</label>
                    <input v-model="name" class="form-control "/>
                </div>
            </div>
            <div class="text-center">
                <router-link to="/cart" class="btn btn-secondary m-1">
                    Back
                </router-link>
                <button class="btn btn-primary m-1" v-on:click="submitOrder">
                    Place Order
                </button>
            </div>
        </div>
    </div>
</template>

<script>

export default {
    data: function() {
        return {
            name: null
        }
    },
    methods: {
        submitOrder() {
            // todo: save order
        }
    }
}
</script>
```

I have started by adding one form element, which allows the user to enter their name. I'll add the remaining form elements shortly, but I started small so I can get everything set up without having to repeat the same code repeatedly in the listings.

There are two features used by this component that I have not used previously because the SportsStore application has been built around a Vuex data store. The first feature is that the component in Listing 6-17 has its own local data, which is not shared with any other component. This is defined using the data property in the script element and must be expressed in unusual way.

```
...
data: function() {
    return {
        name: null
    }
},
...
```

This fragment of code defines a single local data property called name, whose initial value is null. You will become used to this expression as you become experienced in Vue.js development and it soon becomes second nature. As I explain in Chapter 11, you will receive a warning if you forget to set up the data property correctly. In Parts 2 and 3 of this book, I rely on data properties so that I can demonstrate different features without the complication of adding a data store, and you will see lots of examples of how they work.

The second feature in Listing 6-17 is the use of the v-model directive to the input element, which creates a two-way binding with the name property, which keeps the value of the name property and the contents of the input element synchronized. This is a convenient feature for working with form elements, which I describe in more detail in Chapter 15; however, I have not used it in earlier SportsStore components. This is because it cannot be used with values from the data store since Vuex requires changes to be performed using mutations, which the v-model directive doesn't support, as I explain in detail in Chapter 20.

I also need a component that will display a message when an order has been submitted. I added a file called OrderThanks.vue to the src/components folder with the content shown in Listing 6-18.

Listing 6-18. The Contents of the OrderThanks.vue File in the src/components Folder

```
<template>

    <div class="m-2 text-center">
        <h2>Thanks!</h2>
        <p>Thanks for placing your order, which is #{{orderId}}.</p>
        <p>We'll ship your goods as soon as possible.</p>
        <router-link to="/" class="btn btn-primary">Return to Store</router-link>
    </div>

</template>

<script>
    export default {
        computed: {
            orderId() {
                return this.$route.params.id;
            }
        }
    }
</script>
```

This component displays a value that is obtained by the URL of the current route, which it accesses through the this.$route property, which is available in all components when the Vue Router package is enabled. In this case, I get a parameter from the route that will contain the user's order number, which will be the value returned from the HTTP POST request from Listing 6-15.

To incorporate the components into the application, I defined new routes, as shown in Listing 6-19.

Listing 6-19. Adding Routes in the index.js File in the src/router Folder

```
import Vue from "vue";
import VueRouter  from "vue-router";

import Store from "../components/Store";
import ShoppingCart from "../components/ShoppingCart";
import Checkout from "../components/Checkout";
import OrderThanks from "../components/OrderThanks";
```

```
Vue.use(VueRouter);

export default new VueRouter({
    mode: "history",
    routes: [
        { path: "/", component: Store },
        { path: "/cart", component: ShoppingCart },
        { path: "/checkout", component: Checkout},
        { path: "/thanks/:id", component: OrderThanks},
        { path: "*", redirect: "/"}
    ]
})
```

The /checkout URL will display the component from Listing 6-17, which corresponds to the URL I used in the router-link element displayed in the cart, which is presented to the user as a Checkout button.

The /thanks/:id URL displays the thank-you message, presented by the component created in Listing 6-18. The colon in the second segment of the URL tells the routing system that this route should match any two segment URL where the first segment is thanks. The content of the second URL segment will be assigned to a variable named id, which is then displayed to the user by the OrderThanks component, which I defined in Listing 6-18. I explain how to create complex routes and control the URLs they match in Chapters 23–25.

It is the checkout component that is of immediate interest, and you see this by navigating to http://localhost:8080/checkout or by navigating to http://localhost:8080, selecting a product, and then clicking the Checkout button. Regardless of the path you choose, you will see the content in Figure 6-8.

■ **Tip** It is unusual for an online store to allow the customer to jump directly to the checkout part of the process, and I demonstrate how to restrict navigation in Chapter 7.

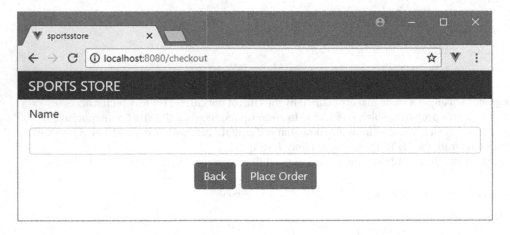

Figure 6-8. *The initial checkout component*

Adding Form Validation

It is important to validate the data that users provide to ensure that the application receives all the data that it requires in a format it is able to process. In Chapter 15, I demonstrate how you can create your own form validation code, but in real projects, it is easier to use a package that handles validation for you, such as Veulidate, which I added to the SportsStore project in Chapter 5. In Listing 6-20, I added statements to the main.js file to declare a dependency on the Veulidate package and add its functionality to the application.

Listing 6-20. Enabling the Veulidate Package in the main.js File in the src Folder

```
import Vue from 'vue'
import App from './App.vue'

Vue.config.productionTip = false

import "bootstrap/dist/css/bootstrap.min.css";
import "font-awesome/css/font-awesome.min.css"

import store from "./store";
import router from "./router";
import Vuelidate from "vuelidate";

Vue.filter("currency", (value) =>  new Intl.NumberFormat("en-US",
    { style: "currency", currency: "USD" }).format(value));

Vue.use(Vuelidate);

new Vue({
  render: h => h(App),
  store,
  router
}).$mount('#app')
```

Vuelidate is distributed as a Vue.js plugin that must be registered with the Vue.use method before the Vue object is created, as shown in the listing. I explain how plugins work and how to create your own in Chapter 26.

A key part of data validation is providing a message to the user when a value cannot be accepted or has not been provided. This requires a number of tests to ensure that the message is useful and isn't displayed until the user submits the data, which can lead to the same code and content being duplicated for each input element to which validation is required. To avoid this duplication, I added a file called ValidationError.vue to the src/components folder, which I used to create the component shown in Listing 6-21.

Listing 6-21. The Contents of the ValidationError.vue File in the src/components Folder

```
<template>
    <div v-if="show" class="text-danger">
        <div v-for="m in messages" v-bind:key="m">{{ m }}</div>
    </div>
</template>

<script>
```

```
export default {
    props: ["validation"],
    computed: {
        show() {
            return this.validation.$dirty && this.validation.$invalid
        },
        messages() {
            let messages = [];
            if (this.validation.$dirty) {
                if (this.hasValidationError("required")) {
                    messages.push("Please enter a value")
                } else if (this.hasValidationError("email")) {
                    messages.push("Please enter a valid email address");
                }
            }
            return messages;
        }
    },
    methods: {
        hasValidationError(type) {
            return this.validation.$params.hasOwnProperty(type)
                && !this.validation[type];
        }
    }
}
```

```
</script>
```

The Vuelidate package provides details about data validation through an object that will be received by this component's validation prop. For the SportsStore application, I require two validators—the required validator that ensures the user has provided a value and the email validator that ensures a value is a correctly formatted e-mail address.

■ **Tip** Vuelidate supports a wide range of validators. See `https://monterail.github.io/vuelidate` for details.

To determine what messages the ValidationError component should display, I use the properties shown in Table 6-1, which are defined on the object that will be received through the prop.

Table 6-1. *The Validation Object Properties*

Name	Description
$invalid	If this property is true, then the element contents have contravened one of the validation rules that has been applied.
$dirty	If this property is true, then the element has been edited by the user.
required	If this property exists, then the required validator has been applied to the element. If the property is false, then the element does not contain a value.
email	If this property exists, then the email validator has been applied to the element. If the property is false, then the element does not contain a valid e-mail address.

The component in Listing 6-21 uses the properties in Table 6-1 to decide whether the object it has received via its prop is reporting validation errors and, if so, which messages should be displayed to the user.

This approach will make more sense when you see how the ValidationError component is applied. In Listing 6-22, I have added data validation to the Checkout component and delegated reporting any problems to the ValidationError component.

Listing 6-22. Validating Data in the Checkout.vue File in the src/components Folder

```
<template>
    <div>
        <div class="container-fluid">
                <div class="row">
                    <div class="col bg-dark text-white">
                        <a class="navbar-brand">SPORTS STORE</a>
                    </div>
                </div>
        </div>
        <div class="m-2">
            <div class="form-group m-2">
                <label>Name</label>
                <input v-model="$v.name.$model" class="form-control "/>
                <validation-error v-bind:validation="$v.name" />
            </div>
        </div>
        <div class="text-center">
            <router-link to="/cart" class="btn btn-secondary m-1">
                Back
            </router-link>
            <button class="btn btn-primary m-1" v-on:click="submitOrder">
                Place Order
            </button>
        </div>
    </div>
</template>
```

```
<script>

import { required } from "vuelidate/lib/validators";
import ValidationError from "./ValidationError";

export default {
    components: { ValidationError },
    data: function() {
        return {
            name: null
        }
    },
    validations: {
        name: {
            required
        }
    },
    methods: {
        submitOrder() {
            this.$v.$touch();
            // todo: save order
        }
    }
}
</script>
```

Vuelidate data validation is applied using a `validations` property in the `script` elements, which has properties that correspond to the name of the data value that will be validated. In the listing, I added a name property and applied the `required` validator, which must be imported from the `veulidate/lib/validators` location.

To connect the validation features to the `input` element, the target of the v-model directive must be changed, like this:

```
...
<input v-model="$v.name.$model" class="form-control "/>
...
```

Validation features are accessed through a property called $v, which has properties that correspond to the validation configuration. In this case, there is a name property, which corresponds to the name data value, and its value is accessed using the $model property.

It is the object returned by the `$v.name` property that I pass to the `ValidationError` component, like this:

```
...
<validation-error v-bind:validation="$v.name" />
...
```

This approach provides access to the properties described in Table 6-1, which are used to display validation error messages without needing any specific details of the data value being processed.

The $v object defines a $touch method, which marks all of the elements as dirty, as though the user had edited them. This is a useful feature to trigger validation as the result of a user action, while not usually displaying validation messages until the user interacts with an input element. To see the effect, navigate to http://localhost:8080/checkout and click the Place Order button without entering anything into the input element. You will see the error message asking you to provide a value, which will disappear when you enter text into the field, as shown in Figure 6-9. Validation is performed live, and you will see the error message again if you remove all the text from the input element.

Figure 6-9. *Validating data*

Adding the Remaining Fields and Validation

In Listing 6-23, I have added the remaining data fields required for an order to the component, along with the validation settings that each requires and the code required to submit an order when all of the data fields are valid.

Listing 6-23. Completing the Form in the Checkout.vue File in the src/components Folder

```
<template>
    <div>
        <div class="container-fluid">
                <div class="row">
                    <div class="col bg-dark text-white">
                        <a class="navbar-brand">SPORTS STORE</a>
                    </div>
                </div>
        </div>
        <div class="m-2">
            <div class="form-group m-2">
                <label>Name</label>
                <input v-model="$v.order.name.$model" class="form-control "/>
                <validation-error v-bind:validation="$v.order.name" />
            </div>
        </div>
```

```
    <div class="m-2">
        <div class="form-group m-2">
            <label>Email</label>
            <input v-model="$v.order.email.$model" class="form-control "/>
            <validation-error v-bind:validation="$v.order.email" />
        </div>
    </div>

    <div class="m-2">
        <div class="form-group m-2">
            <label>Address</label>
            <input v-model="$v.order.address.$model" class="form-control "/>
            <validation-error v-bind:validation="$v.order.address" />
        </div>
    </div>

    <div class="m-2">
        <div class="form-group m-2">
            <label>City</label>
            <input v-model="$v.order.city.$model" class="form-control "/>
            <validation-error v-bind:validation="$v.order.city" />
        </div>
    </div>

    <div class="m-2">
        <div class="form-group m-2">
            <label>Zip</label>
            <input v-model="$v.order.zip.$model" class="form-control "/>
            <validation-error v-bind:validation="$v.order.zip" />
        </div>
    </div>

    <div class="text-center">
        <router-link to="/cart" class="btn btn-secondary m-1">
            Back
        </router-link>
        <button class="btn btn-primary m-1" v-on:click="submitOrder">
            Place Order
        </button>
    </div>
  </div>
</template>

<script>

import { required, email } from "vuelidate/lib/validators";
import ValidationError  from "./ValidationError";
import { mapActions } from "vuex";

export default {
    components: { ValidationError },
```

148

```
    data: function() {
        return {
            order: {
                name: null,
                email: null,
                address: null,
                city: null,
                zip: null
            }
        }
    },
    validations: {
        order: {
            name: { required },
            email: { required, email },
            address: { required },
            city: { required },
            zip: { required }
        }
    },
    methods: {
        ...mapActions({
            "storeOrder": "storeOrder",
            "clearCart": "cart/clearCartData"
        }),
        async submitOrder() {
            this.$v.$touch();
            if (!this.$v.$invalid) {
                let order = await this.storeOrder(this.order);
                this.clearCart();
                this.$router.push(`/thanks/${order}`);
            }
        }
    }
}
</script>
```

I have grouped the data properties together so they are nested under an order object, and I have added email, address, city, and zip fields. In the submitOrder method, I check the $v.$isvalid property, which reports on the validity of all of the validators, and if the form is valid, I invoke the storeOrder action to send the order to the web service, clear the shopping cart, and navigate to the /thanks URL, which displays the component I defined in Listing 6-18. Figure 6-10 shows the checkout sequence.

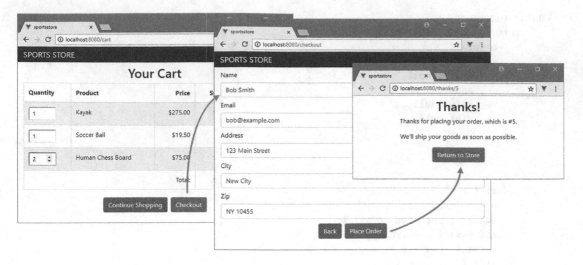

Figure 6-10. *Creating an order through the checkout process*

Once you have completed the checkout process, you can click the Return to Store button and start over. You can't see the order that has been created at the moment because access to that data is restricted, but I will add the required features to the SportsStore application in Chapter 7.

Summary

In this chapter, I added URL routing to the SportsStore application and used it to navigate to different functional areas. I added a shopping cart, which allows users to make their product selection, and persisted the cart data so that manual navigation or reloading the browser doesn't cause data loss. I also created the checkout process, which validates the data provided by the user and sends the order data to the web service for storage. In the next chapter, I scale up the amount of data that the application has to work with and start work on the administration features.

CHAPTER 7

SportsStore: Scaling and Administration

In this chapter, I continue adding features to the SportsStore application that I created in Chapter 5. I add support for dealing with larger amounts of data and begin to implement the features required to administer the application.

■ **Tip**   You can download the example project for this chapter—and for all of the other chapters in this book—from `https://github.com/Apress/pro-vue-js-2`.

Preparing for This Chapter

To prepare for this chapter, I am going to increase the amount of product data that the application has to work with. I used the Faker package, which I added to the project in Chapter 5, to generate a large number of product objects by replacing the contents of the data.js file, as shown in Listing 7-1.

Listing 7-1. Generating Data in the data.js File in the sportsstore Folder

```
var faker = require("faker");

var data = [];
var categories = ["Watersports", "Soccer", "Chess", "Running"];

faker.seed(100);

for (let i = 1; i <= 500; i++) {
    var category = faker.helpers.randomize(categories);
    data.push({
        id: i,
        name: faker.commerce.productName(),
        category: category,
        description: `${category}: ${faker.lorem.sentence(3)}`,
        price: faker.commerce.price()
    })
}
```

```
module.exports = function () {
    return {
        products: data,
        categories: categories,
        orders: []
    }
}
```

The Faker package is an excellent tool for producing randomized data during development, which can be a useful way to find the limits of your application without having to manually create realistic data by hand. The Faker package is described at `http://marak.github.io/faker.js`, and I used it to generate product data with random names, descriptions, and prices.

To start the RESTful web service, open a command prompt and run the following command in the `sportsstore` folder:

```
npm run json
```

Open a second command prompt and run the following command in the `sportsstore` folder to start the development tools and HTTP server:

```
npm run serve
```

Once the initial build process is complete, open a new browser window and navigate to `http://localhost:8080` to see the content shown in Figure 7-1.

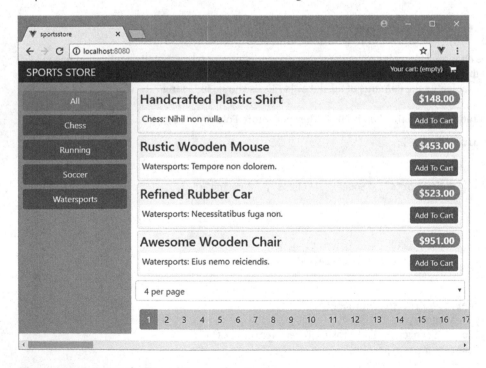

Figure 7-1. *Running the SportsStore application*

Dealing with Larger Amounts of Data

You can already see that the application needs some work to deal with the amount of product data that is provided by the web service, with a line of pagination buttons that is so long that it's useless. In the sections that follow, I'll modify the SportsStore application to present the data in a more useful way and to reduce the amount of data that is requested from the server.

Improving Page Navigation

I am going to start with the most obvious problem, which is that the user is presented with a long list of page numbers, which makes navigation difficult. To address this, I am going to present the user with a restricted list of page buttons that makes navigation easier, albeit without the ability to jump to any page, as shown in Listing 7-2.

Listing 7-2. Improving Navigation in the PageControls.vue File in the /src/components Folder

```
<template>
    <div class="row mt-2">
        <div class="col-3 form-group">
            <select class="form-control" v-on:change="changePageSize">
                <option value="4">4 per page</option>
                <option value="8">8 per page</option>
                <option value="12">12 per page</option>
            </select>
        </div>
        <div class="text-right col">
            <button v-bind:disabled="currentPage == 1"
                v-on:click="setCurrentPage(currentPage - 1)"
                class="btn btn-secondary mx -1">Previous</button>
            <span v-if="currentPage > 4">
                <button v-on:click="setCurrentPage(1)"
                    class="btn btn-secondary mx-1">1</button>
                <span class="h4">...</span>
            </span>
            <span class="mx-1">
                <button v-for="i in pageNumbers" v-bind:key="i"
                        class="btn btn-secpmdary"
                        v-bind:class="{ 'btn-primary': i == currentPage }"
                        v-on:click="setCurrentPage(i)">{{ i }}</button>
            </span>
            <span v-if="currentPage <= pageCount - 4">
                <span class="h4">...</span>
                <button  v-on:click="setCurrentPage(pageCount)"
                    class="btn btn-secondary mx-1">{{ pageCount}}</button>
            </span>
            <button v-bind:disabled="currentPage == pageCount"
                    v-on:click="setCurrentPage(currentPage + 1)"
                    class="btn btn-secondary mx-1">Next</button>
        </div>
    </div>
</template>
```

```
<script>
    import { mapState, mapGetters, mapMutations } from "vuex";

    export default {
        computed: {
            ...mapState(["currentPage"]),
            ...mapGetters(["pageCount"]),
            pageNumbers() {
                if (this.pageCount < 4) {
                    return [...Array(this.pageCount + 1).keys()].slice(1);
                } else if (this.currentPage <= 4) {
                    return [1, 2, 3, 4, 5];
                } else  if (this.currentPage > this.pageCount - 4) {
                    return [...Array(5).keys()].reverse()
                        .map(v => this.pageCount - v);
                } else {
                    return [this.currentPage -1, this.currentPage,
                        this.currentPage + 1];
                }
            }
        },
        methods: {
            ...mapMutations(["setCurrentPage", "setPageSize"]),
            changePageSize($event) {
                this.setPageSize($event.target.value);
            }
        }
    }
</script>
```

There are no new Vue.js features required to change the way that pagination is now presented to the user, and the changes present the user with the currently selected page and the option to select the pages before and after, as well as the first and last pages, producing the result shown in Figure 7-2.

Figure 7-2. *Restricting pagination options*

The navigation model I used for the pages is modeled on Amazon, on the basis that it is an approach that many users will already be familiar with. This is, however, a pagination model that assumes the user is more likely to be interested in the first few pages and makes them easier to access.

Reducing the Amount of Data Requested by the Application

The application makes a single request when it starts and gets all of the data that is available from the web service. This is not an approach that scales well, especially since most of the data is unlikely to be displayed to the user since it will be used for the pages that are unlikely to be viewed. To address this, I am going to request the data as the user requires it, as shown in Listing 7-3, in the expectation that most users will choose products from the early pages.

Listing 7-3. Requesting Data in the index.js File in the src/store Folder

```
import Vue from "vue";
import Vuex from "vuex";
import Axios from "axios";
import CartModule from "./cart";
import OrdersModule from "./orders";

Vue.use(Vuex);

const baseUrl = "http://localhost:3500";
const productsUrl = `${baseUrl}/products`;
const categoriesUrl = `${baseUrl}/categories`;
```

```
export default new Vuex.Store({
    strict: true,
    modules:  { cart: CartModule, orders: OrdersModule },
    state: {
        //products: [],
        categoriesData: [],
        //productsTotal: 0,
        currentPage: 1,
        pageSize: 4,
        currentCategory: "All",
        pages: [],
        serverPageCount: 0
    },
    getters: {
        // productsFilteredByCategory: state => state.products
        //        .filter(p => state.currentCategory == "All"
        //              || p.category == state.currentCategory),
        processedProducts: (state) => {
            return state.pages[state.currentPage];
        },
        pageCount: (state) => state.serverPageCount,
        categories: state => ["All", ...state.categoriesData]
    },
    mutations: {
        _setCurrentPage(state, page) {
            state.currentPage = page;
        },
        _setPageSize(state, size) {
            state.pageSize = size;
            state.currentPage = 1;
        },
        _setCurrentCategory(state, category) {
            state.currentCategory = category;
            state.currentPage = 1;
        },
        // setData(state, data) {
        //      state.products = data.pdata;
        //      state.productsTotal = data.pdata.length;
        //      state.categoriesData = data.cdata.sort();
        // },
        addPage(state, page) {
            for (let i = 0; i < page.pageCount; i++) {
                Vue.set(state.pages, page.number + i,
                    page.data.slice(i * state.pageSize,
                        (i * state.pageSize) + state.pageSize));
            }
        },
        clearPages(state) {
            state.pages.splice(0, state.pages.length);
        },
```

```
        setCategories(state, categories) {
            state.categoriesData = categories;
        },
        setPageCount(state, count) {
            state.serverPageCount = Math.ceil(Number(count) / state.pageSize);
        },
    },
    actions: {
        async getData(context) {
            await context.dispatch("getPage", 2);
            context.commit("setCategories", (await Axios.get(categoriesUrl)).data);
        },
        async getPage(context, getPageCount = 1) {
            let url = `${productsUrl}?_page=${context.state.currentPage}`
                + `&_limit=${context.state.pageSize * getPageCount}`;
            if (context.state.currentCategory != "All") {
                url += `&category=${context.state.currentCategory}`;
            }
            let response = await Axios.get(url);
            context.commit("setPageCount", response.headers["x-total-count"]);
            context.commit("addPage", { number: context.state.currentPage,
                data: response.data, pageCount: getPageCount});
        },
        setCurrentPage(context, page) {
            context.commit("_setCurrentPage", page);
            if (!context.state.pages[page]) {
                context.dispatch("getPage");
            }
        },
        setPageSize(context, size) {
            context.commit("clearPages");
            context.commit("_setPageSize", size);
            context.dispatch("getPage", 2);
        },
        setCurrentCategory(context, category) {
            context.commit("clearPages");
            context.commit("_setCurrentCategory", category);
            context.dispatch("getPage", 2);
        }
    }
})
```

These changes are simpler than they might appear and reflect the strict approach that Vuex takes to data store features. Only actions can perform asynchronous tasks, which means that any activity that leads to an HTTP request for data has to be performed using an action, and actions change state using mutations. As a result, I have created actions with names that were previously used by mutations and added an underscore to the mutation names so that I can still modify the data in the store. This may seem awkward, but the flow of actions to mutations to state is a good model, and enforcing it helps with debugging, as I explain in Chapter 20.

At the heart of the changes in Listing 7-3 is a change in the URLs that are sent to the web service. Previously, the URL requested all of the product data like this:

```
...
http://localhost:3500/products
...
```

The json-server package that is providing the web service includes support for requested pages of data and for filtering data, using URLs like this one:

```
...
http://localhost:3500/products?_page=3&_limit=4&category=Watersports
...
```

The _page and _limit parameters are used to request pages of data, and the category parameter is used to select only objects whose category property is Watersports. This is the format of URL that the changes in Listing 7-3 introduce into the SportsStore application.

The approach I have taken in the listing is to request data in the pages that will be displayed to the user. The application keeps track of the data it has received from the web service and sends an HTTP request when the user navigates to a page for which no data has been requested. The data that has been requested from the server is discarded when the user changes the size of the page or selects a category, and two pages are requested when the application starts to allow the user to navigate to one page without triggering a network request.

■ **Caution**   It can be tempting to implement sophisticated approaches to managing and caching data to minimize the number of HTTP requests that an application makes. Caching is hard to implement effectively, and the complexity it adds to the project can often outweigh any benefits. I recommend starting with a simple approach, such as the one in Listing 7-3, and manage the data more actively only when you are sure that you need it.

Determining the Number of Items

When dealing with data in pages, it is difficult to determine how many objects are available in order to display the pagination buttons. To assist with this issue, the json-server package includes an X-Total-Count header in its responses, which indicates how many objects are in the collection. Each time that an HTTP request is made for a page of data, I get the value of the header from the response and use it to update the page count, like this:

```
...
context.commit("setPageCount", response.headers["x-total-count"]);
...
```

Not all web services will offer this feature, but there is usually something comparable available, such that you can determine how many objects are available without requesting them all.

Adding an Item to the Array of Pages

Vue.js and Vuex both do a good job of tracking changes and ensuring that the data in the application is live. For the most part, this tracking is automatic, and no special actions are required. But this isn't universally true, and there are some limitations in the way that JavaScript works that mean Vue.js requires some assistance for certain operations, one of which is assigning an item to an array index, which won't trigger the change detection process. When I receive a page of data from the server and add it to the array, I use the method that Vue.js provides for this purpose, shown here:

```
...
Vue.set(state.pages, page.number + i, page.data.slice(i * state.pageSize,
    (i * state.pageSize) + state.pageSize));
...
```

The Vue.set method accepts three arguments: the object or array to modify, the property or index to assign to, and the value to assign. Using Vue.set ensures that the change is recognized and handled as an update, as I explain in Chapter 13.

Updating the Components to Use Actions

The changes that I made in Listing 7-3 require corresponding changes in the components that used the mutations that have been replaced with actions. Listing 7-4 shows the changes required to the CategoryControls component.

Listing 7-4. Using Actions in the CategoryControls.vue File in the src/components Folder

```
...
<script>
    import { mapState, mapGetters, mapActions} from "vuex";

    export default {
        computed: {
            ...mapState(["currentCategory"]),
            ...mapGetters(["categories"])
        },
        methods: {
            ...mapActions(["setCurrentCategory"])
        }
    }
</script>
...
```

To update the component, I replaced the mapMutations helper with mapActions. Both helpers add methods to the component, and no changes are required to the rest of the component. In Listing 7-5, I updated the PageControls component.

Listing 7-5. Using Actions in the PageControls.vue File in the src/components Folder

```
...
<script>
    import { mapState, mapGetters, mapActions } from "vuex";

    export default {
        computed: {
            ...mapState(["currentPage"]),
            ...mapGetters(["pageCount"]),
            pageNumbers() {
                if (this.pageCount < 4) {
                    return [...Array(this.pageCount + 1).keys()].slice(1);
                } else if (this.currentPage <= 4) {
                    return [1, 2, 3, 4, 5];
                } else  if (this.currentPage > this.pageCount - 4) {
                    return [...Array(5).keys()].reverse()
                        .map(v => this.pageCount - v);
                } else {
                    return [this.currentPage -1, this.currentPage,
                        this.currentPage + 1];
                }
            }
        },
        methods: {
            ...mapActions(["setCurrentPage", "setPageSize"]),
            changePageSize($event) {
                this.setPageSize($event.target.value);
            }
        }
    }
</script>
...
```

There is no visual change to the content presented to the user, but if you open the browser's F12 developer tools and observe the Network tab as you navigate through the products, you will see the requests sent for the pages of data, as shown in Figure 7-3.

Figure 7-3. *Requesting data in pages*

Adding Search Support

I am going to add the ability to search for products to the SportsStore application, which is always a good idea when dealing with amounts of data are too large for the user to easily page through completely. In Listing 7-6, I have updated the data store so that a search string can be included in the URL used to request data, using the search feature provided by the json-server package that I am using for the web service.

Listing 7-6. Adding Search Support in the index.js File in the src/store Folder

```
import Vue from "vue";
import Vuex from "vuex";
import Axios from "axios";
import CartModule from "./cart";
import OrdersModule from "./orders";

Vue.use(Vuex);

const baseUrl = "http://localhost:3500";
const productsUrl = `${baseUrl}/products`;
const categoriesUrl = `${baseUrl}/categories`;

export default new Vuex.Store({
    strict: true,
    modules:  { cart: CartModule, orders: OrdersModule },
    state: {
        categoriesData: [],
```

```
            currentPage: 1,
            pageSize: 4,
            currentCategory: "All",
            pages: [],
            serverPageCount: 0,
            searchTerm: "",
            showSearch: false
        },
        getters: {
            processedProducts: (state) => {
                return state.pages[state.currentPage];
            },
            pageCount: (state) => state.serverPageCount,
            categories: state => ["All", ...state.categoriesData]
        },
        mutations: {
            _setCurrentPage(state, page) {
                state.currentPage = page;
            },
            _setPageSize(state, size) {
                state.pageSize = size;
                state.currentPage = 1;
            },
            _setCurrentCategory(state, category) {
                state.currentCategory = category;
                state.currentPage = 1;
            },
            addPage(state, page) {
                for (let i = 0; i < page.pageCount; i++) {
                    Vue.set(state.pages, page.number + i,
                        page.data.slice(i * state.pageSize,
                            (i * state.pageSize) + state.pageSize));
                }
            },
            clearPages(state) {
                state.pages.splice(0, state.pages.length);
            },
            setCategories(state, categories) {
                state.categoriesData = categories;
            },
            setPageCount(state, count) {
                state.serverPageCount = Math.ceil(Number(count) / state.pageSize);
            },
            setShowSearch(state, show) {
                state.showSearch = show;
            },
            setSearchTerm(state, term) {
                state.searchTerm = term;
                state.currentPage = 1;
            },
        },
```

```
    actions: {
        async getData(context) {
            await context.dispatch("getPage", 2);
            context.commit("setCategories", (await Axios.get(categoriesUrl)).data);
        },
        async getPage(context, getPageCount = 1) {
            let url = `${productsUrl}?_page=${context.state.currentPage}`
                + `&_limit=${context.state.pageSize * getPageCount}`;

            if (context.state.currentCategory != "All") {
                url += `&category=${context.state.currentCategory}`;
            }

            if (context.state.searchTerm != "") {
                url += `&q=${context.state.searchTerm}`;
            }

            let response = await Axios.get(url);
            context.commit("setPageCount", response.headers["x-total-count"]);
            context.commit("addPage", { number: context.state.currentPage,
                data: response.data, pageCount: getPageCount});
        },
        setCurrentPage(context, page) {
            context.commit("_setCurrentPage", page);
            if (!context.state.pages[page]) {
                context.dispatch("getPage");
            }
        },
        setPageSize(context, size) {
            context.commit("clearPages");
            context.commit("_setPageSize", size);
            context.dispatch("getPage", 2);
        },
        setCurrentCategory(context, category) {
            context.commit("clearPages");
            context.commit("_setCurrentCategory", category);
            context.dispatch("getPage", 2);
        },
        search(context, term) {
            context.commit("setSearchTerm", term);
            context.commit("clearPages");
            context.dispatch("getPage", 2);
        },
        clearSearchTerm(context) {
            context.commit("setSearchTerm", "");
            context.commit("clearPages");
            context.dispatch("getPage", 2);
        }
    }
})
```

Two state properties are required for the SportsStore search feature: the showSearch property will determine if the user is presented with a search box, and the searchTerm property will specify the term that is passed to the web service for searches. The json-server package supports searches through the q parameter, which means that the application will generate URLs like this when searching:

```
...
http://localhost:3500/products?_page=3&_limit=4&category=Soccer&q=car
...
```

This URL requests the third page of four items whose category property is Soccer and have any field that contains the term car. To present the user with the search feature, I added a file called Search.vue to the src/components folder with the content shown in Listing 7-7.

Listing 7-7. The Contents of the Search.vue File in the src/components Folder

```
<template>
    <div v-if="showSearch" class="row my-2">
        <label class="col-2 col-form-label text-right">Search:</label>
        <input class="col form-control"
            v-bind:value="searchTerm" v-on:input="doSearch"
            placeholder="Enter search term..." />
        <button class="col-1 btn btn-sm btn-secondary mx-4"
                v-on:click="handleClose">
            Close
        </button>
    </div>
</template>

<script>

import { mapMutations, mapState, mapActions } from "vuex";

export default {
    computed: {
        ...mapState(["showSearch", "searchTerm"])
    },
    methods: {
        ...mapMutations(["setShowSearch"]),
        ...mapActions(["clearSearchTerm", "search"]),
        handleClose() {
            this.clearSearchTerm();
            this.setShowSearch(false);
        },
        doSearch($event) {
            this.search($event.target.value);
        }
    }
}
</script>
```

This component responds to the data store properties to display an input element to the user that can be used to enter a search term. The v-on directive is used to respond each time the user edits the contents of the input by triggering a search. To bring the search feature into the application, I made the changes shown in Listing 7-8 to the Store component.

Listing 7-8. Enabling Search in the Store.vue File in the src/components Folder

```
<template>
    <div class="container-fluid">
        <div class="row">
            <div class="col bg-dark text-white">
                <a class="navbar-brand">SPORTS STORE</a>
                <cart-summary />
            </div>
        </div>
        <div class="row">
            <div class="col-3 bg-info p-2">
                <CategoryControls class="mb-5" />
                <button class="btn btn-block btn-warning mt-5"
                        v-on:click="setShowSearch(true)">
                    Search
                </button>
            </div>
            <div class="col-9 p-2">
                <Search />
                <ProductList />
            </div>
        </div>
    </div>
</template>

<script>
    import ProductList from "./ProductList";
    import CategoryControls from "./CategoryControls";
    import CartSummary from "./CartSummary";
    import { mapMutations } from "vuex";
    import Search from "./Search";

    export default {
        components: { ProductList, CategoryControls, CartSummary, Search },
        methods: {
            ...mapMutations(["setShowSearch"])
        }
    }
</script>
```

I added a button alongside the list of categories that will cause the search feature to be shown to the user and registered the component I defined in Listing 7-7. The result is that the user can click the Search button and enter text to perform a search, as shown in Figure 7-4. The results are presented in pages and can filtered by category.

Figure 7-4. *Performing a search*

Starting the Administration Features

Any application that presents content to the user requires some degree of administration. In the case of SportsStore, this means managing the product catalog and the orders that customers have placed. In the sections that follow, I start the process of adding administration features to the project, starting with authentication and then building the structure that will present the admin features.

Implementing Authentication

The result of authentication with the RESTful web service is a JSON Web Token (JWT), which is returned by the server and must be included in any subsequent requests to show that the application is authorized to perform protected operations. You can read the JWT specification at https://tools.ietf.org/html/rfc7519, but for the purposes of the SportsStore application, it is enough to know that the application can authenticate the user by sending a POST request to the /login URL, including a JSON-formatted object in the request body that contains name and password properties. There is only one set of valid credentials in the authentication code used in Chapter 5, which is shown in Table 7-1.

Table 7-1. *The Authentication Credentials Supported by the RESTful Web Service*

Name	Description
admin	secret

   As I noted in Chapter 5, you should not hard-code credentials in real projects, but this is the username and password that you will need for the SportsStore application.

   If the correct credentials are sent to the /login URL, then the response from the RESTful web service will contain a JSON object like this:

```
{
  "success": true,
  "token":"eyJhbGciOiJIUzI1NiIsInR5cCI6IkpXVCJ9.eyJkYXRhIjoiYWRtaW4iLCJleHBpcmVz
          SW4iOiIxaCIsImlhdCI6MTQ3ODk1NjI1Mn0.lJaDDrSu-bHBtdWrz0312p_DG5tKypGv6cA
          NgOyzlg8"
}
```

The `success` property describes the outcome of the authentication operation, and the `token` property contains the JWT, which should be included in subsequent requests using the `Authorization` HTTP header in this format:

```
Authorization: Bearer<eyJhbGciOiJIUzI1NiIsInR5cCI6IkpXVCJ9.eyJkYXRhIjoiYWRtaW4iLC
                JleHBpcmVzSW4iOiIxaCIsImlhdCI6MTQ3ODk1NjI1Mn0.lJaDDrSu-bHBtd
                WrzO312p_DG5tKypGv6cANgOyzlg8>
```

If the wrong credentials are sent to the server, then the JSON object returned in the response will just contain a `success` property set to `false`, like this:

```
{
    "success": false
}
```

I configured the JWT tokens returned by the server so they expire after one hour.

Extending the Data Store

To add support for including the authentication header in HTTP requests, I added a file called `auth.js` to the `src/store` folder with the contents shown in Listing 7-9.

Listing 7-9. The Contents of the auth.js File in the src/store Folder

```
import Axios from "axios";

const loginUrl = "http://localhost:3500/login";

export default {
    state: {
        authenticated: false,
        jwt: null
    },
    getters: {
        authenticatedAxios(state) {
            return Axios.create({
                headers: {
                    "Authorization": `Bearer<${state.jwt}>`
                }
            });
        }
    },
    mutations: {
        setAuthenticated(state, header) {
            state.jwt = header;
            state.authenticated = true;
        },
        clearAuthentication(state) {
```

```
                    state.authenticated = false;
                    state.jwt = null;
                }
            },
            actions: {
                async authenticate(context, credentials) {
                    let response = await Axios.post(loginUrl, credentials);
                    if (response.data.success == true) {
                        context.commit("setAuthenticated", response.data.token);
                    }
                }
            }
        }
    }
```

The authenticate action uses Axios to send an HTTP POST request to the web service's /login URL and sets the authenticated and jwt state properties if the request is successful. The Axios create method is used to configure an object that can be used to make requests, and I use this feature in the authenticatedAxious getter to provide an Axios object that will include the Authorization header in all the requests it makes. In Listing 7-10, I added the new module to the data store.

Listing 7-10. Adding a Module in the index.js File in the src/store Folder

```
import Vue from "vue";
import Vuex from "vuex";
import Axios from "axios";
import CartModule from "./cart";
import OrdersModule from "./orders";
import AuthModule from "./auth";

Vue.use(Vuex);

const baseUrl = "http://localhost:3500";
const productsUrl = `${baseUrl}/products`;
const categoriesUrl = `${baseUrl}/categories`;

export default new Vuex.Store({
    strict: true,
    modules: { cart: CartModule, orders: OrdersModule, auth: AuthModule },

    // ...data store features omitted for brevity...
})
```

Adding the Administration Components

To get started with authentication, I need two components, one of which will prompt the user for their credentials and one that will be shown to the user once they have been authenticated and that will present the administration features. To keep the administration features separate from the rest of the application, I created the src/components/admin folder, to which I added a file called Admin.vue with the content shown in Listing 7-11.

Listing 7-11. The Contents of the Admin.vue File in the src/components/admin Folder

```
<template>
    <div class="bg-danger text-white text-center h4 p-2">Admin Features</div>
</template>
```

This is just a placeholder so that I have something to work with while I get the basic features in place, and I'll replace this content with real administration features shortly. To prompt the user for authentication credentials, I added a file called `Authentication.vue` to the `src/components/admin` folder with the content shown in Listing 7-12.

■ **Note** In Listing 7-12, I have set the value of the username and password properties to the credentials from Table 7-1 to make the development process simpler. As you follow the examples and make changes to the project, you will often have to reauthenticate, and this quickly becomes frustrating if you have to type in the credentials every time. In Chapter 8, I will remove the values from the component as I prepare the application for deployment.

Listing 7-12. The Contents of the Authentication.vue File in the src/components/admin Folder

```
<template>
    <div class="m-2">
        <h4 class="bg-primary text-white text-center p-2">
            SportsStore Administration
        </h4>

        <h4 v-if="showFailureMessage"
                class="bg-danger text-white text-center p-2 my-2">
            Authentication Failed. Please try again.
        </h4>

        <div class="form-group">
            <label>Username</label>
            <input class="form-control" v-model="$v.username.$model">
            <validation-error v-bind:validation="$v.username" />
        </div>
        <div class="form-group">
            <label>Password</label>
            <input type="password" class="form-control" v-model="$v.password.$model">
            <validation-error v-bind:validation="$v.password" />
        </div>
        <div class="text-center">
            <button class="btn btn-primary" v-on:click="handleAuth">Log In</button>
        </div>
    </div>
</template>
```

```
<script>

import { required } from "vuelidate/lib/validators";
import { mapActions, mapState } from "vuex";
import ValidationError  from "../ValidationError";

export default {
    components: { ValidationError },
    data: function() {
        return {
            username: "admin",
            password: "secret",
            showFailureMessage: false,
        }
    },
    computed: {
        ...mapState({authenticated: state => state.auth.authenticated })
    },
    validations: {
        username: { required },
        password: { required }
    },
    methods: {
        ...mapActions(["authenticate"]),
        async handleAuth() {
            this.$v.$touch();
            if (!this.$v.$invalid) {
                await this.authenticate({ name: this.username,
                    password: this.password });
                if (this.authenticated) {
                    this.$router.push("/admin");
                } else {
                    this.showFailureMessage = true;
                }
            }
        }
    }
}

</script>
```

This component presents the user with a pair of input elements and a button that performs authentication using the data store features from Listing 7-9, with data validation to ensure that the user provides values for the username and password. If authentication fails, then a warning message is displayed. If authentication is successful, then the routing system is used to navigate to the /admin URL. To configure the routing system to support the new components, I added the routes shown in Listing 7-13.

Listing 7-13. Adding Routes in the index.js File in the src/router Folder

```
import Vue from "vue";
import VueRouter  from "vue-router";
```

```
import Store from "../components/Store";
import ShoppingCart from "../components/ShoppingCart";
import Checkout from "../components/Checkout";
import OrderThanks from "../components/OrderThanks";
import Authentication from "../components/admin/Authentication";
import Admin from "../components/admin/Admin";

Vue.use(VueRouter);

export default new VueRouter({
    mode: "history",
    routes: [
        { path: "/", component: Store },
        { path: "/cart", component: ShoppingCart },
        { path: "/checkout", component: Checkout},
        { path: "/thanks/:id", component: OrderThanks},
        { path: "/login", component: Authentication },
        { path: "/admin", component: Admin},
        { path: "*", redirect: "/"}
    ]
})
```

To test the authentication process, navigate to `http://localhost:8080/login`, enter a username and password, and click the Log In button. If you use the credentials from Table 7-1, authentication will succeed, and you will see the placeholder admin content. If you use different credentials, authentication will fail, and you will see an error. Both outcomes are shown in Figure 7-5.

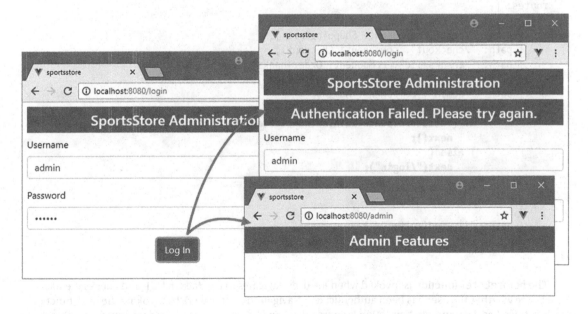

Figure 7-5. *Authenticating the user*

171

Adding the Route Guard

Currently, there is nothing to prevent the user from navigating directly to the /admin URL and bypassing authentication. To prevent this, I added a route *guard*, which is a function that is evaluated when the route is about to change and that can prevent or change navigation. The Vue Router package provides a range of different route guard options, which I describe in Chapter 24. For this chapter, I need a guard that is specific to the route for the /admin URL and that will prevent navigation if the user hasn't been authenticated, as shown in Listing 7-14.

Listing 7-14. Adding a Route Guard in the index.js File in the src/router Folder

```
import Vue from "vue";
import VueRouter  from "vue-router";

import Store from "../components/Store";
import ShoppingCart from "../components/ShoppingCart";
import Checkout from "../components/Checkout";
import OrderThanks from "../components/OrderThanks";
import Authentication from "../components/admin/Authentication";
import Admin from "../components/admin/Admin";

import dataStore from "../store";

Vue.use(VueRouter);

export default new VueRouter({
    mode: "history",
    routes: [
        { path: "/", component: Store },
        { path: "/cart", component: ShoppingCart },
        { path: "/checkout", component: Checkout},
        { path: "/thanks/:id", component: OrderThanks},
        { path: "/login", component: Authentication },
        { path: "/admin", component: Admin,
            beforeEnter(to, from, next) {
                if (dataStore.state.auth.authenticated) {
                    next();
                } else {
                    next("/login");
                }
            }
        },
        { path: "*", redirect: "/"}
    ]
})
```

The beforeEnter function is invoked when the user navigates to the /admin URL and checks the data store to see whether the user has been authenticated. Navigation guards work by invoking the next function that is received as a parameter. Navigation is approved when the guard invokes the next function with no arguments. Navigation is prevented by invoking next with a replacement URL, which in this example is / login to prompt the user for credentials. To see the effect, navigate to http://localhost:8080/admin, and you will see that the route guard redirects the browser to the /login URL instead, as shown in Figure 7-6.

Figure 7-6. *The effect of a route guard*

Notice that I used an `import` statement to access the data store. The `mapState` helper function that I used in earlier examples and the `$store` property that can be used to access the data store directly can be used only in components and isn't available elsewhere in the application, such as in the routing configuration. The `import` statement provides me with access to the data store, through which I can read the value of the `state` property that the route guard needs to determine whether the user has been authenticated.

Adding the Administration Component Structure

Now that the authentication features are in place, I am going to return to the main administration features. The administrator will need the ability to manage the collection of products presented to the user and to see orders and mark them as shipped. I will start by creating placeholder components for each of these areas of functionality, use them to set up the structure that displays them to the user, and then implement the detail of each feature. I added a file called `ProductAdmin.vue` to the `src/components/admin` folder with the content shown in Listing 7-15.

Listing 7-15. The Contents of the ProductAdmin.vue File in the src/components/admin Folder

```
<template>
    <div class="bg-danger text-white text-center h4 p-2">
        Product Admin
    </div>
</template>
```

Next, I added a file called `OrderAdmin.vue` in the same folder with the content shown in Listing 7-16.

Listing 7-16. The Contents of the OrderAdmin.vue File in the src/components/admin Folder

```
<template>
    <div class="bg-danger text-white text-center h4 p-2">
        Order Admin
    </div>
</template>
```

To present these new components to the user, I replaced the content in the `Admin` component with the elements shown in Listing 7-17.

Listing 7-17. Presenting Components in the Admin.vue File in the src/components/admin Folder

```
<template>
    <div class="container-fluid">
        <div class="row">
            <div class="col bg-secondary text-white">
                <a class="navbar-brand">SPORTS STORE Admin</a>
            </div>
        </div>
        <div class="row">
            <div class="col-3 bg-secondary p-2">
                <router-link to="/admin/products" class="btn btn-block btn-primary"
                        active-class="active">
                    Products
                </router-link>
                <router-link to="/admin/orders"  class="btn btn-block btn-primary"
                        active-class="active">
                    Orders
                </router-link>
            </div>
            <div class="col-9 p-2">
                <router-view />
            </div>
        </div>
    </div>
</template>
```

Applications can contain multiple router-view elements, and I have used one here so that I can alternate between the product and order management components using URL routes, which I will configure shortly. To choose the component, I have used router-link elements, which are formatted as buttons. To indicate which button represents the active selection, I have used the active-class attribute, which specifies a class to which the element will be added when the route specified by its to attribute is active, as explained in Chapter 23.

To configure the new router-view element, I added the routes shown in Listing 7-18 to the application's routing configuration.

Listing 7-18. Adding Routes in the index.js File in the src/router Folder

```
import Vue from "vue";
import VueRouter  from "vue-router";
import Store from "../components/Store";
import ShoppingCart from "../components/ShoppingCart";
import Checkout from "../components/Checkout";
import OrderThanks from "../components/OrderThanks";
import Authentication from "../components/admin/Authentication";
import Admin from "../components/admin/Admin";
import ProductAdmin from "../components/admin/ProductAdmin";
import OrderAdmin from "../components/admin/OrderAdmin";

import dataStore from "../store";

Vue.use(VueRouter);
```

```
export default new VueRouter({
    mode: "history",
    routes: [
        { path: "/", component: Store },
        { path: "/cart", component: ShoppingCart },
        { path: "/checkout", component: Checkout},
        { path: "/thanks/:id", component: OrderThanks},
        { path: "/login", component: Authentication },
        { path: "/admin", component: Admin,
            beforeEnter(to, from, next) {
                if (dataStore.state.auth.authenticated) {
                    next();
                } else {
                    next("/login");
                }
            },
            children: [
                { path: "products", component: ProductAdmin },
                { path: "orders", component: OrderAdmin },
                { path: "", redirect: "/admin/products"}
            ]
        },
        { path: "*", redirect: "/"}
    ]
})
```

The new additions use the *child route* feature, which I describe in Chapter 23 and which allows nested
router-view elements to be used. The result is that navigating to /admin/products will display the Admin
component at the top level and then the ProductAdmin component, while the /admin/orders URL will show
the OrderAdmin component, as shown in Figure 7-7. There is also a fallback route that redirects the /admin
URL to /admin/products.

Figure 7-7. *Using child routes and nested router-view elements*

Implementing the Order Administration Feature

To let administrators manage orders, I need to present a list of objects from the server and provide the
means to mark each one as shipped. The starting point for these features is to expand the data store, as
shown in Listing 7-19.

Listing 7-19. Adding Features in the orders.js File in the src/store Folder

```
import Axios from "axios";
import Vue from "vue";

const ORDERS_URL = "http://localhost:3500/orders";

export default {
    state: {
        orders:[]
    },
    mutations: {
        setOrders(state, data) {
            state.orders = data;
        },
        changeOrderShipped(state, order) {
            Vue.set(order, "shipped",
                order.shipped == null || !order.shipped ? true : false);
        }
    },
    actions: {
        async storeOrder(context, order) {
            order.cartLines = context.rootState.cart.lines;
            return (await Axios.post(ORDERS_URL, order)).data.id;
        },
        async getOrders(context) {
            context.commit("setOrders",
                (await context.rootGetters.authenticatedAxios.get(ORDERS_URL)).data);
        },
        async updateOrder(context, order) {
            context.commit("changeOrderShipped", order);
            await context.rootGetters.authenticatedAxios
                .put(`${ORDERS_URL}/${order.id}`, order);
        }
    }
}
```

You have already seen how Vue.js can be used to present data in pages that are requested on-demand, so I have kept the order feature simple: all of the data is requested through the getOrders action, and an order can be modified using the updateOrder action.

To provide a list of the orders and allow them to be marked and shipped, I replaced the placeholder content from the OrderAdmin component and replaced it with the content and code shown in Listing 7-20.

Listing 7-20. Managing Orders in the OrderAdmin.vue File in the src/components/admin Folder

```
<template>
    <div>
        <h4 class="bg-info text-white text-center p-2">Orders</h4>
        <div class="form-group text-center">
            <input class="form-check-input" type="checkbox" v-model="showShipped" />
            <label class="form-check-label">Show Shipped Orders</label>
        </div>
```

```
        <table class="table table-sm table-bordered">
            <thead>
                <tr>
                    <th>ID</th><th>Name</th><th>City, Zip</th>
                    <th class="text-right">Total</th>
                    <th></th>
                </tr>
            </thead>
            <tbody>
                <tr v-if="displayOrders.length == 0">
                    <td colspan="5">There are no orders</td>
                </tr>
                <tr v-for="o in displayOrders" v-bind:key="o.id">
                    <td>{{ o.id }}</td>
                    <td>{{ o.name }}</td>
                    <td>{{ `${o.city}, ${o.zip}` }}</td>
                    <td class="text-right">{{ getTotal(o) | currency }}</td>
                    <td class="text-center">
                        <button class="btn btn-sm btn-danger"
                            v-on:click="shipOrder(o)">
                                {{ o.shipped ? 'Not Shipped' : 'Shipped' }}
                        </button>
                    </td>
                </tr>
            </tbody>
        </table>
    </div>
</template>

<script>

import { mapState, mapActions, mapMutations } from "vuex";

export default {
    data: function() {
        return {
            showShipped: false
        }
    },
    computed: {
        ...mapState({ orders: state => state.orders.orders}),
        displayOrders() {
            return this.showShipped ? this.orders
                : this.orders.filter(o => o.shipped != true);
        }
    },
    methods: {
        ...mapMutations(["changeOrderShipped"]),
        ...mapActions(["getOrders", "updateOrder"]),
        getTotal(order) {
            if (order.cartLines != null && order.cartLines.length > 0) {
                return order.cartLines.reduce((total, line) =>
```

```
                    total + (line.quantity * line.product.price), 0)
            } else {
                return 0;
            }
        },
        shipOrder(order) {
            this.updateOrder(order);
        }
    },
    created() {
        this.getOrders();
    }
}
</script>
```

The component displays a table of orders, each of which has a button that changes the shipping status. To see the effect, navigate to http://localhost:8080 and use the store features to create one or more orders and then navigate to http://localhost:8080/admin, authenticate yourself, and click the Orders button to see and manage the list, as shown in Figure 7-8.

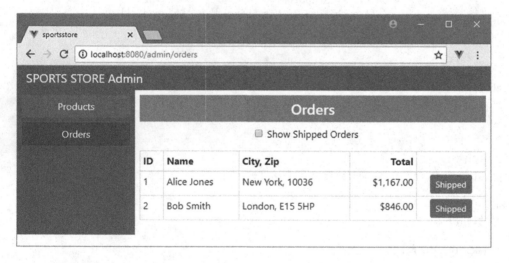

Figure 7-8. *Managing orders*

Summary

In this chapter, I continued building the SportsStore application. I showed you how Vue.js and its core libraries can be used to deal with larger amounts of data, and I put in place the initial administration features, starting with authentication and order management. In the next chapter, I complete the administration features and deploy the completed application.

CHAPTER 8

SportsStore: Administration and Deployment

In this chapter, I complete the SportsStore application by adding the remaining administration features and show you how to prepare and deploy the project. As you will see, the transition from development to production is relatively simple and easy to perform.

Preparing for This Chapter

This chapter uses the SportsStore project from Chapter 7, and no changes are required in preparation for this chapter.

■ **Tip** You can download the example project for this chapter—and for all of the other chapters in this book—from https://github.com/Apress/pro-vue-js-2.

To start the RESTful web service, open a command prompt and run the following command in the sportsstore folder:

```
npm run json
```

Open a second command prompt and run the following command in the sportsstore folder to start the development tools and HTTP server:

```
npm run serve
```

Once the initial build process is complete, open a new browser window and navigate to http://localhost:8080 to see the content shown in Figure 8-1.

© Adam Freeman 2018

A. Freeman, *Pro Vue.js 2*, https://doi.org/10.1007/978-1-4842-3805-9_8

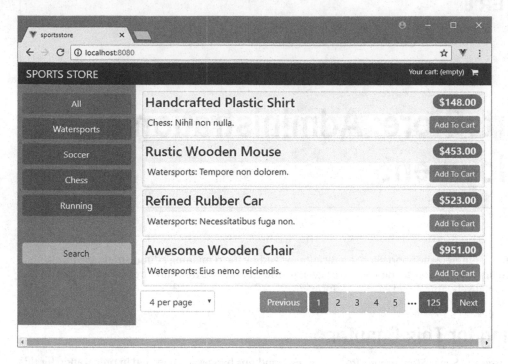

Figure 8-1. *Running the SportsStore application*

Adding the Product Administration Features

To complete the administration features, I need to give the SportsStore application the ability to create, edit, and delete product objects. First, I am going to expand the data store to provide actions that support these operations by sending HTTP requests to the web service and updating the product data, as shown in Listing 8-1.

Listing 8-1. Adding Administration Features in the index.js File in the src/store Folder

```
import Vue from "vue";
import Vuex from "vuex";
import Axios from "axios";
import CartModule from "./cart";
import OrdersModule from "./orders";
import AuthModule from "./auth";

Vue.use(Vuex);

const baseUrl = "http://localhost:3500";
const productsUrl = `${baseUrl}/products`;
const categoriesUrl = `${baseUrl}/categories`;

export default new Vuex.Store({
    strict: true,
    modules:  { cart: CartModule, orders: OrdersModule, auth: AuthModule },
    state: {
```

```
        // ...state properties omitted for brevity...
    },
    getters: {
        processedProducts: (state) => {
            return state.pages[state.currentPage];
        },
        pageCount: (state) => state.serverPageCount,
        categories: state => ["All", ...state.categoriesData],
        productById:(state) => (id) => {
            return state.pages[state.currentPage].find(p => p.id == id);
        }
    },
    mutations: {
        _setCurrentPage(state, page) {
            state.currentPage = page;
        },

        // ...other mutations omitted for brevity...

        setSearchTerm(state, term) {
            state.searchTerm = term;
            state.currentPage = 1;
        },
        _addProduct(state, product) {
            state.pages[state.currentPage].unshift(product);
        },
        _updateProduct(state, product) {
            let page = state.pages[state.currentPage];
            let index = page.findIndex(p => p.id == product.id);
            Vue.set(page, index, product);
        }
    },
    actions: {
        async getData(context) {
            await context.dispatch("getPage", 2);
            context.commit("setCategories", (await Axios.get(categoriesUrl)).data);
        },

        // ...other actions omitted for brevity...

        async addProduct(context, product) {
            let data = (await context.getters.authenticatedAxios.post(productsUrl,
                product)).data;
            product.id = data.id;
            this.commit("_addProduct", product);
        },
        async removeProduct(context, product) {
            await context.getters.authenticatedAxios
                .delete(`${productsUrl}/${product.id}`);
            context.commit("clearPages");
            context.dispatch("getPage", 1);
        },
```

```
    async updateProduct(context, product) {
        await context.getters.authenticatedAxios
            .put(`${productsUrl}/${product.id}`, product);
        this.commit("_updateProduct", product);
    }
  }
})
```

The actions will be invoked by components to store, remove, or change a product, which requires an HTTP request to the web service and a corresponding change to the local data. When a product is changed, I locate the existing object and replace it, but for the other operations, I take slight shortcuts. When a product is added, I insert it at the start of the current page of products, even though this means the page size is incorrect, so that I don't have to figure out which page the new object should be displayed on and get that data from the server. When an object is deleted, I refresh the data so that I don't have to deal with manually repaginating to cover the gap. These shortcuts are performed using the _addProduct and _updateProduct mutations, whose names I have prefixed with an underscore to indicate they are not for wider use. I also added a getter in Listing 8-1 so that I can locate a product in the current page by its id. This type of getter has a parameter, and it is used like a method, which means that I can define the logic that locates the product in the data store, rather than having to get all of the objects in the page and performing the search in a component.

Presenting the Product List

To present the products to the user and provide the means to create, edit, and delete them, I removed the placeholder content from the ProductAdmin component created in Chapter 7 and replaced it with the HTML elements and code shown in Listing 8-2.

Listing 8-2. Adding Features in the ProductAdmin.vue File in the src/components/admin Folder

```
<template>
    <div>
        <router-link to="/admin/products/create" class="btn btn-primary my-2">
            Create Product
        </router-link>
        <table class="table table-sm table-bordered">
            <thead>
                <th>ID</th><th>Name</th><th>Category</th>
                <th class="text-right">Price</th><th></th>
            </thead>
            <tbody>
                <tr v-for="p in products" v-bind:key="p.id">
                    <td>{{ p.id }}</td>
                    <td>{{ p.name }}</td>
                    <td>{{ p.category }}</td>
                    <td class="text-right">{{ p.price | currency }}</td>
                    <td class="text-center">
                        <button class="btn btn-sm btn-danger mx-1"
                            v-on:click="removeProduct(p)">Delete</button>
                        <button class="btn btn-sm btn-warning mx-1"
                            v-on:click="handleEdit(p)">Edit</button>
                    </td>
                </tr>
```

```
            </tbody>
        </table>
        <page-controls />
    </div>
</template>

<script>

import PageControls from "../PageControls";
import { mapGetters, mapActions } from "vuex";

export default {
    components: { PageControls },
    computed: {
        ...mapGetters({
                products: "processedProducts"
            })
    },
    methods: {
        ...mapActions(["removeProduct"]),
        handleEdit(product) {
            this.$router.push(`/admin/products/edit/${product.id}`);
        }
    }
}

</script>
```

This component presents the user with a table of products, populated from the data model using the v-for directive. Each row in the table has Delete and Edit buttons. Clicking a Delete button dispatches the removeProduct action added to the data store in Listing 8-1. Clicking an Edit button or the Create Product button redirects the browser to a URL that I will use to display an editor that can be used to modify or create products.

■ **Tip**   Notice that I am able to use the PageControls component from earlier chapters to handle pagination of products. The administration features build on the same data store features used by the customer-facing features in earlier chapters, which means that common functionality such as pagination can easily be reused.

Adding the Editor Placeholder and URL Routes

Following the pattern used in earlier chapters, I am going to create a placeholder component for the editor and return to add its features once it has been integrated into the application. I added a file called ProductEditor.vue in the src/components/admin folder with the content shown in Listing 8-3.

Listing 8-3. The Contents of the ProductEditor.vue File in the src/components/admin Folder

```
<template>
    <div class="bg-info text-white text-center h4 p-2">
        Product Editor
    </div>
</template>
```

To integrate the editor component into the application, I added the route shown in Listing 8-4, which will match the URLs I used in the ProductAdmin component when the user clicks the Edit or Create Product button.

Listing 8-4. Adding a Route in the index.js File in the src/router Folder

```
import Vue from "vue";
import VueRouter  from "vue-router";
import Store from "../components/Store";
import ShoppingCart from "../components/ShoppingCart";
import Checkout from "../components/Checkout";
import OrderThanks from "../components/OrderThanks";
import Authentication from "../components/admin/Authentication";
import Admin from "../components/admin/Admin";
import ProductAdmin from "../components/admin/ProductAdmin";
import OrderAdmin from "../components/admin/OrderAdmin";
import ProductEditor from "../components/admin/ProductEditor";

import dataStore from "../store";

Vue.use(VueRouter);

export default new VueRouter({
    mode: "history",
    routes: [
        { path: "/", component: Store },
        { path: "/cart", component: ShoppingCart },
        { path: "/checkout", component: Checkout},
        { path: "/thanks/:id", component: OrderThanks},
        { path: "/login", component: Authentication },
        { path: "/admin", component: Admin,
            beforeEnter(to, from, next) {
                if (dataStore.state.auth.authenticated) {
                    next();
                } else {
                    next("/login");
                }
            },
            children: [
                { path: "products/:op(create|edit)/:id(\\d+)?",
                  component: ProductEditor },
                { path: "products", component: ProductAdmin },
                { path: "orders", component: OrderAdmin },
                { path: "", redirect: "/admin/products"}
            ]
        },
        { path: "*", redirect: "/"}
    ]
})
```

As I explain in Chapter 22, the Vue Router package is able to handle complex patterns when it matches URLs and includes support for regular expressions. The route that I added in Listing 8-4 will match the /admin/products/create URL, which will indicate the user wants to add a new product, and the /admin/products/edit/id URL, where the final segment is a numeric value that corresponds to the id property of the product that the user wants to edit.

To see the product administration features, navigate to http://localhost:8080/login and go through the authentication process. Once you are authenticated, you will see the list of products shown in Figure 8-2. If you click one of the Delete buttons, the product you selected will be removed and deleted from the web service. If you click the Create Product button or one of the Edit buttons, you will see the placeholder content.

■ **Tip**   Remember that you can re-create all the test data by restarting the json-server process using the command from the start of the chapter. This will reset the data and discard any changes, additions, or deletions you have made.

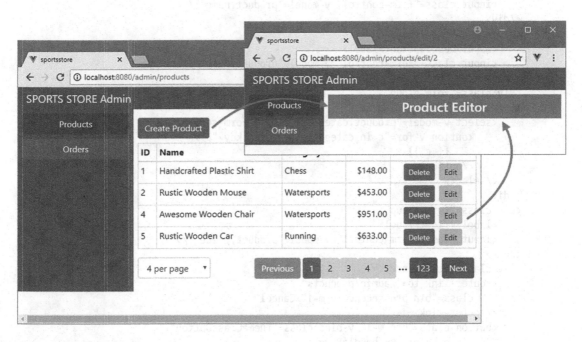

Figure 8-2. *The product administration features*

Implementing the Editor Feature

The editor component will be used to create and edit products and will determine which activity the user requires based on the route that has matched the current URL. In Listing 8-5, I have removed the placeholder content and added the content and code required to create and modify products.

Listing 8-5. Adding Features in the ProductEditor.vue File in the src/components/admin Folder

```
<template>
    <div>
        <h4 class="text-center text-white p-2" v-bind:class="themeClass">
            {{ editMode ? "Edit" : "Create Product" }}
        </h4>
        <h4 v-if="$v.$invalid && $v.$dirty"
                class="bg-danger text-white text-center p-2">
            Values Required for All Fields
        </h4>
        <div class="form-group" v-if="editMode">
            <label>ID (Not Editable)</label>
            <input class="form-control" disabled v-model="product.id" />
        </div>
        <div class="form-group">
            <label>Name</label>
            <input class="form-control" v-model="product.name" />
        </div>
        <div class="form-group">
            <label>Description</label>
            <input class="form-control" v-model="product.description" />
        </div>
        <div class="form-group">
            <label>Category</label>
            <select v-model="product.category" class="form-control">
                <option v-for="c in categories" v-bind:key="c">
                    {{ c }}
                </option>
            </select>
        </div>
        <div class="form-group">
            <label>Price</label>
            <input class="form-control" v-model="product.price" />
        </div>
        <div class="text-center">
            <router-link to="/admin/products"
                class="btn btn-secondary m-1">Cancel
            </router-link>
            <button class="btn m-1" v-bind:class="themeClassButton"
                    v-on:click="handleSave">
                {{ editMode ? "Save Changes" : "Store Product"}}
            </button>
        </div>
    </div>
</template>

<script>

import { mapState, mapActions } from "vuex";
import { required } from "vuelidate/lib/validators";
```

```
export default {
    data: function() {
        return {
            product: {}
        }
    },
    computed: {
        ...mapState({
            pages: state => state.pages,
            currentPage: state => state.currentPage,
            categories: state => state.categoriesData
        }),
        editMode() {
            return this.$route.params["op"] == "edit";
        },
        themeClass() {
            return this.editMode ? "bg-info" : "bg-primary";
        },
        themeClassButton() {
            return this.editMode ? "btn-info" : "btn-primary";
        }
    },
    validations: {
        product: {
            name: { required },
            description: { required },
            category: { required },
            price: { required }
        }
    },
    methods: {
        ...mapActions(["addProduct", "updateProduct"]),
        async handleSave() {
            this.$v.$touch();
            if (!this.$v.$invalid) {
                if (this.editMode) {
                    await this.updateProduct(this.product);
                } else {
                    await this.addProduct(this.product);
                }
                this.$router.push("/admin/products");
            }
        }
    },
    created() {
        if (this.editMode) {
            Object.assign(this.product,
                this.$store.getters.productById(this.$route.params["id"]))
        }
    }
}
</script>
```

The component presents the user with an HTML form with the fields required to create or edit a product. The purpose for which the component has been created is determined by getting details of the active route, and the data store is queried for the product when the user is performing an edit operation, which is done using the created method, which I describe in Chapter 17. I use Object.assign, as described in Chapter 4, to copy the properties from the data store object so that changes can be made without updating the data store, allowing the user to click the Cancel button and discard changes. The form has basic validation and invokes the actions in the data store to store or update a product.

To edit a product, navigate to http://localhost:8080/admin, perform authentication, and click one of the Edit buttons. Use the form to make changes and then click the Save Changes button to see those changes reflected in the product table, as shown in Figure 8-3.

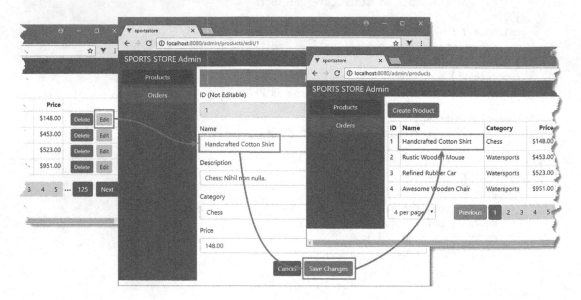

Figure 8-3. *Editing a product*

To create a product, click the Create Product button, populate the form, and click the Store Product button. You will see the new product at the top of the page, as shown in Figure 8-4.

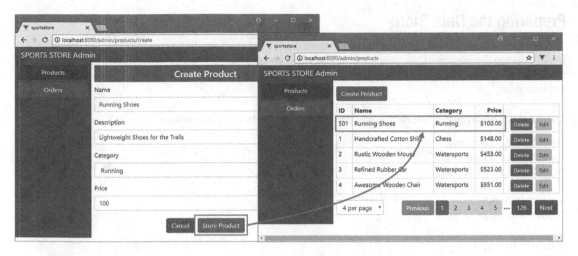

Figure 8-4. *Creating a product*

Deploying SportsStore

In the sections that follow, I go through the process of deploying the SportsStore application. I start by making configuration changes that are required regardless of the platform to which the application is deployed and that prepare SportsStore for production use. I then use Docker to create a container that contains SportsStore and the services it requires to replace the development tools that have been used to run the application during its development.

ALTERNATIVES TO DOCKER

I use Docker in this chapter because it is simple and consistent, and you can follow the example on a reasonably capable development machine, without the need for separate production hardware. There are plenty of alternatives to Docker to consider for your own projects, and Vue.js can be deployed in countless different ways to suit the needs of different applications. You don't have to use Docker, but regardless of how you choose to deploy your applications, remember to make the configuration changes that are shown in the next section.

Preparing the Application for Deployment

To prepare the application for deployment, there are some small changes required. These changes don't alter the behavior of the application, but they are important because they disable features that are useful to developers but that have an impact in production.

Preparing the Data Store

The first change is to disable strict mode in the Vuex data store, as shown in Listing 8-6. This is a useful feature during development because it warns you when you modify state properties directly, rather than through a mutation, but it isn't useful during production and affects performance, especially in complex applications.

Listing 8-6. Preparing for Deployment in the index.js File in the src/store Folder

```
import Vue from "vue";
import Vuex from "vuex";
import Axios from "axios";
import CartModule from "./cart";
import OrdersModule from "./orders";
import AuthModule from "./auth";

Vue.use(Vuex);

const baseUrl = "/api";
const productsUrl = `${baseUrl}/products`;
const categoriesUrl = `${baseUrl}/categories`;

export default new Vuex.Store({
    strict: false,
    modules: { cart: CartModule, orders: OrdersModule, auth: AuthModule },

    // ... data store features omitted for brevity...
})
```

During development, I used a separate process for handling web service requests. For the deployed application, I am going to combine the HTTP requests for the application and its data into a single server, which requires a change to the URLs that the data store uses to get data, which is why I altered the baseUrl value. In Listing 8-7, I have changed the URL used by the authentication module.

Listing 8-7. Changing the URL in the auth.js File in the src/store Folder

```
import Axios from "axios";

const loginUrl = "/api/login";

export default {
    state: {
        authenticated: false,
        jwt: null
    },

    // ... data store features omitted for brevity...

}
```

The URL used to manage orders must also be changed, as shown in Listing 8-8.

Listing 8-8. Changing the URL in the orders.js File in the src/store Folder

```
import Axios from "axios";
import Vue from "vue";

const ORDERS_URL = "/api/orders";

export default {
    state: {
        orders:[]
    },

    // ... data store features omitted for brevity...

}
```

Preparing the Authentication Component

The next change is to remove the credentials for administration authentication from the component, as shown in Listing 8-9, which was useful during development but which should not be included in production.

Listing 8-9. Removing Credentials in the Authentication.vue file in the src/components/admin Folder

```
...
<script>

import { required } from "vuelidate/lib/validators";
import { mapActions, mapState } from "vuex";
import ValidationError  from "../ValidationError";

export default {
    components: { ValidationError },
    data: function() {
        return {
            username: null,
            password: null,
            showFailureMessage: false,
        }
    },
    computed: {
        ...mapState({authenticated: state => state.auth.authenticated })
    },
    validations: {
        username: { required },
        password: { required }
    },
    methods: {
        ...mapActions(["authenticate"]),
        async handleAuth() {
            this.$v.$touch();
            if (!this.$v.$invalid) {
                await this.authenticate({ name: this.username,
```

```
                    password: this.password });
                if (this.authenticated) {
                    this.$router.push("/admin");
                } else {
                    this.showFailureMessage = true;
                }
            }
        }
    }
}

</script>
...
```

Loading the Administration Features On-Demand

Every feature of the SportsStore application is included in the JavaScript bundle that is created by the Vue.js build tools, even though the administration features are likely to be used by a small fraction of the user base. Vue.js makes it easy to break the application into separate bundles that can be loaded only when they are first required. To separate the administration features into their own bundle, I added a file called index.js in the src/components/admin folder with the code shown in Listing 8-10.

Listing 8-10. The Contents of the index.js File in the src/components/admin Folder

```
import Vue from "vue";
import VueRouter  from "vue-router";
import Store from "../components/Store";
import ShoppingCart from "../components/ShoppingCart";
import Checkout from "../components/Checkout";
import OrderThanks from "../components/OrderThanks";

const Authentication = () =>
    import(/* webpackChunkName: "admin" */ "../components/admin/Authentication");
const Admin = () =>
    import(/* webpackChunkName: "admin" */ "../components/admin/Admin");
const ProductAdmin = () =>
    import(/* webpackChunkName: "admin" */ "../components/admin/ProductAdmin");
const OrderAdmin = () =>
    import(/* webpackChunkName: "admin" */ "../components/admin/OrderAdmin");
const ProductEditor = () =>
    import(/* webpackChunkName: "admin" */ "../components/admin/ProductEditor");

import dataStore from "../store";

Vue.use(VueRouter);

export default new VueRouter({
    mode: "history",
    routes: [
        { path: "/", component: Store },
        { path: "/cart", component: ShoppingCart },
```

```
{ path: "/checkout", component: Checkout},
{ path: "/thanks/:id", component: OrderThanks},
{ path: "/login", component: Authentication },
{ path: "/admin", component: Admin,
    beforeEnter(to, from, next) {
        if (dataStore.state.auth.authenticated) {
            next();
        } else {
            next("/login");
        }
    },
    children: [
        { path: "products/:op(create|edit)/:id(\\d+)?",
            component: ProductEditor },
        { path: "products", component: ProductAdmin },
        { path: "orders", component: OrderAdmin },
        { path: "", redirect: "/admin/products"}
    ]
},
{ path: "*", redirect: "/"}
]
})
```

Normal `import` statements create a static dependency on a module, with the effect that importing a component ensures it is included in the JavaScript file that is sent to the browser. As I explain in Chapter 21, the type of `import` statement I used in Listing 8-10 is dynamic, which means that the components required for the administration features will be put into a separate JavaScript file that is loaded the first time any of these components are required. This ensures that the features are available for the small number of users who require them but are not downloaded by the rest of the users.

■ **Note**   You may find that the separate module that is created as a result of Listing 8-10 is loaded anyway, even if the administration features are not used. This is because Vue.js projects are configured to provide the browser with prefetch hints, which are indications that there is content that may be required in the future. The browser is free to ignore these hints but may choose to request the module anyway. In Chapter 21, I demonstrate how to change the configuration of the project so that prefetch hints are not sent to the browser.

The awkward comment that I have included in the `import` statement ensures that the components are packaged into a single separate file. Without these comments, each component would end up in a separate file that would be requested from the server the first time it is required. Since these components provide related features, I have grouped them together. This is a feature that is specific to the tool used by the Vue. js tools to produce bundles of JavaScript code—known as *webpack*—and it may not work unless you have created your project using the Vue.js command-line tools as I did in Chapter 5.

Creating the Data File

I have been working with test data that is generated programmatically when the RESTful web service starts, which has been useful during development because the data is regenerated afresh each time, discarding any modification. For deployment, I am going to switch to data that will be persisted, ensuring that changes are preserved. I added a file called data.json to the sportsstore folder with the content shown in Listing 8-11.

Listing 8-11. The Contents of the data.json File in the sportsstore Folder

```
{
    "products": [
        { "id": 1, "name": "Kayak", "category": "Watersports",
            "description": "A boat for one person", "price": 275 },
        { "id": 2, "name": "Lifejacket", "category": "Watersports",
            "description": "Protective and fashionable", "price": 48.95 },
        { "id": 3, "name": "Soccer Ball", "category": "Soccer",
            "description": "FIFA-approved size and weight", "price": 19.50 },
        { "id": 4, "name": "Corner Flags", "category": "Soccer",
            "description": "Give your playing field a professional touch",
            "price": 34.95 },
        { "id": 5, "name": "Stadium", "category": "Soccer",
            "description": "Flat-packed 35,000-seat stadium", "price": 79500 },
        { "id": 6, "name": "Thinking Cap", "category": "Chess",
            "description": "Improve brain efficiency by 75%", "price": 16 },
        { "id": 7, "name": "Unsteady Chair", "category": "Chess",
            "description": "Secretly give your opponent a disadvantage",
            "price": 29.95 },
        { "id": 8, "name": "Human Chess Board", "category": "Chess",
            "description": "A fun game for the family", "price": 75 },
        { "id": 9, "name": "Bling Bling King", "category": "Chess",
            "description": "Gold-plated, diamond-studded King", "price": 1200 }
    ],
    "categories": ["Watersports", "Soccer", "Chess"],
    "orders": []
}
```

Building the Application for Deployment

To build the SportsStore application so that it can be deployed, run the command shown in Listing 8-12 in the sportsstore folder.

Listing 8-12. Building the Project

```
npm run build
```

The build process generates JavaScript files that are optimized for delivery to the browser and that exclude the development features, such as the automatic reloading of the browser when one of the source files change. The build process can take a while, and when it is complete, you will see a summary of the process, like this:

```
WARNING  Compiled with 2 warnings

 warning

asset size limit: The following asset(s) exceed the recommended size limit (244 KiB).
This can impact web performance.
Assets:
  img/fontawesome-webfont.912ec66d.svg (434 KiB)
```

```
warning

entrypoint size limit: The following entrypoint(s) combined asset size exceeds the
recommended limit (244 KiB). This can impact web performance.

Entrypoints:
  app (346 KiB)
      css/chunk-vendors.291cfd91.css
      js/chunk-vendors.56adf36a.js
      js/app.846b07bf.js


  File                                    Size            Gzipped

  dist\js\chunk-vendors.56adf36a.js       160.98 kb       54.10 kb
  dist\js\app.846b07bf.js                 25.08 kb        6.57 kb
  dist\js\admin.b43c91ef.js               11.62 kb        3.13 kb
  dist\css\chunk-vendors.291cfd91.css     159.97 kb       26.60 kb

Images and other types of assets omitted.

DONE  Build complete. The dist directory is ready to be deployed.
```

The warnings about sizes can be ignored, and the output from the build process is a set of JavaScript and CSS files that contain the content, code, and styles that the application requires, all of which are in the dist folder. (You may see different warnings because the tools that are used in the build process are updated often.)

Testing the Deployment-Ready Application

Before packaging the application for deployment, it is worth performing a quick test just to make sure that everything works as it should. During development, HTTP requests for HTML, JavaScript, and CSS files were handled by the Vue.js development tools, which must not be used in production. As a production-suitable alternative, I am going to install the popular Express package, which is a widely used web server that runs on Node.js. Run the commands shown in Listing 8-13 to install the Express package and a related package that is required to support URL routing.

Listing 8-13. Adding Packages

```
npm install --save-dev express@4.16.3
npm install --save-dev connect-history-api-fallback@1.5.0
```

I added a file called server.js to the sportsstore project folder and added the statements shown in Listing 8-14, which configure the packages installed in Listing 8-13 so they will serve the SportsStore application.

Listing 8-14. The Contents of the server.js File in the sportsstore Folder

```
const express = require("express");
const history = require("connect-history-api-fallback");
const jsonServer = require("json-server");
const bodyParser = require('body-parser');
```

```
const auth = require("./authMiddleware");
const router = jsonServer.router("data.json");

const app = express();
app.use(bodyParser.json());
app.use(auth);
app.use("/api", router);
app.use(history());
app.use("/", express.static("./dist"));

app.listen(80, function () {
    console.log("HTTP Server running on port 80");
});
```

Run the command shown in Listing 8-15 in the sportstore folder to test the application.

Listing 8-15. Testing the Deployment Build

```
node server.js
```

This command executes the statements in the JavaScript file from Listing 8-14, which set up a web server on port 80 and listens for requests. To test the application, navigate to http://localhost:80, and you will see the application running, as illustrated in Figure 8-5.

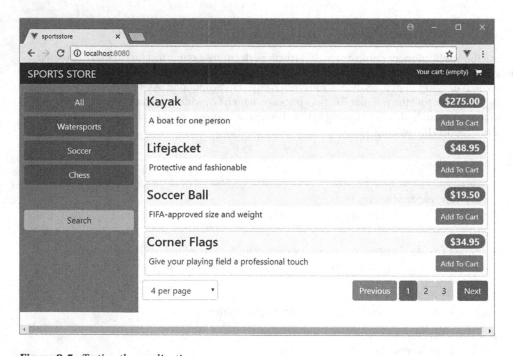

Figure 8-5. *Testing the application*

Deploying the Application

The first step is to download and install the Docker tools on your development machine, which is available from www.docker.com/products/docker. There are versions for macOS, Windows, and Linux, and there are some specialized versions to work with the Amazon and Microsoft cloud platforms. The free Community edition is sufficient for this chapter.

■ **Caution**   The company that produces the Docker software has gained a reputation for making breaking changes. This means that the example that follows may not work as intended with later versions. If you have problems, check the repository for this book for updates (https://github.com/Apress/pro-vue-js-2).

Creating the Package File

To deploy the application to Docker, I need to create a version of the package.js file that will install the packages that are required to run the application. I added a file called deploy-package.json to the sportsstore folder with the content shown in Listing 8-16.

Listing 8-16. The Contents of the deploy-package.json File in the sportsstore Folder

```
{
    "name": "sportsstore",
    "version": "1.0.0",
    "private": true,

    "dependencies": {
        "faker": "^4.1.0",
        "json-server": "^0.12.1",
        "jsonwebtoken": "^8.1.1",
        "express": "4.16.3",
        "connect-history-api-fallback": "1.5.0"
    }
}
```

Creating the Docker Container

To define the container, I added a file called Dockerfile (with no extension) to the sportsstore folder and added the content shown in Listing 8-17.

Listing 8-17. The Contents of the Dockerfile File in the sportsstore Folder

```
FROM node:8.11.2

RUN mkdir -p /usr/src/sportsstore

COPY dist /usr/src/sportsstore/dist
```

```
COPY authMiddleware.js /usr/src/sportsstore/
COPY data.json /usr/src/sportsstore/
COPY server.js /usr/src/sportsstore/server.js
COPY deploy-package.json /usr/src/sportsstore/package.json

WORKDIR /usr/src/sportsstore

RUN npm install

EXPOSE 80

CMD ["node", "server.js"]
```

The contents of the Dockerfile use a base image that has been configured with Node.js and that copies the files required to run the application, including the bundle file containing the application and the package.json file that will be used to install the packages required to run the application in deployment.

Run the command in Listing 8-18 in the sportsstore folder to create an image that will contain the SportsStore application, along with all of the tools and packages it requires.

Listing 8-18. Building the Docker Image

```
docker build . -t sportsstore -f Dockerfile
```

An image is a template for containers. As Docker processes the instructions in the Docker file, the NPM packages will be downloaded and installed, and the configuration and code files will be copied into the image.

Running the Application

Once the image has been created, create and start a new container using the command in Listing 8-19.

Listing 8-19. Creating a Docker Container

```
docker run -p 80:80 sportsstore
```

You can test the application by opening http://localhost in the browser, which will display the response provided by the web server running in the container, as shown in Figure 8-6.

■ **Tip** If you receive an error because port 80 isn't available, you can try a different port by changing the first part of the -p argument. If you want to listen to port 500, for example, then the argument would be -p 500:80.

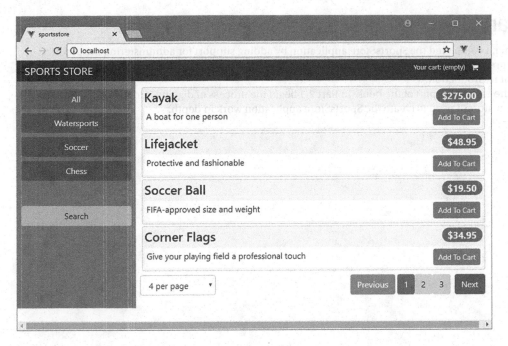

Figure 8-6. Running the containerized SportsStore application

To stop the container, run the command shown in Listing 8-20.

Listing 8-20. Stopping the Docker Container

```
docker ps
```

You will see a list of running containers, like this (I have omitted some fields for brevity):

```
CONTAINER ID        IMAGE           COMMAND             CREATED
ecc84f7245d6        sportsstore     "node server.js"    33 seconds ago
```

Using the value in the Container ID column, run the command shown in Listing 8-21.

Listing 8-21. Stopping the Docker Container

```
docker stop ecc84f7245d6
```

Summary

In this chapter, I completed the SportsStore application by adding support for administering the product catalog and preparing for deployment, which illustrates how easy it is to move a Vue.js project from development to production.

That's the end of this part of the book. In Part 2, I begin the process of digging into the details and show you how the features I used to create the SportsStore application work in depth.

■ ■ ■

PART II

Vue.js in Detail

CHAPTER 9

■ ■ ■

Understanding Vue.js

When you get started with Vue.js, it can be easy to be overwhelmed because there is a lot going on and not all of it makes immediate sense. This chapter explains how Vue.js works and demonstrates that there is no magic involved—something that can be helpful to bear in mind as I dig into the detail of individual Vue.js features in the chapters that follow. Table 9-1 summarizes the chapter.

Table 9-1. *Chapter Summary*

Problem	Solution	Listing
Create a simple web application without Vue.js	Use the DOM API	6
Create a simple web application using Vue.js	Create a Vue object and configure it with el and template properties	7
Present a data value to the user	Define a data property and use a data binding	8
Respond to user interaction through events	Use the v-on directive	9
Generate data values that require calculation	Define a computed property	10
Create a reusable unit of application functionality	Define and apply a component	11–13
Define a component's template as HTML	Use a template element	14–16

Preparing for This Chapter

To create the example project for this chapter, open a new command prompt, navigate to a convenient location, and run the command shown in Listing 9-1. This command depends on the tools that I described in Chapter 1, and you will need to complete the steps in that chapter before you are able to create the project.

■ **Tip** You can download the example project for this chapter—and for all the other chapters in this book—from https://github.com/Apress/pro-vue-js-2.

Listing 9-1. Creating the Example Project

```
vue create nomagic
```

© Adam Freeman 2018
A. Freeman, *Pro Vue.js 2*, https://doi.org/10.1007/978-1-4842-3805-9_9

Select default when prompted to select a preset. The project will be created, and the packages required for the application and the development tools will be downloaded and installed, which can take some time to complete.

■ **Note** At the time of writing, the @vue/cli package has been released in beta. There may be small changes made before the final release, but the core features should remain the same. For details of any breaking changes, check the errata for this book, available at https://github.com/Apress/pro-vue-js-2.

Once the project has been created, add a file called vue.config.js to the nomagic folder with the content shown in Listing 9-2. This file is used to configure the Vue.js development tools, which I describe in Chapter 10.

Listing 9-2. The Contents of the vue.config.js File in the nomagic Folder

```
module.exports = {
    runtimeCompiler: true
}
```

Adding the Bootstrap CSS Framework

Run the command shown in Listing 9-3 in the nomagic folder to add the Bootstrap CSS package to the project. This is the CSS framework that I will use to style the HTML content in this chapter.

Listing 9-3. Adding the Bootstrap Package

```
npm install bootstrap@4.0.0
```

One installation is complete, open the main.js file in the src folder and add the statement shown in Listing 9-4.

Listing 9-4. Adding Bootstrap in the main.js File in the src Folder

```
import Vue from 'vue'
import App from './App.vue'
```

import "bootstrap/dist/css/bootstrap.min.css";

```
Vue.config.productionTip = false

new Vue({
  render: h => h(App)
}).$mount('#app')
```

This statement includes the Bootstrap CSS styles in the content that is sent to the browser.

Running the Example Application

The project that is created by the command in Listing 9-1 includes the tools required for Vue.js development. I explain how to use these tools in more detail in Chapter 10, but to start the development process, run the command shown in Listing 9-5 in the nomagic folder.

Listing 9-5. Starting the Development Tools

```
npm run serve
```

The development HTTP server will start after an initial setup phase. Open a new browser window and navigate to http://localhost:8080, and you will see the placeholder content shown in Figure 9-1.

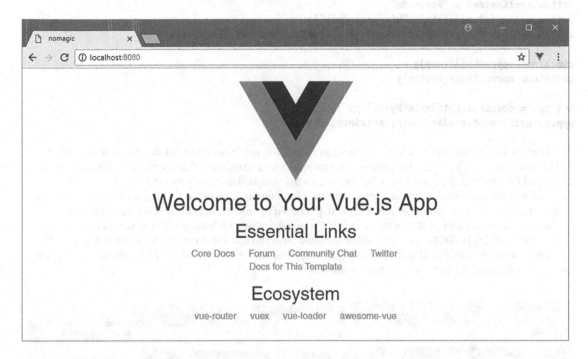

Figure 9-1. *Running the example application*

Creating an Application Using the DOM API

I am going to start by creating a simple web application without using Vue.js at all and then demonstrate how the same functionality can be created using basic Vue.js features.

To do this, I am going to the main.js file, which typically contains the JavaScript code that initializes a Vue.js application. The main.js file is just a JavaScript file, which means that I can remove the code that configures Vue.js and replace it with other statements.

In Listing 9-6, I have replaced the default content of the main.js file with a series of JavaScript statements that use the Domain Object Model (DOM) API. The DOM API is provided by browsers to allow JavaScript access to the HTML document and its content, and it is the foundation for all web applications.

Listing 9-6. Replacing the Contents of the main.js File in the src Folder

```
require('../node_modules/bootstrap/dist/css/bootstrap.min.css')

let counter = 1;

let container = document.createElement("div");
container.classList.add("text-center", "p-3");

let msg = document.createElement("h1");
msg.classList.add("bg-primary", "text-white", "p-3");
msg.textContent = "Button Not Pressed";

let button = document.createElement("button");
button.textContent = "Press Me";
button.classList.add("btn", "btn-secondary");
button.onclick = () => msg.textContent = `Button Presses: ${counter++}`;

container.appendChild(msg);
container.appendChild(button);

let app = document.getElementById("app");
app.parentElement.replaceChild(container, app);
```

Don't worry about understanding this code in detail. You won't need to work directly with the DOM API in most Vue.js projects. The purpose of this example is to demonstrate that the main.js file is a regular JavaScript file and that the code it contains can access the standard features provided by the browser.

The development tools that you started with the command in Listing 9-6 automatically detect changes to the project's files. These changes are compiled, packaged up into a single file that contains all of the application's functionality, and sent to the browser automatically, which means that as soon as you save the change to the main.js file, the browser will be updated, and you will see the content shown in Figure 9-2. An initial message is displayed to the user, which is replaced with a counter when the button is pressed. The counter is incremented with each further button press.

Figure 9-2. *Working directly with the Domain Object Model*

Understanding How the DOM API Application Works

I use the DOM API to create a div element that contains an h1 element and a button element when the code in the main.js file is executed. I add these elements to classes that correspond to styles defined by the Bootstrap CSS framework, which sets their appearance. I then set up an event listener that responds to clicks on the button element by updating a counter and displaying a message in the h1 element.

Once all of that is done, I locate the existing element in the HTML document whose ID is app and replace it with the div element I created.

```
...
let app = document.getElementById("app");
app.parentElement.replaceChild(container, app);
...
```

This is how I present the example application to the user. When the browser sends a request to http://localhost:8000, the development HTTP server responds with the contents of the project's index.html file, which contains these elements:

```
<!DOCTYPE html>
<html>
  <head>
    <meta charset="utf-8">
    <meta name="viewport" content="width=device-width,initial-scale=1.0">
    <title>nomagic</title>
  </head>
  <body>
    <div id="app"></div>
  </body>
</html>
```

I have highlighted the element that the JavaScript code replaces, which is how content is displayed to the user.

When the development server produces a response to the browser's HTTP request, it automatically inserts a script element that loads the JavaScript file that contains all of the project's JavaScript code, which you can see by right-clicking in the browser window and selecting View Page Source from the pop-up menu.

```
<!DOCTYPE html>
<html>
  <head>
    <meta charset="utf-8">
    <meta name="viewport" content="width=device-width,initial-scale=1.0">
    <title>nomagic</title>
  </head>
  <body>
    <div id="app"></div>
    <script type="text/javascript" src="/app.js"></script>
  </body>
</html>
```

The JavaScript file that is provided contains the `main.js` code and any code that it depends on. The browser executes the statements in the JavaScript file, which leads to the content I produced programmatically being inserted into the HTML document.

The combined HTML, consisting of the elements in the `index.html` file and the elements generated by the code in the `main.js` file, can be seen by right-clicking in the browser window and selecting Inspect from the pop-up window, which will show the live view of the HTML document that has been created using the DOM API.

```
<!DOCTYPE html>
<html>
  <head>
    <meta charset="utf-8">
    <meta name="viewport" content="width=device-width,initial-scale=1.0">
    <title>nomagic</title>
  </head>
  <body>
    <div class="text-center p-3">
      <h1 class="bg-primary text-white p-3">Button Not Pressed</h1>
      <button class="btn btn-secondary">Press Me</button>
    </div>
    <script type="text/javascript" src="/app.js"></script>
  </body>
</html>
```

The result isn't especially impressive, but it demonstrates that JavaScript code can be used to access the DOM API to replace elements in HTML documents, to create new content, and to respond to user interaction. These are, as you will see, the foundation for any web application—including those created using Vue.js.

Creating a Vue Object

Vue.js applications also use the DOM API to create HTML content, respond to events, and update data values. The difference is that the approach taken by Vue.js is more elegant, is easier to understand, and scales better.

I used the `main.js` file as a convenient way to get the browser to execute JavaScript code in the previous section, but its regular purpose in a Vue.js application is to create a Vue object, which is the entry point into the features provided by Vue.js. In Listing 9-7, I have replaced the DOM API code in the main.js file with statements that create a Vue object, returning the `main.js` file to its intended purpose.

Listing 9-7. Creating a Vue Object in the main.js File in the src Folder

```
require('../node_modules/bootstrap/dist/css/bootstrap.min.css')

import Vue from "vue"

new Vue({
    el: "#app",
    template: `<div class="text-center p-3">
                    <h1 class="bg-secondary text-white p-3">
                        Vue: Button Not Pressed
                    </h1>
```

```
        <button class="btn btn-secondary">
            Press Me
        </button>
    </div>`
});
```

The import statement is required to import the Vue object from the vue module, which was downloaded and installed into the node_modules folder when the project was created. A Vue object is created using the new keyword and the constructor accepts a configuration object whose properties provide settings that control how the application behaves and define the content that it presents to the user.

In this example, there are two configuration properties: el and template. The Vue object uses the el property to identify the element in index.html that will be replaced to display the application content. The template property is used to provide Vue.js with the HTML content that will replace the element matched by the el property. As you will recall, these are tasks that I had to perform manually when I was working directly with the DOM API in the previous section.

In Listing 9-7, I set the el property to #app, which selects the element whose id attribute is set to app. I set the template property so that it contains the same structure of HTML elements I created programmatically in Listing 9-6, with the advantage that I am able to write the HTML directly, rather than creating them using JavaScript statements. The configuration object is defined using JavaScript, which means that I have to express the HTML content as a JavaScript string. I have used the backtick character (the ` character) so that I can split the string across multiple lines and make it easier to read.

■ **Caution** You can use the template property only if you have overridden the project settings as shown in Listing 9-2. By default, the feature that processes template strings is disabled in Vue.js projects.

When the changes to the main.js file are saved, the browser will reload and present the content shown in Figure 9-3: As the figure shows, I changed the message displayed in the h1 element and its background color to make it obvious that there has been a change.

Figure 9-3. *Using a Vue object*

Adding Data to the Vue Object

My Vue object is displaying HTML content to the user, but that's only part of the functionality that I require. The next step is to add some data and have Vue.js display it to the user. In Listing 9-8, I added a variable called counter to the application and modified the template string so that it is displayed to the user.

Listing 9-8. Adding a Variable in the main/js File in the src Folder

```
require('../node_modules/bootstrap/dist/css/bootstrap.min.css')

import Vue from "vue"

new Vue({
    el: "#app",
    template: `<div class="text-center p-3">
                  <h1 class="bg-secondary text-white p-3">
                      Button Presses: {{ counter }}
                  </h1>
                  <button class="btn btn-secondary">
                      Press Me
                  </button>
              </div>`,
    data: {
        counter: 0
    }
});
```

I added a data property to the Vue object's configuration object. This object defines a counter property, with the initial value of zero. To display the counter value to the user, I used a simple data binding in the h1 element.

```
...
<h1 class="bg-secondary text-white p-3">
    Button Presses: {{ counter }}
</h1>
...
```

Data bindings are an important Vue.js feature that provides the connection between the Vue object's template content and its data object. When Vue.js displays the template content, it looks for data bindings, evaluates them as JavaScript expressions, and includes the result in the HTML that is displayed to the user. In this case, the data binding is just the name of one of the data object's properties, and the result is that the value of the counter property is added to the content of the h1 element.

The data is *live* or *reactive*, meaning that a change to the value of the counter property will be automatically reflected in the contents of the h1 element. When the Vue object is created, it processes the data object and replaces the properties so that it can detect when there are changes.

You can see the effect of the data reactivity using the Vue Devtools. Open the F12 developer tools window, select the Vue tab, and click the <Root> item. In the right pane, move the mouse over the counter item and click the + symbol to increment the value. Vue.js detects the new counter value and evaluates the code in the template again, producing the results shown in Figure 9-4. (See https://github.com/vuejs/vue-devtools for installation instructions if you have not installed the Vue Devtools extension.)

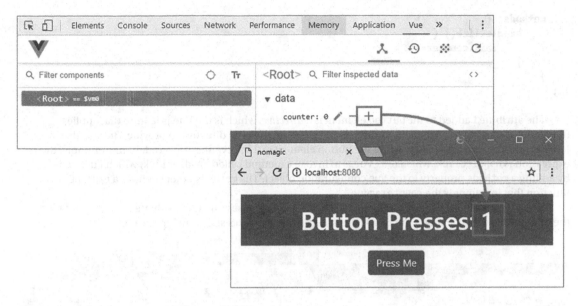

Figure 9-4. *Changing a reactive data variable*

Adding an Event Handler

The next step to re-create the DOM API application in Vue.js is to increment the counter value automatically when the button is clicked. When I used the DOM API, I was able to set up an event handler function directly using a JavaScript statement, but a different approach is required for the Vue object, as shown in Listing 9-9.

Listing 9-9. Handling an Event in the main.js File in the src Folder

```
require('../node_modules/bootstrap/dist/css/bootstrap.min.css')

import Vue from "vue"

new Vue({
    el: "#app",
    template: `<div class="text-center p-3">
                <h1 class="bg-secondary text-white p-3">
                    Button Presses: {{ counter }}
                </h1>
                <button class="btn btn-secondary" v-on:click="handleClick">
                    Press Me
                </button>
            </div>`,
    data: {
        counter: 0
    },
```

211

```
    methods: {
        handleClick() {
            this.counter++;
        }
    }
});
```

The attribute I added to the button element is a *directive*, which is the Vue.js feature that applies functionality to an HTML element. In this case, I have used the v-on directive to provide Vue.js with a JavaScript expression to evaluate when the button element's click event is triggered. In this example, the expression is handleClick, which tells Vue.js to invoke a method called handleClick, which I defined by adding a methods property to the Vue configuration object. The methods object defines a handleClick function that increments the counter value.

Since Vue.js data is reactive, changing the counter value causes Vue.js to evaluate the data binding in the h1 element, which changes the message displayed to the user, as shown in Figure 9-5.

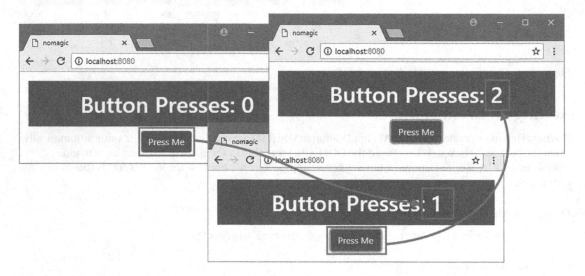

Figure 9-5. *Handling an event*

Correcting the Message

The final change to create parity with the DOM API example 1 is to display a different message when the user has yet to click the button. To create the equivalent using the Vue object, I made the changes shown in Listing 9-10.

Listing 9-10. Displaying a Conditional Message in the main.js File in the src Folder

```
require('../node_modules/bootstrap/dist/css/bootstrap.min.css')

import Vue from "vue"

new Vue({
    el: "#app",
    template: `<div class="text-center p-3">
```

```
                <h1 class="bg-secondary text-white p-3">
                    {{ message }}
                </h1>
                <button class="btn btn-secondary" v-on:click="handleClick">
                    Press Me
                </button>
            </div>`,
    data: {
        counter: 0
    },
    methods: {
        handleClick() {
            this.counter++;
        }
    },
    computed: {
        message() {
            return this.counter == 0 ?
                "Button Not Pressed" : `Button Presses: ${this.counter}`;
        }
    }
});
```

The computed configuration defines data values that require some computation to produce a result. This example uses an expression that checks the value of the counter property and returns the string that should be displayed to the user. The new computed property is called message, and I display its value to the user in the h1 element by putting its name in a data binding, just like I did with the data property earlier.

When the user clicks the button, the v-on directive invokes the handleClick method, which increments the counter value. Vue.js detects the change and re-evaluates the data binding expressions defined in the template content, which produces a new result from the message computed property, which is displayed to the user through the data binding in the h1 element, as shown in Figure 9-6.

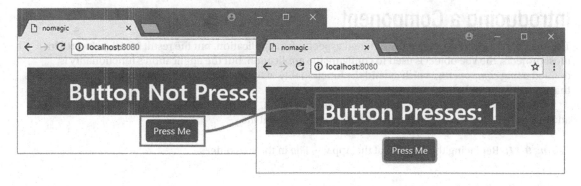

Figure 9-6. Using a computed property

Understanding the Vue Object Structure

The Vue object provides the same functionality as the code that used the DOM API in Listing 9-6, but the result is an application that has better structure, which is easier to develop and maintain than working directly with the DOM. It can be hard to see the advantages of the Vue.js approach when looking at the Vue object in Listing 9-10, but already there is a structure emerging that separates the content, logic, and data in the application, as shown in Figure 9-7.

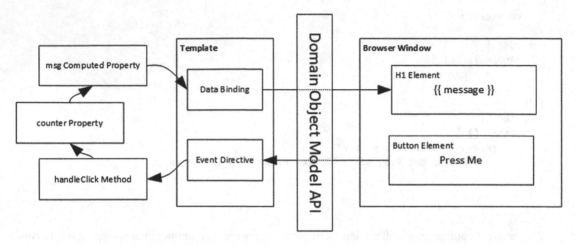

Figure 9-7. *The structure of the application*

The Vue object's template provides the HTML content that is presented to the user and contains the data binding and event directive that provides the application's interactivity. The application's data consists of the counter property and the msg computed property, and the logic that ties them together is contained in the handleClick method.

Introducing a Component

The Vue object helps to separate the different aspects of an application, but the result is still awkward. In most projects, the Vue object is used to configure the application, but the application's functionality is defined using *components*, which extend the functionality of the Vue object and which can be defined in files that contain a more helpful mix of content types.

Components are defined in files with the .vue extension. The project was created with the App.vue file, and in Listing 9-11 I have replaced the default contents of that file.

Listing 9-11. Replacing the Content of the App.vue File in the src Folder

```
<script>
export default {
    template: `<div class="text-center p-3">
                <h1 class="bg-secondary text-white p-3">
                    {{ message }}
                </h1>
```

```
            <button class="btn btn-secondary" v-on:click="handleClick">
                Press Me
            </button>
        </div>`,
    data: function () {
        return {
            counter: 0
        }
    },
    methods: {
        handleClick() {
            this.counter++;
        }
    },
    computed: {
        message() {
            return this.counter == 0 ?
                "Button Not Pressed" : `Button Presses: ${this.counter}`;
        }
    }
}
</script>
```

The component shown in Listing 9-11 contains the same functionality that I defined using the Vue object, except that the JavaScript properties are defined in a `script` element. This may not seem like much of an improvement, but it does demonstrate that components are Vue objects just like the one I created in the `main.js` file. Components allow an application to be composed of multiple components that are combined to provide the user with complex functionality.

The JavaScript code is contained in a `script` element and contains the same functionality as the Vue object. There are two important changes to the JavaScript code when moving from a regular Vue object to a component. The first is that the configuration object must be exported, like this:

```
...
export default {

    // ...configuration properties omitted for brevity...
}
...
```

This allows the object to be imported from its module, which I do in Listing 9-12. The other change is to the `data` property, which must be expressed as a function, like this:

```
...
data: function () {
    return {
        counter: 0
    }
},
...
```

The data property is assigned a function that returns an object whose properties provide the data values for the component. This is an awkward approach, but Vue.js enforces this requirement to ensure that each component has its own data.

Registering and Applying the Component

Components must be registered with Vue.js before they are used, and this is one of the main jobs usually performed in the main.js file. In Listing 9-12, I replaced changed the Vue object's configuration to use the new component.

Listing 9-12. Configuring a Component in the main.js File in the src Folder

```
require('../node_modules/bootstrap/dist/css/bootstrap.min.css')

import Vue from "vue";
import MyComponent from "./App";

new Vue({
    el: "#app",
    components: { "custom": MyComponent },
    template: `<div class="text-center">
                    <h1 class="bg-primary text-white p-3">
                        This is the main.js file
                    </h1>
                    <custom />
            </div>`
});
```

The first new statement uses the import keyword, which imports the module from the App.vue file and gives it the name MyComponent. The convention is to use the file name as the name of the import, but you can use whatever name makes the most sense.

The next change is to add a components property to the Vue object's configuration. This property is assigned an object that provides Vue.js with a list of HTML elements and the components that are associated with them. In this case, I have configured the components property to tell Vue.js that the custom element is associated with MyComponent, which is the name I assigned to the component in the App.vue file.

I also changed the string assigned to the template configuration property so that it contains a simpler set of HTML elements that include a custom element.

When the Vue object processes its template, it will encounter the custom element and replace it with the HTML content provided by the component in the App.vue file. The result that the user is presented with is a combination of HTML from the component's template property and from the Vue object's template property. When you save the changes, the browser will reload, and you will see the content shown in Figure 9-8.

Figure 9-8. *Using a component*

The Vue object doesn't usually display its own content, and the convention is to put just the HTML element for the component in the template, which is what I have done in Listing 9-13.

Listing 9-13. Removing Template Content in the main.js File in the src Folder

```
require('../node_modules/bootstrap/dist/css/bootstrap.min.css')

import Vue from "vue";
import MyComponent from "./App";

new Vue({
    el: "#app",
    components: { "custom": MyComponent },
    template: "<custom />"
});
```

The Vue object replaces the div element in the index.html file with the custom element, which is replaced by the contents of the component's template element. When you save the change to the main.js file, you will see the completed example application, illustrated in Figure 9-9.

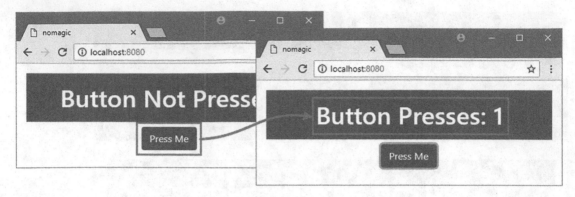

Figure 9-9. *Completing the example application*

Separating the Template from the JavaScript Code

You can define component templates using the `template` property, but there is a different approach that most developers find easier to work with. In Listing 9-14, I have removed the `template` string and replaced it with a `template` element, which is how components are usually defined.

Listing 9-14. Using a Template Element in the App.vue File in the src Folder

```
<template>
    <div class="text-center p-3">
      <h1 class="bg-secondary text-white p-3">
        {{ message }}
      </h1>
      <button class="btn btn-secondary" v-on:click="handleClick">
          Press Me
      </button>
    </div>
</template>

<script>
export default {
    data: function () {
        return {
            counter: 0
        }
    },
    methods: {
        handleClick() {
            this.counter++;
        }
    },
```

```
computed: {
    message() {
        return this.counter == 0 ?
            "Button Not Pressed" : `Button Presses: ${this.counter}`;
    }
}
}
</script>
```

The `template` element contains the same content as the string template it replaces, but this approach means that most programmers' editors are able to recognize the template as HTML content and provide developer support, such as autocompleting element and attribute names and flagging errors. There is no change in the way that the example appears or behaves, and this change is purely to make the development experience more pleasant.

Using Separate JavaScript and HTML Files

Not everyone likes mixing JavaScript and HTML content in the same file. If you just can't bring yourself to use the combined format, then you can create separate files. To demonstrate, I added a file called `App.html` to the `src` folder with the contents shown in Listing 9-15.

Listing 9-15. The Contents of the App.html File in the src Folder

```
<div class="text-center p-3">
    <h1 class="bg-secondary text-white p-3">
      {{ message }}
    </h1>
    <button class="btn btn-secondary" v-on:click="handleClick">
        Press Me
    </button>
</div>
```

In Listing 9-16, I removed the contents of the `template` element and added a `src` attribute that tells Vue. js that the component's content can be found in the HTML file.

Listing 9-16. Specifying an HTML File in the App.vue File in the src Folder

```
<template src="./App.html" />

<script>
export default {
    data: function () {
        return {
            counter: 0
        }
    },
    methods: {
        handleClick() {
            this.counter++;
        }
    },
```

```
    computed: {
        message() {
            return this.counter == 0 ?
                "Button Not Pressed" : `Button Presses: ${this.counter}`;
        }
    }
}
</script>
```

Summary

In this chapter, I explained that Vue.js uses the same DOM API to create web applications that can be accessed by any developer using standard JavaScript, emphasizing that there is nothing mysterious or magical about the way that Vue.js works. As you will see in the chapters that follow, while you could use the DOM API directly, Vue.js provides a compelling set of features and an excellent developer experience that results in more elegant, manageable, and scalable features. In the next chapter, I explain the structure of Vue.js projects and explain how the development tools work.

CHAPTER 10

■ ■ ■

Understanding Vue.js Projects and Tools

In Chapter 9, I briefly described how a Vue.js application works in order to provide context for the rest of the book, and as part of that process, I created a project using the @vue-cli package and then used the tools it contained. In this chapter, I explain how this kind of Vue.js project is structured and what each of the tools does. Table 10-1 puts this chapter in context.

Table 10-1. *Putting Vue.js Projects in Context*

Question	Answer
What are they?	Projects created with the @vue-cli package are designed for the development of complex applications.
Why are they useful?	This kind of project includes a set of tools that simplifies Vue.js development and makes it possible to easily work with some of the advanced features that Vue.js provides.
How are they used?	The project is created using the @vue/cli package, and a series of questions are answered to determine the initial content of the project.
Are there any pitfalls or limitations?	This kind of project can be overkill if you are only experimenting with Vue.js.
Are there any alternatives?	You can create your own projects without using the @vue/cli package, in which case you are free to assemble your own toolchain, although this can be a time-consuming process.

© Adam Freeman 2018
A. Freeman, *Pro Vue.js 2*, https://doi.org/10.1007/978-1-4842-3805-9_10

Table 10-2 summarizes the chapter.

Table 10-2. *Chapter Summary*

Problem	Solution	Listing
Create a new project	Use the vue create command and select the features your application requires	1
Start the development tools	Use the npm run serve command	2–8
Avoid common code and content errors	Use the linter feature	9–11
Debug an application	Use the Vue Devtools browser extension of the browser's JavaScript debugger	12
Change the configuration of the development tools	Add a .vue.config.js file to the project that contains the settings you require	13
Prepare the application for deployment	Use the npm run build command	14–19

Creating a Vue.js Development Project

Modern client-side development frameworks include their own development tools, and Vue.js is no exception. That means you can create a project and start development using tools that have been created specifically for use in Vue.js applications and that have been thoroughly tested by a large and active community.

The @vue/cli package you installed in Chapter 1 is provided by the Vue.js team to simplify the creation of Vue.js projects and install all of the development and build tools that are required. Run the command in Listing 10-1 to create a new project using the vue create command, which is provided by the @vue/cli package.

■ **Note** At the time of writing, the @vue/cli package has been released in beta. There may be small changes made before the final release, but the core features should remain the same. For details of any breaking changes, check the errata for this book, available at https://github.com/Apress/pro-vue-js-2.

Listing 10-1. Creating a New Project

```
vue create projecttools
```

The vue create command uses an interactive process for selecting the options to create a project and will prompt you as shown in Figure 10-1.

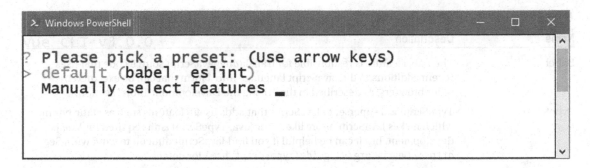

Figure 10-1. *Selecting the project settings*

The text can be hard to read from the image, but the vue create command starts by asking you to choose a preset. There is one preset available—called *default*—that selects the same configuration used in earlier chapters. This is the configuration that I use throughout the rest of the book because it lets me demonstrate how different components are added to the project. There is nothing wrong with using project tools when they are convenient, just as long as you understand what it is they are doing for you behind the scenes. The other option is to manually select the features that you require. Use the arrow keys to select the Manually Select Features option and press Enter, and you will see the list of features shown in Figure 10-2.

```
>_ Windows PowerShell                                          —    □    ×

? Please pick a preset: Manually select features
? Check the features needed for your project:
>(*) Babel
 ( ) TypeScript
 ( ) Progressive Web App (PWA) Support
 ( ) Router
 ( ) Vuex
 ( ) CSS Pre-processors
 (*) Linter / Formatter
 ( ) Unit Testing
 ( ) E2E Testing
```

Figure 10-2. *The project features available for manual selection*

Use the arrow keys to navigate up and down the list of features, which are toggled on and off using the spacebar. Table 10-3 describes the features that are available. I describe the features that are directly related to Vue.js development, either in this chapter or in later chapters. For other features, I have included a URL that provides more details.

Table 10-3. *The Vue.js Project Features*

Name	Description
Babel	The Babel feature is responsible for translating JavaScript source code that uses recent additions to the JavaScript language into a form that can be executed by older browsers, as described in the "Using the Development Tools" section.
TypeScript	TypeScript is a superset of JavaScript that adds useful features such as static typing, which makes JavaScript more like C# or Java. TypeScript isn't required for Vue.js development, but it can be helpful if you find JavaScript difficult to work with. See `https://vuejs.org/v2/guide/typescript.html` for details.
PWA Support	Progressive web apps are web applications that are presented to the user alongside regular applications and that rely on a JavaScript feature called *service workers* to deliver functionality when there is no connectivity. PWAs are not specific to Vue. js, and while support for PWAs is improving, it is a technology that I left out of this edition of the book because it is not yet mature enough for most projects. See `https://developer.mozilla.org/en-US/Apps/Progressive` for details.
Router	This feature installs the Vue Router package that is used to add structure to larger applications using the browser's URL. You can see routing in use in the SportsStore application in Part 1 of this book, and I describe the features provided by Vue Router in detail in Chapters 23–25.
Vuex	This feature installs the Vuex package that is used to create shared data stores. You can see Vuex in use in the SportsStore application in Part 1 of this book, and I describe its features in detail in Chapter 20.
CSS Pre-processors	CSS preprocessors, such as Sass and Less, make it easier to write complex CSS styles, which can be useful if you are not using a CSS framework or want to extend one. Even if you choose not to use a CSS framework, you don't have to use a CSS processor, however, as I explain in later chapters.
Linter/Formatter	The Linter/Formatter feature installs a package that checks your code and content for conformance to best-practice standards, as explained in the "Using the Linter" section.
Unit Testing	This feature installs unit testing tools, as described at `https://cli.vuejs.org/config/#unit-testing`.
E2E Testing	This feature installs end-to-end testing tools, as described at `https://cli.vuejs.org/config/#e2e-testing`.

For the purpose of this chapter, select the Babel, Router, Vuex, and Linter/Formatter features, as shown in Figure 10-3.

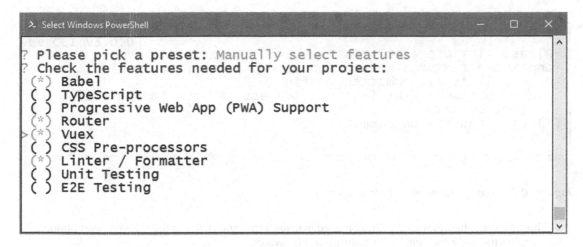

```
>_  Select Windows PowerShell                                    —    □    ✕

? Please pick a preset: Manually select features
? Check the features needed for your project:
 (*) Babel
 ( ) TypeScript
 ( ) Progressive Web App (PWA) Support
 (*) Router
>(*) Vuex
 ( ) CSS Pre-processors
 (*) Linter / Formatter
 ( ) Unit Testing
 ( ) E2E Testing
```

Figure 10-3. *Selecting features for the example project*

Press Enter once you have selected the features. Additional options are presented to configure some of the features you have chosen.

Configuring the Linter

The first option configures the linter, which was selected with the Linter/Formatter feature, as shown in Figure 10-4.

```
>_  Windows PowerShell                                          —    □    ✕

? Please pick a preset: Manually select features
? Check the features needed for your project: Babel, Rou
? Pick a linter / formatter config: (Use arrow keys)
> ESLint with error prevention only
  ESLint + Airbnb config
  ESLint + Standard config
  ESLint + Prettier
```

Figure 10-4. *Configuring the linter*

Choose the "ESLint with error prevention only" option. The linter is responsible for inspecting the project to make sure it conforms to a coding standard, and this question selects the coding rules that are applied to the project. I explain what each option means in the "Using the Linter" section later in the chapter. The next option is to choose when the linter is applied to the source code in the project, as shown in Figure 10-5.

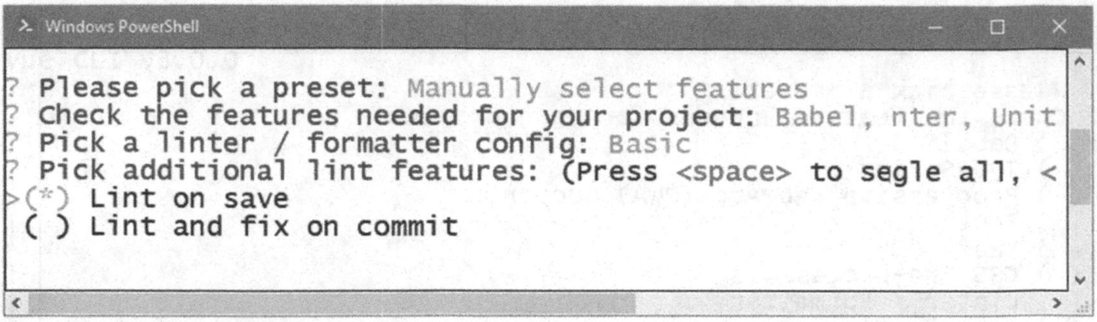

```
>_ Windows PowerShell                                              —    □    ✕
? Please pick a preset: Manually select features
? Check the features needed for your project: Babel, nter, Unit
? Pick a linter / formatter config: Basic
? Pick additional lint features: (Press <space> to segle all, <
>(*) Lint on save
( ) Lint and fix on commit
```

Figure 10-5. *Configuring when the linter is applied*

This option configures when the linter is used to inspect the project. Select the "Lint on save" option, which applies the linter each time a file in the project is saved.

Completing the Project Configuration

Once you have selected the project features, you will be asked what style of configuration you want, as shown in Figure 10-6.

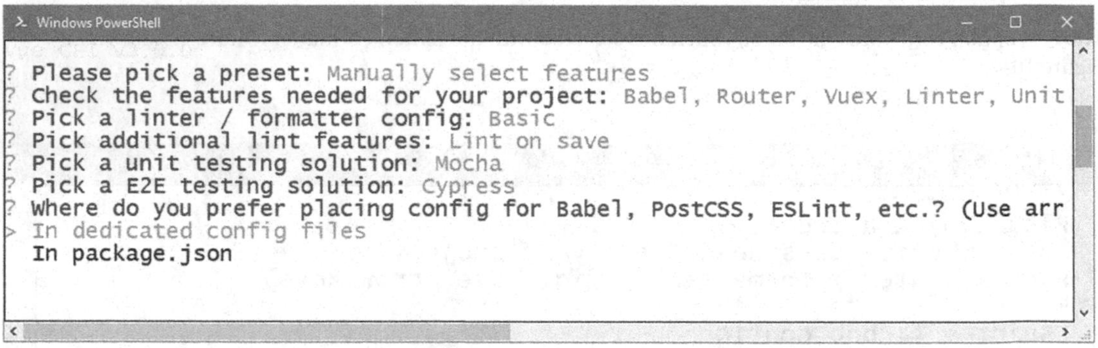

```
>_ Windows PowerShell                                              —    □    ✕
? Please pick a preset: Manually select features
? Check the features needed for your project: Babel, Router, Vuex, Linter, Unit
? Pick a linter / formatter config: Basic
? Pick additional lint features: Lint on save
? Pick a unit testing solution: Mocha
? Pick a E2E testing solution: Cypress
? Where do you prefer placing config for Babel, PostCSS, ESLint, etc.? (Use arr
> In dedicated config files
  In package.json
```

Figure 10-6. *Selecting the style of configuration file*

There are two options. You can choose to use separate configuration files for each of the features that require configuration, or you can choose to include all of the configuration settings in the package.json file, which is also used to keep track of the packages required by the application.

Select the In package.json option, which will add the configuration settings for the project's features to the package.json file, which is the same approach taken by the default configuration used in the other chapters in this book.

Press Enter, and the last step is to decide whether you want to save the configuration you have created so that it can be used to create other projects in the future. Press Enter to select No for this question because this configuration isn't required for any of the other projects I create in this book.

Now that you have answered all the questions, the project will be created, and the packages that are required will be downloaded and installed. A Vue.js project requires a lot of packages, and the initial setup can take a while to complete.

Understanding the Project Structure

Use your preferred editor to open the projecttools folder, and you will see the project structure illustrated in Figure 10-7. The figure shows the way that my preferred editor displays the files and folders created by the vue create command, but you may see some minor differences depending on the editor you have chosen and any changes that have been made to the project template since the time of writing.

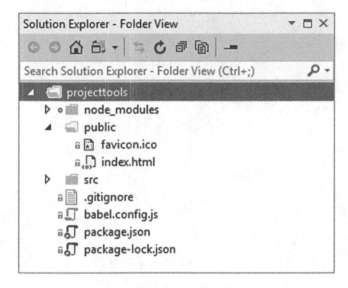

Figure 10-7. *The structure of the example project*

Table 10-4 describes the most important files and folders in the project and the features they support.

Table 10-4. *The Project Files and Folders*

Name	Description
node_modules	This folder contains the packages that the application and development tools require, as described in the "Understanding the Packages Folder" section.
public	This folder contains static project assets, such as images that are not incorporated into the bundle files sent to the browser, as described in the "Using the Development Tools" section.
src	This folder contains the Vue.js application and its resources, and it is the main focus during development, as described in the "Understanding the Source Code Folder" section.
.gitignore	This file contains a list of files and folders that are excluded from version control when using Git.
.babel.config.js	This file contains the configuration settings for the Babel compiler, which I describe in the "Using the Development Tools" section.
package.json	This file contains a list of the packages required for Vue.js development as well as the commands used for the development tools, which are described in the "Understanding the Packages Folder" section.
package-lock.json	This file contains a complete list of the packages required by the project and their dependencies, which ensures that you will receive the same set of packages when you run the npm install command.

Understanding the Source Code Folder

The src folder is the most important part of any Vue.js project and contains the application's HTML content, source code, and other resources. This is the folder that is the focus of most development sessions, and Figure 10-8 shows the contents of the src folder for a project created using the features selected at the start of the chapter.

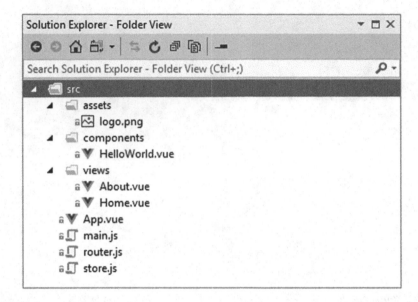

Figure 10-8. *The contents of the src folder*

The structure of the src folder will become more complex as you start to develop a project, but the placeholder content provides just enough functionality to get started and to ensure that the development tools are working. I am not going to describe the contents of the src folder in detail since it is the subject of all the other chapters in this part of the book, but, for completeness, Table 10-5 describes the files that are added when a new project is created.

Table 10-5. *The Initial Contents of the src Folder*

Name	Description
assets	This folder is used for the static resources required by the application and that are included in the bundling process, as described in the "Using the Development Tools" section. The vue create command adds an image file that contains the Vue.js logo to this folder.
components	This folder is used for the application's components. An application can contain many components, and additional folders are often used to group related components. The vue create command adds a placeholder component to this folder called HelloWorld.
views	This folder is used to contain components that are displayed using the URL routing feature. I do not follow this convention in the examples in this book and prefer to group all components in the components folder.
App.vue	This is the root component, which is conventionally used as the point at which custom application content begins.
main.js	This is the JavaScript file that creates the Vue object, as described in Chapter 9.
router.js	This file is used to configure the URL routing system, which is used to select the components that are displayed to the user. I describe the routing feature in detail in Chapters 22–24, where I follow a different convention of creating a router folder that contains an index.js file that contains the configuration statements and that makes it easy to split the configuration into multiple files that are handled as a single JavaScript module.
store.js	This file is used to configure the data store, which is used to share data throughout the application. I describe data stores in Chapter 20 where I follow a different convention of creating a store folder that contains an index.js file, which makes it easy to split the configuration into multiple files in large applications.

Understanding the Packages Folder

JavaScript application development depends on a rich ecosystem of packages, ranging from those that contain the code that will be sent to the browser to small packages that are used behind the scenes during development for a specific task. Lots of packages are required in a Vue.js project. The example project created at the start of this chapter, for example, requires more than 900 packages.

There is a complex hierarchy of dependencies between these packages that is too difficult to manage manually and that is handled using a *package manager*. Vue.js projects can be created using two different package managers: NPM, which is the Node Package Manager and which was installed alongside Node.js in Chapter 1, and Yarn, which is a recent competitor designed to improve package management. I use NPM throughout this book for simplicity.

■ **Tip** You should use NPM to follow the examples in this book, but you can find details of Yarn at https://yarnpkg.com if you want to use it in your own projects.

When a project is created, the package manager is given an initial list of packages required for Vue. js development. The package manager inspects each package to get the set of packages it depends on. The process is performed again to get the dependencies of these packages and repeated until a complete list of the packages required for the project is built up. The package manager downloads and installs all the packages and installs them into the node_modules folder.

The initial set of packages is defined in the package.json file using the dependencies and devDependencies properties. The dependencies property is used to list the packages that the application will require to run. You may see different details in your project, but here is the dependencies section from the package.json file from my example project:

```
...
"dependencies": {
    "vue": "^2.5.16",
    "vue-router": "^3.0.1",
    "vuex": "^3.0.1"
},
...
```

Only three packages are required in the dependencies section for a Vue.js project: the vue package contains the main features, the vue-router package contains navigation features that I describe in Chapters 22–24, and the vuex package contains the data store features that I describe in Chapter 20. For each package, the package.json file includes details of the version numbers that are acceptable, using the format described in Table 10-6.

Table 10-6. *The Package Version Numbering System*

Format	Description
2.5.16	Expressing a version number directly will accept only the package with the exact matching version number, e.g., 2.5.16.
*	Using an asterisk accepts any version of the package to be installed.
>2.5.16 >=2.5.16	Prefixing a version number with > or >= accepts any version of the package that is greater than or greater than or equal to a given version.
<2.5.16 <= 2.5.16	Prefixing a version number with < or <= accepts any version of the package that is less than or less than or equal to a given version.
~2.5.16	Prefixing a version number with a tilde (the ~ character) accepts versions to be installed even if the patch level number (the last of the three version numbers) doesn't match. For example, specifying ~2.5.16 will accept version 2.5.17 or 2.5.18 (which would contain patches to version 2.5.16) but not version 2.6.0 (which would be a new minor release).
^2.5.16	Prefixing a version number with a caret (the ^ character) will accept versions even if the minor release number (the second of the three version numbers) or the patch number doesn't match. For example, specifying ^2.5.16 will allow versions 2.5.17 and 2.6.0, for example, but not version 3.0.0.

The version numbers specified in the dependencies section of the package.json file will accept minor updates and patches. This version flexibility is more important when it comes to the devDependencies section of the file, which contains a list of the packages that are required for development but which will not be part of the finished application. Here is the devDependencies section of my project:

```
...
"devDependencies": {
    "@vue/cli-plugin-babel": "^3.0.0-beta.15",
    "@vue/cli-plugin-e2e-cypress": "^3.0.0-beta.15",
    "@vue/cli-plugin-eslint": "^3.0.0-beta.15",
    "@vue/cli-plugin-unit-mocha": "^3.0.0-beta.15",
    "@vue/cli-service": "^3.0.0-beta.15",
    "@vue/test-utils": "^1.0.0-beta.16",
    "chai": "^4.1.2",
    "vue-template-compiler": "^2.5.16"
},
...
```

These packages provide the development toolset. As I noted at the start of the chapter, the @vue/cli package is in beta at the time of writing, and you can see this reflected in the package version numbers.

UNDERSTANDING GLOBAL AND LOCAL PACKAGES

Package managers can install packages so they are specific to a single project (known as a *local install*) or so they can be accessed from anywhere (known as a *global install*). Few packages require global installs, but one exception is the @vue/cli package that I installed in Chapter 1 as part of the preparations for this book. The @vue/cli package requires a global install because it is used to create new Vue.js projects. The individual packages required for the project are installed locally, into the node_modules folder.

All the packages required to development are automatically downloaded and installed into the node_modules folder when you create a Vue.js project, but Table 10-7 lists some NPM commands that you may find useful during development. All of these commands should be run inside the project folder, which is the one that contains the package.json file.

Table 10-7. *Useful NPM Commands*

Command	Description
`npm install`	This command performs a local install of the packages specified in the `package.json` file.
`npm install package@version`	This command performs a local install of a specific version of a package and updates the `package.json` file to add the package to the `dependencies` section.
`npm install --save-dev package @version`	This command performs a local install of a specific version of a package and updates the `package.json` file to add the package to the `devDependencies` section.
`npm install --global package@ version`	This command performs a global install of a specific version of a package.
`npm list`	This command lists all the local packages and their dependencies.
`npm run`	This command executes one of the scripts defined in the `package.json` file, as described next.

The last command described in Table 10-7 is an oddity, but package managers have traditionally included support for running commands that are defined in the `scripts` section of the `package.json` file. In a Vue.js project, this feature is used to provide access to the tools that are used during development and that prepare the application for deployment. Here is the `scripts` section of the `package.json` file in the example project:

```
...
"scripts": {
    "serve": "vue-cli-service serve",
    "build": "vue-cli-service build",
    "lint": "vue-cli-service lint"
},
...
```

These commands are summarized in Table 10-8, and I demonstrate their use in later sections.

Table 10-8. *The Commands in the Scripts Section of the package.json File*

Name	Description
`serve`	This command starts the development tools, as described in the "Using the Development Tools" section.
`build`	This command performs the build process, as described in the "Building the Application for Deployment" section.
`lint`	This command starts the JavaScript linter, as described in the "Using the Linter" section.

The commands in Table 10-8 are run by using `npm run` followed by the name of the command that you require, and this must be done in the folder that contains the `package.json` file. So, if you want to run the `lint` command in the example project, you would navigate to the `projecttools` folder and type `npm run lint`.

Using the Development Tools

The development tools added to a project automatically detect changes, compile the application, and package the files ready to be used by the browser. These are tasks you could perform manually, but having automatic updates makes for a more pleasant development experience. To start the development tools, open a command prompt, navigate to the projecttools folder, and run the command shown in Listing 10-2.

Listing 10-2. Starting the Development Tools

```
npm run serve
```

The key package used by the development tools is called *webpack*, which is the backbone for many JavaScript development tools and frameworks. Webpack is a module bundler, which means that it packages JavaScript modules for use in a browser, although that's a bland description for an important function, and it is one of the key tools that you will rely on while developing a Vue.js application.

When you run the command in Listing 10-2, you will see a series of messages as webpack prepares the bundles required to run the example application. Webpack starts with the main.js file and loads all the modules for which there are import or require statements to create a set of dependencies. This process is repeated for each of the modules that main.js depends on, and webpack keeps working its way through the application until it has a complete set of dependencies for the entire application, which is then combined into a single file, known as a *bundle*.

During the bundling process, webpack reports on its process as it works its way through the modules and finds the ones that it needs to include in its bundle, like this:

```
...
10% building modules 4/7 modules 3 active ...\node_modules\webpack\hot\emitter.js
...
```

The bundling process can take a moment, but it needs to be performed only when you start the development tools. Once the initial preparation has been completed, you will see a message like this one, which tells you that the application has been compiled and bundled:

```
...
DONE  Compiled successfully in 2099ms

  App running at:
  - Local:   http://localhost:8080/
  - Network: http://192.168.0.77:8080/

Note that the development build is not optimized.
To create a production build, run npm run build.
...
```

Open a new browser tab and navigate to http://localhost:8080 to see the example application, which is shown in Figure 10-9.

■ **Tip** You will notice that the URL displayed by the browser is `http://localhost:8080/#/`. The additional characters are the result of the `vue-router` package that was added to the project at the start of the chapter and that I describe in detail in Chapters 22–24.

Figure 10-9. *Using the development tools*

Understanding the Compilation and Transformation Process

Although webpack focuses on pure JavaScript, its functionality can be extended to deal with other types of content through extensions called *loaders*. The Vue.js development tools include several loaders, but there are two of particular note. You don't have to work directly with these loaders because they are used automatically during development, but knowing what they do helps make sense of the capabilities of the Vue.js development tools.

The first important loader is `vue-loader`, which is responsible for transforming the mixed content in `.vue` files so that it can be compiled and packaged to be consumed by the browser, which is the foundation for being able to define components in a single file that mixes HTML, JavaScript, and CSS content. The other loader of note integrates the Babel compiler, which is responsible for compiling JavaScript code that uses the latest language features into JavaScript that runs on the broadest range of browsers, many of which don't support those features. To demonstrate the effect of Babel, I added statements to the `main.js` file that rely on recent JavaScript features, as shown in Listing 10-3.

Listing 10-3. Adding Statements in the main.js File in the src Folder

```
import Vue from 'vue'
import App from './App.vue'
import router from './router'
import store from './store'
```

```
Vue.config.productionTip = false

let first = "Hello";
const second = "World";
console.log(`Message ${first},${second}`);

new Vue({
  router,
  store,
  render: h => h(App)
}).$mount('#app')
```

These statements use three recent JavaScript features to write a message to the browser's console: the let keyword, the const keyword, and a template string. These are not features that are supported by all browsers, and so Babel is used to transform the JavaScript code.

■ **Tip**　When you save the changes to the main.js file, you will see a warning displayed at the command prompt. This comes from the linter, which I describe in the "Using the Linter" section and can be ignored for the moment.

Seeing the result requires some work because of the way that the application code is bundled by webpack, but if you use the Sources tab of the browser's F12 developer tools, you should be able to explore the contents of the application bundle, which are available in the webpack-internal section.

■ **Tip**　Don't worry if you can't locate the compiled source code. Not all browsers support this feature, and it isn't always available in those that do. The important point to understand is that the compiler transforms the JavaScript so that modern features can be used even when not all of the target browsers support them.

Locate the main.js file in the browser window, and you will see that the statements from Listing 10-3 have been transformed into the following:

```
...
var first = "Hello";
var second = "World";
console.log('Message' + first + ',' + second);
...
```

The compilation process has replaced the let and const keywords with var and replaced the template string with conventional string concatenation. The result is JavaScript code that will run in all of the browsers that Vue.js supports.

UNDERSTANDING THE LIMITS OF BABEL

Babel is an excellent tool, but it deals only with JavaScript language features. Babel is not able to add support for recent JavaScript APIs to browsers that do not implement them. You can still use these APIs—as I demonstrated in Part 1 when I used the local storage API—but doing so restricts the range of browsers that can run the application.

In Listing 10-4, I commented out the statements I added in Listing 10-3 to prevent the warning message displayed by the project tools.

Listing 10-4. Commenting Statements in the main.js File in the src Folder

```
import Vue from 'vue'
import App from './App.vue'
import router from './router'
import store from './store'

Vue.config.productionTip = false

//let first = "Hello";
//const second = "World";
//console.log(`Message ${first},${second}`);

new Vue({
  router,
  store,
  render: h => h(App)
}).$mount('#app')
```

Understanding the Development HTTP Server

To simplify the development process, the project incorporates the webpack-dev-server package, which is an HTTP server that is integrated with webpack. The default port for the development HTTP server is 8080, and the server starts listening for HTTP requests as soon as the initial bundling process is complete.

When an HTTP request is received, the development HTTP server returns the contents of the public/index.html file. As it processes the index.html file, the development server makes an important addition, which you can see by right-clicking in the browser window and selecting View Page Source from the pop-up menu.

```
<!DOCTYPE html>
<html>
  <head>
    <meta charset="utf-8">
    <meta http-equiv="X-UA-Compatible" content="IE=edge">
    <meta name="viewport" content="width=device-width,initial-scale=1.0">
    <link rel="icon" href="/favicon.ico">
    <title>projecttools</title>
    <link as="script" href="/app.js" rel="preload">
  </head>
```

```
<body>
  <noscript>
    <strong>
            We're sorry but projecttools doesn't work properly without
            JavaScript enabled. Please enable it to continue.
    </strong>
  </noscript>
  <div id="app"></div>
  <!-- built files will be auto injected -->
  <script type="text/javascript" src="/app.js"></script></body>
</html>
```

The development server adds a `script` element that tells the browser to load a file called `app.js`, which is the name of the bundle created by webpack during the startup sequence for the development tools. The bundle doesn't contain just the application code, however, and additional features are sent to the browser that are integral to the Vue.js development experience, as described in the sections that follow.

Understanding Hot Model Replacement

The bundle that webpack creates includes support for a feature called Hot Module Replacement (HMR). When you make a change to the application's source or content files, the altered file is processed by webpack and its loaders, bundled, and sent to the browser. In most cases, only a small change is sent to the browser, and the application is updated without resetting the application's state. To demonstrate, I added some HTML elements and some JavaScript code to the App.vue file in the src folder, as shown in Listing 10-5.

Listing 10-5. Changing Content in the App.vue File in the src Folder

```
<template>
    <div id="app">
        <div>Button Clicks: {{ counter }}</div>
        <button v-on:click="incrementCounter">Press Me</button>
        <div id="nav">
            <router-link to="/">Home</router-link> |
            <router-link to="/about">About</router-link>
        </div>
        <router-view />
    </div>
</template>

<script>
export default {
    data() {
        return {
            counter: 0
        }
    },
    methods: {
        incrementCounter() {
            this.counter++;
        }
    }
}
</script>
```

```
<style>

    #app {
        font-family: 'Avenir', Helvetica, Arial, sans-serif;
        -webkit-font-smoothing: antialiased;
        -moz-osx-font-smoothing: grayscale;
        text-align: center;
        color: #2c3e50;
    }

    #nav {
        padding: 30px;
    }

        #nav a {
            font-weight: bold;
            color: #2c3e50;
        }

            #nav a.router-link-exact-active {
                color: #42b983;
            }
</style>
```

The original bundle sent to the browser included code that opens a persistent HTTP connection back to the server and waits for instructions. When you save the changes to the file, you will see messages displayed on the command line as the component file is transformed, compiled, and bundled.

The persistent HTTP connection is then used to tell the browser that there is a replacement module available, which is sent to the browser and used to update the application, as shown in Figure 10-10.

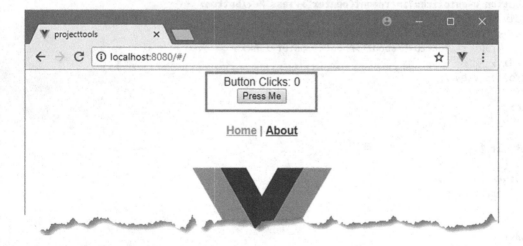

Figure 10-10. *The hot module replacement feature*

For some changes, the HMR feature is able to update the application without resetting its state. This works best for changes to HTML elements. In Listing 10-6, I have changed the element used to display the message to the user.

Listing 10-6. Making an HTML Change in the App.vue File in the src Folder

```
...
<template>
    <div id="app">
        <h1>Button Clicks: {{ counter }}</h1>
        <button v-on:click="incrementCounter">Press Me</button>
        <div id="nav">
            <router-link to="/">Home</router-link> |
            <router-link to="/about">About</router-link>
        </div>
        <router-view />
    </div>
</template>
...
```

Click the button in the browser a few times before saving the changes to the App.vue file, and you will see that the application is updated without losing the application's state, ensuring that the value of the counter property is preserved, as shown in Figure 10-11. Preserving the application's state is useful when you are working on an application feature that requires a navigation process or a form to be filled in and that would otherwise require re-creating the required state each time a change is made.

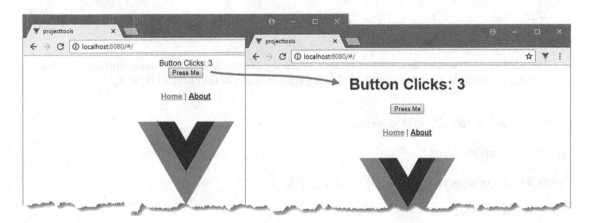

Figure 10-11. *A state-preserving update*

Not all changes can be applied without resetting the application's state. If you change the script part of a component, then Vue.js has to destroy the existing component object and create a new one. The state of the other components in the application remains unaffected, but the state of the component being edited is lost. And, in some cases, the HMR feature just gets it wrong entirely, and you will have to reload the application to see the effect of changes.

Understanding the Error Display

One effect of the immediacy provided by the HMR feature is that you will tend to stop watching the console output during development because your focus will naturally gravitate to the browser window. The risk is that the content displayed by the browser remains static when the code contains errors because the compilation process can't produce a new module to send to the browser through the HMR feature.

To address this, the bundle produced by webpack includes an integrated error display that shows details of problems in the browser window. To demonstrate the way that an error is handled, I added the statement shown in Listing 10-7 to the `script` element of the `App.vue` file.

Listing 10-7. Creating an Error in the App.vue File in the src Folder

```
...
<script>
export default {
    not a valid statement
    data() {
        return {
            counter: 0
        }
    },
    methods: {
        incrementCounter() {
            this.counter++;
        }
    }
}
</script>
...
```

The addition isn't a valid JavaScript statement. When the change to the file is saved, the build process tries to compile the code and generates the following error message at the command prompt:

```
...
ERROR  Failed to compile with 1 errors

 error  in ./src/App.vue

Syntax Error: Unexpected token, expected , (12:8)

  14 | export default {
> 15 |     not a valid statement
     |           ^
  16 |     data() {
  17 |         return {
  18 |             counter: 0
...
```

The same error message is displayed in the browser window, as shown in Figure 10-12, so there is no chance that you won't realize there is a problem even if you are not paying attention to the command-line messages.

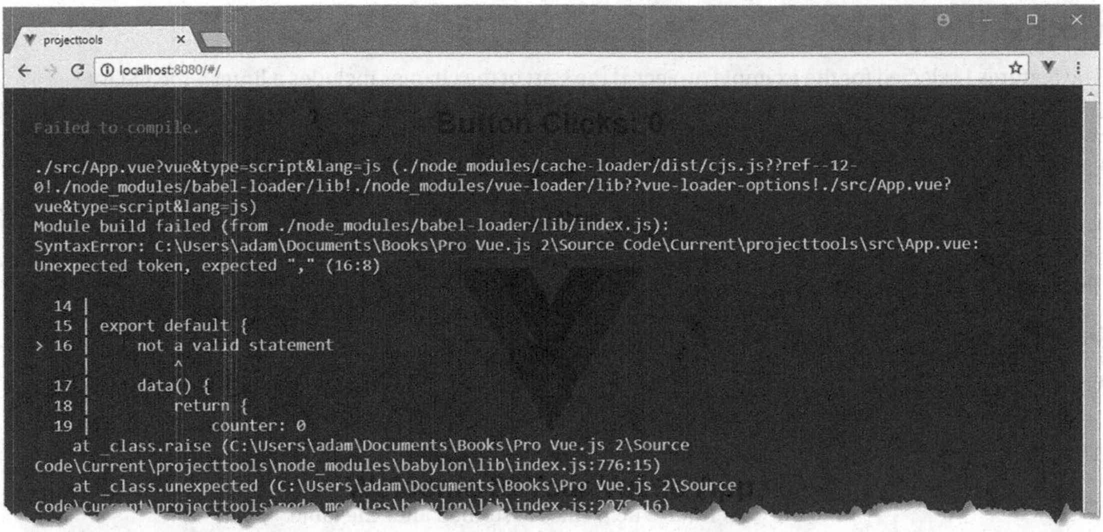

Figure 10-12. *Displaying an error in the browser window*

In Listing 10-8, I have commented out the statement that caused the error, which allows the application to be built without problems.

Listing 10-8. Commenting Out a Problem Statement in the App.vue File in the src Folder

```
...
<script>
export default {
    //not a valid statement
    data() {
        return {
            counter: 0
        }
    },
    methods: {
        incrementCounter() {
            //debugger;
            this.counter++;
        }
    }
}
</script>
...
```

Using the Linter

The features I selected for the example project at the start of the chapter includes a linter—the ESLint package—that is responsible for inspecting the project to make sure the code and content conform to a set of rules. The configuration I chose for the linter means that it performs its checks whenever a change is detected to files in the src folder.

When you choose to add the linter during the setup for a Vue.js project, you are offered a set of options that determine the set of rules that are used to assess the project. These options are described in Table 10-9.

Table 10-9. *The Vue.js Linter Rule Options*

Option	Description
Error Prevention Only	This option applies only the "essential" Vue.js rules and the "recommended" ESLint rules, both of which are described after the table.
Airbnb	This option uses a set of rules developed by Airbnb and that are described at https://github.com/airbnb/javascript. These rules are applied in addition to the "essential" Vue.js rules described after the table.
Standard	This option uses a set of rules known as "standard." The rules are described at https://github.com/standard/standard. These rules are applied in addition to the "essential" Vue.js rules described after the table.
Prettier	This option uses the Prettier tool, which is used to enforce code formatting, as described at https://prettier.io. The formatting is performed in addition to applying the "essential" Vue.js rules described after the table.

I chose the Error Prevention Only option at the start of the chapter, which is the most relaxed set of rules that can be selected and which is focused on identifying problems that may lead to errors. The other options go beyond error prevention to enforce style issues, which is something that I don't get along with and prefer not to use. (I find the "standard" rules especially frustrating because they include a long list of formatting rules; see "The Joy and Misery of Linting" for my views on this kind of linting.)

THE JOY AND MISERY OF LINTING

Linters can be a powerful tool for good, especially in a development team with mixed levels of skill and experience. Linters can detect common problems and subtle errors that lead to unexpected behavior or long-term maintenance issues. I like this kind of linting, and I like to run my code through the linting process after I have completed a major application feature or before I commit my code into version control.

But linters can also be a tool of division and strife. In addition to detecting coding errors, linters can also be used to enforce rules about indentation, brace placement, the use of semicolons and spaces, and dozens of other style issues. Most developers have style preferences that they adhere to and believe that everyone else should, too. I certainly do: I like four spaces for indentation and opening braces to be on the same line as the expression they relate to. I know that these are part of the "one true way" of writing code, and the fact that other programmers prefer two spaces, for example, has been a source of quiet amazement to me since I first started writing code.

Linters allow people with strong views about formatting to enforce them on others, generally under the banner of being "opinionated." The logic is that developers spend too much time arguing about different coding styles and everyone is better off being forced to write in the same way. My experience is that developers will just find something else to argue about and that forcing a code style is often just an excuse to make one person's preferences mandatory for an entire development team.

I often help readers when they can't get book examples working (my e-mail address is adam@adam-freeman.com if you need help), and I see all sorts of coding styles every week. I know, deep in my heart, that anyone who doesn't follow my personal coding preferences is just plain wrong. But rather than forcing them to code my way, I get my code editor to reformat the code, which is a feature that every capable editor provides.

My advice is to use linting sparingly and focus on the issues that will cause real problems. Leave formatting decisions to the individuals and rely on code editor reformatting when you need to read code written by a team member who has different preferences.

There are two groups of rules that are applied when you select the Error Prevention Only option described in Table 10-9. The first set of rules is provided by the ESLint developers and the other by the Vue.js developers.

The ESLint rules are described at `https://eslint.org/docs/rules`, and they focus on general errors that are commonly encountered in JavaScript programming. The Vue.js rules are, as you might imagine, specific to Vue.js development. There are three sets of rules available, as described in Table 10-10. For detailed descriptions of each group of rules, see `https://github.com/vuejs/eslint-plugin-vue`.

Table 10-10. *The Vue.js Linter Rule Levels*

Name	Description
Essential	These are rules are largely related to using directives correctly. Directives are described in Chapters 12–15.
Strongly Recommended	These are rules that are intended to help with the readability of code. They are largely related to formatting and layout issues.
Recommended	These are rules intended to ensure consistency.

The Essential rules are enabled by default, which means the Strongly Recommended and Recommended rules are ignored. You can change the rules used for linting by changing the `esLintConfig` section of the `package.json` file. Here is that section of the `package.json` file as it was created at the start of the chapter:

```
...
"eslintConfig": {
    "root": true,
    "env": {
        "node": true
    },
    "extends": [
        "plugin:vue/essential",
        "eslint:recommended"
    ],
```

```
  "rules": {},
  "parserOptions": {
    "parser": "babel-eslint"
  }
},
...
```

The extends section of the configuration file is used to select the sets of rules that will be applied. The three values for the Vue.js-specific rules are plugin:vue/recommended, plugin:vue/strongly-recommended, and plugin:vue/essential, corresponding to the rules described in Table 10-10. In Listing 10-9, I have enabled the Strongly Recommended rules. When you select a set of rules, the higher-priority rules are also applied so that selecting the Recommended rules will enforce the Strongly Recommended and Essential rules too.

■ **Tip** If you selected the option to store feature settings in separate configuration files when you created the project, then you can make these changes in the .eslintrc.json file instead of the package.json file.

Listing 10-9. Changing Vue.js Linting Rules in the package.json File in the projecttools Folder

```
...
"eslintConfig": {
    "root": true,
    "env": {
        "node": true
    },
    "extends": [
        "plugin:vue/strongly-recommended",
        "eslint:recommended"
    ],
    "rules": {},
    "parserOptions": {
        "parser": "babel-eslint"
    }
},
...
```

Changes to the linter configuration do not take effect until the development tools are restarted. Use Control+C to stop the development tools and start them again by running the command shown in Listing 10-10 in the projecttools folder.

Listing 10-10. Starting the Development Tools

```
npm run serve
```

The linter will be run as part of the build process. Some of the rules that I enabled in Listing 10-9 relate to the number of spaces used as indentation, and if you have followed my coding preferences for the listings, you will see warnings like this one:

```
...
Module Warning (from ./node_modules/eslint-loader/index.js):
error: Expected indentation of 2 spaces but found 4 spaces (vue/html-indent)
at src\App.vue:2:1:
  1 | <template>
> 2 |     <div id="app">
    | ^
  3 |         <h1>Button Clicks: {{ counter }}</h1>
  4 |         <button v-on:click="incrementCounter">Press Me</button>
...
```

You may not see this error depending on your coding style, but you will see this one, which relates changes I made to the App.vue file in Listing 10-5:

```
...
error: Expected '@' instead of 'v-on:' (vue/v-on-style) at src\App.vue:4:17:
  2 |     <div id="app">
  3 |         <h1>Button Clicks: {{ counter }}</h1>
> 4 |         <button v-on:click="incrementCounter">Press Me</button>
    |                 ^
  5 |
  6 |         <div id="nav">
  7 |             <router-link to="/">Home</router-link> |
...
```

As I explain in Chapter 14, there are two ways to register interest in an event—a short form and a long form. One of the rules in the Strongly Recommended set enforces the use of the short form and warns when the long form is used.

■ **Tip**   You can use the npm run lint command to run just the linter, outside of the normal build process.

Customizing the Linter Rules

Neither of the rules for which I have received warnings suit my coding preferences. I am a dedicated four-space coder, and I prefer the long form used to apply Vue.js features to HTML elements. But rather than disable the entire set of rules, I can reconfigure or disable the rules that I don't want and still get the benefit of the ones that I find useful. In Listing 10-11, I have disabled the indentation rule and changed the directive rule so that it checks for the long form and not the short form.

Listing 10-11. Configuring Rules in the package.json File in the projecttools Folder

```
...
"eslintConfig": {
    "root": true,
    "env": {
        "node": true
    },
    "extends": [
        "plugin:vue/strongly-recommended",
        "eslint:recommended"
    ],
    "rules": {
        "vue/html-indent": "off",
        "vue/v-on-style": [ "warn", "longform" ]
    },
    "parserOptions": {
        "parser": "babel-eslint"
    }
},
...
```

Each rule has its own configuration options that can be seen in the summary page for the groups of rules for which I provided URLs in the previous section. In this case, I configured two Vue.js-specific rules. I set the vue/html-indent rule to off, which disables indentation checking for the HTML elements in a component's template element. I left the vue/v-on-style rule enabled but changed its configuration so that it accepts the long form that I prefer and generates a warning when the short form is used. To see the effect of the changes, stop and start the development tools again.

DISABLING LINTING FOR INDIVIDUAL STATEMENTS AND FILES

You may find that there are individual statements that cause the linter to report an error but that you are not able to change. Rather than disable the rule entirely, you can add a comment to the code that tells the linter to ignore the rule for the next line, like this:

```
...
<!-- eslint-disable-next-line vue/v-on-style -->
...
```

If you want to disable every rule for the next statement, then you can omit the rule name, like this:

```
...
<!-- eslint-disable-next-line  -->
...
```

If you want to disable a rule for an entire file, then you can add a comment like this one at the top of the file for Vue.js-specific rules and at the top of the script element for ESLint rules:

```
...
<!-- eslint-disable vue/v-on-style -->
...
```

If you want to disable linting for all rules for a single file, then you can omit the rule name from the comment, like this:

```
...
<!-- eslint-disable -->
...
```

These comments allow you to ignore code that doesn't conform to the rules but that cannot be changed, while still linting the rest of the project. You can also folders and file types to the `package.json` file to exclude them from the linting process.

Debugging the Application

Not all problems can be detected by the compiler or the linter, and code that compiles perfectly can behave in unexpected ways. There are two ways to understand the behavior of your application, as described in the sections that follow.

Exploring the Application State

The Vue Devtools browser extension is an excellent tool for exploring the state of a Vue.js application. There are versions available for Google Chrome and Mozilla Firefox, and you can find details of the project—including support for any additional platforms since the time of writing—at https://github.com/vuejs/vue-devtools. Once you have installed the extension, you will see an additional tab in the browser's developer tools window, which is accessed by pressing the F12 button (which is why these are also known as the F12 tools).

The Vue tab in the F12 tools window allows you to explore and alter the application's structure and state. You can see the set of components that provide the application functionality and the data that each of them provides. For the example application, if you open the Vue tab and expand the application structure in the left pane, you will see the data for the App component in the right pane, including the value of the counter property that I defined in Listing 10-5 and that is shown in Figure 10-13.

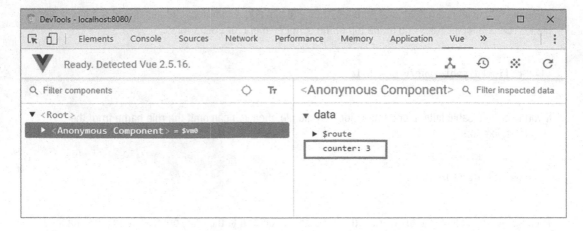

Figure 10-13. *Exploring the application state*

You can click the values to change them. The changes update the application's live data model and will be reflected in the browser immediately if the value you change is displayed through a data binding.

The browser extension also displays information about an application's Vuex store (which I describe in Chapter 20), details of the custom events triggered by the application (which I describe in Chapter 14), and details of the URL routing system, which I describe in Chapters 22–24.

Using the Browser Debugger

Modern browsers include sophisticated debuggers that can be used to control the execution of an application and examine its state. The Vue.js development tools include support for creating source maps, which allow the browser to correlate the minified and bundled code that it is executing with the developer-friendly source code required for productive debugging.

Some browsers let you navigate through the application's source code using these source maps and create breakpoints, which will halt the execution of the application when they are reached and pass control to the debugger. As I write this, the ability to create breakpoints is a fragile feature that doesn't work on Chrome and has mixed reliability in other browsers. As a consequence, the most reliable way to pass control of the application to the debugger is to use the JavaScript debugger keyword, as shown in Listing 10-12.

Listing 10-12. Triggering the Debugger in the App.vue File in the src Folder

```
<template>
    <div id="app">
        <h1>Button Clicks: {{ counter }}</h1>
        <button v-on:click="incrementCounter">Press Me</button>

        <div id="nav">
            <router-link to="/">Home</router-link> |
            <router-link to="/about">About</router-link>
        </div>
        <router-view />
    </div>
</template>
```

```
<script>
export default {
    data() {
        return {
            counter: 0
        }
    },
    methods: {
        incrementCounter() {
            debugger;
            this.counter++;
        }
    }
}
</script>

<style>

    /* ...styles omitted for brevity... */

</style>
```

The application will be executed as normal, but when the button is clicked and the `incrementCounter` method is invoked, the browser will encounter the debugger keyword and halt execution. You can then use the controls in the F12 tools window to inspect the variables and their values at the point at which execution was stopped and manually control execution, as shown in Figure 10-14. The browser is executing the minified and bundled code created by the development tools but displaying the corresponding code from the source map.

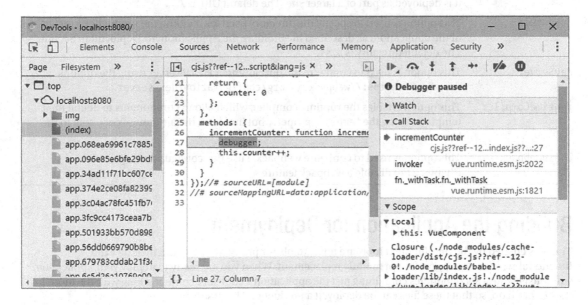

Figure 10-14. Using the browser debugger

Most browsers will ignore the debugger keyword unless the F12 tools window is open, but it is good practice to remove it at the end of a debugging session. The default linter configuration includes a rule that warns when the debugger keyword is left in code when you build the application for production, as described in the next section.

Configuring the Development Tools

The default configuration contains sensible settings, but you can change the configuration to suit your development needs. Configuration changes are defined by adding a file named .vue.config.js in the project folder or by adding a vue section to the package.json file. To demonstrate a configuration change, I created the vue.config.js file in the projecttools folder and added the content shown in Listing 10-13.

Listing 10-13. The Contents of the vue.config.js File in the projecttools Folder

```
module.exports = {
    runtimeCompiler: true
}
```

This is the same configuration change that I made in Chapter 9, and it allows components to define their templates as strings, rather than using template elements. The complete set of configuration options is described at https://cli.vuejs.org/config/#vue-config-js, but Table 10-11 describes the most useful options for most projects.

Table 10-11. Useful Configuration Options

Name	Description
baseUrl	This option is used to specify a URL prefix that is used to reach the application when it is deployed as part of a larger site. The default URL is /.
outputDir	This option is used to specify the directory used for building the production version of the application, as described in "Building the Application for Deployment Section." The default directory is dist.
devServer	This option is used to configure the development HTTP server using the options described at https://webpack.js.org/configuration/dev-server.
runtimeCompiler	This option enables the runtime compiler, which allows components to define their templates using the template property but increases the amount of code sent to the browser.
chainWebpack	This option is used to configure webpack. I use this configuration option in Chapter 21 to disable a webpack feature.

Building the Application for Deployment

The files created by the development tools are not suitable for production use and include extra functionality, such as support for hot module replacement. When you are ready to deploy your application, you must create a set of bundles containing just the application's code and content, along with the modules they depend on, so that these files can be deployed a production HTTP server.

Depending on the features you have selected, you may have to perform some configuration changes to prepare the application for deployment, as I demonstrated for the SportsStore application in Chapter 8.

For the example project for this chapter, as noted in the previous section, it is a good idea to remove the debugger keyword before deployment, so in Listing 10-14, I commented out the debugger statement in the App.vue file.

Listing 10-14. Commenting Out the debugger Keyword in the App.vue File in the src Folder

```
...
<script>
export default {
    data() {
        return {
            counter: 0
        }
    },
    methods: {
        incrementCounter() {
            //debugger;
            this.counter++;
        }
    }
}
</script>
...
```

The linter rules that I enabled in Listing 10-9 perform additional checks that are flagged only when you build for production. You may find these warnings useful, but my personal preference is to disable them, and in Listing 10-15, I have returned to using only the essential Vue.js linting rules.

Listing 10-15. Changing Linter Rules in the package.json File in the projecttools Folder

```
...
"eslintConfig": {
    "root": true,
    "env": {
        "node": true
    },
    "extends": [
        "plugin:vue/essential",
        "eslint:recommended"
    ],
    "rules": {
        "vue/html-indent": "off",
        "vue/v-on-style": [ "warn", "longform" ]
    },
    "parserOptions": {
        "parser": "babel-eslint"
    }
},
...
```

To create the production build, run the command shown in Listing 10-16 in the `projecttools` folder.

Listing 10-16. Creating the Production Build

```
npm run build --modern
```

The `--modern` argument is an optional feature that creates two version of the application, one of which is solely for modern browsers that support the latest JavaScript features and one for older browsers that need extra code and libraries to handle those features. Aside from specifying this option when you build the application, no further action is required, and the selection of the appropriate version is performed automatically, as described at `https://cli.vuejs.org/guide/browser-compatibility.html#modern-mode`.

The build process can take a while to complete, especially for large applications. The result of the build process is a `dist` folder that contains all the files that the application requires in deployment, as shown in Figure 10-15. The name of the individual files will be different in your project.

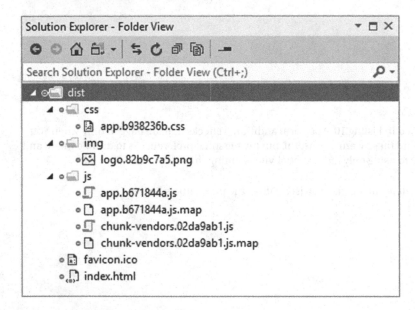

Figure 10-15. *The contents of the dist folder*

The `dist` folder contains the `index.html` file that will be the entry point for the application and that contains `link` and `script` elements that will load the JavaScript and CSS files, like this:

```
<!DOCTYPE html>
<html>
<head>
    <meta charset=utf-8>
    <meta http-equiv=X-UA-Compatible content="IE=edge">
    <meta name=viewport content="width=device-width,initial-scale=1">
    <link rel=icon href=/favicon.ico>
    <title>projecttools</title>
    <link as= style href=/css/app.b938236b.css rel=preload>
    <link as=script href=/js/app.b671844a.js rel=preload>
```

```
<link as=script href=/js/chunk-vendors.02da9ab1.js rel=preload>
<link href=/css/app.b938236b.css rel=stylesheet>
</head>
<body>
    <noscript><strong>We're sorry but projecttools doesn't work properly without JavaScript
    enabled. Please enable it to continue.</strong></noscript><div id=app></div>
    <script src=/js/chunk-vendors.02da9ab1.js></script>
    <script src=/js/app.b671844a.js></script>
</body>
</html>
```

The JavaScript files include the application code and the Vue.js modules that it depends on, and no further additions to the HTML file are required.

Installing and Using an HTTP Server

In a real project, the files in the dist folder would be copied to the production HTTP server, which may be running in a hosted environment or in a local data center. To complete this chapter, I am going to use a simple but powerful HTTP server written in JavaScript that can be downloaded and installed using NPM.

■ **Caution**   The HTTP server used during the development process is not suitable for production use. You must use a different web server to deliver your application to users.

Run the commands shown in Listing 10-17 to install the Express package and a related package that is required to support URL routing.

Listing 10-17. Adding Packages for the Production Build

```
npm install --save-dev express@4.16.3
npm install --save-dev connect-history-api-fallback@1.5.0
```

I added a file called server.js to the projecttools folder and added the statements shown in Listing 10-18, which configure the packages installed in Listing 10-17 so they will serve the example application.

Listing 10-18. The Contents of the server.js File in the projecttools Folder

```
const express = require("express");
const history = require("connect-history-api-fallback");
const bodyParser = require('body-parser');

const app = express();
app.use(bodyParser.json());
app.use(history());
app.use("/", express.static("./dist"));

app.listen(80, function () {
    console.log("HTTP Server running on port 80");
});
```

253

Run the command shown in Listing 10-19 in the `projecttools` folder to test the application.

Listing 10-19. Testing the Deployment Build

```
node server.js
```

This command executes the statements in the JavaScript file from Listing 10-18, which set up a web server on port 80 and listens for requests. To test the application, navigate to `http://localhost`, and you will see the application running, as illustrated in Figure 10-16.

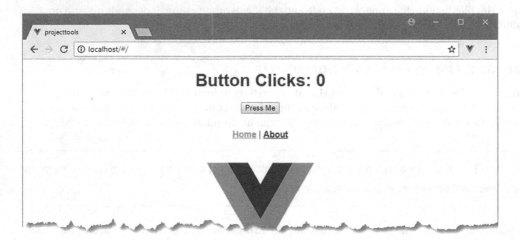

Figure 10-16. *Testing the deployed application*

Summary

In this chapter, I showed you how to create a Vue.js project using the `@vue/cli` package and explained the development tools that it provides. I explained how projects are structured, how applications are compiled and bundled, and how errors are reported, both from the compiler and from the optional linter. I finished the chapter by describing the tools that can be used to debug an application and demonstrated how to build a project in preparation for deployment. In the next chapter, I describe the Vue.js support for data bindings.

CHAPTER 11

■ ■ ■

Understanding Data Bindings

In this chapter, I explain how to perform one of the most basic tasks required in web application development: using a data binding to display a data value. I explain how to add a basic data binding, known as the *text interpolation binding*, to a component's template and how to create the data value for that binding. I explain how Vue.js evaluates a data binding's expression and demonstrate different ways that values can be generated and formatted before they are displayed to the user. Table 11-1 puts the text interpolation data binding in context.

Table 11-1. *Putting Text Interpolation Data Bindings in Context*

Question	Answer
What are they?	Data bindings connect a component's data with the HTML elements in its template. The text interpolation is the simplest of the bindings that Vue.js supports.
Why are they useful?	Data bindings make a Vue.js application interactive. Actions performed by the user alter the application's state, which are reflected back to the user through data bindings.
How are they used?	Text interpolation bindings are created using double curly brace characters, {{ and }}, which is why they are often called *mustache bindings*.
Are there any pitfalls or limitations?	Vue.js allows complex expressions in data bindings. This is a useful feature, but it is easy to get carried away and embed too much logic in data binding, such that the project is hard to test and maintain.
Are there any alternatives?	The text interpolation binding is only one of the bindings that Vue.js supports, and other bindings are described later chapters.

© Adam Freeman 2018
A. Freeman, *Pro Vue.js 2*, https://doi.org/10.1007/978-1-4842-3805-9_11

Table 11-2 summarizes the chapter.

Table 11-2. *Chapter Summary*

Problem	Solution	Listing
Define a new component	Create a file with the .vue extension and add template, script, and style elements.	6, 7
Display a data value	Add a data value and a text interpolation binding	8, 9
Compute a value	Use a computed property or a method	10–14
Format a data property	Use one or more filters	15–18

Preparing for This Chapter

For the examples in this chapter, run the command shown in Listing 11-1 in a convenient location to create a new Vue.js project.

Listing 11-1. Creating a New Project

```
vue create templatesanddata --default
```

This command creates a project called templatesanddata. Once the setup process has finished, run the command shown in Listing 11-2 in the templatesanddata folder to add the Bootstrap CSS package to the project.

■ **Tip**   You can download the example project for this chapter—and for all the other chapters in this book—from https://github.com/Apress/pro-vue-js-2.

Listing 11-2. Adding the Bootstrap CSS Package

```
npm install bootstrap@4.0.0
```

Add the statement shown in Listing 11-3 to the main.js file in the src folder to incorporate the Bootstrap CSS file into the application.

Listing 11-3. Incorporating the Bootstrap Package in the main.js File in the src Folder

```
import Vue from 'vue'
import App from './App.vue'

import "bootstrap/dist/css/bootstrap.min.css";

Vue.config.productionTip = false
```

```
new Vue({
  render: h => h(App)
}).$mount('#app')
```

Add the statement shown in Listing 11-4 to disable the linter rule that warns when the browser's JavaScript console is used, which I rely on later in this chapter.

Listing 11-4. Configuring the Linter in the package.json File in the templatesanddata Folder

```
...
"eslintConfig": {
  "root": true,
  "env": {
    "node": true
  },
  "extends": [
    "plugin:vue/essential",
    "eslint:recommended"
  ],
  "rules": {
    "no-console": "off"
  },
  "parserOptions": {
    "parser": "babel-eslint"
  }
},
"postcss": {
  "plugins": {
    "autoprefixer": {}
  }
},
...
```

Run the command shown in Listing 11-5 in the templatesanddata folder to start the development tools.

Listing 11-5. Navigating to the Project Folder and Starting the Development Tools

```
npm run serve
```

The initial build process will be performed, after which you will see a message telling you that the project has compiled successfully and the HTTP server is listening for requests on port 8080. Open a new browser window and navigate to http://localhost:8080 to see the project's placeholder content, as shown in Figure 11-1.

Figure 11-1. *Running the example application*

Understanding the Elements of a Component

Components are the main building block in Vue.js applications, and all but the simplest projects will contain several components. Components are defined in .vue files that contain HTML content that is displayed to the user, data and JavaScript code to support the content, and CSS styles. The convention in Vue.js projects is to define a root component that orchestrates the rest of the application; this is the App component, and it is defined in a file called App.vue in the src folder. The default project options that I used to create the example project added a root component with the content shown in Listing 11-6.

Listing 11-6. The Initial Contents of the App.vue File in the src Folder

```
<template>
  <div id="app">
    <img src="./assets/logo.png">
    <HelloWorld msg="Welcome to Your Vue.js App"/>
  </div>
</template>

<script>
import HelloWorld from './components/HelloWorld.vue'

export default {
  name: 'app',
  components: {
```

```
    HelloWorld
  }
}
</script>

<style>
#app {
  font-family: 'Avenir', Helvetica, Arial, sans-serif;
  -webkit-font-smoothing: antialiased;
  -moz-osx-font-smoothing: grayscale;
  text-align: center;
  color: #2c3e50;
  margin-top: 60px;
}
</style>
```

Components are defined using three elements: the `template` element, the `script` element, and the `style` element, which I briefly describe in the sections that follow.

Understanding the Template Element

The `template` element contains the component's HTML content. Templates contain a single top-level element (a `div` element in the template in Listing 11-6), which replaces the element that applies the component, as described in Chapter 9. A component's template contains a mix of regular HTML elements and Vue.js enhancements that apply application features, such as data bindings, directives, and custom elements that apply other components. You have seen examples of all these features in earlier chapters, but I describe them in detail in this chapter and throughout the rest of the book.

Understanding the Script Element

The `script` element contains the component's JavaScript module, whose properties configure the component, define its data model, and provide the logic that supports its features. The different roles of the `script` element mean that it can be difficult to understand when you start Vue.js development, but you will soon become familiar with the most useful configuration properties.

Understanding the Style Element

The `style` element defines CSS styles, which can be configured so they apply only to the `template` elements or have a wider effect in the application. Not all components require their own CSS styles, so you will often encounter components that have just `template` and `script` elements, especially when using a CSS framework like Bootstrap, as I do throughout this book. But there are some useful CSS features provided by the `script` element, and it is worth understanding how they can be applied, even when using a CSS framework.

As you will learn, it is the way that the `template`, `script`, and `style` elements are combined that makes components useful, and these elements are the distinctive characteristic of Vue.js development.

Resetting the Component in the Example Application

The component in the App.vue file doesn't do much, but I am still going to strip it right back to the basics so that I can introduce features one by one. In Listing 11-7, I have simplified the template and script elements and removed the style element, giving me a clean slate for the rest of the chapter.

Listing 11-7. Resetting the Contents of the App.vue File in the src Folder

```
<template>
    <div class="bg-primary text-white text-center m-2 p-3">
        <h3>This is the component</h3>
    </div>
</template>

<script>
    export default {
        name: "MyComponent"
    }
</script>
```

The template now contains a top-level div element that I have assigned to several classes that apply Bootstrap CSS styles, which lets me apply styles without using a style element in this component. The div element contains a single h3 element with a simple text message.

When you save the change to the App.vue file, the project will be compiled, the browser will reload, and you will see the content shown in Figure 11-2.

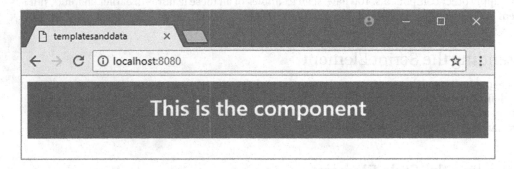

Figure 11-2. *Simplifying the component in the example application*

The only property defined in the script element is name. The Vue Devtools browser extension (described in Chapter 10) uses the optional name property to show the structure of the application, and picking a distinctive and meaningful name can help make sense of what's happening when you inspect the application's state. Open the browser's F12 developer tools and switch to the Vue tab; you will see that the component's name is displayed in the layout, as shown in Figure 11-3. The display itself isn't especially useful at the moment, but it will provide more information as features are added.

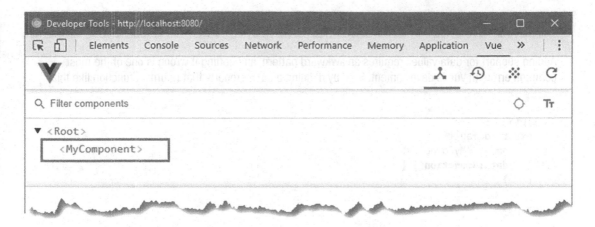

Figure 11-3. *Inspecting the structure of the application*

Displaying a Data Value

One of the most important jobs that a component can do is display data to the user. Displaying a data value requires two steps: defining a data property in the script element and adding a data binding to the template element to present the value to the user, as shown in Listing 11-8.

Listing 11-8. Displaying a Data Value in the App.vue File in the src Folder

```
<template>
    <div class="bg-primary text-white text-center m-2 p-3">
        <h3>Product: {{ name }}</h3>
    </div>
</template>

<script>
    export default {
        name: "MyComponent",
        data: function () {
            return {
                name: "Kayak"
            }
        }
    }
</script>
```

Data values are defined using the data property in the JavaScript module. A specific pattern must be followed to define data values for a component: the data property returns a function, the function returns an object, and the properties defined by the object can be used to display data values to the user.

STEP-BY-STEP GUIDANCE FOR DEFINING DATA VALUES

Adding support for data values requires an awkward pattern, and getting it wrong is one of the most common errors in Vue.js development. Start by defining a `data` property that returns a function like this:

```
...
<script>
    export default {
        name: "MyComponent",
        data: function() {
        }
    }
</script>
...
```

Use `data`, followed by a colon, followed by the `function` keyword, followed by an opening and a closing parenthesis (the (and) characters) and then an opening and a closing curly brace (the { and } characters). The next step is to return an object, using the JavaScript object literal form described in Chapter 4.

```
...
<script>
    export default {
        name: "MyComponent",
        data: function() {
            return {
            }
        }
    }
</script>
...
```

Use the `return` keyword, followed by opening and closing curly braces. The final step is to define the data values that you require. A value is specified using a name, followed by a colon (the : character), followed by the value.

```
...
<script>
    export default {
        name: "MyComponent",
        data: function() {
            return {
                myValue: 10
            }
        }
    }
</script>
...
```

Multiple data values are separated by placing a comma at the end of the previous line and then defining a new value, like this:

```
...
<script>
    export default {
        name: "MyComponent",
        data: function() {
            return {
                myValue: 10, // <-- notice the comma here
                myOtherValue: "Hello, World"
            }
        }
    }
</script>
...
```

This is required only for `data` values, and once you gain a little experience with Vue.js development, you will start to follow this pattern automatically. If you forget to define a function that returns an object, then you will see a warning in the browser's JavaScript console, like this:

```
[Vue warn]: The "data" optionz should be a function that returns a per-instance value in
component definitions.
```

This warning isn't displayed in the main browser window like the compiler errors I demonstrated in Chapter 10, but it will generally cause other warnings and prevent data bindings from working correctly.

Data values in the `script` element are linked to HTML elements in the `template` element using data bindings. There are a number of different types of data binding available, but to get started, I use the simplest, which is the *text interpolation binding*, like this:

```
...
<h3>Product: {{ name }}</h3>
...
```

This type of binding inserts a data value into the text content of an HTML element and is denoted by double curly braces ({{ and }}). The double braces are said to resemble a mustache, which is why this is also known as the *mustache binding*. Save the changes to the App.vue file, and you will see the content displayed in Figure 11-4.

Figure 11-4. *Displaying a data value*

The Vue Devtools tab in the browser's F12 developer tools window will also be updated to show the component's data value. Data values are live, which means that changing the value is automatically reflected throughout the application. For the example application, this means that changing the value of the component's name property will automatically update the text interpolation data binding in the `template` element. The application doesn't have the ability to alter the name value itself yet, but if you move the mouse pointer over the value in the Vue Devtools panel, you will see a pencil icon that can be clicked to activate an editor. Change the value to "Green Kayak" (taking care to retain the quote characters) and click the disk icon to save the change. Vue.js will detect the change to the data property and update the HTML displayed to the user, as shown in Figure 11-5.

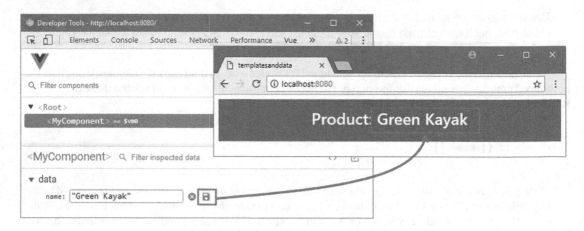

Figure 11-5. *Changing a data property using the Vue Devtools*

Using More Complex Expressions in a Data Binding

When Vue.js displays a data binding, it evaluates its contents as a JavaScript expression. When the contents of the data binding are just the name of a `data` property, then evaluating the expression produces the property's value, which is how the `{{ name }}` binding I used in the example is able to display the value of the data property called name.

Treating data bindings as expressions means you can use more complex JavaScript statements in data bindings. In Listing 11-9, I added two further `data` properties to the `script` element and a more complex data binding to the `template` element.

Listing 11-9. Using a More Complex Data Binding Expression in the App.vue File in the src Folder

```
<template>
    <div class="bg-primary text-white text-center m-2 p-3">
        <h3>Product: {{ name }}</h3>
        <h3>Price: ${{ (price + (price * (taxRate / 100))).toFixed(2) }}</h3>
    </div>
</template>

<script>
    export default {
        name: "MyComponent",
        data: function () {
            return {
                name: "Kayak",
                price: 275,
                taxRate: 12
            }
        }
    }
</script>
```

I added data properties called `price` and `taxRate`, which I used in the new data binding expression to calculate the total price and format the result so that it has two digits after the decimal place, which produces the result shown in Figure 11-6 when the project is compiled and the browser reloads.

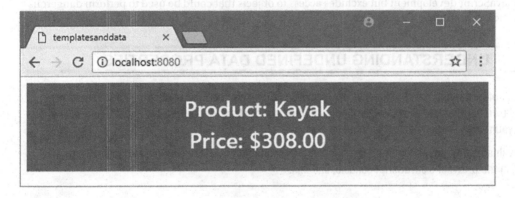

Figure 11-6. Putting a complex data expression in a data binding

Expressions can contain only a single statement, and it must produce a result, which means you cannot invoke functions or perform complex tasks in a data binding. The context of the expression is the component, which means you can only access the data defined by the component whose template contains the data binding. This is how I am able to refer to the `name`, `price`, and `taxRate` properties without needing to qualify the names in any way, but it also prevents me from accessing any of the global objects that browsers provide for JavaScript code (such as `window` and `document`) or data defined by other components.

Expressions can also access commonly used JavaScript global objects and functions, such as the `Math` and `JSON` objects, which are used to access math functions and to deal with JSON data. The most useful global objects and functions that can be accessed from a template are described in Table 11-3.

Table 11-3. *Useful Global Objects and Functions Accessible in Binding Expressions*

Name	Description
parseFloat	This function parses a floating-point number value.
parseInt	This function parses an integer number value.
Math	This object provides math functions.
Number	This object provides methods useful for working with numeric values.
Date	This object provides methods useful for working with dates.
Array	This object provides methods useful for working with arrays.
Object	This object provides methods useful for working with objects.
String	This object provides string-related methods.
RegExp	This object is used to perform regular expression searches.
Map	This object is used to represent a collection of key-value pairs.
Set	This object is used to represent a collection of unique values or objects.
JSON	This object is used to serialize and deserialize JSON data.
Intl	This object provides access to locale-specific formatting as demonstrated in Listing 11-15. Details of the features provided by this object are at https://developer.mozilla.org/en-US/docs/Web/JavaScript/Reference/Global_Objects/Intl.

The list of global objects and functions in Table 11-3 provides access to the most commonly required features for JavaScript development but excludes access to objects that could be used to perform dangerous operations, such as manipulating the DOM.

UNDERSTANDING UNDEFINED DATA PROPERTIES

One result of evaluating data bindings as expressions is that it can be hard to spot mistakes. JavaScript has a relaxed approach to accessing properties that do not exist and will return the special undefined value if you read a property that has not been defined.

Vue.js evaluates the expression but doesn't insert the result into the HTML element and displays a warning in the browser's JavaScript console, like this:

```
...

[Vue warn]: Property or method "category" is not defined on the instance but
referenced during render.
...
```

This is most commonly a problem with typos, where the name of a data property doesn't match the name used in a data binding intended to display its value, and it is worth watching the JavaScript console during development because this problem won't produce a compiler error or be displayed in the browser error overlay.

Calculating Values with Computed Properties

Keeping the expressions in data bindings simple is good practice because it makes the template easier to read, makes it easier to maintain, and maximizes code reuse. To help keep templates simple, Vue.js provides the computed property feature, which is used to generate values based on data properties so that you don't have to include complex expressions in data bindings. In Listing 11-10, I have defined a computed property that calculates the total price for a product using the price and taxRate values.

Listing 11-10. Using a Computed Property in the App.vue File in the src Folder

```
<template>
    <div class="bg-primary text-white text-center m-2 p-3">
        <h3>Product: {{ name }}</h3>
        <h3>Price: ${{ totalPrice.toFixed(2) }}</h3>
    </div>
</template>

<script>
    export default {
        name: "MyComponent",
        data: function () {
            return {
                name: "Kayak",
                price: 275,
                taxRate: 12
            }
        },
        computed: {
            totalPrice: function() {
                return this.price + (this.price * (this.taxRate / 100));
            }
        }
    }
</script>
```

A computed property is added to the component's JavaScript module and assigned a literal object whose property names are the names of the computed properties. Some component features are hard to describe because they depend so heavily on the term *property*, and you may need to read the previous sentence again to make sense of it.

■ **Note**   Notice that I have to use the this keyword in the computed property's function to access the data properties. This is a requirement you will see repeatedly as I describe different component features and you will receive an error telling you that a property is not defined if you omit the this keyword from statements in the script element.

In the listing, I defined a computed property called totalPrice with a function that performs the calculation that was previously included in the data binding. Computed properties are used just like regular data properties in data bindings, which means I am able to simplify the data binding like this:

```
...
<h3>Price: ${{ totalPrice.toFixed(2) }}</h3>
...
```

Understanding Reactivity and Computed Properties

Vue.js optimizes the update process by recalculating a computed property only when there is a change in one of the values it depends on. To demonstrate, I added statements to the computed property's function that indicate when it is invoked, as shown in Listing 11-11.

■ **Tip** You don't need to worry about optimizing reactivity in most projects, but it is useful to understand the different features that are available and how they work together, which is why I have included this example. See Chapter 17 for further details of reactivity in Vue.js applications.

Listing 11-11. Monitoring a Computed Property in the App.vue File in the src Folder

```
<template>
    <div class="bg-primary text-white text-center m-2 p-3">
        <h3>Product: {{ name }}</h3>
        <h3>Price: ${{ totalPrice.toFixed(2) }}</h3>
    </div>
</template>

<script>
    export default {
        name: "MyComponent",
        data: function () {
            return {
                name: "Kayak",
                price: 275,
                taxRate: 12
            }
        },
        computed: {
            totalPrice: function () {
                let tp = this.price + (this.price * (this.taxRate / 100));
                console.log(`Calculated: ${tp} (${this.taxRate})`);
                return tp;
            }
        }
    }
</script>
```

I use the `console.log` method to write a message to the browser's JavaScript console each time the function is invoked.

The application doesn't have the ability to let the user change the data values yet, so save the changes to the file and use the Vue Devtools to increase the value of the `taxRate` property. Each time you increase the property, you will see a message displayed in the browser's JavaScript console that reflects the change you made.

```
...
Calculated: 310.75 (13)
Calculated: 313.5 (14)
Calculated: 316.25 (15)
...
```

Vue.js knows that the `totalPrice` computed property depends on the `taxRate` value and invokes the function to get a new value when `taxRate` is changed so that it can then evaluate the data binding expression.

SIDE EFFECTS IN COMPUTED PROPERTIES

It is bad practice to include statements in a computed property's function that make changes, which is known as a side effect. Side effects make an application harder to understand and can undermine the efficiency of the Vue.js update process.

As a consequence, the Vue.js linter rules, which I described in Chapter 10, include a check for side effects in computed properties. Here is a component that contains a side effect:

```
<template>
    <div class="bg-primary text-white text-center m-2 p-3">
        <h3>Product: {{ name }}</h3>
        <h3>Price: ${{ totalPrice.toFixed(2) }}</h3>
    </div>
</template>

<script>
    export default {
        name: "MyComponent",
        data: function () {
            return {
                name: "Kayak",
                price: 275,
                taxRate: 12,
                counter: 0
            }
        },
        computed: {
            totalPrice: function () {
                let tp = this.price + (this.price * (this.taxRate / 100));
                console.log(`Calculated: (${this.counter++})
                            ${tp}(${this.taxRate})`);
```

269

```
                return tp;
        }
    }
}
</script>
```

I have added a `counter` variable whose value is included in the string passed to the `console.log` method. The side effect in this case is that the `counter` property is incremented with the `++` value. The linter detects the side effect and reports the following error:

```
...
Unexpected side effect in "totalPrice" computed property
    console.log(`Calculated: (${this.counter++})
                                            ^
...
```

You can disable this linter rule, called `vue/no-side-effects-in-computed-properties`, but care is required because side effects can produce unexpected behaviors and should be avoided.

Calculating Data Values with a Method

The main limitation of computed properties is that you can't vary the values that are used to produce the result. If I need to compute the total cost using two tax rates, for example, I have to use two computed properties, each of which performs a similar calculation, as shown in Listing 11-12.

Listing 11-12. Computing Similar Values in the App.vue File in the src Folder

```
<template>
    <div class="bg-primary text-white text-center m-2 p-3">
        <h3>Product: {{ name }}</h3>
        <h4>Price: ${{ lowTotalPrice.toFixed(2) }} (Low Rate)</h4>
        <h4>Price: ${{ highTotalPrice.toFixed(2) }} (High Rate)</h4>
    </div>
</template>

<script>
    export default {
        name: "MyComponent",
        data: function () {
            return {
                name: "Kayak",
                price: 275,
                lowTaxRate: 12,
                highTaxRate: 20
            }
        },
        computed: {
            lowTotalPrice: function () {
                let tp = this.price + (this.price * (this.lowTaxRate / 100));
```

```
            return tp;
        },
        highTotalPrice: function () {
            let tp = this.price + (this.price * (this.highTaxRate / 100));
            return tp;
        }
    }
}
</script>
```

There are now two tax rates, and calculations are performed for each of them, producing the results shown in Figure 11-7.

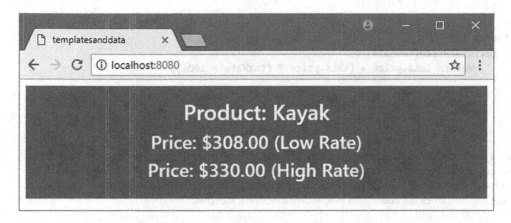

Figure 11-7. *Performing multiple calculations*

This approach in Listing 11-12 works, but it won't scale well. As a rule of thumb, I dislike any approach where the natural way to add a value is to cut and paste the code for an existing one because it is only a matter of time before I duplicate the code but fail to update it to produce the correct value.

A better approach is to define a method, which will allow me to reuse the same code to compute different prices without needing any duplication. In Listing 11-13, I have defined a method that calculates the price of a product.

Listing 11-13. Defining a Method in the App.vue File in the src Folder

```
<template>
    <div class="bg-primary text-white text-center m-2 p-3">
        <h3>Product: {{ name }}</h3>
        <h4>Price: ${{ lowTotalPrice.toFixed(2) }} (Low Rate)</h4>
        <h4>Price: ${{ highTotalPrice.toFixed(2) }} (High Rate)</h4>
    </div>
</template>

<script>
    export default {
        name: "MyComponent",
        data: function () {
```

271

```
            return {
                name: "Kayak",
                price: 275,
                lowTaxRate: 12,
                highTaxRate: 20
            }
        },
        computed: {
            lowTotalPrice: function () {
                return this.getTotalPrice(this.lowTaxRate);
            },
            highTotalPrice: function () {
                return this.getTotalPrice(this.highTaxRate);
            }
        },
        methods: {
            getTotalPrice(taxRate) {
                return this.price + (this.price * (taxRate / 100));
            }
        }
    }
}
</script>
```

To define a method, I added a methods property to the component's configuration object and used it to define a function. Unlike computed properties, a method is able to define parameters. The function in this example is called getTotalPrice, and it defines a taxRate parameter, which it uses to provide a result. I can then invoke the method from the computed properties' functions, like this:

```
...
lowTotalPrice: function () {
    return this.getTotalPrice(this.lowTaxRate);
},
...
```

Notice that I have to prefix the name of the method with the this keyword, just as when I use the data properties. The this keyword isn't required to access the parameter values in methods, which can be read directly, but is required to access data property values.

```
...
getTotalPrice(taxRate) {
    return this.price + (this.price * (taxRate / 100));
}
...
```

Calling Methods Directly from Data Bindings

Using a method allows me to consolidate the code required to calculate the total price, but I can go one step further and simplify the component by removing the computed properties entirely and calling the methods directly from the data bindings, as shown in Listing 11-14.

Listing 11-14. Calling Methods Directly in the App.vue File in the src Folder

```
<template>
    <div class="bg-primary text-white text-center m-2 p-3">
        <h3>Product: {{ name }}</h3>
        <h4>Price: ${{ getTotalPrice(lowTaxRate).toFixed(2) }} (Low Rate)</h4>
        <h4>Price: ${{ getTotalPrice(highTaxRate).toFixed(2) }} (High Rate)</h4>
    </div>
</template>

<script>
    export default {
        name: "MyComponent",
        data: function () {
            return {
                name: "Kayak",
                price: 275,
                lowTaxRate: 12,
                highTaxRate: 20
            }
        },
        methods: {
            getTotalPrice(taxRate) {
                return this.price + (this.price * (taxRate / 100));
            }
        }
    }
</script>
```

This change shows the flexibility in the way that the different component features work together, but it is also a step back because it has increased the complexity of the expressions in the data bindings. As you will find, there are often choices to be made to strike a balance between different Vue.js features.

Formatting Data Values with Filters

To present the user with a dollar amount, I have combined a text character (the dollar sign) with the JavaScript toFixed method, like this:

```
...
<h4>Price: ${{ getTotalPrice(lowTaxRate).toFixed(2) }} (Low Rate)</h4>
...
```

I can improve on this approach by using a filter, which is a function used to format the result of an expression. In Listing 11-15, I have added a filter that formats a number value as a currency amount.

Listing 11-15. Adding a Filter in the App.vue File in the src Folder

```
<template>
    <div class="bg-primary text-white text-center m-2 p-3">
        <h3>Product: {{ name }}</h3>
        <h4>Price: {{ getTotalPrice(lowTaxRate) | currency }} (Low Rate)</h4>
```

```
        <h4>Price: {{ getTotalPrice(highTaxRate) | currency }} (High Rate)</h4>
    </div>
</template>

<script>
    export default {
        name: "MyComponent",
        data: function () {
            return {
                name: "Kayak",
                price: 275,
                lowTaxRate: 12,
                highTaxRate: 20
            }
        },
        methods: {
            getTotalPrice(taxRate) {
                return this.price + (this.price * (taxRate / 100));
            }
        },
        filters: {
            currency(value) {
                return new Intl.NumberFormat("en-US",
                    { style: "currency", currency: "USD" }).format(value);
            }
        }
    }
</script>
```

Filters are defined as functions under a `filters` property in the component's configuration object. Filter functions receive the value through their parameter and return the formatted result. In the listing, I have defined a `currency` filter that formats a value using the global `Intl` object, which provides access to localized formatting. I used the `NumberFormat` method to specify the en-US locale (representing English as it is spoken in the United States) and provided a configuration object that indicates I want to format a U.S. dollar currency amount.

APPLICATION LOCALIZATION

I don't describe localization in this book because it is not a Vue.js-specific feature. But my advice is to think carefully about localization and to give it the time, resources, and attention it deserves.

Localization is a complex topic that is often handled badly, and many applications simply assume that users will understand and accept conventions that are commonly used in the United States. As someone who lives in the United Kingdom, I have become accustomed to seeing dates expressed in the wrong format and amounts in British pounds shown with the U.S. dollar currency symbol. I can, at least, expect to be able to read and understand most written text, which is not the case for non-English speakers.

But doing nothing can be better than doing a poor-quality job of localizing an application, which is what happens if you don't have the services of a fluent speaker for each of the languages you are targeting and if you are not able to commit the time and money required to maintain an application in all of the languages you target. Having access to a localization API such as the one provided by the `Intl` object I used in Listing 11-15 is only a small part of what it takes to localize an application, and there are cultural and linguistic issues that cannot be handled by running your application's content through Google Translate.

Filters are applied using the bar symbol (the | character), like this:

```
...
<h4>Price: {{ getTotalPrice(lowTaxRate) | currency }} (Low Rate)</h4>
...
```

This expression tells Vue.js to format the result from the getTotalPrice method using the currency filter. There is no visible change to the content displayed to the user, but using a filter has made the component more robust by simplifying the data binding expression and helping to ensure that values are formatted consistently. Filters may look like other features in the configuration object, but they have unique characteristics, as I explain in the following sections.

Configuring Filters Using Arguments

The functions used for filters cannot access the rest of the component's data, which means that the formatting result cannot be based on another value. Isolating filters ensures that they do not undermine the change-detection process, such that Vue.js doesn't have to check for changes after calling a filter function, unlike a method call, for example.

But formatting can be a complex task, and so Vue.js filters are allowed to accept arguments. In Listing 11-16, I have added an argument to the currency filter that allows the number of fractional digits to be specified.

Listing 11-16. Adding a Filter Argument in the App.vue File in the src Folder

```
<template>
    <div class="bg-primary text-white text-center m-2 p-3">
        <h3>Product: {{ name }}</h3>
        <h4>Price: {{ getTotalPrice(lowTaxRate) | currency(3) }} (Low Rate)</h4>
        <h4>Price: {{ getTotalPrice(highTaxRate) | currency }} (High Rate)</h4>
    </div>
</template>

<script>
    export default {
        name: "MyComponent",
        data: function () {
            return {
                name: "Kayak",
                price: 275,
                lowTaxRate: 12,
                highTaxRate: 20
            }
        },
```

```
    methods: {
        getTotalPrice(taxRate) {
            return this.price + (this.price * (taxRate / 100));
        }
    },
    filters: {
        currency(value, places) {
            return new Intl.NumberFormat("en-US",
                {
                    style: "currency", currency: "USD",
                    minimumFractionDigits: places || 2,
                    maximumFractionDigits: places || 2
                }).format(value);
        }
    }
}
</script>
```

I have added a parameter named places to the currency function, which I use in the formatting expression to set the minimumFractionDigits and maximumFractionDigits properties of the configuration object passed to the Intl.NumberFormat method, which fixes the number of fractional digits in the result.

When defining parameters for filter functions, it is a good idea to use a default value, and in this example, I default to using the value 2 if the filter is used without an argument.

Arguments are passed to the filter in the data binding expression. I changed one of the bindings in the listing to specify three fractional digits, producing the result shown in Figure 11-8.

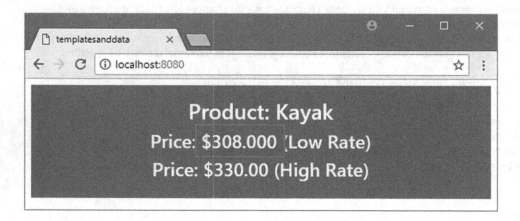

Figure 11-8. *Adding an argument to a filter*

Chaining Filters Together

Filters can be combined so that the output from one filter becomes the input to another, forming a chain of filters. This allows formatting to be composed of several steps and allows fine-grained control over the formatting process. In Listing 11-17, I defined two new filters and chained them together in the template. I also changed the product details to make the effect of the filters easier to see (since Kayak is a palindrome, and one of the filters reverses the characters in a string).

Listing 11-17. Chaining Filters in the App.vue File in the src Folder

```
<template>
    <div class="bg-primary text-white text-center m-2 p-3">
        <h3>Product: {{ name | reverse | capitalize }}</h3>
        <h4>Price: {{ getTotalPrice(lowTaxRate) | currency(3) }} (Low Rate)</h4>
        <h4>Price: {{ getTotalPrice(highTaxRate) | currency }} (High Rate)</h4>
    </div>
</template>

<script>
    export default {
        name: "MyComponent",
        data: function () {
            return {
                name: "Lifejacket",
                price: 48.95,
                lowTaxRate: 12,
                highTaxRate: 20
            }
        },
        methods: {
            getTotalPrice(taxRate) {
                return this.price + (this.price * (taxRate / 100));
            }
        },
        filters: {
            currency(value, places) {
                return new Intl.NumberFormat("en-US",
                    {
                        style: "currency", currency: "USD",
                        minimumFractionDigits: places || 2,
                        maximumFractionDigits: places || 2
                    }).format(value);
            },
            capitalize(value) {
                return value[0].toUpperCase() + value.slice(1);
            },
            reverse(value) {
                return value.split("").reverse().join("");
            }
        }
    }
</script>
```

The new filters are capitalize, which makes the first letter of a string uppercase, and reverse, which reverses the order of a string's characters. Filters are chained together using the pipe character like this:

```
...
<h3>Product: {{ name | reverse | capitalize }}</h3>
...
```

This expression tells Vue.js to format the name value using the reverse filter and then pass the result through the capitalize filter, producing the result shown in Figure 11-9.

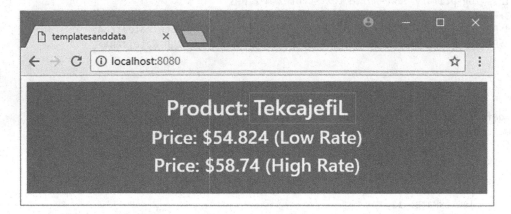

Figure 11-9. *Chaining filters together*

Filters are applied in the order in which they are specified, and changing the order can often produce a different result. To demonstrate, I have changed the order of the chained filters in Listing 11-18

Listing 11-18. Changing Filter Order in the App.vue File in the src Folder

```
...
<template>
    <div class="bg-primary text-white text-center m-2 p-3">
        <h3>Product: {{ name | capitalize | reverse }}</h3>
        <h4>Price: {{ getTotalPrice(lowTaxRate) | currency(3) }} (Low Rate)</h4>
        <h4>Price: {{ getTotalPrice(highTaxRate) | currency }} (High Rate)</h4>
    </div>
</template>
...
```

The name value is passed to the capitalize filter and then to the reverse filter, which produces the result shown in Figure 11-10. The capitalize filter has no discernable effect when the filters are in this order because the first letter of the name value is already an uppercase letter.

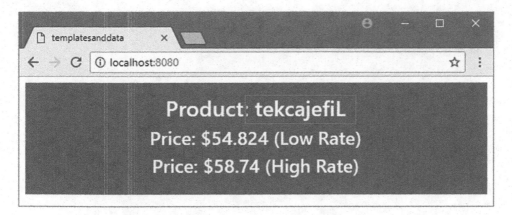

Figure 11-10. *The effect of changing filter ordering*

DEFINING A GLOBAL FILTER

When a filter is defined by a component, it can be used in that component's template and the template of any of its child components (child components are explained in Chapter 16). If you want to define a filter so that it is available throughout the application, then you can use the `Vue.filter` method to register the filter before the `Vue` object is created, like this:

```
...
Vue.filter("currency", (value) =>  new Intl.NumberFormat("en-US",
      { style: "currency", currency: "USD" }).format(value));
...
```

This first argument specifies the name by which the filter will be applied, and the second argument is the function that formats the data value.

Summary

In this chapter, I introduced the text interpolation binding, which is used to present data values to the user. Vue.js supports more advanced ways of connecting the data model to template elements, but the text interpolation binding is the easiest to work with and provides the foundation for understanding how Vue.js works. In the next chapter, I introduce the Vue.js directives feature.

CHAPTER 12

■ ■ ■

Using the Basic Directives

Directives are special attributes that apply Vue.js functionality to HTML elements in a component's template. In this chapter, I explain how to use the basic built-in directives that Vue.js provides, which provide some of the most commonly required features in web application development. In Chapters 13–15, I describe more complex directives, and in Chapter 26, I explain how to create custom directives when the built-in ones don't provide the features you require. Table 12-1 puts the built-in directives in context.

Table 12-1. *Putting the Built-in Directives in Context*

Question	Answer
What are they?	The built-in directives provide features that are commonly required in web application development. The filters that I describe in this chapter are used to manage the text or HTML content of an element, determine whether an element is visible to the user, and manage an element's attributes. There are also directives for responding to user interaction, repeating content, and managing form elements that are described in later chapters.
Why are they useful?	Directives make it easy to connect the data and code in a component's `script` element with the content in its `template`.
How are they used?	Directives are applied to HTML elements as special attributes whose names begin with v-, such as `v-text` and `v-bind`.
Are there any pitfalls or limitations?	Some of the built-in directives are awkward to work with and can produce unexpected results. This is more the case for the directives described in later chapters.
Are there any alternatives?	No. Directives are the Vue.js build block that connects a component's HTML elements and JavaScript code.

© Adam Freeman 2018
A. Freeman, *Pro Vue.js 2*, https://doi.org/10.1007/978-1-4842-3805-9_12

Table 12-2 summarizes the chapter.

Table 12-2. *Chapter Summary*

Problem	Solution	Listing
Set an element's text content	Use the text interpolation binding or the v-text directive	3
Display raw HTML	Use the v-html directive	4–5
Selectively display elements	Use the v-if, v-else, or v-show directive	6, 9–13
Selectively displaying peer elements	Apply the directive to a template element	7–8
Set an attributes and properties	Use the v-bind directive	14–19

Preparing for This Chapter

In this chapter, I continue working with the templatesanddata project created in Chapter 11. To prepare for this chapter, I simplified the application's root component, as shown in Listing 12-1.

■ **Tip**   You can download the example project for this chapter—and for all the other chapters in this book—from https://github.com/Apress/pro-vue-js-2.

Listing 12-1. Simplifying the Content of the App.vue File in the src Folder

```
<template>
    <div class="container-fluid text-center">
        <div class="bg-primary text-white m-2 p-3">
            <h3>Product: {{ name }}</h3>
        </div>
        <button v-on:click="handleClick" class="btn btn-primary">
            Press Me
        </button>
    </div>
</template>

<script>
    export default {
        name: "MyComponent",
        data: function () {
            return {
                name: "Lifejacket"
            }
        },
```

```
        methods: {
            handleClick() {
                // do nothing
            }
        }
    }
</script>
```

I have used the text interpolation binding to display the value of a data property called name, as described in Chapter 11. I have also added a button element, to which I have applied the v-on directive, like this:

```
...
<button v-on:click="handleClick" class="btn btn-primary">
...
```

The v-on directive is used for working with events, as I describe in detail in Chapter 14. Some of the directives that I describe in this chapters have useful features that can be seen only when the state of the application changes and I need a mechanism for triggering those changes. This directive is configured to respond to the click event, which is triggered when the user clicks the button element, by invoking a method called handleClick. I have defined this method in the methods section of the component's script element, but it contains no statements at the moment. Later in the chapter, I'll use the handleClick method to demonstrate some useful directive features. Save the changes to the App.vue file and run the command shown in Listing 12-2 in the templatesanddata folder to start the Vue.js development tools.

Listing 12-2. Starting the Development Tools

```
npm run serve
```

Open a new browser window and navigate to http://localhost:8080 to see the content shown in Figure 12-1.

Figure 12-1. *Running the example application*

Setting an Element's Text Content

A good place to start is the most basic directive, which performs a task you are already familiar with: setting an element's text content. In Listing 12-3, I have replaced the text interpolation binding in the component's template with a directive.

Listing 12-3. Using a Directive in the App.vue File in the src Folder

```
<template>
    <div class="container-fluid text-center">
        <div class="bg-primary text-white m-2 p-3">
            <h3>Product: <span v-text="name"></span></h3>
        </div>
        <button v-on:click="handleClick" class="btn btn-primary">
            Press Me
        </button>
    </div>
</template>

<script>
    export default {
        name: "MyComponent",
        data: function () {
            return {
                name: "Lifejacket"
            }
        },
        methods: {
            handleClick() {
                // do nothing
            }
        }
    }
</script>
```

This is the v-text directive, named after the attribute that is used to apply the directive to an HTML element. Figure 12-2 shows the anatomy of the directive and the element to which it has been applied.

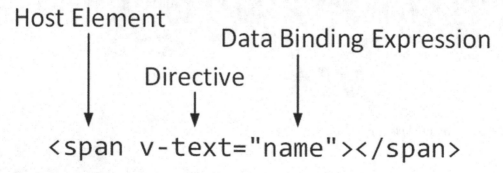

Figure 12-2. *The anatomy of the v-text directive*

The directive is applied using a v-text attribute. The value of the attribute is an expression that Vue.js evaluates to get the content that should be displayed to the user. This is the same type of expression used by the text interpolation binding that I described in Chapter 11, and the result of this binding is to display the value of the data property called name.

Unlike the text interpolation binding, the v-text directive completely replaces the contents of the element to which it is applied, which is why I added a span element to the template in Listing 12-3.

Vue.js re-evaluates a directive's expression when a change is detected, which you can test by using the Vue Devtools to change the value of the name property in the browser, as shown in Figure 12-3.

Figure 12-3. *The effect of a value change on a directive*

Displaying Raw HTML

The text interpolation binding and the v-text directive automatically sanitize the content they display to remove any characters that a browser might interpret as part of the HTML document structure. Sanitizing data values helps prevent cross-site scripting (XSS) attacks, in which the browser interprets a data value as HTML and allows an attacker to insert content or code into the browser. (You can learn more about how XSS attacks work at https://en.wikipedia.org/wiki/Cross-site_scripting.) To demonstrate, I added a data property whose contents are a script element, as shown in Listing 12-4.

Listing 12-4. Adding a Data Property in the App.vue File in the src Folder

```
<template>
    <div class="container-fluid text-center">
        <div class="bg-primary text-white m-2 p-3">
            <h3>Product: <span v-text="name"></span></h3>
            <span v-text="fragment"></span>
        </div>
        <button v-on:click="handleClick" class="btn btn-primary">
            Press Me
        </button>
    </div>
</template>
```

```
<script>
    export default {
        name: "MyComponent",
        data: function () {
            return {
                name: "Lifejacket",
                fragment: `<div class="form-group">
                            Password
                            <input class="form-control" />
                          </div>`
            }
        },
        methods: {
            handleClick() {
                // do nothing
            }
        }
    }
</script>
```

The new data property is called fragment, and its value is a set of HTML elements that include an input element. In the component's template, I added a span element and applied the v-text binding that will replace the element's content with the fragment value. When you save the changes, the application will be updated, and you will see that the fragment of HTML has been made safe, as shown in Figure 12-4.

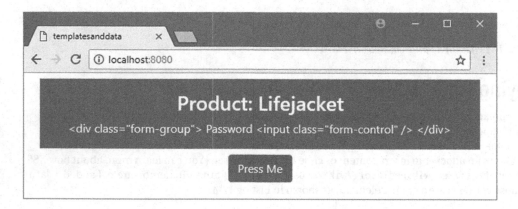

Figure 12-4. Sanitizing data values

Sanitizing data values is a good idea and is essential when you are dealing with data that has been provided by a user. But there may be times when you are dealing with trusted content that you want to be treated as HTML and when sanitization will prevent the data from being displayed correctly. For these situations, Vue.js provides the v-html directive, which I have used in Listing 12-5.

___

■ **Caution**   Don't use this feature unless you trust the source of the data you are displaying.

___

Listing 12-5. Displaying HTML Content in the App.vue File in the src Folder

```
...
<template>
    <div class="bg-primary text-white text-center m-2 p-3">
        <h3 v-text="name" >Product:<span v-text="name"></span></h3>
        <span v-html="fragment"></span>
    </div>
    <button v-on:click="handleClick" class="btn btn-primary">
        Press Me
    </button>
</template>
...
```

The v-html directive is applied in the same way as v-text but displays the data value without sanitization, as shown in Figure 12-5. Without sanitization, the browser interprets the data value as HTML elements and presents the user with an input element.

Figure 12-5. Displaying an HTML data value

Selectively Displaying Elements

The set of elements that a component displays often needs to change to adapt to changes in the component's state. Vue.js includes a set of directives that change the visibility of the HTML elements to which they are applied based on the result of evaluating a data binding expression. In Listing 12-6, I have used the v-if directive to control the visibility of an HTML element.

Listing 12-6. Selectively Displaying Content in the App.vue File in the src Folder

```
<template>
    <div class="container-fluid text-center">
        <div class="bg-primary text-white m-2 p-3">
            <h3>Product: <span v-text="name"></span></h3>
            <h4 v-if="showElements">{{ price }}</h4>
        </div>
```

287

```
        <button v-on:click="handleClick" class="btn btn-primary">
            Press Me
        </button>
    </div>
</template>

<script>
    export default {
        name: "MyComponent",
        data: function () {
            return {
                name: "Lifejacket",
                price: 275,
                showElements: true
            }
        },
        methods: {
            handleClick() {
                this.showElements = !this.showElements;
            }
        }
    }
</script>
```

In this example, I applied the v-if directive to an h4 element, like this:

```
...
<h4 v-if="showElements">{{ price }}</h4>
...
```

The directive will evaluate its expression and use the result to control the visibility of the h4 element. The element will be visible if the expression result is truthy and hidden otherwise (see the "Understanding Truthy and Falsy" sidebar for JavaScript truthiness). The result is that h4 element will be visible when the data property called showElements is true and hidden when it is false.

I added a statement to the handleClick method that toggles the showElements value when the button is clicked, which demonstrates that the v-if directive changes the visibility of the element to which it has been applied when its expression result changes, as shown in Figure 12-6.

■ **Tip** To control visibility, the v-if directive destroys and re-creates elements and their contents or, if the elements are the same type, reuses a single element to display different content. This means that only the elements that are visible are part of the DOM. Use the v-show directive, described later in this chapter, to leave an element in the DOM and manage its visibility using CSS properties.

Figure 12-6. *Controlling the visibility of an element*

UNDERSTANDING TRUTHY AND FALSY

Directives such as v-if evaluate their expressions to determine whether they are truthy or falsy, which is an odd JavaScript feature that often causes confusion and that provides a pitfall for the unwary. The following results are always falsy:

- The false (boolean) value

- The o (number) value

- The empty string ("")

- null

- undefined

- NaN (a special number value)

All other values are truthy, which can be confusing. For example, "false" (a string whose content is the word false) is truthy. The best way to avoid confusion is to only use expressions that evaluate to the boolean values true and false.

Selectively Displaying Adjacent Peer Elements

The standard way to use the v-if directive is to apply it directly to the top-level element whose visibility is to be managed. This approach becomes awkward if there are several elements at the same level whose visibility is controlled by the same expression, as shown in Listing 12-7.

Listing 12-7. Applying the Same Directive to Peer Elements in the App.vue File in the src Folder

```
...
<template>
    <div class="container-fluid text-center">
        <div class="bg-primary text-white m-2 p-3">
            <h3>Product: <span v-text="name"></span></h3>
            <ul class="text-left">
                <li>List item</li>
                <li v-if="showElements">{{name}}</li>
```

289

```
            <li v-if="showElements">{{price}}</li>
            <li>Other list item</li>
        </ul>
    </div>
    <button v-on:click="handleClick" class="btn btn-primary">
        Press Me
    </button>
  </div>
</template>
...
```

I want to control the visibility of two of the four li elements in the list, based on the same data binding expression. Repeatedly applying directives is duplicative and error-prone and is best avoided. For some elements, this problem can be solved by adding a neutral element as a common parent, such as a div or span element, but that won't work here because the result would be illegal HTML (ul elements are not allowed to contain div or span elements).

In these situations, a template element can be used as the common parent, as shown in Listing 12-8.

Listing 12-8. Using a Template Element in the App.vue File in the src Folder

```
...
<template>
    <div class="container-fluid text-center">
        <div class="bg-primary text-white m-2 p-3">
            <h3>Product: <span v-text="name"></span></h3>
            <ul class="text-left">
                <li>List item</li>
                <template v-if="showElements">
                    <li>{{name}}</li>
                    <li>{{price}}</li>
                </template>
                <li>Other list item</li>
            </ul>
        </div>
        <button v-on:click="handleClick" class="btn btn-primary">
            Press Me
        </button>
    </div>
</template>
...
```

The directive is applied to the template element, which is removed during the compilation process and doesn't result in illegal HTML. The result is that the adjacent li elements are managed using a single instance of the v-if directive, with the result shown in Figure 12-7.

■ **Tip** You can use the v-for directive and a computed property to achieve a similar effect with elements that are not next to one another. The v-for directive is described in Chapter 13.

Figure 12-7. *Using a template element to group peer elements*

Choosing Between Sections of Content

If you want to display alternate content based on a data value, then you can repeat the v-if directive and negate one of the expressions, as shown in Listing 12-9.

Listing 12-9. Choosing Content to Display in the App.vue File in the src Folder

```
...
<template>
    <div class="container-fluid text-center">
        <div class="bg-primary text-white m-2 p-3">
            <h3 v-if="showElements">Product: {{name}}</h3>
            <h3 v-if="!showElements">Price: {{price}}</h3>
        </div>
        <button v-on:click="handleClick" class="btn btn-primary">
            Press Me
        </button>
    </div>
</template>
...
```

This approach works, but it is awkward, and you have to remember to update two expressions when the criteria for displaying elements changes. This approach also becomes complex when the expressions are more complex than checking to see whether a value is true. To avoid this kind of expression, Vue. js provides the v-else directive, which works alongside v-if and doesn't require its own expression, as shown in Listing 12-10.

Listing 12-10. Simplifying Content Selection in the App.vue File in the src Folder

```
...
<template>
    <div class="container-fluid text-center">
        <div class="bg-primary text-white m-2 p-3">
```

```
                <h3 v-if="showElements">Product: {{name}}</h3>
                <h3 v-else>Price: {{price}}</h3>
            </div>
            <button v-on:click="handleClick" class="btn btn-primary">
                Press Me
            </button>
        </div>
</template>
...
```

The v-else directive is applied immediately after v-if, and it will automatically change the visibility of the element it has been applied to in opposition to the v-if directive, as shown in Figure 12-8.

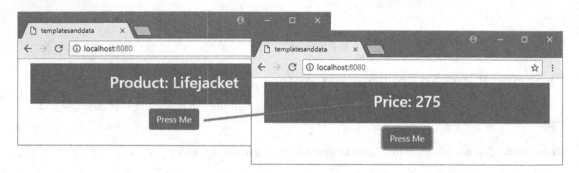

Figure 12-8. *Choosing between content sections*

Performing More Complex Selections

If a basic if/else approach isn't sufficient, then you can also use the v-else-if directive, which is combined with v-if and v-else to select elements and has its own expression. If the result of evaluating the v-if expression is false, then the expression of the v-else-if directive is checked to see whether its elements should be displayed, and if not, the v-else elements are shown. Multiple instances of the v-else-if directive can be used to manage complex selections, as shown in Listing 12-11.

Listing 12-11. Performing a Complex Content Selection in the App.vue File in the src Folder

```
<template>
    <div class="container-fluid text-center">
        <div class="bg-primary text-white m-2 p-3">
            <h3 v-if="counter % 3 == 0">Product: {{name}}</h3>
            <h3 v-else-if="counter % 3 == 1">Price: {{price}}</h3>
            <h3 v-else>Category: {{category}}</h3>
        </div>
        <button v-on:click="handleClick" class="btn btn-primary">
            Press Me
        </button>
    </div>
</template>
```

```
<script>
    export default {
        name: "MyComponent",
        data: function () {
            return {
                name: "Lifejacket",
                price: 275,
                category: "Watersports",
                counter: 0
            }
        },
        methods: {
            handleClick() {
                this.counter++;
            }
        }
    }
</script>
```

The expressions for the v-if and v-else-if directives rely on a counter property whose value is incremented when the button is clicked. There is also a v-else directive whose element will be displayed when both of the other directive expressions are false, producing the results shown in Figure 12-9.

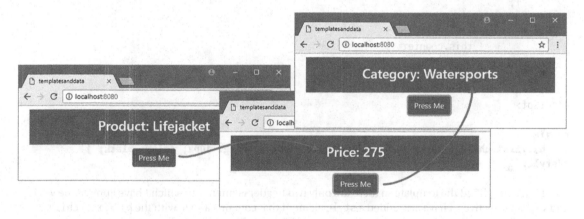

Figure 12-9. *Performing a more complex selection*

Selectively Displaying Elements Using CSS

The v-if, v-else-if, and v-else directives hide elements, removing them from the Document Object Model (DOM) and re-creating them again to make them visible. The result is that the DOM contains only the elements that are visible to the user, which can be a problem, especially when using CSS styles that select elements based on their position within their parent. Listing 12-12 demonstrates the type of problem that can arise.

Listing 12-12. Adding Position-Specific CSS in the App.vue File in the src Folder

```
<template>
    <div class="container-fluid text-center">
        <div class="bg-primary text-white m-2 p-3">
            <h3 v-if="counter % 2 == 0">Product: {{name}}</h3>
            <h3 v-else>Price: {{price}}</h3>
        </div>
        <button v-on:click="handleClick" class="btn btn-primary">
            Press Me
        </button>
    </div>
</template>

<script>
    export default {
        name: "MyComponent",
        data: function () {
            return {
                name: "Lifejacket",
                price: 275,
                counter: 0
            }
        },
        methods: {
            handleClick() {
                this.counter++;
            }
        }
    }
</script>

<style>
    h3:first-child { background-color: aquamarine; padding: 10px; color: black; }
</style>
```

I have simplified the template so there are only two header elements, to which I have applied the v-if and v-else directives. I have also added a style element that contains a style with the h3:first-child selector, which matches h3 elements that are the first children of their parent element.

You can see the problem that results when you save the changes and click the Press Me button. The directives ensure that only one of the h3 elements is visible, but since the invisible elements are removed from the DOM, the visible element is the first—and only—child of its parent and is always matched by the CSS selector, as shown in Figure 12-10.

■ **Tip** You may have to reload the browser to see the effect of the style element.

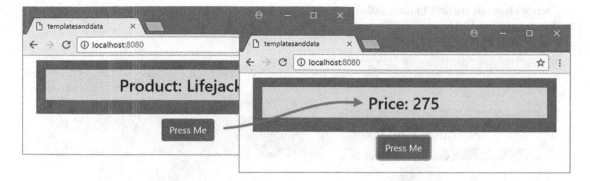

Figure 12-10. *Elements matched by a positional CSS selector*

This sort of behavior is a problem when the intention of the CSS is to change the style properties only of the element that displays the product name. The styles are not intended to affect the element for the price because it is the second child of its parent in the template, but the way the invisible elements are removed from the DOM causes an unexpected result.

In Listing 12-12, I can fix this issue by changing my CSS selector, but this isn't always possible when working with global styles applied to the entire application or when using third-party CSS frameworks such as Bootstrap. In these situations, the v-show directive is a suitable alternative because it has the same effect as v-if but doesn't remove invisible elements from the DOM. In Listing 12-13, I have applied the v-show directive to the component.

Listing 12-13. Leaving Invisible Elements in the DOM in the App.vue File in the src Folder

```
...
<template>
    <div class="container-fluid text-center">
        <div class="bg-primary text-white m-2 p-3">
            <h3 v-show="counter % 2 == 0">Product: {{name}}</h3>
            <h3 v-show="counter % 2 != 0">Price: {{price}}</h3>
        </div>
        <button v-on:click="handleClick" class="btn btn-primary">
            Press Me
        </button>
    </div>
</template>
...
```

The v-show directive is applied in the same way as v-if and can be used as a direct replacement. Save the changes and click the Press Me button to increment the counter and cause the v-show directives to show and hide their content. You can see how the v-show hides an element by examining it in the DOM using the browser's F12 tools, which will show that the elements remain in the DOM and have their display property set to none, like this:

```
...
<h3 style="display: none;">Price: 275</h3>
...
```

Since elements are only hidden, rather than removed, the component's styles are applied as expected, as shown in Figure 12-11.

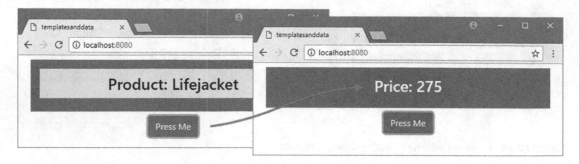

Figure 12-11. *Hiding elements*

Setting the display property can be more efficient than removing an element from the DOM, but the v-show directive can't be used with the template element and has no equivalent to the v-else-if and v-else directives, which is why I have had to apply the v-show directive to both h3 elements.

Setting an Element's Attributes and Properties

The v-bind directive is used to set an element's attributes or properties. I start this section by focusing on attributes, after which I'll explain why properties are different. In Listing 12-14, I have used the v-bind directive to assign elements to classes that correspond to Bootstrap CSS styles, which is the most common use for the v-bind directive.

Listing 12-14. Assigning Elements to Classes in the App.vue File in the src Folder

```
<template>
    <div class="container-fluid text-center">
        <div class="bg-primary text-white m-2 p-3">
            <h3 v-bind:class="elemClasses">Product: {{name}}</h3>
        </div>
        <button v-on:click="handleClick" class="btn btn-primary">
            Press Me
        </button>
    </div>
</template>

<script>
    export default {
        name: "MyComponent",
        data: function () {
            return {
                name: "Lifejacket",
                highlight: false
            }
        },
```

```
        computed: {
            elemClasses() {
                return this.highlight
                    ? ["bg-light", "text-dark", "display-4"]
                    : ["bg-dark", "text-light", "p-2"];
            }
        },
        methods: {
            handleClick() {
                this.highlight = !this.highlight;
            }
        }
    }
</script>
```

This example looks more complicated than it really is. The starting point is the directive, which I applied to the h3 element like this:

```
...
<h3 v-bind:class="elemClasses">Product: {{name}}</h3>
...
```

The v-bind directive is configured with an argument as well as an expression, as shown in Figure 12-12. The argument specifies the element attribute that the directive will configure, and evaluating the expression provides the value for that attribute.

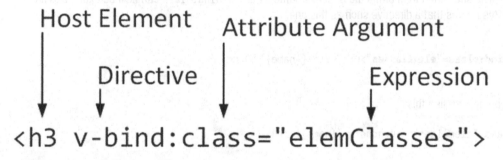

Figure 12-12. *The anatomy of the v-bind directive*

In Listing 12-14, the directive's expression gets the value of a computed property that returns an array of styles whose contents are determined by the value of a data property called highlight. This may seem like an indirect way of setting styles, but it shows the flexible way that Vue.js features can be combined to manage the content presented to the user. To see the effect, save the changes to the App.vue file and click the Press Me button to toggle the value of the highlight property, producing the result shown in Figure 12-13.

Figure 12-13. *Setting an element's class attribute*

Clicking the button changes the membership of the host element between two groups of classes. When the highlight property is true, the host element is a member of the bg-light, text-dark, and display-4 classes (light background color, dark text, and a large font size). When the highlight property is false, the host element is a member of the bg-dark, text-light, and p-2 classes (dark background color, light text, and extra padding).

USING THE DIRECTIVE SHORTHAND

The v-bind directive has two forms. The longhand form is the one that I used in the previous example and combines the directive name, followed by a colon, followed by the name of the attribute to configure. The shorthand form omits the directive name so that v-bind:class can also be expressed as :class. This means that a directive such as this one:

```
...
<h3 v-bind:class="elemClasses">Product: {{name}}</h3>
...
```

can also be applied like this:...

```
<h3 :class="elemClasses">Product: {{name}}</h3>
...
```

The choice between long and shorthand form is one of personal preference and doesn't change the way that the directive behaves.

Using an Object to Configure Classes

The array syntax that I used in the previous section can become awkward to manage if there are multiple inputs that determine the set of classes to which the host element should belong. The v-bind directive can also use an object whose property names correspond to classes and whose value determines class membership for the host element, as shown in Listing 12-15.

Listing 12-15. Using an Object to Control Class Membership with the App.vue File in the src Folder

```
<template>
    <div class="container-fluid text-center">
        <div class="bg-primary text-white m-2 p-3">
            <h3 v-bind:class="elemClasses" class="display-4">Product: {{name}}</h3>
        </div>
        <button v-on:click="handleClick" class="btn btn-primary">
            Press Me
        </button>
        <button v-on:click="handleOtherClick" class="btn btn-primary">
            Or Press Me
        </button>
    </div>
</template>

<script>
    export default {
        name: "MyComponent",
        data: function () {
            return {
                name: "Lifejacket",
                highlight1: false,
                highlight2: false

            }
        },
        computed: {
            elemClasses() {
                return {
                    "text-dark": this.highlight1,
                    "bg-light": this.highlight2
                }
            }
        },
        methods: {
            handleClick() {
                this.highlight1 = !this.highlight1;
            },
            handleOtherClick() {
                this.highlight2 = !this.highlight2;
            }
        }
    }
</script>
```

I added another `button` element and a method that toggles the value of a `data` property. The `elemClasses` computed property returns an object like this:

```
...
return {
    "text-dark": this.highlight1,
    "bg-light": this.highlight2
}
...
```

The object property names control the host element's membership of the `bg-light` and `text-dark` classes based on the values of the two data properties. The `v-bind` directive adds its host element to those classes that correspond to the properties who values are `true` and removes the element from the other classes.

■ **Tip**   I put the property names in quotes in the object returned by the computed property in Listing 12-15. The names of the classes used by the Bootstrap CSS framework contain hyphens, which are allowed in object property names only if they are quoted.

I am still able to use the `class` attribute in the template for those classes that the host element should always be a member of.

```
...
<h3 v-bind:class="elemClasses" class="display-4">Product: {{name}}</h3>
...
```

The result is that the `h3` element will always be a member of the `display-4` class and will belong to the `bg-light` and `text-dark` classes depending on the values toggled by the buttons, as shown in Figure 12-14.

Figure 12-14. *Using an object to configure class memberships*

Setting Individual Styles

The v-bind attribute provides the same features for setting the style attribute as it does for classes, which means it is possible to manage individual CSS style properties. In Listing 12-16, I have used the directive to control the value of separate style properties.

Listing 12-16. Managing the Style Attribute in the App.vue File in the src Folder

```
<template>
    <div class="container-fluid text-center">
        <div class="bg-primary text-white m-2 p-3">
            <h3 v-bind:style="elemStyles" class="display-4">Product: {{name}}</h3>
        </div>
        <button v-on:click="handleClick" class="btn btn-primary">
            Press Me
        </button>
    </div>
</template>

<script>
    export default {
        name: "MyComponent",
        data: function () {
            return {
                name: "Lifejacket",
                highlight: false,
            }
        },
        computed: {
            elemStyles() {
                return {
                    "border": "5px solid red",
                    "background-color": this.highlight ? "coral": ""
                }
            }
        },
        methods: {
            handleClick() {
                this.highlight = !this.highlight;
            }
        }
    }
</script>
```

The elemStyles computed property returns an object whose property names are CSS property names. The border property is a constant value, but the background-color property is determined by the value of the highlighted property, which is changed when the button is clicked. As the data property changes, so does the value of the background-color property on the h3 element, as shown in Figure 12-15.

Figure 12-15. *Setting individual style properties*

Setting Other Attributes

The v-bind directive can be used to set the value of any attribute, although without the special support for the class and style properties that allows objects and arrays to be used. In Listing 12-17, I used the v-bind directive to set the value of a custom attribute that matches selectors defined in the style element.

Listing 12-17. Setting a Custom Attribute in the App.vue File in the src Folder

```
<template>
    <div class="container-fluid text-center">
        <div class="bg-primary text-white m-2 p-3">
            <h3 v-bind:data-size="size" class="display-4">Product: {{name}}</h3>
        </div>
        <button v-on:click="handleClick" class="btn btn-primary">
            Press Me
        </button>
    </div>
</template>

<script>
    export default {
        name: "MyComponent",
        data: function () {
            return {
                name: "Lifejacket",
                highlight: false,
            }
        },
        computed: {
            size() {
                return this.highlight ? "big" : "small";
            }
        },
```

```
        methods: {
            handleClick() {
                this.highlight = !this.highlight;
            }
        }
    }
</script>

<style>
    [data-size=big] { font-size: 40pt; }
    [data-size=small] { font-size: 20pt; }
</style>
```

The HTML specification allows custom attributes whose name begins with data- to be applied to any element. You don't need to prefix custom attributes with data- when using Vue.js, but it is a convention I follow when it is important to easily identify the attributes that are specific to my application.

In this example, I use the v-bind directive to manage the value of a custom data-size attribute, whose value is taken from a computed property called size that returns big or small. These values correspond to the selectors in the style element, which alter the font size, producing the result shown in Figure 12-16.

■ **Tip** You may have to reload the browser to see the effect of the style element in Listing 12-17.

Figure 12-16. Setting a custom attribute

Setting Multiple Attributes

A single v-bind directive can set multiple attributes. No argument is used when applying the directive to its host element. Instead, the expression must produce an object whose property names represent the attributes to be configured, as shown in Listing 12-18.

Listing 12-18. Setting Multiple Attributes in the App.vue File in the src Folder

```
<template>
    <div class="container-fluid text-center">
        <div class="bg-primary text-white m-2 p-3">
            <h3 v-bind="attrValues">Product: {{name}}</h3>
        </div>
```

```
            <button v-on:click="handleClick" class="btn btn-primary">
                Press Me
            </button>
        </div>
</template>

<script>
    export default {
        name: "MyComponent",
        data: function () {
            return {
                name: "Lifejacket",
                highlight: false,
            }
        },
        computed: {
            attrValues() {
                return {
                    class: this.highlight ? ["bg-light", "text-dark"] : [],
                    style: {
                        border: this.highlight ? "5px solid red": ""
                    },
                    "data-size": this.highlight ? "big" : "small"
                }
            }
        },
        methods: {
            handleClick() {
                this.highlight = !this.highlight;
            }
        }
    }
</script>

<style>
    [data-size=big] { font-size: 40pt; }
    [data-size=small] { font-size: 20pt; }
</style>
```

The object returned by the attrValues computed property defines class, style, and data-size properties, the values of which are determined by the value of the data property named highlight, which is toggled by clicking the button. When the highlight value is false, the h3 element to which the directive has been applied is configured like this:

```
...
<h3 class="" style="" data-size="small">Product: Lifejacket</h3>
...
```

When the highlight value is true, the v-bind directive modifies the element like this:

```
...
<h3 class="bg-light text-dark" style="border: 5px solid red;" data-size="big">
    Product: Lifejacket
</h3>
...
```

A single binding manages multiple attributes, producing the result shown in Figure 12-17.

Figure 12-17. *Managing multiple attributes with a single binding*

Setting an HTMLElement Property

By default, the v-bind directive configures the host element's attributes, as shown in the previous example. It is also possible to use the v-bind directive to set the value of a property on the object in the Document Object Model that represents the element.

When a browser processes an HTML document, it creates the Document Object Model and populates it with objects that represent the HTML elements. These objects define properties that do not correspond to attributes supported by the HTML elements, either because they provide specialized features or because of quirks in the HTML and DOM specifications, which have not always been well managed.

You will not need this feature in most projects, but if you do find yourself in the position where setting an attribute doesn't give the required result, then you can use the prop modifier on the v-bind directive, as shown in Listing 12-19.

Listing 12-19. Setting an Element Property in the App.vue File in the src Folder

```
<template>
    <div class="container-fluid text-center">
        <div class="bg-primary text-white m-2 p-3">
            <h3 v-bind:text-content.prop="textContent"></h3>
        </div>
        <button v-on:click="handleClick" class="btn btn-primary">
            Press Me
        </button>
    </div>
</template>
```

```
<script>
    export default {
        name: "MyComponent",
        data: function () {
            return {
                name: "Lifejacket",
                highlight: false,
            }
        },
        computed: {
            textContent() {
                return this.highlight ? "Highlight!" : `Product: ${this.name}`;
            }
        },
        methods: {
            handleClick() {
                this.highlight = !this.highlight;
            }
        }
    }
</script>
```

The modifier is used after the name of the property when applying the directive to its element, separated by a period, like this:

```
...
<h3 v-bind:text-content.prop="textContent">Product: {{name}}</h3>
...
```

This configuration tells the v-bind directive to manage the value of an object property called text-content. The text-content property provides access to an element's text content, and this example sets the content of the h3 element, as shown in Figure 12-18.

GETTING TO KNOW THE ELEMENT PROPERTIES

The Mozilla Foundation provides a useful reference for all the objects that are used to represent HTML elements in the DOM at developer.mozilla.org/en-US/docs/Web/API. For each element, Mozilla provides a summary of the properties that are available and what each is used for. Start with HTMLElement (developer.mozilla.org/en-US/docs/Web/API/HTMLElement), which provides the functionality common to all elements. You can then branch out into the objects that are for specific elements, such as HTMLInputElement, which is used to represent input elements.

Figure 12-18. *Setting an element property*

Summary

In this chapter, I described some of the built-in directives that Vue.js provides for working with HTML elements. I showed you how to manage an element's content using the v-text and v-html directives, how to selectively display content using the v-if and v-show directives, and how to set an element's attributes using the v-bind directive. In the next chapter, I describe the directive that is used to repeat content for each item in an array.

■ ■ ■

CHAPTER 13

Using the Repeater Directive

In this chapter, I continue to describe the built-in Vue.js directives and focus on the v-for directive, which is commonly used to populate lists and generate rows for tables and grid layouts. Table 13-1 puts the v-for directive in context.

Table 13-1. *Putting the v-for Directive in Context*

Question	Answer
What is it?	The v-for directive is used to duplicate a set of HTML elements for each item in an array or for each property defined by an object.
Why is it useful?	The v-for directive defines a variable that provides access to the object being processed, which can be used in data bindings to customize the duplicated HTML elements.
How is it used?	The v-for directive is applied to the top-level element to be duplicated, and its expression specifies the source of the objects and the variable name by which each of them can be referred to in data bindings.
Are there any pitfalls or limitations?	The v-for directive doesn't support JavaScript collections such as Set and Map, and attention must be paid to the order in which properties defined by an object are enumerated.
Are there any alternatives?	You could write a custom directive, as described in Chapter 26, to perform a similar task, but the v-for directive contains a number of optimizations that make it efficient when dealing with large datasets.

Table 13-2 summarizes the chapter.

Table 13-2. *Chapter Summary*

Problem	Solution	Listing
Repeat the same set of elements for each object in an array or each property defined by an object	Use the v-for directive	3, 13, 15–16
Refer to the current object in the set of elements that is duplicated	Use the v-for directive's alias feature	4
Associate an HTML element with a specific object	Define a key attribute using the v-bind directive	5–7
Refer to the current object's position in the array	Use the v-for directive's index feature	8
Ensure that changes to an array index are detected	Use the Vue.set method	9–11
Repeat elements without a data source	Use a number value in place of a data source in the v-for directive's expression	14

Preparing for This Chapter

In this chapter, I continue working with the templatesanddata project from Chapter 12. To prepare for this chapter, I simplified the application's root component, as shown in Listing 13-1.

■ **Tip**   You can download the example project for this chapter—and for all the other chapters in this book—from https://github.com/Apress/pro-vue-js-2.

Listing 13-1. Simplifying the Content of the App.vue File in the src Folder

```
<template>
    <div class="container-fluid">
        <div class="bg-primary text-white m-2 p-3 text-center">
            <h3>Product: {{ name }}</h3>
        </div>
        <div class="text-center">
            <button v-on:click="handleClick" class="btn btn-primary">
                Press Me
            </button>
        </div>
    </div>
</template>

<script>
    export default {
        name: "MyComponent",
        data: function () {
```

```
        return {
            name: "Lifejacket"
        }
    },
    methods: {
        handleClick() {
            // do nothing
        }
    }
}
</script>
```

Save the changes to the App.vue file and run the command shown in Listing 13-2 in the templatesanddata folder to start the Vue.js development tools.

Listing 13-2. Starting the Development Tools

```
npm run serve
```

Open a new browser window and navigate to http://localhost:8080 to see the content shown in Figure 13-1.

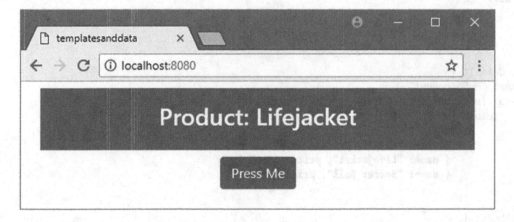

Figure 13-1. *Running the example application*

Enumerating an Array

Most applications deal with arrays of related objects that must be presented to the user, typically to create rows in a table or a grid layout. The v-for directive is used to repeat a set of HTML elements for each object in an array. In Listing 13-3, I have used the v-for directive to enumerate an array of objects to populate a table.

■ **Note** You will see some linter warnings for the examples in this section. The warnings will be addressed as I introduce the features provided by the v-for directive.

Listing 13-3. Enumerating an Array in the App.vue File in the src Folder

```
<template>
    <div class="container-fluid">
        <h2 class="bg-primary text-white text-center p-3">Products</h2>
        <table class="table table-sm table-bordered table-striped text-left">
            <tr><th>Name</th><th>Price</th></tr>
            <tbody>
                <tr v-for="p in products">
                    <td>Name</td>
                    <td>Category</td>
                </tr>
            </tbody>
        </table>
        <div class="text-center">
            <button v-on:click="handleClick" class="btn btn-primary">
                Press Me
            </button>
        </div>
    </div>
</template>

<script>
    export default {
        name: "MyComponent",
        data: function () {
            return {
                products: [
                    { name: "Kayak", price: 275 },
                    { name: "Lifejacket", price: 48.95 },
                    { name: "Soccer Ball", price: 19.50 }]
            }
        },
        methods: {
            handleClick() {
                // do nothing
            }
        }
    }
</script>
```

The value of the data property called products is an array of objects, and the v-for directive processes each of the objects in the array to produce the content shown in Figure 13-2. This isn't an especially useful result yet, but the v-for directive causes confusion and warrants careful explanation.

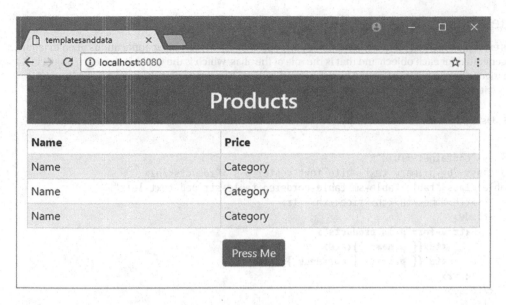

Figure 13-2. Enumerating objects to create table rows

I applied the v-for directive in the template like this:

```
...
<tr v-for="p in products">
    <td>Name</td>
    <td>Category</td>
</tr>
...
```

The v-for directive's expression has to be in a specific form: *<alias> in <source>*. The *source* term is the source of the objects that are to be processed and specifies the data property named products in this example. The in keyword separates the array from *alias*, which is a temporary variable assigned to each object in the array as it is processed.

In the example, the alias is p, and the source is products. Applying the directive tells v-for to duplicate the tr element and the two td elements it contains for each object in the products array, like this:

```
...
<tbody>
    <tr><td>Name</td><td>Category</td></tr>
    <tr><td>Name</td> <td>Category</td></tr>
    <tr><td>Name</td> <td>Category</td></tr>
</tbody>
...
```

The product array contains three objects, and so the v-for directive duplicates the tr and td elements three times.

Using the Alias

The previous example repeated identical content for each object in the source. Most applications need to tailor the content generated for each object, and that is the role of the alias, which is the variable that each object in the array is assigned to when it is processed by the v-for directive. The alias is useful because it can be used in data bindings within the elements that are repeated by the v-for directive, as shown in Listing 13-4.

Listing 13-4. Using the v-for Alias in the App.vue File in the src Folder

```
<template>
    <div class="container-fluid">
        <h2 class="bg-primary text-white text-center p-3">Products</h2>
        <table class="table table-sm table-bordered table-striped text-left">
            <tr><th>Name</th><th>Price</th></tr>
            <tbody>
                <tr v-for="p in products">
                    <td>{{ p.name }}</td>
                    <td>{{ p.price | currency }}</td>
                </tr>
            </tbody>
        </table>
        <div class="text-center">
            <button v-on:click="handleClick" class="btn btn-primary">
                Press Me
            </button>
        </div>
    </div>
</template>

<script>
    export default {
        name: "MyComponent",
        data: function () {
            return {
                products: [
                    { name: "Kayak", price: 275 },
                    { name: "Lifejacket", price: 48.95 },
                    { name: "Soccer Ball", price: 19.50 }]
            }
        },
        filters: {
            currency(value) {
                return new Intl.NumberFormat("en-US",
                    { style: "currency", currency: "USD", }).format(value);
            },
        },
```

```
        methods: {
            handleClick() {
                // do nothing
            }
        }
    }
</script>
```

The name of the alias variable in this example is p, and I have used the text interpolation binding to display the value of each product's name and price properties through the alias, with the binding expressions p.name and p.price.

```
...
<tr v-for="p in products">
    <td>{{ p.name }}</td>
    <td>{{ p.price | currency }}</td>
</tr>
...
```

All the text interpolation features I described in Chapter 11 can be used with a v-for alias, and I have reinstated the currency filter and used it to format the price property, producing the result shown in Figure 13-3.

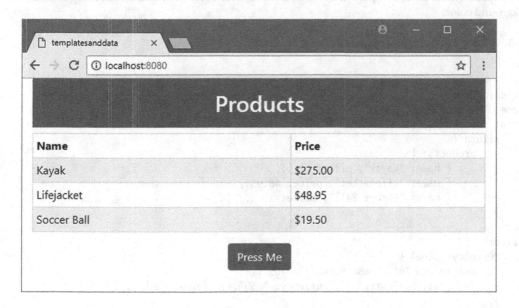

Figure 13-3. *Using the v-for directive alias*

It is the ability to include the object assigned to the alias in data bindings that makes the v-for directive useful, allowing the content that is generated to be differentiated for each object that is processed.

Identifying the Key

If you look at the output from the development tools—either on the command line or in the browser's JavaScript console—you will see that the linter is reporting a warning.

```
...
error: Elements in iteration expect to have 'v-bind:key' directives (vue/require-v-for-key)
    5 |               <tr><th>Name</th><th>Price</th></tr>
    6 |               <tbody>
 >  7 |                   <tr v-for="p in products">
      |                   ^
    8 |                       <td>{{ p.name }}</td>
    9 |                       <td>{{ p.price | currency }}</td>
   10 |                   </tr>
...
```

This warning relates to the way that the v-for directive handles changes to the order of the objects that it processes. By default, the v-for directive responds to changes in the order of the objects it has processed by updating the content displayed by each of the elements it has created. In the example, this means revisiting each tr element that has been created and updating the text contained in the td elements.

Seeing how these changes are performed requires a little work. In Listing 13-5, I have added a statement to the handleClick method that removes the first item from the array and inserts it again at the end. I have also added a style element to the component with a style that selects an element with an id of tagged and sets its background color.

Listing 13-5. Adding a Style in the App.vue File in the src Folder

```
...
<script>
    export default {
        name: "MyComponent",
        data: function () {
            return {
                products: [
                    { name: "Kayak", price: 275 },
                    { name: "Lifejacket", price: 48.95 },
                    { name: "Soccer Ball", price: 19.50 }]
            }
        },
        filters: {
            currency(value) {
                return new Intl.NumberFormat("en-US",
                    { style: "currency", currency: "USD", }).format(value);
            },
        },
        methods: {
            handleClick() {
                this.products.push(this.products.shift());
            }
        }
    }
</script>
```

```
<style>
    #tagged { background-color: coral; }
</style>
...
```

Save the change, and once the application has updated, open the browser's F12 developer tools, switch to the Console panel, and execute the statement shown in Listing 13-6.

Listing 13-6. Marking an Element

```
document.querySelector("tbody > tr").id = "tagged"
```

This statement uses the DOM API to select the first tr element that is a child of a tbody element and sets its ID to tagged, which corresponds to the selector for the style in Listing 13-6. As soon as the command is executed, the first row in the table body is shown in a different background color.

Click the Press Me button to see the default way the v-for directive deals with a change in the order of its objects. Each time the handleClick method changes the order of the objects in the array, the v-for directive updates the contents of the elements it has created, as shown in Figure 13-4.

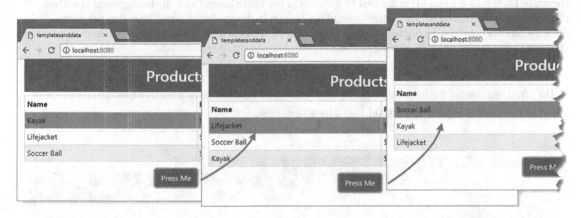

Figure 13-4. *Updating the contents of elements in place*

The v-for directive has to update all the elements that it created because it doesn't know how to correlate them with the objects now that the array has been modified.

Providing the directive with a hint about which object is related to which element means selecting a property and using it as a unique key, which is then identified using the v-bind directive, as shown in Listing 13-7.

Listing 13-7. Selecting a Key in the App.vue File in the src Folder

```
...
<template>
    <div class="container-fluid">
        <h2 class="bg-primary text-white text-center p-3">Products</h2>
        <table class="table table-sm table-bordered table-striped text-left">
            <tr><th>Name</th><th>Price</th></tr>
```

317

```
        <tbody>
            <tr v-for="p in products" v-bind:key="p.name">
                <td>{{ p.name }}</td>
                <td>{{ p.price | currency }}</td>
            </tr>
        </tbody>
    </table>
    <div class="text-center">
        <button v-on:click="handleClick" class="btn btn-primary">
            Press Me
        </button>
    </div>
</div>
</template>
...
```

The v-bind directive is used to set an attribute named key, whose value is expressed using the alias defined in the v-for directive expression. In this case, I have used p as the v-for alias, and I want to use the name property as the key for the data objects, so I used p.name as the v-bind expression.

Save the changes to the component and, once the application has updated, execute the statement shown in Listing 13-6 again to tag the first tr element in the table body. Once the background color has changed, click the button to change the order of the objects in the products array. Now that the v-for directive knows how to work out which object is associated with each set of elements, it is able to respond to changes in the array's order by moving elements around, as shown in Figure 13-5.

■ **Tip** You can disable the linter rule that requires keys if you want the default behavior, which can be faster for small numbers of objects. See Listing 13-14 for an example.

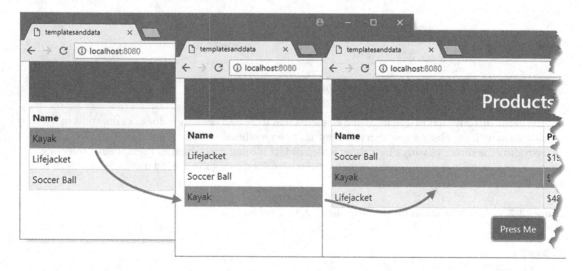

Figure 13-5. Moving elements to respond to a change

Getting the Item Index

The v-for directive supports an additional variable that is assigned the index of the current object in the array and that can be used for a range of purposes, such as displaying a row number in tables or targeting elements with styles. In Listing 13-8, I added a new column to the table that displays the index and used the v-bind directive to set an attribute on the table rows to which I apply a style.

Listing 13-8. Using a v-for Index in the App.vue File in the src Folder

```
<template>
    <div class="container-fluid">
        <h2 class="bg-primary text-white text-center p-3">Products</h2>
        <table class="table table-sm table-bordered  text-left">
            <tr><th>Index</th><th>Name</th><th>Price</th></tr>
            <tbody>
                <tr v-for="(p, i) in products"
                        v-bind:key="p.name" v-bind:odd="i % 2 == 0">
                    <td>{{ i + 1 }}</td>
                    <td>{{ p.name }}</td>
                    <td>{{ p.price | currency }}</td>
                </tr>
            </tbody>
        </table>
        <div class="text-center">
            <button v-on:click="handleClick" class="btn btn-primary">
                Press Me
            </button>
        </div>
    </div>
</template>

<script>
    export default {
        name: "MyComponent",
        data: function () {
            return {
                products: [
                    { name: "Kayak", price: 275 },
                    { name: "Lifejacket", price: 48.95 },
                    { name: "Soccer Ball", price: 19.50 },
                    { name: "Corner Flags", price: 39.95 },
                    { name: "Stadium", price: 79500 },
                    { name: "Thinking Cap", price: 16 }
                ]
            }
        },
```

```
        filters: {
            currency(value) {
                return new Intl.NumberFormat("en-US",
                    { style: "currency", currency: "USD", }).format(value);
            },
        },
        methods: {
            handleClick() {
                this.products.push(this.products.shift());
            }
        }
    }
</script>

<style>
    [odd]{ background-color: lightblue; }
</style>
```

To use the index feature, an additional variable is defined when applying the v-for expression, like this:

```
...
<tr v-for="(p, i) in products" v-bind:key="p.name" v-bind:odd="i % 2 == 0">
...
```

The index variable is separated from the alias using a comma (the , character), and both variables are surrounded by parentheses. As the v-for directive enumerates objects, it assigns the current object to p and sets i to be the position of the current object in the array, starting at zero. The index variable can be used in data bindings, just like any other data value. In the listing, I have used the text interpolation binding to set the contents of a new table column, using an expression to present the user with a sequence that begins with one, rather than zero:

```
...
<td>{{ i + 1 }}</td>
...
```

I also used the index to set a custom attribute named odd on each tr element that is created and used the modulo operator to indicate whether a row is odd.

```
...
<tr v-for="(p, i) in products" v-bind:key="p.name" v-bind:odd="i % 2 == 0">
...
```

The effect is that the odd-numbered rows are made members of the odd class, which matches the selector in the style element and stripes the rows in the table, as shown in Figure 13-6. I added more items to the products array in Listing 13-8 to emphasize the result.

THE EXPANDED FORM OF THE V-FOR DIRECTIVE

It may seem odd that I am able to access the index variable in Listing 13-8 using a v-bind directive that is applied to the same element as v-for. This works because I have used the concise form of the v-for directive, where it is applied to the outermost element that should be duplicated for each data object. This is equivalent to using a template item, like this:

```
...
<tbody>
    <template v-for="(p, i) in products" >
        <tr v-bind:key="p.name"  v-bind:odd="i % 2 == 0">
            <td>{{ i + 1 }}</td>
            <td>{{ p.name }}</td>
            <td>{{ p.price | currency }}</td>
        </tr>
    </template>
</tbody>
...
```

This is equivalent to the directive applied in Listing 13-8 but more clearly shows the way that the directive and its contents interact. You don't need to use a template element with the v-for directive unless you need to duplicate multiple peer elements for each data object. If you do use a template element, bear in mind that the v-bind directive for the key attribute must be applied to the elements that are duplicated and not to the template.

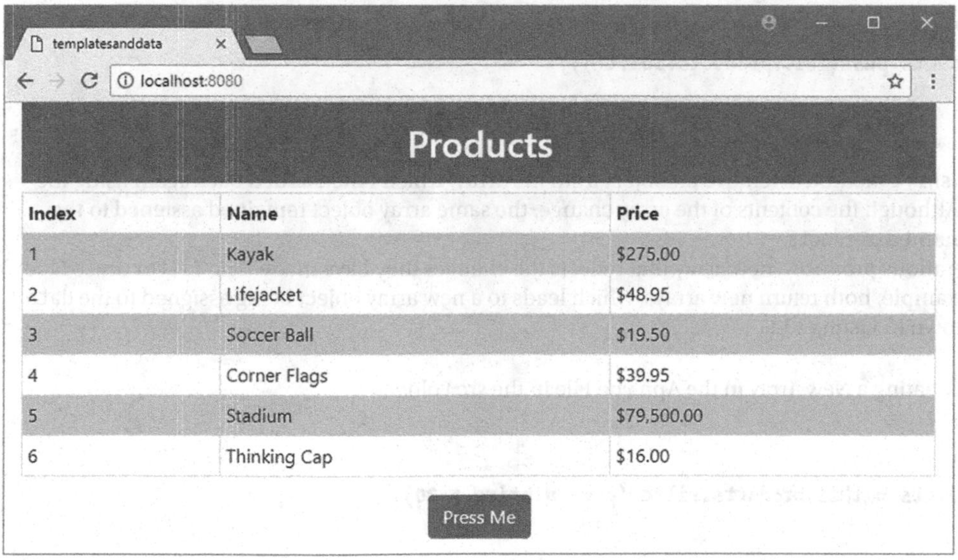

---

templatesanddata	Products	

← → C ① localhost:8080

Index	Name	Price
1	Kayak	$275.00
2	Lifejacket	$48.95
3	Soccer Ball	$19.50
4	Corner Flags	$39.95
5	Stadium	$79,500.00
6	Thinking Cap	$16.00

Press Me

Figure 13-6. *Using the v-for directive's index feature*

```
┌─────────────────────────────────────────────────────────────────────┐
│                    USING CSS TO STRIPE TABLE ROWS                     │
└─────────────────────────────────────────────────────────────────────┘
```

Alternating colors in a table or grid layout is a common requirement, but there is an easier way to do it than relying on the index feature provided by the v-for directive. Most CSS frameworks, including Bootstrap, implement table striping, but if you are relying on custom styles, then you can use CSS selectors like this in your component's style element:

```
...
<style>
    tbody > tr:nth-child(even) { background-color: coral; }
    tbody > tr:nth-child(odd) { background-color: lightblue; }
</style>
...
```

The selectors for these styles match the odd and even tr elements that are children of a tbody element. The important part of these selectors is :n-child(odd) and :nth-child(even), which can be used to select any odd and even elements.

Understanding Array Change Detection

Vue.js will detect changes made to an array using the following methods: push, pop, shift, unshift, splice, sort, and reverse. These are known as the mutating array methods because they change the content of the array, which allows Vue.js to keep a reference to the array object and observe the changes. This is the type of change I made in Listing 13-8 to demonstrate the key feature:

```
...
handleClick() {
    this.products.push(this.products.shift());
}
...
```

I used the shift method to remove an object from the array, which I then added back again using the push method. Although the contents of the array change, the same array object remained assigned to the data property named products.

Other operations produce a new array that reflects the changes they have made. The filter and slice methods, for example, both return new arrays, which leads to a new array object being assigned to the data property, as shown in Listing 13-9.

Listing 13-9. Creating a New Array in the App.vue File in the src Folder

```
...
handleClick() {
    this.products = this.products.filter(p => p.price > 20);
}
...
```

I replaced the statement in the handleClick method with one that uses the filter method to create a new array that contains only those objects whose price value is greater than 20. I assign the new array returned by the filter method to the products property, but this is an operation that Vue.js is designed to cope with, and if there is overlap between the objects in the old array and the new array, the existing content will be reused for efficiency. But, regardless of the amount of overlap, replacing the array with a new object will update the content presented to the user, as shown in Figure 13-7.

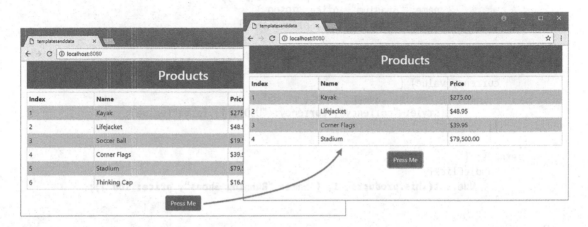

Figure 13-7. *Assigning a new array*

Understanding Update Problems

There are two types of array change that Vue.js can't detect and won't respond to. The first is when an item in the array is replaced, as shown in Listing 13-10.

Listing 13-10. Replacing an Array Item in the App.vue File in the src Folder

```
...
handleClick() {
    this.products[1] = { name: "Running Shoes", price: 100 };
}
...
```

The method uses the array index notation to assign a new object to position 1 in the array. Vue.js won't detect the change, and any changes made to the property values of the new object won't be detected either.

To work around this limitation, Vue.js provides a method that replaces an object in an array and triggers the change detection process. This method must be imported from its module before it can be used, as shown in Listing 13-11.

Listing 13-11. Safely Replacing an Array Item in the App.vue File in the src Folder

```
...
<script>
    import Vue from "vue";

    export default {
        name: "MyComponent",
```

```
        data: function () {
            return {
                products: [
                    { name: "Kayak", price: 275 },
                    { name: "Lifejacket", price: 48.95 },
                    { name: "Soccer Ball", price: 19.50 },
                    { name: "Corner Flags", price: 39.95 },
                    { name: "Stadium", price: 79500 },
                    { name: "Thinking Cap", price: 16 }]
            }
        },
        filters: {
            currency(value) {
                return new Intl.NumberFormat("en-US",
                    { style: "currency", currency: "USD", }).format(value);
            },
        },
        methods: {
            handleClick() {
                Vue.set(this.products, 1, { name: "Running Shoes", price: 100 });
            }
        }
    }
}
</script>
...
```

The Vue.set method accepts three arguments: the array to modify, the index of the object to be replaced, and the new object. The effect is to perform the update and trigger the change detection process so that the content presented to the user is updated, as shown in Figure 13-8.

■ **Tip** The Vue.set method can also be accessed as this.$set in components. I prefer to use Vue.set because not all arrays are performed in components, and I like to keep the updates consistent.

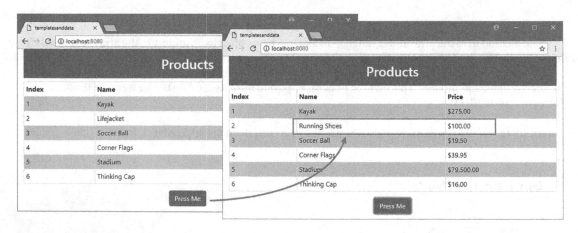

Figure 13-8. *Safely replacing an object in an array*

The other change to an array that Vue.js cannot detect is when the array is shortened by changing the value of the length property. This problem can be avoided by using the array splice method to remove unwanted elements in a way that Vue.js can see.

Enumerating Object Properties

Although the most common use of the v-for directive is to enumerate the contents of an array, it can also be used to enumerate the properties of an object, which is more useful than it may first appear. In Listing 13-12, I have replaced the array of objects with a single object whose property names and values contain the information I require.

Listing 13-12. Using an Object for Enumeration in the App.vue File in the src Folder

```
<template>
    <div class="container-fluid">
        <h2 class="bg-primary text-white text-center p-3">Products</h2>
        <table class="table table-sm table-bordered  text-left">
            <tr><th>Index</th><th>Name</th><th>Price</th></tr>
            <tbody>
                <tr v-for="(p, key, i) in products" v-bind:key="p.name">
                    <td>{{ i + 1 }}</td>
                    <td>{{ p.name }}</td>
                    <td>{{ p. price | currency }}</td>
                </tr>
            </tbody>
        </table>
        <div class="text-center">
            <button v-on:click="handleClick" class="btn btn-primary">
                Press Me
            </button>
        </div>
    </div>
</template>

<script>
    import Vue from "vue";

    export default {
        name: "MyComponent",
        data: function () {
            return {
                products: {
                    1: { name: "Kayak", price: 275 },
                    2: { name: "Lifejacket", price: 48.95 },
                    3: { name: "Soccer Ball", price: 19.50 },
                    4: { name: "Corner Flags", price: 39.95 }
                }
            }
        },
```

```
        filters: {
            currency(value) {
                return new Intl.NumberFormat("en-US",
                    { style: "currency", currency: "USD", }).format(value);
            },
        },
        methods: {
            handleClick() {
                Vue.set(this.products, 5, { name: "Running Shoes", price: 100});
            }
        }
    }
</script>
```

In this listing, I changed the products property so that it returns an object. This object defines properties whose values are themselves objects with name and price properties. To enumerate the properties of the products object, I applied the v-for directive like this:

```
...
<tr v-for="(p, key, i) in products" v-bind:key="p.name">
...
```

When processing an object, the directive provides an alias, a new variable that contains the key, and the index variable. Vue.js can detect when a property is modified but can't tell when a new property is added to the object, which is why I have used the Vue.set method in the handleClick method, like this:

```
...
Vue.set(this.products, 5, { name: "Running Shoes", price: 100});
...
```

The result is that the v-for directive will enumerate the properties of the object and duplicate content for each of them, as shown in Figure 13-9.

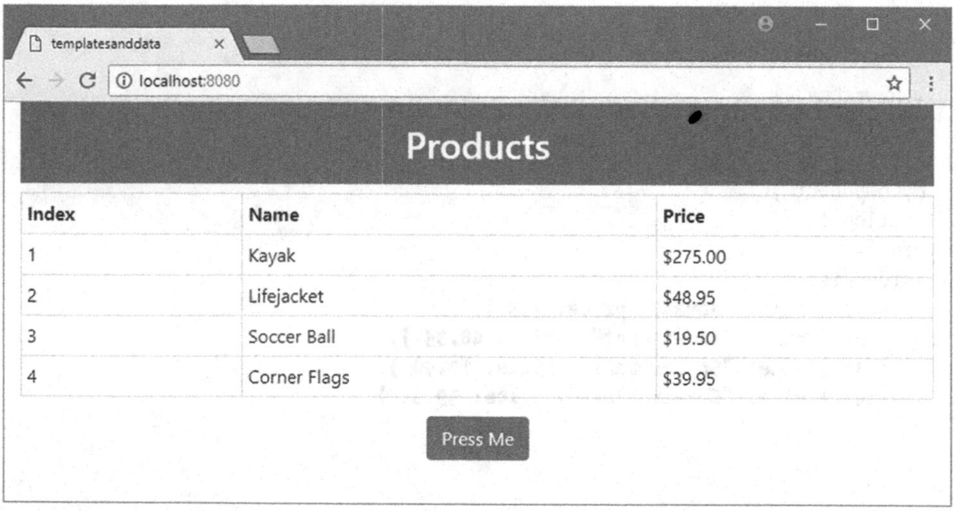

Figure 13-9. Enumerating the properties of an object

Understanding Object Property Ordering

Properties are enumerated in the order returned by the JavaScript Object.keys method, which usually sorts properties as follows:

1. Keys with an integer value, including values that can be parsed to an integer, in ascending order

2. Keys with a string value, in the order they were defined

3. All other keys, in the order they were defined

■ **Caution** This is the order that you will usually encounter, but there can be differences between JavaScript implementations. Use a computed property to sort the objects to ensure consistency, as demonstrated in the next section.

To demonstrate the way that properties are sorted, I changed the keys for the products object and added a column to the HTML table to display each key value, as shown in Listing 13-13.

Listing 13-13. Working with Object Keys in the App.vue File in the src Folder

```
<template>
    <div class="container-fluid">
        <h2 class="bg-primary text-white text-center p-3">Products</h2>
        <table class="table table-sm table-bordered  text-left">
            <tr><th>Index</th><th>Key</th><th>Name</th><th>Price</th></tr>
            <tbody>
                <tr v-for="(p, key, i) in products" v-bind:key="p.name">
                    <td>{{ i + 1 }}</td>
                    <td>{{ key }}</td>
                    <td>{{ p.name }}</td>
                    <td>{{ p. price | currency }}</td>
                </tr>
            </tbody>
        </table>
        <div class="text-center">
            <button v-on:click="handleClick" class="btn btn-primary">
                Press Me
            </button>
        </div>
    </div>
</template>

<script>
    import Vue from "vue";

    export default {
        name: "MyComponent",
        data: function () {
            return {
```

```
                products: {
                    "kayak": { name: "Kayak", price: 275 },
                    22: { name: "Lifejacket", price: 48.95 },
                    3: { name: "Soccer Ball", price: 19.50 },
                    "4": { name: "Corner Flags", price: 39.95 }
                }
            }
        },
        filters: {
            currency(value) {
                return new Intl.NumberFormat("en-US",
                    { style: "currency", currency: "USD", }).format(value);
            },
        },
        methods: {
            handleClick() {
                Vue.set(this.products, 5, { name: "Running Shoes", price: 100 });
            }
        }
    }
</script>
```

When the v-for directive enumerates the products object's properties, they will be processed in the following order: 3, 4, 22, kayak. When the button is clicked, and a new property is added to the object using 5 as a key, a new table row will be shown between the 4 and 22 keys, as shown in Figure 13-10.

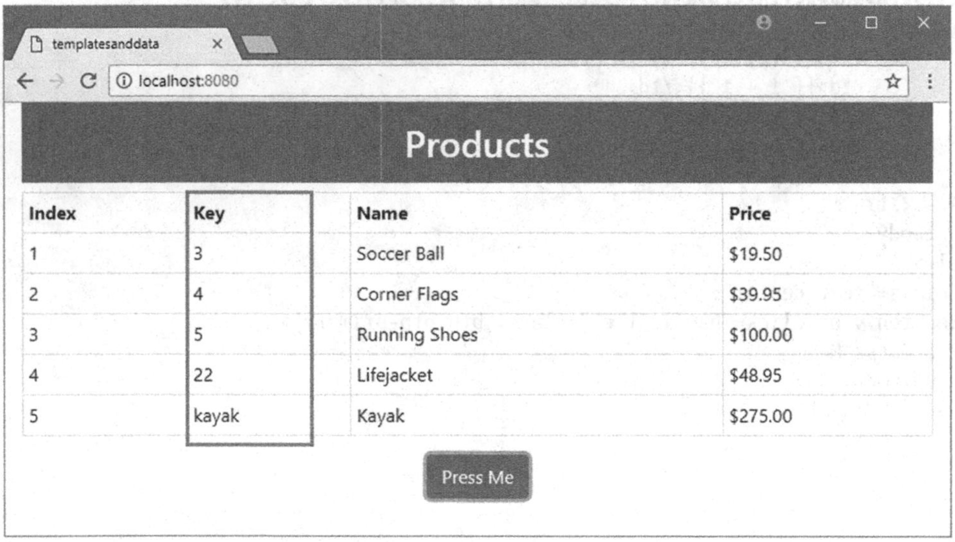

Figure 13-10. *The effect of object property ordering*

Repeating HTML Elements Without a Data Source

The v-for directive can be used to duplicate HTML elements a specific number of times without needing to use a data array or object as the data source. This feature is useful for creating content that isn't tied to a specific data item, such as pagination buttons, as demonstrated in Listing 13-14.

Listing 13-14. Repeating Content in the App.vue File in the src Folder

```
...
<template>
    <div class="container-fluid">
        <h2 class="bg-primary text-white text-center p-3">Products</h2>
        <table class="table table-sm table-bordered  text-left">
            <tr><th>Index</th><th>Key</th><th>Name</th><th>Price</th></tr>
            <tbody>
                <tr v-for="(p, key, i) in products" v-bind:key="p.name">
                    <td>{{ i + 1 }}</td>
                    <td>{{ key }}</td>
                    <td>{{ p.name }}</td>
                    <td>{{ p. price | currency }}</td>
                </tr>
            </tbody>
        </table>
        <div class="text-center">
            <!-- eslint-disable-next-line vue/require-v-for-key -->
            <button v-for="i in 5" v-on:click="handleClick(i)"
                    class="btn btn-primary m-1">
                {{ i }}
            </button>
        </div>
    </div>
</template>
...
```

When the source in the v-for expression is an integer value, the directive will repeat the HTML elements the specified number of times and assign the current value to the alias. In this listing, I have specified the number 5 when applying the v-for directive to the button element and used the alias as the element's content. The first value assigned to the alias is 1, which produces the result shown in Figure 13-11.

■ **Tip** Notice that I disabled the linter rule that requires a key to be identified. Since the sequence of values is generated by the directive, there is no need to worry about the strategy for dealing with changes in the order of array items.

329

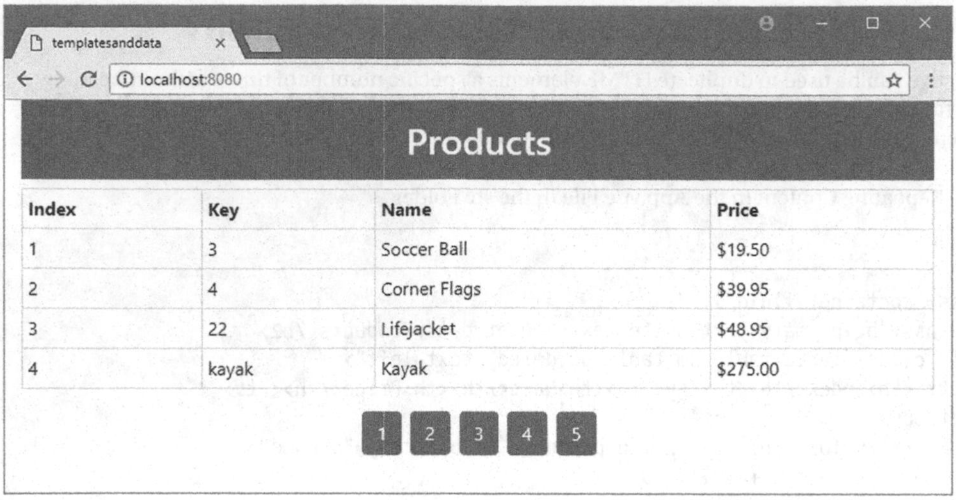

Figure 13-11. *Repeating elements without a data source*

Using Computed Properties with the v-for Directive

All the examples so far have used data properties, but the v-for directive will also work with computed properties and methods, which makes it possible to use JavaScript to filter or sort the objects for which content is duplicated. In the following sections, I demonstrate different ways in which you can manage the data that is processed by the v-for directive.

Paging Data

Most applications need to present a subset of the available data to the user, which is typically done by presenting pages of data. Combining a computed property with the feature for repeating content without a data source makes it easy to implement pagination, as shown in Listing 13-15.

■ **Tip** You can see a more complex pagination example in the SportsStore application in Part 1 of this book.

Listing 13-15. Paging Data in the App.vue File in the src Folder

```
<template>
    <div class="container-fluid">
        <h2 class="bg-primary text-white text-center p-3">Products</h2>
        <table class="table table-sm table-bordered  text-left">
            <tr><th>Name</th><th>Price</th></tr>
            <tbody>
                <tr v-for="p in pageItems" v-bind:key="p.name">
                    <td>{{ p.name }}</td>
                    <td>{{ p. price | currency }}</td>
                </tr>
            </tbody>
        </table>
```

```
        <div class="text-center">
            <!-- eslint-disable-next-line vue/require-v-for-key -->
            <button v-for="i in pageCount" v-on:click="selectPage(i)"
                    class="btn btn-secondary m-1"
                    v-bind:class="{'bg-primary': currentPage == i}">
                {{ i }}
            </button>
        </div>
    </div>
</template>
<script>
    export default {
        name: "MyComponent",
        data: function () {
            return {
                pageSize: 3,
                currentPage: 1,
                products: [
                    { name: "Kayak", price: 275 },
                    { name: "Lifejacket", price: 48.95 },
                    { name: "Soccer Ball", price: 19.50 },
                    { name: "Corner Flags", price: 39.95 },
                    { name: "Stadium", price: 79500 },
                    { name: "Thinking Cap", price: 16 },
                    { name: "Unsteady Chair", price: 29.95 },
                    { name: "Human Chess Board", price: 75 },
                    { name: "Bling Bling King", price: 1200 }
                ]
            }
        },
        computed: {
            pageCount() {
                return Math.ceil(this.products.length / this.pageSize);
            },
            pageItems() {
                let start = (this.currentPage - 1) * this.pageSize;
                return this.products.slice(start, start + this.pageSize);
            }
        },
        filters: {
            currency(value) {
                return new Intl.NumberFormat("en-US",
                    { style: "currency", currency: "USD", }).format(value);
            },
        },
        methods: {
            selectPage(page) {
                this.currentPage = page;
            }
        }
    }
</script>
```

I have changed back to using an array for this example and added some objects so there is more data to work with. There are two new data properties: the pageSize property specifies the number of items per page, and the currentPage property is used to keep track of the page that is being displayed to the user. There are also two new computed properties: the pageCount property returns the number of pages that the application requires, and the pageItems property returns just the data objects required for the current page.

To generate the pagination buttons, I use the pageItems property in the v-for expression, which allows me to repeat the button element for each page that the user can select. I want to highlight the button that represents the current page, which I do by using the v-bind directive to assign the element to a class based on the v-for alias value. Finally, I use the v-on directive—which I describe in Chapter 14—to invoke a method called selectPage when the user clicks a button, which allows me to change the currentPage value, allowing the user to navigate between pages, as shown in Figure 13-12.

Figure 13-12. *Paging data*

Filtering and Sorting Data

Computed properties can also be used to filter and sort data before it is received by the v-for directive. In Listing 13-16, I have added select elements whose values are used to alter the data that is displayed to the user.

Listing 13-16. Filtering and Sorting Data in the App.vue File in the src Folder

```
<template>
    <div class="container-fluid">
        <h2 class="bg-primary text-white text-center p-3">Products</h2>
        <table class="table table-sm table-bordered  text-left">
            <tr><th>Name</th><th>Price</th></tr>
            <tbody>
                <tr v-for="p in pageItems" v-bind:key="p.name">
                    <td>{{ p.name }}</td>
                    <td>{{ p. price | currency }}</td>
                </tr>
            </tbody>
        </table>
```

```
        <div class="text-center">
            <button class="btn btn-secondary m-1" v-on:click="toggleSort"
                    v-bind:class="{'bg-primary': sort}">
                Toggle Sort
            </button>
            <button class="btn btn-secondary m-1" v-on:click="toggleFilter"
                    v-bind:class="{'bg-primary': filter}">
                Toggle Filter
            </button>
            <!-- eslint-disable-next-line vue/require-v-for-key -->
            <button v-for="i in pageCount" v-on:click="selectPage(i)"
                    class="btn btn-secondary m-1"
                    v-bind:class="{'bg-primary': currentPage == i}">
                {{ i }}
            </button>
        </div>
    </div>
</template>
<script>
    export default {
        name: "MyComponent",
        data: function () {
            return {
                pageSize: 3,
                currentPage: 1,
                filter: false,
                sort: false,
                products: [
                    { name: "Kayak", price: 275 },
                    { name: "Lifejacket", price: 48.95 },
                    { name: "Soccer Ball", price: 19.50 },
                    { name: "Corner Flags", price: 39.95 },
                    { name: "Stadium", price: 79500 },
                    { name: "Thinking Cap", price: 16 },
                    { name: "Unsteady Chair", price: 29.95 },
                    { name: "Human Chess Board", price: 75 },
                    { name: "Bling Bling King", price: 1200 }
                ]
            }
        },
        computed: {
            pageCount() {
                return Math.ceil(this.dataItems.length / this.pageSize);
            },
            pageItems() {
                let start = (this.currentPage - 1) * this.pageSize;
                return this.dataItems.slice(start, start + this.pageSize);
            },
```

```
            dataItems() {
                let data = this.filter
                    ? this.products.filter(p => p.price > 100) : this.products;
                return this.sort
                    ? data.concat().sort((p1, p2) => p2.price - p1.price) : data;
            }
        },
        filters: {
            currency(value) {
                return new Intl.NumberFormat("en-US",
                    { style: "currency", currency: "USD", }).format(value);
            },
        },
        methods: {
            selectPage(page) {
                this.currentPage = page;
            },
            toggleFilter() {
                this.filter = !this.filter
                this.currentPage = 1;
            },
            toggleSort() {
                this.sort = !this.sort;
                this.currentPage = 1;
            }
        }
    }
}
</script>
```

This example uses a new computed property named dataItems to prepare the data for display based on the data properties named sort and filter. The data property values are toggled by clicking the new button elements, and the number of pagination buttons is updated based on the user's choices, as shown in Figure 13-13.

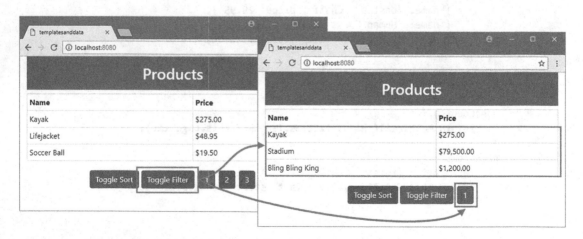

Figure 13-13. Paging and sorting data

Summary

In this chapter, I explained the use of the `v-for` directive and demonstrated how it can enumerate arrays, the properties of an object, and a numeric sequence. I showed you how to use the alias, how to make updates more efficient using a key, and how to get the index of the item being processed. I also demonstrated how the `v-for` directive can be used with computed properties so that data can be paged, sorted, and filtered. In the next chapter, I show you how to handle events using a Vue.js directive.

CHAPTER 14

■ ■ ■

Handling Events

In this chapter, I continue describing the built-in Vue.js directives, focusing on the v-on directive, which is used for event handling and which Table 14-1 puts in context.

Table 14-1. Putting the v-on Directive in Context

Question	Answer
What is it?	The v-on directive is used to listen and respond to events.
Why is it useful?	This directive makes it easy to access component data or invoke methods when responding to an event and makes event handling an integrated part of Vue.js development.
How is it used?	The v-on directive is applied to the HTML element whose events you in which you are interested, and its expression is evaluated when the events you specify are triggered.
Are there any pitfalls or limitations?	The v-on directive works consistently and is generally easy to use, just as long as you bear the DOM event propagation model in mind when applying the directive, as described in the "Managing Event Propagation" section.
Are there any alternatives?	If you are interested in events triggered by form elements, then the v-model directive, described in Chapter 15, may be more suitable.

Table 14-2 summarizes the chapter.

Table 14-2. Chapter Summary

Problem	Solution	Listing
Handle an event emitted by an element	Use the v-on directive	3, 7
Get details about an event	Use the event object	4
Respond to an event outside of a directive expression	Handle the event using a method and receive the event object as a parameter	5, 6
Handle multiple events from the same element	Apply the v-on directive for each event you want to receive or detect the event type using the event object	8, 9
Manage event propagation	Use the event propagation modifiers	10–14
Filter events based on key or mouse activity	Use the mouse and keyboard modifiers	15–17

© Adam Freeman 2018
A. Freeman, *Pro Vue.js 2*, https://doi.org/10.1007/978-1-4842-3805-9_14

Preparing for This Chapter

In this chapter, I continue working with the templatesanddata project from Chapter 14. To prepare for this chapter, I simplified the application's root component, as shown in Listing 14-1.

■ **Tip** You can download the example project for this chapter—and for all the other chapters in this book—from https://github.com/Apress/pro-vue-js-2.

Listing 14-1. Simplifying the Content of the App.vue File in the src Folder

```
<template>
    <div class="container-fluid">
        <div class="bg-primary text-white m-2 p-3 text-center">
            <h3>{{ name }}</h3>
        </div>
    </div>
</template>

<script>
    export default {
        name: "MyComponent",
        data: function () {
            return {
                name: "Lifejacket"
            }
        }
    }
</script>
```

Save the changes to the App.vue file and run the command shown in Listing 14-2 in the templatesanddata folder to start the Vue.js development tools.

Listing 14-2. Starting the Development Tools

```
npm run serve
```

Open a new browser window and navigate to http://localhost:8080 to see the content shown in Figure 14-1.

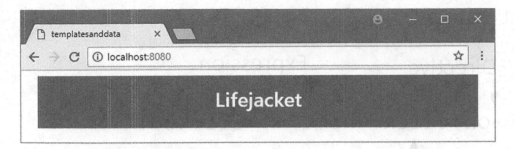

Figure 14-1. *Running the example application*

Handling Events

Vue.js provides the v-on directive, which is used to create bindings for events. Events are triggered as the result of user interaction with the HTML elements. There is a core set of events that all elements support, and these are supplemented by events that are specific to the features that are unique to specific elements. In Listing 14-3, I have used the v-on directive to tell Vue.js how I want it to respond when the user clicks the h3 element in the component's template.

Listing 14-3. Handling an Event in the App.vue File in the src Folder

```
<template>
    <div class="container-fluid">
        <div class="bg-primary text-white m-2 p-3 text-center">
            <h3 v-on:click="name = 'Clicked!'">{{ name }}</h3>
        </div>
    </div>
</template>

<script>
    export default {
        name: "MyComponent",
        data: function () {
            return {
                name: "Lifejacket"
            }
        }
    }
</script>
```

The application of the v-on directive follows the pattern established in earlier chapters and that I have broken down in Figure 14-2.

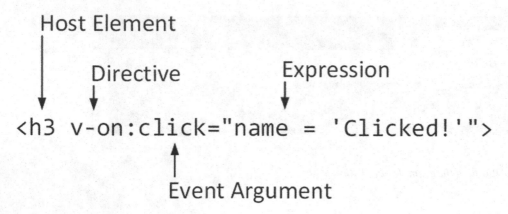

Figure 14-2. *The anatomy of the v-on directive*

The name of the directive is followed by a colon and then an argument that specifies the name of the event. The expression will be invoked when the event is triggered, and the expression for this example is a fragment of JavaScript code that changes the value of the name property. To see the result, save the changes and click the h3 element's content in the browser window, producing the effect shown in Figure 14-3.

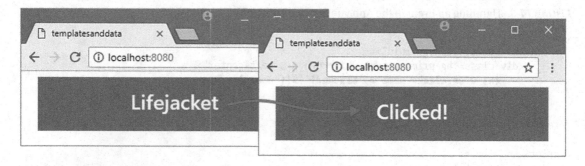

Figure 14-3. *Handling an event*

Clicking the element triggers the click event, which Vue.js responds to by evaluating the directive's expression. There is a visible change only for the first click, and you must reload the browser to reset the application to its original state.

Understanding Events and Event Objects

There are a lot of different types of events available, and the ones that I use in this chapter are described in Table 14-3.

■ **Note** See https://developer.mozilla.org/en-US/docs/Web/Events for detailed information about all of the available events.

Table 14-3. *The Events Used in This Chapter*

Event	Description
click	This event is triggered when the mouse button is pressed and released inside the bounds of an element.
mousedown	This event is triggered when the mouse button is pressed within the bounds of an element.
mousemove	The event is triggered when the mouse pointer moves within the bounds of the element.
mouseleave	This event is triggered when the mouse pointer leaves the bounds of the element.
keydown	This event is triggered when a key is pressed.

When browsers trigger events, they produce an object that describes the event, known as the *event object*. The event object defines properties and methods that provide information about the event and can be used to control how the event is processed. In Table 14-4, I have described the most useful event object properties for Vue.js development. (If you are familiar with web development, you might be wondering about the methods and other properties defined by event objects. As you will learn, you don't need to use these directly with the v-on directive, which takes care of a lot of event handling detail.)

Table 14-4. *Useful Event Object Properties*

Property	Description
target	This property returns the DOM object that represents the HTML element that triggered the event
currentTarget	This property returns the DOM object that represents the HTML element that is handling the event. The difference from the target property is explained in the "Managing Event Propagation" section.
type	This property returns the event type.
key	For keyboard events, this property returns the key that the event relates to.

The v-on directive makes the event object available through a variable named $event. In Listing 14-4, I have updated the directive's expression so that the value of the type property is displayed when the event is triggered.

Listing 14-4. *Using an Event Object in the App.vue File in the src Folder*

```
<template>
    <div class="container-fluid">
        <div class="bg-primary text-white m-2 p-3 text-center">
            <h3 v-on:click="name = $event.type">{{ name }}</h3>
        </div>
    </div>
</template>
```

```
<script>
    export default {
        name: "MyComponent",
        data: function () {
            return {
                name: "Lifejacket"
            }
        }
    }
</script>
```

The v-on directive handles the click event cause by clicking the h3 element and assigns the event object created by the browser to the $event variable before evaluating the expression, producing the result shown in Figure 14-4.

Figure 14-4. *Using an event object*

Using a Method to Handle Events

The v-on directive will evaluate fragments of JavaScript when an event is triggered, as the previous examples demonstrated, but a more common approach is to invoke a method. Using methods minimizes the amount of code in the template and allows events to be handled consistently. In Listing 14-5, I have added a method to the component and updated the v-on directive's binding so that the method will be invoked when the h3 element's click event is triggered.

Listing 14-5. Using a Method in the App.vue File in the src Folder

```
<template>
    <div class="container-fluid">
        <div class="bg-primary text-white m-2 p-3 text-center">
            <h3 v-on:click="handleEvent">{{ name }}</h3>
        </div>
    </div>
</template>

<script>
    export default {
        name: "MyComponent",
        data: function () {
```

```
            return {
                name: "Lifejacket"
            }
        },
        methods: {
            handleEvent($event) {
                this.name = $event.type;
            }
        }
    }
</script>
```

I have set the directive's expression to handleEvent, which tells v-on to invoke the method and pass it the $event object when the click event is triggered, which produces the result shown in Figure 14-5. (You don't have to use $event as the name of the method parameter, but I tend to because it makes the purpose of the parameter obvious.)

■ **Tip** Vue.js is generally relaxed about the names of methods that are invoked when an event is triggered, but you will receive an error if you use a method name that is also a built-in JavaScript keyword, such as delete.

Specifying just a method name is useful, but the real advantage in using methods comes when you have multiple sources of the same event type that produce different results. In these situations, the v-for directive can invoke a method with arguments that are used to determine the way that the event is handled, as shown in Listing 14-6.

Listing 14-6. Using Method Arguments in the App.vue File in the src Folder

```
<template>
    <div class="container-fluid">
        <div class="bg-primary text-white m-2 p-3 text-center">
            <h3 v-on:click="handleEvent('Soccer Ball', $event)">{{ name }}</h3>
        </div>
        <div class="bg-primary text-white m-2 p-3 text-center">
            <h3 v-on:click="handleEvent('Stadium', $event)">{{ name }}</h3>
        </div>
    </div>
</template>

<script>
    export default {
        name: "MyComponent",
        data: function () {
            return {
                name: "Lifejacket"
            }
        },
```

```
        methods: {
            handleEvent(name, $event) {
                this.name = `${name} - ${$event.type}`;
            }
        }
    }
}
</script>
```

I have added another h3 element with the v-on binding. Both binding expressions call the handleEvent method, but they provide different values for the first argument. The result is that a different message is displayed to the user based on which element is clicked, as shown in Figure 14-5.

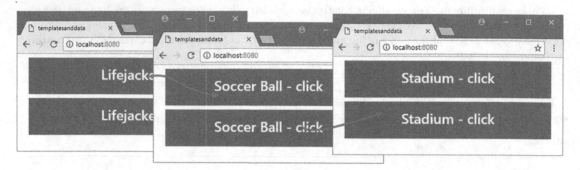

Figure 14-5. *Calling a method with an argument*

USING THE DIRECTIVE SHORTHAND

The v-on directive has two forms. The longhand form, as shown in Figure 14-2, combines the directive name, followed by a colon, followed by the name of the event. The short form combines the @ sign with the event name, such that v-on:click can also be expressed as @click. This means that a directive such as this one:

```
...
<h3 v-on:click="handleEvent('Soccer Ball', $event)">{{ name }}</h3>
...
```

can also be expressed like this:

```
...
<h3 @click="handleEvent('Soccer Ball', $event)">{{ name }}</h3>
...
```

The choice between long and shorthand form is one of personal preference and doesn't change the way that the directive behaves.

Combining Events, Methods, and Repeated Elements

The ability to provide arguments when invoking the v-on directive becomes much more useful when combined with the v-for directive. In Listing 14-7, I have used the v-for directive to repeat a set of elements for objects in an array and used the v-on directive to set up event handlers for each one.

Listing 14-7. Repeating Elements in the App.vue File in the src Folder

```
<template>
    <div class="container-fluid">
        <h3 class="bg-primary text-white text-center mt-2 p-2">{{message}}</h3>
        <table class="table table-sm table-striped table-bordered">
            <tr><th>Index</th><th>Name</th><th>Actions</th></tr>
            <tr v-for="(name, index) in names" v-bind:key="name">
                <td>{{index}}</td>
                <td>{{name}}</td>
                <td>
                    <button class="btn btn-sm bg-primary text-white"
                            v-on:click="handleClick(name)">
                        Select
                    </button>
                </td>
            </tr>
        </table>
    </div>
</template>

<script>
    export default {
        name: "MyComponent",
        data: function () {
            return {
                message: "Ready",
                names: ["Kayak", "Lifejacket", "Soccer Ball", "Stadium"]
            }
        },
        methods: {
            handleClick(name) {
                this.message = `Select: ${name}`;
            }
        }
    }
</script>
```

The v-for directive duplicates rows in the table for each object in the names array. The duplication includes all of the data bindings and directives, which means that there is a button element with a v-on binding for the click event in each table row, like this:

```
...
<button class="btn btn-sm bg-primary text-white" v-on:click="handleClick(name)">
    Select
</button>
...
```

The v-on binding expression is set up using the value of the v-for alias, which means that each button element will invoke the handleClick method using the object that was being processed when it was created. The handleClick method uses its parameter value to set the value of the message property, which is displayed to the user in the h3 element. The effect is that clicking a button in the table displays the corresponding value from the names array, as illustrated in Figure 14-6.

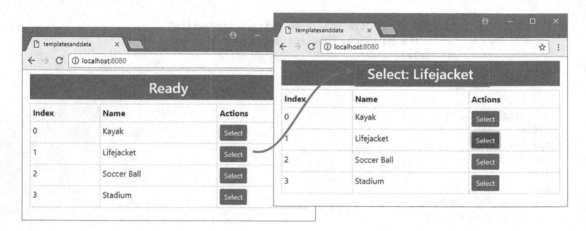

Figure 14-6. *Event handling in repeated content*

Listening for Multiple Events from the Same Element

There are two ways to handle different types of event on the same element. The first approach is to apply the v-on directive separately for each event, as shown in Listing 14-8.

Listing 14-8. Handling Multiple Event Types in the App.vue File in the src Folder

```
<template>
    <div class="container-fluid">
        <h3 class="bg-primary text-white text-center mt-2 p-2">{{message}}</h3>
        <table class="table table-sm table-striped table-bordered">
            <tr><th>Index</th><th>Name</th><th>Actions</th></tr>
            <tr v-for="(name, index) in names" v-bind:key="name">
                <td>{{index}}</td>
                <td>{{name}}</td>
                <td>
```

```
                    <button class="btn btn-sm bg-primary text-white"
                            v-on:click="handleClick(name)"
                            v-on:mousemove="handleMouseEvent(name, $event)"
                            v-on:mouseleave="handleMouseEvent(name, $event)">
                        Select
                    </button>
                </td>
            </tr>
        </table>
    </div>
</template>

<script>
    export default {
        name: "MyComponent",
        data: function () {
            return {
                counter: 0,
                message: "Ready",
                names: ["Kayak", "Lifejacket", "Soccer Ball", "Stadium"]
            }
        },
        methods: {
            handleClick(name) {
                this.message = `Select: ${name}`;
            },
            handleMouseEvent(name, $event) {
                if ($event.type == "mousemove") {
                    this.message = `Move in ${name} ${this.counter++}`;
                } else {
                    this.counter = 0;
                    this.message = "Ready";
                }
            }
        }
    }
</script>
```

I added v-on directives to handle the mousemove and mouseleave events. The mousemove event is triggered when the mouse pointer is moved over an element, and the mouseleave event is triggered when the pointer moves away from the element. Both events are processed by the handleMouseEvent method, which uses the $event variable to determine the event type and updates the message and counter properties. The result is that a message and counter are displayed when the pointer is moved over the button elements, which are then reset when the pointer leaves the screen area that the button occupies, as shown in Figure 14-7.

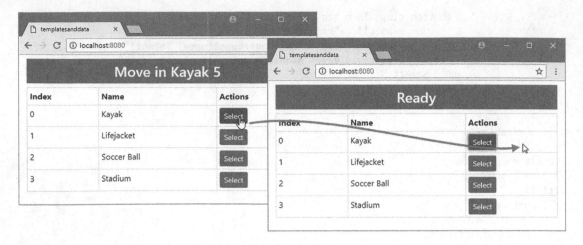

Figure 14-7. *Responding to several types of events*

The second way to listen for multiple events is to apply the v-on directive without an event argument and set the directive's expression to an object whose property names are the event types and whose values specify the methods that should be invoked, as shown in Listing 14-9.

Listing 14-9. Handling Multiple Events in a Single Directive in the App.vue File in the src Folder

```
<template>
    <div class="container-fluid">
        <h3 class="bg-primary text-white text-center mt-2 p-2">{{message}}</h3>
        <table class="table table-sm table-striped table-bordered">
            <tr><th>Index</th><th>Name</th><th>Actions</th></tr>
            <tr v-for="(name, index) in names" v-bind:key="name">
                <td>{{index}}</td>
                <td>{{name}}</td>
                <td>
                    <button class="btn btn-sm bg-primary text-white"
                            v-on="buttonEvents"
                            v-bind:data-name="name">
                        Select
                    </button>
                </td>
            </tr>
        </table>
    </div>
</template>

<script>
    export default {
        name: "MyComponent",
        data: function () {
            return {
```

```
                buttonEvents: {
                    click: this.handleClick,
                    mousemove: this.handleMouseEvent,
                    mouseleave: this.handleMouseEvent
                },
                counter: 0,
                message: "Ready",
                names: ["Kayak", "Lifejacket", "Soccer Ball", "Stadium"]
            }
        },
        methods: {
            handleClick($event) {
                let name = $event.target.dataset.name;
                this.message = `Select: ${name}`;
            },
            handleMouseEvent($event) {
                let name = $event.target.dataset.name;
                if ($event.type == "mousemove") {
                    this.message = `Move in ${name} ${this.counter++}`;
                } else {
                    this.counter = 0;
                    this.message = "Ready";
                }
            }
        }
    }
}
</script>
```

The data property named buttonEvents returns an object that has click, mousemove, and mouseleave properties, corresponding to the event that I want to process, and the value of these properties is the method that should be invoked for each event. The limitation of this approach is that it doesn't support passing arguments to the methods, which receive only the $event argument. To work around this, I used the v-bind directive to add a data-name attribute to each button element, like this:

```
...
<button class="btn btn-sm bg-primary text-white" v-on="buttonEvents"
    v-bind:data-name="name">
...
```

The $event object provides access to the HTML element that triggered the event, and I use the dataset property to access the custom data- attributes to get the data-name value when processing an event like this:

```
...
let name = $event.target.dataset.name;
...
```

The result is the same as Listing 14-8 but without needing to define multiple v-on directives on the button elements, which can produce a template that is hard to read.

■ **Tip**   You can define the event mapping object as a string literal directly in the v-on directive's expression if you prefer, although can still produce a template that is difficult to make sense of.

Using Event Handling Modifiers

To keep event processing methods simple and focused, the v-on directive supports a set of modifiers that are used to perform common tasks that usually require JavaScript statements. Table 14-5 describes the set of v-on event handling modifiers.

Table 14-5.   *The v-on Event Handling Modifiers*

Modifier	Description
stop	This modifier is equivalent to calling the stopPropagation method on the event object, as described in the "Stopping Event Propagation" section.
prevent	This modifier is equivalent to calling the preventDefault method on the event object. This modifier is demonstrated in Chapter 15.
capture	This modifier enables capture mode for event propagation, as described in the "Receiving Events in the Capture Phase" section.
self	This modifier will invoke the handler method only if the event originated from the element to which the directive has been applied, as demonstrated in the "Handling Only Target Phase Events" section.
once	This modifier will prevent subsequent events of the same type from invoking the handler method, as demonstrated in the "Preventing Duplicate Events" section.
passive	This modifier will enable passive event listening, which improves the performance of touch events and is especially useful on mobile devices. See https://developer.mozilla.org/en-US/docs/Web/API/EventTarget/addEventListener for a good description of when this option is used.

Managing Event Propagation

The stop, capture, and self modifiers are used to manage the propagation of an event through the hierarchy of HTML elements. When an event is triggered, the browser goes through three phases to locate handlers for the event: the capture, target, and bubble phases. To demonstrate how these phases work—and how they can be controlled using v-on modifiers—I have updated the component in the example application, as shown in Listing 14-10.

Listing 14-10.   Handling Events in the App.vue File in the src Folder

```
<template>
    <div class="container-fluid">
        <div id="outer-element" class="bg-primary p-4 text-white h3"
            v-on:click="handleClick">
            Outer Element
```

```
        <div id="middle-element" class="bg-secondary p-4"
            v-on:click="handleClick">
            Middle Element
            <div id="inner-element" class="bg-info p-4"
                v-on:click="handleClick">
                Inner Element
            </div>
        </div>
      </div>
    </div>
  </template>

<script>
    export default {
        name: "MyComponent",
        methods: {
            handleClick($event) {
                console.log(`handleClick target: ${$event.target.id}`
                    + ` currentTarget: ${$event.currentTarget.id}`);
            }
        }
    }
</script>
```

The template contains three nested div elements, with an id attribute and the v-on directive configured to process the click event using the handleClick method. The method receives the $event object and uses the target property to get details of the element that triggered the event and use the currentTarget property to get details of the element whose v-on directive is processing the event.

To understand why there are two properties involved in handling an event, save the changes to the component and then click the part of the browser window occupied by the inner element, as shown in Figure 14-8.

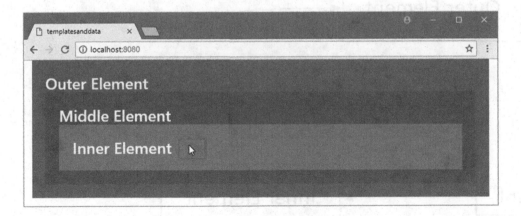

Figure 14-8. *Triggering an event in a set of nested elements*

By default, a v-on directive will receive events in the target and bubble phases, which means that an event will be received first by the v-on element on the element that triggered the event—the target—and then by each of its antecedents in turn, all the way from the immediate parent element to the body element. You can see this in the messages that have been written to the JavaScript console.

```
...
handleClick target: inner-element currentTarget: inner-element
handleClick target: inner-element currentTarget: middle-element
handleClick target: inner-element currentTarget: outer-element
...
```

The first message shows the target phase of the event, where the v-on directive on the element that triggered the event invokes the handleClick method. In the target phase, the target and currentTarget properties of the $event object are the same.

The second and third messages show the bubble phase, where the event propagates up the HTML document to each parent element, causing each element's v-on directive for that event type to invoke its method. In this phase, the target property of the $event object returns the element that triggered the event, and the currentTarget property returns the element whose v-on directive is currently processing the event. Figure 14-9 shows the flow of events in the target and bubble phases.

■ **Tip** Not all types of event have a bubble phase. As a rule of thumb, events that are specific to a single element—such as gaining and losing focus—do not bubble. Events that apply to multiple elements—such as clicking a region of the screen that is occupied by multiple elements—will bubble. You can check to see whether a specific event is going to go through the bubble phase by reading the bubbles property of the $event object.

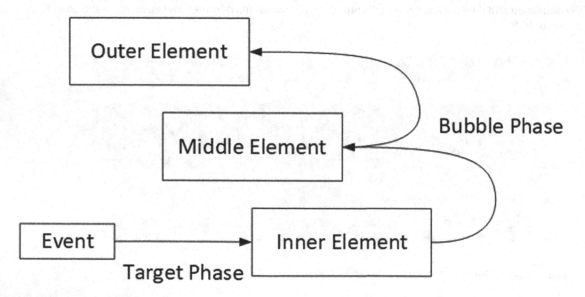

Figure 14-9. The target and bubble phases

Receiving Events in the Capture Phase

The capture phase provides an opportunity for elements to process events before the target phase. During the capture phase, the browser starts with the body element and works its way down the hierarchy of elements toward the target, following the opposite path to the bubble phase, and gives each element the change to process the event, as shown in Figure 14-10.

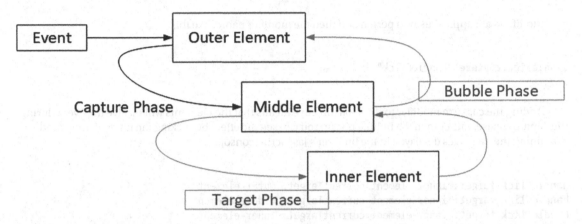

Figure 14-10. *The capture phase*

The v-on directive doesn't receive events during the capture phase unless the `capture` modifier is applied, as shown in Listing 14-11.

Listing 14-11. Using the Capture Phase in the App.vue File in the src Folder

```
<template>
    <div class="container-fluid">
        <div id="outer-element" class="bg-primary p-4 text-white h3"
            v-on:click.capture="handleClick">
            Outer Element
            <div id="middle-element" class="bg-secondary p-4"
                v-on:click.capture="handleClick">
            Middle Element
            <div id="inner-element" class="bg-info p-4"
                v-on:click="handleClick">
                Inner Element
            </div>
        </div>
        </div>
    </div>
</template>

<script>
    export default {
        name: "MyComponent",
        methods: {
```

```
        handleClick($event) {
            console.log(`handleClick target: ${$event.target.id}`
                + ` currentTarget: ${$event.currentTarget.id}`);
        }
    }
}
</script>
```

Modifiers are applied using a period and then the modifier name, like this:

```
...
v-on:click.capture="handleClick"
...
```

Adding the capture modifier to the v-on directive means that the elements will receive the event during the capture phase, rather than the bubble phase. You can see the effect by clicking the inner element and examining the messages displayed in the browser's JavaScript console.

```
...
handleClick target: inner-element currentTarget: outer-element
handleClick target: inner-element currentTarget: middle-element
handleClick target: inner-element currentTarget: inner-element
...
```

The messages show that the event has worked its way down the HTML document, triggering the v-on directive on the outer element and then the middle element.

Handling Only Target Phase Events

You can restrict the v-on directive so that it will only respond to events in the target phase. The self modifier ensures that only events triggered by the element to which the directive has been applied will be processed, as shown in Listing 14-12.

Listing 14-12. Selecting Target Phase Events in the App.vue File in the src Folder

```
<template>
    <div class="container-fluid">
        <div id="outer-element" class="bg-primary p-4 text-white h3"
            v-on:click.capture="handleClick">
            Outer Element
            <div id="middle-element" class="bg-secondary p-4"
                v-on:click.self="handleClick">
                Middle Element
                <div id="inner-element" class="bg-info p-4"
                    v-on:click="handleClick">
                    Inner Element
                </div>
            </div>
        </div>
    </div>
</template>
```

```
<script>
    export default {
        name: "MyComponent",
        methods: {
            handleClick($event) {
                console.log(`handleClick target: ${$event.target.id}`
                    + ` currentTarget: ${$event.currentTarget.id}`);
            }
        }
    }
</script>
```

I have applied the self modifier to the v-on directive on the middle element. If you click the inner element, you will see the following messages displayed in the browser's JavaScript console:

```
...
handleClick target: inner-element currentTarget: outer-element
handleClick target: inner-element currentTarget: inner-element
...
```

The first message is received from the outer element, whose v-on directive uses the capture modifier and so receives the event during the capture phase. The second message is from the inner element, which is the target and received the event during the target phase. There is no message from the middle element because the self modifier has prevented it from receiving the event during the bubble phase. You will see these messages if you click the middle element:

```
...
handleClick target: middle-element currentTarget: outer-element
handleClick target: middle-element currentTarget: middle-element
...
```

The first of these messages is from the outer element again, which gets the event first during the capture phase. The second message is from the middle element during the target phase, which is allowed by the self modifier.

Stopping Event Propagation

The stop modifier halts the propagation of an event, preventing it from being processed by any subsequent element's v-on directive. In Listing 14-13, I have applied the stop directive to the middle element's v-on directive.

Listing 14-13. Stopping Event Propagation in the App.vue File in the src Folder

```
<template>
    <div class="container-fluid">
        <div id="outer-element" class="bg-primary p-4 text-white h3"
            v-on:click.capture="handleClick">
            Outer Element
            <div id="middle-element" class="bg-secondary p-4"
                v-on:click.stop="handleClick">
                Middle Element
```

```
            <div id="inner-element" class="bg-info p-4"
                v-on:click="handleClick">
                Inner Element
            </div>
        </div>
    </div>
    </div>
</template>
<script>
    export default {
        name: "MyComponent",
        methods: {
            handleClick($event) {
                console.log(`handleClick target: ${$event.target.id}`
                    + ` currentTarget: ${$event.currentTarget.id}`);
            }
        }
    }
</script>
```

The stop modifier prevents an event from continuing its usual progress but doesn't stop propagation until it reaches the element to which it has been applied. In the example, this means that an element triggered by the middle element will still go through the capture phase before being stopped during the target phase. Since the outer element's v-on directive is configured with the capture modifier, the following messages are displayed in the browser's JavaScript console:

```
...
handleClick target: middle-element currentTarget: outer-element
handleClick target: middle-element currentTarget: middle-element
...
```

COMBINING EVENT HANDLING MODIFIERS

You can apply multiple modifiers to a single v-on directive. The modifiers are processed in the order in which they are specified, which means that different effects are achieved by using the same modifiers in different combinations. This combination will process events during the target phase and then stop them from being propagated any further.

```
...
v-on:click.self.stop="handleClick"
...
```

But if these modifiers are reversed, then events will be stopped in the target and bubble phases (because the stop modifier is first).

```
...
v-on:click.stop.self="handleClick"
...
```

As a consequence, it is important to think through the consequences of combining modifiers, to test combinations thoroughly, and to apply them consistently.

Preventing Duplicate Events

The once modifier stops a v-on directive from invoking its method more than once. This doesn't stop the normal event propagation process, but it does prevent an element from participating in it after the first event has been processed. In Listing 14-14, I have applied the once modifier to the inner element in the component's template.

Listing 14-14. Stopping Duplicate Events in the App.vue File in the src Folder

```
<template>
    <div class="container-fluid">
        <div id="outer-element" class="bg-primary p-4 text-white h3"
            v-on:click.capture="handleClick">
            Outer Element
            <div id="middle-element" class="bg-secondary p-4"
                v-on:click.stop="handleClick">
                Middle Element
                <div id="inner-element" class="bg-info p-4"
                    v-on:click.once="handleClick">
                    Inner Element
                </div>
            </div>
        </div>
    </div>
</template>

<script>
    export default {
        name: "MyComponent",
        methods: {
            handleClick($event) {
                console.log(`handleClick target: ${$event.target.id}`
                    + ` currentTarget: ${$event.currentTarget.id}`);
            }
        }
    }
</script>
```

The first time you click inside the inner element, you will see all the v-on directives respond, like this:

```
...
handleClick target: inner-element currentTarget: outer-element
handleClick target: inner-element currentTarget: inner-element
handleClick target: inner-element currentTarget: middle-element
...
```

The outer element is configured with the capture modifier, so it gets the event during the capture phase. This is the first time that the click event has been handled by the inner element, so the target phase of the event is just like normal. Finally, the middle element receives the event during the bubble phase, where the stop modifier prevents it from going any further.

When you click the inner element again, you will see a different set of messages:

```
...
handleClick target: inner-element currentTarget: outer-element
handleClick target: inner-element currentTarget: middle-element
...
```

The once modifier prevents the inner element's v-on directive from invoking the `handleClick` method but doesn't prevent the event from propagating to the other elements.

Using Mouse Event Modifiers

The v-on directive provides a set of modifiers that simplify processing mouse events when you need to be specific about the conditions that trigger the event. Table 14-6 describes the set of v-on mouse event modifiers.

Table 14-6. The v-on Mouse Event Modifiers

Modifier	Description
left	This modifier selects only events that are triggered by the left mouse button.
middle	This modifier selects only events that are triggered by the middle mouse button.
right	This modifier selects only events that are triggered by the right mouse button.

When applied to the v-on directive, these modifiers restrict the events that are processed to those triggered with the specified mouse button, as shown in Listing 14-15.

Listing 14-15. Using a Mouse Modifier in the App.vue File in the src Folder

```
<template>
    <div class="container-fluid">
        <div id="outer-element" class="bg-primary p-4 text-white h3"
            v-on:mousedown="handleClick">
            Outer Element
            <div id="middle-element" class="bg-secondary p-4"
                v-on:mousedown="handleClick">
                Middle Element
                <div id="inner-element" class="bg-info p-4"
                    v-on:mousedown.right="handleClick">
                    Inner Element
                </div>
            </div>
        </div>
    </div>
</template>
```

```
<script>
    export default {
        name: "MyComponent",
        methods: {
            handleClick($event) {
                console.log(`handleClick target: ${$event.target.id}`
                    + ` currentTarget: ${$event.currentTarget.id}`);
            }
        }
    }
</script>
```

In the listing, I have changed the v-on directives so they listen for the mousedown event, which is triggered when any mouse button is pressed over an element, and applied the right modifier to the v-on directive on the inner element so it will receive events only for the right mouse button.

The modifiers described do not prevent an event from being propagated. Instead, they prevent the v-on directive to which they are applied from processing events that are triggered using other mouse buttons. If you left-click the inner element, you will see the following messages in the browser's JavaScript console, which show that the v-on directives applied to the middle and outer elements receive the event, even though it is not processed by the inner element's directive:

```
...
handleClick target: inner-element currentTarget: middle-element
handleClick target: inner-element currentTarget: outer-element
...
```

If you right-click the inner element, then all three v-on directives will process the event, resulting in the following messages:

```
...
handleClick target: inner-element currentTarget: inner-element
handleClick target: inner-element currentTarget: middle-element
handleClick target: inner-element currentTarget: outer-element
...
```

Using Keyboard Event Modifiers

Vue.js provides a set of keyboard event modifiers that are used to limit the keyboard events processed by a v-on directive in a similar way to the mouse modifiers described in the previous section. In Listing 14-16, I have modified the component so that it has an input element that I use to receive keyboard events.

Listing 14-16. Receiving Keyboard Events in the App.vue File in the src Folder

```
<template>
    <div class="container-fluid">
        <div class="bg-primary p-4 text-white h3">
            {{message}}
        </div>
        <input class="form-control bg-light" placeholder="Type here..."
            v-on:keydown.ctrl="handleKey" />
    </div>
</template>
```

```
<script>
    export default {
        name: "MyComponent",
        data: function () {
            return {
                message: "Ready"
            }
        },
        methods: {
            handleKey($event) {
                this.message = $event.key;
            }
        }
    }
</script>
```

This example applies the ctrl modifier to the keydown event, which means that the handleKey event will be invoked only for keydown event when the Control key is being held down. You can see the effect by typing into the input element and observing the characters that are displayed in the text interpolation binding in the div element. The data binding shows that the handleKey method is invoked when the Control key is pressed on its own or in combination with another key but not otherwise, as shown in Figure 14-11.

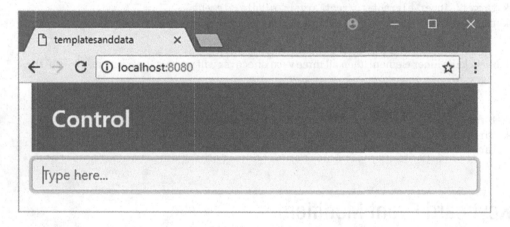

Figure 14-11. *Using a modifier to filter key events*

Table 14-7 shows the set of key event modifiers provided by Vue.js. Some of these modifiers are for keys that can be used in conjunction with others, such as the Shift and Control keys, and the rest make it easy to specify commonly required keys such as Tab and the spacebar.

Table 14-7. *The v-on Keyboard Event Modifiers*

Modifier	Description
enter	This modifier selects the Enter key.
tab	This modifier selects the Tab key.
delete	This modifier selects the Delete key.
esc	This modifier selects the Escape key.
space	This modifier selects the spacebar.
up	This modifier selects the up arrow key.
down	This modifier selects the down arrow key.
left	This modifier selects the left arrow key.
right	This modifier selects the right arrow key.
ctrl	This modifier selects the Control key.
alt	This modifier selects the Alt key.
shift	This modifier selects the Shift key.
meta	This modifier selects the meta key.
exact	This modifier selects only the specified modifier key, as described after the table.

The exact modifier further restricts an event binding so that it will be invoked only when the specified keys are pressed. The modifier in Listing 14-17, for example, will invoke the handleKey method only when just the Control key is pressed and not when the Control key is pressed along with, say, the Shift key.

Listing 14-17. Matching Keys Exactly in the App.vue File in the src Folder

```
<template>
    <div class="container-fluid">
        <div class="bg-primary p-4 text-white h3">
            {{message}}
        </div>
        <input class="form-control bg-light" placeholder="Type here..."
               v-on:keydown.ctrl.exact="handleKey" />
    </div>
</template>

<script>
    export default {
        name: "MyComponent",
        data: function () {
            return {
                message: "Ready"
            }
        },
```

```
        methods: {
            handleKey($event) {
                this.message = $event.key;
            }
        }
    }
</script>
```

Summary

In this chapter, I demonstrated the different ways the v-on directive can be used to respond to events. I showed you how to specify one or more events when applying the directive, how to invoke methods and receive arguments when generating repeated content, and how to use modifiers to change event behavior and select specific mouse buttons or keys. In the next chapter, I describe the Vue.js features for working with form elements.

CHAPTER 15

■ ■ ■

Working with Form Elements

In this chapter, I describe v-model, which is the built-in directive used for HTML form elements. The v-model directive creates a two-way data binding between a form element and a data value and ensures that the application remains consistent, regardless of how the data is changed. I also show you how to combine the v-model directive with some of the built-in directives described in earlier chapters to validate the data entered into a form by the user. Table 15-1 puts the v-model directive in context.

Table 15-1. *Putting the v-model Directive in Context*

Question	Answer
What is it?	The v-model directive creates a two-way binding between an HTML form element and a data property, ensuring that the two remain consistent.
Why is it useful?	Working with form elements is an important part of most web applications, and the v-model directive takes care of creating data bindings without needing to worry about the differences that exist in the way that different form elements work.
How is it used?	The v-model directive is applied to input, select, and textarea elements, and its expression is the name of the data property to which the bindings should be created.
Are there any pitfalls or limitations?	The v-model directive cannot be used with Vuex data stores, which I describe in Chapter 20.
Are there any alternatives?	You can create the required bindings manually if you prefer, as described in the "Creating Two-Way Model Bindings" section of this chapter.

A. Freeman, *Pro Vue.js 2*, https://doi.org/10.1007/978-1-4842-3805-9_15

Table 15-2 summarizes the chapter.

Table 15-2. *Chapter Summary*

Problem	Solution	Listing
Create a two-way data binding between a data property and a form element	Use the v-model directive	1–9
Format input values as numbers	Use the number modifier	10, 11
Delay binding updates	Use the lazy modifier	12
Trim whitespace from input values	Use the trim modifier	13
Populate an array with the user's form selections	Use the v-model directive to bind to an array	14
Bind indirectly to values	Use a custom value with the v-model directive	15–17
Ensure that the user provides values that the application can use	Validate the form data gathered using the v-model directive	18–21

Preparing for This Chapter

In this chapter, I continue working with the templatesanddata project from Chapter 14. To prepare for this chapter, I simplified the application's root component, as shown in Listing 15-1.

■ **Tip** You can download the example project for this chapter—and for all the other chapters in this book—from https://github.com/Apress/pro-vue-js-2.

Listing 15-1. Simplifying the Content of the App.vue File in the src Folder

```
<template>
    <div class="container-fluid">

        <div class="bg-info m-2 p-2 text-white">
            Value: {{ dataValue }}
        </div>

        <div class="bg-primary m-2 p-2 text-white">
            <div class="form-check">
                <label class="form-check-label">
                    <input class="form-check-input" type="checkbox"
                            v-on:change="handleChange" />
                    Data Value
                </label>
            </div>
        </div>
```

```
        <div class="text-center m-2">
            <button class="btn btn-secondary" v-on:click="reset">
                Reset
            </button>
        </div>
    </div>
</template>

<script>
    export default {
        name: "MyComponent",
        data: function () {
            return {
                dataValue: false
            }
        },
        methods: {
            reset() {
                this.dataValue= false;
            },
            handleChange($event) {
                this.dataValue = $event.target.checked;
            }
        }
    }
</script>
```

Save the changes to the App.vue file and run the command shown in Listing 15-2 in the templatesanddata folder to start the Vue.js development tools.

Listing 15-2. Starting the Development Tools

```
npm run serve
```

Open a new browser window and navigate to http://localhost:8080 to see the content shown in Figure 15-1.

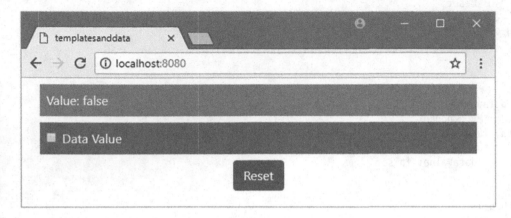

Figure 15-1. *Running the example application*

Creating Two-Way Model Bindings

All the data bindings I have created so far in this part of the book have been one-way, meaning that the data flows from the component's script element to the template element so that it can be displayed to the user.

The example application shows the one-way flow of data. When the state of the checkbox is changed, the v-on directive invokes the handleChange method, which sets the dataValue property. This data change triggers an update, which is displayed by the text interpolation data binding, as illustrated in Figure 15-2.

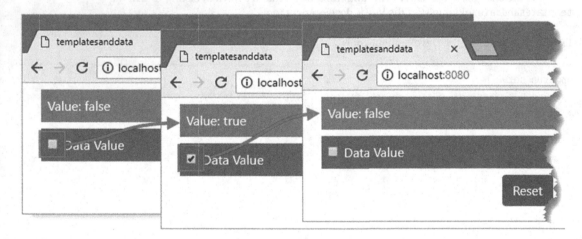

Figure 15-2. *Using a one-way data binding*

A one-way data binding works well when form elements are the only source of changes in an application. They are less effective when the user has other means to make changes, such as the Reset button in the example, whose v-on directive invokes the reset method, which sets dataValue to false. The text interpolation binding reflects the new value correctly, but the input element isn't aware of the change and gets out of sync, as shown in Figure 15-3.

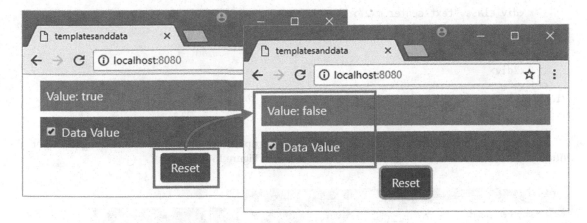

Figure 15-3. *The limitations of a one-way data binding*

Adding a Two-Way Binding

Form elements need data to flow in two directions. The data must flow from the form to the data model
when the user manipulates the element, such as when typing into a field or checking a checkbox. The data
must also flow in the other direction when the data model is modified by other means—such as the Reset
button in the example—to ensure that the user is always presented with consistent data. In Listing 15-3,
I have created a binding between the checkbox and the data property.

Listing 15-3. Creating a Binding in the App.vue File in the src Folder

```
...
<template>
    <div class="container-fluid">

        <div class="bg-info m-2 p-2 text-white">
            Value: {{ dataValue }}
        </div>

        <div class="bg-primary m-2 p-2 text-white">
            <div class="form-check">
                <label class="form-check-label">
                    <input class="form-check-input" type="checkbox"
                            v-on:change="handleChange"
                            v-bind:checked="dataValue" />
                    Data Value
                </label>
            </div>
        </div>
```

```
        <div class="text-center m-2">
            <button class="btn btn-secondary" v-on:click="reset">
                Reset
            </button>
        </div>
    </div>
</template>
...
```

I used the v-bind directive to set the element's checked property, which ensures that clicking the Reset button has the effect of unchecking the checkbox, as shown in Figure 15-4.

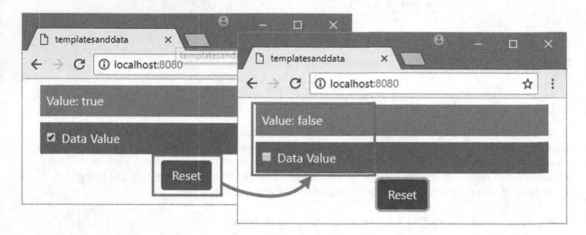

Figure 15-4. *The effect of an additional data binding*

There is now a two-way binding between the dataValue property and the checkbox. When the checkbox is checked and unchecked, the input element sends the change event, which leads the v-on directive to invoke the handleChange method, which sets the dataValue value. In the other direction, when dataValue is changed as a result of clicking the Reset button, the v-bind directive sets the input element's checked attribute, which checks or unchecks the checkbox.

Two-way data bindings are the foundation for the effective use of HTML forms. In a Vue.js application, the data model is authoritative, and changes to it can originate in different ways, all of which must be accurately reflected in the form elements that the user sees.

Adding Another Input Element

The HTML and DOM specification for form elements isn't consistent, and there are differences in the way that different element types work that must be reflected in the v-on and v-bind directives used to create two-way data bindings. In Listing 15-4, I have added a text input element, which shows the difference between just two different form elements.

Listing 15-4. Expanding the Form Elements in the App.vue File in the src Folder

```
<template>
    <div class="container-fluid">

        <div class="bg-info m-2 p-2 text-white">
            <div>Data Value: {{ dataValue }}</div>
            <div>Other Value: {{ otherValue || "(Empty)" }}</div>
        </div>

        <div class="bg-primary m-2 p-2 text-white">
            <div class="form-check">
                <label class="form-check-label">
                    <input class="form-check-input" type="checkbox"
                        v-on:change="handleChange"
                        v-bind:checked="dataValue" />
                    Data Value
                </label>
            </div>
        </div>

        <div class="bg-primary m-2 p-2">
            <input type="text" class="form-control"
                v-on:input="handleChange"
                v-bind:value="otherValue" />
        </div>

        <div class="text-center m-2">
            <button class="btn btn-secondary" v-on:click="reset">
                Reset
            </button>
        </div>
    </div>
</template>

<script>
    export default {
        name: "MyComponent",
        data: function () {
            return {
                dataValue: false,
                otherValue: ""
            }
        },
        methods: {
            reset() {
                this.dataValue = false;
                this.otherValue = "";
            },
```

```
        handleChange($event) {
            if ($event.target.type == "checkbox") {
                this.dataValue = $event.target.checked;
            } else {
                this.otherValue = $event.target.value;
            }
        }
    }
}
</script>
```

This example shows the differences that are required to create two-way bindings for different types of element. When dealing with the checkbox, I have to listen to the change event and bind to the checked attribute, but for the text input, I listen to the input event and bind to the value attribute. I have to make similar adaptations in the handleChange event, setting the checked property for the checkbox and the value property for the text input. The result is that there are now two form elements, each of which has two-way bindings with a data property, as shown in Figure 15-5.

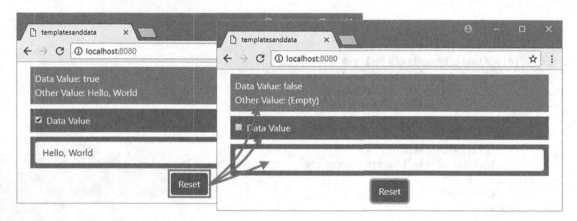

Figure 15-5. *Adding another input element*

Simplifying Two-Way Bindings

The differences required to create the bindings complicates the process of setting up the bindings, and it is easy to get confused about the needs of different element types and end up using the wrong events, attributes, or properties.

Vue.js provides the v-model directive; it simplifies two-way bindings, automatically deals with the differences between element types, and can be used on input, select, and textarea elements. In Listing 15-5, I have simplified the bindings using the v-model directive.

Listing 15-5. Simplifying Two-Way Bindings in the App.vue File in the src Folder

```
<template>
    <div class="container-fluid">

        <div class="bg-info m-2 p-2 text-white">
            <div>Data Value: {{ dataValue }}</div>
            <div>Other Value: {{ otherValue || "(Empty)" }}</div>
        </div>
```

```
    <div class="bg-primary m-2 p-2 text-white">
        <div class="form-check">
            <label class="form-check-label">
                <input class="form-check-input" type="checkbox"
                    v-model="dataValue" />
                Data Value
            </label>
        </div>
    </div>

    <div class="bg-primary m-2 p-2">
        <input type="text" class="form-control" v-model="otherValue" />
    </div>

    <div class="text-center m-2">
        <button class="btn btn-secondary" v-on:click="reset">
            Reset
        </button>
    </div>
    </div>
</template>

<script>
    export default {
        name: "MyComponent",
        data: function () {
            return {
                dataValue: false,
                otherValue: ""
            }
        },
        methods: {
            reset() {
                this.dataValue = false;
                this.otherValue = "";
            }
            //handleChange($event) {
            //    if ($event.target.type == "checkbox") {
            //        this.dataValue = $event.target.checked;
            //    } else {
            //        this.otherValue = $event.target.value;
            //    }

            //}
        }
    }
</script>
```

The expression for the v-model directive is a property for which two-way bindings are created. There is no need to receive events in a method, which allows me to remove the handleChange method, and the effect is to refocus the component on its data and content, rather than the plumbing that connects them.

Binding to Form Elements

Before moving on, I am going to demonstrate how to use the v-model directive to create bindings for different types of form element. Most of the differences between elements are handled by the v-model directive, but a simple catalog of bindings means you can copy and paste into your own projects without having to figure out the exact approach required for each of them.

Binding to Text Fields

The simplest bindings are created to input elements configured to allow the user to enter text. In Listing 15-6, I have used input elements set up for plain text and passwords, along with two-way bindings using the v-model directive.

Listing 15-6. Binding to Text Fields in the App.vue File in the src Folder

```
<template>
    <div class="container-fluid">
        <div class="bg-info m-2 p-2 text-white">
            <div>Name: {{ name }} </div>
            <div>Password: {{ password }}</div>
            <div>Details: {{ details }}</div>
        </div>
        <div class="bg-primary m-2 p-2 text-white">
            <div class="form-group">
                <label>Name</label>
                <input class="form-control" v-model="name" />
            </div>
            <div class="form-group">
                <label>Password</label>
                <input type="password" class="form-control" v-model="password" />
            </div>
            <div class="form-group">
                <label>Details</label>
                <textarea   class="form-control" v-model="details" />
            </div>
        </div>
    </div>
</template>

<script>
    export default {
        name: "MyComponent",
        data: function () {
            return {
                name: "Bob",
                password: "secret",
                details: "Has admin access"
            }
        }
    }
</script>
```

I have created two `input` elements, one of which defaults to a regular text field and one of which is configured as a password field, and a `textarea` element. All three elements use the `v-model` directive to create a two-way data binding to a data property defined by the component, producing the result shown in Figure 15-6.

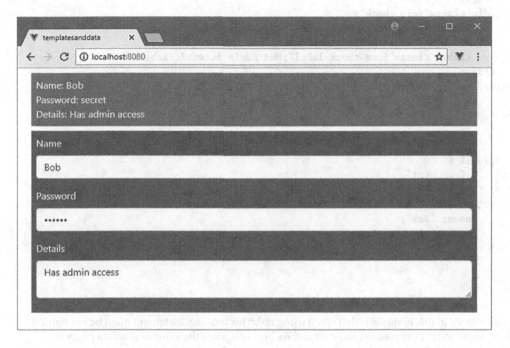

Figure 15-6. *Binding to text fields*

Binding to Radio Buttons and Checkboxes

In Listing 15-7, I have replaced the elements from the previous example with checkboxes and radio buttons that present the user with a constrained set of choices. As with the previous example, each element uses the `v-model` directive to create a two-way data binding with a data property.

Listing 15-7. Binding to Checkboxes and Radio Buttons in the App.vue File in the src Folder

```
<template>
    <div class="container-fluid">

        <div class="bg-info m-2 p-2 text-white">
            <div>Name: {{ name }} </div>
            <div>Has Admin Access: {{ hasAdminAccess }}</div>
        </div>
        <div class="bg-primary m-2 p-2 text-white">
            <div class="form-check">
                <input class="form-check-input" type="radio"
                    v-model="name" value="Bob" />
                <label class="form-check-label">Bob</label>
            </div>
```

```
        <div class="form-check">
            <input class="form-check-input" type="radio"
                v-model="name" value="Alice" />
            <label class="form-check-label">Alice</label>
        </div>
        <div class="form-check">
            <input class="form-check-input" type="checkbox"
                v-model="hasAdminAccess" />
            <label class="form-check-label">Has Admin Access?</label>
        </div>
    </div>
</div>
</template>

<script>
    export default {
        name: "MyComponent",
        data: function () {
            return {
                name: "Bob",
                hasAdminAccess: true
            }
        }
    }
</script>
```

The key difference in this example is that when using radio buttons, each element must be configured with a value attribute so that the v-model directive knows how to update the value of the data property. The elements in Listing 15-7 produce the result shown in Figure 15-7.

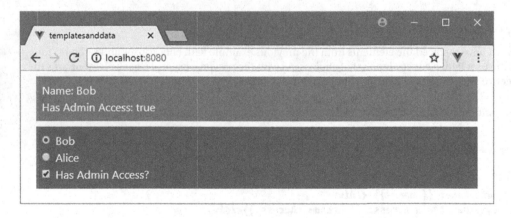

Figure 15-7. *Binding to radio buttons and checkboxes*

The v-model directive can be combined with the v-for and v-bind directives to generate form elements from an array of values, as shown in Listing 15-8, which is useful when the options presented to the user are known only at runtime.

Listing 15-8. Generating Radio Buttons in the App.vue File in the src Folder

```
<template>
    <div class="container-fluid">
        <div class="bg-info m-2 p-2 text-white">
            <div>Name: {{ name }} </div>
        </div>
        <div class="bg-primary m-2 p-2 text-white">
            <div class="form-check" v-for="n in allNames" v-bind:key="n">
                <input class="form-check-input" type="radio"
                    v-model="name" v-bind:value="n" />
                <label class="form-check-label">{{ n }}</label>
            </div>
        </div>
    </div>
</template>

<script>
    export default {
        name: "MyComponent",
        data: function () {
            return {
                allNames: ["Bob", "Alice", "Joe"],
                name: "Bob"
            }
        }
    }
</script>
```

The v-bind directive must be used to set the value attribute of the input elements; otherwise, Vue.js won't evaluate the attribute value as an expression. Figure 15-8 shows the result from Listing 15-8.

Figure 15-8. *Generating form elements from data values*

Binding to Select Elements

Select elements allow the user to be presented with a limited number of choices in a compact way, as shown in Listing 15-9. The option elements that define the choices available to the user can be defined statically or using the v-for directive or, as shown in the listing, by a mix of both.

Listing 15-9. Binding to a Select Element in the App.vue File in the src Folder

```
<template>
    <div class="container-fluid">
        <div class="bg-info m-2 p-2 text-white">
            <div>Name: {{ name }} </div>
        </div>
        <div class="bg-primary m-2 p-2 text-white">
            <div class="form-group">
                <label>Selected Names</label>
                <select class="form-control" v-model="name">
                    <option value="all">Everyone</option>
                    <option v-for="n in allNames" v-bind:key="n"
                        v-bind:value="n">Just {{ n }}</option>
                </select>
            </div>
        </div>
    </div>
</template>

<script>
    export default {
        name: "MyComponent",
        data: function () {
            return {
                allNames: ["Bob", "Alice", "Joe"],
                name: "Bob"
            }
        }
    }
</script>
```

As with radio buttons, the v-bind directive must be used to set the value attribute. Figure 15-9 shows the result of Listing 15-9.

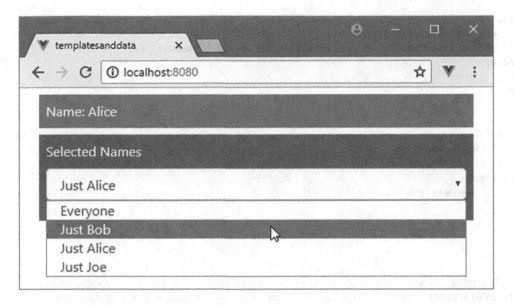

Figure 15-9. *Binding to a select element*

Using the v-model Modifiers

The v-model directive provides three bindings that alter the two-way bindings it creates. These modifiers are described in Table 15-3 and demonstrated in the sections that follow.

Table 15-3. *The Modifiers for the v-model Directive*

Modifier	Description
number	This modifier parses the value from the input into a number before assigning it to the data property.
trim	This modifier removes any leading and trailing whitespace from the input before assigning it to the data property.
lazy	This modifier changes the event to which the v-model directive listens so that the data property is updated only when the user navigates away from the input element.

Formatting Values as Numbers

The number modifier addresses an oddity in the way that input elements work when the type attribute is set to number and is demonstrated in Listing 15-10.

Listing 15-10. Using a Numeric Input Element in the App.vue File in the src Folder

```
<template>
    <div class="container-fluid">
        <div class="bg-info m-2 p-2 text-white">
            <div>Amount: {{ amount }}, Amount + 10 = {{ amount + 10 }}</div>
        </div>
```

```
        <div class="form-group">
            <label>Amount</label>
            <input type="number" class="form-control" v-model="amount" />
        </div>
    </div>
</template>

<script>
    export default {
        name: "MyComponent",
        data: function () {
            return {
                amount: 100
            }
        }
    }
</script>
```

The HTML5 specification added a range of values for the type attribute, and the number value tells the browser only to accept keystrokes for digits and decimal points. But the value entered by the user is presented as a string by the browser. This combines with the dynamic JavaScript typing system to create a problem, which you can see by changing the value in the Amount field to any number, such as 101. The v-model directive responds to the events generated by the input element as the value is changed and updates the data property named amount using the string value it receives, producing the effect shown on the left in Figure 15-10.

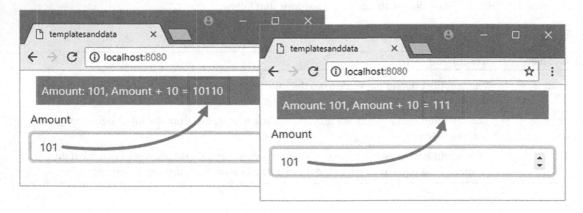

Figure 15-10. *The effect of the number modifier*

The problem is seen in the text interpolation binding that adds 10 to the amount value. Since the v-model directive has updated amount with a string, JavaScript interprets the data binding's expression as string concatenation, rather than addition, which means that 101 + 10 produces a result of 10110. In Listing 15-11, I added the number modifier to the v-model directive, which avoids this problem.

Listing 15-11. Applying a Modifier in the App.vue File in the src Folder

```
...
<template>
    <div class="container-fluid">
        <div class="bg-info m-2 p-2 text-white">
            <div>Amount: {{ amount }}, Amount + 10 = {{ amount + 10 }}</div>
        </div>
        <div class="form-group">
            <label>Amount</label>
            <input type="number" class="form-control" v-model.number="amount" />
        </div>
    </div>
</template>
...
```

The number modifier tells the v-model directive to convert the value entered by the user to a number before using it to update the application.

■ **Caution**   The number modifier doesn't apply any restrictions on the characters that the input element allows, and it will allow the directive to update the data model with a string if the value entered by the user contains nondigit characters. When using this modifier, you must ensure that the user can enter only digits by setting the type attribute of the input element to number.

Delaying Updates

By default, the v-model directive updates the data model after every keypress made into input or textarea elements. The lazy modifier changes the event that the v-model directive listens to so that an update is performed only when the navigates to another component. In Listing 15-12, I have applied the modifier to the input element in the component's template.

Listing 15-12. Applying a Modifier in the App.vue File in the src Folder

```
...
<template>
    <div class="container-fluid">
        <div class="bg-info m-2 p-2 text-white">
            <div>Amount: {{ amount }}, Amount + 10 = {{ amount + 10 }}</div>
        </div>
        <div class="form-group">
            <label>Amount</label>
            <input type="number" class="form-control" v-model.number.lazy="amount" />
        </div>
    </div>
</template>
...
```

The lazy modifier will prevent the amount property from being updated until the input element loses the focus, typically when the user tabs to another form element or clicks the mouse button outside of the element.

Removing Whitespace Characters

The trim modifier removes leading and trailing whitespace characters from the text entered by the user and can help avoid validation errors that are hard for the user to see. In Listing 15-13, I added a text input element to the component and used the trim modifier on its v-model directive.

■ **Note** The trim modifier affects only the values entered into the element by the user. If another part of the application sets the data property to a string that has leading or trailing whitespace, those characters will be displayed to the user by the input element.

Listing 15-13. Trimming Whitespace in the App.vue File in the src Folder

```
<template>
    <div class="container-fluid">
        <div class="bg-info m-2 p-2 text-white">
            <div>Name: **{{name}}** </div>
        </div>
        <div class="form-group">
            <label>Name</label>
            <input type="text" class="form-control" v-model.trim="name" />
        </div>
    </div>
</template>

<script>
    export default {
        name: "MyComponent",
        data: function () {
            return {
                name: "Bob"
            }
        }
    }
</script>
```

I have surrounded the text interpolation binding that displays the value with asterisks to help emphasize any leading or trailing whitespace. To test the modifier, save the changes to the component and enter a string that begins or ends with spaces. These characters will be trimmed from the string that is assigned to the data property, producing the result shown in Figure 15-11.

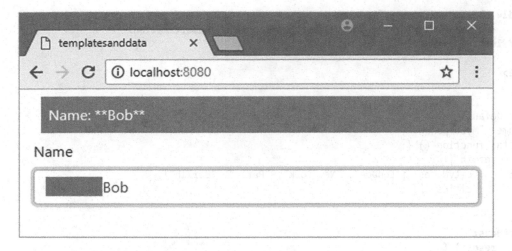

Figure 15-11. *Trimming whitespace characters*

Binding to Different Data Types

The v-model directive is able to adapt the way it binds to the data model, which makes it possible to use form elements in ways that are often useful for web application development, as described in the following sections.

Selecting an Array of Items

If the v-model directive is applied to a checkbox and bound to a data property that is an array, then checking and unchecking the box will add and remove a value from the array. This is easier to demonstrate than explain, and in Listing 15-14 I have used the v-for directive to generate a set of checkboxes and used the v-model directive to bind them to an array.

Listing 15-14. Creating a Binding to an Array in the App.vue File in the src Folder

```
<template>
    <div class="container-fluid">
        <div class="bg-info m-2 p-2 text-white">
            <div>Selected Cities: {{ cities }}</div>
        </div>

        <div class="form-check m-2" v-for="city in cityNames" v-bind:key="city">
            <label class="form-check-label">
                <input type="checkbox" class="form-check-input"
                        v-model="cities" v-bind:value="city" />
                {{city}}
            </label>
        </div>
```

```
        <div class="text-center">
            <button v-on:click="reset" class="btn btn-info">Reset</button>
        </div>
    </div>
</template>

<script>
    export default {
        name: "MyComponent",
        data: function () {
            return {
                cityNames: ["London", "New York", "Paris", "Berlin"],
                cities: []
            }
        },
        methods: {
            reset() {
                this.cities = [];
            }
        }
    }
</script>
```

The v-for directive creates a checkbox element for each of the values in the cityName array, which provides the set of values from which the user can select. Each input element is configured with a value attribute that specifies the city name that will be added to the cities array when it is checked and removed when it is unchecked. The v-model directive is configured to create a two-way data binding to the cities array, which will be populated with the selected values. The two-way binding means that if another part of the application—such as the reset method in this example—removes the value from the array, the v-model directive will automatically uncheck the box. I used a text interpolation binding to display the selected values, as shown in Figure 15-12.

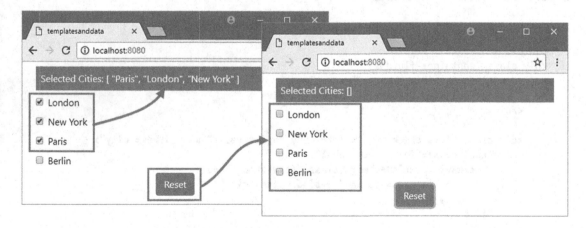

Figure 15-12. Creating a data binding to an array

BINDING TO AN ARRAY USING A SELECT ELEMENT

A similar effect can be achieved using a select element that is configured to allow multiple selections, like this:

```
...
<div class="form-control">
    <label>City</label>
    <select multiple class="form-control" v-model="cities">
        <option v-for="city in cityNames" v-bind:key="city">
            {{city}}
        </option>
    </select>
</div>
...
```

The v-for directive is applied to the option element and populates the select element with the choices that will be presented to the user. The v-model directive is configured to bind to an array and works in the same way as the group of checkboxes demonstrated in Listing 15-14.

My preference is for the checkboxes because most users are unaware of the need to hold a modifier key—such as the Shift or Control keys on Windows to make contiguous and noncontiguous selections. Presenting the user with a collection of checkboxes presents a more obvious approach that I prefer to explanatory text alongside the select element.

Using Custom Values for Form Elements

A common pattern with checkboxes is to toggle a value indirectly so that the true/false value provided by the input element and its v-model binding is translated into different values by a computed property or a data binding expression. In Listing 15-15, I have demonstrated this pattern by using the v-bind directive to assign an element to classes that correspond to Bootstrap CSS classes.

Listing 15-15. Indirect Values in the App.vue File in the src Folder

```
<template>
    <div class="container-fluid">
        <div class="m-2 p-2 text-white" v-bind:class="elemClass">
            <div>Value: {{ elemClass }}</div>
        </div>
        <div class="form-check m-2">
            <label class="form-check-label">
                <input type="checkbox" class="form-check-input"
                        v-model="dataValue" />
                Dark Color
            </label>
        </div>
    </div>
</template>
```

```
<script>
    export default {
        name: "MyComponent",
        data: function () {
            return {
                dataValue: false,
            }
        },
        computed: {
            elemClass() {
                return this.dataValue ? "bg-primary" : "bg-info";
            }
        }
    }
</script>
```

The v-model directive on the checkbox sets the data property named dataValue, which is used solely by the elemClass computed property, which the v-bind directive on the div element uses to set class membership. The effect is that toggling the checkbox moves the div element between the bg-primary and bg-info classes, which Bootstrap uses to set the background color, as shown in Figure 15-13.

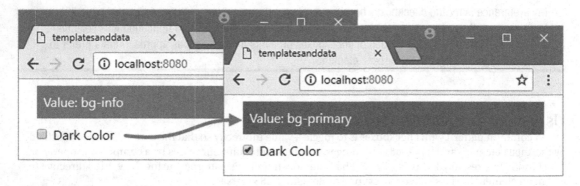

Figure 15-13. *Using an indirect value set by a checkbox*

When the data property set by the checkbox is used this way, the computed property that converts the true/false value can be eliminated by applying true-value and false-value attributes, as shown in Listing 15-16.

Listing 15-16. Simplifying Bindings in the App.vue File in the src Folder

```
<template>
    <div class="container-fluid">
        <div class="m-2 p-2 text-white" v-bind:class="dataValue">
            <div>Value: {{ dataValue }}</div>
        </div>
        <div class="form-check m-2">
            <label class="form-check-label">
                <input type="checkbox" class="form-check-input"
                    v-model="dataValue" true-value="bg-primary"
                    false-value="bg-info" />
```

```
            Dark Color
        </label>
    </div>
</div>
</template>

<script>
    export default {
        name: "MyComponent",
        data: function () {
            return {
                dataValue: "bg-info"
            }
        }
    }
</script>
```

The `true-value` and `false-value` attributes are used by the `v-model` directive to set `dataValue`, which means that a computed property isn't required to translate the user's choice into class names that can be used by the `v-bind` directive. The result is the same—toggling the checkbox changes the class membership of the `div` element—but the code is simpler and cleaner.

Using Custom Values for Radio Buttons and Select Elements

The `v-model` directive can be combined with the `v-bind` directive to support values that can also be used for radio buttons and select elements. In Listing 15-17, I have added both types of element and configured them so they use the class names introduced in the previous section.

Listing 15-17. Using Custom Values for Other Elements in the App.vue File in the src Folder

```
<template>
    <div class="container-fluid">
        <div class="m-2 p-2 text-white" v-bind:class="dataValue">
            <div>Value: {{ dataValue }}</div>
        </div>
        <div class="form-check m-2">
            <label class="form-check-label">
                <input type="checkbox" class="form-check-input"
                       v-model="dataValue" v-bind:true-value="darkColor"
                       v-bind:false-value="lightColor" />
                Dark Color
            </label>
        </div>

        <div class="form-group m-2 p-2 bg-secondary">
            <label>Color</label>
            <select v-model="dataValue" class="form-control">
                <option v-bind:value="darkColor">Dark Color</option>
                <option v-bind:value="lightColor">Light Color</option>
            </select>
        </div>
```

```
            <div class="form-check-inline m-2">
                <label class="form-check-label">
                    <input type="radio" class="form-check-input"
                            v-model="dataValue" v-bind:value="darkColor" />
                    Dark Color
                </label>
            </div>
            <div class="form-check-inline m-2">
                <label class="form-check-label">
                    <input type="radio" class="form-check-input"
                            v-model="dataValue" v-bind:value="lightColor" />
                    Light Color
                </label>
            </div>
        </div>
</template>

<script>
    export default {
        name: "MyComponent",
        data: function () {
            return {
                darkColor: "bg-primary",
                lightColor: "bg-info",
                dataValue: "bg-info"
            }
        }
    }
</script>
```

To avoid duplicating the class names on each element, I use the v-bind directive to set the value attribute for the input and option elements using the data properties named darkColor and lightColor. The result is a set of form elements that manage the class membership of the div element without needing a computed property to convert true/false values, as shown in Figure 15-14.

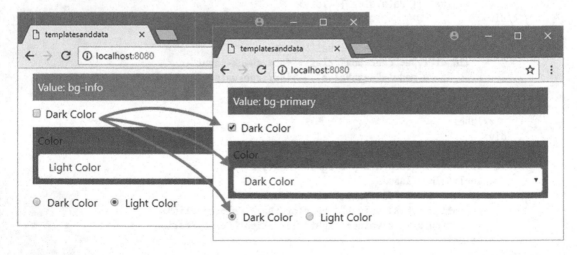

Figure 15-14. *Using custom values for other elements*

Validating Form Data

As soon as you begin using form elements, you need to start thinking about data validation. Users will enter anything into text fields, and it is important to ensure that your application receives the data it requires to function. In the following sections, I explain how form data can be validated, and to prepare, I have updated the component so that it contains a simple form, as shown in Listing 15-18.

■ **Note**   I am showing you how to write your own validation code in this section because it is interesting and because it demonstrates how some of the features described in this chapter and earlier chapters can be combined to produce useful features. In real projects, I suggest you rely on one of the excellent and widely used open source packages for Vue.js form validation, such as vuelidate (https://github.com/monterail/vuelidate), which I used in Part 1 for the SportsStore project, or VeeValidate (http://vee-validate.logaretm.com).

Listing 15-18. Creating a Form in the App.Vue File in the src Folder

```
<template>
    <div class="container-fluid">

        <div class="btn-primary text-white my-2 p-2">
            Name: {{ name }}, Category: {{ category }}, Price: {{ price }}
        </div>

        <form v-on:submit.prevent="handleSubmit">
            <div class="form-group">
                <label>Name</label>
                <input v-model="name" class="form-control" />
            </div>
            <div class="form-group">
                <label>Category</label>
                <input v-model="category" class="form-control" />
            </div>
            <div class="form-group">
                <label>Price</label>
                <input type="number" v-model.number="price" class="form-control" />
            </div>

            <div class="text-center">
                <button class="btn btn-primary" type="submit">Submit</button>
            </div>

        </form>
    </div>

</template>
```

```
<script>
    export default {
        name: "MyComponent",
        data: function () {
            return {
                name: "",
                category: "",
                price: 0
            }
        },
        methods: {
            handleSubmit() {
                console.log(`FORM SUBMITTED: ${this.name} ${this.category} `
                    + ` ${this.price}`);
            }
        }
    }
</script>
```

The component defines data properties named name, category, and price that are presented to the user through input elements, to which the v-model directive has been applied. Details of the values entered are displayed above the form elements, as shown in Figure 15-15.

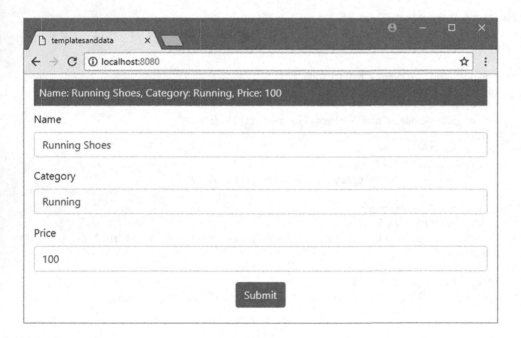

Figure 15-15. *Presenting a form to the user*

The input elements are contained within a form element to which the v-on directive has been applied like this:

```
...
<form v-on:submit.prevent="handleSubmit">
...
```

The submit event is triggered when the user clicks the button element, whose type has been set to submit. The prevent modifier is required to stop the browser from submitting the form to the HTTP server, which is the default action for this event. The directive's expression invokes a method called handleSubmit, which would send the data to a web service in a real application but which simply writes out a message to the browser's JavaScript console in this example. Click the Submit button, and you will see a message like this one in the JavaScript console:

```
...
FORM SUBMITTED: Running Shoes Running  100
...
```

I explain how to work with web services in Chapter 19, but for this chapter, the emphasis is on validating the data entered by the user. The goal for this part of the chapter is to control the message displayed by the handleSubmit method so that it is displayed only when the user has entered valid data for all the form fields. When performing validation, it is important to have a clear set of requirements, and for this example, the validation requirements for each property are described in Table 15-4.

Table 15-4. *The Validation Requirements*

Name	Description
name	The user must provide a value that contains at least three characters.
category	The user must provide a value that contains only letters.
price	The user must provide a value that contains only digits and that is between 1 and 1,000.

Defining the Validation Rules

When you validate data, you will find that the same set of rules are applied repeatedly to different data values provided by the user. To reduce code duplication, it is a good idea to define validation rules once and reuse them. To define the validation rules that are required in Table 15-4, I added a JavaScript file called validationRules.js to the src folder and added the code shown in Listing 15-19.

UNDERSTANDING WHY USERS ENTER BAD DATA

There are several reasons why users enter bad data into an application, requiring data validation. The first type of bad data occurs when the user doesn't understand the data that is required or the format in which it must be expressed. A common example that I encounter is requiring credit cards to be expressed with or without spaces between the number groups. You should make it clear to the user if you require common data values to be expressed in a specific format. Better still, avoid the issue entirely, accept all of the common formats, and convert them into the one you like automatically.

The second type of bad data occurs when the user doesn't care about the process and just wants to get to the result. If you make the user endure long and complex forms or repeat a process over and over, then you can expect to see a lot of results containing nonsense. To minimize this type of issue, ask the user only for the data you really need, provide sensible default values where possible, and try to bear in mind that few users will care as much about your products as services as you would like them to.

There is nothing you can do about the final reason for bad data, which is where a user is trying to subvert the application. There will always be malicious users, and the more valuable your products and services are, the more malicious users you will attract. Data validation on its own isn't enough to avoid this type of issue, and you must give proper effort to end-to-end security reviews, monitoring, and remediation.

Listing 15-19. The Contents of the validationRules.js File in the src Folder

```
function required(name) {
    return {
        validator: (value) => value != "" && value !== undefined && value !== null,
        message: `A value is required for ${name}`
    }
}

function minLength(name, minlength) {
    return {
        validator: (value) => String(value).length >= minlength,
        message: `At least ${minlength} characters are required for ${name}`
    }
}

function alpha(name) {
    return {
        validator: (value) => /^[a-zA-Z]*$/.test(value),
        message: `${name} can only contain letters`
    }
}

function numeric(name) {
    return {
        validator: (value) => /^[0-9]*$/.test(value),
        message: `${name} can only contain digits`
    }
}

function range(name, min, max) {
    return {
        validator: (value) => value >= min && value <= max,
        message: `${name} must be between ${min} and ${max}`
    }
}
```

```
export default {
    name: [minLength("Name", 3)],
    category: [required("Category"), alpha("Category")],
    price: [numeric("Price"), range("Price", 1, 1000)]
}
```

This JavaScript file defines the validation functions that I will use to check the values entered by the user and the combination of these functions for each of the properties that will be validated.

Performing Validation

The next step is to add the code that will perform the validation. In Listing 15-20, I have added the methods and properties that are required to use the validation rules defined in the following section.

Listing 15-20. Performing Validation in the App.vue File in the src Folder

```
<template>
    <div class="container-fluid">

        <div class="bg-danger text-white my-2 p-2" v-if="errors">
            <h5>The following problems have been found:</h5>
            <ul>
                <template v-for="(errors) in validationErrors">
                    <li v-for="error in errors" v-bind:key="error">{{error}}</li>
                </template>
            </ul>
        </div>

        <form v-on:submit.prevent="handleSubmit">
            <div class="form-group">
                <label>Name</label>
                <input v-model="name" class="form-control" />
            </div>
            <div class="form-group">
                <label>Category</label>
                <input v-model="category" class="form-control" />
            </div>
            <div class="form-group">
                <label>Price</label>
                <input type="number" v-model.number="price" class="form-control" />
            </div>

            <div class="text-center">
                <button class="btn btn-primary" type="submit">
                    Submit
                </button>
            </div>
        </form>
    </div>
</template>
```

```
<script>

    import validation from "./validationRules";
    import Vue from "vue";

    export default {
        name: "MyComponent",
        data: function () {
            return {
                name: "",
                category: "",
                price: 0,
                validationErrors: {},
            }
        },
        computed: {
            errors() {
                return Object.values(this.validationErrors).length > 0;
            }
        },
        methods: {
            validate(propertyName, value) {
                let errors = [];
                Object(validation)[propertyName].forEach(v => {
                    if (!v.validator(value)) {
                        errors.push(v.message);
                    }
                });
                if (errors.length > 0) {
                    Vue.set(this.validationErrors, propertyName, errors);
                } else {
                    Vue.delete(this.validationErrors, propertyName);
                }
            },
            validateAll() {
                this.validate("name", this.name);
                this.validate("category", this.category);
                this.validate("price", this.price);
                return this.errors;
            },
            handleSubmit() {
                if (this.validateAll()) {
                    console.log(`FORM SUBMITTED: ${this.name} ${this.category} `
                        + ` ${this.price}`);
                }
            }
        }
    }
</script>
```

The validate method is used to validate an individual data property using the rules defined in Listing 15-20, which are accessed through an import statement. Details of validation errors are stored in the data property named validationErrors, which will have a property for each input field set to an array of the validation messages that need to be presented to the user.

■ **Tip** The Vue.delete method that I use in Listing 15-20 is the counterpart to the Vue.set method described in Chapter 13 and is used to remove a property from an object so that Vue.js is aware of the change.

When the user clicks the Submit button, the handleSubmit method calls the validateAll method, which calls the validate method for each of the data properties and performs the action—logging a message in this example—only if there are no validation problems.

In the component's template, I use the v-if directive to control the visibility of a div element, which then relies on the v-for directive to enumerate the properties of the validationErrors object and then again to create li elements for each message.

The result is that the values that the user has entered into the form are checked when the Submit button is clicked, as shown in Figure 15-16, which illustrates the errors shown when the button is clicked without changing any of the input fields.

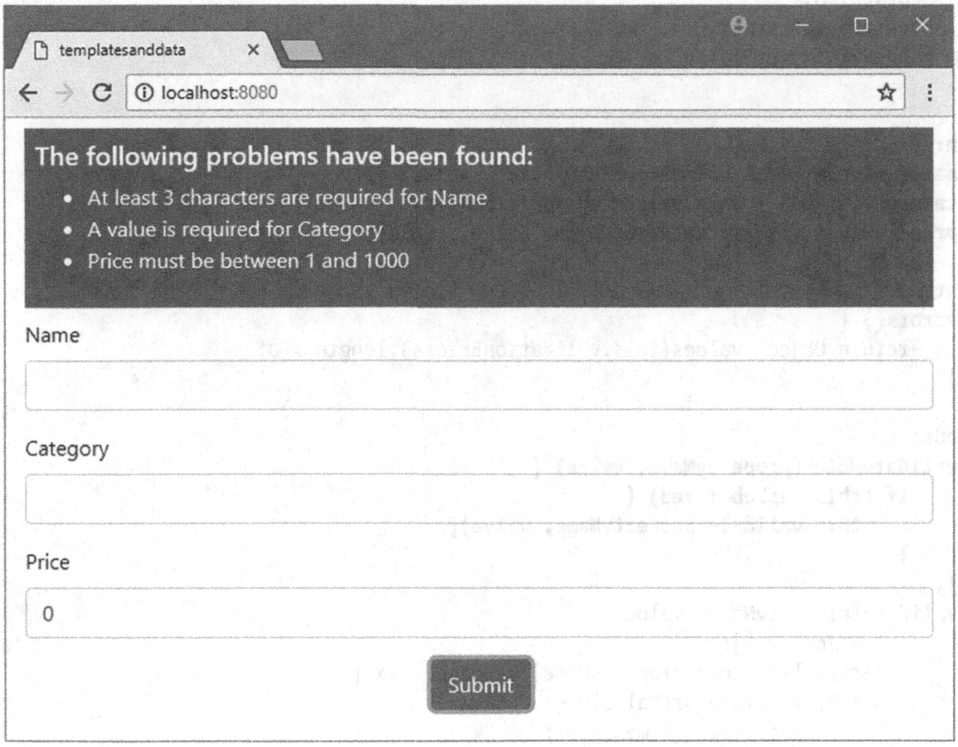

Figure 15-16. *Validating form data*

Responding to Live Changes

The basic validation works, but the checks are performed only when the user clicks the Submit button. A smoother approach is to validate the data as the user enters data into the input elements, providing more immediate feedback. I don't want to start showing errors immediately, so I'll wait until the user has clicked Submit once before responding to changes, as shown in Listing 15-21.

Listing 15-21. Responding to Changes in the App.vue File in the src Folder

```
...
<script>

    import validation from "./validationRules";
    import Vue from "vue";

    export default {
        name: "MyComponent",
        data: function () {
            return {
                name: "",
                category: "",
                price: 0,
                validationErrors: {},
                hasSubmitted: false
            }
        },
        watch: {
            name(value) { this.validateWatch("name", value) },
            category(value) { this.validateWatch("category", value) },
            price(value) { this. validateWatch("price", value) }
        },
        computed: {
            errors() {
                return Object.values(this.validationErrors).length > 0;
            }
        },
        methods: {
            validateWatch(propertyName, value) {
                if (this.hasSubmitted) {
                    this.validate(propertyName, value);
                }
            },
            validate(propertyName, value) {
                let errors = [];
                Object(validation)[propertyName].forEach(v => {
                    if (!v.validator(value)) {
                        errors.push(v.message);
                    }
                });
                if (errors.length > 0) {
                    Vue.set(this.validationErrors, propertyName, errors);
                } else {
```

```
            Vue.delete(this.validationErrors, propertyName);
        }
    },
    validateAll() {
        this.validate("name", this.name);
        this.validate("category", this.category);
        this.validate("price", this.price);
        return this.errors;
    },
    handleSubmit() {
        this.hasSubmitted = true;
        if (this.validateAll()) {
            console.log(`FORM SUBMITTED: ${this.name} ${this.category} `
                + ` ${this.price}`);
        }
    }
    }
  }
}
</script>
...
```

I have added a watch section in the script element, which is used to define watchers. I explain watchers in Chapter 17, but this feature allows a component to receive notifications when one of its data values changes. In this example, I have added functions to the watch section so that I will receive notifications when the name, category, and price properties change and use this to invoke a method named validateWatch, which will validate the property value only after the Submit button has been clicked at least once, which is managed through a new data property named hasSubmitted. The result is that the error messages displayed to the user are updated immediately on edit once the Submit button has been clicked, as shown in Figure 15-17.

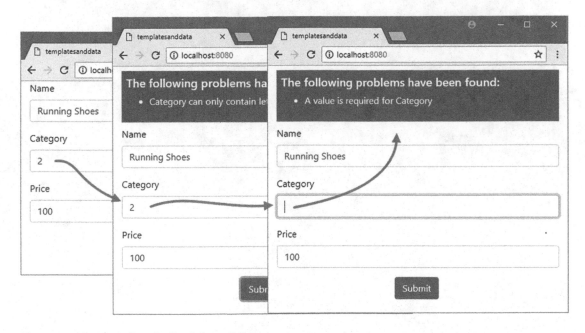

Figure 15-17. *Immediate feedback for validation errors*

Summary

In this chapter, I explained the use of two-way data bindings and described how they can be created using the `v-model` directive. I also demonstrated how to validate the data that a user enters into an HTML form using the v-model directive and other key Vue.js features. In the next chapter, I describe how components can be used to add structure to an application.

■ ■ ■

CHAPTER 16

Using Components

In this chapter, I explain how components form the building blocks in a Vue.js application and allow related content and code to be grouped together to make development easier. I show you how to add components to a project, how to communicate between components, and how components can work together to present content to the user. Table 16-1 puts components in context.

Table 16-1. *Putting Components in Context*

Question	Answer
What are they?	Components can be composed to create complex functionality from smaller building blocks.
Why are they useful?	Building a complex application using a single component makes it hard to tell which content and code relate to each feature. Breaking an application into several components means that each can be developed and tested individually.
How are they used?	Components are declared using a `components` property in the `script` element and applying using a custom HTML element.
Are there any pitfalls or limitations?	Components are isolated from one another by default, and the features that allow them to communicate can be complex to master.
Are there any alternatives?	You don't have to use multiple components to build an application, and a single component may be acceptable for simple projects.

Table 16-2 summarizes the chapter.

Table 16-2. *Chapter Summary*

Problem	Solution	Listing
Group related features	Add components to the project	1–9
Communicate with a child component	Use the props feature	10–12
Communicate with a parent component	Use the custom event feature	13–14
Mix parent and child component content	Use the slots feature	15–20

Preparing for This Chapter

I continue working with the templatesanddata project from Chapter 15. To prepare for this chapter, I simplified the application's root component, as shown in Listing 16-1.

■ **Tip** You can download the example project for this chapter—and for all the other chapters in this book—from https://github.com/Apress/pro-vue-js-2.

Listing 16-1. Simplifying the Content of the App.vue File in the src Folder

```
<template>

    <div class="bg-secondary text-white text-center m-2 p-2 h5">
        Root Component
    </div>

</template>

<script>

export default {
    name: 'App'
}

</script>
```

Run the command shown in Listing 16-2 in the templatesanddata folder to start the development tools.

Listing 16-2. Navigating to the Project Folder and Starting the Development Tools

---

```
npm run serve
```

The initial bundling process will be performed, after which you will see a message telling you that the project has compiled successfully and the HTTP server is listening for requests on port 8080. Open a new browser window and navigate to http://localhost:8080 to see the project's placeholder content, as shown in Figure 16-1.

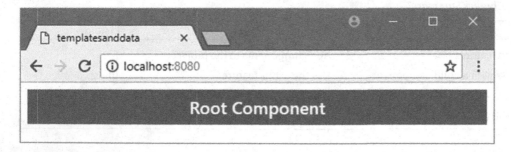

Figure 16-1. Running the example application

Understanding Components as Building Blocks

Using a single component becomes increasingly difficult as the complexity of an application increases. You saw an example of this in Chapter 15, where a form and its validation logic existed side by side, with the result that it is hard to work out which parts of the template and script elements are responsible for dealing with the form and which are related to validation. A component that has multiple responsibilities is hard to understand, hard to test, and hard to maintain.

Components are the building block for Vue.js applications, and using multiple components in an application allows for smaller units of functionality that are more easily written, maintained, and reused throughout an application.

When using components to build an application, the effect is a parent-child relationship where one component (the *parent*) delegates part of its template to another component (the *child*). The best way to see how this works is by creating an example that demonstrates this relationship. Components are conventionally defined in files with the .vue extension in the src/components folder, and I added a file called Child.vue in that folder, with the content shown in Listing 16-3.

■ **Note**   The project was created with a HelloWorld.vue file in the src/components, but I don't use that file in this chapter, and you can ignore—or delete—this file.

Listing 16-3. The Contents of the Child.vue File in the src/components Folder

```
<template>
    <div class="bg-primary text-white text-center m-2 p-3 h6">
        Child Component
    </div>
</template>
```

A component has to provide at least a template element, which is at the heart of the delegation process. The next step is to set up the delegation and create the relationship between the parent and the child, as shown in Listing 16-4.

Listing 16-4. Delegating to a Child Component in the App.vue File in the src Folder

```
<template>
    <div class="bg-secondary text-white text-center m-2 p-2 h5">
        Root Component
        <ChildComponent></ChildComponent>
    </div>
</template>

<script>
import ChildComponent from "./components/Child";

export default {
    name: 'App',
    components: {
        ChildComponent
    }
}
</script>
```

Three steps are required to set up the child component in the parent. The first step is to use an `import` statement for the child component, like this:

```
...
import ChildComponent from "./components/Child";
...
```

The source used in the `import` statement must start with a period, which indicates that this is a local import statement, rather than one that targets a package installed using a package manager. The most important part of the import statement is the name to which the child component is assigned, which I have marked in bold and which is `ChildComponent` in this example.

The name in the `import` statement is used to register the component, using a property named `components` in the `script` element, like this:

```
...
export default {
    name: 'App',
    components: {
        ChildComponent
    }
}
...
```

The `components` property is assigned using an object whose properties are the components it uses, and it is important to make sure you use the same name in the `components` object as you did in the `import` statement. The final step is to add an HTML element to the parent component's template with a tag that matches the name used in the `import` statement and the `components` object, like this:

```
...
<div class="bg-secondary text-white text-center m-2 p-2 h5">
    Root Component
    <ChildComponent></ChildComponent>
</div>
...
```

When Vue.js processes the parent component's template, it finds the custom HTML element and replaces it with the content in the `template` element of the child component, producing the result shown in Figure 16-2.

■ **Note** This example shows an important aspect of parent-child relationships: it is the parent that determines the name by which a child component is defined. This may seem odd at first, but it allows meaningful names to be used, reflecting the way that the child component is being applied. As you will see in later examples, a single component can be used in different parts of the application, and allowing the parent to name its child means that each use of the component can be given a name that suggests its use.

Figure 16-2. *Adding a component to the example application*

If you use the browser's F12 tools to examine the HTML document, you will see how the child component has been used to replace the ChildComponent element.

```
...
<body>
    <div class="bg-secondary text-white text-center m-2 p-2 h5">
        Root Component
        <div class="bg-primary text-white text-center m-2 p-3 h6">
            Child Component
        </div>
    </div>
    <script type="text/javascript" src="/app.js"></script>
</body>
...
```

The result is that part of the content presented by the App component, defined in the App.vue file, has been delegated to the Child component, defined in the Child.vue file, as illustrated in Figure 16-3.

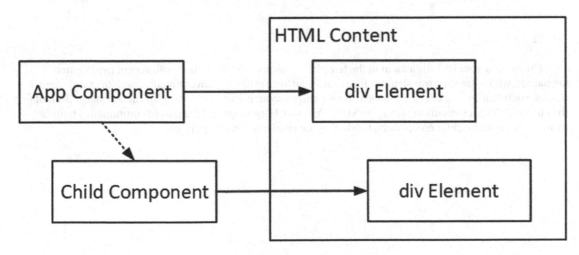

Figure 16-3. *The parent-child component relationship*

Understanding Child Component Names and Elements

In Listing 16-4, I used the name in the `import` statement to set up the child component, which led to this awkward-looking custom HTML element:

```
...
<div class="bg-secondary text-white text-center m-2 p-2 h5">
    Root Component
    <ChildComponent></ChildComponent>
</div>
...
```

This was a useful approach to demonstrate that it is the parent that names its child components, but Vue.js has a more sophisticated approach to names, which can lead to more elegant HTML.

The first name feature is that Vue.js will automatically reformat custom HTML element tag names when it looks for the child component to use, as shown in Listing 16-5.

Listing 16-5. Tag Name Reformatting in the App.vue File in the src Folder

```
<template>
    <div class="bg-secondary text-white text-center m-2 p-2 h5">
        Root Component
        <ChildComponent></ChildComponent>
        <child-component></child-component>
    </div>
</template>

<script>
import ChildComponent from "./components/Child";

export default {
    name: 'App',
    components: {
        ChildComponent
    }
}
</script>
```

The new custom HTML element in the template demonstrates that Vue.js will accept hyphenated tag names, which are then translated to the camel case format that is conventionally used for component names, such that the tag `child-component` is recognized as an instruction to use `ChildComponent`. Both of the custom HTML elements in Listing 16-5 tells Vue.js to delegate part of the parent component's template to an instance of the child component, producing the result shown in Figure 16-4.

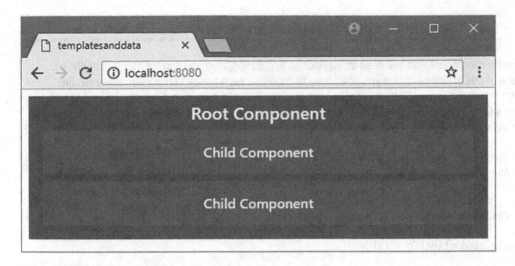

Figure 16-4. Flexible custom element tag formatting

The components property is a map that Vue.js uses to translate custom HTML element tag names into child component names, and this means that you can specify a completely different tag name when you register a component, as shown in Listing 16-6.

Listing 16-6. Specifying a Tag Name in the App.vue File in the src Folder

```
<template>
    <div class="bg-secondary text-white text-center m-2 p-2 h5">
        Root Component
        <MyFeature></MyFeature>
        <my-feature></my-feature>
    </div>
</template>

<script>
import ChildComponent from "./components/Child";

export default {
    name: 'App',
    components: {
        MyFeature: ChildComponent
    }
}
</script>
```

When you specify a property and value for a child component, the property name is used for the custom HTML elements. In this example, I have set the name of the property to MyFeature, which means I can apply the ChildComponent using the MyFeature and my-feature tags.

REGISTERING COMPONENTS GLOBALLY

If you have a component that you need throughout an application, then you can register it globally. The advantage of this approach is that you don't have to configure each parent component; however, the drawback is that the same HTML element is used to apply the child component, which can lead to less meaningful templates. To register a component globally, you add an import statement in the main.js file and use the Vue.component method, like this:

```
import Vue from 'vue'
import App from './App'

import "../node_modules/bootstrap/dist/css/bootstrap.min.css";
import ChildComponent from "./components/Child";

Vue.config.productionTip = false

Vue.component("child-component", ChildComponent);

new Vue({
  render: h => h(App)
}).$mount('#app')
```

The Vue.component method must be called before the application's Vue object is created, and its arguments are the HTML element tag that will be used to apply the component and the component object named in the import statement. The result is that the child-component element can be used throughout the application to apply the component without any further configuration.

Using Component Features in Child Components

The child component I defined in Listing 16-6 contains just a template element, but Vue.js supports the full range of features described in previous chapters in child components, including one-way and two-way data bindings, event handlers, data and computed properties, and methods. In Listing 16-7, I have added a script element to the child component and used it to support data bindings in the template.

Listing 16-7. Adding Features in the Child.vue File in the src/components Folder

```
<template>
    <div class="bg-primary text-white text-center m-2 p-3 h6">
        {{ message }}
        <div class="form-group m-1">
            <input v-model="message" class="form-control" />
        </div>
    </div>
</template>
```

```
<script>
export default {
    data: function() {
        return {
            message: "This is the child component"
        }
    }
}
</script>
```

The `script` element I added defines a data property named `message`, which I use in the `template` element with a text interpolation binding and the `v-model` directive. The result is the child component displays an `input` element whose contents are reflected in the text data binding, as shown in Figure 16-5.

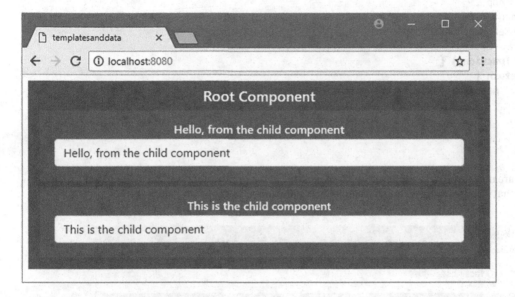

Figure 16-5. *Adding features to a child component*

Understanding Component Isolation

Components are isolated from one another, which means you don't have to worry about picking unique property and method names or binding to a value that is owned by a different component.

In Figure 16-5, you can see that editing the contents of one `input` element has no effect on the other child component, even though they both define and use a `message` property. This isolation also applies to the parent and child components, which can be demonstrated by adding a `message` property to the parent component in the example application, as shown in Listing 16-8.

Listing 16-8. Adding a Data Property in the App.vue File in the src Folder

```
<template>
    <div class="bg-secondary text-white text-center m-2 p-2 h5">
        {{ message }}
        <MyFeature></MyFeature>
        <my-feature></my-feature>
    </div>
</template>

<script>
import ChildComponent from "./components/Child";

export default {
    name: 'App', ·
    components: {
        MyFeature: ChildComponent
    },
    data: function() {
        return {
            message: "This is the parent component"
        }
    }
}
</script>
```

There are now three data properties named message in the application, but Vue.js keeps each of them isolated so that changes made to one have no effect on the other, as shown in Figure 16-6.

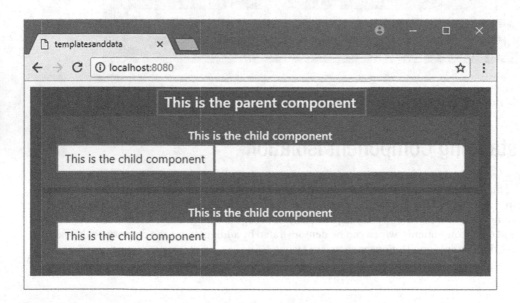

Figure 16-6. *Isolation between parent and child components*

```
┌──────────────────────────────────────────────────────────────────────┐
│                    UNDERSTANDING CSS SCOPING                           │
└──────────────────────────────────────────────────────────────────────┘
```

If you define custom styles in a component, you will find they are applied to elements defined by any component. For example, this style:

```
...
<style>
    div { border: 5px solid red ; }
</style>
...
```

will match any `div` element in the application and apply a solid red border. If you want to restrict your custom CSS styles to the component that defines them, you can add the `scoped` attribute to the `style` element, like this:

```
...
<style scoped>
    div { border: 5px solid red ; }
</style>
...
```

The `scoped` attribute tells Vue.js that the styles should be applied only to the elements in the current component's `template` element and not to elements in the templates of other components.

Using Component Props

Keeping components isolated is a good default policy because it avoids unexpected interactions. If components were not isolated from one another, making a change to one `message` property would affect all the components. On the other hand, in most applications, components have to work together to deliver features for the user, and this means breaking through the barrier that separates components. One feature for component collaboration is the *prop*, which allows a parent to provide a child with a data value. In Listing 16-9, I have added a prop to the child component.

Listing 16-9. Adding a Prop in the Child.vue File in the src/components Folder

```
<template>
    <div class="bg-primary text-white text-center m-2 p-3 h6">
        {{ message }}
        <div class="form-group m-1 text-left">
            <label>{{ labelText }}</label>
            <input v-model="message" class="form-control" />
        </div>
    </div>
</template>
```

```
<script>
    export default {
        props: ["labelText"],
        data: function () {
            return {
                message: "This is the child component"
            }
        }
    }
</script>
```

Props are defined using an array of strings assigned to a props property in the component's script element. In this case, the prop name is labelText. Once you have defined a prop, you can use it elsewhere in the component, such as in the text interpolation binding. If you need to modify the value once it has been received from the parent component, then you must use a data or computed property whose initial value is obtained from the prop, as shown in Listing 16-10.

■ **Note** This approach is required because the flow of data in a prop is in one direction: from the parent component to the child component. If you modify a prop value, the changes you make are likely to be overwritten by the parent component.

Listing 16-10. Setting a Mutable Value from a Prop in the Child.vue File in the src/components Folder

```
<template>
    <div class="bg-primary text-white text-center m-2 p-3 h6">
        {{ message }}
        <div class="form-group m-1 text-left">
            <label>{{ labelText }}</label>
            <input v-model="message" class="form-control" />
        </div>
    </div>
</template>

<script>
    export default {
        props: ["labelText", "initialValue"],
        data: function () {
            return {
                message: this.initialValue
            }
        }
    }
</script>
```

The component defines a second prop, named initialValue, that is used to set the value of the message property.

Using a Prop in a Parent Component

When a component defines a prop, its parent can send it data values by using attributes on the custom HTML element, as shown in Listing 16-11.

Listing 16-11. Using a Prop in the App.vue File in the src Folder

```
<template>
    <div class="bg-secondary text-white text-center m-2 p-2 h5">
        {{ message }}
        <MyFeature labelText="Name" initialValue="Kayak"></MyFeature>
        <my-feature label-text="Category" initial-value="Watersports"></my-feature>
    </div>
</template>

<script>
    import ChildComponent from "./components/Child";

    export default {
        name: 'App',
        components: {
            MyFeature: ChildComponent
        },
        data: function () {
            return {
                message: "This is the parent component"
            }
        }
    }
</script>
```

Vue.js applies the same flexibility when matching attribute names to props as it does when matching custom HTML elements to components. This means I can use `labelText` or `label-text` to set the value for the prop, for example. The attributes in Listing 16-11 configure the child components to produce the result shown in Figure 16-7.

■ **Tip** You may have to reload the browser to see the results of this example.

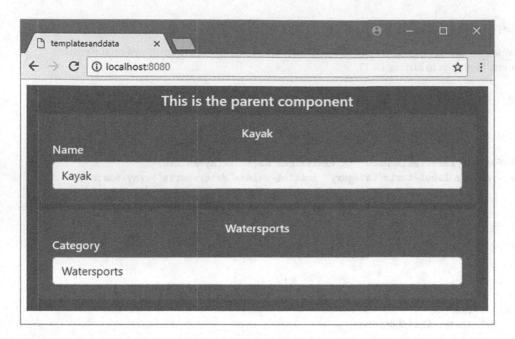

Figure 16-7. *Using a prop to configure a child component*

■ **Tip** Prop attribute values are literal, which means that the value is not evaluated as an expression. If you want to pass a string to the child component, then you can do so like this: `my-attr="Hello"`. You do not need to use double quotes: `my-attr="'Hello'"`. If you want a prop attribute value to be evaluated as an expression, then use the `v-bind` directive. If you want the child component to respond to prop changes in data bindings, then you can use a watcher, as described in Chapter 17.

When using a prop, it is important to bear in mind that the flow of data is only from the parent component to the child, as shown in Figure 16-8. You will receive a warning if you attempt to modify a prop value, reminding you that the prop should be used to initialize a data property, as shown in Listing 16-10.

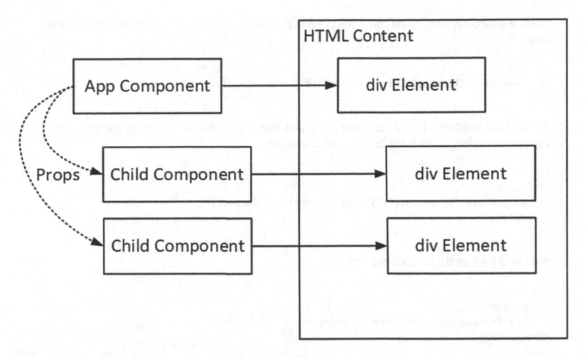

Figure 16-8. *The flow of data when using a prop*

SETTING REGULAR ATTRIBUTES ON CUSTOM HTML ELEMENTS

When Vue.js replaces a custom HTML element with a child component's template, it transfers any nonprop attributes to the top-level template element, which can lead to confusing results, especially if the element in the child's template already has this attribute. For example, if this is the child's template element:

```
...
<template>
    <div id="childIdValue">This is the child's element</div>
</template>
...
```

and this is the parent's template element:

```
...
<template>
    <my-feature id="parentIdValue"></my-feature>
</template>
...
```

then the attribute applied by the parent will override the child's attribute, producing HTML like this in the browser:

```
...
<div id="parentIdValue">This is the child's element</div>
...
```

The behavior is different for the `class` and `style` attributes, which browsers handle by combining the two attribute values. If this is the child's template element:

```
...
<template>
    <div class="bg-primary">This is the child's element</div>
</template>
...
```

and this is the parent's template element:

```
...
<template>
    <my-feature class="text-white"></my-feature>
</template>
...
```

then the browser will combine the `class` attribute values to produce the following HTML in the browser:

```
...
<div class="bg-primary text-white">This is the child's element</div>
...
```

Care must be taken when both the parent and child components set the same attribute, and ideally this situation should be avoided. If you want to make the parent responsible for specifying the HTML content presented by a child element, then use the slots feature, which I describe in the "Using Component Slots" section.

Using Prop Value Expressions

Prop attribute values are not evaluated as expressions unless the v-bind directive is used, as shown in Listing 16-12.

Listing 16-12. Using an Expression in the App.vue File in the src Folder

```
<template>
    <div class="bg-secondary text-white text-center m-2 p-2 h5">
        <div class="form-group">
            <input class="form-control" v-model="labelText" />
        </div>
        <my-feature v-bind:label-text="labelText" initial-value="Kayak"></my-feature>
    </div>
</template>
```

```
<script>
    import ChildComponent from "./components/Child";

    export default {
        name: 'App',
        components: {
            MyFeature: ChildComponent
        },
        data: function () {
            return {
                message: "This is the parent component",
                labelText: "Name"
            }
        }
    }
</script>
```

The parent component's template includes an `input` element that uses the `v-model` directive to bind to the `labelText` property. The same property is specified on the custom element for the child directive, which tells Vue.js to set up a one-way binding between the child component's `labelText` prop and the parent component's data property.

```
...
<my-feature v-bind:label-text="labelText" initial-value="Kayak"></my-feature>
...
```

The result is that when the parent component's `input` element is edited, the new value is received by the child component, where it is displayed by a text interpolation binding, as shown in Figure 16-9.

■ **Caution** The flow of changes remains one-way, even when using the `v-bind` directive. Changes made to the prop value by the child component are not received by the parent and will be discarded when the property used by the `v-bind` directive changes. See the next section for details of how to send data from a child component to its parent.

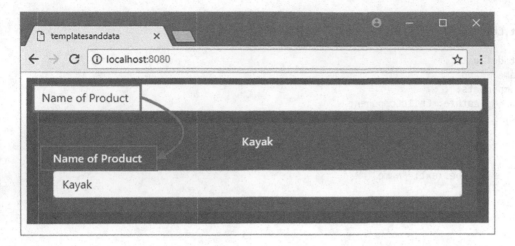

Figure 16-9. *Using a prop value expression*

Creating Custom Events

The counterpart to the props feature is custom events, which allow a child component to send data to its parent. To demonstrate the use of custom events, I expanded the functionality of the child component so that it provides some self-contained functionality, as shown in Listing 16-13, which is more typical of how components are used in real projects.

COMBINING PROPS AND CUSTOM EVENTS

At some point, most developers who are new to Vue.js development will try to get a parent and child component to both display and change the same data value by combining custom events, props, and the v-model directive. With a little effort, you will be able to get something working, but it goes against the purpose of these features and will always be a brittle solution that will occasionally act unpredictably and in ways that confuse the user. Use shared application state If you want multiple components to be able to display and change the same data values, as described in Chapter 20. For simpler applications, an event bus may suffice, as described in Chapter 18.

Listing 16-13. Adding Features to the Child.vue File in the src/components Folder

```
<template>
    <div class="bg-primary text-white text-center m-2 p-3 h6">
        <div class="form-group m-1 text-left">
            <label>Name</label>
            <input v-model="product.name" class="form-control" />
        </div>
        <div class="form-group m-1 text-left">
            <label>Category</label>
            <input v-model="product.category" class="form-control" />
        </div>
```

```
        <div class="form-group m-1 text-left">
            <label>Price</label>
            <input v-model.number="product.price" class="form-control" />
        </div>
        <div class="mt-2">
            <button class="btn btn-info" v-on:click="doSubmit">Submit</button>
        </div>
    </div>
</template>

<script>
    export default {
        props: ["initialProduct"],
        data: function () {
            return {
                product: this.initialProduct || {}
            }
        },
        methods: {
            doSubmit() {
                this.$emit("productSubmit", this.product);
            }
        }
    }
</script>
```

The component is a basic editor for product objects, with input elements that edit name, category, and price properties of an object assigned to the data property named product, whose initial data values are received using a prop called initialProduct.

There is also a button element that uses the v-on directive to respond to the click event by invoking a method called doSubmit. It is this method that allows the component to communicate with its parent, which it does like this:

```
...
doSubmit() {
    this.$emit("productSubmit", this.product);
}
...
```

The $emit method, which is called using the this keyword, is used to send a custom event. The first argument is the event type, expressed as a string, and the optional second argument is a payload for the event, which can be any value that the parent might find useful. In this case, I have sent an event called productSubmit and included the product object as the payload.

Receiving a Custom Event from a Child Component

The v-on directive is used by a parent component to receive events from its child components, just like with regular DOM events. In Listing 16-14, I have updated the App.vue file so that it provides the child component with the initial data to edit and responds to its event when it is triggered.

Listing 16-14. Responding to Child Component Events in the App.vue File in the src Folder

```
<template>
    <div class="bg-secondary text-white text-center m-2 p-2 h5">
        <h6>{{ message }}</h6>
        <my-feature v-bind:initial-product="product"
                    v-on:productSubmit="updateProduct">
        </my-feature>
    </div>
</template>

<script>
    import ChildComponent from "./components/Child";

    export default {
        name: 'App',
        components: {
            MyFeature: ChildComponent
        },
        data: function () {
            return {
                message: "Ready",
                product: {
                    name: "Kayak",
                    category: "Watersports",
                    price: 275
                }
            }
        },
        methods: {
            updateProduct(newProduct) {
                this.message = JSON.stringify(newProduct);
            }
        }
    }
</script>
```

The v-on directive is used to listen for the child component's custom event, using the name that was passed as the first argument to the $emit method, which is productSubmit in this example:

```
...
<my-feature v-bind:initial-product="product" v-on:productSubmit="updateProduct">
...
```

In this case, the v-on binding is used to respond to the productSubmit event by invoking the updateProduct method. The method used by the parent component receives the optional payload that the child component used as the second argument to the $emit method, and in this example, a JSON representation of the payload is assigned to the data property named message, which is displayed to the user through a text interpolation binding. The result is that you can edit the values displayed by the child component, click the Submit button, and see the data that is received by the parent component, as shown in Figure 16-10.

■ **Note** Custom events do not behave like regular DOM events, even though the v-on directive is used to process both of them. Custom events are passed only to the parent component and are not propagated through the hierarchy of HTML elements in the DOM, and they do not have capture, target, and bubble phases. If you want to communicate beyond the parent-child relationship, then you can use an event bus, as described in Chapter 18, or shared state, as described in Chapter 20.

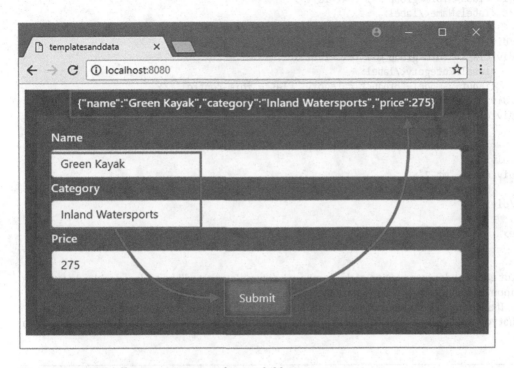

Figure 16-10. *Handling a custom event from a child component*

Using Component Slots

If you are using a component in different parts of the application, you may want to tailor the appearance of the HTML elements it presents to the user to suit the context.

For simple content changes, a prop can be used, or the parent component can directly style the custom HTML element that is used to apply the child component.

For more complex content changes, Vue.js provides a feature called *slots*, which allow a parent component to provide content through which the features provided by the child component will be displayed. In Listing 16-15, I have added a slot to the child component, which will be used to display content provided by the parent.

Listing 16-15. Adding a Slot in the Child.vue File in the src/components Folder

```
...
<template>
    <div class="bg-primary text-white text-center m-2 p-3 h6">
        <slot>
            <h4>Use the form fields to edit the data</h4>
        </slot>
        <div class="form-group m-1 text-left">
            <label>Name</label>
            <input v-model="product.name" class="form-control" />
        </div>
        <div class="form-group m-1 text-left">
            <label>Category</label>
            <input v-model="product.category" class="form-control" />
        </div>
        <div class="form-group m-1 text-left">
            <label>Price</label>
            <input v-model.number="product.price" class="form-control" />
        </div>
        <div class="mt-2">
            <button class="btn btn-info" v-on:click="doSubmit">Submit</button>
        </div>
    </div>
</template>
...
```

The slot element denotes a region of the component's template that will be replaced with whatever the parent component includes between the start and end tags of the custom element used to apply the child component. If the parent component doesn't provide any content, then Vue.js will ignore the slot element, which is what you will see if you save the Child.vue file and examine the content in the browser, as shown in Figure 16-11.

■ **Tip** You may have to reload the browser to see the effect of this example.

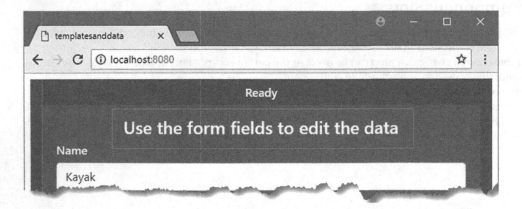

Figure 16-11. *Displaying the default content in a slot*

418

This provides a fallback that allows the child component to display useful content to the user. To override the default content, the parent component has to include elements in its template, as shown in Listing 16-16.

Listing 16-16. Providing Elements for a Slot in the App.vue File in the src Folder

```
...
<template>
    <div class="bg-secondary text-white text-center m-2 p-2 h5">
        <h6>{{ message }}</h6>
        <my-feature v-bind:initial-product="product"
                    v-on:productSubmit="updateProduct">
            <div class="bg-warning m-2 p-2 h3 text-dark">Product Editor</div>
        </my-feature>
    </div>
</template>
...
```

The div element that appears between the start and end tags of the my-feature element is used as the content for the slot element in the child component's template, producing the result shown in Figure 16-12.

Figure 16-12. *Providing content for a child component's slot*

Using Named Slots

If a child component can receive several regions of content from its parents, then it can assign names to its slots, as shown in Listing 16-17.

Listing 16-17. Adding Named Slots in the Child.vue File in the src/components Folder

```
...
<template>
    <div class="bg-primary text-white text-center m-2 p-3 h6">
        <slot name="header">
            <h4>Use the form fields to edit the data</h4>
        </slot>
```

```
            <div class="form-group m-1 text-left">
                <label>Name</label>
                <input v-model="product.name" class="form-control" />
            </div>
            <div class="form-group m-1 text-left">
                <label>Category</label>
                <input v-model="product.category" class="form-control" />
            </div>
            <div class="form-group m-1 text-left">
                <label>Price</label>
                <input v-model.number="product.price" class="form-control" />
            </div>
            <slot name="footer"></slot>
            <div class="mt-2">
                <button class="btn btn-info" v-on:click="doSubmit">Submit</button>
            </div>
        </div>
</template>
...
```

The name attribute is used to assign names to each slot element. In this example, I have assigned the name header to the element that appears above the input element and the name footer to the slot that appears below them. The footer slot contains no elements, which means that nothing will be displayed unless the parent component provides content.

To use a named slot, the parent adds a slot attribute to one of the elements contained between the custom start and end tags, as shown in Listing 16-18.

Listing 16-18. Using Names Slots in the App.vue File in the src Folder

```
...
<template>
    <div class="bg-secondary text-white text-center m-2 p-2 h5">
        <h6>{{ message }}</h6>
        <my-feature v-bind:initial-product="product"
                    v-on:productSubmit="updateProduct">
            <div slot="header" class="bg-warning m-2 p-2 h3 text-dark">
                Product Editor
            </div>
            <div slot="footer" class="bg-warning p-2 h3 text-dark">
                Check Details Before Submitting
             </div>
        </my-feature>
    </div>
</template>
...
```

The parent has provided div elements for each of the named slots, which produces the result shown in Figure 16-13.

■ **Tip** If the child component defines an unnamed slot, then it will display any elements from the parent's template that are not assigned to a slot with a `slot` attribute. If the child component doesn't define an unnamed slot, then the parent's unassigned elements will be discarded.

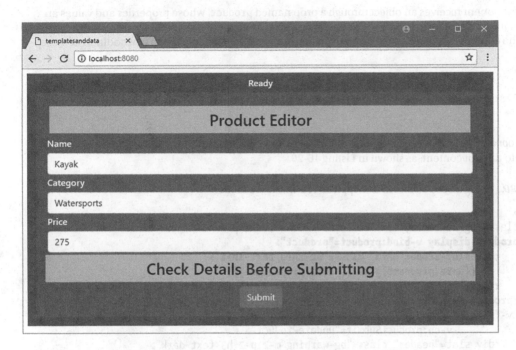

Figure 16-13. *Using named slots*

Using Scoped Slots

A scoped slot allows the parent component to provide a template into which the child component can insert data, which can be useful when a child component performs a transformation using data that it receives from the parent and the parent needs to control the formatting. To demonstrate the scoped slots feature, I added a file called `ProductDisplay.vue` in the `src/components` folder and added the content shown in Listing 16-19.

Listing 16-19. The Contents of the ProductDisplay.vue File in the src/components Folder

```
<template>
    <ul>
        <li v-for="prop in Object.keys(product)" v-bind:key="prop">
            <slot v-bind:propname="prop" v-bind:propvalue="product[prop]">
                {{ prop }}: {{ product[prop] }}
            </slot>
        </li>
    </ul>
</template>
```

```
<script>
export default {
    props: ["product"]
}
</script>
```

This component receives an object through a prop named `product`, whose properties and values are enumerated in the template using the `v-for` directive. The `slot` element provides the parent with a chance to replace the content that displays the property name and value but with the important addition of these attributes:

```
...
<slot v-bind:propname="prop" v-bind:propvalue="product[prop]">
...
```

The `propname` and `propvalue` attributes allow the parent component to incorporate the values they are assigned into the slot content, as shown in Listing 16-20.

Listing 16-20. Using a Scoped Slot in the App.vue File in the src Folder

```
<template>
    <div class="bg-secondary text-white text-center m-2 p-2 h5">
        <product-display v-bind:product="product">
            <div slot-scope="data" class="bg-info text-left">
                {{data.propname}} is {{ data.propvalue }}
            </div>
        </product-display>
        <my-feature v-bind:initial-product="product"
                    v-on:productSubmit="updateProduct">
            <div slot="header" class="bg-warning m-2 p-2 h3 text-dark">
                Product Editor
            </div>
            <div slot="footer" class="bg-warning p-2 h3 text-dark">
                Check Details Before Submitting
            </div>
        </my-feature>
    </div>
</template>

<script>
    import ChildComponent from "./components/Child";
    import ProductDisplay from"./components/ProductDisplay";

    export default {
        name: 'App',
        components: {
            MyFeature: ChildComponent,
            ProductDisplay
        },
```

```
        data: function () {
            return {
                message: "Ready",
                product: {
                    name: "Kayak",
                    category: "Watersports",
                    price: 275
                }
            }
        },
        methods: {
            updateProduct(newProduct) {
                this.message = JSON.stringify(newProduct);
            }
        }
    }
}
</script>
```

The slot-scope attribute is used to select a name for a temporary variable that is created when the templates are processed, and it will be assigned a property for each attribute that the child has defined on its slot element, which can then be used in data bindings and directives in the slot content, like this:

```
...
<product-display v-bind:product="product">
    <div slot-scope="data" class="bg-info text-left">
        {{data.propname}} is {{ data.propvalue }}
    </div>
</product-display>
...
```

The result is that the HTML elements from the parent component are mixed with the data provided by the child component, producing the result shown in Figure 16-14.

■ **Tip** Expressions and data bindings in scoped slot content are evaluated in the context of the parent, which means that Vue.js will look for any value you refer to that isn't prefixed with the variable named in the slot-scope attribute in the parent component's script element.

Figure 16-14. Using a scoped slot

Summary

In this chapter, I described the way that components are used as the building blocks for a Vue.js application, allowing related content and code to be grouped for ease of development and maintenance. I explained how components are isolated by default, how the prop and custom event features allow components to communicate, and how the slots feature allows a parent component to provide content to a child component. In Part 3 of this book, I describe the advanced Vue.js features.

PART III

■ ■ ■

Advanced Vue.js Features

CHAPTER 17

■ ■ ■

Understanding the Component Lifecycle

When Vue.js creates a component, it begins a well-defined lifecycle that includes preparing the data values, rendering the HTML content in the Document Object Model (DOM), and dealing with any updates. In this chapter, I describe the different stages in the component lifecycle and demonstrate the various ways a component can respond to them.

The component lifecycle is worth your attention for two reasons. First, the more you understand about how Vue.js works, the better prepared you are to diagnose problems when you don't get the results you expect. The second reason is that some of the advanced features that I describe in the chapters that follow are more easily understood and applied when you appreciate the context in which they operate. Table 17-1 puts the component lifecycle in context.

Table 17-1. *Putting the Component Lifecycle in Context*

Question	Answer
What is it?	Each component follows a well-defined lifecycle that begins when Vue.js creates it and ends when it is destroyed.
Why is it useful?	A well-defined lifecycle makes Vue.js components predictable, and there are notification methods that allow a component to respond to the different lifecycle stages.
How is it used?	Vue.js follows the lifecycle automatically, and no direct action is required. If a component wants to receive notifications about its lifecycle, then it can implement the methods described in Table 17-3.
Are there any pitfalls or limitations?	One of the main reasons for implementing the lifecycle notification methods is to use the DOM API to access the component's HTML content directly, rather than using directives or other Vue.js features. This can undermine the design of the application and make it harder to test and maintain.
Are there any alternatives?	You don't have to pay any attention to the component lifecycle, and many projects won't need to implement the notification methods at all.

© Adam Freeman 2018

A. Freeman, *Pro Vue.js 2*, https://doi.org/10.1007/978-1-4842-3805-9_17

Table 17-2 summarizes the chapter.

Table 17-2. *Chapter Summary*

Problem	Solution	Listing
Receive a notification when a component is created	Implement the beforeCreate or created method	8
Receive a notification when access to the DOM is permitted	Implement the beforeMount or mounted method	9, 10
Receive a notification when a data property changes	Implement the beforeUpdate or updated method	11–12
Perform a task after an update	Use the Vue.nextTick method	13
Receive notifications for individual data properties	Use a watcher	14
Receive a notification when a component is destroyed	Implement the beforeDestroy or destroyed method	15, 16
Receive a notification when there is an error	Implement the errorCaptured method	17, 18

Preparing for This Chapter

For the examples in this chapter, run the command shown in Listing 17-1 in a convenient location to create a new Vue.js project.

■ **Tip** You can download the example project for this chapter—and for all the other chapters in this book—from https://github.com/Apress/pro-vue-js-2.

Listing 17-1. Creating a New Project

```
vue create lifecycles --default
```

This command creates a project called *lifecycles*. Once the project has been created, add a file called vue.config.js to the lifecycles folder with the content shown in Listing 17-2. This file is used to enable the ability to define templates as strings, as described in Chapter 10, and I use it for one of the examples in this chapter.

Listing 17-2. The Contents of the vue.config.js File in the nomagic Folder

```
module.exports = {
    runtimeCompiler: true
}
```

Add the statement shown in Listing 17-3 to the linter section of the package.json file to disable the rule that warns when the JavaScript console is used. I rely on the console for many of the examples in this chapter.

Listing 17-3. Disabling a Linter Rule in the package.json File in the lifecycles Folder

```
...
"eslintConfig": {
    "root": true,
    "env": {
      "node": true
    },
    "extends": [
        "plugin:vue/essential",
        "eslint:recommended"
    ],
    "rules": {
        "no-console": "off"
    },
    "parserOptions": {
        "parser": "babel-eslint"
    }
},
...
```

Run the command shown in Listing 17-4 in the lifecycles folder to add the Bootstrap CSS package to the project.

Listing 17-4. Adding the Bootstrap CSS Package

```
npm install bootstrap@4.0.0
```

Add the statement shown in Listing 17-5 to the main.js file in the src folder to incorporate the Bootstrap CSS file into the application.

Listing 17-5. Incorporating the Bootstrap Package in the main.js File in the src Folder

```
import Vue from 'vue'
import App from './App.vue'

import "bootstrap/dist/css/bootstrap.min.css";

Vue.config.productionTip = false

new Vue({
  render: h => h(App)
}).$mount('#app')
```

The final preparatory step is to replace the contents of the root component, as shown in Listing 17-6.

Listing 17-6. Replacing the Contents of the App.vue File in the src Folder

```
<template>
    <div class="bg-primary text-white m-2 p-2">
        <div class="form-check">
            <input class="form-check-input" type="checkbox" v-model="checked" />
            <label>Checkbox</label>
        </div>
        Checked Value: {{ checked }}
    </div>
</template>

<script>

export default {
    name: 'App',
    data: function () {
        return {
            checked: true
        }
    }
}
</script>
```

Run the command shown in Listing 17-7 in the productapp folder to start the development tools.

Listing 17-7. Starting the Development Tools

```
npm run serve
```

The initial bundling process will be performed, after which you will see a message telling you that the project has compiled successfully and the HTTP server is listening for requests on port 8080. Open a new browser window and navigate to http://localhost:8080 to see the project's placeholder content, as shown in Figure 17-1.

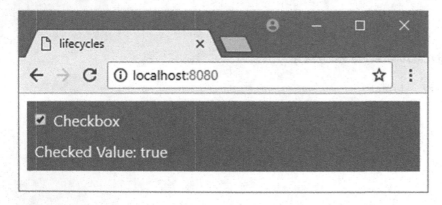

Figure 17-1. *Running the example application*

Understanding the Component Lifecycle

The component lifecycle starts when Vue.js first initializes a component. The lifecycle incorporates preparing the data properties, processing templates, dealing with data changes, and, ultimately, destroying a component when it is no longer required. For each stage in the lifecycle, Vue.js provides methods that it will invoke if implemented by a component. In Table 17-3, I describe each of the component lifecycle methods.

Table 17-3. *The Component Lifecycle Methods*

Name	Description
beforeCreate	This method is invoked before Vue.js initializes a component, as described in the "Understanding the Creation Phase" section.
created	This method is invoked after Vue.js initializes a component, as described in the "Understanding the Creation Phase" section.
beforeMount	This method is invoked before Vue.js processes the component's template, as described in the "Understanding the Mounting Phase" section.
mounted	This method is invoked after Vue.js processes the component's template, as described in the "Understanding the Mounting Phase" section.
beforeUpdate	This method is invoked before Vue.js processes an update to the component's data, as described in the "Understanding the Update Phase" section.
updated	This method is invoked after Vue.js processes an update to the component's data, as described in the "Understanding the Update Phase" section.
activated	This method is invoked when a component that has been kept alive with the keep-alive element is activated, as described in Chapter 22.
deactivated	This method is invoked when a component that has been kept alive with the keep-alive element is deactivated, as described in Chapter 22.
beforeDestroy	This method is invoked before Vue.js destroys a component, as described in the "Understanding the Destruction Phase" section.
destroyed	This method is invoked after Vue.js destroys a component, as described in the "Understanding the Destruction Phase" section.
errorCaptured	This method allows a component to handle an error thrown by one of its children, as described in the "Handling Component Errors" section.

Understanding the Creation Phase

This is the initial phase of the lifecycle, where Vue.js creates a new instance of a component and prepares it for use, including processing the properties in the script element, such as the data and computed properties. After it has created the component—but before it has processed its configuration object—Vue. js invokes the beforeCreate method. Once Vue.js has processed the configuration properties, including the data properties, the created method is invoked. In Listing 17-8, I have added both of the methods for this phase to the component.

Listing 17-8. Adding Creation Lifecycle Methods in the App.vue File to the src Folder

```
<template>
    <div class="bg-primary text-white m-2 p-2">
        <div class="form-check">
            <input class="form-check-input" type="checkbox" v-model="checked" />
            <label>Checkbox</label>
        </div>
        Checked Value: {{ checked }}
    </div>
</template>

<script>

export default {
    name: 'App',
    data: function () {
        return {
            checked: true
        }
    },
    beforeCreate() {
        console.log("beforeCreate method called" + this.checked);
    },
    created() {
        console.log("created method called" + this.checked);
    }
}
</script>
```

In the listing, the beforeCreate and created methods both write a message to the browser's JavaScript console that includes the value of the checked property.

■ **Note**   The lifecycle methods are defined directly on the object in the script element and not under the methods property.

Between the beforeCreate and created methods, Vue.js sets up the features that make components useful, including methods and data properties, and you can see the messages shown in the browser's JavaScript console.

```
...
beforeCreate method called undefined
created method called true
...
```

When the beforeCreate method is called, Vue.js has yet to set up the component's data properties and so the value of the checked property is undefined. By the time the created method is called, the setup has been performed, and the checked property has been created and assigned its initial value.

Understanding Component Object Creation

The message displayed by the beforeCreate method shows that Vue.js has created the component and assigned it to this before invoking the method. The object assigned to this is the component, and if there are multiple instances of a component used in an application, then there will be an object for each of them. As Vue.js goes through the initialization process, it is this object to which the data properties, computed properties, and methods are assigned. When you define a method, for example, you use the methods property on configuration object used to create the component; during initialization, Vue.js assigns the function you defined to the component object so that you can invoke it as this.myMethod(), without needing to worry about the structure of the configuration object. When Vue.js first creates the component object, it has few useful features, and most projects won't need to implement the beforeCreate event.

Understanding the Reactivity Preparations

One of the key Vue.js features is reactivity, where a change to a data property is automatically propagated throughout the application, triggering updates to computed properties, data bindings, and props to ensure that everything is up-to-date.

During the creation phase, Vue.js processes the component's configuration object from its script element. A property is added to the component object for each of the data properties, with a getter and setter so that Vue.js can detect when a property is read or modified. This means Vue.js is able to detect when a property is used and update the affected parts of the application—but it also means that you must ensure that you have defined all the data properties you require before Vue.js performs the creation phase.

■ **Tip** If an application requires external data, such as from a RESTful API, then the created method provides a good opportunity to request the data, as demonstrated in Chapter 20.

Understanding the Mounting Phase

During the second phase of the component lifecycle, Vue.js deals with the component's template, handling the data bindings, directives, and other application features.

Accessing the Document Object Model

If a component requires access to the Document Object Model (DOM), then the mounted event indicates that the component's content has been processed and can be accessed through a property called $el, which Vue.js defines on the component object.

In Listing 17-9, I have accessed the DOM to get data values that have been provided through an attribute on the HTML element that applies the component. As I explained in Chapter 16, any attributes applied to the HTML element that applies a component will be transferred to the top-level element in the component's template.

■ **Caution** Accessing the DOM directly should be done only when there is no alternative approach that fits better into the Vue.js model. This example, where data is provided through attributes, can be useful when integrating Vue.js into an environment that generates HTML documents programmatically. Such approaches should be used as an interim measure until a better approach can be implemented, such as using a RESTful API, as described in Chapter 20.

Listing 17-9. Accessing the DOM in the App.vue File in the src Folder

```
<template>
    <div class="bg-primary text-white m-2 p-2">
        <div class="form-check">
            <input class="form-check-input" type="checkbox" v-model="checked" />
            <label>Checkbox</label>
        </div>
        Checked Value: {{ checked }}
        <div class="bg-info p-2">
            Names:
            <ul>
                <li v-for="name in names" v-bind:key="name">
                    {{ name }}
                </li>
            </ul>
        </div>
    </div>
</template>

<script>

    export default {
        name: 'App',
        data: function () {
            return {
                checked: true,
                names: []
            }
        },
        beforeCreate() {
            console.log("beforeCreate method called" + this.checked);
        },
        created() {
            console.log("created method called" + this.checked);
        },
        mounted() {
            this.$el.dataset.names.split(",")
                .forEach(name => this.names.push(name));
        }
    }
</script>
```

The mounted method will be called after the template has been processed and its content added to the DOM, by which time the attributes added to the custom HTML element that applies the component will have been transferred to the top-level div element from Listing 17-9. Within the mounted method, I use the this.$el property to access the set of data- attributes to read the value of the data-names attribute, create an array, and push each item into the names data property, whose values are displayed in a list using the v-for directive.

■ **Tip** Notice that I have defined the `names` property and assigned it an empty array in Listing 17-9. It is important to define all the `data` properties before they are processed to set up reactivity; otherwise, the changes will not be detected.

In Listing 17-10, I have added a `data-name` attribute to the HTML element that applies the component.

Listing 17-10. Adding an Attribute in the main.js File in the src Folder

```
import Vue from 'vue'
import App from './App'

import "bootstrap/dist/css/bootstrap.min.css";

Vue.config.productionTip = false

new Vue({
  el: '#app',
  components: { App },
  template: '<App data-names="Bob, Alice, Peter, Dora" />'
})
```

The result is that the component uses the DOM API provided by the browser to read the attribute applied to its element and uses its contents to set a data property, as shown in Figure 17-2.

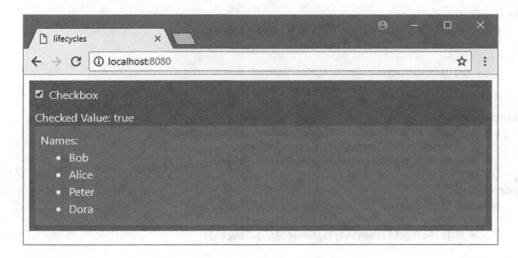

Figure 17-2. Accessing the DOM during the mounting lifecycle phase

Understanding Update Phase

Once the component has been initialized and its content has been mounted, it will enter the update phase, where Vue.js reacts to changes made to the data properties. When a change is detected, Vue.js will call a component's beforeUpdate method and call the component's updated method once the update has been performed and the HTML content has been updated to reflect the change.

Most projects don't need to use the beforeUpdate and updated methods, which are provided so that a component can access the DOM directly before and after a change. As with direct DOM access in the previous section, this is not something to be done lightly and should be performed only when none of the standard Vue.js features are suitable. For completeness, in Listing 17-11, I have implemented both methods for this phase.

Listing 17-11. Implementing the Update Phase Methods in the App.vue File in the src Folder

```
...
<script>
    export default {
        name: 'App',
        data: function () {
            return {
                checked: true,
                names: []
            }
        },
        beforeCreate() {
            console.log("beforeCreate method called" + this.checked);
        },
        created() {
            console.log("created method called" + this.checked);
        },
        mounted() {
            this.$el.dataset.names.split(",")
                .forEach(name => this.names.push(name));
        },
        beforeUpdate() {
            console.log(`beforeUpdate called. Checked: ${this.checked}`
                + ` Name: ${this.names[0]} List Elements: `
                + this.$el.getElementsByTagName("li").length);
        },
        updated() {
            console.log(`updated called. Checked: ${this.checked}`
                + ` Name: ${this.names[0]} List Elements: `
                + this.$el.getElementsByTagName("li").length);
        }
    }
</script>
...
```

The beforeUpdate and updated methods write out a message to the browser's JavaScript console that includes the values of the checked property, which include the first value in the names array and the number of li elements in the component's HTML content, which I access through the DOM. You will see the following messages displayed in the browser's JavaScript console when you save the changes to the component:

```
...
beforeCreate method called undefined
created method called true
beforeUpdate called. Checked: true Name: Bob List Elements: 0
updated called. Checked: true Name: Bob List Elements: 4
...
```

This sequence of messages reveals the initialization process that Vue.js goes through for the component. In the created method, I add values to one of the component's data properties, which leads to a corresponding change in the HTML content presented to the user. When the beforeUpdate method is called, there are no li elements in the component's content, and there are four li elements by the time the updated method is called and Vue.js has finished processing the update.

Understanding Update Consolidation

Notice there is only one call to the beforeUpdate and updated methods, even though I add four items to the names array. Vue.js doesn't respond to individual data changes, which would lead to a string of individual DOM updates, which are expensive to perform. Instead, Vue.js maintains a queue of pending updates that removes duplicate updates and allows changes to be batched together. To provide a clearer demonstration, I added a button element to the component that leads to changes to both data properties, as shown in Listing 17-12.

Listing 17-12. Making Multiple Changes in the App.vue File in the src Folder

```
<template>
    <div class="bg-primary text-white m-2 p-2">
        <div class="form-check">
            <input class="form-check-input" type="checkbox" v-model="checked" />
            <label>Checkbox</label>
        </div>
        Checked Value: {{ checked }}
        <div class="bg-info p-2">
            Names:
            <ul>
                <li v-for="name in names" v-bind:key="name">
                    {{ name }}
                </li>
            </ul>
        </div>
        <div class="text-white center my-2">
            <button class="btn btn-light" v-on:click="doChange">
                Change
            </button>
        </div>
    </div>
</template>
```

```
<script>
    export default {
        name: 'App',
        data: function () {
            return {
                checked: true,
                names: []
            }
        },
        beforeCreate() {
            console.log("beforeCreate method called" + this.checked);
        },
        created() {
            console.log("created method called" + this.checked);
        },
        mounted() {
            this.$el.dataset.names.split(",")
                .forEach(name => this.names.push(name));
        },
        beforeUpdate() {
            console.log(`beforeUpdate called. Checked: ${this.checked}`
                + ` Name: ${this.names[0]} List Elements: `
                + this.$el.getElementsByTagName("li").length);
        },
        updated() {
            console.log(`updated called. Checked: ${this.checked}`
                + ` Name: ${this.names[0]} List Elements: `
                + this.$el.getElementsByTagName("li").length);
        },
        methods: {
            doChange() {
                this.checked = !this.checked;
                this.names.reverse();
            }
        }
    }
</script>
```

Clicking the button invokes the doChange method, which toggles the value of the checked property and reverses the order of the items in the names array, as shown in Figure 17-3.

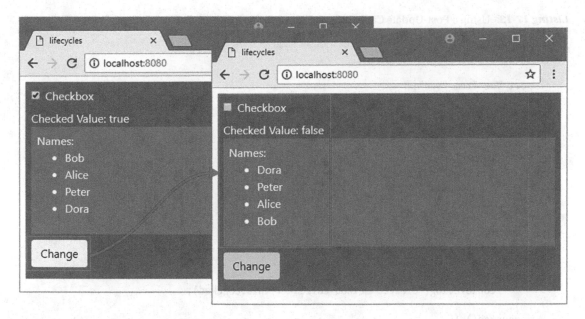

Figure 17-3. *Making multiple changes*

Despite changes to two different data properties, the messages displayed in the browser's JavaScript console show that only one update was performed to the component's HTML content.

```
...
beforeUpdate called. Checked: false Name:  Dora List Elements: 4
updated called. Checked: false Name:  Dora List Elements: 4
...
```

■ **Tip** The `beforeUpdate` and `updated` methods are called only if a change to one or more HTML elements is required. If you make a change to a data property that doesn't require a corresponding change to the component's HTML content, then these methods will not be invoked.

Using a Post-Update Callback

One consequence of the way that Vue.js consolidates and defers updates is that you cannot make a data change and then work directly with the DOM in the expectation that the effect of the change will have been applied to the component's HTML elements. Vue.js provides the `Vue.nextTick` method, which can be used to perform a task after all of the pending changes have been applied. In Listing 17-13, I have used `nextTick` in the `doChange` method to illustrate the sequence of actions and method calls.

Listing 17-13. Using a Post-Update Callback in the App.vue File in the src Folder

```
...
<script>

    import Vue from "vue";

    export default {
        name: 'App',
        data: function () {
            return {
                checked: true,
                names: []
            }
        },
        beforeCreate() {
            console.log("beforeCreate method called" + this.checked);
        },
        created() {
            console.log("created method called" + this.checked);
        },
        mounted() {
            this.$el.dataset.names.split(",")
                .forEach(name => this.names.push(name));
        },
        beforeUpdate() {
            console.log(`beforeUpdate called. Checked: ${this.checked}`
                + ` Name: ${this.names[0]} List Elements: `
                + this.$el.getElementsByTagName("li").length);
        },
        updated() {
            console.log(`updated called. Checked: ${this.checked}`
                + ` Name: ${this.names[0]} List Elements: `
                + this.$el.getElementsByTagName("li").length);
        },
        methods: {
            doChange() {
                this.checked = !this.checked;
                this.names.reverse();
                Vue.nextTick(() => console.log("Callback Invoked"));
            }
        }
    }
</script>
...
```

The nextTick method accepts a function and an optional context object as its arguments, and the function will be invoked at the end of the next update cycle. Save the changes, click the button, and you will see the following sequence of messages displayed in the browser's JavaScript console:

```
...
beforeUpdate called. Checked: false Name:  Dora List Elements: 4
updated called. Checked: false Name:  Dora List Elements: 4
Callback Invoked
...
```

The change that has led to the update is triggered by the doChange method, but the use of the nextTick method ensures that the callback isn't invoked until the effect of the change has been dealt with and the DOM has been updated.

Observing Data Changes Using Watchers

The beforeUpdate and update methods tell you when a component's HTML elements are updated but don't tell you what change was made, and these methods won't be called at all if the change is to a data property that isn't referred to in a directive expression or data binding.

If you want to receive a notification when a data property changes, then you can use a watcher. In Listing 17-14, I have added a watcher that will provide notifications when the data property named checked is changed.

Listing 17-14. Using a Watcher in the App.vue File in the src Folder

```
...
<script>

    import Vue from "vue";

    export default {
        name: 'App',
        data: function () {
            return {
                checked: true,
                names: []
            }
        },
        beforeCreate() {
            console.log("beforeCreate method called" + this.checked);
        },
        created() {
            console.log("created method called" + this.checked);
        },
        mounted() {
            this.$el.dataset.names.split(",")
                .forEach(name => this.names.push(name));
        },
        beforeUpdate() {
            console.log(`beforeUpdate called. Checked: ${this.checked}`
                + ` Name: ${this.names[0]} List Elements: `
                + this.$el.getElementsByTagName("li").length);
        },
```

```
            updated() {
                console.log(`updated called. Checked: ${this.checked}`
                    + ` Name: ${this.names[0]} List Elements: `
                    + this.$el.getElementsByTagName("li").length);
            },
            methods: {
                doChange() {
                    this.checked = !this.checked;
                    this.names.reverse();
                    Vue.nextTick(() => console.log("Callback Invoked"));
                }
            },
            watch: {
                checked: function (newValue, oldValue) {
                    console.log(`Checked Watch, Old: ${oldValue}, New: ${newValue}`);
                }
            }
        }
    }
</script>
...
```

Watchers are defined using a watch property on the component's configuration object, which is assigned an object containing a property for each property that is to be observed. A watch requires the property's name and a handler function that will be invoked with the new value and the previous value. In the listing, I have defined a watcher for the checked property that writes out both the new and old values to the browser's JavaScript console. Save the changes and uncheck the checkbox, and you will see the following sequence of messages, including the one from the watcher:

```
...
Checked Watch, Old: true, New: false
beforeUpdate called. Checked: false Name: Bob List Elements: 4
updated called. Checked: false Name: Bob List Elements: 4
...
```

Notice that the watcher's handler function is invoked before the beforeUpdate and updated methods.

USING THE WATCH OPTIONS

There are two options that can be used to change the behavior of watchers, although they require the watch to be expressed in a different way. The first option is immediate, which tells Vue.js to invoke the handler as soon as the watcher is set up, during the creation phase, between the period when the beforeCreate and created methods are invoked. To use this feature, the watcher is expressed as an object with a handler property and an immediate property, like this:

```
...
watch: {
    checked: {
        handler: function (newValue, oldValue) {
            // respond to changes here
        },
```

```
        immediate: true
    }
}
...
```

The other option is deep, which will monitor all the properties defined by an object assigned to a data property, which is more convenient than having to set up a separate watcher for each of them. The deep option is applied like this:

```
...
watch: {
    myObject: {
        handler: function (newValue, oldValue) {
            // respond to changes here
        },
        deep: true
    }
}
...
```

The deep option cannot be used to create a watcher for all the data properties, only individual properties that have been assigned an object. When you use a function for a watcher, you must not use an arrow expression because this won't be assigned to the component whose value has changed. Instead, use the traditional function keyword as shown.

Understanding the Destruction Phase

The final phase of the component lifecycle is its destruction, which typically happens when a component is being displayed dynamically and is no longer required, as demonstrated in Chapter 22. Vue.js will invoke the beforeDestroy method to give a component the opportunity to prepare itself and will invoke the destroy method after the destruction process, which removes watchers, event handlers, and any child components.

To help demonstrate this part of the lifecycle, I added a file called MessageDisplay.vue to the src/components folder with the content shown in Listing 17-15.

Listing 17-15. The Contents of the MessageDisplay.vue File in the src/components Folder

```
<template>
    <div class="bg-dark text-light text-center p-2">
        <div>
            Counter Value: {{ counter }}
        </div>
        <button class="btn btn-secondary" v-on:click="handleClick">
            Increment
        </button>
    </div>
</template>
```

```
<script>
export default {
    data: function () {
        return {
            counter: 0
        }
    },
    created: function() {
        console.log("MessageDisplay: created");
    },
    beforeDestroy: function() {
        console.log("MessageDisplay: beforeDestroy");
    },
    destroyed: function() {
        console.log("MessageDisplay: destroyed");
    },
    methods: {
        handleClick() {
            this.counter++;
        }
    }
}
</script>
```

This component displays a counter that can be incremented by clicking a button. It also implements the created, beforeDestroy, and destroyed methods so that the start and end of the component's lifecycle can be seen in messages written to the browser's JavaScript console. In Listing 17-16, I have simplified the example application's root component and applied the new component so that it is displayed only when the data value named checked is true.

Listing 17-16. Applying a Child Component in the App.vue File in the src Folder

```
<template>
    <div class="bg-primary text-white m-2 p-2">
        <div class="form-check">
            <input class="form-check-input" type="checkbox" v-model="checked" />
            <label>Checkbox</label>
        </div>
        Checked Value: {{ checked }}
        <div class="bg-info p-2" v-if="checked">
            <message-display></message-display>
        </div>
    </div>
</template>

<script>
    import MessageDisplay from "./components/MessageDisplay"

    export default {
        name: 'App',
        components: { MessageDisplay },
        data: function () {
```

444

```
        return {
            checked: true,
            names: []
        }
    }
}
</script>
```

As the checkbox is toggled, Vue.js creates and destroys the `MessageDisplay` component, as shown in Figure 17-4.

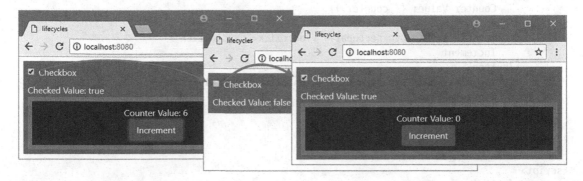

Figure 17-4. *Creating and destroying a component*

■ **Caution**   You should not rely on the destruction phase to perform important tasks because Vue.js won't always be able to complete the lifecycle. If the user navigates to another URL, for example, the complete application will be terminated without the opportunity to complete the lifecycle of the components.

When you uncheck the checkbox, the child component is destroyed, and its content is removed from the DOM. When you check the checkbox, a new component is created, and the lifecycle starts again. If you examine the browser's JavaScript console, you will see messages like these as one component is destroyed and another is created:

```
...
MessageDisplay: beforeDestroy
MessageDisplay: destroyed
MessageDisplay: created
...
```

If you click the Increment button before you toggle the checkbox, you will be able to see that the component's state is lost when it is destroyed. See Chapter 21 for details of how to create a shared state for an application that will survive individual component lifecycle changes.

Handling Component Errors

There is one phase that falls outside of the standard lifecycle, and it occurs when an error arises in a child component. To demonstrate this phase, I added the elements and code shown in Listing 17-17 to the MessageDisplay component to generate an error when a button is clicked.

Listing 17-17. Generating an Error in the MessageDisplay.vue File in the src/components Folder

```
<template>
    <div class="bg-dark text-light text-center p-2">
        <div>
            Counter Value: {{ counter }}
        </div>
        <button class="btn btn-secondary" v-on:click="handleClick">
            Increment
        </button>
        <button class="btn btn-secondary" v-on:click="generateError">
            Generate Error
        </button>
    </div>
</template>

<script>
export default {
    data: function () {
        return {
            counter_base: 0,
            generate_error: false
        }
    },
    created: function() {
        console.log("MessageDisplay: created");
    },
    beforeDestroy: function() {
        console.log("MessageDisplay: beforeDestroy");
    },
    destroyed: function() {
        console.log("MessageDisplay: destroyed");
    },
    methods: {
        handleClick() {
            this.counter_base++;
        },
        generateError() {
            this.generate_error = true;
        }
    },
    computed: {
        counter() {
            if (this.generate_error) {
                throw "My Component Error";
```

```
            } else {
                return this.counter_base;
            }
        }
    }
}
</script>
```

The component error-handling support can deal with errors that arise when a component's data is modified, when a watch function is executed, or when one of the lifecycle methods is invoked. It doesn't work when an error arises handling an event, which is why the code in Listing 17-17 responds to the button click by setting a data property that causes the counter computed property to generate an error using the throw keyword.

To handle errors from its children, a component implements the errorCaptured method, which defines three parameters: the error, the component that threw the error, and an information string that describes what Vue.js was doing when the error occurred. If the errorCaptured method returns false, the error won't be propagated further up the hierarchy of components, which is a useful way to stop multiple components from responding to the same error. In Listing 17-18, I have implemented the errorCaptured method in the application's root component and added elements to its template to display details of the error it receives.

Listing 17-18. Handling an Error in the App.vue File in the src Folder

```
<template>
    <div class="bg-danger text-white text-center h3 p-2" v-if="error.occurred">
        An Error Has Occurred
        <h4>
            Error : "{{ error.error }}" ({{ error.source }})
        </h4>
    </div>
    <div v-else class="bg-primary text-white m-2 p-2">
        <div class="form-check">
            <input class="form-check-input" type="checkbox" v-model="checked" />
            <label>Checkbox</label>
        </div>
        Checked Value: {{ checked }}
        <div class="bg-info p-2" v-if="checked">
            <message-display></message-display>
        </div>
    </div>
</template>

<script>
    import MessageDisplay from "./components/MessageDisplay"

    export default {
        name: 'App',
        components: { MessageDisplay },
        data: function () {
            return {
                checked: true,
                names: [],
```

447

```
                error: {
                    occurred: false,
                    error: "",
                    source: ""
                }
            }
        },
        errorCaptured(error, component, source) {
            this.error.occurred = true;
            this.error.error = error;
            this.error.source = source;
            return false;
        }
    }
}
</script>
```

The errorCaptured method responds to an error by setting properties of a data object named error, which is displayed to the user through the v-if and v-else directives. When you save the changes and click the Generate Error button, you will see the error message shown in Figure 17-5.

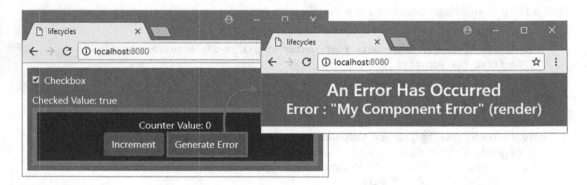

Figure 17-5. Handling an error

DEFINING A GLOBAL ERROR HANDLER

Vue.js also provides a global error handler, which is used to deal with errors that are not dealt with by the components in the application. The global handler is a function that receives the same arguments as the errorCaptured method but is defined on the application's top-level Vue object in the main.js file, rather than in one of its components.

The global error handler allows you to receive a notification when no other part of the application has dealt with a problem, which usually means you won't be able to do anything especially useful to recover from the situation. But if you need to perform a task when an error hasn't been handled elsewhere, then you can define a handler in the main.js file like this:

```
...
import Vue from 'vue'
import App from './App'
```

```
import "bootstrap/dist/css/bootstrap.min.css";

Vue.config.productionTip = false

Vue.config.errorHandler = function (error, component, source) {
    console.log(`Global Error Handler: ${error}, ${component}, ${source}`);
}

new Vue({
    el: '#app',
    components: { App },
    template: `<div><App data-names="Bob, Alice, Peter, Dora" /></div>`
})
...
```

This handler writes a message to the browser's JavaScript console, which is similar to the default behavior. There are error tracking services that allow developers to collate and inspect errors by pushing them to a central server for later analysis, and some of these provide out-of-the-box support for Vue.js applications using the global error handler, although they can become expensive to use if you have large numbers of users.

Summary

In this chapter, I described the lifecycle that Vue.js provides for its components and the methods that allow to you receive notifications at each stop. I explained how changes to data values are processed, how to access the component's HTML content in the DOM, how to observe data values using watchers, and how to handle errors. In the next chapter, I explain how to add structure to a Vue.js application using loosely coupled components.

CHAPTER 18

■ ■ ■

Loosely Coupled Components

As a Vue.js application grows, the need to pass data and events between parent and child components becomes harder to arrange, especially when components in different parts of the application need to communicate. The result can be components whose own functionality is overtaken by the need to pass on props for their descendants and relay events to their antecedents. In this chapter, I describe an alternative approach, known as *dependency injection*, which allows components to communicate without being tightly coupled to one another. I show you the different ways in which dependency injection can be used and demonstrate how it frees up the structure of an application. I also show you how to use an event bus, which combines dependency injection with the ability to register interest in custom events programmatically, allowing a component to send a custom event to any interested receiver, rather than just its parent. Table 18-1 puts dependency injection and event buses in context.

Table 18-1. Putting Dependency Injection and Event Buses in Context

Question	Answer
What are they?	Dependency injection allows any component to provide services to any of its descendants, where services can be values, objects, or functions. Event buses build on the dependency injection feature to provide a common mechanism for sending and receiving custom events.
Why are they useful?	These features allow the structure of an application to become more complex without being bogged down in managing parent-child relationship features that are used only to relay data to distant descendants and antecedents.
How are they used?	A component defines a service using the provide property and declares a dependency on a service using the inject property. Event buses are services that distribute a Vue object, which is used to send and receive events using the $emit and $on methods.
Are there any pitfalls or limitations?	Care must be taken to ensure that service and event names are consistently used throughout the application. Without care, different components will end up reusing a name that already has meaning to another part of the application.
Are there any alternatives?	Simple applications don't need the features described in this chapter and can rely on props and standard custom events. Complex applications can benefit from shared application state, which is a complementary approach that is described in Chapter 20.

© Adam Freeman 2018
A. Freeman, *Pro Vue.js 2*, https://doi.org/10.1007/978-1-4842-3805-9_18

Table 18-2 summarizes the chapter.

Table 18-2. *Chapter Summary*

Problem	Solution	Listing
Define functionality that can be used by a component's descendants	Use the dependency injection feature to define a service	10–12
Provide functionality that responds to changes	Create a reactive service by defining a data property and using it as the source for data values	13–14
Define functionality that will be used if no service is provided	Specify a fallback using an object with the inject property	15–16
Distribute custom events outside the parent-child relationship	Use an event bus	17
Send events using an event bus	Call the event bus $emit method	18
Receive events from an event bus	Call the event bus $on method	19, 20
Distribute events to only part of an application	Create a local event bus	21, 22

Preparing for This Chapter

For the examples in this chapter, run the command shown in Listing 18-1 in a convenient location to create a new Vue.js project.

■ **Tip** You can download the example project for this chapter—and for all the other chapters in this book—from https://github.com/Apress/pro-vue-js-2.

Listing 18-1. Creating a New Project

```
vue create productapp --default
```

This command creates a project called *productapp*. Once the setup process has finished, add the statement shown in Listing 18-2 to the linter section of the package.json file to disable the rules that warn when the JavaScript console is used and when variables are defined but not used. I rely on the console for many of the examples in this chapter and define placeholder variables that are used only when later features are introduced.

Listing 18-2. Disabling a Linter Rule in the package.json File in the lifecycles Folder

```
...
"eslintConfig": {
    "root": true,
    "env": {
      "node": true
    },
```

```
    "extends": [
        "plugin:vue/essential",
        "eslint:recommended"
    ],
    "rules": {
        "no-console": "off",
        "no-unused-vars": "off"
    },
    "parserOptions": {
        "parser": "babel-eslint"
    }
},
...
```

Next, run the command shown in Listing 18-3 in the `productapp` folder to add the Bootstrap CSS package to the project.

Listing 18-3. Adding the Bootstrap CSS Package

```
npm install bootstrap@4.0.0
```

Add the statement shown in Listing 18-4 to the `main.js` file in the `src` folder to incorporate the Bootstrap CSS file into the application.

Listing 18-4. Incorporating the Bootstrap Package in the main.js File in the src Folder

```
import Vue from 'vue'
import App from './App.vue'

import "../node_modules/bootstrap/dist/css/bootstrap.min.css";

Vue.config.productionTip = false

new Vue({
  render: h => h(App)
}).$mount('#app')
```

Run the command shown in Listing 18-5 in the `productapp` folder to start the development tools.

Listing 18-5. Starting the Development Tools

```
npm run serve
```

The initial bundling process will be performed, after which you will see a message telling you that the project has compiled successfully and the HTTP server is listening for requests on port 8080. Open a new browser window and navigate to `http://localhost:8080` to see the project's placeholder content, as shown in Figure 18-1.

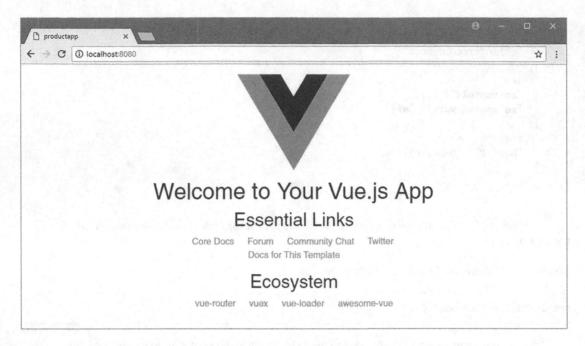

Figure 18-1. *Running the example application*

Creating the Product Display Component

The core of the example application will be a component that displays a table containing details of product objects, with buttons that will be used to edit or delete objects. I added a file called ProductDisplay.vue to the src/components folder with the content shown in Listing 18-6.

Listing 18-6. The Contents of the ProductDisplay.vue File in the src/components Folder

```
<template>
    <div>
        <table class="table table-sm table-striped table-bordered">
            <tr>
                <th>ID</th><th>Name</th><th>Price</th><th></th>
            </tr>
            <tbody>
                <tr v-for="p in products" v-bind:key="p.id">
                    <td>{{ p.id }}</td>
                    <td>{{ p.name }}</td>
                    <td>{{ p.price | currency }}</td>
                    <td>
                        <button class="btn btn-sm btn-primary"
                                v-on:click="editProduct(p)">
                            Edit
                        </button>
                    </td>
                </tr>
            </tbody>
        </table>
```

```
        <div class="text-center">
            <button class="btn btn-primary" v-on:click="createNew">
                Create New
            </button>
        </div>
    </div>
</template>

<script>
    export default {
        data: function () {
            return {
                products: [
                    { id: 1, name: "Kayak", price: 275 },
                    { id: 2, name: "Lifejacket", price: 48.95 },
                    { id: 3, name: "Soccer Ball", price: 19.50 },
                    { id: 4, name: "Corner Flags", price: 39.95 },
                    { id: 5, name: "Stadium", price: 79500 }]
            }
        },
        filters: {
            currency(value) {
                return `$${value.toFixed(2)}`;
            }
        },
        methods: {
            createNew() {
            },
            editProduct(product) {
            }
        }
    }
</script>
```

This component defines a data property named `products`, which is assigned an array of objects that are enumerated in the template using the `v-for` directive. Each `products` object produces a row in a table with columns for `id`, `name`, and `price` values, and a `button` element that will be used to edit the object. There is another button under the table that the user will click to create a new product, and the `v-on` directive has been applied to both `button` elements so that the `createNew` and `editProduct` methods are invoked when the buttons are clicked. These methods are empty at the moment.

Creating the Product Editor Component

I need an editor to allow the user to edit existing objects and create new ones. I started by adding a file called `EditorField.vue` to the `src/components` folder and added the content shown in Listing 18-7.

Listing 18-7. The Contents of the EditorField.vue File in the src/components Folder

```
<template>

    <div class="form-group">
        <label>{{label}}</label>
        <input v-model.number="value" class="form-control" />
    </div>

</template>

<script>

export default {
    props: ["label"],
    data: function () {
        return {
            value: ""
        }
    }
}

</script>
```

This component displays a label element and an input element. To combine the editor into a larger unit of functionality, I added a file called ProductEditor.vue to the src/components folder and added the content shown in Listing 18-8.

Listing 18-8. The Contents of the ProductEditor.vue File in the src/components Folder

```
<template>

    <div>
        <editor-field label="ID" />
        <editor-field label="Name" />
        <editor-field label="Price" />

        <div class="text-center">
            <button class="btn btn-primary" v-on:click="save">
                {{ editing ? "Save" : "Create" }}
            </button>
            <button class="btn btn-secondary" v-on:click="cancel">Cancel</button>
        </div>
    </div>

</template>
<script>

    import EditorField from "./EditorField";
```

```
    export default {
        data: function () {
            return {
                editing: false,
                product: {
                    id: 0,
                    name: "",
                    price: 0
                }
            }
        },
        components: { EditorField },
        methods: {
            startEdit(product) {
                this.editing = true;
                this.product = {
                    id: product.id,
                    name: product.name,
                    price: product.price
                }
            },
            startCreate() {
                this.editing = false;
                this.product = {
                    id: 0,
                    name: "",
                    price: 0
                };
            },
            save() {
                // TODO - process edited or created product
                console.log(`Edit Complete: ${JSON.stringify(this.product)}`);
                this.startCreate();
            },
            cancel() {
                this.product = {};
                this.editing = false;
            }
        }
    }
}
</script>
```

The editor presents a collection of editor components that can be used to edit or create objects. There are fields for the id, name, and price values, along with button elements that use the v-on directive to complete or cancel operations.

Displaying the Child Components

To complete the preparations for this chapter, I edited the root component to display the components created in the previous sections, as shown in Listing 18-9.

457

Listing 18-9. Displaying Components in the App.vue File in the src Folder

```
<template>
    <div class="container-fluid">
        <div class="row">
            <div class="col-8 m-3">
                <product-display></product-display>
            </div>
            <div class="col m-3">
                <product-editor></product-editor>
            </div>
        </div>
    </div>
</template>

<script>
    import ProductDisplay from "./components/ProductDisplay";
    import ProductEditor from "./components/ProductEditor";

    export default {
        name: 'App',
        components: { ProductDisplay, ProductEditor }
    }
</script>
```

The component displays its children side by side, as shown in Figure 18-2. Clicking the button elements has no real effect because the components are not yet wired up to work together.

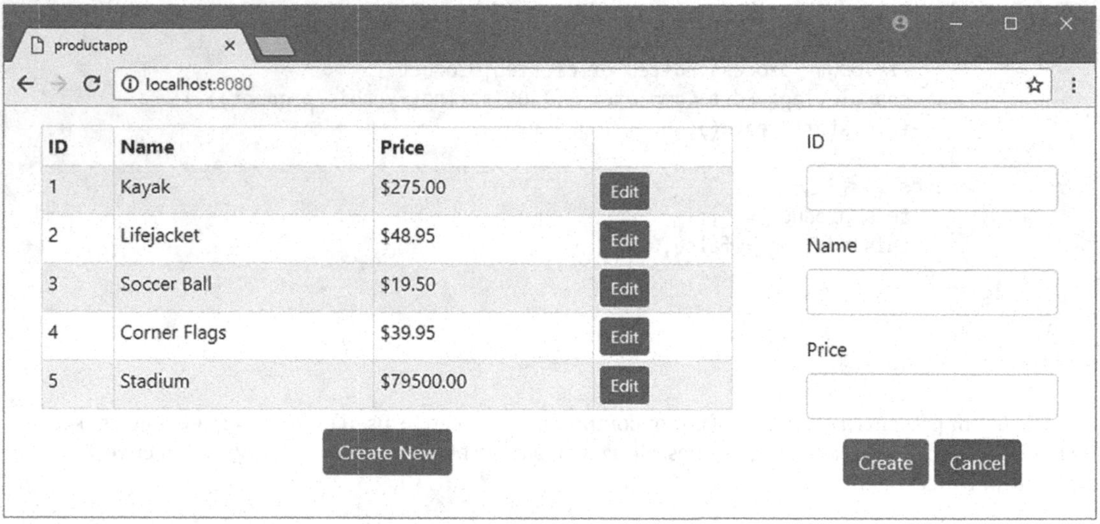

Figure 18-2. Adding features and components to the example application

Understanding Dependency Injection

Dependency injection allows a component to define a service, which can be any value, function, or object, and make it available to any of its descendants. Services provided through dependency injection are not limited to just children and avoid the need to pass data through a chain of props to distribute it to the part of the application where it is needed.

Defining a Service

In Listing 18-10, I have added a service to the root component that provides details of the Bootstrap CSS classes that should be used for background and text. This service will be available to all the components in the application since they are all descendants of the root component.

Listing 18-10. Defining a Service in the App.vue File in the src Folder

```
<template>
    <div class="container-fluid">
        <div class="row">
            <div class="col-8 m-3">
                <product-display></product-display>
            </div>
            <div class="col m-3">
                <product-editor></product-editor>
            </div>
        </div>
    </div>
</template>

<script>
    import ProductDisplay from "./components/ProductDisplay";
    import ProductEditor from "./components/ProductEditor";

    export default {
        name: 'App',
        components: { ProductDisplay, ProductEditor },
        provide: function() {
            return {
                colors: {
                    bg: "bg-secondary",
                    text: "text-white"
                }
            }
        }
    }
</script>
```

The provide property follows the same pattern as the data property and returns a function that produces an object whose properties are the names of the services that will be available to descendant components. In this example, I defined a service called colors whose bg and text properties provide the names of classes associated with Bootstrap CSS styles.

459

Consuming a Service via Dependency Injection

When a component wants to consume a service provided by its antecedents, it uses the inject property, as shown in Listing 18-11, where I have configured the EditorField component so it consumes the colors service defined in Listing 18-10.

Listing 18-11. Consuming a Service in the EditorField.vue File in the src/components Folder

```
<template>

    <div class="form-group">
        <label>{{label}}</label>
        <input v-model.number="value" class="form-control"
                v-bind:class="[colors.bg, colors.text]" />
    </div>

</template>

<script>

export default {
    props: ["label"],
    data: function () {
        return {
            value: ""
        }
    },
    inject: ["colors"]
}

</script>
```

The inject property is assigned an array that contains string values for the name of each service that the component requires. When the component is initialized, Vue.js works its way up through the component's antecedents until it finds a service with the specified name, gets the service value, and assigns it to a property with the service name on the component's object. In this example, Vue.js works its way up through the components looking for a service called colors, which it finds on the root component, and uses the object that the root component has provided as the value for a component called colors on the EditorField component. Creating a property that corresponds to the service allows me to use its properties in a directive expression like this:

```
...
<input v-model.number="value" class="form-control"
    v-bind:class="[colors.bg, colors.text]" />
...
```

The result is that the root component is able to provide the names of the classes that should be used to style elements without having to pass them through the chain of components. These classes names are applied to the EditorField component's input elements, producing the result shown in Figure 18-3. (You will have to enter some text into the input elements to see the text color.)

■ **Tip**   You may have to reload the browser before you see the effect of this example.

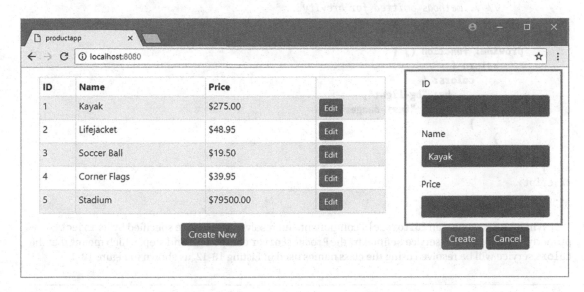

Figure 18-3. Using dependency injection

Overriding Antecedent Services

When Vue.js creates a component with an `inject` property, it resolves the dependencies on the services that are required, working its way up the chain of components and examining each to see whether there is a provide property with a service that matches the required name. This approach means a component can override one or more services that its antecedents provide, which can be a useful way to create more specialized services that apply to only part of the application. To demonstrate, I added a `provide` property to the `ProductEditor` component that defines a `colors` service, as shown in Listing 18-12.

Listing 18-12. Defining a Service in the ProductEditor.vue File in the src/components Folder

```
...
<script>

    import EditorField from "./EditorField";

    export default {
        data: function () {
            return {
                editing: false,
                product: {
                    id: 0,
                    name: "",
                    price: 0
                }
            }
        },
```

```
        components: { EditorField },
        methods: {

            // ...methods omitted for brevity...

        },
        provide: function () {
            return {
                colors: {
                    bg: "bg-light",
                    text: "text-danger"
                }
            }
        }
    }
}
</script>
...
```

When Vue.js creates an EditorField component and resolved the service specified by its inject property, it will reach the service defined by the ProductEditor component and stop, which means that the colors service will be resolved using the class names used in Listing 18-12, as shown in Figure 18-4.

▪ **Tip**   Each service is resolved independently, which means a component can choose to override only some of the services provided by its antecedents.

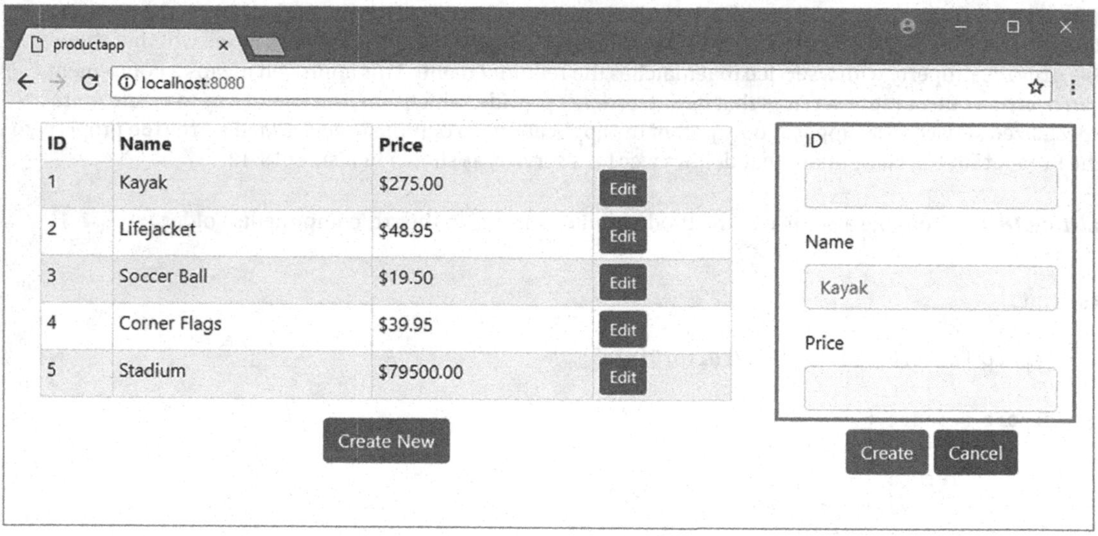

Figure 18-4. *The effect of overriding a service*

UNDERSTANDING THE ANONYMITY OF SERVICES

Dependency injection makes it possible to create loosely coupled applications because services are provided and consumed anonymously. When a component defines a service, it doesn't know which of its descendants will use it, whether it will be overridden by one another component, or even if it will be used at all.

Equally, when a component uses a service, it doesn't know which of its antecedents has provided it. This approach allows components that need data or functionality to receive it from those components that are able to provide it without needing to define rigid relationships or worry about passing it down through a series of parent-child relationships.

Creating Reactive Services

Vue.js services are not reactive by default, which means that any changes made to the properties of the object provided by the color service won't be propagated to the rest of the application. But, since Vue.js resolves dependencies for services each time a component is created, components created after a change will receive the new values.

If you want to create a service that does propagate changes, then you must assign an object to a data property and use this as the value for the service, as shown in Listing 18-13.

Listing 18-13. Creating a Reactive Service in the App.vue File in the src Folder

```
<template>
    <div class="container-fluid">
        <div class="text-right m-2">
            <button class="btn btn-primary" v-on:click="toggleColors">
                Toggle Colors
            </button>
        </div>
        <div class="row">
            <div class="col-8 m-3">
                <product-display></product-display>
            </div>
            <div class="col m-3">
                <product-editor></product-editor>
            </div>
        </div>
    </div>
</template>

<script>
    import ProductDisplay from "./components/ProductDisplay";
    import ProductEditor from "./components/ProductEditor";

    export default {
        name: 'App',
        components: { ProductDisplay, ProductEditor },
```

```
    data: function () {
        return {
            reactiveColors: {
                bg: "bg-secondary",
                text: "text-white"
            }
        }
    },
    provide: function() {
        return {
            colors: this.reactiveColors
        }
    },
    methods: {
        toggleColors() {
            if (this.reactiveColors.bg == "bg-secondary") {
                this.reactiveColors.bg = "bg-light";
                this.reactiveColors.text = "text-danger";
            } else {
                this.reactiveColors.bg = "bg-secondary";
                this.reactiveColors.text = "text-white";
            }
        }
    }
}
</script>
```

The component defines a data property named reactiveColors, which has been assigned an object with bg and text properties. During the component's creation phase, Vue.js processes the data property before the provide property, which means that the reactiveColors object is made reactive and subsequently used as the value for the colors service. To help demonstrate a reactive service, I have also added a button element that uses the v-on directive to invoke the toggleColors method, which changes the bg and text values.

For this example to work, I need to comment out the provide property in the ProductEditor component, as shown in Listing 18-14; otherwise, the service it provides will be used in preference to the one in Listing 18-13.

■ **Tip** You may have to reload the browser to see the changes in this example.

Listing 18-14. Removing a Service in the ProductEditor.vue File in the src Folder

```
...
<script>

    import EditorField from "./EditorField";

    export default {
        data: function () {
            return {
```

```
            editing: false,
            product: {
                id: 0,
                name: "",
                price: 0
            }
        }
    },
    components: { EditorField },
    methods: {

        // ...methods omitted for brevity...

    },
//      provide: function () {
//          return {
//              colors: {
//                  bg: "bg-light",
//                  text: "text-danger"
//              }
//          }
//      }
    }
</script>
...
```

The result is that when the button is clicked, the values of the service object's properties are changed and propagated throughout the application, as shown in Figure 18-5.

■ **Caution**   Any component can make changes to a reactive service and not just the component that defines it. This can be a useful feature, but it can also cause unexpected behavior.

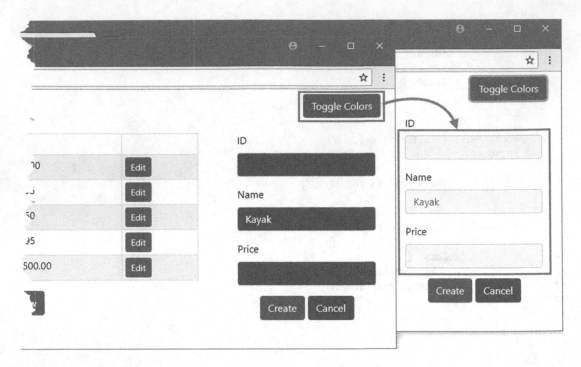

Figure 18-5. *Creating a reactive service*

Using Advanced Dependency Injection Features

There are two useful advanced features that can be used when consuming services. The first feature is providing a default value that will be used if no antecedents define a service that a component requires. The second feature is the ability to change the name by which the service will be known by the component. I have applied both of these features in Listing 18-15.

Listing 18-15. Using Advanced Features in the EditorField.vue File in the src/components Folder

```
<template>

    <div class="form-group">
        <label>{{ formattedLabel }}</label>
        <input v-model.number="value" class="form-control"
                v-bind:class="[colors.bg, colors.text]" />
    </div>

</template>

<script>

    export default {
        props: ["label"],
```

```
        data: function () {
            return {
                value: "",
                formattedLabel: this.format(this.label)
            }
        },
        inject: {
            colors: "colors",
            format: {
                from: "labelFormatter",
                default: () => (value) => `Default ${value}`
            }
        }
    }
```

```
</script>
```

These features require the value of the `inject` property to be an object. The name of each property is the name by which the service will be used inside the component. If no advanced features are required, then the value of the property is the name of the service that is required, like this:

```
...
"colors": "colors",
...
```

This property tells Vue.js that the component requires a service called `colors` and wants to refer to it as `colors`, which produces the same result as the earlier examples. The second property uses both of the advanced features.

```
...
inject: {
    colors: "colors",
    format: {
        from: "labelFormatter",
        default: () => (value) => `Default ${value}`
    }
}
...
```

The `from` property tells Vue.js that it should look for a service called `labelFormatter` provided by the component's antecedents but that the service will be known as `format` when it is used by the component. The `default` property provides a default value that will be used if none of the component's antecedents provides a `labelFormatter` service.

■ **Note**   A factory function is required when you provide default values for services, which is why the value of the `default` property in Listing 18-15 is assigned a function that returns another function as its result. When Vue.js creates the component, it will invoke the `default` function to get the object that will be used as the service.

The default value in this example is a function that prefixes the value it receives with Default so that it is obvious when the default service is used, producing the result shown on the left side of Figure 18-6.

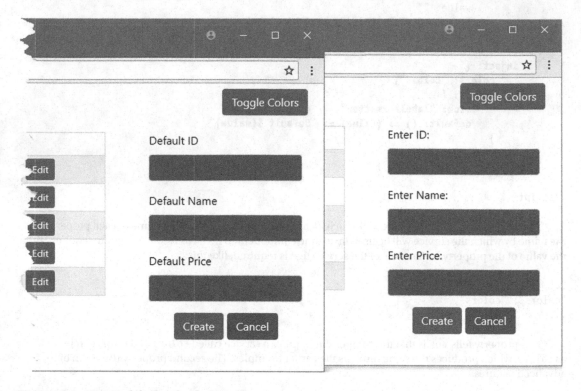

Figure 18-6. *Using a default value for a service*

The default value for the service has been used because none of the component's antecedents provides a service called labelFormatter. To demonstrate that a provided service will be used when it is available, I created a service with this name, as shown in Listing 18-16.

Listing 18-16. Defining a Service in the App.vue File in the src Folder

```
...
<script>
    import ProductDisplay from "./components/ProductDisplay";
    import ProductEditor from "./components/ProductEditor";

    export default {
        name: 'App',
        components: { ProductDisplay, ProductEditor },
        data: function () {
            return {
                reactiveColors: {
                    bg: "bg-secondary",
                    text: "text-white"
                }
            }
        },
```

```
        provide: function() {
            return {
                colors: this.reactiveColors,
                labelFormatter: (value) => `Enter ${value}:`
            }
        },
        methods: {
            toggleColors() {
                if (this.reactiveColors.bg == "bg-secondary") {
                    this.reactiveColors.bg = "bg-light";
                    this.reactiveColors.text = "text-danger";
                } else {
                    this.reactiveColors.bg = "bg-secondary";
                    this.reactiveColors.text = "text-white";
                }
            }
        }
    }
</script>
...
```

The new service is a function that transforms the values it receives by prefixing them with the word *Enter*, producing the result shown on the right side of Figure 18-6. Since this isn't a default value for a service, I don't need to define a factory function.

Using an Event Bus

Dependency injection can be combined with another advanced Vue.js feature to allow components to send and receive events outside beyond the parent-child relationship, producing a result known as the *event bus*. The first step in creating an event bus is to define the service in the Vue object, as shown in Listing 18-17.

Listing 18-17. Creating an Event Bus Service in the main.js File in the src Folder

```
import Vue from 'vue'
import App from './App.vue'

import "../node_modules/bootstrap/dist/css/bootstrap.min.css";

Vue.config.productionTip = false

new Vue({
  render: h => h(App),
  provide: function () {
      return {
          eventBus: new Vue()
      }
  }
}).$mount('#app')
```

The value for the service is a new Vue object. This may seem strange, but it produces an object that can be used to send and receive custom Vue.js events programmatically without relying on the application's hierarchy of components.

Sending Events Using an Event Bus

The $emit method is used to send events through an event bus, following the same basic approach that I demonstrated in Chapter 16 when I showed you how to send events to a component's parent. In Listing 18-18, I have updated the ProductDisplay component so that it uses the event bus to send custom events when the user clicks the Create New or Edit button.

Listing 18-18. Using the Event Bus in the ProductDisplay.vue File in the src/components Folder

```
...
<script>
    export default {
        data: function () {
            return {
                products: [
                        { id: 1, name: "Kayak", price: 275 },
                        { id: 2, name: "Lifejacket", price: 48.95 },
                        { id: 3, name: "Soccer Ball", price: 19.50 },
                        { id: 4, name: "Corner Flags", price: 39.95 },
                        { id: 5, name: "Stadium", price: 79500 }]
            }
        },
        filters: {
            currency(value) {
                return `$${value.toFixed(2)}`;
            }
        },
        methods: {
            createNew() {
                this.eventBus.$emit("create");
            },
            editProduct(product) {
                this.eventBus.$emit("edit", product);
            }
        },
        inject: ["eventBus"]
    }
</script>
...
```

The inject property is used to declare a dependency on the eventBus service, whose $emit method is used to send custom events called create and edit in the methods that are invoked when the user clicks the button elements presented by the component.

■ **Note** One drawback of the event bus model is that you must ensure that event names are unique within the application so that the meaning of events is not confused. If your application becomes too large to allow easy management of event names, then you should consider the shared state approach that I describe in Chapter 20.

Receiving Events from the Event Bus

The feature that allows the event bus model to work is that Vue.js supports registering for events programmatically, using the $on method, which can be performed once the component has been initialized and its dependencies on services have been resolved. In Listing 18-19, I have used the event bus in the ProductEditor component to receive the events sent in the previous section.

Listing 18-19. Receiving Events in the ProductEditor.vue File in the src/components Folder

```
...
<script>

    import EditorField from "./EditorField";

    export default {
        data: function () {
            return {
                editing: false,
                product: {
                    id: 0,
                    name: "",
                    price: 0
                }
            }
        },
        components: { EditorField },
        methods: {
            startEdit(product) {
                this.editing = true;
                this.product = {
                    id: product.id,
                    name: product.name,
                    price: product.price
                }
            },
            startCreate() {
                this.editing = false;
                this.product = {
                    id: 0,
                    name: "",
                    price: 0
                };
            },
```

```
        save() {
            this.eventBus.$emit("complete", this.product);
            this.startCreate();
            console.log(`Edit Complete: ${JSON.stringify(this.product)}`);
        },
        cancel() {
            this.product = {};
            this.editing = false;
        }
    },
    inject: ["eventBus"],
    created() {
        this.eventBus.$on("create", this.startCreate);
        this.eventBus.$on("edit", this.startEdit);
    }
}
</script>
...
```

The inject property is used to declare a dependency on the eventBus service, and the created method is used to register handler methods for the create and edit events, which are used to invoke the startCreate and startEdit method defined at the start of the chapter.

Components can both send and receive events through the event bus, and in Listing 18-19, I have used the $emit method to send an event called complete when the save method is called. This two-way communication allows me to easily compose complex behaviors, and in Listing 18-20, I have further updated the ProductDisplay component to update the data displayed to the user in response to the complete event, which signals that the user either has finished editing an existing product or has created a new one.

Listing 18-20. Receiving Events in the ProductDisplay.vue File in the src/components Folder

```
...
<script>

    import Vue from "vue";

    export default {
        data: function () {
            return {
                products: [
                    { id: 1, name: "Kayak", price: 275 },
                    { id: 2, name: "Lifejacket", price: 48.95 },
                    { id: 3, name: "Soccer Ball", price: 19.50 },
                    { id: 4, name: "Corner Flags", price: 39.95 },
                    { id: 5, name: "Stadium", price: 79500 }]
            }
        },
        filters: {
            currency(value) {
                return `$${value.toFixed(2)}`;
            }
        },
```

```
        methods: {
            createNew() {
                this.eventBus.$emit("create");
            },
            editProduct(product) {
                this.eventBus.$emit("edit", product);
            },
            processComplete(product) {
                let index = this.products.findIndex(p => p.id == product.id);
                if (index == -1) {
                    this.products.push(product);
                } else {
                    Vue.set(this.products, index, product);
                }
            }
        },
        inject: ["eventBus"],
        created() {
            this.eventBus.$on("complete", this.processComplete);
        }
    }
}
</script>
...
```

The created method is used to listen for the complete event and call the processComplete method when it is received. The processComplete method uses the id property as a key to update objects that have been edited or to add new objects.

The result is that the ProductDisplay and ProductEditor components are able to send and receive events that allow them to respond to each other's actions, outside of the parent-child relationship. There is still some key functionality missing, but if you click the Edit or Create New button, you will see that the text in the editor buttons will adapt accordingly, as shown in Figure 18-7.

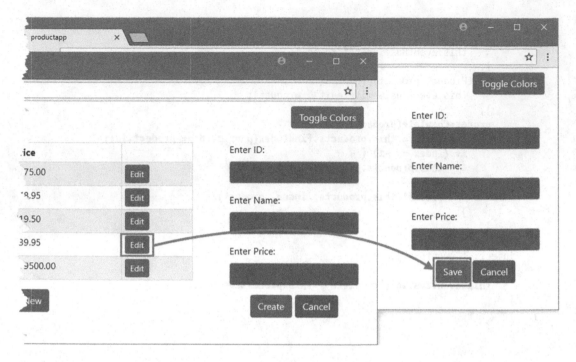

Figure 18-7. *Using an event bus*

Creating Local Event Buses

You don't have to use a single event bus for the entire application, and sections of the application can have their own bus and use custom events without distributing them to components that perform unrelated tasks. In Listing 18-21, I have added a separate event bus, called editingEventBus, to the ProductEditor component and used it to send and receive custom events that will wire up the individual editor fields with the rest of the application.

Listing 18-21. Creating a Local Event Bus in the ProductEditor.vue File in the src/components Folder

```
<template>

    <div>
        <editor-field label="ID" editorFor="id" />
        <editor-field label="Name" editorFor="name" />
        <editor-field label="Price" editorFor="price" />

        <div class="text-center">
            <button class="btn btn-primary" v-on:click="save">
                {{ editing ? "Save" : "Create" }}
            </button>
            <button class="btn btn-secondary" v-on:click="cancel">Cancel</button>
        </div>
    </div>

</template>
```

474

```
<script>

    import EditorField from "./EditorField";
    import Vue from "vue";

    export default {
        data: function () {
            return {
                editing: false,
                product: {
                    id: 0,
                    name: "",
                    price: 0
                },
                localBus: new Vue()
            }
        },
        components: { EditorField },
        methods: {
            startEdit(product) {
                this.editing = true;
                this.product = {
                    id: product.id,
                    name: product.name,
                    price: product.price
                }
            },
            startCreate() {
                this.editing = false;
                this.product = {
                    id: 0,
                    name: "",
                    price: 0
                };
            },
            save() {
                this.eventBus.$emit("complete", this.product);
                this.startCreate();
                console.log(`Edit Complete: ${JSON.stringify(this.product)}`);
            },
            cancel() {
                this.product = {};
                this.editing = false;
            }
        },
        inject: ["eventBus"],
        provide: function () {
            return {
                editingEventBus: this.localBus
            }
        },
```

```
        created() {
            this.eventBus.$on("create", this.startCreate);
            this.eventBus.$on("edit", this.startEdit);
            this.localBus.$on("change",
                (change) => this.product[change.name] = change.value);
        },
        watch: {
            product(newValue, oldValue) {
                this.localBus.$emit("target", newValue);
            }
        }
    }
}
</script>
```

There are a number of changes in this listing, but they all work toward providing a local event bus dedicated to events for editing a product object, combining features from previous sections and previous chapters. When the user starts to edit or create a new object, a target event is sent on the local event bus, and when a change event is received on that bus, the product object is updated, reflecting a change made by the user. Complementary changes are required in the component responsible for displaying the editor fields, as shown in Listing 18-22.

Listing 18-22. Using a Local Event Bus in the EditorField.vue File in the src/components Folder

```
<template>

    <div class="form-group">
        <label>{{ formattedLabel }}</label>
        <input v-model.number="value" class="form-control"
                v-bind:class="[colors.bg, colors.text]" />
    </div>

</template>

<script>

    export default {
        props: ["label", "editorFor"],
        data: function () {
            return {
                value: "",
                formattedLabel: this.format(this.label)
            }
        },
        inject: {
            colors: "colors",
            format: {
                from: "labelFormatter",
                default: () => (value) => `Default ${value}`
            },
            editingEventBus: "editingEventBus"
        },
```

```
    watch: {
        value(newValue) {
            this.editingEventBus.$emit("change",
                { name: this.editorFor, value: this.value});
        }
    },
    created() {
        this.editingEventBus.$on("target",
            (p) => this.value = p[this.editorFor]);
    }
}
```

</script>

The result is that clicking an Edit button allows the user to edit an existing object, clicking the Create New button allows the user to create a new object, and clicking the Create/Save button applies any changes that are made, as shown in Figure 18-8.

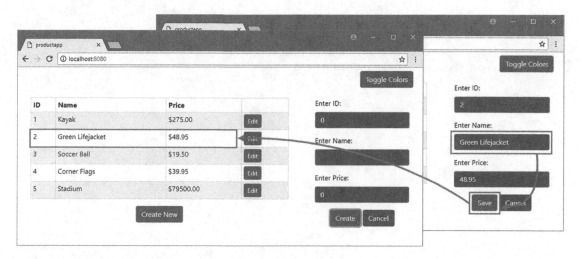

Figure 18-8. *Wiring up the editor components using a local event bus*

Summary

In this chapter, I explained how the Vue.js dependency injection and event bus features can be used to break through the parent-child relationship and create components that are loosely coupled. I demonstrated how to define and consume services, how to make services reactive, and how to create an event bus to distribute custom events throughout an application. In the next chapter, I explain how to use RESTful web services in Vue.js applications.

CHAPTER 19

■ ■ ■

Using RESTful Web Services

In this chapter, I demonstrate how to consume a RESTful web service in a Vue.js application. I explain the different ways that HTTP requests can be made and extend the example application so that it reads and stores its data from a server. Table 19-1 puts using web services n context.

Table 19-1. *Putting RESTful Web Services in Context*

Question	Answer
What are they?	RESTful web services provide data to web applications over HTTP requests.
Why are they useful?	Many applications need to access data and allow users to create, modify, and delete objects from a persistent data store.
How are they used?	The web application sends an HTTP request to the server, using the request type and the URL to identify the data and the operation that is required.
Are there any pitfalls or limitations?	There is no standard for RESTful web services, which means there is variation in the way that web services work. Within the Vue.js application, HTTP requests are performed asynchronously, which many developers find confusing. Special attention is required to deal with errors because Vue.js won't detect them automatically.
Are there any alternatives?	You don't have to use HTTP requests in a web application, especially if you have only small amounts of data to work with.

Table 19-2 summarizes the chapter.

Table 19-2. *Chapter Summary*

Problem	Solution	Listing
Get data from a web service	Create `Axios.get` method and read the response object's `data` property	10–14
Consolidate the code that accesses a web service	Create an HTTP service	15–17
Perform other HTTP operations	Use the Axios method that corresponds to the HTTP request type you require	18–19
Respond to errors	Consolidate the requests and use a `try/catch` block to trap and handle the error	20–23

© Adam Freeman 2018
A. Freeman, *Pro Vue.js 2*, https://doi.org/10.1007/978-1-4842-3805-9_19

Preparing for This Chapter

In this chapter, I continue working with the productapp project from Chapter 18. Follow the instructions in the following sections to prepare the example application for working with HTTP requests.

■ **Tip** You can download the example project for this chapter—and for all the other chapters in this book—from `https://github.com/Apress/pro-vue-js-2`.

Preparing the HTTP Server

I need an additional package to receive the HTTP requests made by the example application in this chapter. Run the command shown in Listing 19-1 in the productapp folder to install a package called json-server.

Listing 19-1. Installing a Package

```
npm install json-server@0.12.1
```

To provide the server with the data it will use to handle HTTP requests, add a file called restData.js in the productapp folder with the contents shown in Listing 19-2.

Listing 19-2. The Contents of the restData.js File in the productapp Folder

```
module.exports = function () {
    var data = {
        products: [
            { id: 1, name: "Kayak", category: "Watersports", price: 275 },
            { id: 2, name: "Lifejacket", category: "Watersports", price: 48.95 },
            { id: 3, name: "Soccer Ball", category: "Soccer", price: 19.50 },
            { id: 4, name: "Corner Flags", category: "Soccer", price: 34.95 },
            { id: 5, name: "Stadium", category: "Soccer", price: 79500 },
            { id: 6, name: "Thinking Cap", category: "Chess", price: 16 },
            { id: 7, name: "Unsteady Chair", category: "Chess", price: 29.95 },
            { id: 8, name: "Human Chess Board", category: "Chess", price: 75 },
            { id: 9, name: "Bling Bling King", category: "Chess", price: 1200 }
        ]
    }
    return data
}
```

To allow NPM to run the json-server package, add the statement shown in Listing 19-3 to the scripts section of the package.json file.

Listing 19-3. Adding a Script in the package.json File in the productapp Folder

```
...
  "scripts": {
    "serve": "vue-cli-service serve",
    "build": "vue-cli-service build",
    "lint": "vue-cli-service lint",
    "json": "json-server restData.js -p 3500"
  },
...
```

Preparing the Example Application

To prepare the example application for this chapter, I am going to remove some features that are no longer required, remove the data that was hard-coded into the application, and prepare for working with objects that have a category property in addition to the id, name, and price properties I used in Chapter 18.

Installing the HTTP Package

First, however, I am going to add the package that I will use to make HTTP requests. Run the command shown in Listing 19-4 in the productapp folder to install a package called Axios.

Listing 19-4. Installing a Package

```
npm install axios@0.18.0
```

Axios is a popular library for making HTTP requests in web applications. It isn't specifically written for Vue.js applications, but it has become the most common HTTP library used in Vue.js applications because it is reliable and easy to use. You don't have to use Axios in your own projects, and I describe the range of options in the "Choosing an HTTP Request Mechanism" sidebar.

Simplifying the Components

I simplified the ProductEditor component so that is displays the input elements for editing directly to the user, rather than through a separate component, which I used in Chapter 18 to demonstrate how to wire up different parts of an application. Listing 19-5 shows the simplified component.

Listing 19-5. Simplifying the Component in the ProductEditor.vue File in the src/components Folder

```
<template>

    <div>
        <div class="form-group">
            <label>ID</label>
            <input class="form-control" v-model="product.id" />
        </div>
        <div class="form-group">
            <label>Name</label>
            <input class="form-control" v-model="product.name" />
        </div>
```

```
        <div class="form-group">
            <label>Category</label>
            <input class="form-control" v-model="product.category" />
        </div>
        <div class="form-group">
            <label>Price</label>
            <input class="form-control" v-model.number="product.price" />
        </div>
        <div class="text-center">
            <button class="btn btn-primary" v-on:click="save">
                {{ editing ? "Save" : "Create" }}
            </button>
            <button class="btn btn-secondary" v-on:click="cancel">Cancel</button>
        </div>
    </div>

</template>

<script>

    export default {
        data: function () {
            return {
                editing: false,
                product: {}
            }
        },
        methods: {
            startEdit(product) {
                this.editing = true;
                this.product = {
                    id: product.id,
                    name: product.name,
                    category: product.category,
                    price: product.price
                }
            },
            startCreate() {
                this.editing = false;
                this.product = {};
            },
            save() {
                this.eventBus.$emit("complete", this.product);
                this.startCreate();
            },
            cancel() {
                this.product = {};
                this.editing = false;
            }
        },
```

```
        inject: ["eventBus"],
        created() {
            this.eventBus.$on("create", this.startCreate);
            this.eventBus.$on("edit", this.startEdit);
        }
    }
</script>
```

Next, I simplified the ProductDisplay component to remove the hard-coded data and add support for displaying category values, as shown in Listing 19-6.

Listing 19-6. Simplifying the Component in the ProductDisplay.vue File in the src/components Folder

```
<template>
    <div>
        <table class="table table-sm table-striped table-bordered">
            <tr>
                <th>ID</th><th>Name</th><th>Category</th><th>Price</th><th></th>
            </tr>
            <tbody>
                <tr v-for="p in products" v-bind:key="p.id">
                    <td>{{ p.id }}</td>
                    <td>{{ p.name }}</td>
                    <td>{{ p.category }}</td>
                    <td>{{ p.price }}</td>
                    <td>
                        <button class="btn btn-sm btn-primary"
                                v-on:click="editProduct(p)">
                            Edit
                        </button>
                    </td>
                </tr>
                <tr v-if="products.length == 0">
                    <td colspan="5" class="text-center">No Data</td>
                </tr>
            </tbody>
        </table>
        <div class="text-center">
            <button class="btn btn-primary" v-on:click="createNew">
                Create New
            </button>
        </div>
    </div>
</template>
```

```
<script>

    import Vue from "vue";

    export default {
        data: function () {
            return {
                products: []
            }
        },
        methods: {
            createNew() {
                this.eventBus.$emit("create");
            },
            editProduct(product) {
                this.eventBus.$emit("edit", product);
            }
        },
        inject: ["eventBus"]
    }
</script>
```

Finally, I simplified the App component by removing the button that was used to toggle the input element colors and the method and services that it used, as shown in Listing 19-7.

Listing 19-7. Simplifying the Component in the App.vue File in the src Folder

```
<template>
    <div class="container-fluid">
        <div class="row">
            <div class="col-8 m-3"><product-display/></div>
            <div class="col m-3"><product-editor/></div>
        </div>
    </div>
</template>

<script>
    import ProductDisplay from "./components/ProductDisplay";
    import ProductEditor from "./components/ProductEditor";

    export default {
        name: 'App',
        components: { ProductDisplay, ProductEditor }
    }
</script>
```

Running the Example Application and HTTP Server

Two command prompts are required for this chapter: one to run the HTTP server and the other to run the Vue.js development tools. Open a new command prompt in the productapp folder and run the command shown in Listing 19-8 to start the HTTP server.

Listing 19-8. Starting the RESTful Server

```
npm run json
```

The server will start listening for requests on port 3500. To test that the server is running, open a new web browser and request the URL `http://localhost:3500/products/1`. If the server is running and has been able to find the data file, then the browser will show the following JSON data:

```
...
{
  "id": 1,
  "name": "Kayak",
  "category": "Watersports",
  "price": 275
}
...
```

Leave the HTTP server running and open another command prompt. Navigate to the `productapp` folder and run the command shown in Listing 19-9 to start the Vue.js development tools.

Listing 19-9. Starting the Vue.js Development Tools

```
npm run serve
```

Once the initial bundling process is complete, open a new browser window and navigate to `http://localhost:8080`, where you will see the example application, as shown in Figure 19-1.

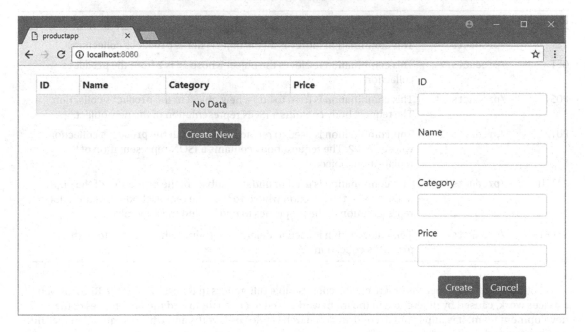

Figure 19-1. *Running the example application*

Understanding RESTful Web Services

The most common approach for delivering data to an application is to use the Representational State Transfer pattern, known as REST, to create a data web service. There is no detailed specification for REST, which leads to a lot of different approaches that fall under the RESTful banner. There are, however, some unifying ideas that are useful in web application development.

The core premise of a RESTful web service is to embrace the characteristics of HTTP so that request methods—also known as *verbs*—specify an operation for the server to perform, and the request URL specifies one or more data objects to which the operation will be applied.

As an example, here is a URL that might refer to a specific product in the example application:

```
http://localhost:3500/products/2
```

The first segment of the URL—products—indicates the collection of objects that will be operated on and allows a single server to provide multiple services, each of which with its own data. The second segment—2—selects an individual object within the products collection. In the example, it is the value of the id property that uniquely identifies an object and would be used in the URL, in this case, specifying the Lifejacket object.

The HTTP verb or method used to make the request tells the RESTful server what operation should be performed on the specified object. When you tested the RESTful server in the previous section, the browser sent an HTTP GET request, which the server interprets as an instruction to retrieve the specified object and send it to the client. It is for this reason that the browser displayed a JSON representation of the Lifejacket object.

Table 19-3 shows the most common combination of HTTP methods and URLs and explains what each of them does when sent to a RESTful server.

Table 19-3. *Common HTTP Methods and Their Effect in a RESTful Web Service*

Method	URL	Description
GET	/products	This combination retrieves all the objects in the products collection.
GET	/products/2	This combination retrieves the object whose id is 2 from the products collection.
POST	/products	This combination is used to add a new object to the products collection. The request body contains a JSON representation of the new object.
PUT	/products/2	This combination is used to replace the object in the products collection whose id is 2. The request body contains a JSON representation of the replacement object.
PATCH	/products/2	This combination is used to update a subset of the properties of the object in the products collection whose id is 2. The request body contains a JSON representation of the properties to update and the new values.
DELETE	/products/2	This combination is used to delete the product whose id is 2 from the products collection.

Caution is required because there can be considerable differences in the way that some RESTful web services work, caused by differences in the frameworks used to create them and the preferences of the development team. It is important to confirm how a web service uses verbs and what is required in the URL and request body to perform operations.

Some common variations include web services that won't accept any request bodies that contain id values (to ensure they are generated uniquely by the server's data store) and web services that don't support all of the verbs (it is common to ignore PATCH requests and only accept updates using the PUT verb).

CHOOSING AN HTTP REQUEST MECHANISM

There are three different ways of making asynchronous HTTP requests. The first approach is to use the XMLHttpRequest object, which is the original mechanism for asynchronous requests and dates from when XML was the standard data format for web applications. Here is a fragment of code that sends an HTTP request to the RESTful web service used throughout this chapter:

```
...
let request = new XMLHttpRequest();
request.onreadystatechange = () => {
    if (request.readyState == XMLHttpRequest.DONE && request.status == 200) {
        this.products.push(...JSON.parse(request.responseText));
    }
};
request.open("GET", "http://localhost:3500/products");
request.send();
...
```

The API presented by the XMLHttpRequest object uses an event handler to receive updates, including details of the response from the server when the request completes. The XMLHttpRequest is awkward to use, and there is no support for modern features like the async/await keywords, but you can rely on it being available in all of the browsers that can run Vue.js applications. You can learn more about the XMLHttpRequest API at https://developer.mozilla.org/en-US/docs/Web/API/XMLHttpRequest.

The second approach is to use the Fetch API, which is a recent replacement for the XMLHttpRequest object. The Fetch API uses promises, rather than events, and is generally easier to work with. Here is a fragment of code that gets the product data, equivalent to the XMLHttpRequest example:

```
...
fetch("http://localhost:3500/products")
    .then(response => response.json())
    .then(data => this.products.push(...data));
...
```

If anything, the Fetch API uses too many promises. The fetch method is used to make the HTTP request, which returns a promise that yields a result object, whose json method yields the eventual results of the request parsed from the JSON data. The Fetch API can be used with the async and await keywords, but dealing with the multiple promises requires care and can result in tortured statements like this one:

```
...
this.products.push(
    ...await (await fetch("http://localhost:3500/products")).json());
...
```

The Fetch API is an improvement on XMLHttpRequest, but it isn't supported in all browsers that can run Vue.js applications. You can find details of the Fetch API at https://developer.mozilla.org/en-US/docs/Web/API/Fetch_API.

The third approach is to use a package that uses the XMLHttpRequest object but hides the details and presents an API that is more consistent with the rest of the Vue.js development experience. I used the Axios package in this chapter because it is the most popular, but there are many choices available. Vue.js doesn't have an "official" HTTP package, but there are plenty of choices, and even packages that are not specifically written for Vue.js are easy to use, as this chapter demonstrates. The drawback of using an HTTP package is that the size of your application will increase because additional code will be required by the browser.

Consuming a RESTful Web Service

The most important thing to understand about the HTTP requests that a web application makes is they are asynchronous. This may seem obvious, but it causes confusion because the response from the server won't be available immediately. As a consequence, the code required for HTTP requests has to be written carefully and requires the JavaScript features for dealing with asynchronous operations. Because HTTP requests cause so much confusion, I am going to build up the code for the first request in a step-by-step fashion in the sections that follow.

MAKING CROSS-ORIGIN REQUESTS

By default, browsers enforce a security policy that only allows JavaScript code to make asynchronous HTTP requests within the same origin as the document that contains them. This policy is intended to reduce the risk of cross-site scripting (CSS) attacks, where the browser is tricked into executing malicious code, which is well-described at http://en.wikipedia.org/wiki/Cross-site_scripting. For web application developers, the same-origin policy can be a problem when using web services because they are typically outside of the origin that contains the application's JavaScript code. Two URLs are considered to be in the same origin if they have the same protocol, host, and port and have different origins if this is not the case. The URL that I use for the RESTful web service in this chapter has a different origin than the URL used by the main application because they use different TCP ports.

The Cross-Origin Resource Sharing (CORS) protocol is used to send requests to different origins. With CORS, the browser includes headers in the asynchronous HTTP request that provide the server with the origin of the JavaScript code. The response from the server includes headers that tell the browser whether it is willing to accept the request. The details of CORS are outside the scope of this book, but there is an introduction to the topic at https://en.wikipedia.org/wiki/Cross-origin_resource_sharing, and the CORS specification is available at www.w3.org/TR/cors.

CORS is something that happens automatically in this chapter. The json-server package that provides the RESTful web service supports CORS and will accept requests from any origin, while the Axios package that I use to make HTTP requests automatically applies CORS. When you select software for your own projects, you must either select a platform that will allow all requests to be handled through a single origin or configure CORS so that the server will accept the application's requests for data.

Handling the Response Data

It may seem counterintuitive, but the best place to start is with the code that will handle the data you expect to receive from the server. In Listing 19-10, I have added a method to the script element of the ProductDisplay component that will process the product data when it is received from the RESTful web service.

Listing 19-10. Adding a Method in the ProductDisplay.vue File in the src/components Folder

```
...
<script>

    import Vue from "vue";

    export default {
        data: function () {
            return {
                products: []
            }
        },
        methods: {
            createNew() {
                this.eventBus.$emit("create");
            },
            editProduct(product) {
                this.eventBus.$emit("edit", product);
            },
            processProducts(newProducts) {
                this.products.splice(0);
                this.products.push(...newProducts);
            }
        },
        inject: ["eventBus"]
    }
</script>
...
```

The processProducts method will receive an array of product objects and use them to replace the contents of the data property named products. As I explained in Chapter 13, Vue.js has some difficulties detecting changes in arrays, so I used the splice method to remove any existing objects. I then used the destructuring operator to unpack the values in the method's argument and used the push method to repopulate the array. Since the products array is a reactive data property, Vue.js will detect the changes automatically and update the data bindings to reflect the new data.

Making the HTTP Request

The next step is to make the HTTP request and ask the RESTful web service for data. In Listing 19-11, I have imported the Axios package and used it to send an HTTP request.

Listing 19-11. Making an HTTP Request in the ProductDisplay.vue File in the src/components Folder

```
...
<script>

    import Vue from "vue";
    import Axios from "axios";

    const baseUrl = "http://localhost:3500/products/";

    export default {
        data: function () {
            return {
                products: []
            }
        },
        methods: {
            createNew() {
                this.eventBus.$emit("create");
            },
            editProduct(product) {
                this.eventBus.$emit("edit", product);
            },
            processProducts(newProducts) {
                this.products.splice(0);
                this.products.push(...newProducts);
            }
        },
        inject: ["eventBus"],
        created() {
            Axios.get(baseUrl);
        }
    }
</script>
...
```

Axios provides methods for each of the HTTP request types, such that GET requests are made using the get method, POST requests are made using the post method, and so on. There is also a request method that accepts a configuration object and can be used to make all types of requests; I use it in the "Creating an Error Handling Service" section.

I make the HTTP request in the component's created method. I want the result from my request to trigger the Vue.js change mechanism when the data is received, and using the created method ensures that the component's data properties have been processed before I make the request to the HTTP server.

■ **Tip** Some developers prefer to use the mounted method to make initial HTTP requests. It doesn't matter which method you use, but it is a good idea to be consistent so that all of your components behave the same.

Receiving the Response

The result from the Axios get method is a Promise that will produce the response from the server when the HTTP request has completed. As I explained in Chapter 4, the then method is used to specify what will happen when the work represented by a Promise is complete, and in Listing 19-12, I have used the then method to process the HTTP response.

Listing 19-12. Receiving the HTTP Response in the ProductDisplay.vue File in the src/components Folder

```
...
<script>

    import Vue from "vue";
    import Axios from "axios";

    const baseUrl = "http://localhost:3500/products/";

    export default {
        data: function () {
            return {
                products: []
            }
        },
        methods: {
            createNew() {
                this.eventBus.$emit("create");
            },
            editProduct(product) {
                this.eventBus.$emit("edit", product);
            },
            processProducts(newProducts) {
                this.products.splice(0);
                this.products.push(...newProducts);
            }
        },
        inject: ["eventBus"],
        created() {
            Axios.get(baseUrl).then(resp => {
                console.log(`HTTP Response: ${resp.status}, ${resp.statusText}`);
                console.log(`Response Data: ${resp.data.length} items`);
            });
        }
    }
</script>
...
```

The then method receives an object from Axios that represents the response from the server and that defines the properties shown in Table 19-4.

Table 19-4. *The Axios Response Properties*

Name	Description
status	This property returns the status code for the response, such as 200 or 404.
statusText	This property returns the explanatory text that accompanies the status code, such as OK or Not Found.
headers	This property returns an object whose properties represent the response headers.
data	This property returns the payload from the response.
config	This property returns an object that contains the configuration options used to make the request.
request	This property returns the XMLHttpRequest object that was used to make the request.

In Listing 19-12, I use the status and statusText properties to write out details of the response to the browser's JavaScript console. Of more interest is the data property, which returns the payload sent by the server and which Axios automatically decodes for JSON responses, which means I can read the length property to find out how many objects have been included in the response. Save the changes to the component and examine the browser's JavaScript console, and you will see the following messages:

```
...
HTTP Response: 200, OK
Response Data: 9 items
...
```

Processing the Data

The final step is to read the data property from the response object and pass it to the processProducts method so that the objects obtained from the RESTful web service will update the application, as shown in Listing 19-13.

Listing 19-13. Processing the Response in the ProductDisplay.vue File in the src/components Folder

```
...
<script>

    import Vue from "vue";
    import Axios from "axios";

    const baseUrl = "http://localhost:3500/products/";

    export default {
        data: function () {
            return {
                products: []
            }
        },
        methods: {
            createNew() {
                this.eventBus.$emit("create");
            },
```

```
        editProduct(product) {
            this.eventBus.$emit("edit", product);
        },
        processProducts(newProducts) {
            this.products.splice(0);
            this.products.push(...newProducts);
        }
    },
    inject: ["eventBus"],
    created() {
        Axios.get(baseUrl).then(resp => this.processProducts(resp.data));
    }
}
</script>
...
```

The effect is that the component will initiate an HTTP GET request in its created method. When the response is received from the server, Axios parses the JSON data it contains and makes it available as part of the response. The response data is used to populate the component's products array, and the consequent update evaluates the v-for directive in the template and displays the data shown in Figure 19-2.

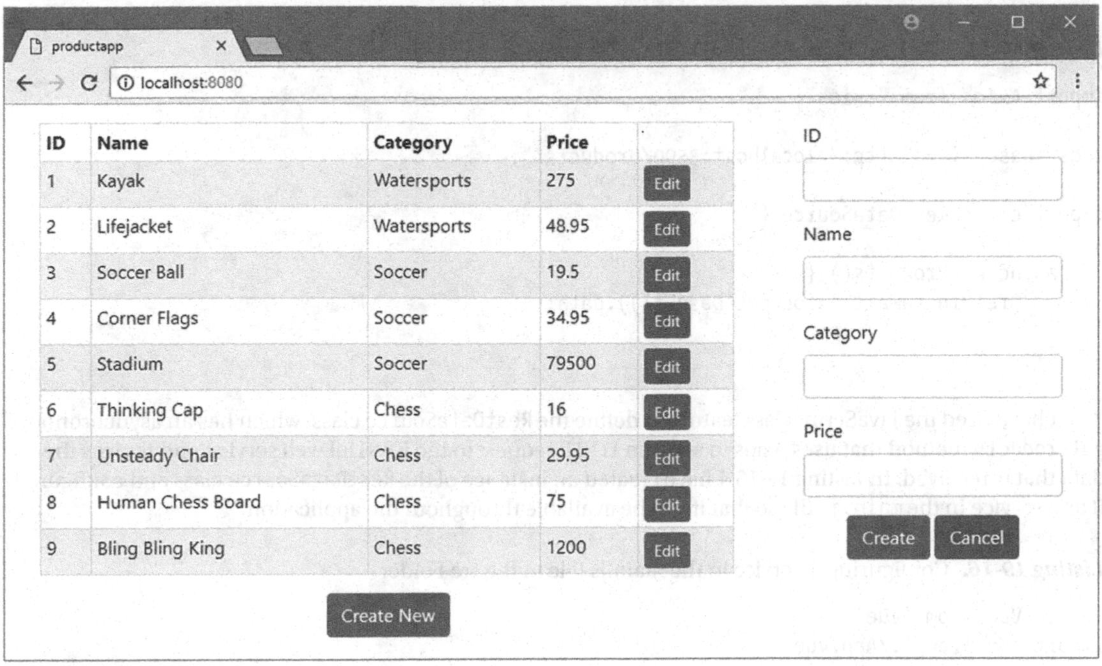

Figure 19-2. Getting data from the web service

I can streamline this code using the async/await keywords, which will let me make HTTP requests without having to rely on the then method, which some developers find confusing. In Listing 19-14, I have applied the async keyword to the create method and have used the await keyword to make the HTTP request.

Listing 19-14. Streamlining the Request Code in the ProductDisplay.vue File in the src/components Folder

```
...
async created() {
    let data = (await Axios.get(baseUrl)).data;
    this.processProducts(data);
}
...
```

This code works in the same way as the code in Listing 19-13 but without the use of the then method to specify the statements that will be executed when the HTTP request has completed.

Creating an HTTP Service

Before I go any further, I am going to change the structure of the application. The approach I took in the previous section demonstrated how easy it is to make HTTP requests in a component, but the result is that the functionality provided by the component to the user has been diluted with the code required to communicate with the server. As the range of request types increases, the component will become increasingly dedicated to dealing with HTTP.

I added a JavaScript file called restDataSource.js to the src folder and used it to define the JavaScript class shown in Listing 19-15.

Listing 19-15. The Contents of the restDataSource.js File in the src Folder

```
import Axios from "axios";

const baseUrl = "http://localhost:3500/products/";

export class RestDataSource {

    async getProducts() {
        return (await Axios.get(baseUrl)).data;
    }
}
```

I have used the JavaScript class feature to define the RestDataSource class, which has an asynchronous getProducts method that uses Axios to send an HTTP request to the RESTful web service and returns the data that is received. In Listing 19-16, I have created an instance of the RestDataSource class and configured it as a service in the main.js file so that it will be available throughout the application.

Listing 19-16. Configuring a Service in the main.js File in the src Folder

```
import Vue from 'vue'
import App from './App.vue'

import "../node_modules/bootstrap/dist/css/bootstrap.min.css";
import { RestDataSource } from "./restDataSource";

Vue.config.productionTip = false
```

```
new Vue({
  render: h => h(App),
  provide: function () {
    return {
        eventBus: new Vue(),
        restDataSource: new RestDataSource()
    }
  }
}).$mount('#app')
```

The new service is called restDataSource, and it will be available for use by all the components in the application.

Consuming the HTTP Service

Now that I have defined a service, I can remove the Axios code from the ProductDisplay code and use the service instead, as shown in Listing 19-17.

Listing 19-17. Using the HTTP Service in the ProductDisplay.vue File in the src/components Folder

```
...
<script>

    import Vue from "vue";

    //import Axios from "axios";
    //const baseUrl = "http://localhost:3500/products/";

    export default {
        data: function () {
            return {
                products: []
            }
        },
        methods: {
            createNew() {
                this.eventBus.$emit("create");
            },
            editProduct(product) {
                this.eventBus.$emit("edit", product);
            },
            processProducts(newProducts) {
                this.products.splice(0);
                this.products.push(...newProducts);
            }
        },
        inject: ["eventBus", "restDataSource"],
        async created() {
            this.processProducts(await this.restDataSource.getProducts());
        }
    }
</script>
...
```

The inject property declares a dependency on the restDataSource service, which is used in the created method to get the data from the RESTful web service and populate the data property named products.

Adding Other HTTP Operations

Now that I have a basic structure in place, I can add the complete set of HTTP operations that the application requires, expanding the service to use the methods provided by Axios, as shown in Listing 19-18.

Listing 19-18. Adding Operations in restDataSource.js in the src Folder

```
import Axios from "axios";

const baseUrl = "http://localhost:3500/products/";

export class RestDataSource {

    async getProducts() {
        return (await Axios.get(baseUrl)).data;
    }

    async saveProduct(product) {
        await Axios.post(baseUrl, product);
    }

    async updateProduct(product) {
        await Axios.put(`${baseUrl}${product.id}`, product);
    }

    async deleteProduct(product) {
        await Axios.delete(`${baseUrl}${product.id}`, product);
    }
}
```

I have added methods for saving new objects, updating existing objects, and deleting objects. All of these methods use the async/await keywords, which will allow the component that requires the operation to wait for the outcome. This is important because it means that the component can ensure that the local representation of the data isn't updated unless the HTTP operation completes successfully.

■ **Tip** Stop and start the json-server package to reset the example data to its original state after you have deleted or edited items. The contents of the JavaScript file created in Listing 19-2 will be used to repopulate the database when the process starts.

In Listing 19-19, I have changed the ProductDisplay component to use the methods defined in Listing 19-18 and added support for deleting objects.

Listing 19-19. Adding Data Operations in the ProductDisplay.vue File in the src/components Folder

```
<template>
    <div>
        <table class="table table-sm table-striped table-bordered">
            <tr>
                <th>ID</th>
                <th>Name</th>
                <th>Category</th>
                <th>Price</th>
                <th></th>
            </tr>
            <tbody>
                <tr v-for="p in products" v-bind:key="p.id">
                    <td>{{ p.id }}</td>
                    <td>{{ p.name }}</td>
                    <td>{{ p.category }}</td>
                    <td>{{ p.price }}</td>
                    <td>
                        <button class="btn btn-sm btn-primary"
                                v-on:click="editProduct(p)">
                            Edit
                        </button>
                        <button class="btn btn-sm btn-danger"
                                v-on:click="deleteProduct(p)">
                            Delete
                        </button>
                    </td>
                </tr>
                <tr v-if="products.length == 0">
                    <td colspan="5" class="text-center">No Data</td>
                </tr>
            </tbody>
        </table>
        <div class="text-center">
            <button class="btn btn-primary" v-on:click="createNew">
                Create New
            </button>
        </div>
    </div>
</template>

<script>

    import Vue from "vue";

    export default {
        data: function () {
            return {
                products: []
            }
        },
```

```
    methods: {
        createNew() {
            this.eventBus.$emit("create");
        },
        editProduct(product) {
            this.eventBus.$emit("edit", product);
        },
        async deleteProduct(product) {
            await this.restDataSource.deleteProduct(product);
            let index = this.products.findIndex(p => p.id == product.id);
            this.products.splice(index, 1);
        },
        processProducts(newProducts) {
            this.products.splice(0);
            this.products.push(...newProducts);
        },
        async processComplete(product) {
            let index = this.products.findIndex(p => p.id == product.id);
            if (index == -1) {
                await this.restDataSource.saveProduct(product);
                this.products.push(product);
            } else {
                await this.restDataSource.updateProduct(product);
                Vue.set(this.products, index, product);
            }
        }
    },
    inject: ["eventBus", "restDataSource"],
    async created() {
        this.processProducts(await this.restDataSource.getProducts());
        this.eventBus.$on("complete", this.processComplete);
    }
}
</script>
```

It is important to use the await keyword when calling the asynchronous methods defined by the HTTP service. If the await keyword is omitted, the subsequent statements in the component's method will be executed immediately regardless of the outcome of the HTTP request. For operations that ask the RESTful web service to store or delete objects, that means the data that the application shows to the user will suggest that the operation has completed immediately and successfully, even if an error occurs. For example, the use of the await keyword in this method prevents the component from removing the object from the products array until the HTTP request has completed:

```
...
async deleteProduct(product) {
    await this.restDataSource.deleteProduct(product);
    let index = this.products.findIndex(p => p.id == product.id);
    this.products.splice(index, 1);
},
...
```

When you use the `await` keyword, any error that occurs during the execution of the asynchronous operation will cause an exception to be thrown in the component's method, which will stop the execution of the statements in the component's method and, in this case, prevent the user's data from getting out of sync with the data on the server.

■ **Tip** When you use the `await` keyword in a component's method, you must remember to also apply the `async` keyword, as shown in Listing 19-19.

The result of these changes is that the application reads its data from the RESTful web service and is able to create new products and edit and delete existing products, as illustrated in Figure 19-3.

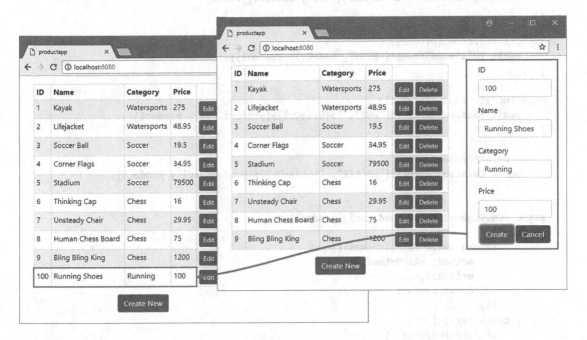

Figure 19-3. *Performing HTTP operations*

Creating an Error Handling Service

Vue.js can't detect exceptions that arise during asynchronous HTTP operations, and some additional work is required to indicate to the user that an error has occurred. My preference is to create a component that is dedicated to display the errors and have the `RestDataSource` class provide error notifications by sending custom events through the event bus. In Listing 19-20, I have added support to the `RestDataSource` class for handling exceptions by dispatching a custom event.

Listing 19-20. Handling Errors in the restDataSource.js File in the src Folder

```
import Axios from "axios";

const baseUrl = "http://localhost:3500/products/";

export class RestDataSource {

    constructor(bus) {
        this.eventBus = bus;
    }

    async getProducts() {
        return (await this.sendRequest("GET", baseUrl)).data;
    }

    async saveProduct(product) {
        await this.sendRequest("POST", baseUrl, product);
    }

    async updateProduct(product) {
        await this.sendRequest("PUT", `${baseUrl}${product.id}`, product);
    }

    async deleteProduct(product) {
        await this.sendRequest("DELETE", `${baseUrl}${product.id}`, product);
    }

    async sendRequest(httpMethod, url, product) {
        try {
            return await Axios.request({
                method: httpMethod,
                url: url,
                data: product
            });
        } catch (err) {
            if (err.response) {
                this.eventBus.$emit("httpError",
                    `${err.response.statusText} - ${err.response.status}`);
            } else {
                this.eventBus.$emit("httpError", "HTTP Error");
            }
            throw err;
        }
    }
}
```

Regular classes don't go through the component lifecycle and can't use the inject property to receive services. With this in mind, I added a constructor that accepts an event bus, and I rewrote the class so that all of the methods perform their work by calling the sendRequest method, which uses the Axios request method. This method allows the details of the request to be specified using a configuration object and allows me to consolidate the code that performs HTTP requests so that I can handle errors consistently.

Axios won't always be able to provide an object that contains the response, such as when the request times out. For these situations, I provide a general description that indicates that the problem is related to an HTTP request.

The Axios methods throw an error when an HTTP request returns a status code from the 400 and 500 ranges, which indicate a problem. In Listing 19-20, I use a try/catch block to catch the exception and send a custom event called httpError. The object that is received in the catch block is a response property that returns an object representing the response from the server. This object defines the properties described in Table 19-4, and I have used it to formulate a simple message to accompany the custom event.

■ **Tip** Notice that I still throw the event after sending the custom event. This is so that the component that initiated the HTTP request receives the exception and doesn't proceed to update the local representation of the data. Without the throw statement, only recipients of the custom event would know that there was a problem.

The constructor that I added in Listing 19-20 requires an event bus, which I provided in the main.js file, as shown in Listing 19-21.

Listing 19-21. Configuring a Service in the main.js File in the src Folder

```
import Vue from 'vue'
import App from './App.vue'

import "../node_modules/bootstrap/dist/css/bootstrap.min.css";
import { RestDataSource } from "./restDataSource";

Vue.config.productionTip = false

new Vue({
  render: h => h(App),
  data: {
    eventBus: new Vue()
  },
  provide: function () {
      return {
          eventBus: this.eventBus,
          restDataSource: new RestDataSource(this.eventBus)
      }
  }
}).$mount('#app')
```

The properties that define services cannot refer to other services, so I have defined a data property that creates the event bus, which I then expose directly through its own provide property and as a constructor argument to the RestDataSource class.

Creating an Error Display Component

I need a component that will receive the custom events and display an error message to the user. I added a file called ErrorDisplay.vue to the src/components folder and added the content shown in Listing 19-22.

Listing 19-22. The Contents of the ErrorDisplay.vue File in the src/components Folder

```
<template>
    <div v-if="error" class="bg-danger text-white text-center p-3 h3">
        An Error Has Occurred
        <h6>{{ message }}</h6>
        <a href="/" class="btn btn-secondary">OK</a>
    </div>
</template>

<script>

export default {
    data: function () {
        return {
            error: false,
            message: ""
        }
    },
    methods: {
        handleError(err) {
            this.error = true;
            this.message = err;
        }
    },
    inject: ["eventBus"],
    created() {
        this.eventBus.$on("httpError", this.handleError);
    }
}
</script>
```

This component registers its interest in the custom event in its `created` method by using the event bus and responds when the event is received by revealing an element through the `v-if` directive. To apply the component to the user, I made the changes shown to the application's root component, as shown in Listing 19-23.

Listing 19-23. Applying a Component in the App.vue File in the src Folder

```
<template>
    <div class="container-fluid">
        <div class="row">
            <div class="col"><error-display /></div>
        </div>
        <div class="row">
            <div class="col-8 m-3"><product-display/></div>
            <div class="col m-3"><product-editor/></div>
        </div>
    </div>
</template>
```

```
<script>
    import ProductDisplay from "./components/ProductDisplay";
    import ProductEditor from "./components/ProductEditor";
    import ErrorDisplay from "./components/ErrorDisplay";

    export default {
        name: 'App',
        components: { ProductDisplay, ProductEditor, ErrorDisplay }
    }
</script>
```

An import statement assigns the name ErrorDisplay to the component, which is used to register it with Vue.js and allows an error-display element to be added to the root component's template. The result is that any errors encountered during the HTTP request are displayed to the user, as shown in Figure 19-4.

■ **Tip** If you want to test the error handling, then the easiest ways are to stop the json-server process and to change the baseUrl value in the RestDataSource class so that it refers to a URL that doesn't exist, such as http://localhost:3500/hats/.

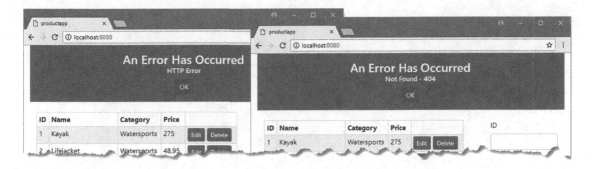

Figure 19-4. *Displaying errors*

RECOVERING FROM HTTP ERRORS

The approach that I have taken in the error handling component is an all-or-nothing approach, where the user is presented with an OK button that navigates to the root URL, which effectively reloads the application and gets fresh data. The drawback of this approach is that the user will lose any local state, which can cause frustration, especially if the user tries to repeat a complex task only to end up in the same state again.

A better approach is to allow the user to correct the problem and retry the HTTP request, but this is something that should be attempted only if the cause of the problem is clear and the solution is obvious. It isn't always easy to diagnose problems from an HTTP request, even if the server provides extra error information.

Summary

In this chapter, I demonstrated how a Vue.js application can access a RESTful web service using the Axios package. I demonstrated how to perform data operations using HTTP requests, I showed you how to create a separate class to separate details of the HTTP requests from the rest of the application, and I explained how to deal with errors when they arise. In the next chapter, I explain how to use the Vuex package to create a shared data store.

CHAPTER 20

■■■

Using a Data Store

In this chapter, I show you how to use the Vuex package to create a data store, which provides an alternative approach to sharing data in an application and arranging coordination between components. Table 20-1 puts the Vuex data store in context.

Table 20-1. *Putting the Vuex Data Store in Context*

Question	Answer
What is it?	A data store is a common repository for an application state, managed by the Vuex package, which is an official part of the Vue.js project.
Why is it useful?	A data store can simplify the management of data by making it readily available through an application.
How is it used?	A data store is created using the Vuex package and registered in the main.js file such that every component is given access to the data store through a special $store property.
Are there any pitfalls or limitations?	Vuex data stores work in a specific way that is counterintuitive when you first start using them. Until you get used to the Vuex approach, it is better to enable strict mode, although you must remember to disable this feature before deploying your application.
Are there any alternatives?	If you can't get on with Vuex, then you can use the dependency injection feature and the event bus pattern, as described in Chapter 18, to achieve similar results.

Table 20-2 summarizes the chapter.

A. Freeman, *Pro Vue.js 2*, https://doi.org/10.1007/978-1-4842-3805-9_20

Table 20-2. *Chapter Summary*

Problem	Solution	Listing
Create a data store	Define a new module and use it to register the Vuex plugin and create a Vuex.Store object	6
Register a data store	Import the data store module and add a store property to the Vue object's configuration	7
Access a data store in a component	Use the $store property	8
Make a change in a data store	Invoke a mutation	9
Define a computed property in a data store	Use a getter	10–13
Perform an asynchronous task in a data store	Use an action	14–16
Observe a data store for changes	Use a watcher	17–19
Map data store features into component computed properties and methods	Use the mapping functions	20
Break a data store into separate files	Create additional data store modules	21–24
Separate the features in a module from the rest of a data store	Use the namespace feature	25, 26

Preparing for This Chapter

In this chapter, I continue using the productapp project from Chapter 19. To start the RESTful web service, open a command prompt and run the command shown in Listing 20-1 in the productapp folder.

■ **Tip** You can download the example project for this chapter—and for all the other chapters in this book—from https://github.com/Apress/pro-vue-js-2.

Listing 20-1. Starting the Web Service

```
npm run json
```

Open a second command prompt, navigate to the productapp directory, and run the command shown in Listing 20-2 to download and install the Vuex package.

Listing 20-2. Installing the Vuex Package

```
npm install vuex@3.0.1
```

To prepare for this chapter, I removed all the statements from the ProductDisplay component that manage the product data and use the event bus, leaving only empty methods that are invoked when the user clicks a button, as shown in Listing 20-3.

Listing 20-3. Simplifying the Contents of the ProductDisplay.vue File in the src/components Folder

```
<template>
    <div>
        <table class="table table-sm table-striped table-bordered">
            <tr>
                <th>ID</th><th>Name</th><th>Category</th><th>Price</th><th></th>
            </tr>
            <tbody>
                <tr v-for="p in products" v-bind:key="p.id">
                    <td>{{ p.id }}</td>
                    <td>{{ p.name }}</td>
                    <td>{{ p.category }}</td>
                    <td>{{ p.price }}</td>
                    <td>
                        <button class="btn btn-sm btn-primary"
                                v-on:click="editProduct(p)">
                            Edit
                        </button>
                        <button class="btn btn-sm btn-danger"
                                v-on:click="deleteProduct(p)">
                            Delete
                        </button>
                    </td>
                </tr>
                <tr v-if="products.length == 0">
                    <td colspan="5" class="text-center">No Data</td>
                </tr>
            </tbody>
        </table>
        <div class="text-center">
            <button class="btn btn-primary" v-on:click="createNew">
                Create New
            </button>
        </div>
    </div>
</template>

<script>
    export default {
        data: function () {
            return {
                products: []
            }
        },
        methods: {
            createNew() { },
            editProduct(product) { },
            deleteProduct(product) { }
        }
    }
</script>
```

I also removed the event bus from the ProductEditor component, as shown in Listing 20-4.

Listing 20-4. Simplifying the Contents of the ProductEditor.vue File in the src/components Folder

```
<template>

    <div>
        <div class="form-group">
            <label>ID</label>
            <input class="form-control" v-model="product.id" />
        </div>
        <div class="form-group">
            <label>Name</label>
            <input class="form-control" v-model="product.name" />
        </div>
        <div class="form-group">
            <label>Category</label>
            <input class="form-control" v-model="product.category" />
        </div>
        <div class="form-group">
            <label>Price</label>
            <input class="form-control" v-model.number="product.price" />
        </div>
        <div class="text-center">
            <button class="btn btn-primary" v-on:click="save">
                {{ editing ? "Save" : "Create" }}
            </button>
            <button class="btn btn-secondary" v-on:click="cancel">Cancel</button>
        </div>
    </div>

</template>
<script>
    export default {
        data: function () {
            return {
                editing: false,
                product: {}
            }
        },
        methods: {
            save() { },
            cancel() { }
        }
    }
</script>
```

Save the changes and run the command shown in Listing 20-5 in the productapp directory to start the Vue.js development tools.

Listing 20-5. Starting the Development Tools

```
npm run serve
```

Once the initial bundling process is complete, open a new browser window and navigate to http://localhost:8080, where you will see the example application, as shown in Figure 20-1.

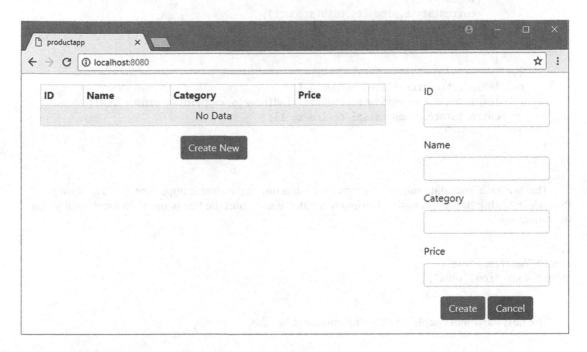

Figure 20-1. *Running the example application*

Creating and Using a Data Store

The process for getting started with shared application state involves several steps, but once the basic data store is in place, the application can be readily scaled up, and the initial investment in time pays off. The convention is to create the Vuex store in a folder called store. I created the src/store folder and added to it a file called index.js with the contents shown in Listing 20-6.

Listing 20-6. The Contents of the index.js File in the src/store Folder

```
import Vue from "vue";
import Vuex from "vuex";

Vue.use(Vuex);
```

```
export default new Vuex.Store({
    state: {
        products: [
            { id: 1, name: "Product #1", category: "Test", price: 100 },
            { id: 2, name: "Product #2", category: "Test", price: 150 },
            { id: 3, name: "Product #3", category: "Test", price: 200 }]
    },
    mutations: {
        saveProduct(currentState, product) {
            let index = currentState.products.findIndex(p => p.id == product.id);
            if (index == -1) {
                currentState.products.push(product);
            } else {
                Vue.set(currentState.products, index, product);
            }
        },
        deleteProduct(currentState, product) {
            let index = currentState.products.findIndex(p => p.id == product.id);
            currentState.products.splice(index, 1);
        }
    }
})
```

This is a basic Vuex data store. Getting the basic structure of the store is important, so I'll go through the code in Listing 20-6 step-by-step. The first two statements import the Vue.js and Vuex functionality from their modules.

```
...
import Vue from "vue";
import Vuex from "vuex";
...
```

The next statement enables the Vuex functionality, like this:

```
...
Vue.use(Vuex);
...
```

Vuex is provided as a Vue.js *plugin*, which allows the core Vue.js features to be extended as I describe in Chapter 26, and plugins are installed with the Vue.use method. The next statement creates the data store and makes it the default export from the JavaScript module:

```
...
export default new Vuex.Store({
...
```

The new keyword is used to create a new Vuex.Store object, which accepts a configuration object as its argument.

Understanding Separate State and Mutations

One of the most challenging aspects of working with data stores is that the data is read-only, and all changes are made using separate functions called *mutations*. When creating the data store, the application's data is defined using a `state` property, and the set of changes that can be made to that data is specified using a `mutations` property. For the data store defined in Listing 20-6, there is one data item.

```
...
state: {
    products: [
        { id: 1, name: "Product #1", category: "Test", price: 100 },
        { id: 2, name: "Product #2", category: "Test", price: 150 },
        { id: 3, name: "Product #3", category: "Test", price: 200 }]
},
...
```

The `state` property has been used to define a `products` property, to which I have assigned an array of objects. The data store in Listing 20-6 also defines two mutations.

```
...
mutations: {
    saveProduct(currentState, product) {
        let index = currentState.products.findIndex(p => p.id == product.id);
        if (index == -1) {
            currentState.products.push(product);
        } else {
            Vue.set(currentState.products, index, product);
        }
    },
    deleteProduct(currentState, product) {
        let index = currentState.products.findIndex(p => p.id == product.id);
        currentState.products.splice(index, 1);
    }
}
...
```

Mutations are functions that receive the current state of the data store and an optional payload argument that provides context to make changes. In this example, the `saveProduct` mutation is a function that receives an object and adds it to the `products` array or replaces an existing object in the array, while the `deleteProduct` mutation is a function that receives an object and uses the `id` value to locate and remove the corresponding object from the `products` array.

■ **Tip**   Notice that I have used `Vue.set` to replace an item in an array in the `saveProduct` mutation in Listing 20-6. Data stores have the same change-detection limitations as the rest of a Vue.js application, as described in Chapter 13.

511

Mutation functions access the current state of the data store using the first function parameter, like this:

```
...
saveProduct(currentState, product) {
    let index = currentState.products.findIndex(p => p.id == product.id);
    if (index == -1) {
        currentState.products.push(product);
    } else {
        Vue.set(currentState.products, index, product);
    }
},
...
```

You don't use the this keyword in mutations, and access to data is available only through the first parameter. Most developers are used to freely reading and writing data, so it can feel awkward to define separate functions to make changes. But, as you will learn, there are benefits to this approach that are especially valuable in large and complex applications.

Providing Access to the Vuex Data Store

Once you have created a data store, the next step is to make it available to the application's components. This is done by configuring the Vue object in the main.js file, as shown in Listing 20-7.

Listing 20-7. Configuring the Vuex Data Store in the main.js File in the src Folder

```
import Vue from 'vue'
import App from './App.vue'

import "../node_modules/bootstrap/dist/css/bootstrap.min.css";
import { RestDataSource } from "./restDataSource";
import store from "./store";

Vue.config.productionTip = false

new Vue({
  render: h => h(App),
  data: {
    eventBus: new Vue()
  },
  store,
  provide: function () {
      return {
          eventBus: this.eventBus,
          restDataSource: new RestDataSource(this.eventBus)
      }
  }
}).$mount('#app')
```

The import statement is used to import the module from the store folder (which will load the index.js file automatically) and assign it the name store, which is then used to define a property on the configuration object used to create the Vue object. This has the effect of taking the Vuex store object created in the index.js file and making it available in all components as the special variable $store, as demonstrated in the following section.

Using the Data Store

The separation of data and its mutations feels awkward when you create the data store, but it fits well with the structure of components. In Listing 20-8, I have updated the ProductDisplay component so that it reads its data from the data store and uses the deleteProduct mutation when a Delete button is clicked.

Listing 20-8. Using the Data Store in the ProductDisplay.vue File in the src/components Folder

```
...
<script>
    export default {
        //data: function () {
        //    return {
        //        products: []
        //    }
        //},
        computed: {
            products() {
                return this.$store.state.products;
            }
        },
        methods: {
            createNew() { },
            editProduct(product) { },
            deleteProduct(product) {
                this.$store.commit("deleteProduct", product);
            }
        }
    }
</script>
...
```

Accessing the data in the store is done through the $store property that is created by the addition to the Vue configuration object shown in Listing 20-7. Because data store values are read-only, they are integrated into the component as computed properties, and in the example, I have replaced the products data property with a computed property of the same name that returns the value from the data store.

```
...
products() {
    return this.$store.state.products;
}
...
```

The $store property returns the data store, and the state property is used to access individual data properties, such as the products property used in this example.

USING STRICT MODE TO AVOID DIRECT STATE CHANGES

Vuex doesn't enforce the separation between state and the operations by default, which means that components are able to access and modify properties defined in the store's `state` section. It is easy to forget that changes should not be made directly, and doing so means that debugging tools like Vue Devtools won't detect the changes that are made.

To help avoid accidental changes, Vuex provides a `strict` setting that monitors the store's state properties and throws an error if a direct change is made. This feature is enabled by adding a `strict` property to the configuration object used to create the store, like this:

```
import Vue from "vue";
import Vuex from "vuex";

Vue.use(Vuex);

export default new Vuex.Store({
    strict: true,
    state: {
        products: [
            { id: 1, name: "Product #1", category: "Test", price: 100 },
            { id: 2, name: "Product #2", category: "Test", price: 150 },
            { id: 3, name: "Product #3", category: "Test", price: 200 }]
    },
    mutations: {
        saveProduct(currentState, product) {
            let index = currentState.products
                .findIndex(p => p.id == product.id);
            if (index == -1) {
                currentState.products.push(product);
            } else {
                Vue.set(currentState.products, index, product);
            }
        },
        deleteProduct(currentState, product) {
            let index = currentState.products
                .findIndex(p => p.id == product.id);
            currentState.products.splice(index, 1);
        }
    }
})
```

This setting should only be used during development because it relies on expensive operations that may hinder the performance of an application.

Applying mutations to a data store is done through the $store.commit methods and is similar to triggering an event. The first argument to the comment method is the name of the mutation that should be applied, expressed as a string, followed by an optional payload argument to provide context for the mutation. In this example, I have set the body of the component's deleteProduct method, which is triggered when the user clicks a Delete method, to apply the mutation of the same name:

```
...
deleteProduct(product) {
    this.$store.commit("deleteProduct", product);
}
...
```

Once you understand how values are read and modified, you can integrate the data store into the application. In Listing 20-9, I have updated the ProductEditor component so that it modifies the data store to create new products.

Listing 20-9. Using the Data Store in the ProductEditor.vue File in the src/components Folder

```
...
<script>

    export default {
        data: function () {
            return {
                editing: false,
                product: {}
            }
        },
        methods: {
            save() {
                this.$store.commit("saveProduct", this.product);
                this.product = {};
            },
            cancel() { }
        }
    }
</script>
...
```

The save method has been updated to apply the data store's addProduct mutation, which will add a new product to the products array in the state section of the data store. The result of the changes to the components is that the user can fill out the form fields and click the Create button to add new products and click the Delete buttons to remove them, as shown in Figure 20-2.

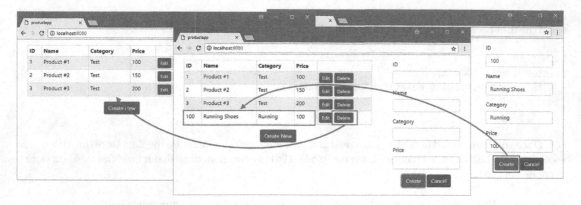

Figure 20-2. *Using the data store*

ACCESSING THE DATA STORE OUTSIDE OF COMPONENTS

The data store can be accessed using the `$store` property in any component in the application. If you want to access the data store in part of the application that isn't a component, then you can use the `import` statement, like this:

```
...
import dataStore from "../store";
...
```

This statement is from a later example in Chapter 24, where I use the data store in a code file that doesn't contain a component. This statement assigns the data store to the name `dataStore`, and the expression that follows the `from` keyword is the path to the `store` folder that contains the `index.js` file. Once you have used the `import` statement, you can access the data store functionality like this:

```
...
dataStore.commit("setComponentLoading", true);
...
```

This is another statement from the same example in Chapter 24, where you can see this feature used in context.

Inspecting Data Store Changes

The main advantage of using a data store is that it separates the application's data from the components, which keeps the components simple, allows them to interact easily, and makes the entire project easier to understand and test.

Performing changes only through mutations makes it possible to keep track of the changes that are made to the store's data. The Vue Devtools browser plugin has integrated support for working with Vuex, and if you open the browser's F12 tools and navigate to the Vue tab, you will see a button with a clock icon, which will show the data in the Vuex store when it is clicked, as shown in Figure 20-3.

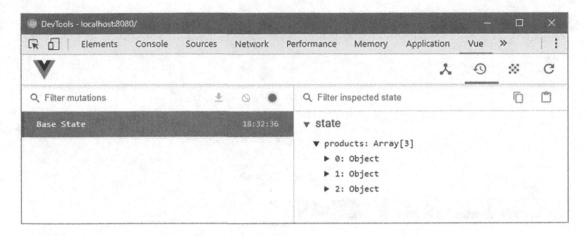

Figure 20-3. *Examining the data store*

You can see the state section contains a products property whose value is an array of three objects. You can explore each object in the array and see the properties it defines.

Leaving the F12 tools window open, use the main browser window to create three new items by entering the details shown in Table 20-3. Click the Create button after entering each set of details so that a new item is displayed in the table of products shown by the ProductDisplay component.

Table 20-3. *The Products for Testing the Vuex Store*

ID	Name	Category	Price
100	Running Shoes	Running	100
101	Snowboard	Winter Sports	500
102	Gloves	Winter Sports	35

Once you have created all three products, click the Delete button for the Gloves product, which will remove it from the list.

As you make each change, the Vuex section of the Vue Devtools tab will show the effect of each mutation that was applied to the data, along with a snapshot of the store's data and details of the payload argument that was provided for each change, as shown in Figure 20-4.

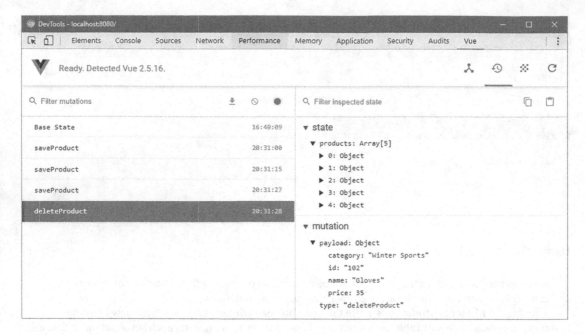

Figure 20-4. *The evolving state of the data store*

Each change can be undone to unwind the state of the data store and return it to an earlier stage, and the entire state can be exported and then reimported again later. Being able to see every change that is made to the store and what effect those changes had is a powerful tool that makes simplifies debugging complex problems, although it does require a degree of discipline to ensure that changes are applied only through mutations because changes made directly to state properties are not detected (see the "Using Strict Mode to Avoid Direct State Changes" sidebar about the Vuex strict mode if you find it difficult to remember to use mutations).

Defining Computed Properties in the Data Store

When you move an application's data into a store, you will often find that several components have to perform the same operation on a state value to get the data they require. Rather than duplicate the same code in every component, you can use the Vuex *getters* feature, which is the equivalent of a computed property in a component. In Listing 20-10, I have added two getters to the data store that transform the product data.

Listing 20-10. Adding Getters in the index.js File in the src/store Folder

```
import Vue from "vue";
import Vuex from "vuex";

Vue.use(Vuex);

export default new Vuex.Store({
    state: {
        products: [
```

```
            { id: 1, name: "Product #1", category: "Test", price: 100 },
            { id: 2, name: "Product #2", category: "Test", price: 150 },
            { id: 3, name: "Product #3", category: "Test", price: 200 }]
    },
    mutations: {
        saveProduct(currentState, product) {
            let index = currentState.products.findIndex(p => p.id == product.id);
            if (index == -1) {
                currentState.products.push(product);
            } else {
                Vue.set(currentState.products, index, product);
            }
        },
        deleteProduct(currentState, product) {
            let index = currentState.products.findIndex(p => p.id == product.id);
            currentState.products.splice(index, 1);
        }
    },
    getters: {
        orderedProducts(state) {
            return state.products.concat().sort((p1, p2) => p2.price - p1.price);
        },
        filteredProducts(state, getters) {
            return getters.orderedProducts.filter(p => p.price > 100);
        }
    }
})
```

Getters are defined by adding a `getters` property to the store's configuration object. Each getter is a function that receives an object that provides access to the data store's state properties and whose result is the computed value. The first getter I defined sorts the product data by accessing the products array through the state parameter.

```
...
orderedProducts(state) {
    return state.products.concat().sort((p1, p2) => p2.price - p1.price);
},
...
```

One getter can build on the result of another getter by defining a second parameter, which allows the getter's function to receive an object that provides access to the other getters in the store. The second getter that I defined gets the sorted products produced by the `orderedProducts` getter and then filters them to select only those whose `price` property is greater than 100.

```
...
filteredProducts(state, getters) {
    return getters.orderedProducts.filter(p => p.price > 100);
}
...
```

Being able to compose getters to create more complex results is a useful feature that helps reduce code duplication.

■ **Caution**　Getters should not make changes to the data in the store. It is for this reason that I have used the concat method in the orderedProducts getter because the sort method sorts the objects in an array in place. The concat method generates a new array and ensures that reading the value of the getter doesn't cause a change in the store's state data.

Using a Getter in a Component

Reading a getter is done through the this.$store.getters property and uses the name of the getter to read so that a getter called myGetter is read using this.$store.getters.myGetter. In Listing 20-11, I have changed the computed property defined by the ProductDisplay component so that it obtains its data from the filteredProducts getter.

Listing 20-11. Using a Getter in the ProductDisplay.vue File in the src/components Folder

```
...
<script>
    export default {
        computed: {
            products() {
                return this.$store.getters.filteredProducts;
            }
        },
        methods: {
            createNew() { },
            editProduct(product) { },
            deleteProduct(product) {
                this.$store.commit("deleteProduct", product);
            }
        }
    }
</script>
...
```

The v-for binding in the component's template reads the value of the products computed property, which gets its value from the getter in the data store. The result is a filtered and ordered set of products displayed to the user, as shown in Figure 20-5.

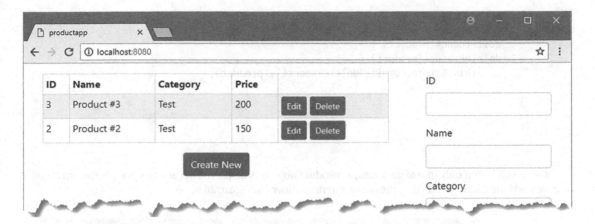

Figure 20-5. *Using a data store getter*

Providing Arguments to Getters

Getters can also receive additional arguments that are provided by the component and that can be used to influence the value that it generated. In Listing 20-12, I have changed the `filteredProducts` getter so that the amount used to filter product objects can be specified as an argument.

Listing 20-12. Using a Getter Argument in the index.js File in the src/store Folder

```
...
getters: {
    orderedProducts(state) {
        return state.products.concat().sort((p1, p2) => p2.price - p1.price);
    },
    filteredProducts(state, getters) {
        return (amount) => getters.orderedProducts.filter(p => p.price > amount);
    }
}
...
```

The syntax is awkward, but to receive an argument a getter must return a function, which will be invoked when the getter is read and provided with the argument by the component. In this example, the result of the getter is a function that receives an `amount` argument to be applied when the product objects are filtered. In Listing 20-13, I have updated the computed property defined by the `ProductDisplay` component to pass a value to the getter.

Listing 20-13. Using a Getter Argument in the ProductDisplay.vue File in the src/components Folder

```
...
<script>
    export default {
        computed: {
            products() {
                return this.$store.getters.filteredProducts(175);
            }
        },
```

521

```
        methods: {
            createNew() { },
            editProduct(product) { },
            deleteProduct(product) {
                this.$store.commit("deleteProduct", product);
            }
        }
    }
}
</script>
...
```

The result is that only one of the example product objects is displayed because its price is the only one that exceeds the value specified by the component, as shown in Figure 20-6.

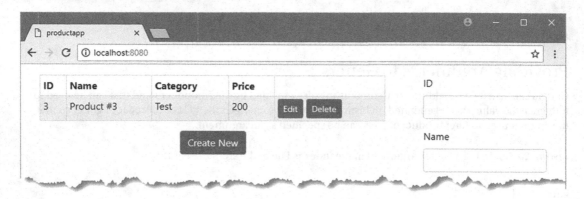

Figure 20-6. *Using a getter argument*

Performing Asynchronous Operations

Mutations perform synchronous operations, which means they are perfect for dealing with local data but are not suitable for working with a RESTful web service. For asynchronous tasks, Vuex provides a feature called *actions*, which allow tasks to be performed and changes fed back into the data store through mutations. In Listing 20-14, I have added actions to the data store that consume the RESTful web service.

Listing 20-14. Adding Actions in the index.js File in the src/store Folder

```
import Vue from "vue";
import Vuex from "vuex";
import Axios from "axios";

Vue.use(Vuex);

const baseUrl = "http://localhost:3500/products/";

export default new Vuex.Store({
    state: {
        products: []
    },
```

```
    mutations: {
        saveProduct(currentState, product) {
            let index = currentState.products.findIndex(p => p.id == product.id);
            if (index == -1) {
                currentState.products.push(product);
            } else {
                Vue.set(currentState.products, index, product);
            }
        },
        deleteProduct(currentState, product) {
            let index = currentState.products.findIndex(p => p.id == product.id);
            currentState.products.splice(index, 1);
        }
    },
    getters: {
        orderedProducts(state) {
            return state.products.concat().sort((p1, p2) => p2.price - p1.price);
        },
        filteredProducts(state, getters) {
            return (amount) => getters.orderedProducts.filter(p => p.price > amount);
        }
    },
    actions: {
        async getProductsAction(context) {
            (await Axios.get(baseUrl)).data
                .forEach(p => context.commit("saveProduct", p));
        },
        async saveProductAction(context, product) {
            let index = context.state.products.findIndex(p => p.id == product.id);
            if (index == -1) {
                await Axios.post(baseUrl, product);
            } else {
                await Axios.put(`${baseUrl}${product.id}`, product);
            }
            context.commit("saveProduct", product);
        },
        async deleteProductAction(context, product) {
            await Axios.delete(`${baseUrl}${product.id}`);
            context.commit("deleteProduct", product);
        }
    }
})
```

Actions are defined by adding an `actions` property to the store's configuration object, and each action is a function that receives a context object that provides access to the state, getters, and mutations. Actions are not permitted to modify the state data directly and must work through mutations, using the `commit` method. In the listing, I have removed the dummy data from the `products` array and defined three actions that use Axios to communicate with the RESTful web service and update the data store using its mutations.

■ **Tip** You don't have to include the term Action in the names you give your actions. I like to make sure my actions and mutations are clearly differentiated, but that's just personal preference and isn't a requirement.

In Listing 20-15, I have updated the ProductDisplay component so that it uses the store's actions to get the initial data from the web service when the user clicks a Delete button.

Listing 20-15. Using Actions in the ProductDisplay.vue File in the src/components Folder

```
...
<script>
    export default {
        computed: {
            products() {
                return this.$store.state.products;
            }
        },
        methods: {
            createNew() { },
            editProduct(product) { },
            deleteProduct(product) {
                this.$store.dispatch("deleteProductAction", product);
            }
        },
        created() {
            this.$store.dispatch("getProductsAction");
        }
    }
</script>
...
```

Actions are invoked using the dispatch method, which accepts the name of the argument to use and an optional argument that will be passed on to the action, similar to the way that mutations are used. There is no direct support for populating a Vuex store when it is created, so I have used the component's created method, described in Chapter 17, to invoke the getProductsAction action and get the initial data from the web service. (I have also changed the data used for the products computed property so that it is read from the state data rather than the getters, ensuring that all of the data received from the server is displayed.)

In Listing 20-16, I have updated the ProductEditor component so that it uses actions to store or update data in the web service.

Listing 20-16. Using Action in the ProductEditor.vue File in the src/components Folder

```
...
<script>

    export default {
        data: function () {
            return {
                editing: false,
                product: {}
            }
        },
```

```
    methods: {
        save() {
            this.$store.dispatch("saveProductAction", this.product);
            this.product = {};
        },
        cancel() { }
    }
  }
</script>
...
```

The result is that the data is obtained from the web service, as shown in Figure 20-7, and creating or deleting objects results in a corresponding change at the server.

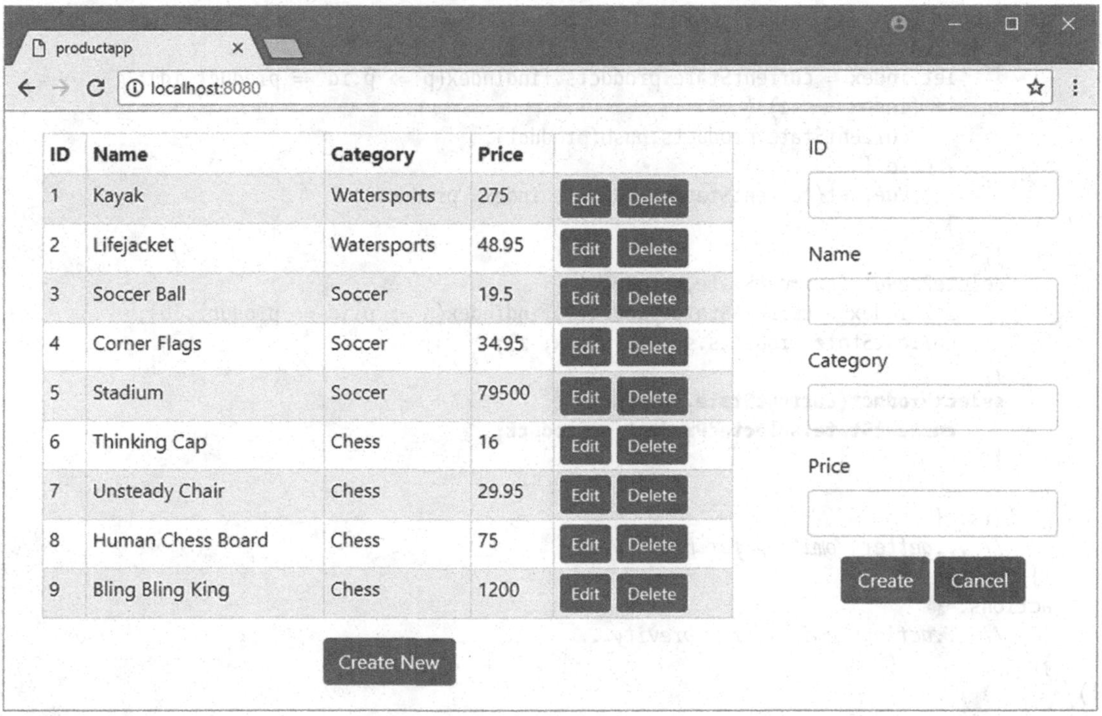

Figure 20-7. *Using data store actions*

Receiving Change Notifications

The Vuex data store can be used for all of an application's state and not just the data that is displayed to the user. In the example application, the user selects a product for editing by clicking a button provided by the ProductDisplay component, but the ProductEditor component provides the editing features. To enable this type of coordination between components, Vuex provides watchers that trigger notifications when a data value changes, equivalent to the watchers provided by Vue.js components (described in Chapter 17). In Listing 20-17, I have added a state property to the data store that indicates which product the user has chosen, along with a mutation that sets its value.

Listing 20-17. Adding a State Property and Mutation in the index.js File in the src/store Folder

```
import Vue from "vue";
import Vuex from "vuex";
import Axios from "axios";

Vue.use(Vuex);

const baseUrl = "http://localhost:3500/products/";

export default new Vuex.Store({
    state: {
        products: [],
        selectedProduct: null
    },
    mutations: {
        saveProduct(currentState, product) {
            let index = currentState.products.findIndex(p => p.id == product.id);
            if (index == -1) {
                currentState.products.push(product);
            } else {
                Vue.set(currentState.products, index, product);
            }
        },
        deleteProduct(currentState, product) {
            let index = currentState.products.findIndex(p => p.id == product.id);
            currentState.products.splice(index, 1);
        },
        selectProduct(currentState, product) {
            currentState.selectedProduct = product;
        }
    },
    getters: {
        // ...getters omitted for brevity...
    },
    actions: {
        // ...actions omitted for brevity...
    }
})
```

In Listing 20-18, I have updated the ProductDisplay component so that it invokes the selectProduct mutation when the user clicks the Create New button or one of the Edit buttons.

Listing 20-18. Using a Mutation in the ProductDisplay.vue File in the src/components Folder

```
...
<script>
    export default {
        computed: {
            products() {
                return this.$store.state.products;
            }
        },
```

```
        methods: {
            createNew() {
                this.$store.commit("selectProduct");
            },
            editProduct(product) {
                this.$store.commit("selectProduct", product);
            },
            deleteProduct(product) {
                this.$store.dispatch("deleteProductAction", product);
            }
        },
        created() {
            this.$store.dispatch("getProductsAction");
        }
    }
</script>
...
```

When the user clicks the Create New button, the component's createNew method is invoked, which triggers the selectProduct mutation without an argument, setting the selectedProduct state property to null, which signals that the user has not selected an existing product to be edited. When the user clicks one of the Edit buttons, the editProduct method is invoked, which triggers the same mutation but provides a product object, signaling that this is the object the user wants to edit.

To respond to the signals that the ProductDisplay component is sending through the data store, I added a Vuex watcher to the ProductEditor component, as shown in Listing 20-19.

Listing 20-19. Watching a Data Store Value in the ProductEditor.vue File in the src/components Folder

```
...
<script>

    export default {
        data: function () {
            return {
                editing: false,
                product: {}
            }
        },
        methods: {
            save() {
                this.$store.dispatch("saveProductAction", this.product);
                this.product = {};
            },
            cancel() {
                this.$store.commit("selectProduct");
            }
        },
```

```
        created() {
            this.$store.watch(state => state.selectedProduct,
                (newValue, oldValue) => {
                    if (newValue == null) {
                        this.editing = false;
                        this.product = {};
                    } else {
                        this.editing = true;
                        this.product = {};
                        Object.assign(this.product, newValue);
                    }
                });
        }
    }
</script>
...
```

I used the component's created lifecycle method, described in Chapter 17, to create the watcher; this is done using the watch method, which is accessed as this.$store.watch. The watch method accepts two functions: the first function is used to select the data value to watch, and the second function is invoked when there is a change to the selected data, using the same function style used by component watches.

■ **Tip** The result of the watch method is a function that can be invoked to stop receiving notifications. You can see an example of this function in use in Chapter 21.

The effect is that the component reacts to the signals that are sent through the data store by changing its local state and copying the values from the selected product if there is one. You can test the changes by clicking the Create New or Edit buttons and checking that the form fields respond, as shown in Figure 20-8.

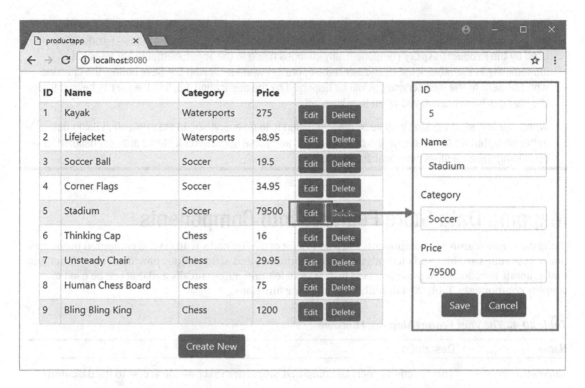

Figure 20-8. *Using a data store watcher*

UNDERSTANDING INDIRECTION AND LOCAL COMPONENT STATE

There is an oddity in the code in Listing 20-19 that is worth attention: I use `Object.assign` to copy the values from the object in the data store to the local `product` property, like this:

```
...
} else {
    this.editing = true;
    this.product = {};
    Object.assign(this.product, newValue);
}
...
```

You may wonder why I didn't simply work directly with the state property in the data store. The first reason is using the `v-bind` directive to create two-way bindings on Vuex data values is awkward. It can be done, but it requires using separate data and event bindings or creating computed properties that have both setters and getters. The result isn't ideal, and my preference is to use local state in the component, as in this example.

529

The second reason is that working directly with the object in the data store can cause confusion for the user. Since this object in the data store is the same object that is displayed by the v-for directive used by the ProductDisplay component, any changes made in the input elements are reflected immediately in the table. If the user cancels the operation without clicking the Save button, the changes won't be sent to the web service but will be displayed by the application, leading the user to believe that the changes have been saved when they have not.

When you first start working with Vuex, the temptation is to do everything in the application using data in the store, but that isn't always the best approach, and some application features are best handled by combining the data store with local state data.

Mapping Data Store Features into Components

Using data store features in components can lead to a lot of similar code, with several computed properties that access state variables and methods that trigger mutations and actions. Vuex provides a set of functions that generate functions that provide access to data store features automatically and that can be used to simplify components. Table 20-4 describes the mapping functions.

Table 20-4. *The Vuex Feature Mapping Functions*

Name	Description
mapState	This function generates computed properties that provide access to the data store's state values.
mapGetters	This function generates computed properties that provide access to the data store's getters.
mapMutations	This function generates methods that provide access to the data store's mutations.
mapActions	This function generates methods that provide access to the data store's actions.

These functions add features from the data store alongside a component's local properties and methods. In Listing 20-20, I have used the functions from Table 20-4 to provide access to the data store in the ProductDisplay component.

Listing 20-20. Generating Members in the ProductDisplay.vue File in the src/components Folder

```
<template>
    <div>
        <table class="table table-sm table-striped table-bordered">
            <tr>
                <th>ID</th><th>Name</th><th>Category</th><th>Price</th><th></th>
            </tr>
            <tbody>
                <tr v-for="p in products" v-bind:key="p.id">
                    <td>{{ p.id }}</td>
                    <td>{{ p.name }}</td>
                    <td>{{ p.category }}</td>
                    <td>{{ p.price }}</td>
                    <td>
```

```
                    <button class="btn btn-sm btn-primary"
                            v-on:click="editProduct(p)">
                        Edit
                    </button>
                    <button class="btn btn-sm btn-danger"
                            v-on:click="deleteProduct(p)">
                        Delete
                    </button>
                </td>
            </tr>
            <tr v-if="products.length == 0">
                <td colspan="5" class="text-center">No Data</td>
            </tr>
        </tbody>
    </table>
    <div class="text-center">
        <button class="btn btn-primary" v-on:click="createNew()">
            Create New
        </button>
    </div>
</div>
</template>

<script>

    import { mapState, mapMutations, mapActions } from "vuex";

    export default {
        computed: {
            ...mapState(["products"])
        },
        methods: {
            ...mapMutations({
                editProduct: "selectProduct",
                createNew: "selectProduct",
            }),
            ...mapActions({
                getProducts: "getProductsAction",
                deleteProduct: "deleteProductAction"
            })
        },
        created() {
            this.getProducts();
        }
    }
</script>
```

The functions described in Table 20-4 are imported from the vuex module and are applied with the JavaScript spread operator (the ... expression) to create properties and methods that map onto the data store.

There are two ways to create data store mappings. The first way is to pass a string array to the mapping function, which tells Vuex to create properties or methods with the name that matches the one used in the data store, like this:

```
...
computed: {
    ...mapState(["products"])
},
...
```

This tells Vuex to create a computed property called products that returns the value of the products data store state property. If you don't want to use the names from the data store, then you can pass a map object to the functions in Table 20-4, which provides Vuex with names that should be used in the component, like this:

```
...
...mapActions({
    getProducts: "getProductsAction",
    deleteProduct: "deleteProductAction"
})
...
```

This example tells Vuex to create methods called getProducts and deleteProduct that invoke the data store actions called getProductsAction and deleteProductAction.

INVOKING MAPPED METHODS WITHOUT ARGUMENTS

The methods generated by the mapping functions for mutations and actions will accept arguments, which are then passed on to the data store. Care is required if you want to invoke one of these methods directly from an event binder without an argument. In Listing 20-20, I had to make a change to the event binding for the Create New button.

```
...
<button class="btn btn-primary" v-on:click="createNew()">
...
```

Previously, the expression for the v-on directive specified only the method name. This has the effect of invoking the mapped method created by Vuex with the event object provided by the directive, which is passed on to the mapped mutation. The example application depends on the mutation being invoked without an argument, so I added empty parentheses to the v-on directive's expression to prevent an argument from being provided.

Using Data Store Modules

As the complexity of an application increases, so does the amount of data and code in the store. Vuex provides support for modules, which allows a data store to be broken up into self-contained sections that are easier to write, understand, and manage.

Each module is defined in a separate file. To demonstrate, I added a file called preferences.js to the src/store folder with the content shown in Listing 20-21.

Listing 20-21. The Contents of the preferences.js File in the src/store Folder

```
export default {
    state: {
        stripedTable: true,
        primaryEditButton: false,
        dangerDeleteButton: false
    },
    getters: {
        editClass(state) {
            return state.primaryEditButton ? "btn-primary" : "btn-secondary";
        },
        deleteClass(state) {
            return state.dangerDeleteButton ? "btn-danger" : "btn-secondary";
        },
        tableClass(state, payload, rootState) {
            return rootState.products.length > 0
                && rootState.products[0].price > 500 ? "table-striped" : ""
        }
    },
    mutations: {
        setEditButtonColor(currentState, primary) {
            currentState.primaryEditButton = primary;
        },
        setDeleteButtonColor(currentState, danger) {
            currentState.dangerDeleteButton = danger;
        }
    }
}
```

When you define a module, you define a JavaScript object that has the same state, getters, mutations, and actions properties that you have seen in earlier sections of this chapter. The difference is that the context objects that are passed to the functions defined in the module provide access only to the state data and other features in the local module. If you want to access data store features in the main module, then you can define an additional argument, like this:

```
...
tableClass(state, payload, rootState) {
    return rootState.products.length > 0
        && rootState.products[0].price > 500 ? "table-striped" : ""
}
...
```

This getter defines a rootState parameter that is used to access the products property, allowing the result from the getter to be determined based on the price value of the first product in the array.

■ **Tip**   When accessing the root data store module, you must define the payload argument even if you are not going to use it, as shown in Listing 20-21.

Registering and Using a Data Store Module

To incorporate a module in the data store, you must use the import statement and configure the data store using the modules property, as shown in Listing 20-22.

Listing 20-22.   Registering a Module in the index.js File in the src/store Folder

```
import Vue from "vue";
import Vuex from "vuex";
import Axios from "axios";

import PrefsModule from "./preferences";

Vue.use(Vuex);

const baseUrl = "http://localhost:3500/products/";

export default new Vuex.Store({
    modules: {
        prefs: PrefsModule
    },
    state: {
        products: [],
        selectedProduct: null
    },

    // ...other data store features omitted for brevity...
})
```

Vuex combines the state, getters, mutations, and actions defined in the module with those defined directly in the index.js file, which means that components don't have to worry about where different parts of the data store have been defined. In Listing 20-23, I have updated the ProductDisplay component so that it uses the data and mutations defined in the module.

Listing 20-23.   Using Module Features in the ProductDisplay.vue File in the src/components Folder

```
<template>
    <div>
        <table class="table table-sm table-bordered" v-bind:class="tableClass">
            <tr>
                <th>ID</th><th>Name</th><th>Category</th><th>Price</th><th></th>
            </tr>
```

```
        <tbody>
            <tr v-for="p in products" v-bind:key="p.id">
                <td>{{ p.id }}</td>
                <td>{{ p.name }}</td>
                <td>{{ p.category }}</td>
                <td>{{ p.price }}</td>
                <td>
                    <button class="btn btn-sm"
                            v-bind:class="editClass"
                            v-on:click="editProduct(p)">
                        Edit
                    </button>
                    <button class="btn btn-sm"
                            v-bind:class="deleteClass"
                            v-on:click="deleteProduct(p)">
                        Delete
                    </button>
                </td>
            </tr>
            <tr v-if="products.length == 0">
                <td colspan="5" class="text-center">No Data</td>
            </tr>
        </tbody>
    </table>
    <div class="text-center">
        <button class="btn btn-primary" v-on:click="createNew()">
            Create New
        </button>
    </div>
  </div>
</template>

<script>

    import { mapState, mapMutations, mapActions, mapGetters } from "vuex";

    export default {
        computed: {
            ...mapState(["products"]),
            ...mapGetters(["tableClass", "editClass", "deleteClass"])
        },
        methods: {
            ...mapMutations({
                editProduct: "selectProduct",
                createNew: "selectProduct",
            }),
            ...mapMutations(["setEditButtonColor", "setDeleteButtonColor"]),
            ...mapActions({
                getProducts: "getProductsAction",
                deleteProduct: "deleteProductAction"
            })
        },
```

```
        created() {
            this.getProducts();
            this.setEditButtonColor(false);
            this.setDeleteButtonColor(false);
        }
    }
</script>
```

I have used the mapping functions to map the getters and mutations provided by the data store module and tied their values into the component's template using the v-bind directive. I invoke the mutations in the component's created method, and you can see the effect of the getter that accesses the root data store state by changing the price property of the first product in the table to more than 500, as shown in Figure 20-9. When the value is less than 500, the table rows are not striped; when the value is greater than 500, the rows are displayed in alternating colors.

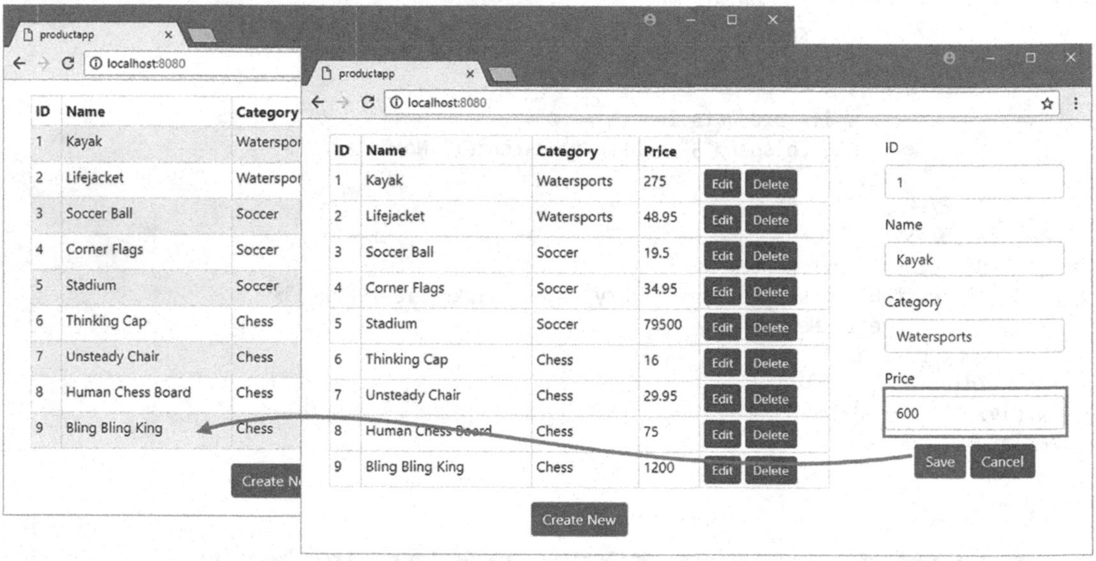

Figure 20-9. *Using features provided by a data store module*

Accessing Module State

A different approach is required if you want to access the state properties defined in a module. Although the getters, mutations, and actions are seamlessly merged with the rest of the data store, the state data is kept separate and must be accessed using the name assigned to the module when it is imported, as shown in Listing 20-24.

Listing 20-24. Accessing Module State Data in the ProductDisplay.vue File in the src Folder

```
<template>
    <div>
        <table class="table table-sm table-bordered"
               v-bind:class="'table-striped' == useStripedTable">
```

```
            <tr>
                <th>ID</th><th>Name</th><th>Category</th><th>Price</th><th></th>
            </tr>
            <tbody>
                <tr v-for="p in products" v-bind:key="p.id">
                    <td>{{ p.id }}</td>
                    <td>{{ p.name }}</td>
                    <td>{{ p.category }}</td>
                    <td>{{ p.price }}</td>
                    <td>
                        <button class="btn btn-sm"
                                v-bind:class="editClass"
                                v-on:click="editProduct(p)">
                            Edit
                        </button>
                        <button class="btn btn-sm"
                                v-bind:class="deleteClass"
                                v-on:click="deleteProduct(p)">
                            Delete
                        </button>
                    </td>
                </tr>
                <tr v-if="products.length == 0">
                    <td colspan="5" class="text-center">No Data</td>
                </tr>
            </tbody>
        </table>
        <div class="text-center">
            <button class="btn btn-primary" v-on:click="createNew()">
                Create New
            </button>
        </div>
    </div>
</template>

<script>

    import { mapState, mapMutations, mapActions, mapGetters } from "vuex";

    export default {
        computed: {
            ...mapState(["products"]),
            ...mapState({
                useStripedTable: state => state.prefs.stripedTable
            }),
            ...mapGetters(["tableClass", "editClass", "deleteClass"])
        },
        methods: {
            ...mapMutations({
                editProduct: "selectProduct",
                createNew: "selectProduct",
            }),
```

```
            ...mapMutations(["setEditButtonColor", "setDeleteButtonColor"]),
            ...mapActions({
                getProducts: "getProductsAction",
                deleteProduct: "deleteProductAction"
            })
        },
        created() {
            this.getProducts();
            this.setEditButtonColor(false);
            this.setDeleteButtonColor(false);
        }
    }
</script>
```

The mapState method is passed an object whose properties are the names that will be used as the local properties and whose values are functions that receive a state object and select the data store value that is required. In the example, I have used this feature to create a computed property called useStripedTable that is mapped to the stripedTable state property defined in the prefs module.

Using Module Namespaces

The default behavior for modules is to merge the getters, mutations, and actions they offer into the data store so that components are unaware of the store structure but keep the state data separate so that it must be accessed using a prefix. If you enable the namespace feature, as shown in Listing 20-25, then all the features must be accessed using a prefix.

Listing 20-25. Enabling the Namespace Feature in the preferences.js File in the src/store Folder

```
export default {
    namespaced: true,
    state: {
        stripedTable: true,
        primaryEditButton: true,
        dangerDeleteButton: false
    },
    getters: {
        editClass(state) {
            return state.primaryEditButton ? "btn-primary" : "btn-secondary";
        },
        deleteClass(state) {
            return state.dangerDeleteButton ? "btn-danger" : "btn-secondary";
        },
        tableClass(state, payload, rootState) {
            return rootState.products.length > 0
                && rootState.products[0].price > 500 ? "table-striped" : ""
        }
    },
    mutations: {
        setEditButtonColor(currentState, primary) {
            currentState.primaryEditButton = primary;
        },
```

```
        setDeleteButtonColor(currentState, danger) {
            currentState.dangerDeleteButton = danger;
        }
    }
}
```

When you map the features defined by the module into a component, the name of the feature you want must be prefixed with the name that was used to register the module with the data store, as shown in Listing 20-26.

Listing 20-26. Using a Module Namespace in the ProductDisplay.vue File in the src/components Folder

```
...
<script>
    import { mapState, mapMutations, mapActions, mapGetters } from "vuex";

    export default {
        computed: {
            ...mapState(["products"]),
            ...mapState({
                striped: state => state.prefs.stripedTable
            }),
            ...mapGetters({
                tableClass: "prefs/tableClass",
                editClass: "prefs/editClass",
                deleteClass: "prefs/deleteClass"
            })
        },
        methods: {
            ...mapMutations({
                editProduct: "selectProduct",
                createNew: "selectProduct",
                setEditButtonColor: "prefs/setEditButtonColor",
                setDeleteButtonColor: "prefs/setDeleteButtonColor"
            }),
            ...mapActions({
                getProducts: "getProductsAction",
                deleteProduct: "deleteProductAction"
            })
        },
        created() {
            this.getProducts();
            this.setEditButtonColor(false);
            this.setDeleteButtonColor(false);
        }
    }
</script>
...
```

To select getters, mutations, and actions, the namespace is used, followed by a forward slash (the / character) followed by the function name, like this:

```
...
...mapGetters({
    tableClass: "prefs/tableClass",
    editClass: "prefs/editClass",
    deleteClass: "prefs/deleteClass"
})
...
```

This fragment maps the tableClass, editClass, and deleteClass getters in the prefs namespace.

Summary

In this chapter, I showed you how to use Vuex to create a data store for a Vue.js application. I showed you how to modify state data using mutations, how to synthesize values using getters, and how to perform asynchronous tasks using actions. I also demonstrated the Vuex functions for mapping data store features into components and how you can structure the data store using modules and namespaces. In the next chapter, I describe the Vue.js dynamic components feature.

CHAPTER 21

■■■

Dynamic Components

Simple applications can present all their content to the user at once, but more complex projects will need to be more selective and display different components to the user at different times. In this chapter, I explain the built-in Vue.js features that allow components to be displayed dynamically based on user interaction and to load components only when they are required, which can help reduce the amount of data users consume. Table 21-1 puts dynamic components in context.

■ **Tip** The features described in this chapter are often used with URL routing, which I describe in Chapter 22.

Table 21-1. *Putting Dynamic Components in Context*

Question	Answer
What are they?	Dynamic components are displayed to the user only when they are required.
Why are they useful?	Complex applications have too many features to present to the user at once. Being able to change the components that are shown to the user allows an application to present complex content without overwhelming the user.
How are they used?	The Vue.js is directive can be used to select components dynamically.
Are there any pitfalls or limitations?	Care must be taken to ensure that dynamic components do not make assumptions about their lifecycle, which can be an issue when introducing dynamic components to an existing project. See the "Preparing Components for Dynamic Lifecycles" section for details.
Are there any alternatives?	Applications do not have to display their components dynamically. Simple applications can display all of their content at once, as demonstrated by the example applications in earlier chapters.

© Adam Freeman 2018

A. Freeman, *Pro Vue.js 2*, https://doi.org/10.1007/978-1-4842-3805-9_21

Table 21-2 summarizes the chapter.

Table 21-2. *Chapter Summary*

Problem	Solution	Listing
Select a component dynamically	Use the is attribute and the v-bind directive	6–12
Load a component only when it is required	Define an asynchronous component	13–14
Disable prefetch hints	Change the application configuration	15
Fine-tune asynchronous components	Use the lazy loading configuration options	16, 17

Preparing for This Chapter

I continue using the productapp example in this chapter from Chapter 21. To start the RESTful web service, open a command prompt and run the command shown in Listing 21-1 in the productapp folder.

Listing 21-1. Starting the Web Service

```
npm run json
```

Open a second command prompt, navigate to the productapp directory, and run the command shown in Listing 21-2 to start the Vue.js development tools.

Listing 21-2. Starting the Development Tools

```
npm run serve
```

Once the initial bundling process is complete, open a new browser window and navigate to http://localhost:8080, where you will see the example application, as shown in Figure 21-1.

■ **Tip** You can download the example project for this chapter—and for all the other chapters in this book—from https://github.com/Apress/pro-vue-js-2.

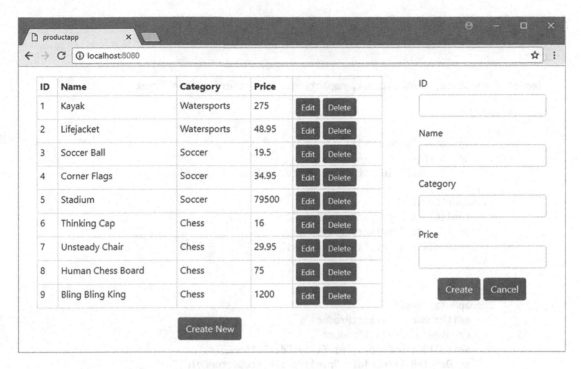

Figure 21-1. *Running the example application*

Preparing Components for Dynamic Lifecycles

The ProductDisplay and ProductEditor components were written with the assumption that they will be created when the application is initialized and exist until the application is terminated. That can be a problem when components are displayed dynamically because Vue.js won't create components until they are needed and will destroy them once they are not visible to the user. The result is that watchers and event handlers may miss important notifications and expensive tasks, such as getting data from a web service, will be repeated each time a component is created even though the application has already received the data it requires.

Getting the Application Data

In Listing 21-3, I have removed the statement in the ProductDisplay component's created method that gets the initial data from the web service. As I start to display components to the user dynamically, Vue.js will create a new instance of this component each time the user wants to see the table of products, and the instance that is created will have its own lifecycle that includes invoking its created method.

Listing 21-3. Avoiding Duplicate Requests in the ProductDisplay.vue File in the src/components Folder

```
...
<script>

    import { mapState, mapMutations, mapActions, mapGetters } from "vuex";

    export default {
        computed: {
            ...mapState(["products"]),
            ...mapState({
                useStripedTable: state => state.prefs.stripedTable
            }),
            ...mapGetters({
                tableClass: "prefs/tableClass",
                editClass: "prefs/editClass",
                deleteClass: "prefs/deleteClass"
            })
        },
        methods: {
            ...mapMutations({
                editProduct: "selectProduct",
                createNew: "selectProduct",
                setEditButtonColor: "prefs/setEditButtonColor",
                setDeleteButtonColor: "prefs/setDeleteButtonColor"
            }),
            ...mapActions({
                //getProducts: "getProductsAction",
                deleteProduct: "deleteProductAction"
            })
        },
        created() {
            //this.getProducts();
            this.setEditButtonColor(false);
            this.setDeleteButtonColor(false);
        }
    }
</script>
...
```

Tasks that should be performed only once must be handled by components that are not going to be displayed dynamically. In most Vue.js projects, the top-level component is used to coordinate the visibility of the application's other components and will always be visible to the user. In Listing 21-4, I have made the App component responsible for getting the initial data from the web service.

Listing 21-4. Getting Data in the App.vue File in the src Folder

```
<template>
    <div class="container-fluid">
        <div class="row">
            <div class="col"><error-display /></div>
        </div>
```

```
            <div class="row">
                <div class="col-8 m-3"><product-display /></div>
                <div class="col m-3"><product-editor /></div>
            </div>
        </div>
    </template>

<script>
    import ProductDisplay from "./components/ProductDisplay";
    import ProductEditor from "./components/ProductEditor";
    import ErrorDisplay from "./components/ErrorDisplay";

    export default {
        name: 'App',
        components: { ProductDisplay, ProductEditor, ErrorDisplay },
        created() {
            this.$store.dispatch("getProductsAction");
        }
    }
</script>
```

I have used the Vuex dispatch method to invoke the action called getProductsAction, which I defined in Chapter 20. Since I will not be displaying the App component dynamically, I can rely on this task being performed only once.

Managing Watch Events

The ProductEditor component uses a data store watcher to determine when the user clicks a Create New or Edit button. When components are created dynamically, it can be difficult to ensure that changes to the application's state are handled before Vue.js creates the components it requires, with the result that a component can miss the events that configure it for use. In Listing 21-5, I have changed the ProductEditor component to use existing data store values in its created method.

Listing 21-5. Preparing for Dynamic Display in the ProductEditor.vue File in the src/components Folder

```
...
<script>

    let unwatcher;

    export default {
        data: function () {
            return {
                editing: false,
                product: {}
            }
        },
        methods: {
            save() {
                this.$store.dispatch("saveProductAction", this.product);
                this.product = {};
            },
```

```
            cancel() {
                this.$store.commit("selectProduct");
            },
            selectProduct(selectedProduct) {
                if (selectedProduct == null) {
                    this.editing = false;
                    this.product = {};
                } else {
                    this.editing = true;
                    this.product = {};
                    Object.assign(this.product, selectedProduct);
                }
            }
        },
        created() {
            unwatcher = this.$store.watch(state =>
                state.selectedProduct, this.selectProduct);
            this.selectProduct(this.$store.state.selectedProduct);
        },
        beforeDestroy() {
            unwatcher();
        }
    }
}
</script>
...
```

The created method processes the current data values in the data store and uses the watch method to create a watcher to observe future changes. The result of the watch method is a function that can be used to stop receiving notifications, and I have used this function in the beforeDestroy lifecycle method to ensure that the watcher doesn't linger around when Vue.js has destroyed the component.

Displaying Components Dynamically

Now that the components have been updated so they can be created and destroyed without causing any problems, I can change the way the application presents its content. In this section, I demonstrate how to work directly with the Vue.js support for dynamically selecting components, which will provide the foundation for explaining how to use the popular Vue-Router package.

Presenting Different Components in an HTML Element

Vue.js supports a special attribute on HTML elements to specify the component whose content will be used to replace that element when the application is running. The special attribute is called is, and it can be used on any element, although the convention is to use the component element, as shown in Listing 21-6.

■ **Tip** You will see a linter warning when you save the changes in Listing 21-6. This will be resolved in the next section.

Listing 21-6. Using the is Attribute in the App.vue File in the src Folder

```
<template>
    <div class="container-fluid">
        <div class="row">
            <div class="col"><error-display /></div>
        </div>
        <div class="row">
            <div class="col">
                <component is="ProductDisplay"></component>
            </div>
        </div>
    </div>
</template>

<script>
    import ProductDisplay from "./components/ProductDisplay";
    import ProductEditor from "./components/ProductEditor";
    import ErrorDisplay from "./components/ErrorDisplay";

    export default {
        name: 'App',
        components: { ProductDisplay, ProductEditor, ErrorDisplay },
        created() {
            this.$store.dispatch("getProductsAction");
        }
    }
</script>
```

At runtime, Vue.js will encounter the is attribute on the component element and evaluate the attribute's value to determine which component should be displayed. In the listing, the is attribute is set to ProductDisplay, which is the name assigned by an import statement in the script element and which has been used with the components configuration property, with the result that the user is presented with the table of products, as shown in Figure 21-2.

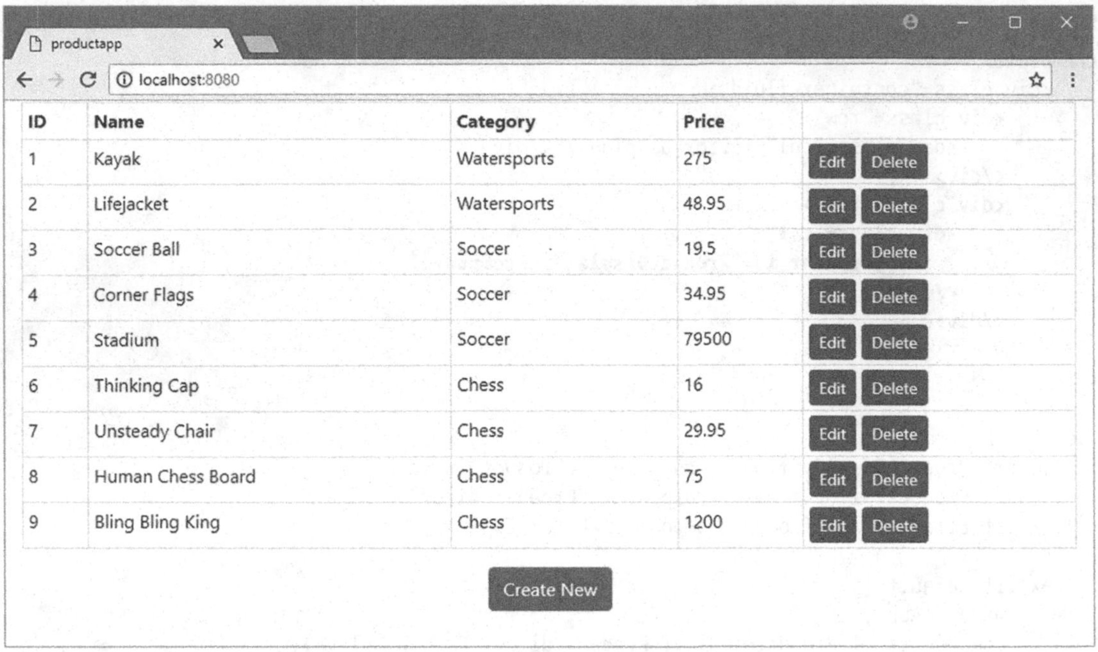

Figure 21-2. *Displaying a component*

Selecting Components Using a Data Binding

The is attribute becomes interesting when it is used with a data binding, which allows the components presented to the user to be changed while the application is running. In Listing 21-7, I have added a data binding to the App component's template that sets the value of the is attribute based on the user's selection.

Listing 21-7. Using a Data Binding in the App.vue File in the src Folder

```
<template>
    <div class="container-fluid">
        <div class="row">
            <div class="col text-center m-2">
                <div class="btn-group btn-group-toggle">
                    <label class="btn btn-info"
                            v-bind:class="{active: (selected == 'table') }">
                        <input type="radio" v-model="selected" value="table" />
                        Table
                    </label>
                    <label class="btn btn-info"
                            v-bind:class="{active: (selected == 'editor') }">
                        <input type="radio" v-model="selected" value="editor" />
                        Editor
                    </label>
                </div>
            </div>
        </div>
```

```
        <div class="row">
            <div class="col">
                <component v-bind:is="selectedComponent"></component>
            </div>
        </div>
    </div>
</template>

<script>
    import ProductDisplay from "./components/ProductDisplay";
    import ProductEditor from "./components/ProductEditor";
    import ErrorDisplay from "./components/ErrorDisplay";

    export default {
        name: 'App',
        components: { ProductDisplay, ProductEditor, ErrorDisplay },
        created() {
            this.$store.dispatch("getProductsAction");
        },
        data: function() {
            return {
                selected: "table"
            }
        },
        computed: {
            selectedComponent() {
                return this.selected == "table" ? ProductDisplay : ProductEditor;
            }
        }
    }
</script>
```

The input elements in this example allow the user to select which component is displayed by changing the data property named selected using the v-model directive. The value of the is attribute on the component element reflects the chosen value using the v-bind directive, which reads the value of a computed property that uses the selected value to identify the component that the user requires, producing the result shown in Figure 21-3.

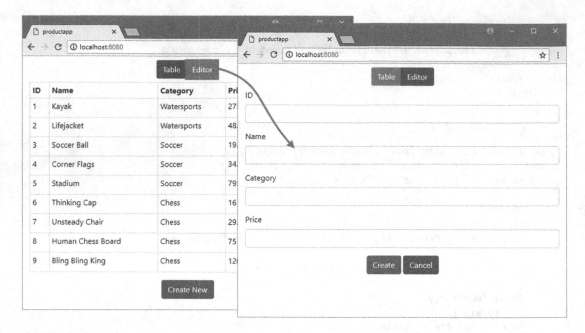

Figure 21-3. *Selecting components using a data binding*

The user is presented with a button group that allows the component displayed by the application to be selected: clicking the Table button shows the `ProductDisplay` component, and clicking the Editor button shows the `ProductEditor` button.

Understanding the Component Lifecycle

It is worth taking a moment to inspect the state of the application to see how Vue.js is dealing with the dynamic changes. Click the Table and Editor buttons while viewing the application's components using Vue Devtools, and you will see that components are being created and destroyed as they are required, with the result that the App component has only one child at any given moment, as shown in Figure 21-4.

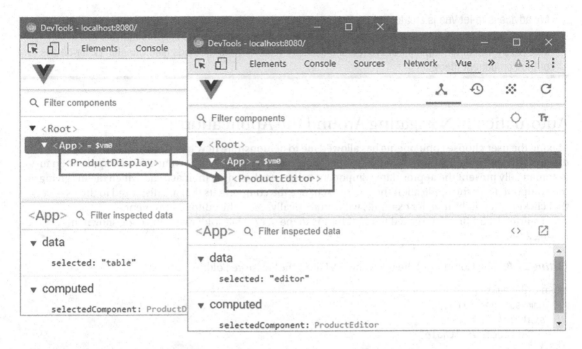

Figure 21-4. *Creating and destroying components*

REUSING DYNAMIC COMPONENTS

Vue.js provides an alternative approach to managing dynamic components that does not require them to be created each time they are required and destroyed when they are not. If you surround the element that displays the component—the element with the is attribute—with a keep-alive element, Vue.js will make components inactive when they are not required instead of destroying them. Here is an example of applying the keep-alive element:

```
...
<div class="row">
    <div class="col">
        <keep-alive>
            <component v-bind:is="selectedComponent"></component>
        </keep-alive>
    </div>
</div>
...
```

The advantage of this feature is you don't have to worry about updating components to avoid repeating one-off tasks or missing important events. The disadvantage is that resources are consumed by components that are not active and that may not be required again.

My advice is to let Vue.js create and destroy components as they are needed, but if you do use the keep-alive element, then you can receive notifications when components become activate and inactive by implementing the activated and deactivated lifecycle methods (see Chapter 17 for details of the component lifecycle).

Automatically Navigating Around the Application

Making the user choose components has allowed me to demonstrate how components are displayed dynamically, but it isn't the way that most applications need to work. What I want is for the application to automatically present the appropriate component to the user based on their actions, which means giving all the components in the application the ability to change the components that are displayed to the user, such that clicking an Edit button, for example, will automatically select the editor component.

I started by adding a file called navigation.js to the src/store folder with the code shown in Listing 21-8.

Listing 21-8. The Contents of the navigation.js File in the src/store Folder

```
export default {
    namespaced: true,
    state: {
        selected: "table"
    }
    ,
    mutations: {
        selectComponent(currentState, selection) {
            currentState.selected = selection;
        }
    }
}
```

This Vuex module will extend the data store so that I can navigate around the application. I will use the selected state property as the value of the is attribute and change its value using the selectComponent mutation. In Listing 21-9, I have imported the module into the main data store.

Listing 21-9. Adding a Module in the index.js File in the src/store Folder

```
import Vue from "vue";
import Vuex from "vuex";
import Axios from "axios";

import PrefsModule from "./preferences";
import NavModule from "./navigation";

Vue.use(Vuex);

const baseUrl = "http://localhost:3500/products/";
```

```
export default new Vuex.Store({
    modules: {
        prefs: PrefsModule,
        nav: NavModule
    },
    state: {
        products: [],
        selectedProduct: null
    },

    // ...other data store features omitted for brevity...

})
```

The next step is to use the new data store state property as the value of the is attribute in the App component's template, as shown in Listing 21-10. In addition to using the data store, I have removed the button elements that allow the user to explicitly select the component to display.

Listing 21-10. Using the Data Store in the App.vue File in the src Folder

```
<template>
    <div class="container-fluid">
        <!-- <div class="row">
            <div class="col text-center m-2">
                <div class="btn-group btn-group-toggle">
                    <label class="btn btn-info"
                            v-bind:class="{active: (selected == 'table') }">
                        <input type="radio" v-model="selected" value="table" />
                        Table
                    </label>
                    <label class="btn btn-info"
                            v-bind:class="{active: (selected == 'editor') }">
                        <input type="radio" v-model="selected" value="editor" />
                        Editor
                    </label>
                </div>
            </div>
        </div> -->
        <div class="row">
            <div class="col">
                <component v-bind:is="selectedComponent"></component>
            </div>
        </div>
    </div>
</template>

<script>
    import ProductDisplay from "./components/ProductDisplay";
    import ProductEditor from "./components/ProductEditor";
    import ErrorDisplay from "./components/ErrorDisplay";

    import { mapState } from "vuex";
```

```
    export default {
        name: 'App',
        components: { ProductDisplay, ProductEditor, ErrorDisplay },
        created() {
            this.$store.dispatch("getProductsAction");
        },
        // data: function() {
        //     return {
        //         selected: "table"
        //     }
        // },
        computed: {
            ...mapState({
                selected: state => state.nav.selected
            }),
            selectedComponent() {
                return this.selected == "table" ? ProductDisplay : ProductEditor;
            }
        }
    }
}
</script>
```

All that remains is to invoke the data store mutation to change the component displayed to the user. In Listing 21-11, I have updated the ProductDisplay component so that the user will be presented with the editor when clicking a Create New or Edit button.

Listing 21-11. Adding Navigation in the ProductDisplay.vue File in the src/components Folder

```
...
<script>
    import { mapState, mapMutations, mapActions, mapGetters } from "vuex";

    export default {
        computed: {
            ...mapState(["products"]),
            ...mapState({
                useStripedTable: state => state.prefs.stripedTable
            }),
            ...mapGetters({
                tableClass: "prefs/tableClass",
                editClass: "prefs/editClass",
                deleteClass: "prefs/deleteClass"
            })
        },
        methods: {
            editProduct(product) {
                this.selectProduct(product);
                this.selectComponent("editor");
            },
            createNew() {
                this.selectProduct();
                this.selectComponent("editor");
            },
```

```
        ...mapMutations({
            selectProduct: "selectProduct",
            selectComponent: "nav/selectComponent",
            //editProduct: "selectProduct",
            //createNew: "selectProduct",
            setEditButtonColor: "prefs/setEditButtonColor",
            setDeleteButtonColor: "prefs/setDeleteButtonColor"
        }),
        ...mapActions({
            deleteProduct: "deleteProductAction"
        })
    },
    created() {
        this.setEditButtonColor(false);
        this.setDeleteButtonColor(false);
    }
  }
}
</script>
...
```

I have redefined the editProduct and createNew methods so they are no longer directly mapped to the selectProduct data store mutation. Instead, I have created local methods that invoke the selectProduct and selectComponent mutations to identify the object that will be edited and then display the editor components. In Listing 21-12, I have updated the ProductEditor component so that it navigates to the table display once the user has completed or canceled an editing task.

SEPARATING NAVIGATION FROM OTHER OPERATIONS

Notice that I have handled navigation in the example application's components, rather than incorporating it directly into the data store mutations such as selectProduct. It can be tempting to perform navigation as part of other state changes, but this assumes that the components will always be displayed when a given mutation or action is performed. This may be the case when you start displaying components dynamically, but it often changes as a project becomes more complex and the user is presented with different paths through the application's features. Performing navigation in each component may seem more complex, but it results in an application that more readily accommodates new features.

Listing 21-12. Adding Navigation in the ProductEditor.vue File in the src/components Folder

```
...
<script>

    let unwatcher;

    export default {
        data: function () {
            return {
                editing: false,
                product: {}
            }
        },
```

```
        methods: {
            async save() {
                await this.$store.dispatch("saveProductAction", this.product);
                this.$store.commit("nav/selectComponent", "table");
                this.product = {};
            },
            cancel() {
                this.$store.commit("selectProduct");
                this.$store.commit("nav/selectComponent", "table");
            },
            selectProduct(selectedProduct) {
                if (selectedProduct == null) {
                    this.editing = false;
                    this.product = {};
                } else {
                    this.editing = true;
                    this.product = {};
                    Object.assign(this.product, selectedProduct);
                }
            }
        },
        created() {
            unwatcher = this.$store.watch(state =>
                state.selectedProduct, this.selectProduct);
            this.selectProduct(this.$store.state.selectedProduct);
        },
        beforeDestroy() {
            unwatcher();
        }
    }
</script>
...
```

This component uses the data store features directly, without using the Vuex mapping functions. I added the async keyword to the save method, which allows me to use the await keyword when saving a product so that navigation isn't performed until after the HTTP operation has completed.

The result is that the user's actions automatically select the component that will be displayed, automatically switching between the table and editor, as shown in Figure 21-5.

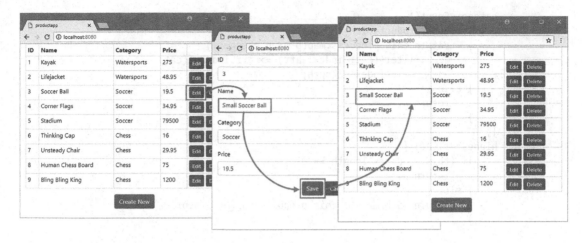

Figure 21-5. *Navigating between components*

Using Asynchronous Components

In larger applications, there are often features that are not required by all users or are required only occasionally, such as advanced settings or administration tools. By default, these unused components are included in the JavaScript bundle sent to the browser, which wastes bandwidth and increases the time taken for the application to start. To avoid this problem, Vue.js provides the asynchronous component feature, which is used to defer the loading of components until they are required—a feature that is also known as *lazy loading*. To demonstrate the asynchronous component feature, I added a file called DataSummary.vue to the src/components folder with the content shown in Listing 21-13.

Listing 21-13. The Contents of the DataSummary.vue File in the src/components Folder

```
<template>
    <div>
        <h3 class="bg-success text-center text-white p-2">
        Summary
        </h3>
        <table class="table">
            <tr><th>Number of Products:</th><td> {{ products.length}} </td></tr>
            <tr><th>Number of Categories:</th><td> {{ categoryCount }} </td></tr>
            <tr>
                <th>Highest Price:</th><td> {{ highestPrice | currency }} </td>
            </tr></table>
    </div>
</template>

<script>

    import { mapState, } from "vuex";

    export default {
        computed: {
            ...mapState(["products"]),
```

```
        categoryCount() {
            if (this.products.length > 0) {
                return this.products.map(p => p.category)
                    .filter((cat, index, arr) => arr.indexOf(cat)
                        == index).length;
            } else {
                return 0;
            }
        },
        highestPrice() {
            if (this.products.length == 0) {
                return 0;
            } else {
                return Math.max(...this.products.map(p => p.price));
            }
        }
    },
    filters: {
        currency(value) {
            return new Intl.NumberFormat("en-US",
                { style: "currency", currency: "USD" }).format(value);
        }
    }
}
</script>
```

This component displays a summary of the data in the store, which, for the purposes of this chapter, is a feature I don't want the browser to load until it is required. In Listing 21-14, I have registered the new component so that it will be lazily loaded.

UNDERSTANDING THE COST OF LAZY LOADING

The term *lazy* refers to the fact that the component won't be loaded from the HTTP server until it is required. This is in contrast to the default strategy of eager loading, where components are loaded as part of the main application bundle, even though they may not be required.

Both approaches represent a compromise. Eager loading requires a larger initial download and trades bandwidth and startup speed for a smoother user experience because all the code and content that the user could require is always available. Lazy loading reduces the size of the initial download but trades this against the need to make additional HTTP requests for components if they are required.

You can make the initial assessment of which components should be lazily loaded based on how you expect the application to be used, but it is important to validate your expectations once you have deployed your application. If you find that most users are performing actions that lazily load components, then you should change the configuration of the application because you are incurring the downsides of both approaches, such that there is no bandwidth saving and the user has to wait while lazy loading is performed.

Listing 21-14. Lazily Loading a Component in the App.vue File in the src/components Folder

```
<template>
    <div class="container-fluid">
        <div class="col">
            <div class="col text-center m-2">
                <button class="btn btn-primary"
                        v-on:click="selectComponent('table')">
                    Standard Features
                </button>
                <button class="btn btn-success"
                        v-on:click="selectComponent('summary')">
                    Advanced Features
                </button>
            </div>
        </div>
        <div class="row">
            <div class="col">
                <component v-bind:is="selectedComponent"></component>
            </div>
        </div>
    </div>
</template>

<script>
    import ProductDisplay from "./components/ProductDisplay";
    import ProductEditor from "./components/ProductEditor";
    import ErrorDisplay from "./components/ErrorDisplay";

    const DataSummary = () => import("./components/DataSummary");

    import { mapState, mapMutations } from "vuex";

    export default {
        name: 'App',
        components: { ProductDisplay, ProductEditor, ErrorDisplay, DataSummary },
        created() {
            this.$store.dispatch("getProductsAction");
        },
        methods: {
            ...mapMutations({
                selectComponent: "nav/selectComponent"
            })
        },
        computed: {
            ...mapState({
                selected: state => state.nav.selected
            }),
            selectedComponent() {
                switch (this.selected) {
                    case "table":
                        return ProductDisplay;
```

559

```
                case "editor":
                    return ProductEditor;
                case "summary":
                    return  DataSummary;
            }
        }
    }
}
</script>
```

There are a number of changes in the listing, but this one that tells Vue.js that this is a component that should be loaded only when it is required:

```
...
const DataSummary = () => import("./components/DataSummary");
...
```

The standard use of the import keyword creates a static dependency, which webpack processes by including the component in the JavaScript bundle it creates. But this form of import, where it is used as a function and the component is specified as the argument, creates a dynamic dependency, which webpack handles by putting the component in its own bundle. The result of the import function is a JavaScript Promise that is fulfilled when the component is loaded. The loading process begins as soon as the import function is invoked, so it is important to assign the component reference, which is DataSummary in this example, a function that, in turn, invokes import.

```
...
const DataSummary = () => import("./components/DataSummary");
...
```

When DataSummary is selected for use with the is attribute, Vue.js detects the function, which signifies an asynchronous component. The function is invoked to start the loading process, and the component is displayed once it is complete.

Disabling Prefetch Hints

By default, the project is configured to provide the browser with prefetch hints that indicate that there is application content that may be required in the future. The intention of this feature is that it allows the browser to decide whether it makes sense to get the content before it is needed. This tends to undermine the idea of lazy loading for Vue.js modules that are likely to be required by a small number of users since the JavaScript file will be downloaded and then discarded without being used. To disable the prefetch hint feature, I added a file called vue.config.js in the productapp folder and added the statements shown in Listing 21-15.

Listing 21-15. Disabling Prefetch Hints in the vue.config.js File in the productapp Folder

```
module.exports = {
    chainWebpack: config => {
        config.plugins.delete('prefetch');
    }
}
```

To apply the configuration change, stop the development tools and restart them by running the command shown in Listing 21-16 in the `productapp` folder.

Listing 21-16. Starting the Vue.js Development Tools

```
npm run serve
```

To test the asynchronous component, navigate to `http://localhost:8080` and click the Advanced Features button, which will show component defined in Listing 21-13, as shown in Figure 21-6.

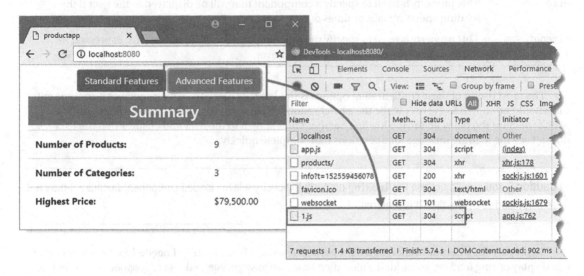

Figure 21-6. *Lazily loading a component*

You are unlikely to see any delay in loading the component because the browser and HTTP server are running on the same workstation. But if you open the browser's F12 development tools and switch to the Network tab, you will see that there is an HTTP request for a JavaScript file when you click the Advanced Features button. This is the file that contains the `DataSummary` component and is called `1.js` for me, although you may see a different name.

Configuring Lazy Loading

Vue.js provides a set of configuration options that can be used to fine-tune the loading process for asynchronous components, as described in Table 21-3.

Table 21-3. *The Lazy Loading Configuration Options*

Name	Description
component	This property is used to define the import function that will load the asynchronous component.
loading	This property is used to specify a component that will be displayed to the user during the loading process.
delay	This property is used to specify a delay, expressed in milliseconds, before the loading component is shown to the user. The default value is 200.
error	This property is used to specify a component that will be displayed to the user if the loading operation fails or times out.
timeout	This property is used to specify the timeout period for load operations, expressed in milliseconds. The default value waits forever.

The most useful of these configuration options is the loading property, which specifies a component that should be shown to the user while the asynchronous component is loading, and the delay option, which specifies the delay before the loading component is shown to the user and ensures that the user doesn't see the loading message for operations that complete quickly.

■ **Caution**   You should not use the loading property to specify a lazily loaded component because it may not have been loaded by the time it is required.

To prepare for a demonstration of the properties described in Table 21-3, I needed a component that I can display during loading, so I added a file called LoadingMessage.vue to the src/components folder with the content shown in Listing 21-17.

Listing 21-17. The Contents of the LoadingMessage.vue File in the src/components Folder

```
<template>
    <h3 class="bg-info text-white text-center m-2 p-2">
        Lazily Loading Component...
    </h3>
</template>
```

This component consists of just a template that will display a message to the user. In Listing 21-18, I have used this component to configure the lazy loading of the DataSummary component.

Listing 21-18. Configuring Lazy Loading in the App.vue File in the src Folder

```
...
<script>
    import ProductDisplay from "./components/ProductDisplay";
    import ProductEditor from "./components/ProductEditor";
    import ErrorDisplay from "./components/ErrorDisplay";
    import LoadingMessage from "./components/LoadingMessage";
```

```
const DataSummary = () => ({
    component: import("./components/DataSummary"),
    loading: LoadingMessage,
    delay: 100
});

import { mapState, mapMutations } from "vuex";

export default {
    name: 'App',
    components: { ProductDisplay, ProductEditor, ErrorDisplay, DataSummary },
    created() {
        this.$store.dispatch("getProductsAction");
    },
    methods: {
        ...mapMutations({
            selectComponent: "nav/selectComponent"
        })
    },
    computed: {
        ...mapState({
            selected: state => state.nav.selected
        }),
        selectedComponent() {
            switch (this.selected) {
                case "table":
                    return ProductDisplay;
                case "editor":
                    return ProductEditor;
                case "summary":
                    return  DataSummary;
            }
        }
    }
}
</script>
...
```

The component property is assigned the import function that load will the component, and I have specified that the user will see the LoadingMessage component if the load operation takes more than 100 milliseconds. To see the effect, navigate to http://localhost:8080 and click the Advanced Features button, which will produce the loading sequence shown in Figure 21-7.

■ **Note**   It can be hard to test the configuration features during development because the asynchronous component will be loaded too quickly to see the component specified by the component property. My approach is to use the Google Chrome developer tools to create a network profile that adds several seconds of latency to HTTP requests and to enable this profile before triggering the lazy load.

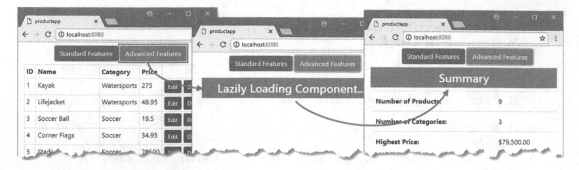

Figure 21-7. *Configuring the lazy loading process*

COMBINING COMPONENTS INTO A SHARED BUNDLE

By default, each asynchronous component will be put into its own file and loaded only when it is required. An alternative approach is to group related components so they are all loaded the first time that any of them is required. This is done by adding a comment that is detected by webpack during the build process, like this:

```
...
const DataSummary = () => ({
    component:
        import(/* webpackChunkName: "advanced" */ "./components/DataSummary"),
    loading: LoadingMessage,
    delay: 100
});
...
```

The comment sets the value of a property called webpackChunkName, and webpack will package all asynchronous components with the same webpackChunkName value into a single bundle. The name you specify won't be used as the name of the bundle file, which is selected dynamically during the build process.

Summary

In this chapter, I demonstrated how components can be displayed dynamically. I showed you how to use the is attribute to select a component, which is a good approach for simpler projects. I also showed you how to load components on demand, which can be a good way to deal with components that are not required by all users. In the next chapter, I introduce URL routing, which builds on the features described in this chapter.

CHAPTER 22

■ ■ ■

URL Routing

In this chapter, I start to describe the URL routing feature, which builds on the dynamic components that I described in Chapter 21 but uses the current URL to select the components that are displayed to the user. URL routing is a complex topic, and I continue to describe different aspects of this feature in Chapters 23 and 24. Table 22-1 puts URL routing in context.

Table 22-1. *Putting URL Routing in Context*

Question	Answer
What is it?	URL routing selects components to display to the user based on the current URL.
Why is it useful?	Using the URL to select components allows the user to navigate directly to a specific part of the application and allows complex applications to be composed in a way that is easier to maintain than selecting components in code.
How is it used?	The Vue Router package is added to a project, and a router-view element is used to display the component selected by the application's routing configuration.
Are there any pitfalls or limitations?	It can be difficult to find the appropriate balance between concisely expressing routes and creating routes that are easy to read and understand.
Are there any alternatives?	URL routing is optional, and the features described in this chapter are required only for complex applications.

Table 22-2 summarizes the chapter.

© Adam Freeman 2018
A. Freeman, *Pro Vue.js 2*, https://doi.org/10.1007/978-1-4842-3805-9_22

Table 22-2. *Chapter Summary*

Problem	Solution	Listing
Configure URL routing	Create a VueRouter object and provide it with a configuration object that has a routes property	4, 5
Display a routed component	Use the router-view element	6
Navigate in code	Use the $router.push method	7
Navigate in a template	Use the router-link element	8
Configure the routing mode	Use the mode property when creating the VuewRouter object	9
Define a catchall route	Define a route with * as the path	10
Define an alias for a route	Use the route property	11
Get details of the route in code	Use the $route object	12–14
Control the URLs matched by a route	Add a dynamic segment, use regular expressions, or use optional segments	15–20
Assign a name to a route	Use the name property	21–23
Receive notifications when the active route changes	Implement one or more guard methods	24

Preparing for This Chapter

In this chapter, I continue using the productapp project from Chapter 21. The URL routing feature requires a package called vue-router to be added to the project. Run the command shown in Listing 22-1 in the productapp folder to install the package.

■ **Tip** You can download the example project for this chapter—and for all the other chapters in this book—from https://github.com/Apress/pro-vue-js-2.

Listing 22-1. Installing the Routing Package

```
npm install vue-router@3.0.1
```

To start the RESTful web service, open a command prompt and run the command shown in Listing 22-2 in the productapp folder.

Listing 22-2. Starting the Web Service

```
npm run json
```

Open a second command prompt, navigate to the productapp directory, and run the command shown in Listing 22-3 to start the Vue.js development tools.

Listing 22-3. Starting the Development Tools

```
npm run serve
```

Once the initial bundling process is complete, open a new browser window and navigate to http://localhost:8080, where you will see the example application, as shown in Figure 22-1.

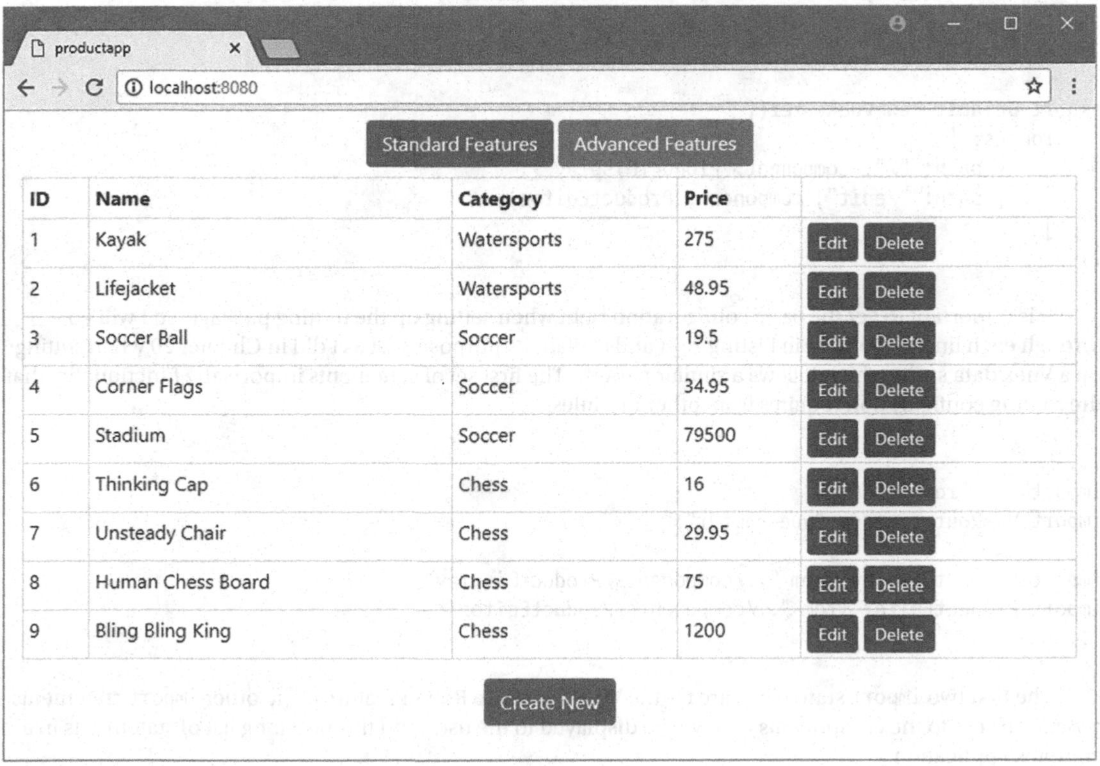

Figure 22-1. *Running the example application*

Getting Started with URL Routing

Before I get into the detail of how to use and configure URL routing, I am going to provide a quick introduction to the main features so that you have some context for more detailed topics. The first step when you start using URL routing is to configure the set of *routes*, which are mappings between the URLs that the application will support and the components that each will display. The convention is to put the routing configuration in a folder called router, so I created the src/router folder in the example project and added to it a file called index.js with the code shown in Listing 22-4.

Listing 22-4. The Contents of the index.js File in the src/router Folder

```
import Vue from "vue";
import VueRouter  from "vue-router";

import ProductDisplay from "../components/ProductDisplay";
import ProductEditor from "../components/ProductEditor";

Vue.use(VueRouter);

export default new VueRouter({
    routes: [
        { path: "/", component: ProductDisplay },
        { path: "/edit", component: ProductEditor}
    ]
})
```

It is important to get the basic configuration right when setting up the routing package, so I will go through each line of the code in Listing 22-4 and explain its purpose, just as I did in Chapter 20 when setting up a Vuex data store, which follows a similar pattern. The first set of statements imports the functionality that the routing configuration requires from other modules.

```
...
import Vue from "vue";
import VueRouter  from "vue-router";

import ProductDisplay from "../components/ProductDisplay";
import ProductEditor from "../components/ProductEditor";
...
```

The first two `import` statements are for the Vue.js and Vue Router features. The other `import` statements provide access to the components that will be displayed to the user, and this be a long list of statements in a complex application.

```
The next statement enables the Vue Router functionality:...
Vue.use(VueRouter);
...
```

Vue Router is provided as a Vue.js plugin, which allows the Vue.js core functionality to be extended, as I describe in Chapter 26, and plugins are installed with the `Vue.use` method.

CHAPTER 22 ■ URL ROUTING

The next statement creates the routing configuration and makes it the default export from the module in the routes folder:

```
...
export default new VueRouter({
...
```

The new keyword is used to create a VueRouter object, which accepts a configuration object. The configuration in this example provides a basic set of instructions for how to display two components.

```
...
routes: [
    { path: "/", component: ProductDisplay },
    { path: "/edit", component: ProductEditor}
]
...
```

The routes property is used to define mappings between URLs and components. The mappings in this example tell Vue Router to display the ProductDisplay component for the application's default route and to display the ProductEditor component for the /edit URL. Don't worry about the URL routes at the moment because they will be easier to understand once you see how they are applied and used.

Providing Access to the Routing Configuration

The next step is to add the routing functionality to the application so that it can be used by components, as shown in Listing 22-5.

Listing 22-5. Enabling the Routing Configuration in the main.js File in the src Folder

```
import Vue from 'vue'
import App from './App.vue'

import "../node_modules/bootstrap/dist/css/bootstrap.min.css";
import { RestDataSource } from "./restDataSource";
import store from "./store";
import router from "./router";

Vue.config.productionTip = false

new Vue({
  render: h => h(App),
  data: {
    eventBus: new Vue()
  },
  store,
  router,
  provide: function () {
      return {
          eventBus: this.eventBus,
          restDataSource: new RestDataSource(this.eventBus)
      }
  }
}).$mount('#app')
```

To add the URL routing functionality to the application, I used an import statement that specifies the router module and gives it the name router (I don't have to specify the index.js file because this is the default name that is looked for when a module is imported). The import statement loads the routing configuration from the index.js file in the router folder. I added a router property to the Vue configuration object, which makes the URL routing functionality available to the application's components.

■ **Caution**   If you forget to add the router property shown in Listing 22-5, the URL routing package won't be set up properly, and you will encounter errors in the examples that follow.

Using the Routing System to Display Components

Now that the routing system is enabled, I can use it to display components to the user, as shown in Listing 22-6, where I have used URL routing to replace the existing content and code that displayed components dynamically.

Listing 22-6.   Using URL Routing in the App.vue File in the src Folder

```
<template>
    <div class="container-fluid">
        <div class="row">
            <div class="col m-2">
                <router-view></router-view>
            </div>
        </div>
    </div>
</template>

<script>
    // import ProductDisplay from "./components/ProductDisplay";
    // import ProductEditor from "./components/ProductEditor";
    // import ErrorDisplay from "./components/ErrorDisplay";

    //import { mapState } from "vuex";

    export default {
        name: 'App',
        // components: { ProductDisplay, ProductEditor, ErrorDisplay },
        created() {
            this.$store.dispatch("getProductsAction");
        },
        // computed: {
        //     ...mapState({
        //         selected: state => state.nav.selected
        //     }),
        //     selectedComponent() {
        //         return this.selected == "table" ? ProductDisplay : ProductEditor;
        //     }
        // }
    }
</script>
```

The Vue Router uses the `router-view` element to display content, replacing the previous element that used the `is` attribute. Because the Vue Router package will be responsible for selecting the component displayed by the `router-view` element, I am able to simplify the component's configuration object, removing the `components` property, the computed properties, and all of the `import` statements. The result of these changes is that responsibility for the content presented by the `router-view` element is delegated to Vue Router, producing the result shown in Figure 22-2. (The Create New and Edit buttons have no effect yet, but I'll wire them up shortly.)

■ **Tip** When adding and changing routing features, you may not always get the response you expect. If that happens, the first thing to try is to reload the browser to get a fresh copy of the application, which will often sort out the problem.

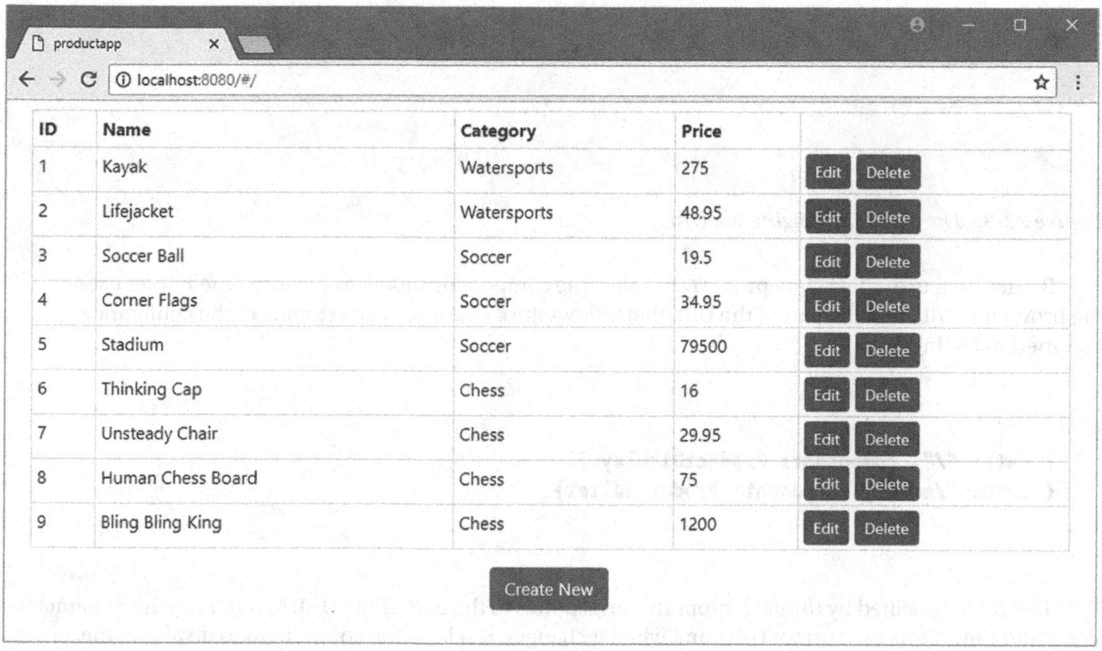

Figure 22-2. *Using the Vue Router package*

This may look like the previous examples, but there is an important difference, which can be seen by examining the browser's URL bar. When you navigate to `http://localhost:8080`, the browser actually displays this URL:

```
http://localhost:8080/#/
```

The important part to note is the last part of the URL, which is #/. Carefully edit the URL in the browser's URL bar to navigate to this URL:

```
http://localhost:8080/#/edit
```

This is the same URL that was previously displayed but with edit appended to the end. Press Enter and the content displayed by the browser will change, as shown in Figure 22-3.

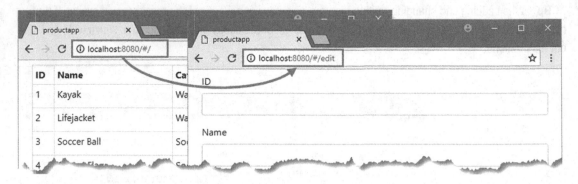

Figure 22-3. *The effect of changing the URL*

Rather than use a data store property to select the component shown to the user, Vue Router uses the browser's URL, and the part of the URL that follows the # character corresponds to the configuration I defined in Listing 22-4.

```
...
routes: [
    { path: "/", component: ProductDisplay },
    { path: "/edit", component: ProductEditor}
]
...
```

The value specified by the path property corresponds to the part of the URL that follows the # character. Vue Router monitors the current URL, and when it changes, it selects the component to display in the router-view element by finding the corresponding routes configuration item based on its path property and displaying the component specified by its component property.

Navigating to Different URLs

To change the component that is displayed to the user, I have to change the browser's URL, at which point Vue Router will compare the new URL to its configuration and display the corresponding component. Vue Router provides features for navigating to new URLs, and in Listing 22-7, I have updated the ProductDisplay component to use them.

Listing 22-7. Navigating Programatically in the ProductDisplay.vue File in the src/components Folder

```
...
<script>
    import { mapState, mapMutations, mapActions, mapGetters } from "vuex";

    export default {
        computed: {
            ...mapState(["products"]),
            ...mapState({
                useStripedTable: state => state.prefs.stripedTable
            }),
            ...mapGetters({
                tableClass: "prefs/tableClass",
                editClass: "prefs/editClass",
                deleteClass: "prefs/deleteClass"
            })
        },
        methods: {
            editProduct(product) {
                this.selectProduct(product);
                //this.selectComponent("editor");
                this.$router.push("/edit");
            },
            createNew() {
                this.selectProduct();
                //this.selectComponent("editor");
                this.$router.push("/edit");
            },
            ...mapMutations({
                selectProduct: "selectProduct",
                //selectComponent: "nav/selectComponent",
                setEditButtonColor: "prefs/setEditButtonColor",
                setDeleteButtonColor: "prefs/setDeleteButtonColor"
            }),
            ...mapActions({
                deleteProduct: "deleteProductAction"
            })
        },
        created() {
            this.setEditButtonColor(false);
            this.setDeleteButtonColor(false);
        }
    }
</script>
...
```

The effect of adding the router property in Listing 22-7 is that all the components in the application are given access to Vue Router features through a $router variable, similar to the way that components are able to access the Vuex data store using the $store property. The $router property returns an object that defines the navigation methods described in Table 22-3.

Table 22-3. *The Vue Router Navigation Methods*

Name	Description
push(location)	This method navigates to the specified URL. This method accepts optional callback arguments that are invoked when the navigation is complete or if there is an error.
replace(location)	This method performs the same task as the push method but doesn't leave an entry in the browser's history, as discussed after the table.
back()	This method navigates to the previous URL in the browser's history.
forward()	This method navigates to the next URL in the browser's history.

The difference between these methods is that navigation performed with the push method results in an entry in the browser's history with the effect that clicking the browser's back button will return to the previous route. The replace method changes the URL without adding to the browser's history, which means that moving backward may cause the browser to navigate away from the Vue.js application. In the listing, I disabled the selectComponent method, which applied to a mutation to the data store, and replaced it with calls to the Vue Router push method to navigate to the /edit URL.

```
...
this.$router.push("/edit");
...
```

The result is that clicking the Create New button or an Edit button tells Vue Router to ask the browser to navigate to the #/edit URL. URL routing is a two-stage process. The push method changes the URL, which Vue Router observes and uses to change the component displayed to the user. Put another way, clicking a button changes the URL, which in turn changes the component displayed to the user, as shown in Figure 22-4.

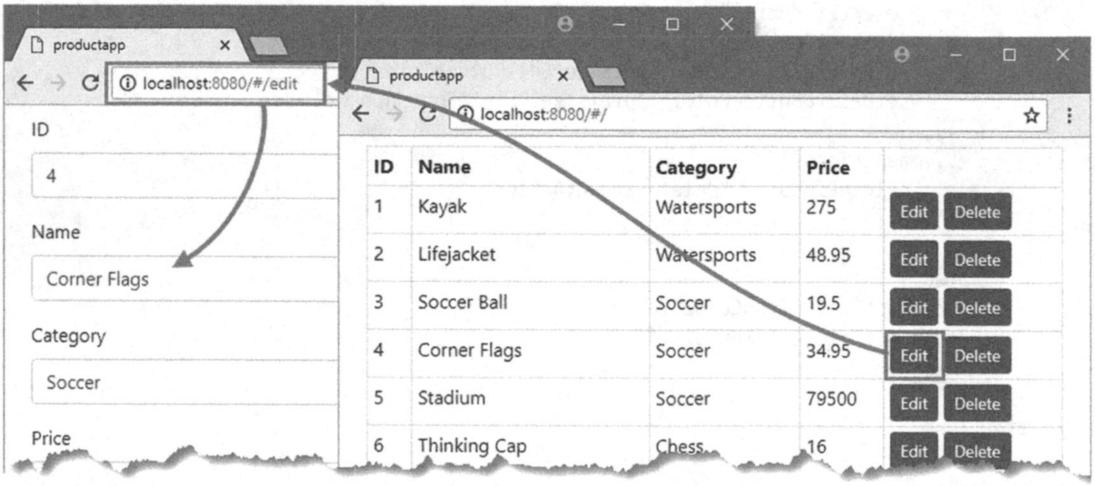

Figure 22-4. *Navigating around the application*

Navigating Using HTML Elements

The $router methods are not the only way to navigate around the application. Vue Router also supports a custom HTML element that triggers navigation when it is clicked. The $router methods and the custom HTML element can be freely mixed in a component, as shown in Listing 22-8.

Listing 22-8. Adding URL Navigation in the ProductEditor.vue File in the src/components Folder

```
<template>

    <div>
        <div class="form-group">
            <label>ID</label>
            <input class="form-control" v-model="product.id" />
        </div>
        <div class="form-group">
            <label>Name</label>
            <input class="form-control" v-model="product.name" />
        </div>
        <div class="form-group">
            <label>Category</label>
            <input class="form-control" v-model="product.category" />
        </div>
        <div class="form-group">
            <label>Price</label>
            <input class="form-control" v-model.number="product.price" />
        </div>
        <div class="text-center">
            <button class="btn btn-primary" v-on:click="save">
                {{ editing ? "Save" : "Create" }}
            </button>
            <router-link to="/" class="btn btn-secondary">Cancel</router-link>
        </div>
    </div>

</template>

<script>

    let unwatcher;

    export default {
        data: function () {
            return {
                editing: false,
                product: {}
            }
        },
```

575

```
    methods: {
        async save() {
            await this.$store.dispatch("saveProductAction", this.product);
            //this.$store.commit("nav/selectComponent", "table");
            this.$router.push("/");
            this.product = {};
        },
        // cancel() {
        //     this.$store.commit("selectProduct");
        //     //this.$store.commit("nav/selectComponent", "table");
        //     this.$router.push("/");
        // },
        selectProduct(selectedProduct) {
            if (selectedProduct == null) {
                this.editing = false;
                this.product = {};
            } else {
                this.editing = true;
                this.product = {};
                Object.assign(this.product, selectedProduct);
            }
        }
    },
    created() {
        unwatcher = this.$store.watch(state =>
            state.selectedProduct, this.selectProduct);
        this.selectProduct(this.$store.state.selectedProduct);
    },
    beforeDestroy() {
        unwatcher();
    }
}
</script>
```

In the component's template, I have used the router-link element to create an HTML element that will trigger navigation when it is clicked. The URL that will be navigated to is specified using the to attribute, like this:

```
...
<router-link to="/" class="btn btn-secondary">Cancel</router-link>
...
```

In this case, I have specified /, which is the first route defined in the configuration. When the template is processed and displayed to the user, the result is an anchor (a) element like this:

```
...
<a href="#/" class="btn btn-secondary router-link-active">Cancel</a>
...
```

The href attribute is specified so that the URL that the browser navigates to is relative to the # part of the URL, although you should not specify this in the to attribute because there are other ways that URL navigation can be implemented, as I explain shortly. The Bootstrap CSS framework that I use throughout this book supports styling anchor elements so they appear as buttons, which allows me to present the routing link as a seamless replacement for the button element that it replaces. Since the URL navigation is handled directly by the anchor element, I have been able to remove the cancel method.

Not all navigation can be performed just using an HTML element because some additional tasks must be performed in response to the user's action, as the save method demonstrates. The Save/Create button in the component's template cannot be replaced with a router-link element because the data that the user has entered must be sent to the web service. For this type of activity, the $router.push method can be used, as shown in the listing. The changes in Listing 22-8 allow the user to navigate back from the editor to the table, either by clicking the Save/Create button to save their changes or by clicking Cancel to abandon them, as shown in Figure 22-5.

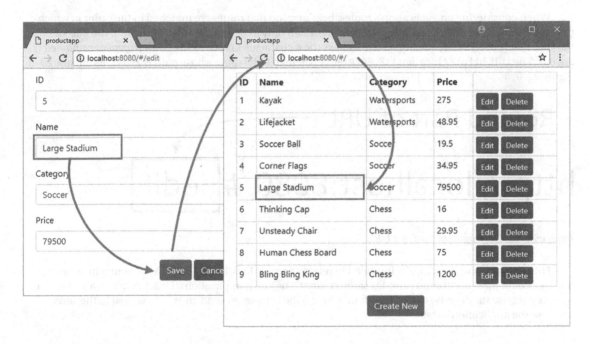

Figure 22-5. *Navigating back to the display of products*

Understanding and Configuring URL Route Matching

The examples in the previous section have given you a brief overview of how URL routing works, including defining the routes and the different ways of navigating around the application. In the sections that follow, I dig a little deeper and explain how to change the format of URLs to make them friendlier to the user and different ways that routes can be expressed to match URLs.

Understanding URL Matching and Formatting

Vue Router examines the current URL and works its way down through the list of routes in its configuration until it finds a match. To match a route, a URL must contain the same number of segments, and each segment must contain the value specified in the routing configuration. Here are the routes I defined in the index.js file in the src/router folder in Listing 22-4:

```
...
routes: [
    { path: "/", component: ProductDisplay },
    { path: "/edit", component: ProductEditor}
]
...
```

When considering an application's routes, bear in mind that routes are matched in the order in which they are defined and that the routing system is interested only in part of the URL. By default, the part of the URL that is used by the routing system follows the # character, known as the URLs *fragment* or *named anchor*. The URL http://localhost:8080/#/edit will match the route whose path is /edit, as illustrated in Figure 22-6.

Figure 22-6. *The fragment part of a URL*

URL fragments were originally intended to refer to specific locations in an HTML document so that the user could navigate around complex static content. For Vue.js applications, URL fragments are used for routing because they can be changed without causing the browser to send an HTTP request to the server and lose the application's state.

Using the HTML5 History API for Routing

URL fragments are supported by all browsers, but the result is application URLs that have an odd structure and that can be confusing to users. One of the attractions of using URL routing is that users can navigate directly to a specific part of the application by changing the URL, but this can be an error-prone process if the importance of the # character isn't understood. If the user navigates to /edit instead of /#/edit, for example, the browser will assume that the user is trying to navigate to a new URL and will send an HTTP request to the server, with the result that the browser will navigate away from the Vue.js application.

A better alternative is to configure Vue Router so that it uses the HTML 5 History API, which allows for more robust and elegant URLs but which isn't supported by older browsers, although Vue Router will automatically fall back to using fragments in browsers that don't support the History API. In Listing 22-9, I have updated the routing configuration so that Vue Router will use the History API.

Listing 22-9. Enabling the History API in the index.js File in the src/router Folder

```
import Vue from "vue";
import VueRouter  from "vue-router";

import ProductDisplay from "../components/ProductDisplay";
import ProductEditor from "../components/ProductEditor";

Vue.use(VueRouter);

export default new VueRouter({
    mode: "history",
    routes: [
        { path: "/", component: ProductDisplay },
        { path: "/edit", component: ProductEditor}
    ]
})
```

The mode property is added to the Vue Router configuration object to specify the mechanism used for URL routing, using the values shown in Table 22-4.

Table 22-4. *The mode Property Configuration Values*

Name	Description
hash	This mode uses the URL fragment for routing, which offers the widest browser support but produces awkward URLs. This is the default mode that is used if the mode property is not specified.
history	This mode uses the History API for routing, which offers the most natural URLs but is not supported by older browsers.

In the listing, I specified the history value for the mode property, which tells Vue Router to use the History API. To see the effect, reload the browser and click one of the Edit buttons once the application has reloaded, as shown in Figure 22-7.

■ **Tip**   With many of the examples in this chapter, you may have to reload the browser window or manually navigate to http://localhost:8080 to see the changes.

Figure 22-7. *Using the History API for routing*

Instead of a URL that includes a fragment, such as http://localhost:8080/#/edit, the application has navigated to http://localhost:8080/edit. The History API allows navigation using complete URLs without triggering a browser reload, with the effect that the part of the URL used for routing changes, as shown in Figure 22-8.

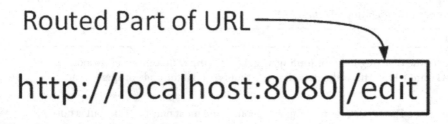

Figure 22-8. *The effect of using the History API*

■ **Note** For browsers that don't support the History API, which includes older versions of Internet Explorer, Vue Router will automatically try to use the hash setting instead, which will return the application to using the URL fragment to define the route. To disable this behavior, you can set the fallback property to false in the routing configuration object.

Providing a Catchall Route

Using the History API requires additional work to ensure a smooth experience for the user, who may navigate directly to a URL that has meaning to the application but for which there is no HTML document on the server. In the case of the example application, that means the user may type http://localhost:8080/edit into the URL bar, which will lead the browser to send an HTTP request for a document called edit. There is no such HTML document on the server, but the webpack development server has been configured to respond to any request with the index.html file.

It doesn't matter what URL has been requested; if there is no content available, the server will always return the contents of the index.html file and will never return a 404 – Not Found error. This is useful when the user requests a URL that corresponds to one of the routes defined by the application, such as /edit in the case of the example application, but it leaves the user looking at an empty window when the URL doesn't correspond to a route.

■ **Caution** You must ensure that you configure your production HTTP server to return the contents of the index.html file if you are using the History API for routing. The Vue.js team provides instructions for commonly used production servers at `https://router.vuejs.org/en/essentials/history-mode.html`.

To address this problem, a catchall route can be defined that matches any request and redirects it to another URL, as shown in Listing 22-10

Listing 22-10. Creating a Catchall Route in the index.js File in the src/router Folder

```
import Vue from "vue";
import VueRouter  from "vue-router";

import ProductDisplay from "../components/ProductDisplay";
import ProductEditor from "../components/ProductEditor";

Vue.use(VueRouter);

export default new VueRouter({
    mode: "history",
    routes: [
        { path: "/", component: ProductDisplay },
        { path: "/edit", component: ProductEditor},
        { path: "*", redirect: "/" }
    ]
})
```

The path property of this route is an asterisk (the * character), which allows it to match any URL. Instead of a component property, this route has a redirect property, which tells Vue.js to perform a redirection to the specified URL. The overall effect is combined with the fallback feature of the HTTP server, which mean that requests for which there is no content will be handled with the contents of the index. html file, and if the URL doesn't correspond to a route, the browser will then be redirected to the / URL. To test this feature, open a new browser window and request the http://localhost:8080/does/not/exist URL. As Figure 22-9 shows, the browser will display the application, even though the requested URL doesn't correspond to any of the application's routes.

■ **Tip** Redirections can also be defined as a function, which allows aspects of the URL that the user has requested to be incorporated into the redirected URL. See Chapter 23 for an example.

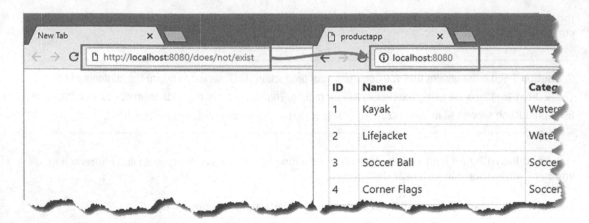

Figure 22-9. *The effect of a catchall route*

When the Vue.js application starts, Vue Router inspects the current URL and starts working its way through its routes to find a match. The first and second routes do match the current URL because that URL is neither / nor /edit. Vue Router reaches the final URL, which matches anything and which causes a redirection to /. The matching process begins again, but now the first route matches, which causes the application to display the ProductDisplay component.

Using a Route Alias

One potential pitfall of using redirection is that the user will see that the URL they typed into the browser will be immediately replaced with the redirected URL, which may be confusing. An alternative is to create an alias for a route, which allows it to match more than one URL without needing a redirection. In Listing 22-11, I have added an alias to the routing configuration to change the way that unmatched URLs are handled.

Listing 22-11. Using a Route Alias in the index.js File in the src/router Folder

```
import Vue from "vue";
import VueRouter from "vue-router";

import ProductDisplay from "../components/ProductDisplay";
import ProductEditor from "../components/ProductEditor";

Vue.use(VueRouter);

export default new VueRouter({
    mode: "history",
    routes: [
        { path: "/", component: ProductDisplay, alias: "/list" },
        { path: "/edit", component: ProductEditor } ,
        { path: "*", redirect: "/" }
    ]
})
```

The alias property is used to create an alias for a route, which allows it to match multiple URLs without using redirection. The alias I created defines the /list URL as an alias of the root URL, which can be tested by navigating to http://localhost:8080/list. As Figure 22-10 shows, the ProductDisplay component is displayed without the current URL being modified.

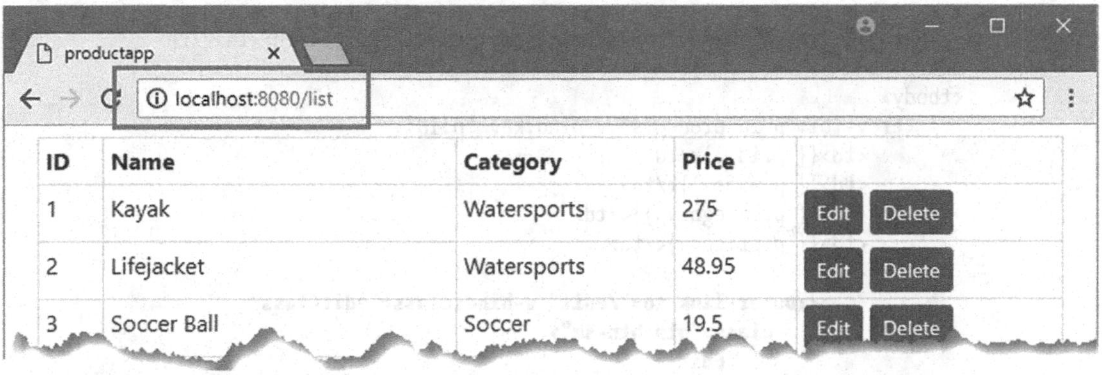

Figure 22-10. *Using a routing alias*

Getting Routing Data in Components

In addition to the $router property, the Vue Router package also provides components with a $route property that describes the current route and that can be used to adapt the content or behavior of components. To demonstrate, I added a new route to the example application, as shown in Listing 22-12.

Listing 22-12. Adding a Route in the index.js File in the src/router Folder

```
import Vue from "vue";
import VueRouter from "vue-router";

import ProductDisplay from "../components/ProductDisplay";
import ProductEditor from "../components/ProductEditor";

Vue.use(VueRouter);

export default new VueRouter({
    mode: "history",
    routes: [
        { path: "/", component: ProductDisplay, alias: "/list" },
        { path: "/edit", component: ProductEditor },
        { path: "/create", component: ProductEditor },
        { path: "*", redirect: "/" }
    ]
})
```

The new route matches the /create URL and targets the ProductEditor component, which means that there are two different URLs—/edit and /create—that will lead the application to display the editor feature. In Listing 22-13, I have replaced the button elements in the ProductDisplay component's template with a router-link element that targets the /edit and /create URLs.

Listing 22-13. Targeting Routes in the ProductDisplay.vue File in the src/components Folder

```
...
<template>
    <div>
        <table class="table table-sm table-bordered" v-bind:class="tableClass">
            <tr>
                <th>ID</th><th>Name</th><th>Category</th><th>Price</th><th></th>
            </tr>
            <tbody>
                <tr v-for="p in products" v-bind:key="p.id">
                    <td>{{ p.id }}</td>
                    <td>{{ p.name }}</td>
                    <td>{{ p.category }}</td>
                    <td>{{ p.price }}</td>
                    <td>
                        <router-link to="/edit" v-bind:class="editClass"
                            class="btn btn-sm">
                                Edit
                        </router-link>
                        <button class="btn btn-sm"
                                v-bind:class="deleteClass"
                                v-on:click="deleteProduct(p)">
                            Delete
                        </button>
                    </td>
                </tr>
                <tr v-if="products.length == 0">
                    <td colspan="5" class="text-center">No Data</td>
                </tr>
            </tbody>
        </table>
        <div class="text-center">
            <router-link to="/create" class="btn btn-primary">
                Create New
            </router-link>
        </div>
    </div>
</template>
...
```

Notice that the component doesn't know what the result of navigating to the /edit or /create URL will be. This is similar to the effect of using a data store to coordinate components, as described in Chapter 21, with the advantage that you can easily reconfigure the application just by editing the routing configuration. Now that there are two different URLs that display the ProductEditor component, I can use the $route property to see which of them has been used and change the content that is presented to the user, as shown in Listing 22-14.

Listing 22-14. Accessing Route Information in the ProductEditor.vue File in the src/components Folder

```
<template>

    <div>
        <h3 class="btn-primary text-center text-white p-2">
            {{ editing ? "Edit" : "Create"}}
        </h3>
        <div class="form-group">
            <label>ID</label>
            <input class="form-control" v-model="product.id" />
        </div>
        <div class="form-group">
            <label>Name</label>
            <input class="form-control" v-model="product.name" />
        </div>
        <div class="form-group">
            <label>Category</label>
            <input class="form-control" v-model="product.category" />
        </div>
        <div class="form-group">
            <label>Price</label>
            <input class="form-control" v-model.number="product.price" />
        </div>
        <div class="text-center">
            <button class="btn btn-primary" v-on:click="save">
                {{ editing ? "Save" : "Create" }}
            </button>
            <router-link to="/" class="btn btn-secondary">Cancel</router-link>
        </div>
    </div>

</template>

<script>

    let unwatcher;

    export default {
        data: function () {
            return {
                editing: false,
                product: {}
            }
        },
        methods: {
            async save() {
                await this.$store.dispatch("saveProductAction", this.product);
                this.$router.push("/");
                this.product = {};
            },
```

```
            selectProduct(selectedProduct) {
                if (this.$route.path == "/create") {
                    this.editing = false;
                    this.product = {};
                } else {
                    this.product = {};
                    Object.assign(this.product, selectedProduct);
                    this.editing = true;
                }
            }
        },
        created() {
            unwatcher = this.$store.watch(state =>
                state.selectedProduct, this.selectProduct);
            this.selectProduct(this.$store.state.selectedProduct);
        },
        beforeDestroy() {
            unwatcher();
        }
    }
}
</script>
```

When the selectProduct method is called, the component inspects the $route object to get details of the route. The $route property is assigned an object that describes the current route. Table 22-5 describes the most useful properties provided by the $route object.

Table 22-5. Useful $route Properties

Name	Description
name	This property returns the name of the route, as described in the "Creating Named Routes" section.
path	This property returns the URL path, such as /edit/4.
params	This property returns a map object for the parameters matched by a dynamic route, as described in the "Matching Routes Dynamically" section.
query	This property returns a map object containing the query string values. For the URL /edit/4?validate=true, for example, the query property would return an object with a validate property whose value is true.

In the listing, I use the path property to determine whether the /create or /edit URL has been used and configure the component accordingly. To make the difference more obvious, I have added an h3 element that uses a text interpolation binding to display a header. To test these changes, you can click a Create New or Edit button displayed by the ProductDisplay component or navigate directly to the http://localhost:8080/create and http://localhost:8080/edit URLs, which produce the result shown in Figure 22-11.

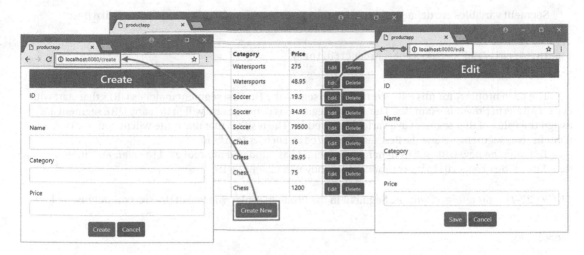

Figure 22-11. *Responding to different routes in a component*

Matching Routes Dynamically

The problem with the changes I made in the previous section is that the /edit URL tells the ProductEditor component that the user wants to perform an edit operation but doesn't specify which object should be edited.

I can address this using a *dynamic segment*, which is added to a route when a component needs to receive data from the URL. In Listing 22-15, I extended the routing configuration so that it includes a dynamic segment.

Listing 22-15. Using a Dynamic Segment in the index.js File in the src/router Folder

```
import Vue from "vue";
import VueRouter from "vue-router";

import ProductDisplay from "../components/ProductDisplay";
import ProductEditor from "../components/ProductEditor";

Vue.use(VueRouter);

export default new VueRouter({
    mode: "history",
    routes: [
        { path: "/", component: ProductDisplay, alias: "/list" },
        { path: "/edit/:id", component: ProductEditor },
        { path: "/create", component: ProductEditor },
        { path: "*", redirect: "/" }
    ]
})
```

Segment variables are defined by prefixing the segment with a colon (the : character), like this:

```
...
{ path: "/edit/:id", component: ProductEditor },
...
```

The path property for this route contains two segments. The first segment matches URLs that start with /edit, just as in previous examples. The second segment is dynamic and will match any URL segment and assign the value of that segment to a variable named id. The result is that this route will match any URL that contains two segments where the first segment is /edit, such as /edit/10.

To target the new URL and its dynamic segment, I have updated the router-link elements in the template of the ProductDisplay component, as shown in Listing 22-16.

Listing 22-16. Targeting a Dynamic Segment in the ProductDisplay.vue File in the src/components Folder

```
...
<template>
    <div>
        <table class="table table-sm table-bordered" v-bind:class="tableClass">
            <tr>
                <th>ID</th><th>Name</th><th>Category</th><th>Price</th><th></th>
            </tr>
            <tbody>
                <tr v-for="p in products" v-bind:key="p.id">
                    <td>{{ p.id }}</td>
                    <td>{{ p.name }}</td>
                    <td>{{ p.category }}</td>
                    <td>{{ p.price }}</td>
                    <td>
                        <router-link v-bind:to="'/edit/' +  p.id "
                            v-bind:class="editClass" class="btn btn-sm">
                                Edit
                        </router-link>
                        <button class="btn btn-sm"
                                v-bind:class="deleteClass"
                                v-on:click="deleteProduct(p)">
                            Delete
                        </button>
                    </td>
                </tr>
                <tr v-if="products.length == 0">
                    <td colspan="5" class="text-center">No Data</td>
                </tr>
            </tbody>
        </table>
        <div class="text-center">
            <router-link to="/create" class="btn btn-primary">
                Create New
            </router-link>
        </div>
    </div>
</template>
...
```

588

This change means that clicking an Edit button will navigate to a URL that includes the corresponding object's id property so that clicking the button for the Stadium product, for example, will navigate to /edit/5.

Components can access dynamic segment variables through the $route.params property. In Listing 22-17, I have updated the ProductEditor component to retrieve the product object from the data store based on the value of the id dynamic segment.

Listing 22-17. Using a Dynamic Segment Value in the ProductEditor.vue File in the src/components Folder

```
...
<script>

    let unwatcher;

    export default {
        data: function () {
            return {
                editing: false,
                product: {}
            }
        },
        methods: {
            async save() {
                await this.$store.dispatch("saveProductAction", this.product);
                this.$router.push("/");
                this.product = {};
            },
            selectProduct() {
                if (this.$route.path == "/create") {
                    this.editing = false;
                    this.product = {};
                } else {
                    let productId = this.$route.params.id;
                    let selectedProduct
                        = this.$store.state.products.find(p => p.id == productId);
                    this.product = {};
                    Object.assign(this.product, selectedProduct);
                    this.editing = true;
                }
            }
        },
        created() {
            unwatcher = this.$store.watch(state => state.products,
                this.selectProduct);
            this.selectProduct();
        },
        beforeDestroy() {
            unwatcher();
        }
    }
</script>
...
```

In the selectProduct method, I get the value of the id segment through the $route object and get the object that the user has selected through the data store.

It may be hard to spot, but I have also changed the target of the data store watcher in this listing. The ProductDisplay component no longer uses the data store for the user's editing selection, which may have led you to expect that the watcher is now redundant. The watcher is still required, however, but it observes the products array of objects.

```
...
unwatcher = this.$store.watch(state => state.products, this.selectProduct);
...
```

The user can now navigate directly to a URL that will edit an object, and the result is that the ProductEditor component will be displayed to the user before the data store is populated with the data from the HTTP request sent to the web service by the App component. To ensure that the user sees the data they require, I use a data store watcher that invokes the selectProduct method.

■ **Tip** The Vue Router package provides a more elegant way of waiting for data, which I describe in Chapter 24.

The effect of these changes is that clicking one of the Edit buttons presented by the ProductDisplay component navigates to a URL such as /edit/4, which the user can also navigate to directly using the browser's URL bar.

When the URL is matched by the routing system, the ProductEditor component reads the value of the dynamic segment, locates the corresponding object from the data store, and displays it to the user for editing, as shown in Figure 22-12.

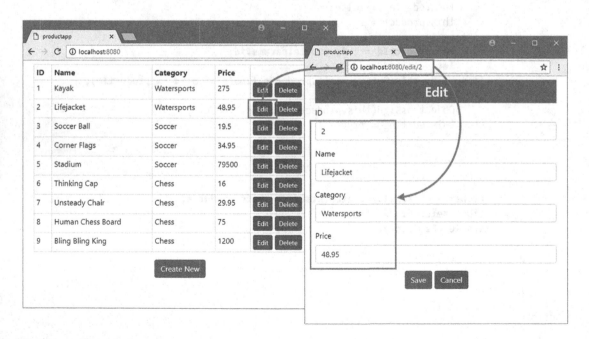

Figure 22-12. Using a dynamic segment

Using Regular Expressions to Match URLs

Dynamic segments expand the range of URLs that a route will match, but the result can be a route that matches URLs that you want to handle later in the routing configuration. To help increase the precision of routes, Vue Router supports the use of regular expressions for dynamic segments that provide fine-grained control of the URLs that will be matched.

In Listing 22-18, I have revised the routing configuration to add a dynamic segment with a regular expression and to apply a regular expression to the existing id segment.

Listing 22-18. Using Regular Expressions in the index.js File in the src/router Folder

```
import Vue from "vue";
import VueRouter from "vue-router";

import ProductDisplay from "../components/ProductDisplay";
import ProductEditor from "../components/ProductEditor";

Vue.use(VueRouter);

export default new VueRouter({
    mode: "history",
    routes: [
        { path: "/", component: ProductDisplay, alias: "/list" },
        { path: "/:op(create|edit)/:id(\\d+)", component: ProductEditor },
        //{ path: "/create", component: ProductEditor },
        { path: "*", redirect: "/" }
    ]
})
```

Regular expressions are applied in parentheses after the name of a dynamic segment. The new dynamic segment is called op, and the regular expression that I have applied allows it to match segments that contain create or edit, which has allowed me to combine two routes into one and comment out the dedicated /create route.

```
...
{ path: "/:op(create|edit)/:id(\\d+)", component: ProductEditor },
...
```

The regular expression I applied to the id segment will match segments that consist of only one or more digits. The d character in this expression has to be escaped with two backslashes (the \ character) to prevent it from being interpreted as a literal d character, and the plus sign (the + character) specifies that the expression should match only one or more digits.

```
...
{ path: "/:op(create|edit)/:id(\\d+)", component: ProductEditor },
...
```

The result is that this route will now match two segment URLs where the first segment is /create or /edit and the second segment contains one or more digits.

Defining Optional Segments

The route that I defined in Listing 22-18 doesn't work exactly as I would like because it doesn't match /create, which is the URL that the ProductDisplay component navigates to when the user clicks the Create New button. Dynamic segments can be marked as optional using a question mark (the ? character), which is the symbol for matching zero or more instances of an expression. In Listing 22-19, I have applied a question mark to make the id segment optional.

Listing 22-19. Using an Optional Segment in the index.js File in the src/router Folder

```
import Vue from "vue";
import VueRouter from "vue-router";

import ProductDisplay from "../components/ProductDisplay";
import ProductEditor from "../components/ProductEditor";

Vue.use(VueRouter);

export default new VueRouter({
    mode: "history",
    routes: [
        { path: "/", component: ProductDisplay, alias: "/list" },
        { path: "/:op(create|edit)/:id(\\d+)?", component: ProductEditor },
        { path: "*", redirect: "/" }
    ]
})
```

Since the id segment is optional, this route will now match any one-segment URLs like /edit and /create and any two-segment URLs where the first segment is /edit or /create and the second segment consists of one or more digits.

This routing configuration will match a URL such as /create/10, which the existing code in the ProductEditor component will treat as though it is a request to edit the object whose id is 10. This shows the importance of updating components when you change an application's routing configuration, and in Listing 22-20, I have modified the ProductEditor component to avoid this issue by examining the new dynamic segment introduced in Listing 22-19.

Listing 22-20. Using a New Segment in the ProductEditor.vue File in the src/components Folder

```
...
<script>

    let unwatcher;

    export default {
        data: function () {
            return {
                editing: false,
                product: {}
            }
        },
```

```
    methods: {
        async save() {
            await this.$store.dispatch("saveProductAction", this.product);
            this.$router.push("/");
            this.product = {};
        },
        selectProduct() {
            if (this.$route.params.op == "create") {
                this.editing = false;
                this.product = {};
            } else {
                let productId = this.$route.params.id;
                let selectedProduct
                    = this.$store.state.products.find(p => p.id == productId);
                this.product = {};
                Object.assign(this.product, selectedProduct);
                this.editing = true;
            }
        }
    },
    created() {
        unwatcher = this.$store.watch(state => state.products,
            this.selectProduct);
        this.selectProduct();
    },
    beforeDestroy() {
        unwatcher();
    }
}
</script>
...
```

As a result of the regular expressions added to the routing configuration, URLs such as /edit/apples won't be matched by the route that selects the ProductEditor component. Instead, the routing system will continue working its way through the routing configuration until it reaches the catch-all route, which performs a redirection to the application's root URL, as shown in Figure 22-13.

593

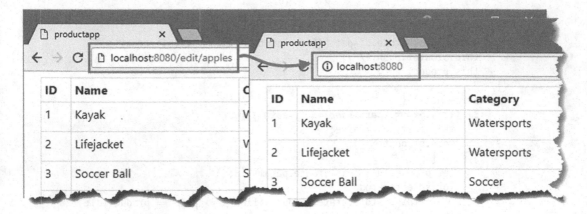

Figure 22-13. *Using regular expressions in a route*

Creating Named Routes

If you don't want to embed URLs into your component's code and templates, then you can assign your names to your routes and use these instead. The advantage of this approach is that it is easy to change the URLs used by an application, without having to change all of the navigation elements and code in its components, which you can see demonstrated in Chapter 23. The disadvantage is that using named routes requires an awkward syntax. In Listing 22-21, I have added names to the routes that target the `ProductDisplay` and `ProductEditor` components.

Listing 22-21. Naming a Route in the index.js File in the src/router Folder

```
import Vue from "vue";
import VueRouter from "vue-router";

import ProductDisplay from "../components/ProductDisplay";
import ProductEditor from "../components/ProductEditor";

Vue.use(VueRouter);

export default new VueRouter({
    mode: "history",
    routes: [
        { name: "table", path: "/", component: ProductDisplay, alias: "/list" },
        { name: "editor", path: "/:op(create|edit)/:id(\\d+)?",
            component: ProductEditor },
        { path: "*", redirect: "/" }
    ]
})
```

The `name` property is used to assign a name to a route, and I have used the names `table` and `editor`. In Listing 22-22, I have used a route's name for navigation instead of its URL.

Listing 22-22. Navigating by Route Name in the ProductEditor.vue File in the src/components Folder

```
<template>

    <div>
        <h3 class="btn-primary text-center text-white p-2">
            {{ editing ? "Edit" : "Create"}}
        </h3>
        <div class="form-group">
            <label>ID</label>
            <input class="form-control" v-model="product.id" />
        </div>
        <div class="form-group">
            <label>Name</label>
            <input class="form-control" v-model="product.name" />
        </div>
        <div class="form-group">
            <label>Category</label>
            <input class="form-control" v-model="product.category" />
        </div>
        <div class="form-group">
            <label>Price</label>
            <input class="form-control" v-model.number="product.price" />
        </div>
        <div class="text-center">
            <button class="btn btn-primary" v-on:click="save">
                {{ editing ? "Save" : "Create" }}
            </button>
            <router-link v-bind:to="{name: 'table'}" class="btn btn-secondary">
                Cancel
            </router-link>
        </div>
    </div>

</template>

<script>

    let unwatcher;

    export default {
        data: function () {
            return {
                editing: false,
                product: {}
            }
        },
        methods: {
            async save() {
                await this.$store.dispatch("saveProductAction", this.product);
                this.$router.push({name: "table"});
                this.product = {};
            },
```

```
        selectProduct() {
            if (this.$route.params.op == "create") {
                this.editing = false;
                this.product = {};
            } else {
                let productId = this.$route.params.id;
                let selectedProduct
                    = this.$store.state.products.find(p => p.id == productId);
                this.product = {};
                Object.assign(this.product, selectedProduct);
                this.editing = true;
            }
        }
    },
    created() {
        unwatcher = this.$store.watch(state => state.products,
            this.selectProduct);
        this.selectProduct();
    },
    beforeDestroy() {
        unwatcher();
    }
    }
}
</script>
```

To navigate to a route by name, an object that has a name property is passed to the $router.push method or assigned to a router-link element's to attribute. The value of the name property is the name of the required route, and the v-bind directive must be used to ensure that Vue.js interprets the attribute value as a JavaScript expression.

If a route has dynamic segments, then the object that is used for navigation defines a params property that is used to provide segment values. In Listing 22-23, I have changed the navigation element and code to use names and provide parameter values.

Listing 22-23. Navigating with Parameters in the ProductDisplay.vue File in the src/components Folder

```
...
<template>
    <div>
        <table class="table table-sm table-bordered" v-bind:class="tableClass">
            <tr>
                <th>ID</th>
                <th>Name</th>
                <th>Category</th>
                <th>Price</th>
                <th></th>
            </tr>
            <tbody>
                <tr v-for="p in products" v-bind:key="p.id">
                    <td>{{ p.id }}</td>
                    <td>{{ p.name }}</td>
                    <td>{{ p.category }}</td>
                    <td>{{ p.price }}</td>
```

```
            <td>
                <router-link v-bind:to="{name: 'editor',
                                params: { op: 'edit', id: p.id}}"
                        v-bind:class="editClass" class="btn btn-sm">
                        Edit
                </router-link>
                <button class="btn btn-sm"
                        v-bind:class="deleteClass"
                        v-on:click="deleteProduct(p)">
                    Delete
                </button>
            </td>
        </tr>
        <tr v-if="products.length == 0">
            <td colspan="5" class="text-center">No Data</td>
        </tr>
        </tbody>
    </table>
    <div class="text-center">
        <router-link v-bind:to="{name: 'editor', params: { op: 'create'}}"
                    class="btn btn-primary">
            Create New
        </router-link>
    </div>
    </div>
</template>
...
```

The v-bind directive is required when using a name and providing parameters with a router-link element; otherwise, Vue.js won't interpret the value of the to attribute as a JavaScript object and will treat the value as a URL instead.

Dealing with Navigation Changes

When a route change requires new content, the existing component is destroyed, and an instance of the new component is created, following the lifecycle I described in Chapter 17 and Chapter 21. When a route change displays the same component, the Vue Router package simply reuses the existing component and notifies it that there has been a change. To demonstrate the problem, I added new navigation features to the ProductEditor component that allow the user to move through the objects available for editing, as shown in Listing 22-24.

Listing 22-24. Adding Navigation Features in the ProductEditor.vue File in the src/components Folder

```
<template>

    <div>
        <h3 class="btn-primary text-center text-white p-2">
            {{ editing ? "Edit" : "Create"}}
        </h3>
        <div class="form-group">
            <label>ID</label>
            <input class="form-control" v-model="product.id" />
        </div>
```

```
            <div class="form-group">
                <label>Name</label>
                <input class="form-control" v-model="product.name" />
            </div>
            <div class="form-group">
                <label>Category</label>
                <input class="form-control" v-model="product.category" />
            </div>
            <div class="form-group">
                <label>Price</label>
                <input class="form-control" v-model.number="product.price" />
            </div>
            <div class="text-center">

                <button class="btn btn-primary" v-on:click="save">
                    {{ editing ? "Save" : "Create" }}
                </button>
                <router-link to="{name: 'table'}" class="btn btn-secondary">
                    Cancel
                </router-link>

                <router-link v-if="editing" v-bind:to="nextUrl" class="btn btn-info">
                    Next
                </router-link>
            </div>
        </div>
    </div>

</template>

<script>

    let unwatcher;

    export default {
        data: function () {
            return {
                editing: false,
                product: {}
            }
        },
        computed: {
            nextUrl() {
                if (this.product.id != null && this.$store.state.products != null) {
                    let index = this.$store.state.products
                        .findIndex(p => p.id == this.product.id);
                    let target = index < this.$store.state.products.length - 1
                        ? index + 1 : 0
                    return `/edit/${this.$store.state.products[target].id}`;
                }
                return "/edit";
            }
        },
```

```
        methods: {
            async save() {
                await this.$store.dispatch("saveProductAction", this.product);
                this.$router.push({name: "table"});
                this.product = {};
            },
            selectProduct(route) {
                if (route.params.op == "create") {
                    this.editing = false;
                    this.product = {};
                } else {
                    let productId = route.params.id;
                    let selectedProduct
                        = this.$store.state.products.find(p => p.id == productId);
                    this.product = {};
                    Object.assign(this.product, selectedProduct);
                    this.editing = true;
                }
            }
        },
        created() {
            unwatcher = this.$store.watch(state => state.products,
                () => this.selectProduct(this.$route));
            this.selectProduct(this.$route);
        },
        beforeDestroy() {
            unwatcher();
        },
        beforeRouteUpdate(to, from, next) {
            this.selectProduct(to);
            next();
        }
    }
}
</script>
```

I added a router-link element that is displayed when a product is edited and that navigates to the next product in the data store. The component displayed to the user doesn't change, which means that Vue Router won't destroy the existing instance of the ProductEditor component and create a new one.

Components can implement methods to receive notifications from the routing system. I describe the full range of methods in Chapter 24, but for this chapter, it the beforeRouteUpdate method that is important because it is called when the route is about to change without destroying the component. The beforeRouteUpdate method defines three parameters, which are described in Table 22-6.

Table 22-6. *The beforeRouteUpdate Parameters*

Name	Description
to	This parameter is assigned an object that describes the route that the application is about to navigate to.
from	This parameter is assigned an object that describes the current route, which the application is about to navigate away from.
next	This parameter is assigned a function that must be invoked to allow the notification to be processed by other components. It can also be used to take control of the navigation process, which I describe in Chapter 24.

The objects received through the to and from parameters define the same set of properties as the $route object, as described in Table 22-5. In the listing, the implementation of the beforeRouteUpdate method passes the to object to the selectProduct method so that the component can update its state. Bear in mind that the active route has not yet changed, so I can't use the $route object to respond to the update. Once I have processed the change, I invoke the next function, which allows other components in the application to receive the notification (this may seem like an odd requirement, but the next function can also be used to prevent or alter navigation, which I describe in Chapter 24).

To test the routing notifications, navigate to http://localhost:8080, click one of the Edit buttons, and then click the Next button to navigate through the product objects, as shown in Figure 22-14.

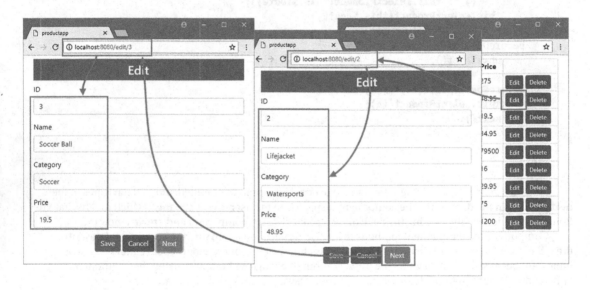

Figure 22-14. *Responding to routing notifications*

Summary

In this chapter, I showed you how to select components dynamically using URL routing. I showed you different ways to define routes, how to enable the HTML5 History API to route without URL fragments, how to provide a catchall route, and how to name routes and creates aliases for them. I also demonstrated the use of dynamic segments to get data from a URL and showed you how to receive notifications when a route change will display the same component. In the next chapter, I describe the HTML elements used to manage routing in more detail.

CHAPTER 23

■ ■ ■

URL Routing Element Features

In this chapter, I describe some of the features provided by the `router-link` and `router-view` elements.
I will show you how to change the way that `router-link` elements are processed, how to use different events
for navigation, and how to respond to route activation by changing the styles applied to navigation elements.
I'll also show you how to use more than one `router-view` element in an application and how to manage two
or more `router-view` elements when they appear in the same template. Table 23-1 puts this chapter into
context.

Table 23-1. *Putting Routing Element Features in Context*

Question	Answer
What are they?	The `router-link` element provides features that control the HTML that is generated, the events that trigger navigation, and the classes to which the element will be added to indicate the active route. The `router-view` element provides features that allow multiple elements to exist in a single component's template.
Why are they useful?	The `router-link` features are useful when you need to present navigation through nonstandard elements or when you want to provide feedback using styles from a CSS framework. The `router-view` features are useful in complex applications because they allow more advanced compositions of content to be created.
How are they used?	These features are applied using attributes on the `router-link` and `router-view` elements, with corresponding support in the application's routes.
Are there any pitfalls or limitations?	Care must be taken to ensure that there are suitable catchall routes and redirections defined to ensure that the application doesn't present the user with an empty window or provide confusing feedback through navigation elements.
Are there any alternatives?	These features are optional, and you don't have to use them.

A. Freeman, *Pro Vue.js 2*, https://doi.org/10.1007/978-1-4842-3805-9_23

Table 23-2 summarizes the chapter.

Table 23-2. *Chapter Summary*

Problem	Solution	Listing
Configure the elements used for navigation	Use the attributes provided by the router-link element	4–7
Style an element when it matches the active URL	Define styles that select the router-link-active and router-link-exact-active classes	8
Ensure that an element is styled only when it exactly matches the active route	Apply the exact attribute	9
Change the classes used to indicate the active route	Use the exact-active-class and active-class attributes	10
Create nested routes	Apply multiple router-view elements in the application and target them with routes defined using the children property	11–17

Preparing for This Chapter

In this chapter, I continue using the productapp project from Chapter 23. To prepare for this chapter, I have commented out the create method in the ProductDisplay component, as shown in Listing 23-1. The statements in this method were used to demonstrate the use of the data store in Chapter 20 and are not required for this chapter because they cause the data store values to be reset each time a new instance of the ProductDisplay component is created.

Listing 23-1. Disabling a Method in the ProductDisplay.vue File in the src/components Folder

```
...
<script>
    import { mapState, mapMutations, mapActions, mapGetters } from "vuex";

    export default {
        computed: {
            ...mapState(["products"]),
            ...mapState({
                useStripedTable: state => state.prefs.stripedTable
            }),
            ...mapGetters({
                tableClass: "prefs/tableClass",
                editClass: "prefs/editClass",
                deleteClass: "prefs/deleteClass"
            })
        },
        methods: {
            editProduct(product) {
                this.selectProduct(product);
                this.$router.push("/edit");
            },
```

```
            createNew() {
                this.selectProduct();
                this.$router.push("/edit");
            },
            ...mapMutations({
                selectProduct: "selectProduct",
                setEditButtonColor: "prefs/setEditButtonColor",
                setDeleteButtonColor: "prefs/setDeleteButtonColor"
            }),
            ...mapActions({
                deleteProduct: "deleteProductAction"
            })
        },
        //created() {
        //    this.setEditButtonColor(false);
        //    this.setDeleteButtonColor(false);
        //}
    }
</script>
...
```

To start the RESTful web service, open a command prompt and run the command shown in Listing 23-2 in the productapp folder.

Listing 23-2. Starting the Web Service

```
npm run json
```

Open a second command prompt, navigate to the productapp directory, and run the command shown in Listing 23-3 to start the Vue.js development tools.

Listing 23-3. Starting the Development Tools

```
npm run serve
```

Once the initial bundling process is complete, open a new browser window and navigate to http://localhost:8080, where you will see the example application, as shown in Figure 23-1.

■ **Tip** You can download the example project for this chapter—and for all the other chapters in this book—from https://github.com/Apress/pro-vue-js-2.

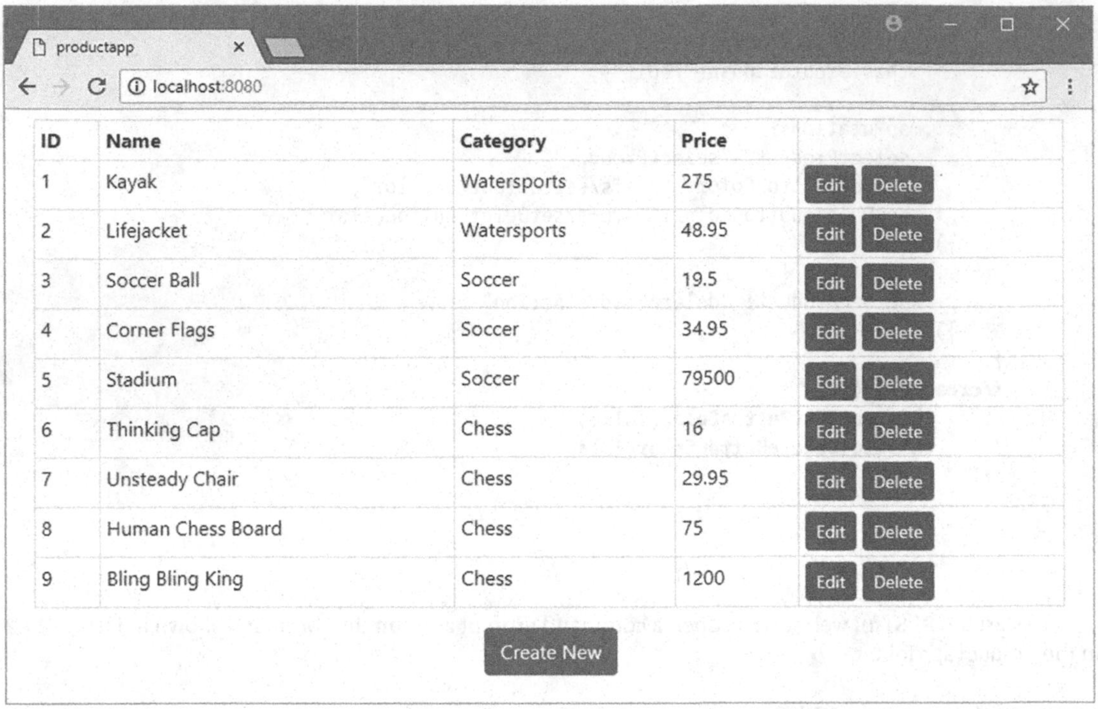

ID	Name	Category	Price		
1	Kayak	Watersports	275	Edit	Delete
2	Lifejacket	Watersports	48.95	Edit	Delete
3	Soccer Ball	Soccer	19.5	Edit	Delete
4	Corner Flags	Soccer	34.95	Edit	Delete
5	Stadium	Soccer	79500	Edit	Delete
6	Thinking Cap	Chess	16	Edit	Delete
7	Unsteady Chair	Chess	29.95	Edit	Delete
8	Human Chess Board	Chess	75	Edit	Delete
9	Bling Bling King	Chess	1200	Edit	Delete

Create New

Figure 23-1. *Running the example application*

Working with Router-Link Elements

The router-link element is more flexible than it first appears and supports some useful options for customizing the HTML element that it generates and for providing useful feedback to the user. To prepare for the sections that follow, I added router-link elements to the template of the App component, as shown in Listing 23-4.

Listing 23-4. Adding Navigation Elements in the App.vue File in the src Folder

```
<template>
    <div class="container-fluid">
        <div class="row">
            <div class="col text-center m-2">
                <router-link to="/list" class="m-1">List</router-link>
                <router-link to="/create" class="m-1">Create</router-link>
            </div>
        </div>
        <div class="row">
            <div class="col m-2">
                <router-view></router-view>
            </div>
        </div>
    </div>
</template>
```

```
<script>

    export default {
        name: 'App',
        created() {
            this.$store.dispatch("getProductsAction");
        }
    }
</script>
```

These router-link elements are processed as part of the component's template and transformed into anchor elements, as shown in Figure 23-2.

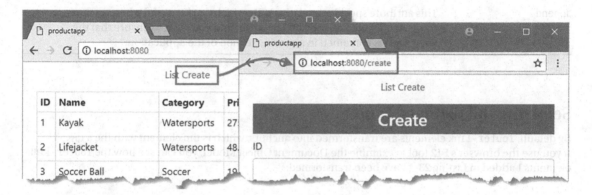

Figure 23-2. *Navigating using router-link elements*

The router-link element is configured by applying the attributes described in Table 23-3, the most useful of which I demonstrate in the sections that follow.

Table 23-3. *The Router Link Attributes*

Name	Description
tag	This attribute specifies the tag type of the HTML element that will be generated when the router-link element is transformed, as described in the "Selecting the Element Type" section.
event	This attribute specifies the event that will trigger navigation, as described in the "Selecting the Navigation Event" section.
exact	This attribute specifies whether partial URL matching will be used when identifying the element that corresponds to the active route, as described in the "Styling Router Link Elements" section.
active-class	This attribute specifies the class that the element will be added to when the active URL starts with the navigation target of the element, as described in the "Styling Router Link Elements" section.

(*continued*)

Table 23-3. (*continued*)

Name	Description
exact-active-class	This attribute specifies the class that the element will be added to when the active URL matches the navigation target of the element, as described in the "Styling Router Link Elements" section.
to	This attribute specifies the navigation location and will add an entry to the browser's history, equivalent to the push navigation method described in Chapter 22.
replace	This attribute specifies the navigation location but will not add an entry to the browser's history, equivalent to the replace navigation method described in Chapter 22.
append	This attribute specifies a relative URL, which can be useful when you are navigating using data provided by a user and you want to ensure that the navigation is contained in a specific section of the application.

Selecting the Element Type

By default, router-link elements are transformed into anchors, which is the element with the a tag. If you use the browser's F12 tool to examine the Document Object Model, you can see how the router-link elements I added in Listing 23-4 have been transformed.

```
...
<div class="col text-center m-2">
    <a href="/list" class="m-1">List</a>
    <a href="/create" class="m-1">Create</a>
</div>
...
```

■ **Tip** If you have clicked one of the a elements, you may see that it has been added to the router-link-active and router-link-exact-active classes. I explain what these represent in the "Styling Router Link Elements" section.

The tag attribute can be used to choose a different element type that will be used instead of the anchors when the router-link element is transformed. This can be useful when you want to present a series of navigation elements in ways where a elements cannot be used or where you want to apply CSS styles where the selectors will not match anchor elements. In Listing 23-5, I have used the tag attribute to populate a list with navigation elements.

Listing 23-5. Specifying Tag Type in the App.vue File in the src Folder

```
<template>
    <div class="container-fluid">
        <div class="row">
            <div class="col text-center m-2">
                <ol>
                    <router-link tag="li" to="/list">List</router-link>
                    <router-link tag="li" to="/create">Create</router-link>
                </ol>
            </div>
        </div>
        <div class="row">
            <div class="col m-2">
                <router-view></router-view>
            </div>
        </div>
    </div>
</template>

<script>

    export default {
        name: 'App',
        created() {
            this.$store.dispatch("getProductsAction");
        }
    }
</script>
```

The tag attribute specifies that the router-link elements should be replaced with li elements when the component's template is processed. If you save the changes and use the browser's F12 development tools to examine the Document Object Model, you will see these elements:

```
...
<ol>
    <li class="">List</li>
    <li class="">Create</li>
</ol>
...
```

Navigation occurs when you click one of the li elements, as shown in Figure 23-3.

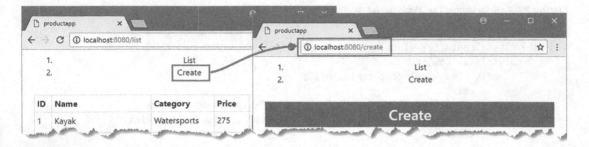

Figure 23-3. *Changing the navigation element type*

Selecting the Navigation Event

The default navigation event is click, which means that navigation is performed when the user clicks the element created by the router-link element. The event attribute is used to specify an alternative event, which allows navigation to be performed in different ways. In Listing 23-6, I have used the event attribute so that navigation will be performed when the user moves the mouse pointer over the navigation element.

■ **Caution**   Users will expect navigation to occur when they click an element because that is how most web applications work. Use the event attribute with caution because you can easily confuse your users and create unexpected results.

Listing 23-6. Specifying the Navigation Event in the App.vue File in the src Folder

```
<template>
    <div class="container-fluid">
        <div class="row">
            <div class="col text-center m-2">
                <ol>
                    <router-link tag="li" event="mouseenter" to="/list">
                        List
                    </router-link>
                    <router-link tag="li" event="mouseenter" to="/create">
                        Create
                    </router-link>
                </ol>
            </div>
        </div>
        <div class="row">
            <div class="col m-2">
                <router-view></router-view>
            </div>
        </div>
    </div>
</template>
```

```
<script>

    export default {
        name: 'App',
        created() {
            this.$store.dispatch("getProductsAction");
        }
    }
</script>
```

The mouseenter event is triggered when the mouse pointer enters the region of the browser window occupied by the HTML element, which means that navigation occurs without the user having to click a mouse button.

Styling Router Link Elements

When you apply styles to router-link elements, it is important to remember you are styling the element into which the router-link has been transformed and not the router-link element itself. In Listing 23-7, I have added a style attribute to the App component that is used to defines styles for the navigation elements.

Listing 23-7. Styling Navigation Elements in the App.vue File in the src Folder

```
<template>
    <div class="container-fluid">
        <div class="row">
            <div class="col text-center m-2">
                <ol>
                    <router-link tag="li" event="mouseenter" to="/list">
                        List
                    </router-link>
                    <router-link tag="li" event="mouseenter" to="/create">
                        Create
                     </router-link>
                </ol>
            </div>
        </div>
        <div class="row">
            <div class="col m-2">
                <router-view></router-view>
            </div>
        </div>
    </div>
</template>

<script>

    export default {
        name: 'App',
        created() {
            this.$store.dispatch("getProductsAction");
        }
    }
</script>
```

```
<style scoped>
    router-link { text-align: right; color: yellow; background-color: red; }
    li { text-align: left; color:blue; background-color: lightblue; }
</style>
```

It is important to remember that it is the browser that evaluates style selectors and does so after the router-link elements have been transformed to the element type specified by the tag attribute. For this reason, the first style defined in Listing 23-7 won't match any elements because there are no router-link elements to select after the component's template has been processed. This is a common cause of confusion, especially when using tools that manage CSS styles automatically. The selector of the second style matches the transformed elements and will be applied to the component's content, as shown in Figure 23-4.

■ **Tip** You may have to reload the browser to see the new styles shown in Figure 23-4.

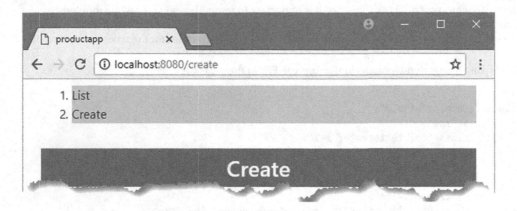

Figure 23-4. *Styling navigation elements*

Responding to the Active Route

When the current URL matches the target of a navigation element, the Vue Router package adds the element to the router-link-active and router-link-exact-active classes, which can be used to apply styles that provide feedback to the user. In Listing 23-8, I have defined styles that use these classes in their selectors. I have also removed the event attributes so that navigation occurs when the user clicks, and I have added new router-link elements that navigate to the /edit and /edit/1 URLs.

Listing 23-8. Styling the Active Navigation Element in the App.vue File in the src Folder

```
<template>
    <div class="container-fluid">
        <div class="row">
            <div class="col text-center m-2">
                <ol>
                    <router-link tag="li" to="/list">List</router-link>
                    <router-link tag="li" to="/create">Create</router-link>
```

```
                    <router-link tag="li" to="/edit">Edit</router-link>
                    <router-link tag="li" to="/edit/1">Edit Kayak</router-link>
                </ol>
            </div>
        </div>
        <div class="row">
            <div class="col m-2">
                <router-view></router-view>
            </div>
        </div>
    </div>
</template>

<script>

    export default {
        name: 'App',
        created() {
            this.$store.dispatch("getProductsAction");
        }
    }
</script>

<style scoped>
    li { text-align: left; color:blue; background-color: lightblue; }
    .router-link-active { font-size: xx-large; }
    .router-link-exact-active { font-weight: bolder; }
</style>
```

The navigation elements are automatically added and removed from the classes when the route changes. If the target specified by the to attribute matches the current URL exactly, then the element is added to the router-link-exact-active class, which applies the style that makes the element text bold. The element is added to the router-link-active class if the current URL starts with the target specified by the to attribute. You can see the difference by clicking the Edit Kayak link, which will navigate to the /edit/1 URL. The Edit element, whose target is /edit, is added to the router-link-active class because the current URL starts with its target: /edit/1 starts with /edit. The Edit Kayak link is added to both classes because the current URL starts with its target and matches its target exactly. The result is that the Edit element is shown with larger text, while the Edit Kayak link is shown with larger text that is also bold, as illustrated in Figure 23-5.

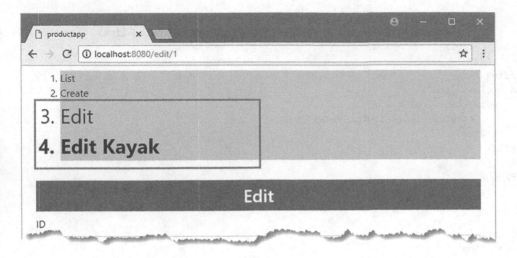

Figure 23-5. *Responding to the active route classes*

Using the router-link-active classes for partial URL matches isn't always helpful and can be disabled by adding the exact attribute to the router-link element, as shown in Listing 23-9.

Listing 23-9. Disabling Partial URL Matching in the App.vue File in the src Folder

```
...
<template>
    <div class="container-fluid">
        <div class="row">
            <div class="col text-center m-2">
                <ol>
                    <router-link tag="li" to="/list">List</router-link>
                    <router-link tag="li" to="/create">Create</router-link>
                    <router-link tag="li" to="/edit" exact>Edit</router-link>
                    <router-link tag="li" to="/edit/1">Edit Kayak</router-link>
                </ol>
            </div>
        </div>
        <div class="row">
            <div class="col m-2">
                <router-view></router-view>
            </div>
        </div>
    </div>
</template>
...
```

The exact attribute will take effect regardless of the value assigned to it, and it is the presence of the attribute, rather than its value, that disables the partial matching feature. The attribute applied in the listing prevents the Edit element from being added to the router-link-active class when the user has navigated to the /edit/1 URL, as shown in Figure 23-6.

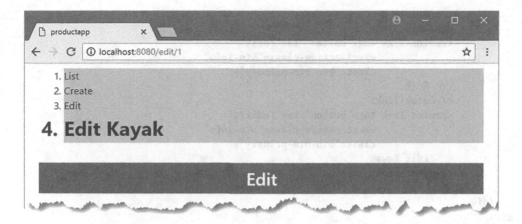

Figure 23-6. *Disabling partial URL mapping*

Changing the Active Route Classes

When you are using a CSS framework, such as the Bootstrap framework that I have used throughout this book, you will find there are often classes that are used to indicate when an element is active and that these do not correspond to the names of the classes used by Vue Router. The active-class and exact-active-class attributes can be used to specify the names of classes to which elements should be added when their target matches the current URL. In Listing 23-10, I have replaced the list of navigation elements with a set of more conventional button elements and used the active-class-exact attribute to specify the name of the Bootstrap class used to indicate an active button. I have also removed the style element since I no longer require custom CSS styles.

■ **Tip** You can change the classes used to indicate routes globally by using linkActiveClass and linkExactActiveClass properties in the routing configuration object, which means you don't have to specify these classes on every element.

Listing 23-10. Specifying Active Class Names in the App.vue File in the src Folder

```
<template>
    <div class="container-fluid">
        <div class="row">
            <div class="col text-center m-2">
                <div class="btn-group">
                    <router-link tag="button" to="/list"
                                exact-active-class="btn-info"
                                class="btn btn-primary">
                        List
                    </router-link>
                    <router-link tag="button" to="/create"
                                exact-active-class="btn-info"
                                class="btn btn-primary">
```

615

```
                    Create
                </router-link>
                <router-link tag="button" to="/edit"
                            exact-active-class="btn-info"
                            class="btn btn-primary">
                    Edit
                </router-link>
                <router-link tag="button" to="/edit/1"
                            exact-active-class="btn-info"
                            class="btn btn-primary">
                    Edit Kayak
                </router-link>
            </div>
        </div>
    </div>
    <div class="row">
        <div class="col m-2">
            <router-view></router-view>
        </div>
    </div>
</div>
</template>

<script>

    export default {
        name: 'App',
        created() {
            this.$store.dispatch("getProductsAction");
        }
    }
</script>
```

The new router-link elements are all assigned to the btn and btn-primary classes, which are Bootstrap classes for styling buttons and will be assigned to the btn-info class when they represent the active route, with the effect shown in Figure 23-7.

Figure 23-7. *Changing the active route classes*

616

Creating Nested Routes

So far, the routing examples have assumed that the application has only one set of components to display and that when one of them is selected, it will always present the same content. In complex applications, one top-level component may need to display different child components, and to support this requirement, the Vue Router package supports nested routes, which are also known as *child routes*.

Planning the Application Layout

When using nested routes, it is important to understand your objective. For the example application, I am going to provide the user with a top level of navigation elements that allows the user to choose between the product-related features and a component that will set the application's preferences. Figure 23-8 shows the application structure I intend to create.

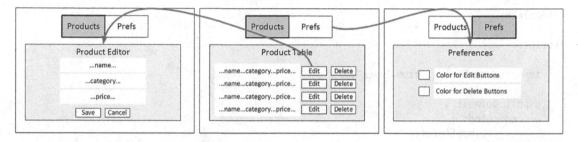

***Figure 23-8.** The structure of the application*

Deciding on the set of URLs that the application will support makes creating the routes simpler. The URLs that I am going to use in the example application are described in Table 23-4 and follow the same basic approach that I have used in earlier examples.

***Table 23-4.** The URLs for the Example Application*

URL	Description
/products/table	This URL will display the table of products.
/products/create	This URL will display the editor to create a new product.
/products/edit/10	This URL will display the editor to modify the specified product.
/preferences	This URL will display the preference settings.

Adding Components to the Project

To create the structure I require, I need to add a component to the project. First, I added a file called Preferences.vue to the src/components folder with the content shown in Listing 23-11.

Listing 23-11. The Contents of the Preferences.vue File in the src/components Folder

```
<template>
    <div>
        <h4 class="bg-info text-white text-center p-2">Preferences</h4>
        <div class="form-check">
            <input class="form-check-input" type="checkbox"
                v-bind:checked="primaryEdit" v-on:input="setPrimaryEdit">
            <label class="form-check-label">Primary Color for Edit Buttons</label>
        </div>
        <div class="form-check">
            <input class="form-check-input" type="checkbox"
                v-bind:checked="dangerDelete" v-on:input="setDangerDelete">
            <label class="form-check-label">Danger Color for Delete Buttons</label>
        </div>
    </div>
</template>

<script>

    import { mapState } from "vuex";

    export default {
        computed: {
            ...mapState({
                primaryEdit: state => state.prefs.primaryEditButton,
                dangerDelete: state => state.prefs.dangerDeleteButton
            })
        },
        methods: {
            setPrimaryEdit() {
                this.$store.commit("prefs/setEditButtonColor", !this.primaryEdit);
            },
            setDangerDelete() {
                this.$store.commit("prefs/setDeleteButtonColor", !this.dangerDelete);
            }
        }
    }
</script>
```

This is the component that will display the preferences to the user. It presents the values of two state properties from the data store using checkboxes and updates those values when the user toggles the controls. These are the same data store state properties that are used to set the color of the Edit and Delete buttons shown by the ProductDisplay component.

Next, I added a file called Products.vue to the src/components folder with the content shown in Listing 23-12.

Listing 23-12. The Contents of the Products.vue file in the src/component Folder

```
<template>
    <router-view></router-view>
</template>
```

This component contains only a `template` element that, in turn, contains only a `router-view` element. This component will allow me to display the list of products or the editor.

Defining the Routes

With the components in place, I can define the application's routing configuration to implement the set of URLs described in Table 23-4, as shown in Listing 23-13.

Listing 23-13. Defining Routes in the index.js File in the src/router Folder

```
import Vue from "vue";
import VueRouter from "vue-router";

import ProductDisplay from "../components/ProductDisplay";
import ProductEditor from "../components/ProductEditor";
import Preferences from "../components/Preferences";
import Products from "../components/Products";

Vue.use(VueRouter);

export default new VueRouter({
    mode: "history",
    routes: [
        { path: "/preferences", component: Preferences},
        { path: "/products", component: Products,
            children: [
                { name: "table", path: "list", component: ProductDisplay},
                { name: "editor", path: ":op(create|edit)/:id(\\d+)?",
                    component: ProductEditor},
                { path: "", redirect: "list" }
            ]
        },
        { path: "/edit/:id", redirect: to => `/products/edit/${to.params.id}`},
        { path: "*", redirect: "/products/list" }
    ]
})
```

These routes contain a lot of information, so I am going to unpack each of them and explain how it contributes toward the structure that I described at the start of this section. The first route follows the format you have seen in earlier examples, shown here:

```
...
{ path: "/preferences", component: Preferences},
...
```

This route tells Vue Router to display the Preferences component when the URL is /preferences. There are no dynamic segments, names, redirections, or other special features used in this route, and the selected component will be displayed in the `router-view` element defined in the App component's template.

The next route is more complex and is best approached in steps. The first part is simple enough.

```
...
{ path: "/products", component: Products,
...
```

The path and component properties tell Vue Router that the Products component should be displayed when the URL is /products. As with the previous route, the Products component will be displayed in the router-view element in the App component's template. But the Product component's template also contains a router-view element, for which a component must be selected, and that is the purpose of the children property that this route defines:

```
...
{ path: "/products", component: Products,
    children: [
        { name: "table", path: "list", component: ProductDisplay},
        { name: "editor", path: ":op(create|edit)/:id(\\d+)?",
            component: ProductEditor},
        { path: "", redirect: "list" }
    ]
},
...
```

The children property is used to define a set of routes that will be applied to the router-view element in the Products component's template. The value of each child route's path property is combined with the path of its parent to match a URL and select a component so that the ProductDisplay component will be selected for the /products/list URL. Child routes can include dynamic segments and regular expressions, which you can see in the route that selects the ProductEditor component for the /create and /edit/id URLs.

The final route in the children section is a catchall route that will perform a redirection, such that any URL that starts with /products but is not matched by the first two routes will be redirected to /products/list. Notice that the path for this route is an empty string, rather than an asterisk, because I want to match URLs that don't have a value for this segment.

Handling Old URLs

When the set of URLs supported by an existing application changes, it is important to ensure that you either update the URLs used in components or create redirections or aliases between the old and new URLs. The editing feature was previously accessed through the /edit/:id path but is now accessed through /products/edit/:id. To ensure that the old URL still functions, I defined the redirection route in Listing 23-13.

```
...
{ path: "/edit/:id", redirect: to => `/products/edit/${to.params.id}`},
...
```

In Chapter 22, I created a redirection using a fixed URL. That won't work in this situation because I need to pass along the value of the dynamic id segment to the new route. As the listing shows, redirections can also be expressed as a function, which receives the matched route and returns the redirection URL. In this example, the redirection function receives the route and composes the redirection URL so that it includes the id value.

Creating the Navigation Elements

In Listing 23-14, I replaced the navigation buttons in the App component's template with ones that target the URLs described in Table 23-4.

Listing 23-14. Navigating to the New URLs in the App.vue File in the src Folder

```
<template>
    <div class="container-fluid">
        <div class="row">
            <div class="col text-center m-2">
                <div class="btn-group">
                    <router-link tag="button" to="/products" active-class="btn-info"
                            class="btn btn-primary">
                        Products
                    </router-link>
                    <router-link tag="button" to="/preferences"
                            active-class="btn-info" class="btn btn-primary">
                        Preferences
                    </router-link>
                </div>
            </div>
        </div>
        <div class="row">
            <div class="col m-2">
                <router-view></router-view>
            </div>
        </div>
    </div>
</template>

<script>

    export default {
        name: 'App',
        created() {
            this.$store.dispatch("getProductsAction");
        }
    }
</script>
```

These router-link elements will be transformed into button elements that navigate to the /products and /preferences URLs and that are styled using the Bootstrap btn and btn-primary classes, which apply basic button styles in the primary color of the Bootstrap color scheme.

To indicate when the button represents the active route, I add the elements to the btn-info class, which applies a different Bootstrap color to the button, using the active-class attribute.

Testing the Nested Routes

All the changes required to support the nested router-view element are in place. You can see the effect by navigating to http://localhost:8080 and using the Products and Preferences button to change the content of the router-view element in the template of the App component, which produces the results shown in Figure 23-9.

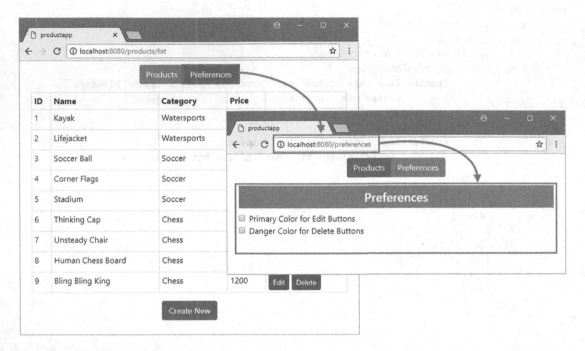

Figure 23-9. *Selecting components for the top-level router-view element*

To see the nested router-view element in action, click the Products button and then click one of the Edit buttons shown in the table. The component displayed by the router-view element in the Products component will change to show the editor, and you can return to the table view by clicking the Save or Cancel button, as shown in Figure 23-10.

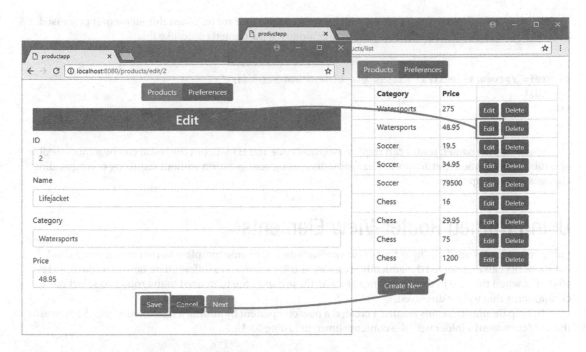

Figure 23-10. *Selecting components for the nested router-view element*

Notice that the router-link elements and code that uses named routes automatically target URLs that work with the new routes. When I defined the routes in Listing 23-13, I applied the names I defined in Chapter 22 to corresponding routes in the new configuration.

```
...
{ path: "/products", component: Products,
    children: [
        { name: "table", path: "list", component: ProductDisplay},
        { name: "editor", path: ":op(create|edit)/:id(\\d+)?",
            component: ProductEditor},
        { path: "", redirect: "list" }
    ]
},
...
```

When router-link elements that use named routes are processed, the result is a URL that will target the specified route, and this means that names keep working even when the routes they relate to change. You can see this in the Edit buttons that are presented in the table view, which are created with this router-link element:

```
...
<router-link v-bind:to="{name: 'editor', params: { op: 'edit', id: p.id}}"
        v-bind:class="editClass" class="btn btn-sm">
    Edit
</router-link>
...
```

The to attribute is set using a name, which specifies the editor route. When this element is processed, the result is an anchor element whose target corresponds to the named route, like this:

```
...
<a href="/products/edit/1" class="btn btn-sm btn-secondary">
    Edit
</a>
...
```

Working with named routes can require awkward code and HTML, but the result can be a more flexible and robust application that adapts to changes in its routing configuration without requiring corresponding changes in its components.

Using Named Router-View Elements

Some components need multiple router-view elements in the same template so that two or more child components can be selected dynamically. The name attribute is used to differentiate between router-view elements when they are in the same template, and these names are then used in the routes to select the components that will be displayed.

To help demonstrate this feature, I created a new component by adding a file called SideBySide.vue in the src/components folder with the content shown in Listing 23-15.

Listing 23-15. The Contents of the SideBySide.vue File in the src/components Folder

```
<template>
    <div class="container-fluid">
        <div class="row">
            <div class="col text-center m-2">
                <h3 class="bg-secondary text-white text-center p-2">Left View</h3>
                <router-view name="left" class="border border-secondary p-2" />
            </div>
            <div class="col text-center m-2">
                <h3 class="bg-secondary text-white text-center p-2">Right View</h3>
                <router-view name="right" class="border border-secondary p-2" />
            </div>
        </div>
    </div>
</template>
```

This component has a template element that contains two router-view elements, which are differentiated using the name attribute so that one is named left and the other is named right. The Bootstrap classes and the structural elements will present the user with contents of the router-view elements side by side. To target the new router-view elements, I am going to add support for the URLs described in Table 23-5.

Table 23-5. *The URLs for the Named Router View Elements*

URL	Description
/named/tableleft	This URL will display the table of products in the left element and the editor in the right element.
/named/tableright	This URL will display the table of products in the right element and the editor in the left element.

To target these URLs, I added the navigation elements shown in Listing 23-16 to the top-level App component's template.

Listing 23-16. Adding Navigation Elements in the App.vue File in the src Folder

```
<template>
    <div class="container-fluid">
        <div class="row">
            <div class="col text-center m-2">
                <div class="btn-group">
                    <router-link tag="button" to="/products"
                        active-class="btn-info" class="btn btn-primary">
                            Products
                    </router-link>
                    <router-link tag="button" to="/preferences"
                        active-class="btn-info" class="btn btn-primary">
                            Preferences
                    </router-link>
                    <router-link to="/named/tableleft" class="btn btn-primary"
                            active-class="btn-info">
                        Table Left
                    </router-link>
                    <router-link to="/named/tableright" class="btn btn-primary"
                            active-class="btn-info">
                        Table Right
                    </router-link>
                </div>
            </div>
        </div>
        <div class="row">
            <div class="col m-2">
                <router-view></router-view>
            </div>
        </div>
    </div>
</template>
```

```
<script>

    export default {
        name: 'App',
        created() {
            this.$store.dispatch("getProductsAction");
        }
    }
</script>
```

To complete the support for the new URLs and target the named router-view elements, I created the routes shown in Listing 23-17.

Listing 23-17. Adding Routes in the index.js File in the src/router Folder

```
import Vue from "vue";
import VueRouter from "vue-router";

import ProductDisplay from "../components/ProductDisplay";
import ProductEditor from "../components/ProductEditor";
import Preferences from "../components/Preferences";
import Products from "../components/Products";
import SideBySide from "../components/SideBySide";

Vue.use(VueRouter);

export default new VueRouter({
    mode: "history",
    routes: [
        { path: "/preferences", component: Preferences},
        { path: "/products", component: Products,
            children: [
                { name: "table", path: "list", component: ProductDisplay},
                { name: "editor", path: ":op(create|edit)/:id(\\d+)?",
                        component: ProductEditor},
                { path: "", redirect: "list" }
            ]
        },
        { path: "/edit/:id", redirect: to => `/products/edit/${to.params.id}`},

        { path: "/named", component: SideBySide,
            children:[
                {   path: "tableleft",
                    components: {
                        left: ProductDisplay,
                        right: ProductEditor
                    }
                },
                {   path: "tableright",
                        components: {
                        left: ProductEditor,
                        right: ProductDisplay
```

```
                }
            }
        ]
    },
    { path: "*", redirect: "/products" }
    ]
})
```

The components property is used when defining routes that target named router-view elements. This property is assigned an object whose properties are the names of the router-view elements and whose values are the component that should be displayed, like this:

```
...
{ path: "tableleft",
  components: {
      left: ProductDisplay,
      right: ProductEditor
  }
},
...
```

The components property tells the Vue Router package to display ProductComponent in the router-view element named left and the ProductEditor component in the router-view element named right.

■ **Note**   The property that targets named elements is components (plural) and not the component (singular) property used in the other routes in Listing 23-17.

To see the result, navigate to http://localhost:8080 and click the Table Left and Table Right buttons, which target the URLs for the routes defined in Listing 23-17, producing the result shown in Figure 23-11.

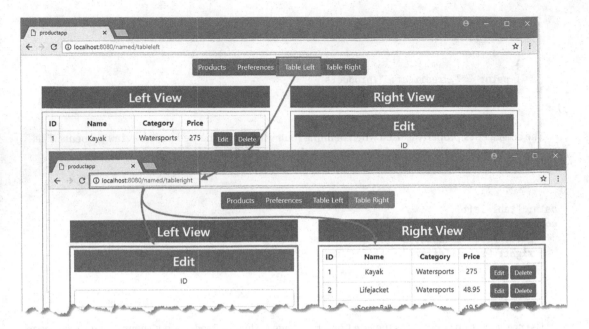

Figure 23-11. *Using named router-view elements*

Summary

In this chapter, I described some of the advanced features that are available when using use URL routing in a Vue.js application. I explained how the router-link element can be configured to produce different HTML elements and respond to different events and how to style navigation elements to provide feedback to the user. For the router-view element, I showed you how to use nested routes so that an application can contain more than element and how to name those elements when they are defined in the same template. In the next chapter, I describe the advanced URL routing features.

CHAPTER 24

■ ■ ■

Advanced URL Routing

In this chapter, I describe the more advanced URL routing features. I start by showing you how to structure a complex routing configuration using multiple files, how to use router guards to control navigation, and how to lazily load components when they are selected by a route. I finish this chapter by showing you how to work with components that have not been written to work with the Vue Router package. Table 24-1 summarizes the chapter.

Table 24-1. *Chapter Summary*

Problem	Solution	Listing
Group related routes	Define separate modules for each group of routes	3–5
Inspect and intercept navigation	Use a route guard	6, 9–11
Change the target of navigation	Supply a replacement URL in the route guard's next function	7, 8
Access a component before navigation is complete	Use the callback feature in the beforeRouteEnter guard method	12–15
Lazily load components	Use dynamic dependencies for components	16–21
Use components that are unaware of the routing system	Use the props feature when defining routes	22–23

Preparing for This Chapter

In this chapter, I continue using the productapp project from Chapter 23. No changes are required for this chapter. To start the RESTful web service, open a command prompt and run the command shown in Listing 24-1 in the productapp folder.

Listing 24-1. Starting the Web Service

```
npm run json
```

Open a second command prompt, navigate to the productapp directory, and run the command shown in Listing 24-2 to start the Vue.js development tools.

A. Freeman, *Pro Vue.js 2*, https://doi.org/10.1007/978-1-4842-3805-9_24

Listing 24-2. Starting the Development Tools

```
npm run serve
```

Once the initial bundling process is complete, open a new browser window and navigate to http://localhost:8080, where you will see the example application, as shown in Figure 24-1.

■ **Tip** You can download the example project for this chapter—and for all the other chapters in this book—from https://github.com/Apress/pro-vue-js-2.

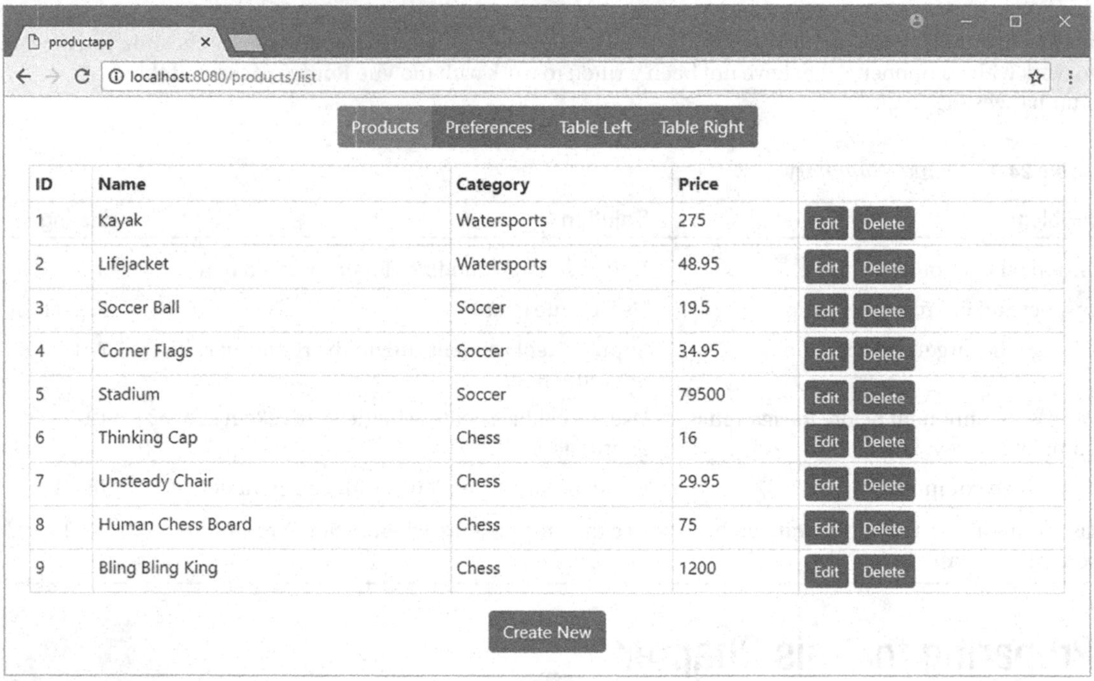

Figure 24-1. *Running the example application*

Using Separate Files for Related Routes

As the number of URLs supported by an application increases, it becomes more difficult to keep track of the routes and the part of the application they support. Additional JavaScript files can be used to group related routes, which can then be imported into the main routing configuration.

There is no hard-and-fast way to group routes, and the approach that I am going to take in this chapter is to separate the routes that deal with the side-by-side presentation of components using named router-view elements from those that deal with the basic functionality presented by the rest of the application. I added a file called basicRoutes.js in the src/router folder and added the code shown in Listing 24-3.

Listing 24-3. The Contents of the basicRoutes.js File in the src/router Folder

```
import ProductDisplay from "../components/ProductDisplay";
import ProductEditor from "../components/ProductEditor";
import Preferences from "../components/Preferences";
import Products from "../components/Products";

export default [

    { path: "/preferences", component: Preferences },
    { path: "/products", component: Products,
      children: [ { name: "table", path: "list", component: ProductDisplay },
                  { name: "editor", path: ":op(create|edit)/:id(\\d+)?",
                      component: ProductEditor
                  },
                  { path: "", redirect: "list" }]
    },
    { path: "/edit/:id", redirect: to => `/products/edit/${to.params.id}` },
]
```

This file exports an array of routes that deal with the basic URLs supported by the application. Next, I added a file called sideBySideRoutes.js in the src/router folder and added the code shown in Listing 24-4.

Listing 24-4. The Contents of the sideBySideRoutes.js File in the src/router Folder

```
import ProductDisplay from "../components/ProductDisplay";
import ProductEditor from "../components/ProductEditor";
import SideBySide from "../components/SideBySide";

export default {
    path: "/named", component: SideBySide,
    children: [
        { path: "tableleft",
          components: { left: ProductDisplay, right: ProductEditor }
        },
        { path: "tableright",
          components: { left: ProductEditor, right: ProductDisplay }
        }
    ]
}
```

Moving these groups of routes into dedicated files allows me to simplify the index.js file, as shown in Listing 24-5, which shows how I have imported the routes defined in the basicRoutes.js and sideBySideRoutes.js files.

Listing 24-5. Importing Routes in the index.js File in the src/router Folder

```
import Vue from "vue";
import VueRouter from "vue-router";

//import ProductDisplay from "../components/ProductDisplay";
```

```
//import ProductEditor from "../components/ProductEditor";
//import Preferences from "../components/Preferences";
//import Products from "../components/Products";
//import SideBySide from "../components/SideBySide";

import BasicRoutes from "./basicRoutes";
import SideBySideRoutes from "./sideBySideRoutes";

Vue.use(VueRouter);

export default new VueRouter({
    mode: "history",
    routes: [
        ...BasicRoutes,
        SideBySideRoutes,
        { path: "*", redirect: "/products" }
    ]
})
```

I import the contents of each file using an `import` statement and give the contents a name that I use in the `routes` property. The `basicRoutes.js` file exports an array, which must be unpacked using the spread operator, which I described in Chapter 4. The `sideBySideRoutes.js` file exports a single object and can be used without the spread operator. There is no visible change to the way that the application functions, but the routing configuration has been broken up, which will make managing related routes simpler.

Guarding Routes

One drawback of allowing the user to navigate around the application using URLs is they may try to access parts of the application under undesirable circumstances, such as accessing administration features when they are unauthenticated or accessing editing features before the data has been loaded from the server. Navigation guards control access to routes, and they can respond to an attempt at navigation by redirecting it to another URL or canceling the navigation completely. Navigation guards can be applied in different ways, as I explain in the sections that follow.

Defining Global Navigation Guards

Global navigation guards are methods that are defined as part of the routing configuration and are used to control access to all of the routes in the application. There are three global navigation guard methods that are used to register functions to control navigation, as described in Table 24-2.

Table 24-2. *The Global Navigation Guard Methods*

Name	Description
beforeEach	This method is called before the active route is changed.
afterEach	This method is called after the active route is changed.
beforeResolve	This method is similar to beforeEach, but it is called after all the route-specific and component guards, which I describe in the next section, have been checked, as described in the "Understanding Guard Ordering" section.

Each of these methods is called on the VueRouter object and accepts a function that is invoked during navigation. This is easier to explain with an example, and in Listing 24-6, I have used the beforeEach method to prevent navigation from routes whose path starts with /named to the /preferences URL.

Listing 24-6. Guarding a Route in the index.js File in the src/router Folder

```
import Vue from "vue";
import VueRouter from "vue-router";

import BasicRoutes from "./basicRoutes";
import SideBySideRoutes from "./sideBySideRoutes";

Vue.use(VueRouter);

const router = new VueRouter({
    mode: "history",
    routes: [
        ...BasicRoutes,
        SideBySideRoutes,
        { path: "*", redirect: "/products" }
    ]
});

export default router;

router.beforeEach((to, from, next) => {
    if (to.path == "/preferences" && from.path.startsWith("/named")) {
        next(false);
    } else {
        next();
    }
});
```

The global route guards are the most flexible type of guard because they can be used to intercept all navigation, but they are awkward to set up, as Listing 24-6 shows. The VueRouter object is created with the new keyword, and then the function you want to be invoked is passed to the corresponding method from Table 24-2. In this example, I have passed a function to the beforeEach method, which means it will be invoked before each navigation attempt.

The function receives three arguments. The first two arguments are objects that represent the route that the application is navigating to and the route that the application is about to navigate away from. These objects define the properties I described in Chapter 22, and I use their path properties in the listing to check to see whether the application is navigating to /preferences from /named.

The third argument is a function that is invoked to accept, redirect, or cancel the navigation and will pass on the navigation requests to the next route guard for processing, which is why this argument is usually called next. The different outcomes are specified by passing different arguments to the function, as described in Table 24-3.

Table 24-3. *Uses of the Next Function for Navigation Guards*

Method Use	Description
next()	When the function is invoked with no arguments, navigation will proceed.
next(false)	When the function is passed false as its argument, navigation will be canceled.
next(url)	When the function is passed a string, it is interpreted as a URL and becomes the new navigation target.
next(object)	When the function is passed an object, it is interpreted as the new navigation target, which is useful for selecting routes by name, as shown in the "Redirecting to a Named Route" section.
next(callback)	This is a special version of the next function that can be used in only one situation, as described in the "Accessing the Component in the beforeRouteEnter Method" section, and that is not otherwise supported.

In the listing, I pass the next function false if the current URL starts with /named and the target URL is /preferences, which cancels the navigation request. For all other navigation, I call the next method without an argument, which allows the navigation to proceed.

■ **Caution**　You must remember to call the next function in your guards. There can be multiple guards defined in an application, and they won't be invoked if you forget to call the function, which can lead to unexpected results.

Redirecting the Navigation Request to Another URL

An alternative to canceling navigation is to redirect it to another URL. In Listing 24-7, I have added an additional guard function that intercepts requests for the /named/tableright URL and redirects them to /products.

■ **Tip**　When there are multiple global guard functions, they are executed in the order in which they are passed to the beforeEach or beforeAfter method.

Listing 24-7. Defining Another Guard in the index.js File in the src/router Folder

```
import Vue from "vue";
import VueRouter from "vue-router";

import BasicRoutes from "./basicRoutes";
import SideBySideRoutes from "./sideBySideRoutes";

Vue.use(VueRouter);

const router = new VueRouter({
    mode: "history",
    routes: [
        ...BasicRoutes,
```

```
        SideBySideRoutes,
        { path: "*", redirect: "/products" }
    ]
});

export default router;

router.beforeEach((to, from, next) => {
    if (to.path == "/preferences" && from.path.startsWith("/named")) {
        next(false);
    } else {
        next();
    }
});

router.beforeEach((to, from, next) => {
    if (to.path == "/named/tableright") {
        next("/products");
    } else {
        next();
    }
});
```

I could have implemented this check in the existing guard function, but I wanted to demonstrate support for multiple guards, which can be a useful way of grouping related checks in complex applications. To see the effect of the redirection, navigate to http://localhost:8080/preferences and then click the Table Right button. Instead of showing the components side by side, the application navigates to the /products URL, as shown in Figure 24-2.

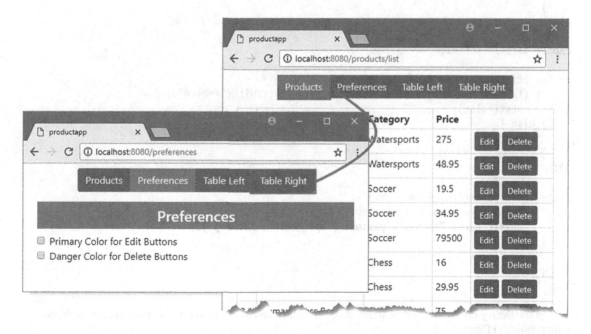

Figure 24-2. *Redirecting navigation with a route guard*

■ **Tip** When you perform a redirection in a route guard, a new navigation request is started and invokes all of the guard functions again. For this reason, it is important not to create a redirection loop where two guard functions cause the application to bounce between the same two URLs.

Redirecting to a Named Route

If you want to redirect a navigation request to a named route, then you can pass an object that has a name property to the next function, as shown in Listing 24-8.

Listing 24-8. Redirecting to a Named Route in the index.js File in the src/router Folder

```
import Vue from "vue";
import VueRouter from "vue-router";

import BasicRoutes from "./basicRoutes";
import SideBySideRoutes from "./sideBySideRoutes";

Vue.use(VueRouter);

const router = new VueRouter({
    mode: "history",
    routes: [
        ...BasicRoutes,
        SideBySideRoutes,
        { path: "*", redirect: "/products" }
    ]
});

export default router;

router.beforeEach((to, from, next) => {
    if (to.path == "/preferences" && from.path.startsWith("/named")) {
        next(false);
    } else {
        next();
    }
});

router.beforeEach((to, from, next) => {
    if (to.path == "/named/tableright") {
        next({ name: "editor", params: { op: "edit", id: 1 } });
    } else {
        next();
    }
});
```

In the listing, I used the next function to redirect the navigation to the route named editor, with the effect shown in Figure 24-3.

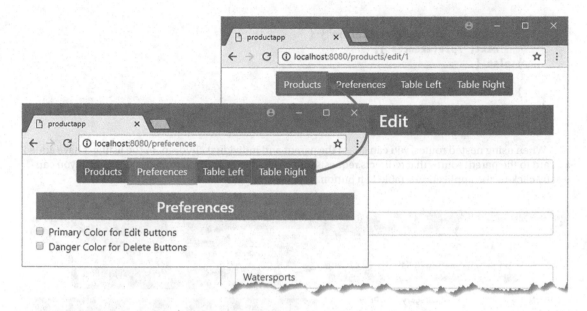

Figure 24-3. Redirecting navigation to a named route

Defining Route-Specific Guards

Individual routes can implement their own guards, which can offer a more natural way to manage navigation. The only one-guard method available for use directly in routes is beforeEnter, and I have used it in Listing 24-9 to guard two routes.

Listing 24-9. Guarding Individual Routes in the sideBySideRoutes.js File in the src/router Folder

```
import ProductDisplay from "../components/ProductDisplay";
import ProductEditor from "../components/ProductEditor";
import SideBySide from "../components/SideBySide";

export default {

    path: "/named", component: SideBySide,
    children: [
        {
            path: "tableleft",
            components: { left: ProductDisplay, right: ProductEditor }
        },
        {
            path: "tableright",
            components: { left: ProductEditor, right: ProductDisplay },
            beforeEnter: (to, from, next) => {
                next("/products/list");
            }
        }
    ],
```

```
    beforeEnter: (to, from, next) => {
        if (to.path == "/named/tableleft") {
            next("/preferences");
        } else {
            next();
        }
    }
}
```

When using nested routes, you can guard the parent and individual children. In the listing, I have added a guard to the parent routes that redirects requests for /named/tableleft to /preferences, which you can test by clicking the application's Table Left button, as shown in Figure 24-4.

Figure 24-4. *Guarding a single route*

Understanding Guard Ordering

In Listing 24-9, I added a guard to one of the child routes that redirects requests for /named/tableright to /products/list. But if you click the Table Right button, you will see that this guard doesn't have the intended effect.

This happens because the global route guards are executed before the route-specific ones, and one of the global guards is already redirecting requests for /named/tableright. When a guard performs a redirection, the processing of the current route change is abandoned, and a new navigation begins, meaning that any guards that would be executed after the one that performs the redirection won't be able to inspect the request.

As noted in Table 24-2, the global beforeResolve method is executed after all the other types of guard, which is a useful way to define a global guard as a final check after the route-specific guards have been checked. In Listing 24-10, I have used the beforeResolve method to change the guard function that was blocking the route guard defined in Listing 24-9.

Listing 24-10. Changing a Guard in the index.js File in the src/router Folder

```
import Vue from "vue";
import VueRouter from "vue-router";

import BasicRoutes from "./basicRoutes";
import SideBySideRoutes from "./sideBySideRoutes";

Vue.use(VueRouter);
```

```
const router = new VueRouter({
    mode: "history",
    routes: [
        ...BasicRoutes,
        SideBySideRoutes,
        { path: "*", redirect: "/products" }
    ]
});

export default router;

router.beforeEach((to, from, next) => {
    if (to.path == "/preferences" && from.path.startsWith("/named")) {
        next(false);
    } else {
        next();
    }
});

router.beforeResolve((to, from, next) => {
    if (to.path == "/named/tableright") {
        next({ name: "editor", params: { op: "edit", id: 1} });
    } else {
        next();
    }
})
```

In real projects, this would be a useful change to make only if there were a set of URLs for which the route-specific guard would not intercept, but you can see the effect of the timing change by clicking the Table Right button. The application will start navigating to /named/tableright, which will be intercepted by the route-specific guard, which redirects the application to /products/list instead, as shown in Figure 24-5.

Figure 24-5. *The effect of route guard ordering*

Defining Component Route Guards

In Chapter 22, I used the beforeRouteUpdate method in the ProductEditor component to respond to route changes, like this:

```
...
beforeRouteUpdate(to, from, next) {
    this.selectProduct(to);
    next();
}
...
```

This is one of the route guard methods that components can implement to participate in guarding the routes that select them to be displayed. The use of the beforeRouteUpdate method to receive a change notification is a useful technique, but this method forms part of the set of the component guard methods, which are described in Table 24-4.

Table 24-4. *The Component Guard Methods*

Name	Description
beforeRouteEnter	This method is called before the component that has been selected by the target route is confirmed, and it is used to control access to routes before they lead to components being created. A specific technique is required to access the component in this method, as described in the "Accessing the Component in the beforeRouteEnter Method" section.
beforeRouteUpdate	This method is called when the route that has selected the current component changes, and this component has also been selected by the new route.
beforeRouteLeave	This method is called when the application is about to navigate away from the route that has selected the current component.

These methods receive the same three arguments as the other guards and can be used to accept, redirect, or cancel navigation. In Listing 24-11, I have implemented the beforeRouterLeave method to ask the user to confirm navigation when the route is about to change.

Listing 24-11. Route Guarding in the Preferences.vue File in the src/components Folder

```
<template>
    <div>
        <div v-if="displayWarning" class="text-center m-2">
            <h5 class="bg-danger text-white p-2">
                Are you sure?
            </h5>
            <button class="btn btn-danger" v-on:click="doNavigation">
                Yes
            </button>
            <button class="btn btn-danger" v-on:click="cancelNavigation">
                Cancel
            </button>
        </div>
        <h4 class="bg-info text-white text-center p-2">Preferences</h4>
        <div class="form-check">
```

```
            <input class="form-check-input" type="checkbox"
                   v-bind:checked="primaryEdit" v-on:input="setPrimaryEdit">
            <label class="form-check-label">Primary Color for Edit Buttons</label>
        </div>
        <div class="form-check">
            <input class="form-check-input" type="checkbox"
                   v-bind:checked="dangerDelete" v-on:input="setDangerDelete">
            <label class="form-check-label">Danger Color for Delete Buttons</label>
        </div>
    </div>
</template>

<script>

    import { mapState } from "vuex";

    export default {
        data: function() {
            return {
                displayWarning: false,
                navigationApproved: false,
                targetRoute: null
            }
        },
        computed: {
            ...mapState({
                primaryEdit: state => state.prefs.primaryEditButton,
                dangerDelete: state => state.prefs.dangerDeleteButton
            })
        },
        methods: {
            setPrimaryEdit() {
                this.$store.commit("prefs/setEditButtonColor", !this.primaryEdit);
            },
            setDangerDelete() {
                this.$store.commit("prefs/setDeleteButtonColor", !this.dangerDelete);
            },
            doNavigation() {
                this.navigationApproved = true;
                this.$router.push(this.targetRoute.path);
            },
            cancelNavigation() {
                this.navigationApproved = false;
                this.displayWarning = false;
            }
        },
        beforeRouteLeave(to, from, next) {
            if (this.navigationApproved) {
                next();
            } else {
                this.targetRoute = to;
                this.displayWarning = true;
```

```
                next(false);
            }
        }
    }
</script>
```

The beforeRouteLeave method is invoked when the application is going to navigate to a route that will display a different component. In this example, I prompt the user for confirmation and prevent navigation until it is received. To see the effect, click the Preferences button and then click the Products button. The route guard will prevent navigation until you click the Yes button, as shown in Figure 24-6.

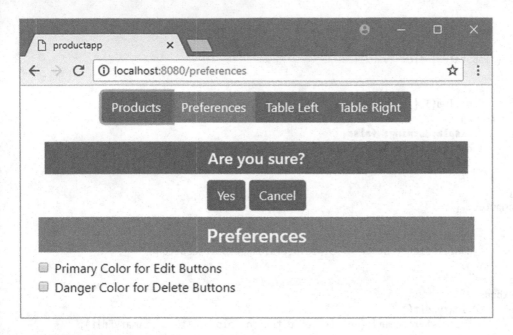

Figure 24-6. *Using a component route guard*

Accessing the Component in the beforeRouteEnter Method

The beforeRouteEnter method is invoked before the component is created, which ensures that navigation can be canceled before the component lifecycle begins. This can cause a problem if you want to use this method to perform a task that requires access to the component's properties and methods, such as requesting data from a web service. To address this limitation, the next function passed to the beforeRouteEnter method can accept a callback function that is invoked once the component has been created, which allows the beforeRouteEnter method to access the component but only once the opportunity to cancel or redirect the navigation has passed. To demonstrate, I created a component that uses the beforeRouteEnter method to access a method defined by the component by adding a file called FilteredData.vue in the src/component folder with the contents shown in Listing 24-12.

Listing 24-12. The Contents of the FilteredData.vue File in the src/components Folder

```
<template>
    <div>
        <h3 class="bg-primary text-center text-white p-2">
            Data for {{ category }}
        </h3>

        <div class="text-center m-2">
            <label>Category:</label>
            <select v-model="category">
                <option>All</option>
                <option>Watersports</option>
                <option>Soccer</option>
                <option>Chess</option>
            </select>
        </div>

        <h3 v-if="loading" class="bg-info text-white text-center p-2">
            Loading Data...
        </h3>

        <table v-else class="table table-sm table-bordered">
            <tr>
                <th>ID</th>
                <th>Name</th>
                <th>Category</th>
                <th>Price</th>
            </tr>
            <tbody>
                <tr v-for="p in data" v-bind:key="p.id">
                    <td>{{ p.id }}</td>
                    <td>{{ p.name }}</td>
                    <td>{{ p.category }}</td>
                    <td>{{ p.price }}</td>
                </tr>
            </tbody>
        </table>
    </div>
</template>

<script>

    import Axios from "axios";

    const baseUrl = "http://localhost:3500/products/";

    export default {
        data: function () {
            return {
                loading: true,
                data: [],
```

```
                    category: "All"
                }
            },
            methods: {
                async getData(route) {
                    if (route.params != null && route.params.category != null) {
                        this.category = route.params.category;
                    } else {
                        this.category = "All";
                    }
                    let url = baseUrl
                        + (this.category == "All" ? "" : `?category=${this.category}`);
                    this.data.push(...(await Axios.get(url)).data);
                    this.loading = false;
                }
            },
            watch: {
                category() {
                    this.$router.push(`/filter/${this.category}`);
                }
            },
            async beforeRouteEnter(to, from, next) {
                next(async component => await component.getData(to));
            },
            async beforeRouteUpdate(to, from, next) {
                this.data.splice(0, this.data.length);
                await this.getData(to);
                next();
            }
        }
    }
</script>
```

This component allows the user to filter product data by category, which is retrieved fresh from the web service each time, which is requested using Axios, which is described in Chapter 19. (For simplicity, I have used Axios directly and store the data in the component, rather than modify the repository and the data store.)

This component presents the user with a select element to choose the category that is used to filter the data. When the select element is used, the category property is modified, which causes the watcher to perform a navigation to a URL that includes the category name, so selecting the Soccer category, for example, will navigate to the /filter/Soccer URL.

The component implements two of the component route guard methods, both of which are used to invoke the component's asynchronous getData method, which accepts a route object and uses it to get the appropriate data from the web service. The json-server package that I added in Chapter 19 supports filtering data, so a request for http://localhost:3500/products?category=Soccer, for example, will return only those objects whose category property is Soccer. One of the route guard methods is easy to understand, as shown here:

```
...
async beforeRouteUpdate(to, from, next) {
    this.data.splice(0, this.data.length);
    await this.getData(to);
    next();
}
...
```

This is the pattern of working with components that I have used throughout this book, which uses `this` to refer to the component object, so `this.getData` is used to invoke the `getData` method defined by the component, for example. Achieving the same effect in the `beforeRouteEnter` method requires a different approach.

```
...
async beforeRouteEnter(to, from, next) {
    next(component => component.getData(to));
},
...
```

The `beforeRouteEnter` method is invoked before the component is created and its regular lifecycle begins, which means that `this` cannot be used to access the component. Instead, the `next` method can be passed a function that will be invoked once the component has been created and that receives the component object as its argument. In the listing, I use the `next` function to invoke the `getData` method on the component once it has been created.

This may seem like an oddly complex approach to requesting data, which could as easily be done using the `created` method as part of the component's lifecycle, which I described in Chapter 17. The reason that the `beforeRouteEnter` method is useful is that it allows for navigation to be canceled before the component is created, which is something that cannot be done in the `created` method, which is invoked only after navigation has been completed and the component has already been created. To demonstrate, I added a check in the `beforeRouteEnter` method that will redirect navigation if the user has specified a category value other than `All` in the URL, as shown in Listing 24-13.

Listing 24-13. Guarding a Component in the FilteredData.vue File in the src/components Folder

```
...
async beforeRouteEnter(to, from, next) {
    if (to.params.category != "All") {
        next("/filter/All");
    } else {
        next(async component => await component.getData(to));
    }
},
...
```

The method redirects any attempts to navigate to a URL that displays the component unless that URL targets the All category, which requests all the data from the server. Once the component is displayed, navigation to other components is permitted because those changes are guarded by the `beforeRouteUpdate` method.

This is an example that is more readily understood when you can see it working. To add support for the new component, I added the statements shown in Listing 24-14 to the set of basic routes.

Listing 24-14. Adding a Route in the basicRoutes.js File in the src/router Folder

```
import ProductDisplay from "../components/ProductDisplay";
import ProductEditor from "../components/ProductEditor";
import Preferences from "../components/Preferences";
import Products from "../components/Products";
import FilteredData from "../components/FilteredData";

export default [
```

```
    { path: "/preferences", component: Preferences },
    {
        path: "/products", component: Products,
        children: [{ name: "table", path: "list", component: ProductDisplay },
        {
            name: "editor", path: ":op(create|edit)/:id(\\d+)?",
            component: ProductEditor
        },
        { path: "", redirect: "list" }]
    },
    { path: "/edit/:id", redirect: to => `/products/edit/${to.params.id}` },
    { path: "/filter/:category", component: FilteredData }
]
```

To make it easy to navigate to the new route, I added the navigation element shown in Listing 24-15 to the top-level App component's template.

Listing 24-15. Adding a Navigation Element in the App.vue File in the src Folder

```
<template>
    <div class="container-fluid">
        <div class="row">
            <div class="col text-center m-2">
                <div class="btn-group">
                    <router-link tag="button" to="/products"
                                 active-class="btn-info" class="btn btn-primary">
                        Products
                    </router-link>
                    <router-link tag="button" to="/preferences"
                                 active-class="btn-info" class="btn btn-primary">
                        Preferences
                    </router-link>
                    <router-link to="/named/tableleft" class="btn btn-primary"
                                 active-class="btn-info">
                        Table Left
                    </router-link>
                    <router-link to="/named/tableright" class="btn btn-primary"
                                 active-class="btn-info">
                        Table Right
                    </router-link>
                    <router-link to="/filter/All" class="btn btn-primary"
                                 active-class="btn-info">
                        Filtered Data
                    </router-link>
                </div>
            </div>
        </div>
        <div class="row">
            <div class="col m-2">
                <router-view></router-view>
            </div>
        </div>
```

```
    </div>
</template>

<script>

    export default {
        name: 'App',
        created() {
            this.$store.dispatch("getProductsAction");
        }
    }
</script>
```

The result is a new button element that navigates to a route that selects the FilteredData component. The route guard method will allow navigation only when the category dynamic segment is All and will redirect other requests. Once the component has been displayed, picking a difference component using the select element will navigate to a URL that is guarded by the beforeRouteUpdate method, which responds to the route change by getting the data in the specified category, as shown in Figure 24-7.

Figure 24-7. *Accessing a component object in the route guard*

DEVELOPING WITH COMPONENT ROUTE GUARDS

Working with component route guards can be difficult. The Vue.js development tools dynamically update the application, but this happens in a way that doesn't correctly trigger the route guard methods, and you may have to reload the browser window to see your route guards working.

Similarly, when the browser and the web service are both running on the same development workstation, the response from the web service can be so quick that you don't have a chance to see the feedback that the component presents to the user while waiting for data. If you want to slow down the data loading so you can see how the component behaves while waiting for data, then add this statement before making the HTTP request:

```
...
await new Promise(resolve => setTimeout(resolve, 3000));
...
```

For the component in Listing 24-15, for example, this statement would be inserted into the `getData` method immediately before the statement that uses Axios to send the HTTP request and will introduce a three-second pause before sending the request.

Loading Components on Demand

The components required by a route can be excluded from the application's JavaScript bundle and loaded only when required, using the same basic features that I described in Chapter 21. When using URL routing, only the basic lazy loading feature is supported, and the configuration options, such as `loading` or `delay`, are ignored (however, I demonstrate how to display a loading message using route guards in the next section). In Listing 24-16, I have changed the statement that imports the `FilteredData` component so that it is lazily loaded.

Listing 24-16. Lazily Loading a Component in the basicRoutes.js File in the src/router Folder

```
import ProductDisplay from "../components/ProductDisplay";
import ProductEditor from "../components/ProductEditor";
import Preferences from "../components/Preferences";
import Products from "../components/Products";

const FilteredData = () => import("../components/FilteredData");

export default [

    { path: "/preferences", component: Preferences },
    {
        path: "/products", component: Products,
        children: [{ name: "table", path: "list", component: ProductDisplay },
        {
            name: "editor", path: ":op(create|edit)/:id(\\d+)?",
            component: ProductEditor
        },
        { path: "", redirect: "list" }]
    },
    { path: "/edit/:id", redirect: to => `/products/edit/${to.params.id}` },
    { path: "/filter/:category", component: FilteredData }
]
```

This is the `import` function that I used in Chapter 21, and it has the same effect. The `FilteredData` component is excluded from the main application JavaScript bundle and is placed in its own bundle that is loaded the first time it is required.

To ensure that the `FilteredData` is being loaded only when it is required, navigate to http:// localhost:8080 and open the browser's F12 developer's tools to the Network tab. In the main browser window, click the Filtered Data button, and you will see that an HTTP request is sent to the server for a file named 0.js, as shown in Figure 24-8. (You may see a different file name in the request, but that isn't important.)

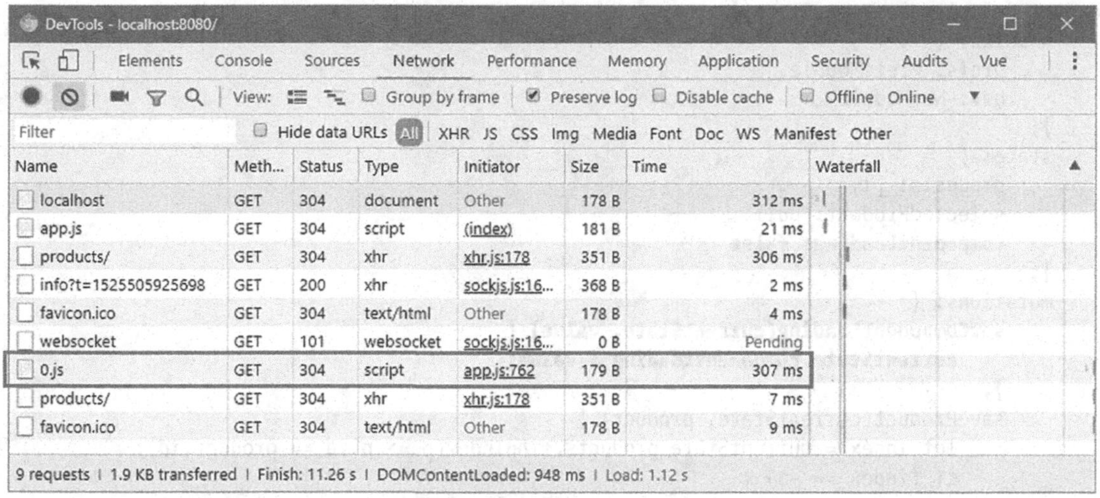

Figure 24-8. Lazily loading a component

During the build process, two separate bundles of JavaScript code have been created. The app.js file contains the main part of the application, and the 0.js file contains just the FilteredData component. (The other requests shown by the F12 tools are the initial HTTP request, requests for data from the web service, and the connection back to the server that the development tools use to update the browser.)

■ **Tip** The lazy loading feature for URL routing will provide prefetch hints by default. See Chapter 21 for details and the configuration instructions for disabling this feature.

Displaying a Component Loading Message

At the time of writing, the features described in Chapter 21 to display a loading or error component are not supported by the Vue Router package. To create a comparable feature, I am going to combine a data store property with router guards to display a message to the user while lazily loading a component. To start, I added a property to the data store that will indicate when a component is being loaded and a mutation to change its value, as shown in Listing 24-17.

Listing 24-17. Adding a Data Property and Mutation in the index.js File in the src/store Folder

```
import Vue from "vue";
import Vuex from "vuex";
import Axios from "axios";

import PrefsModule from "./preferences";
import NavModule from "./navigation";

Vue.use(Vuex);

const baseUrl = "http://localhost:3500/products/";
```

649

```
export default new Vuex.Store({
    modules: {
        prefs: PrefsModule,
        nav: NavModule
    },
    state: {
        products: [],
        selectedProduct: null,
        componentLoading: false
    },
    mutations: {
        setComponentLoading(currentState, value) {
            currentState.componentLoading = value;
        },
        saveProduct(currentState, product) {
            let index = currentState.products.findIndex(p => p.id == product.id);
            if (index == -1) {
                currentState.products.push(product);
            } else {
                Vue.set(currentState.products, index, product);
            }
        },

        // ...other data store features omitted for brevity...


    }
})
```

To indicate when a component is being loaded, I added the elements shown in Listing 24-18 to the App component's template, along with a mapping to the data store property created in Listing 24-17.

Listing 24-18. Displaying a Loading Message in the App.vue File in the src Folder

```
<template>
    <div class="container-fluid">
        <div class="row">
            <div class="col text-center m-2">
                <div class="btn-group">
                    <router-link tag="button" to="/products"
                                 active-class="btn-info" class="btn btn-primary">
                        Products
                    </router-link>
                    <router-link tag="button" to="/preferences"
                                 active-class="btn-info" class="btn btn-primary">
                        Preferences
                    </router-link>
                    <router-link to="/named/tableleft" class="btn btn-primary"
                                 active-class="btn-info">
                        Table Left
                    </router-link>
                    <router-link to="/named/tableright" class="btn btn-primary"
                                 active-class="btn-info">
```

```
                        Table Right
                    </router-link>
                    <router-link to="/filter/All" class="btn btn-primary"
                            active-class="btn-info">
                        Filtered Data
                    </router-link>
                </div>
            </div>
        </div>
        <div class="row">
            <div class="col m-2">
                <h3 class="bg-warning text-white text-center p-2"
                        v-if="componentLoading">
                    Loading Component...
                </h3>
                <router-view></router-view>
            </div>
        </div>
    </div>
</template>

<script>
    import { mapState } from "vuex";

    export default {
        name: 'App',
        computed: {
            ...mapState(["componentLoading"]),
        },
        created() {
            this.$store.dispatch("getProductsAction");
        }
    }
</script>
```

To set the value of the data store property and display the message to the user, I added a guard to the route that targets the lazily loaded component, as shown in Listing 24-19.

Listing 24-19. Adding a Route Guard in the basicRoutes.js File in the src/router Folder

```
import ProductDisplay from "../components/ProductDisplay";
import ProductEditor from "../components/ProductEditor";
import Preferences from "../components/Preferences";
import Products from "../components/Products";

const FilteredData = () => import("../components/FilteredData");

import dataStore from "../store";

export default [

    { path: "/preferences", component: Preferences },
```

```
    {
        path: "/products", component: Products,
        children: [{ name: "table", path: "list", component: ProductDisplay },
        {
            name: "editor", path: ":op(create|edit)/:id(\\d+)?",
            component: ProductEditor
        },
        { path: "", redirect: "list" }]
    },
    { path: "/edit/:id", redirect: to => `/products/edit/${to.params.id}` },
    { path: "/filter/:category", component: FilteredData,
        beforeEnter: (to, from, next) => {
            dataStore.commit("setComponentLoading", true);
            next();
        }
    }
}
]
```

The import statement in this example provides access to the data store. The $store that I used in the examples in Chapter 20 is available only in components, and access to the data store is available through an import statement in the rest of the application. The guard method in Listing 24-19 uses the setComponentLoading mutation to update the data store and then calls the next function.

DEALING WITH LOADING ERRORS

The lazy loading feature for URL routing doesn't support an error component. To deal with errors when loading components or when invoking route guards, you can use the onError method defined by the VueRouter object to register a callback function that will be invoked when there is a problem.

The guard method defined in Listing 24-19 indicates when the loading process starts, but I also need to indicate when it is complete so that the user no longer sees the loading message. In Listing 24-20, I have updated the route guard in the component that will be lazily loaded.

■ **Caution** You might be tempted to put both mutation statements in the beforeRouteEnter guard method in the component. This will not work because the component's code is what the application is loading, and the route guard method can't be invoked before the loading process is complete.

Listing 24-20. Updating a Route Guard in the FilteredData.vue File in the src/components Folder

```
...
async beforeRouteEnter(to, from, next) {
    if (to.params.category != "All") {
        next("/filter/All");
    } else {
        next(async component => {
            component.$store.commit("setComponentLoading", false);
```

```
            await component.getData(to)
        });
    }
},
...
```

I added a statement to the callback function that is invoked once navigation has been confirmed and the component has been created. Using the component parameter, I update the data store and apply the mutation that signals the loading process is complete, producing the effect shown in Figure 24-9.

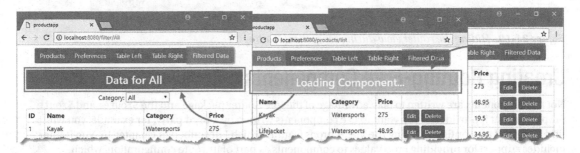

Figure 24-9. *Displaying a message while lazily loading a component*

Hiding the Outgoing Component During Loading

If you examine Figure 24-9, you will see that the component that is about to be removed is displayed to the user throughout the loading process. While this is acceptable for many projects, care must be taken to use the v-show directive if you want to hide the old component while waiting for the new one to be loaded, as shown in Listing 24-21.

Listing 24-21. Hiding an Element in the App.vue File in the src Folder

```
...
<div class="row">
    <div class="col m-2">
        <h3 class="bg-warning text-white text-center p-2"
                v-if="componentLoading">
            Loading Component...
        </h3>
        <router-view v-show="!componentLoading"></router-view>
    </div>
</div>
...
```

As I explained in Chapter 12, the v-show hides an element without removing it. This is important because if you use the v-if or v-else directive, the router-view element will be removed from the Document Object Model, and the loaded component will never be initialized and displayed to the user. Using the v-show directive leaves the router-view element in the document and available as a target to display the lazily loaded component, as shown in Figure 24-10.

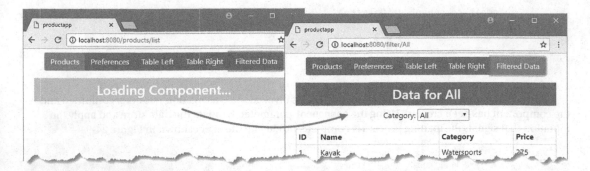

Figure 24-10. Hiding the router view during component loading

Creating Routing-Free Components

Not all components are written to take advantage of the Vue Router package and the $router and $route properties that it provides. If you want to use components written by a third party, for example, you will find that most are configured using the Vue.js props feature, which I described in Chapter 16. Vue Router includes support for providing prop values to components as part of its route configuration, which makes it possible to integrate components into an application that uses URL routing without having to modify them or write awkward wrappers to adapt them. To demonstrate this feature, I added a file called MessageDisplay.vue in the src/components folder with the content shown in Listing 24-22.

Listing 24-22. The Contents of the MessageDisplay.vue File in the src/components Folder

```
<template>
    <h3 class="bg-success text-white text-center p-2">
        Message: {{ message }}
    </h3>
</template>

<script>
    export default {
        props: ["message"]
    }
</script>
```

This component displays a message using a prop, which is all that I need to demonstrate this feature. In Listing 24-23, I have added two routes to the application's configuration that target the new component and configure it using different prop values.

Listing 24-23. Adding Routes in the basicRoutes.js File in the src/router Folder

```
import ProductDisplay from "../components/ProductDisplay";
import ProductEditor from "../components/ProductEditor";
import Preferences from "../components/Preferences";
import Products from "../components/Products";
import MessageDisplay from "../components/MessageDisplay";

const FilteredData = () => import("../components/FilteredData");
```

```
import dataStore from "../store";

export default [

    { path: "/preferences", component: Preferences },
    {
        path: "/products", component: Products,
        children: [{ name: "table", path: "list", component: ProductDisplay },
        {
            name: "editor", path: ":op(create|edit)/:id(\\d+)?",
            component: ProductEditor
        },
        { path: "", redirect: "list" }]
    },
    { path: "/edit/:id", redirect: to => `/products/edit/${to.params.id}` },
    { path: "/filter/:category", component: FilteredData,
        beforeEnter: (to, from, next) => {
            dataStore.commit("setComponentLoading", true);
            next();
        }
    },
    { path: "/hello", component: MessageDisplay, props: { message: "Hello, Adam"}},
    { path: "/hello/:text", component: MessageDisplay,
        props: (route) => ({ message: `Hello, ${route.params.text}`})},
    { path: "/message/:message", component: MessageDisplay, props: true},
]
```

Props are passed to a component using a props property when defining the route. The routes added in Listing 24-23 show three different ways of passing props to a component using the props property. In the first route, the prop value is entirely independent of the route and will always be set to the same value, which you can see by navigating to http://localhost:8080/hello, where you will see the result shown in Figure 24-11.

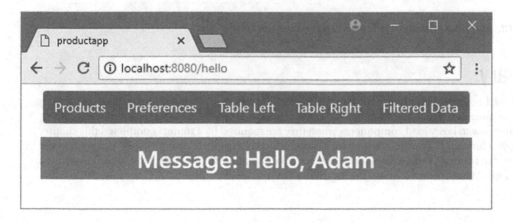

Figure 24-11. *Passing fixed prop values*

The other two routes use the values of the path's dynamic segment to set the prop value. The props value can be assigned a function that receives the current route as its parameter and returns an object containing the props value, like this:

```
...
{ path: "/hello/:text", component: MessageDisplay,
  props: (route) => ({ message: `Hello, ${route.params.text}`})},
...
```

This example takes the value from the text segment and uses it to set the value of the message prop, which is a useful technique if the values from the URL need to be processed. If you don't need to process the dynamic segment, then you can use the final technique, which is to set the props value to true, like this:

```
...
{ path: "/message/:message", component: MessageDisplay, props: true},
...
```

This has the effect of using the params values from the current route as prop values, which avoids the need to explicitly define mappings for each of the dynamic segments and props (although the names of the segments must match the names of the props expected by the component). To see the effect, navigate to http://localhost:8080/hello/adam and http://localhost:8080/message/Hello%20Adam, which will produce the results shown in Figure 24-12.

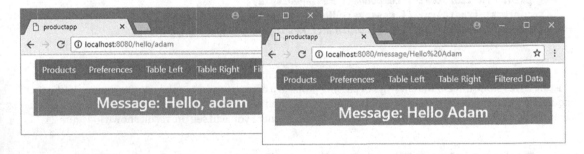

Figure 24-12. *Mapping dynamic segment values to component props*

Summary

In this chapter, I explained how to use multiple JavaScript files to group related routes to make the routing configuration more manageable. I also showed you how to guard routes to control their activation and demonstrated how to lazily load components when they are required by a route. I completed this chapter by showing you how to configure a component's props, which is a useful technique when you want to use components that have not been written to get their configuration information from the routing system. In the next chapter, I show you how to use the transitions feature.

CHAPTER 25

■ ■ ■

Transitions

The Vue.js transition feature allows you to respond when an HTML element is added or removed or changes position. When combined with the features provided by modern browsers, transitions can be used to draw the user's attention to the part of the application that has been affected by their actions. In this chapter, I show you the different ways that transitions can be used, demonstrate how to use third-party CSS and JavaScript animation packages, and show you how to draw the user's attention to other types of change, such as when a data value is modified. Table 25-1 puts this chapter in context.

Table 25-1. *Putting Transitions in Context*

Question	Answer
What are they?	Transitions are instructions to add and remove elements from classes at key moments, such as when they are added and removed from the DOM. The classes are used to gradually apply changes in the element's style to create animation effects.
Why are they useful?	Transitions can be a useful way to draw the user's attention to important changes or to make changes less jarring.
How are they used?	Transitions are applied with the transition and transition-group elements.
Are there any pitfalls or limitations?	It is easy to get carried away and create an application that contains effects that frustrate the user and disrupt effective workflows.
Are there any alternatives?	Transitions are an optional feature, and you do not have to use them in your projects.

Table 25-2 summarizes the chapter.

Table 25-2. *Chapter Summary*

Problem	Solution	Listing
Apply a transition	Use the transition element and define styles that match the transition classes	13, 15, 16, 20–22
Use an animation library	Use the transition element attributes to specify the classes that will apply the animation	14, 17
Determine how the transition between elements is presented	Use the mode attribute	15
Apply a transition to a group of repeated elements	Use the transition-group element	18
Receive notifications for transitions	Handle the transition events	19

Preparing for This Chapter

To create the project required for the examples in this chapter, run the command shown in Listing 25-1 in a convenient location to create a new Vue.js project.

Listing 25-1. Creating the Example Project

```
vue create transitions --default
```

This command creates a project called transitions. Once the setup process has finished, run the commands shown in Listing 25-2 in the transitions folder to add the Bootstrap CSS and Vue Router packages to the project.

Listing 25-2. Adding Packages

```
npm install bootstrap@4.0.0
npm install vue-router@3.0.1
```

To provide the effects for the examples in this chapter, I use the animate.css and popmotion packages. Run the commands shown in Listing 25-3 in the transitions folder to download and install the packages.

Listing 25-3. Adding the Animation Packages

```
npm install animate.css@3.6.1
npm install popmotion@8.1.24
```

Add the statements shown in Listing 25-4 to the main.js file in the src folder to incorporate the Bootstrap and the animation packages into the application.

Listing 25-4. Incorporating the Packages in the main.js File in the src Folder

```
import Vue from 'vue'
import App from './App.vue'

import "bootstrap/dist/css/bootstrap.min.css";
import "animate.css/animate.min.css";
import "popmotion/dist/popmotion.global.min.js";

Vue.config.productionTip = false

new Vue({
  render: h => h(App)
}).$mount('#app')
```

Creating the Components

I need some basic components for this chapter. I started by adding a file called SimpleDisplay.vue to the src/components folder with the contents shown in Listing 25-5.

Listing 25-5. The Contents of the SimpleDisplay.vue File in the src/components Folder

```
<template>
    <div class="mx-5 border border-dark p-2">
        <h3 class="bg-warning text-white text-center p-2">Display</h3>

        <div v-if="show" class="h4 bg-info text-center p-2">Hello, Adam</div>

        <div class="text-center">
            <button class="btn btn-primary" v-on:click="toggle">
                Toggle Visibility
            </button>
        </div>
    </div>
</template>

<script>

    export default {
        data: function () {
            return {
                show: true
            }
        },
        methods: {
            toggle() {
                this.show = !this.show;
            }
        }
    }

</script>
```

This component displays a message whose visibility is managed using the v-if directive. Next, I added a file called Numbers.vue to the src/components folder with the content shown in Listing 25-6.

Listing 25-6. The Contents of the Numbers.vue File in the src/components Folder

```
<template>
    <div class="mx-5 p-2 border border-dark">
        <h3 class="bg-success text-white text-center p-2">Numbers</h3>

        <div class="container-fluid">
            <div class="row">
                <div class="col">
                    <input class="form-control" v-model.number="first" />
                </div>
                <div class="col-1 h3">+</div>
                <div class="col">
                    <input class="form-control" v-model.number="second" />
                </div>
                <div class="col h3">= {{ total }} </div>
            </div>
        </div>
    </div>
</template>

<script>
    export default {
        data: function () {
            return {
                first: 10,
                second: 20
            }
        },
        computed: {
            total() {
                return this.first + this.second;
            }
        }
    }
</script>
```

This component displays two input elements that use the v-model directive to update data properties, which are summed by a computed property, which is also displayed in the template. Next, I added a file called ListMaker.vue to the src/components folder with the content shown in Listing 25-7.

Listing 25-7. The Contents of the ListMaker.vue File in the src/components Folder

```
<template>
    <div class="mx-5 p-2 border border-dark">
        <h3 class="bg-info text-white text-center p-2">My List</h3>
        <table class="table table-sm">
            <tr><th>#</th><th>Item</th><th width="20%" colspan="2"></th></tr>
            <tr v-for="(item, i) in items" v-bind:key=item>
```

```
            <td>{{i}}</td>
            <td>{{item}}</td>
            <td>
                <button class="btn btn-sm btn-info" v-on:click="moveItem(i)">
                    Move
                </button>
                <button class="btn btn-sm btn-danger" v-on:click="removeItem(i)">
                    Delete
                </button>
            </td>
        </tr>
        <controls v-on:add="addItem" />
    </table>
</div>
</template>

<script>

    import Controls from "./ListMakerControls";

    export default {
        components: { Controls },
        data: function () {
            return {
                items: ["Apples", "Oranges", "Grapes"]
            }
        },
        methods: {
            addItem(item) {
                this.items.push(item);
            },
            removeItem(index) {
                this.items.splice(index, 1);
            },
            moveItem(index) {
                this.items.push(...this.items.splice(index, 1));
            }
        }
    }
</script>
```

This component displays an array of items. New items can be added to the array, and the existing items can be moved to the end of the array or removed from it. I will be making changes to the component's template later in the chapter, and to avoid having to list HTML elements that are not directly related to the examples, I created a supporting component by adding a file called ListMakerControls.vue in the src/ components folder with the content shown in Listing 25-8.

Listing 25-8. The Contents of the ListMakerControls.vue in the src/components Folder

```
<template>
    <tfoot>
        <tr v-if="showAdd">
```

```
            <td></td>
            <td><input class="form-control" v-model="currentItem" /></td>
            <td>
                <button id="add" class="btn btn-sm btn-info" v-on:click="handleAdd">
                    Add
                </button>
                <button id="cancel" class="btn btn-sm btn-secondary"
                        v-on:click="showAdd = false">
                    Cancel
                </button>
            </td>
        </tr>
        <tr v-else>
            <td colspan="4" class="text-center p-2">
                <button class="btn btn-info" v-on:click="showAdd = true">
                    Show Add
                </button>
            </td>
        </tr>
    </tfoot>
</template>

<script>
    export default {
        data: function () {
            return {
                showAdd: false,
                currentItem: ""
            }
        },
        methods: {
            handleAdd() {
                this.$emit("add", this.currentItem);
                this.showAdd = false;
            }
        }
    }
</script>
```

This component allows new items to be added to the list and is a dependency of the component I created in Listing 25-7.

Configuring URL Routing

To set up the URL routing system, I created the src/router folder and added to it a file called index.js with the content shown in Listing 25-9.

Listing 25-9. The Contents of the index.js File in the src/router Folder

```
import Vue from "vue"
import Router from "vue-router"
```

```
import SimpleDisplay from "../components/SimpleDisplay";
import ListMaker from "../components/ListMaker";
import Numbers from "../components/Numbers";

Vue.use(Router)

export default new Router({
    mode: "history",
    routes: [
        { path: "/display", component: SimpleDisplay },
        { path: "/list", component: ListMaker },
        { path: "/numbers", component: Numbers },
        { path: "*", redirect: "/display" }
    ]
})
```

This configuration enables the History API mode and defines /display, /numbers, and /list routes that target the components created in the previous section. There is also a catchall route that redirects the browser to the /display URL. In Listing 25-10, I imported the router into the main.js file and added the property that will make the routing features available.

Listing 25-10. Enabling Routing in the main.js File in the src Folder

```
import Vue from 'vue'
import App from './App.vue'

import "bootstrap/dist/css/bootstrap.min.css";
import "animate.css/animate.min.css";
import "popmotion/dist/popmotion.global.min.js";
import router from "./router";

Vue.config.productionTip = false

new Vue({
  router,
  render: h => h(App)
}).$mount('#app')
```

Creating the Navigation Elements

The final preparatory step is to add navigation elements to the root component's template that will target the URLs defined in the routing configuration, as shown in Listing 25-11.

Listing 25-11. Adding Navigation Elements in the App.vue File in the src Folder

```
<template>
    <div class="m-2">
        <div class="text-center m-2">
            <div class="btn-group">
                <router-link tag="button" to="/display"
                        exact-active-class="btn-warning" class="btn btn-secondary">
                    Simple Display
                </router-link>
```

```
        <router-link tag="button" to="/list"
                exact-active-class="btn-info" class="btn btn-secondary">
            List Maker
        </router-link>
        <router-link tag="button" to="/numbers"
                exact-active-class="btn-success" class="btn btn-secondary">
            Numbers
        </router-link>
      </div>
    </div>
    <router-view />
  </div>
</template>

<script>
    export default {
        name: 'App'
    }
</script>
```

Run the command shown in Listing 25-12 in the transitions folder to start the development tools.

Listing 25-12. Starting the Development Tools

```
npm run serve
```

The initial bundling process will be performed, after which you will see a message telling you that the project has compiled successfully and the HTTP server is listening for requests on port 8080. Open a new browser window and navigate to http://localhost:8080 to see the content shown in Figure 25-1.

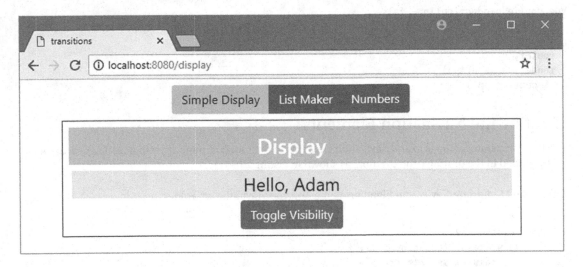

Figure 25-1. *Running the example application*

GUIDANCE FOR APPLYING TRANSITIONS

Developers often get carried away when applying transitions, and the result is applications that users find frustrating. These features should be applied sparingly, they should be simple, and they should be quick. Use transitions to help the user make sense of your application and not as a vehicle to demonstrate your artistic skills. Users, especially for corporate line-of-business applications, have to perform the same task repeatedly, and excessive and long animations just get in the way.

I suffer from this tendency, and, unchecked, my applications behave like Las Vegas slot machines. I have two rules that I follow to keep the problem under control. The first is that I perform the major tasks or workflows in the application 20 times in a row. In the case of the example application, that might mean adding 20 items to the list, moving them around, and then deleting them. I remove or shorten any effect that I find myself having to wait to complete before I can move on to the next step in the process.

The second rule is that I don't disable effects during development. It can be tempting to comment out a transition or animation when I am working on a feature because I will be performing a series of quick tests as I write the code. But any animation that gets in my way will also get in the user's way, so I leave the transitions in place and adjust them—generally reducing their duration—until they become less obtrusive and annoying.

You don't have to follow my rules, of course, but it is important to make sure that the transitions are helpful to the user and not a barrier to working quickly or a distracting annoyance.

Getting Started with Transitions

By default, the changes that are made to HTML elements in a component's template take effect immediately, which you can see by clicking the Toggle Visibility button shown by the `SimpleDisplay` component. Each time you click the button, the `show` data property is modified, which causes the `v-if` directive to immediately show and hide the element to which it has been applied, as shown in Figure 25-2.

■ **Note** Static screenshots are not ideally suited to showing changes in the application. The examples in this chapter are best experienced firsthand to help appreciate how the Vue.js transition features work.

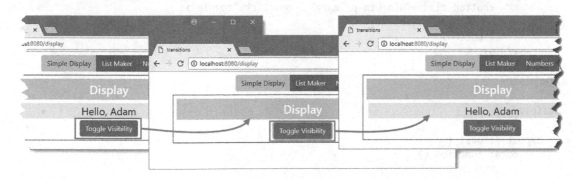

Figure 25-2. *The default behavior for state changes*

The Vue.js transition feature can be used to manage the change from one state to the other, which is done using the `transition` component. The basic use of the transition component is to apply a CSS transition, which I have done in Listing 25-13.

VUE.JS TRANSITIONS VERSUS CSS TRANSITIONS AND ANIMATIONS

There is a clash of terms for the features I describe in this chapter. The Vue.js transition feature is used to respond to changes in the application state. This is most typically related to HTML elements being added and removed from the DOM, but it can also be responding to a change in a data value.

The most common way to respond to a change in an HTML element is to use the Vue.js transition feature to apply a *CSS transition*. A CSS transition is a gradual change between one set of CSS property values and another, which has the effect of animating the change in the element. You can see an example of a CSS transition in Listing 25-13. A CSS animation is similar to a CSS transition but provides more options over how the CSS property values are changed. The other term you may encounter is *CSS transforms*, which allows you to move, rotate, scale, and skew HTML elements. Transforms are often combined with CSS transitions or animations to create more complex effects.

If you find yourself getting bogged down with these terms, remember that it is the Vue.js transition feature that is most important for Vue.js application development. After the initial examples that allow me to demonstrate how the Vue.js features work, I don't use the CSS features directly and rely on third-party packages to provide the effects that are shown to the user. I recommend you do this in your own projects as well because the results are more predictable—and less frustrating—than trying to create your own complex effects working directly with the CSS transition, animation, and transform features.

Listing 25-13. Applying a Transition in the SimpleDisplay.vue File in the src/components Folder

```
<template>
    <div class="mx-5 border border-dark p-2">
        <h3 class="bg-warning text-white text-center p-2">Display</h3>

        <transition>
            <div v-if="show" class="h4 bg-info text-center p-2">Hello, Adam</div>
        </transition>

        <div class="text-center">
            <button class="btn btn-primary" v-on:click="toggle">
                Toggle Visibility
            </button>
        </div>
    </div>
</template>

<script>

    export default {
        data: function () {
            return {
                show: true
```

```
            }
        },
        methods: {
            toggle() {
                this.show = !this.show;
            }
        }
    }

</script>

<style>
    .v-leave-active {
        opacity: 0;
        font-size: 0em;
        transition: all 250ms;
    }

    .v-enter {
        opacity: 0;
        font-size: 0em;
    }

    .v-enter-to {
        opacity: 1;
        font-size: x-large;
        transition: all 250ms;
    }
</style>
```

This example is easier to understand once you have seen it work. Once you have saved the changes shown in the listing, reload the browser and click the Toggle Visibility button. Instead of the instantaneous change, the visibility of the element changes gradually, as shown in Figure 25-3. (It may be hard to discern from the figure, but the HTML element becomes smaller and fades from view gradually.)

■ **Tip** You may find that you have to reload the browser to see the expected results for the examples in this chapter. This is a consequence of the way that the webpack bundling process deals with changes.

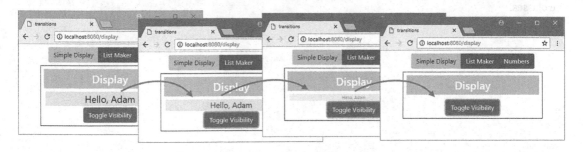

Figure 25-3. *The effect of a transition*

The transition is applied by wrapping the element you want to handle in a transition element, like this:

```
...
<transition>
    <div v-if="show" class="h4 bg-info text-center p-2">Hello, Adam</div>
</transition>
...
```

Vue.js doesn't animate the element itself—instead, it adds the element to a number of classes and leaves the browser to apply any effects that are associated with those classes. This isn't as complex as it might seem once you understand the steps that are involved, which I describe in the following sections.

Understanding the Transition Classes and CSS Transition

The effect of the transition element is to add the element it contains to a series of classes during its transition, which for the case of the example is when the element is added or removed from the DOM. Table 25-3 describes these classes.

Table 25-3. *The Transition Classes*

Name	Description
v-enter	The element is added to this class before it is added to the DOM and removed immediately afterward.
v-enter-active	The element is added to this class before it is added to the DOM and is removed when the transition is complete.
v-enter-to	The element is added to this class immediately after it has been added to the DOM and is removed when the transition is complete.
v-leave	The element is added to this class at the start of the transition and is removed after one frame.
v-leave-active	The element is added to this class when the transition begins and removed when it finishes.
v-leave-to	The element is added to this class one frame into the transition and is removed when it is complete.

The element that is being transitioned is added and removed from the classes shown in the table as the transition starts and stops and always in the same order. Figure 25-4 shows the sequence of class memberships when the element is added to the DOM, showing the relationship between the transition and the classes.

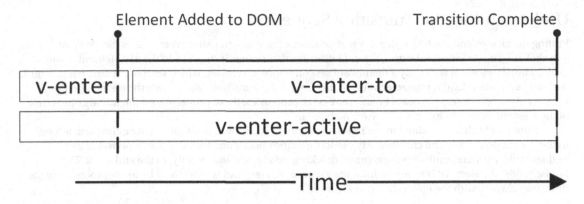

Figure 25-4. *The entering transition*

The v-enter class is used to define the initial state of the HTML element before it is added to the DOM. In Listing 25-13, I defined a CSS style with a selector that matches elements in the v-enter class like this:

```
...
.v-enter {
    opacity: 0;
    font-size: 0em;
}
...
```

When an element is a member of the v-enter class, its opacity will be zero (making the element transparent), and its text will have zero height (which will set the height of the element for this example). This represents the starting state for the element before it is added to the DOM, such that it is transparent and has zero height.

In Listing 25-13, I used a CSS style with a selector that matches elements in the v-enter-to class like this:

```
...
.v-enter-to {
    opacity: 1;
    font-size: x-large;
    transition: all 250ms;
}
...
```

The value for the opacity property makes the element fully opaque, and the value of font-size property specifies large text. The properties defined by the v-enter-to style represent the end state of the transition, and this is the part that many developers find confusing. The key is the transition property, which tells the browser to gradually change the values of all the CSS properties applied to the element from their current values to the values defined by this style and to do so over a period of 250 milliseconds. Browsers can gradually alter the value of CSS properties that can be expressed using numeric values, which includes font sizes, padding and margins, and even colors.

Understanding the Transition Sequence

Putting the classes and the CSS styles together produces the Vue.js transition that reveals the element. When you click the Toggle Visibility button, the v-if directive determines it should add the div element to the DOM. The div element is already a member of several Bootstrap classes, which set the text size, background, padding, and other display characteristics. To prepare for the transition, Vue.js adds the element to the v-enter class, which sets the opacity and font-size properties; these properties set the initial appearance of the element to be transparent and give it no height.

Immediately after it is added to the DOM, the element is removed from the v-enter class and added to the v-enter-to class. The change in styles increases the opacity and font size over a period of 250 milliseconds, with the result that the element quickly grows in size and opacity. At the end of the 250 milliseconds, the element is removed from the v-enter-to class and is styled only by its membership of the Bootstrap classes, with the effect shown in Figure 25-5.

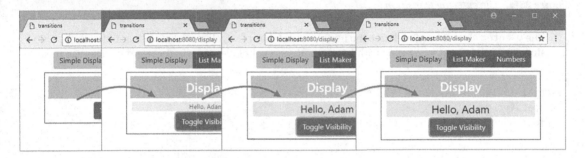

Figure 25-5. *The effect of the enter transition*

Using an Animation Library

You can use the CSS transition, animation, and translation features directly, but they are difficult to use, and it takes experience and careful testing to get good results for anything but the most basic of effects. A better approach is to use an animation library such as the animate.css package that I added to the project at the start of the chapter. There are lots of good-quality animation libraries to use, and they contain effects that are ready to use and easy to apply.

In Listing 25-14, I have replaced my custom effects for the div element in the SimpleDisplay component with ones provided by the animate.css library.

■ **Tip** You don't have to use animate.css, but I recommend it as a good place to start if you are new to transitions. You can see the complete range of effects that the package includes at https://github.com/daneden/animate.css.

Listing 25-14. Using Library Animations in the SimpleDisplay.vue File in the src/components Folder

```
<template>
    <div class="mx-5 border border-dark p-2">
        <h3 class="bg-warning text-white text-center p-2">Display</h3>

        <transition enter-to-class="fadeIn" leave-to-class="fadeOut">
            <div v-if="show" class="animated h4 bg-info text-center p-2">
                Hello, Adam
            </div>
        </transition>

        <div class="text-center">
            <button class="btn btn-primary" v-on:click="toggle">
                Toggle Visibility
            </button>
        </div>
    </div>
</template>

<script>

    export default {
        data: function () {
            return {
                show: true
            }
        },
        methods: {
            toggle() {
                this.show = !this.show;
            }
        }
    }

</script>
```

The animate.css package requires that the elements it is applied to are members of the animated class, which I have applied directly to the div element in Listing 25-14. To apply the individual effects, I have used the enter-to-class and leave-to-class attributes, which allow the names of the classes that elements are added to during a transition to be changed. Table 25-4 lists the attributes that allow classes to be selected.

Table 25-4. *The Transition Class Selection Attributes*

Name	Description
enter-class	This attribute is used to specify the name of the class that will be used instead of v-enter.
enter-active-class	This attribute is used to specify the name of the class that will be used instead of v-enter-active.
enter-to-class	This attribute is used to specify the name of the class that will be used instead of v-enter-to.
leave-class	This attribute is used to specify the name of the class that will be used instead of v-leave.
leave-active-class	This attribute is used to specify the name of the class that will be used instead of v-leave-active.
leave-to-class	This attribute is used to specify the name of the class that will be used instead of v-leave-to.

In the listing, I used the enter-to-class and leave-to-class attributes to specify animation classes provided by the animate.css package. As the class names suggest, the fadeIn class applies an effect where the element fades into view, while the fadeOut class applies an effect that makes the element fade away.

Switching Between Multiple Elements

The effect of a transition can be applied to multiple elements that are displayed by a combination of the v-if, v-else-if, and v-else directives. A single transition element is required, and Vue.js will automatically add the elements to the correct classes when they are added or removed from the DOM. In Listing 25-15, I have added an element whose visibility is managed by the v-else directive and that is contained by the same transition element as the element to which the v-if directive has been applied.

Listing 25-15. Adding an Element in the SimpleDisplay.vue File in the src/components Folder

```
<template>
    <div class="mx-5 border border-dark p-2">
        <h3 class="bg-warning text-white text-center p-2">Display</h3>

        <transition enter-active-class="fadeIn"
                leave-active-class="fadeOut" mode="out-in">
            <div v-if="show" class="animated h4 bg-info text-center p-2"
                    key="hello">
                Hello, Adam
            </div>
            <div v-else class="animated h4 bg-success text-center p-2"
                    key="goodbye">
                Goodbye, Adam
            </div>
        </transition>

        <div class="text-center">
            <button class="btn btn-primary" v-on:click="toggle">
```

```
            Toggle Visibility
        </button>
    </div>
</div>
</template>

<script>

    export default {
        data: function () {
            return {
                show: true
            }
        },
        methods: {
            toggle() {
                this.show = !this.show;
            }
        }
    }

</script>
```

When want to apply transitions to multiple elements of the same type, like the two div elements in this example, then the key attribute must be applied so that Vue.js can tell the elements apart:

```
...
<div v-if="show" class="animated h4 bg-info text-center p-2" key="hello">
    Hello, Adam
</div>
...
```

■ **Tip** Notice that I have applied the effect using the enter-active-class and leave-active-class attributes. When using an animation library to transition between elements, it can be important to apply the animation throughout the transition; otherwise, there is an unfortunate glitch where the outgoing element snaps back into view for a fraction of a second before being removed.

By default, Vue.js transitions both elements at the same time, which means that one element is fading in as the other is fading out. This doesn't create the desired effect for this example because one element is intended to be the replacement for the other. I have told Vue.js to stagger the transitions for the elements using the mode attribute on the transition element, which can be given the values described in Table 25-5.

Table 25-5. The mode Attribute Values

Name	Description
in-out	The incoming element is transitioned first, followed by the outgoing element.
out-in	This outgoing element is transitioned first, followed by the incoming element.

I have chosen the out-in mode in Listing 25-15, which means that Vue.js will wait until the outgoing element completes its transition before starting the transition for the incoming element, with the results shown in Figure 25-6.

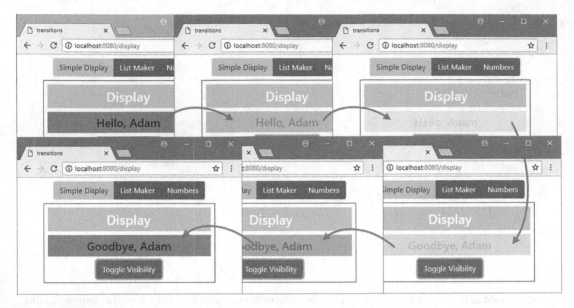

Figure 25-6. Transitioning multiple elements

ADJUSTING THE SPEED OF ANIMATION LIBRARY EFFECTS

Using an animation library is a good way to apply transitions, but they won't always be perfectly suited to your needs. A common problem that I encounter is that they can take too long to complete, which becomes an issue when you are switching between multiple elements and have to wait for several effects to be performed.

Some animation libraries allow you to specify a speed for an effect, but for other packages—including animate.css—you can change the amount of time by creating a class that sets the animation-duration property, like this:

```
...
<style>
    .quick { animation-duration: 250ms }
</style>
...
```

You can then add the element to this class during the transition, like this:

```
...
<transition enter-active-class="fadeIn quick"
    leave-active-class="fadeOut quick" mode="out-in">
...
```

Each transition will be performed in the time span you specify, which is 250 milliseconds in this example.

Applying a Transition to URL Routed Elements

The same approach can be used to apply an effect when the element displayed by a router-view element changes, as shown in Listing 25-16.

Listing 25-16. Applying a Transition in the App.vue File in the src Folder

```
<template>
    <div class="m-2">
        <div class="text-center m-2">
            <div class="btn-group">
                <router-link tag="button" to="/display"
                        exact-active-class="btn-warning" class="btn btn-secondary">
                    Simple Display
                </router-link>
                <router-link tag="button" to="/list"
                        exact-active-class="btn-info" class="btn btn-secondary">
                    List Maker
                </router-link>
                <router-link tag="button" to="/numbers"
                        exact-active-class="btn-success" class="btn btn-secondary">
                    Numbers
                </router-link>
            </div>
        </div>
        <transition enter-active-class="animated fadeIn"
                    leave-active-class=" animated fadeOut" mode="out-in">
            <router-view />
        </transition>
    </div>
</template>

<script>
    export default {
        name: 'App'
    }
</script>
```

You don't need to provide a key attribute when using the router-view element because the URL routing system is able to differentiate between components. You can see the effect of the transition in Listing 25-16 by using the navigation buttons, as shown in Figure 25-7.

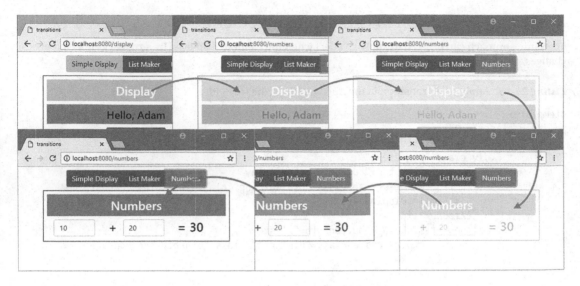

Figure 25-7. *Applying a transition to URL routed elements*

Applying a Transition for an Element's Appearance

By default, Vue.js doesn't apply a transition to the initial display of an element. You can override this by adding the appear attribute to the transition element. By default, Vue.js will use the enter classes, but you can also use classes specifically for the initial appearance or specify classes using the attributes, as described in Table 25-6.

Table 25-6. *The VueTransition Classes for an Element's Appearance*

Name	Description
v-appear	The element is added to this class before its initial appearance and is removed immediately after it is added to the DOM. A custom class can be specified using the appear-class attribute.
v-appear-active	The element is added to this class before its initial appearance and removed when the transition is complete. A custom class can be specified using the appear-active-class attribute.
v-appear-to	The element is added to this class immediately after it has been added to the DOM and is removed when the transition is complete. A custom class can be specified using the appear-to-class attribute.

In Listing 25-17, I have applied a transition that will be applied only when the element first appears.

Listing 25-17. *Adding a Transition in the App.vue File in the src Folder*

```
<template>

    <div class="m-2">
        <div class="text-center m-2">
            <div class="btn-group">
                <router-link tag="button" to="/display"
                    exact-active-class="btn-warning" class="btn btn-secondary">
```

```
                Simple Display
            </router-link>
            <router-link tag="button" to="/list"
                exact-active-class="btn-info" class="btn btn-secondary">
                List Maker
            </router-link>
            <router-link tag="button" to="/numbers"
                exact-active-class="btn-success" class="btn btn-secondary">
                Numbers
            </router-link>
        </div>
    </div>
    <transition enter-active-class="animated fadeIn"
            leave-active-class=" animated fadeOut" mode="out-in"
            appear appear-active-class="animated zoomIn">
        <router-view />
    </transition>
    </div>

</template>

<script>
    export default {
        name: 'App'
    }
</script>
```

I added the appear attribute, which does not require a value, and used the appear-active-class attribute to tell Vue.js that the element should be assigned to the animated and zoomIn classes throughout the transition. The result is that the component displayed by the router-view element zooms into view when the application first starts, as shown in Figure 25-8.

■ **Tip** You will have to reload the browser to see this transition.

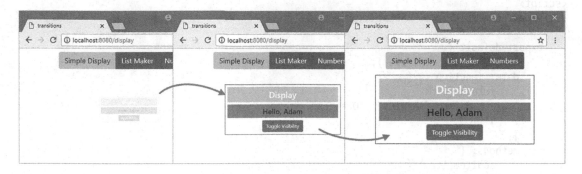

Figure 25-8. *Applying a transition for an element's initial appearance*

Applying Transitions for Collection Changes

Vue.js includes support for applying transitions to elements generated using the v-for directive, allowing effects to be specified for when an element is added, removed, or moved. In Listing 25-18, I have applied transitions to the ListMaker component.

Listing 25-18. Applying a Transition in the ListMaker.vue File in the src/components Folder

```
<template>
    <div class="mx-5 p-2 border border-dark">
        <h3 class="bg-info text-white text-center p-2">My List</h3>
        <table class="table table-sm">
            <tr><th>#</th><th>Item</th><th width="20%" colspan="2"></th></tr>
            <transition-group enter-active-class="animated fadeIn"
                              leave-active-class="animated fadeOut"
                              move-class="time"
                              tag="tbody">
                <tr v-for="(item, i) in items" v-bind:key=item>
                    <td>{{i}}</td>
                    <td>{{item}}</td>
                    <td>
                        <button class="btn btn-sm btn-info" v-on:click="moveItem(i)">
                            Move
                        </button>
                        <button class="btn btn-sm btn-danger"
                                v-on:click="removeItem(i)">
                            Delete
                        </button>
                    </td>
                </tr>
            </transition-group>
            <controls v-on:add="addItem" />
        </table>
    </div>
</template>

<script>
    import Controls from "./ListMakerControls";

    export default {
        components: { Controls },
        data: function () {
            return {
                items: ["Apples", "Oranges", "Grapes"]
            }
        },
        methods: {
            addItem(item) {
                this.items.push(item);
            },
```

```
        removeItem(index) {
            this.items.splice(index, 1);
        },
        moveItem(index) {
            this.items.push(...this.items.splice(index, 1));
        }
    }
}
</script>

<style>
    .time {
        transition: all 250ms;
    }
</style>
```

The transition-group element requires some care when it is applied because it adds an element to the DOM, unlike the transition element. To ensure that the component produces valid HTML, the tag attribute is used to specify the type of HTML element that will be generated. Since the example component uses the v-for directive to generate a set of table rows, I specified the tbody element, which represents a table body.

```
...
<transition-group enter-active-class="animated fadeIn"
    leave-active-class="animated fadeOut" move-class="time" tag="tbody">
...
```

The enter and leave transitions are applied in the same way as in earlier examples, and I used the enter-active-class and leave-active-class attributes to put the elements generated by the v-for directive into the animated, fadeIn, and fadeOut classes as they are added and removed. The remaining attribute is move-class, which is used to apply a class when an element is moved from one position to another. Vue.js will automatically transition the element from its existing position to its new one, and if that is the only effect you require, then the move-class attribute can be used to associate the element with a style that specifies the time that the move will take. In the listing, I specified a class called time and defined a corresponding CSS style that uses the transition property to specify that all of the element's properties should be changed over a period of 250 milliseconds.

■ **Note** The elements managed by a transition-group attribute must have a key, as described in Chapter 13.

The attributes I used with the transition-group element result in new elements fading into place, deleted elements fading away, and elements moving into place when the Move button is clicked, the last of which is shown in Figure 25-9.

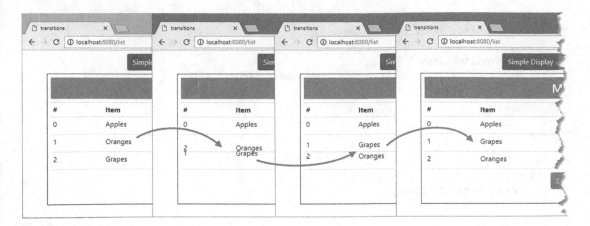

Figure 25-9. Animating collection item moves

Using Transition Events

The transition and transition-group elements emit events that can be handled to provide fine-grained control over transitions, including adapting them based on the state of the application. Table 25-7 describes the events.

Table 25-7. The Transition Events

Name	Description
before-enter	This method is invoked before an enter transition starts and receives the HTML element that is affected.
enter	This method is invoked before an enter transition starts and receives the HTML element that is affected and a callback that must be invoked to tell Vue.js that the transition has completed.
after-enter	This method is invoked before an enter transition completes and receives the HTML element that is affected.
before-leave	This method is invoked before a leave transition starts and receives the HTML element that is affected.
leave	This method is invoked before a leave transition starts and receives the HTML element that is affected and a callback that must be invoked to tell Vue.js that the transition has completed.
after-leave	This method is invoked before a leave transition completes and receives the HTML element that is affected.

In Listing 25-19, I have defined handlers for transition events using the v-on directive and used them to apply an effect programmatically.

Listing 25-19. Handling Transition Events in the ListMakerControls.vue File in the src/components Folder

```
<template>
    <tfoot>
```

```
<transition v-on:beforeEnter="beforeEnter"
    v-on:after-enter="afterEnter" mode="out-in">
    <tr v-if="showAdd" key="addcancel">
        <td></td>
        <td><input class="form-control" v-model="currentItem" /></td>
        <td>
            <button id="add" class="btn btn-sm btn-info"
                    v-on:click="handleAdd">
                Add
            </button>
            <button id="cancel" class="btn btn-sm btn-secondary"
                    v-on:click="showAdd = false">
                Cancel
            </button>
        </td>
    </tr>
    <tr v-else key="show">
        <td colspan="4" class="text-center p-2">
            <button class="btn btn-info" v-on:click="showAdd = true">
                Show Add
            </button>
        </td>
    </tr>
</transition>
    </tfoot>
</template>

<script>
    export default {
        data: function () {
            return {
                showAdd: false,
                currentItem: ""
            }
        },
        methods: {
            handleAdd() {
                this.$emit("add", this.currentItem);
                this.showAdd = false;
            },
            beforeEnter(el) {
                if (this.showAdd) {
                    el.classList.add("animated", "fadeIn");
                }
            },
            afterEnter(el) {
                el.classList.remove("animated", "fadeIn");
            }
        }
    }
</script>
```

681

In the handler for the before-enter event, I check the value of the showAdd data property to see whether the change should be animated. The result is that the transition effect is applied when the user clicks the Show Add button, while there is no effect when the user clicks the Add or Cancel button.

Using the Enter and Leave Events

The enter and leave events are useful when you want to perform a custom transition from start to end, typically where you want to generate a sequence of values for an element property programmatically or use a JavaScript library that does that for you. In Listing 25-20, I have handled the event method by adding the HTML element to animate.css classes and then listening for the DOM event that indicates when the animation is complete.

Listing 25-20. Using the Enter Event in the ListMakeControls.vue File in the src/components Folder

```
<template>
    <tfoot>
        <transition v-on:enter="enter" mode="out-in">
            <tr v-if="showAdd" key="addcancel">
                <td></td>
                <td><input class="form-control" v-model="currentItem" /></td>
                <td>
                    <button id="add" class="btn btn-sm btn-info"
                            v-on:click="handleAdd">
                        Add
                    </button>
                    <button id="cancel" class="btn btn-sm btn-secondary"
                            v-on:click="showAdd = false">
                        Cancel
                    </button>
                </td>
            </tr>
            <tr v-else key="show">
                <td colspan="4" class="text-center p-2">
                    <button class="btn btn-info" v-on:click="showAdd = true">
                        Show Add
                    </button>
                </td>
            </tr>
        </transition>
    </tfoot>
</template>

<script>
    import { styler, tween } from "popmotion";

    export default {
        data: function () {
            return {
                showAdd: false,
                currentItem: ""
            }
        },
```

```
    methods: {
        handleAdd() {
            this.$emit("add", this.currentItem);
            this.showAdd = false;
        },
        enter(el, done) {
            if (this.showAdd) {
                let t = tween({
                    from: { opacity: 0 },
                    to: { opacity: 1 },
                    duration: 250
                });
                t.start({
                    update: styler(el).set,
                    complete: done
                })
            }
        }
    }
}
</script>
```

This example uses the popmotion package, which is an animation library that uses JavaScript rather than CSS. The details of how popmotion works are not important for this chapter—see http://popmotion. io for details—and the listing serves only to demonstrate that you can use the enter and leave events to perform transitions using JavaScript.

■ **Note** Notice that the enter method in Listing 25-20 defines a done parameter. This is a callback function that is used to tell Vue.js that the transition is complete. Vue.js won't trigger the after-enter event until the done function is invoked, so it is important to ensure that you call this method directly or use it as the completion callback for your JavaScript library, as I did in the listing.

Drawing Attention to Other Changes

If you want to draw the user's attention when there is a change in the application's data, then you can use a watcher to respond to new values. In Listing 25-21, I have used the popmotion package to create a transition effect when the user enters new values into the input elements presented by the Numbers component.

Listing 25-21. Responding to Changes in the Numbers.vue File in the src/components Folder

```
<template>
    <div class="mx-5 p-2 border border-dark">
        <h3 class="bg-success text-white text-center p-2">Numbers</h3>

        <div class="container-fluid">
            <div class="row">
                <div class="col">
                    <input class="form-control" v-model.number="first" />
```

```
                </div>
                <div class="col-1 h3">+</div>
                <div class="col">
                    <input class="form-control" v-model.number="second" />
                </div>
                <div class="col h3">= {{ displayTotal }} </div>
            </div>
        </div>
    </div>
</template>

<script>

    import { tween } from "popmotion";

    export default {
        data: function () {
            return {
                first: 10,
                second: 20,
                displayTotal: 30
            }
        },
        computed: {
            total() {
                return this.first + this.second;
            }
        },
        watch: {
            total(newVal, oldVal) {
                let t = tween({
                    from: Number(oldVal),
                    to: Number(newVal),
                    duration: 250
                });
                t.start((val) => this.displayTotal = val.toFixed(0));
            }
        }
    }
</script>
```

When the value of the total computed property changes, the watcher responds by using the popmotion package to generate a series of values between the old and new values, each of which is used to update the displayTotal property that is displayed in the component's template.

This type of update can be combined with a CSS animation by using the $el property to get the component's DOM element, using it to locate the element you want to animate, and adding it to the appropriate classes, as shown in Listing 25-22.

Listing 25-22. Adding an Animation in the Numbers.vue File in the src/components Folder

```
<template>
    <div class="mx-5 p-2 border border-dark">
        <h3 class="bg-success text-white text-center p-2">Numbers</h3>

        <div class="container-fluid">
            <div class="row">
                <div class="col">
                    <input class="form-control" v-model.number="first" />
                </div>
                <div class="col-1 h3">+</div>
                <div class="col">
                    <input class="form-control" v-model.number="second" />
                </div>
                <div id="total" class="col h3">= {{ displayTotal }} </div>
            </div>
        </div>
    </div>
</template>

<script>

    import { tween } from "popmotion";

    export default {
        data: function () {
            return {
                first: 10,
                second: 20,
                displayTotal: 30
            }
        },
        computed: {
            total() {
                return this.first + this.second;
            }
        },
        watch: {
            total(newVal, oldVal) {
                let classes = ["animated", "fadeIn"]
                let totalElem = this.$el.querySelector("#total");
                totalElem.classList.add(...classes);
                let t = tween({
                    from: Number(oldVal),
                    to: Number(newVal),
                    duration: 250
                });
                t.start({
                    update: (val) => this.displayTotal = val.toFixed(0),
                    complete: () => totalElem.classList.remove(...classes)
                });
```

```
            }
        }
    }
</script>
```

To ensure that the animation can be applied again, I remove the element from the animation classes when the change has been completed. The result is that new results are displayed as a smooth transition, as shown in Figure 25-10, although this is an effect that is difficult to capture in a screenshot.

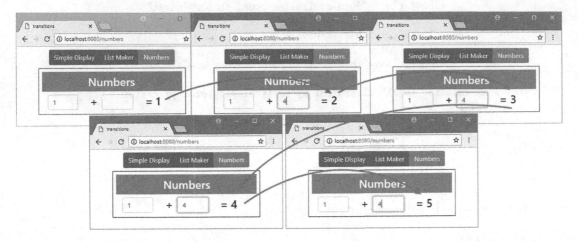

Figure 25-10. *Using a watcher to respond to value changes*

Summary

In this chapter, I explained the different ways in which Vue.js transitions can be used. I demonstrated how to use the `transition` and `transition-group` elements, how to assign elements to classes, how to use third-party packages, and how to respond to the transition events. I also showed you how to draw the user's attention to other types of change, such as when a data value changes. In the next chapter, I describe the different ways you can extend Vue.js.

CHAPTER 26

■ ■ ■

Extending Vue.js

Vue.js provides all the features that are required for most web application projects. But if you find that you need to extend Vue.js, then there are several different techniques available, and they are the topic of this chapter. I show you how to supplement the built-in directives with your own custom code, how to define common features for components using mixins, and how to group a wider range of related features using a plugin. Table 26-1 puts this chapter in context.

Table 26-1. *Putting the Vue.js Features in Context*

Question	Answer
What are they?	The features described in this chapter allow you to extend the functionality provided by Vue.js.
Why are they useful?	These features can be useful if you have common code that is required throughout an application and for which you cannot use dependency injection. These features can also be useful if you have common functionality that is required by multiple application projects.
How are they used?	Directives are created using a series of functions that are invoked as the state of the element they are applied to changes. Mixins are defined as groups of features that are merged with those defined by a component when a new instance is created. Plugins are JavaScript modules that can contain a wide range of Vue.js features that can be used throughout an application.
Are there any pitfalls or limitations?	These are advanced features that should be used with care and that are not required by most features. Before using these features, consider whether the desired result can be achieved using the features from earlier chapters.
Are there any alternatives?	These are optional features that are not required in most projects, where the built-in functionality provided by Vue.js will be sufficient.

© Adam Freeman 2018
A. Freeman, *Pro Vue.js 2*, https://doi.org/10.1007/978-1-4842-3805-9_26

Table 26-2 summarizes the chapter.

Table 26-2. *Chapter Summary*

Problem	Solution	Listing
Define a custom directive	Implement one or more hook functions and register the directive using the `directives` property of a component	7–8, 16–18
Get information about how a custom directive has been applied	Read the properties of the binding object	9–14
Pass data between hook functions	Use data properties on the HTML element to which the component has been applied	15
Define base features for components	Define a mixin	19–22
Create a mixed set of related features	Create a plugin	23–31

Preparing for This Chapter

To create the project required for the examples in this chapter, run the command shown in Listing 26-1 in a convenient location.

Listing 26-1. Creating the Example Project

```
vue create extendingvue --default
```

Once the setup process has finished, run the command shown in Listing 26-2 in the extendingvue folder to add the Bootstrap CSS package to the project.

Listing 26-2. Adding the Bootstrap CSS Package

```
npm install bootstrap@4.0.0
```

Add the statement shown in Listing 26-3 to the main.js file in the src folder to incorporate the Bootstrap package into the application.

Listing 26-3. Incorporating the Bootstrap Package in the main.js File in the src Folder

```
import Vue from 'vue'
import App from './App.vue'
import "bootstrap/dist/css/bootstrap.min.css";

Vue.config.productionTip = false

new Vue({
  render: h => h(App)
}).$mount('#app')
```

688

I added a file called Numbers.vue to the src/components folder with the content shown in Listing 26-4.

Listing 26-4. The Contents of the Numbers.vue File in the src/components Folder

```
<template>
    <div class="mx-5 p-2 border border-dark">
        <h3 class="bg-success text-white text-center p-2">Numbers</h3>

        <div class="container-fluid">
            <div class="row">
                <div class="col">
                    <input class="form-control" v-model.number="first" />
                </div>
                <div class="col-1 h3">+</div>
                <div class="col">
                    <input class="form-control" v-model.number="second" />
                </div>
                <div class="col h3">= {{ total }} </div>
            </div>
        </div>
    </div>
</template>

<script>
    export default {
        data: function () {
            return {
                first: 10,
                second: 20
            }
        },
        computed: {
            total() {
                return this.first + this.second;
            }
        }
    }
</script>
```

This is the same component I used at the start of Chapter 25, without the transitions that I added in later examples. To integrate this component into the application, replace the contents in the App.vue file, as shown in Listing 26-5.

Listing 26-5. The Contents of the App.vue File in the src Folder

```
<template>
    <div class="m-2">
        <numbers />
    </div>
</template>

<script>
```

```
import Numbers from "./components/Numbers"

export default {
    name: 'App',
    components: { Numbers }
}
</script>
```

Run the command shown in Listing 26-6 in the `transitions` folder to start the development tools.

Listing 26-6. Starting the Development Tools

```
npm run serve
```

The initial bundling process will be performed, after which you will see a message telling you that the project has compiled successfully and the HTTP server is listening for requests on port 8080. Open a new browser window and navigate to `http://localhost:8080` to see the content shown in Figure 26-1.

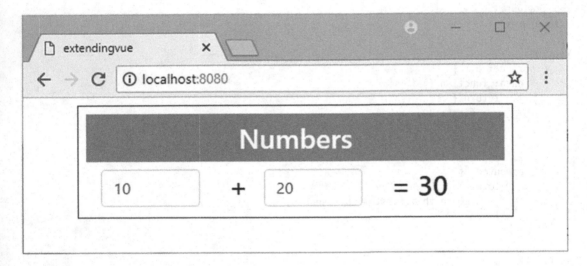

Figure 26-1. *Running the example application*

Creating Custom Directives

The built-in directives provided by Vue.js cover the key tasks that are required in most applications, but you can also create your own directives if you need to work directly with the HTML elements presented by an application and you need to do so across the application. I added a `src/directives` folder and added to it a file called `colorize.js` with the content shown in Listing 26-7.

■ **Tip** Notice that I have created a JavaScript file. Only components are written using `.vue` files, which allow a mix of HTML, CSS, and JavaScript. Directives are written using only JavaScript.

Listing 26-7. The Contents of the colorize.js File in the src/directives Folder

```
export default {
    update(el, binding) {
        if (binding.value > 100) {
            el.classList.add("bg-danger", "text-white");
        } else {
            el.classList.remove("bg-danger", "text-white");
        }
    }
}
```

I'll explain how custom directives work shortly, but it helps to show what this code does before digging into how it does it. In Listing 26-8, I registered the directive and applied it to an HTML element.

WHY YOU PROBABLY DON'T NEED A CUSTOM DIRECTIVE

The basic building block in a Vue.js application is the component, and this is what you should create when you want to add features to your project. Directives are harder to work with, have more limited features available, and can require manipulating HTML elements using JavaScript APIs, which can be a tedious process.

Directives can be useful if you want to manipulate an HTML element at a low level, but this is something that can be done using the built-in directives in most cases since the most common changes needed are supported by directives such as v-bind, as described in Chapter 12. If you find yourself creating a custom directive, it is worth taking a moment to ask yourself if you are able to achieve the same result using one of the other Vue.js features.

Listing 26-8. Registering and Applying a Directive in the Numbers.vue File in the src/components Folder

```
<template>
    <div class="mx-5 p-2 border border-dark">
        <h3 class="bg-success text-white text-center p-2">Numbers</h3>

        <div class="container-fluid">
            <div class="row">
                <div class="col">
                    <input class="form-control" v-model.number="first" />
                </div>
                <div class="col-1 h3">+</div>
                <div class="col">
                    <input class="form-control" v-model.number="second" />
                </div>
                <div v-colorize="total" class="col h3">= {{ total }} </div>
            </div>
        </div>
    </div>
</template>

<script>
```

```
import Colorize from "../directives/colorize";

export default {
    data: function () {
        return {
            first: 10,
            second: 20
        }
    },
    computed: {
        total() {
            return this.first + this.second;
        }
    },
    directives: { Colorize }
}
</script>
```

Custom directives are registered using the directives property, which is assigned an object. In this example, I have used the import keyword to give the directive the name Colorize, which I then apply to an HTML in the component's template as an attribute whose name is prefixed with v-, like this:

```
...
<div v-colorize="total" class="col h3">= {{ total }} </div>
...
```

I have specified the total property as the attribute's value, which I'll return to when I explain how the directive works. To test the directive, reload the browser and enter values that provide a total that is greater than 100. When you do this, the background and text colors of the result are changed, as shown in Figure 26-2.

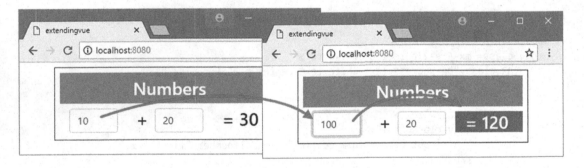

Figure 26-2. *The effect of the custom directive*

Understanding How Directives Work

Directives define methods, known as *hook functions*, that are invoked at key moments in the lifecycle of the component whose template they have been applied to. Table 26-3 describes the directive hook functions.

Table 26-3. *The Directive Hook Functions*

Name	Description
bind	This method is called when the directive is first initialized and provides an opportunity to perform any initial tasks.
inserted	This method is called when the element to which the directive has been applied is inserted into its parent.
update	This method is called when the component whose template contains the element to which the directive has been applied is updated. This method may be called before the component's children have been updated.
componentUpdated	This method is called when the component whose template contains the element to which the directive has been applied is updated and after its children have been updated.
unbind	This method is called to provide an opportunity to clean up before the directive is no longer associated with the element.

In Listing 26-7, the custom directive implements the update hook, which allows it to update the HTML element when the component whose template contains the HTML element is updated. When you entered a new value in one of the input elements, the change triggered an update for the component, which led to the directive's update hook function being invoked, providing the directive with an opportunity to modify the HTML element to which it has been applied.

The first argument to the hook functions is an HTMLElement object that implements the standard DOM API and that can be used to modify the HTML content presented to the user. I used this object in the hook function to add and remove classes that correspond to Bootstrap CSS styles, like this:

```
...
export default {
    update(el, binding) {
        if (binding.value > 100) {
            el.classList.add("bg-danger", "text-white");
        } else {
            el.classList.remove("bg-danger", "text-white");
        }
    }
}
...
```

This is the standard DOM API, which I don't describe in this book but which you can learn about at https://developer.mozilla.org/en-US/docs/Web/API/HTMLElement.

REGISTERING DIRECTIVES GLOBALLY

In Listing 26-8, I registered the custom directive for use in a single component. You can also register directives so they can be used globally so that you don't have to register them for individual components. Global registration is done in the main.js file, using the Vue.directive method, like this:

```
...
import Vue from 'vue'
import App from './App'

import "bootstrap/dist/css/bootstrap.min.css";

import Colorize from "./directives/colorize";
Vue.directive("colorize", Colorize);

Vue.config.productionTip = false

new Vue({
    el: '#app',
    components: { App },
    template: '<App/>'
})
...
```

The first argument is the name by which the directive will be applied, and the second argument is the object or function imported from the custom directive's JavaScript file. The `Vue.directive` method must be called before you create the `new Vue` object for the application, as shown in the code fragment, and the result is that you can use the directive throughout the application without needing to use the `directives` property.

The second argument passed to the hook functions is an object that represents the directive's binding to the HTML element and that defines the properties shown in Table 26-4.

■ **Tip** The hook functions are also provided with the `VNode` objects that Vue.js uses to keep track of HTML elements internally, but I do not describe them in this chapter because they are not that useful. See `https://vuejs.org/v2/api/#VNode-Interface` for details.

Table 26-4. *The Properties Defined by the Binding Object*

Name	Description
name	This property returns the name used to apply the directive to the HTML element without the v- prefix. This would be `colorize` for the directive applied in Listing 26-8.
expression	This property returns the expression used to apply the directive, expressed as a string. In the example, this would be `total`. You don't have to process the expression to get a result, which is provided through the `value` property.
value	This property returns the current value produced by evaluating the expression used to apply the directive. For the example, this will be the current value of the component's `total` property
oldValue	This property returns the previous expression value but is available only for the `update` and `componentUpdated` hook functions.
arg	This property returns the argument used to apply the directive if there is one.
modifiers	This property returns the modifiers used to apply the directive if there are any.

The custom directive I defined in Listing 26-7 uses the `value` property to get the current value of the expression, which it uses to decide whether to add or remove the element from the Bootstrap CSS classes.

```
...
export default {
    update(el, binding) {
        if (binding.value > 100) {
            el.classList.add("bg-danger", "text-white");
        } else {
            el.classList.remove("bg-danger", "text-white");
        }
    }
}
...
```

Note that the directive doesn't have any direct relationship to the component and that it receives its value through the expression without any context about the meaning of that value.

■ **Caution**   The properties described in Table 26-4 are read-only. Custom directives should make changes only through the HTML element.

Using Custom Directive Expressions

The temptation when creating custom directives is to put too much logic into the directive and not rely on the core Vue.js features and, as a result, create a directive that cannot be widely applied. The directive that I defined in Listing 26-7 falls into this trap because it hard-codes the value that triggers the element coloring in the JavaScript code. A better approach is to rely on the Vue.js expression feature to let the component control the directive's behavior, as shown in Listing 26-9.

Listing 26-9. Using an Expression in the Numbers.vue File in the src/components Folder

```
...
<template>
    <div class="mx-5 p-2 border border-dark">
        <h3 class="bg-success text-white text-center p-2">Numbers</h3>

        <div class="container-fluid">
            <div class="row">
                <div class="col">
                    <input v-colorize="first > 45" class="form-control"
                        v-model.number="first" />
                </div>
                <div class="col-1 h3">+</div>
                <div class="col">
                    <input class="form-control" v-model.number="second" />
                </div>
                <div v-colorize="total > 50" class="col h3">= {{ total }} </div>
            </div>
```

```
            </div>
        </div>
</template>
...
```

Instead of providing the directive with the `total` value, I have used expressions that allow the value that triggers the classes, meaning that I am able to apply the same directive to different elements with different trigger values. In Listing 26-10, I have made the corresponding change to the directive.

Listing 26-10. Removing the Trigger Value in the colorize.js File in the src/directives Folder

```
export default {
    update(el, binding) {
        if (binding.value) {
            el.classList.add("bg-danger", "text-white");
        } else {
            el.classList.remove("bg-danger", "text-white");
        }
    }
}
```

The result is that the directive will change the background and font color of the first `input` element if its value exceeds 45 and the `div` element if the total exceeds 50, as shown in Figure 26-3.

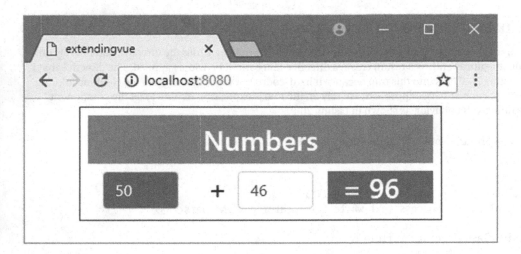

Figure 26-3. *Applying the same directive to multiple elements*

Using Custom Directive Arguments

A directive can be provided with arguments that provide additional information to shape its behavior, such as the way that the event you want to handle is specified when using the v-on directive, as described in Chapter 14. Custom directives can also receive an argument, and in Listing 26-11 I have used an argument to specify the name of the class that will be used to change the background color of the element that the directive is applied to.

Listing 26-11. Receiving an Argument in the colorize.js File in the src/directives Folder

```
export default {
    update(el, binding) {
        const bgClass = binding.arg || "bg-danger";
        if (binding.value) {
            el.classList.add(bgClass, "text-white");
        } else {
            el.classList.remove(bgClass, "text-white");
        }
    }
}
```

I use the arg property to get the class name, falling back to the bg-danger class if no argument is provided. In Listing 26-12, I have added an argument to one of the directives to specify the bg-info class.

Listing 26-12. Adding an Argument in the Numbers.vue File in the src/components Folder

```
...
<template>
    <div class="mx-5 p-2 border border-dark">
        <h3 class="bg-success text-white text-center p-2">Numbers</h3>

        <div class="container-fluid">
            <div class="row">
                <div class="col">
                    <input v-colorize:bg-info="first > 45" class="form-control"
                        v-model.number="first" />
                </div>
                <div class="col-1 h3">+</div>
                <div class="col">
                    <input class="form-control" v-model.number="second" />
                </div>
                <div v-colorize="total > 50" class="col h3">= {{ total }} </div>
            </div>
        </div>
    </div>
</template>
...
```

As a result, entering a value that exceeds 45 into the first input element puts the element into a class for which Bootstrap uses a different background color, as shown in Figure 26-4.

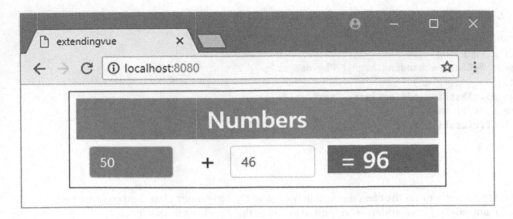

Figure 26-4. Using an argument in a custom directive

Using Custom Directive Modifiers

Modifiers provide directives with additional instructions, which can be used to supplement arguments. In Listing 26-13, I have updated the custom directive so that it checks for modifiers that specify whether the background and text colors should be changed.

Listing 26-13. Receiving Modifiers in the colorizer.js File in the src/directives Folder

```
export default {
    update(el, binding) {
        const bgClass = binding.arg || "bg-danger";
        const noMods = Object.keys(binding.modifiers).length == 0;
        if (binding.value) {
            if (noMods || binding.modifiers.bg) {
                el.classList.add(bgClass);
            }
            if (noMods || binding.modifiers.text) {
                el.classList.add("text-white");
            }
        } else {
            el.classList.remove(bgClass, "text-white");
        }
    }
}
```

Modifiers are accessed through the object returned by the modifiers property of the binding parameter. If no modifiers have been applied, then the object will have no properties, but for each modifier that has been applied, there will be a property whose name is the modifier and whose value is true. For my example directive, I want to change both the background and text colors if there are no modifiers. If modifiers have been used, then the bg modifier will indicate that the background color should be changed, and the text modifier will indicate that the text color should be changed. In Listing 26-14, I have used different combinations of modifiers to the directive and applied the directive to the second input element.

Listing 26-14. Using Directive Modifiers in the Numbers.vue File in the src/components Folder

```
...
<template>
    <div class="mx-5 p-2 border border-dark">
        <h3 class="bg-success text-white text-center p-2">Numbers</h3>

        <div class="container-fluid">
            <div class="row">
                <div class="col">
                    <input v-colorize:bg-info.bg="first > 45" class="form-control"
                            v-model.number="first" />
                </div>
                <div class="col-1 h3">+</div>
                <div class="col">
                    <input v-colorize:bg-info="second > 30"
                        class="form-control" v-model.number="second" />
                </div>
                <div v-colorize.bg.text="total > 50" class="col h3">
                    = {{ total }}
                </div>
            </div>
        </div>
    </div>
</template>
...
```

The modifiers for the example directive are optional, so I am able to use the v-colorizer attribute with no modifiers, with just the bg modifier, and with both the bg and text modifiers. This has the effect that I am able to configure each HTML element to which the directive has been applied separately, as shown in Figure 26-5.

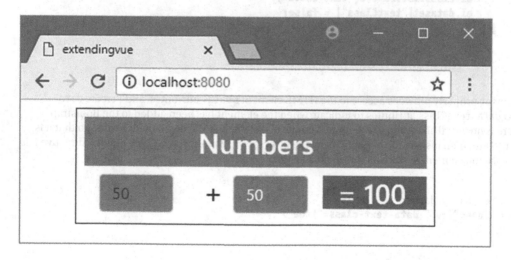

Figure 26-5. *Using modifiers to configure the directive*

699

Communicating Between Hook Functions

The nature of custom directives is simple and stateless, and it requires some effort if you want to pass data between the hook functions so that some result produced in the bind hook, for example, can be reused in the update hook or so that the outcome of one invocation of the update hook can be used in the next update. The solution to this problem is to use the HTML element to store the data you require using data attributes. In Listing 26-15, I have modified the custom directive so it uses the data attribute to keep track of whether the element has been added to the Bootstrap classes.

Listing 26-15. Using Data Attributes in the colorize.js File in the src/directives Folder

```
export default {
    update(el, binding) {
        const bgClass = binding.arg || "bg-danger";
        const noMods = Object.keys(binding.modifiers).length == 0;
        if (binding.value) {
            if (noMods || binding.modifiers.bg) {
                el.classList.add(bgClass);
                el.dataset["bgClass"] = true;
            }
            if (noMods|| binding.modifiers.text) {
                el.classList.add("text-white");
                el.dataset["textClass"] = true;
            }
        } else {
            if (el.dataset["bgClass"]) {
                el.classList.remove(bgClass);
                el.dataset["bgClass"] = false;
            }
            if (el.dataset["textClass"]) {
                el.classList.remove("text-white");
                el.dataset["textClass"] = false;
            }
        }
    }
}
```

The dataset property provides access to the HTML element's data- attributes, and I create data-bgClass and data-textClass attributes to indicate when the element has been added to the Bootstrap classes. There is no visual change in this example, but if you set the first HTML element's value so that it is greater than 45 and then inspect the element using the browser's F12 tools, you will see that the directive has been able to use the element to store its state data, like this:

```
...
<div class="col h3 bg-danger text-white"
    data-bg-class="true" data-text-class="true">
        = 70
</div>
...
```

This may seem like an odd approach, but it means that the HTML element provides the consistent source of data used by the directive without having the need to add features for local state data and a separate directive lifecycle.

Defining Single Function Directives

Directives are prone to code duplication if they need to perform the same task during setup and again when there is a change, as shown in Listing 26-16.

Listing 26-16. Adding a Hook in the colorizer.js File in the src/directives Folder

```
export default {
    bind(el, binding) {
        if (binding.value) {
            el.classList.add("bg-danger", "text-white");
        } else {
            el.classList.remove("bg-danger", "text-white");
        }
    },
    update(el, binding) {
        if (binding.value) {
            el.classList.add("bg-danger", "text-white");
        } else {
            el.classList.remove("bg-danger", "text-white");
        }
    }
}
```

I have simplified the directive so that it no longer uses arguments, modifiers, or data attributes, and I have added the bind hook. The result is that the initial value of the expression used to apply the directive is used to configure the HTML element, albeit by duplicating the same statements in each hook.

This is such a common pattern that Vue.js supports an optimization, which allows the directives that require only the bind and update hooks to be expressed as a single function, as shown in Listing 26-17.

Listing 26-17. Using a Single Function in the colorizer.js File in the src/directives Folder

```
export default function (el, binding) {
    if (binding.value) {
        el.classList.add("bg-danger", "text-white");
    } else {
        el.classList.remove("bg-danger", "text-white");
    }
}
```

The drawback of this approach is that you cannot specify any other hooks, but it does allow most directives to be expressed as a single function without having to duplicate any code. To show that Vue.js applies the directive as though it had a bind hook, I increased the initial value of one of the Numbers component's data properties, as shown in Listing 26-18.

Listing 26-18. Increasing a Data Property in the Numbers.vue File in the src/components Folder

```
...
<script>

    import Colorize from "../directives/colorize";

    export default {
        data: function () {
```

```
            return {
                first: 50,
                second: 20
            }
        },
        computed: {
            total() {
                return this.first + this.second;
            }
        },
        directives: { Colorize }
    }
</script>
...
```

The new value exceeds the threshold used to apply the directive, which produces the result shown in Figure 26-6.

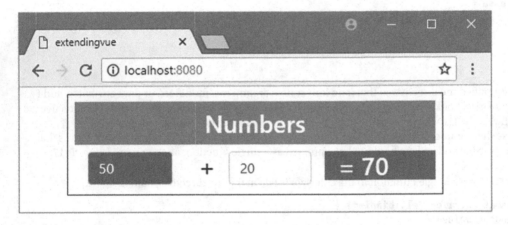

Figure 26-6. *Using a single function to provide the bind hook*

Creating Component Mixins

Mixins are a useful way to provide shared features to components to help reduce code duplication. The advantage of mixins is simplicity, but the drawback is that they cannot be used to share state, for which features like dependency injection or a data store are required.

I like to define mixins in their own folder to keep them separate from the rest of the project. To demonstrate a mixin, I created the src/mixins directory and added to it a file called numbersMixin.js with the content shown in Listing 26-19.

Listing 26-19. The Contents of the numbersMixin.js File in the src/mixins Folder

```
import Colorize from "../directives/colorize";

export default {
    data: function () {
        return {
```

```
            first: 50,
            second: 20
        }
    },
    computed: {
        total() {
            return 0;
        }
    },
    directives: { Colorize },
}
```

A mixin can contain any component code feature, including data and computed properties, methods, filters, and directives. If you are building a set of related components that share common functionality, then a mixin can be a good way to avoid copying and pasting the same code into the script element of .vue files. The mixin in Listing 26-19 contains data properties, a computed property, and a directive registration, all of which I took from the existing Numbers component, albeit the total computed property returns zero, which I have done to show how mixins work.

In Listing 26-20, I have updated the Numbers component so it uses the mixin and only defines the functionality that is different.

Listing 26-20. Using a Mixin in the Numbers.vue File in the src/components Folder

```
...
<script>
    import mixin from "../mixins/numbersMixin";

    export default {
        computed: {
            total() {
                return this.first + this.second;
            }
        },
        mixins: [ mixin ]
    }
</script>
...
```

Mixins are applied using the mixins property, which is assigned an array of the mixin objects. When a mixin is used, Vue.js treats the component as though it had defined the features provided by the mixins. When the component defines a feature that has the same name, such as the total computed property in Listing 26-20, then the component's feature overrides the one provided by the mixin.

APPLYING A MIXIN TO ALL COMPONENTS

Mixins can be registered globally, which applies their features to all the components in an application. This is not something that should be done lightly because its effects are wide-ranging and usually cause expected behavior. Mixins are registered globally in the main.js file using the Vue.mixin method, like this:

```
...
import Vue from 'vue'
import App from './App'

import "bootstrap/dist/css/bootstrap.min.css";

Vue.config.productionTip = false

import mixin from "./mixins/numbersMixin";

Vue.mixin(mixin);

new Vue({
    el: '#app',
    components: { App },
    template: '<App/>'
})
...
```

The `Vue.mixin` method must be called before you create the `new Vue` object for the application, as shown in the code fragment. When you register a mixin like this, you don't need to use the `mixins` property in individual components.

This allows the mixin to provide generic functionality that is overridden by more specialized behavior. To show how a single mixin can be used to provide the foundation for related components, I created a file called `Subtraction.vue` in the `src/components` folder with the content shown in Listing 26-21.

■ **Tip** When a mixin and a component both implement a lifecycle method, as described in Chapter 17, Vue.js invokes the mixin's method and then invokes the method defined by the component.

Listing 26-21. The Contents of the Subtraction.vue File in the src/components Folder

```
<template>
<div class="mx-5 p-2 border border-dark">
    <h3 class="bg-info text-white text-center p-2">Subtraction</h3>

    <div class="container-fluid">
        <div class="row">
            <div class="col">
                <input class="form-control" v-model.number="first" />
            </div>
            <div class="col-1 h3">-</div>
            <div class="col">
                <input class="form-control" v-model.number="second" />
            </div>
            <div v-colorize.bg.text="total > 50" class="col h3">= {{ total }}</div>
        </div>
    </div>
</div>
```

```
    </div>
</template>

<script>

    import mixin from "../mixins/numbersMixin";

    export default {

        computed: {
            total() {
                return this.first - this.second;
            }
        },
        mixins: [ mixin ]
    }
</script>
```

This component has the same basic structure as the Numbers component but overrides the total computed property so that the value of one data property is subtracted from the other, instead of the addition performed by the original component. All of the other component features are provided by the mixin. In Listing 26-22, I have updated the top-level App component to display the new component.

Listing 26-22. Adding a Component in the App.vue File in the src Folder

```
<template>
    <div class="m-2">
        <numbers />
        <subtraction />
    </div>
</template>

<script>

import Numbers from "./components/Numbers";
import Subtraction from "./components/Subtraction";

export default {
    name: 'App',
    components: { Numbers, Subtraction }
}
</script>
```

I have displayed the new component alongside the existing one, producing the result shown in Figure 26-7.

■ **Note**   Each component that uses a mixin gets its own data properties, which are not shared with the other components. If you want components to operate on the same data values, then see Chapter 18 for details of dependency injection or Chapter 20 for information about data stores.

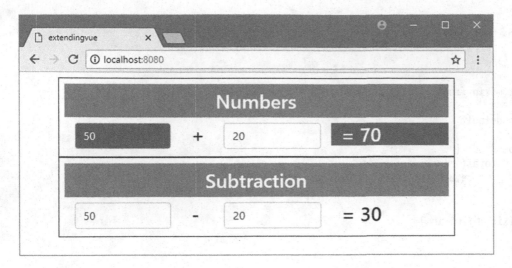

Figure 26-7. Creating similar components using the same mixin

Creating a Vue.js Plugin

Plugins allow broad sets of features to be applied globally throughout an application without needing to configure each feature individually. These features include directives and mixins but also allow methods and properties to be defined globally, which is how package like Vuex (Chapter 20) and Vue Router (Chapter 22) provide access to their functionality.

To demonstrate how plugins are created and used, I am going to define a set of global features that will support the simple math operations performed by the components in the example application.

To get started, I created the src/plugins/maths folder and added to it a file called filters.js with the content shown in Listing 26-23.

Listing 26-23. The Contents of the filters.js File in the src/plugins/maths Folder

```
export default {

    currency: function (value) {
        return new Intl.NumberFormat("en-US",
            { style: "currency", currency: "USD" }).format(value);
    },

    noDecimal: function (value) {
        return Number(value).toFixed(0);
    }
}
```

This file defines two filter functions that format numeric values and assigns them to properties whose names I will use to register the filters shortly. The purpose of these filters isn't as important as the way they can be included in a plugin. See Chapter 11 for details of how filters work.

Plugins can also include directives, so I created a file called `directives.js` in the `src/plugins/maths` folder with the content shown in Listing 26-24.

Listing 26-24. The Contents of the directives.js File in the src/plugins/maths Folder

```
export default {

    borderize: function (el, binding) {
        if (binding.value) {
            el.classList.add("border", "border-dark");
        } else {
            el.classList.remove("border", "border-dark");
        }
    }
}
```

This file defines a single-function directive that applies a border to its HTML element when its expression is true. This isn't an especially useful directive, but, as noted earlier, custom directives are rarely useful and are not needed in most applications.

Plugins can also define global methods and properties that can be accessed throughout the application. I added a file called `globals.js` in the `src/plugins/maths` folder with the content shown in Listing 26-25.

Listing 26-25. The Contents of the globals.js File in the src/plugins/maths Folder

```
export default {
    sumValues(...vals) {
        return vals.reduce((val, total) => total += val, 0);
    },

    getSymbol(operation) {
        switch (operation.toLowerCase()) {
            case "add": return "+";
            case "subtract": return "-";
            case "multiply": return "*";
            default: return "/";
        }
    }
}
```

In the listing, I have defined a `sumValues` function that uses a rest argument to receive an array of values that are summed to produce a result and a `getSymbol` method that takes the name of a math operation and returns the symbol that represents it.

You can also use a plugin to add properties and methods to every component, similar to the way that Vuex provides the $store property and Vue Router provides $route and $router. I added a file called `componentFeatures.js` in the `src/plugins/maths` folder with the content shown in Listing 26-26.

Listing 26-26. The Contents of the componentFeatures.js File in the src/plugins/maths Folder

```
export default {
    $calc: {
        add(first, second) {
            return first + second;
        },
```

```
        subtract(first, second) {
            return first - second;
        },
        multiply(first, second) {
            return first * second;
        },
        divide(first, second) {
            return first / second;
        }
    }
}
```

The convention is that features provided to components have names that begin with a dollar sign, and in the listing, I have defined a $calc object with add, subtract, multiply, and divide methods that perform basic math operations.

Plugins can contain components, which is a useful way to ensure that common functionality is available throughout the application. I added a file called Operation.vue to the src/plugins/maths folder with the content shown in Listing 26-27.

Listing 26-27. The Contents of the Operation.vue File in the src/plugins/maths Folder

```
<template>
    <div class="mx-5 p-2 border border-dark">
        <h3 class="bg-info text-white text-center p-2">{{ operation }}</h3>

        <div class="container-fluid">
            <div class="row">
                <div class="col">
                    <input class="form-control" v-model.number="first" />
                </div>
                <div class="col-1 h3">{{ symbol }}</div>
                <div class="col">
                    <input class="form-control" v-model.number="second" />
                </div>
                <div class="col h3" v-borderize="total > 25">= {{ total }}</div>
            </div>
        </div>
    </div>
</template>

<script>

import Vue from "vue";

export default {
        props: ["firstVal", "secondVal", "operation"],
        data: function () {
            return {
                first: Number(this.firstVal),
                second: Number(this.secondVal)
            }
        },
```

```
    computed: {
        symbol() {
            return Vue.getSymbol(this.operation);
        },
        total() {
            switch (this.operation.toLowerCase()) {
                case "add":
                    return this.$calc.add(this.first, this.second);
                case "subtract":
                    return this.$calc.subtract(this.first, this.second);
                case "multiply":
                    return this.$calc.multiply(this.first, this.second);
                case "divide":
                    return this.$calc.divide(this.first, this.second);
            }
        }
    }
}
</script>
```

This component presents a standardized interface for performing simple operations on two numbers and builds on some of the other features in the plugin, which I will explain shortly.

Creating the Plugin

The features that I have defined in the previous section have to be combined to create a plugin. I added a file called index.js in the src/plugins/maths folder and added the code shown in Listing 26-28, which brings together the different features to create a plugin.

Listing 26-28. The Contents of the index.js File in the src/plugins/maths Folder

```
import filters from "./filters";
import directives from "./directives";
import globals from "./globals";
import componentFeatures from "./componentFeatures";
import Operation from "./Operation";

export default {
    install: function (Vue) {

        Vue.filter("currency", filters.currency);
        Vue.filter("noDecimal", filters.noDecimal);
        Vue.directive("borderize", directives.borderize);
        Vue.component("maths", Operation);

        Vue.sumValues = globals.sumValues;
        Vue.getSymbol = globals.getSymbol;

        Vue.prototype.$calc = componentFeatures.$calc;
    }
}
```

Plugins are objects that define an `install` function, which receives a Vue object and an optional configuration object. The methods provided by the Vue object are used to register each feature, which I have imported from the JavaScript files that I created in the previous section, as described in Table 26-5.

Table 26-5. *The Vue Methods for Registering Plugin Features*

Name	Description
Vue.directive	This method is used to register a directive. The arguments are the name by which the directive will be applied and the directive object.
Vue.filter	This method is used to register a filter. The arguments are the name by which the filter will be applied and the filter object.
Vue.component	This method is used to register a component. The arguments are the name by which the component will be applied and the component object.
Vue.mixin	This method is used to register a mixin. The argument to this method is the mixin object.

In Listing 26-28, I have used the `filter`, `directive`, and `component` methods to register the features that were defined in the previous section. To register the global methods and properties, new members are added to the Vue object, like this:

```
...
Vue.getSymbol = globals.getSymbol;
...
```

This statement makes the getSymbol method available throughout the application, which means it can be accessed through the Vue object, as this statement from the component in Listing 26-27 demonstrates:

```
...
symbol() {
    return Vue.getSymbol(this.operation);
},
...
```

Methods and properties that you want to access in each component are added to the Vue.prototype object, like this:

```
...
Vue.prototype.$calc = componentFeatures.$calc;
...
```

This statement sets up the $calc object so that it can be accessed as `this.$calc` in components, as this statement from the component Listing 26-27 shows:

```
...
return this.$calc.add(this.first, this.second);
...
```

Through a combination of these techniques and the methods in Table 26-5, a plugin is able to provide a Vue.js application with a wide range of features.

Using a Plugin

Plugins are enabled with the Vue.use method, which is the same method that I used to register the data store and URL routing plugins in earlier chapters, the only difference being that those plugins were in their own NPM packages. In Listing 26-29, I have imported the custom package in the example application and enabled it with the Vue.use method.

Listing 26-29. Using the Plugin in the main.js File in the src Folder

```
import Vue from 'vue'
import App from './App.vue'
import "bootstrap/dist/css/bootstrap.min.css";

Vue.config.productionTip = false

import MathsPlugin from "./plugins/maths";
Vue.use(MathsPlugin);

new Vue({
  render: h => h(App)
}).$mount('#app')
```

Once a plugin has been enabled, its features can be used throughout the application. In Listing 26-30, I have added the component I defined to the top-level App component's template.

Listing 26-30. Using a Plugin's Component in the App.vue File in the src Folder

```
<template>
    <div class="m-2">
        <numbers />
        <subtraction />
        <maths operation="Divide" firstVal="10"  secondVal="20" />
    </div>
</template>

<script>

import Numbers from "./components/Numbers";
import Subtraction from "./components/Subtraction";

export default {
    name: 'App',
    components: { Numbers, Subtraction }
}
</script>
```

Notice that I don't have to register the component and that I can just add a maths element to the template because the features provided by the plugin are available throughout the application. In Listing 26-31, for example, I have used one of the filters and a global method in the Numbers component.

Listing 26-31. Using Plugin Features in the Numbers.vue File in the src/components Folder

```
<template>
    <div class="mx-5 p-2 border border-dark">
        <h3 class="bg-success text-white text-center p-2">Numbers</h3>

        <div class="container-fluid">
            <div class="row">
                <div class="col">
                    <input v-colorize:bg-info.bg="first > 45" class="form-control"
                            v-model.number="first" />
                </div>
                <div class="col-1 h3">+</div>
                <div class="col">
                    <input v-colorize:bg-info="second > 30"
                        class="form-control" v-model.number="second" />
                </div>
                <div v-colorize.bg.text="total > 50" class="col h3">
                    = {{ total | currency }}
                </div>
            </div>
        </div>
    </div>
</template>

<script>
    import mixin from "../mixins/numbersMixin";
    import Vue from "vue";

    export default {

        computed: {
            total() {
                return Vue.sumValues(this.first, this.second);
            }
        },
        mixins: [ mixin ]
    }
</script>
```

The result is that the value displayed by the component is formatted as a currency amount, and a new component is displayed to the user, as shown in Figure 26-8.

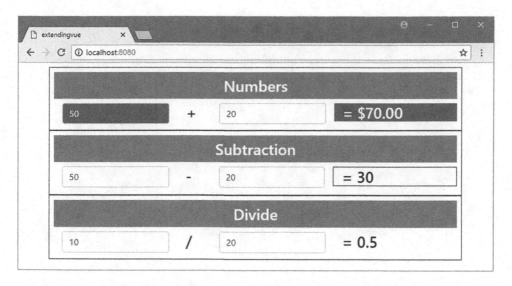

Figure 26-8. *Using plugin features*

Summary

In this chapter, I described the different ways that the functionality provided by Vue.js can be extended. I showed you how to create a custom directive, with the caveat that this is rarely the best approach; how to provide components with common features using a mixin; and how to provide a range of related features by creating a plugin.

And that is all I have to teach you about Vue.js. I started by creating a simple application and then took you on a comprehensive tour of the different building blocks in the framework, showing you how they can be created, configured, and applied to create web applications.

I wish you every success in your Vue.js projects, and I can only hope that you have enjoyed reading this book as much as I enjoyed writing it.

Index

A

Angular and Vue.js, 30
Axios
  errors, 500
  installing, 481
  making requests, 490, 496
  response data, 492
  responses, 491

B

Bootstrap CSS, 45
  applying classes, 46
  contextual classes, 46
  forms, 50
  framework, 11
  grid layout, 47
  margin, 47
  padding, 47
  tables, 48

C

Change detection process
  limitations, 323
  Vue.delete method, 393
  Vue.set method, 323
Components, 9, 214
  asynchronous, 557
  as building blocks, 399
  child element names, 402
  computed properties, 267
  CSS scoping, 407
  custom events, 414
    $this method, 415
    v-on directive, 416
  data properties, 261
  dynamic, 546
    data binding, 548
    keep-alive element, 551
  errors, 446
  filters, 273
    arguments, 276
    chaining, 276
    global filters, 279
  inject property, 460
  is attribute, 546
  isolation from other
      components, 405
  lazy loading, 557
  lifecycle, 431
    creation phase, 432
    destruction phase, 443
    error handling, 446
    methods, 24, 431
    mounting phase, 433
    update consolidation, 437
    watchers, 441
  methods, 270
  mixins, 702
  parent-child relationships, 399
  props, 407
    defining, 408
    expressions, 412
    using, 409
  provide property, 459
  registering, 216
  slots, 418
    named slots, 419
    scoped slots, 421
  $store property, 513
  templates (see Templates)
  update phase, 436
  using in templates, 216
  Vue.nextTick method, 440
  watchers, 441
Computed properties, 212, 267
CSS style scoping, 407
Custom events, 414

D

Data bindings, 210
  binding to an array, 381
  input element bindings, 372

Data bindings, 210 (*cont.*)
    one-way bindings, 366
    text interpolation binding, 13, 263
    two-way bindings, 17, 367
    v-model directive, 17
Data properties, 210
Data store
    actions, 522
    change notifications, 525
    commit method, 515
    defining, 509
    dispatch method, 524
    getters, 518
        additional arguments, 521
    inspecting, 516
    installing Vuex package, 506
    mapActions helper, 530
    mapGetters helper, 530
    mapMutations helper, 530
    mapState helper, 530
    modules, 533
        namespaces, 538
    mutations, 515
    namespaces, 538
    registering, 512
    $store property, 513
    strict mode, 514
    Vuex.Store object, 509
    watchers, 526
Dependency injection, 459
    consuming a service, 460
    defining a service, 459
    fallback services, 466
    inject property, 460
    overriding services, 461
    provide property, 459
    reactive services, 463
Directives
    custom, 690
        arguments, 696
        binding object, 695
        expressions, 695
        global registration, 693
        modifiers, 698
        values, 696
    hook functions, 692
    is attribute, 546
    v-bind, 15, 296
        classes, 296
        configuration object, 299
        data attributes, 302
        multiple attributes, 303
        properties, 305
        styles, 301
    v-else, 25, 292

v-for, 15, 311
    alias, 314
    change detection, 322
    index, 319
    key, 316
    no data source, 329
    update limitations, 323
    Vue.set method, 323
v-html, 286
v-if, 25, 287
v-model, 17, 370
    binding to an array, 381
    lazy modifier, 379
    number modifier, 377
v-on, 23, 211, 339
    capture modifier, 353
    custom events, 416
    event objects, 340
    event propagation, 350, 352
    handling events with
        methods, 342
    keyboard modifiers, 359
    mouse modifiers, 358
    multiple events, 346
    once modifier, 357
    self modifier, 354
    stop modifier, 355
v-show, 295
v-text, 284
Docker, 197
Domain Object Model
    (DOM) API, 205
Dynamic components, 546

E

Error handling, 446
Event bus, 469
    $emit method, 470
    local event buses, 474
    $on method, 471
    receiving events, 471
    sending events, 470
Events, 339
    creating custom events, 414
    event bus, 469
    handling, 211

F

Filtering data, 332
Filters, 273
    creating a global filter, 131
Form elements
    binding

to checkboxes, 373
to radio buttons, 373
to select elements, 376
to text fields, 372
creating data bindings, 372
validating data, 387

■ G

GitHub repository, 35

■ H, I

History API, 579
HTML
attributes, 42
literal values, 43
element content, 41
element structure, 40
live HTML document, viewing, 44
tags, 40
void elements, 42

■ J, K

JavaScript
arrays, 71
accessing values, 71
built-in methods, 74
enumerating, 72
literal arrays, 71
spread operator, 73
arrow functions, 61
closure, 64
conditional statements
equality operator, 68
identity operator, 68
if/else, 67
switch, 67
constants, defining, 62
const keyword, 62
functions, 57
default parameters, 59
fat arrow functions, 61
rest parameters, 59
results, 60
using functions as arguments, 61
let keyword, 62
modules, 79
composing modules, 83
importing, 82
import locations, 80
multiple features, 81
renaming features, 82
objects, 75
literal objects, 76

methods, 77
properties, 76
primitive types
boolean, 64
numbers, 66
strings, 65
promises, 84
async keyword, 86
await keyword, 86
statements, 56
parameters, 58
template strings, 66
truthy and falsy, 289
type conversion, 69
variables
closure, 64
defining, 62
jQuery, 32

■ L

Lazy loading, 557
Linting, 225, 242
Localization, 275
Local storage API, 24

■ M

Methods, data values, 270–272
Mixins, 702

■ N, O

npm run build command, 252
npm run serve command, 233

■ P, Q

Projects
Babel compiler, 234
basic project structure, 6
configuring development
tools, 250
creating, 222
debugging, 247
development tools, 233
ESLint package, 243
features, 223
hot module replacement, 237
linting, 225, 242
package management, 229
NPM, 229
Yarn, 229
src folder, 228
vue.confuig.js file, 250
webpack, 233

■ R

React and Vue.js, 30
Round-trip applications, 30

■ S

script element, 259
Server-side rendering, 31
Single-page applications, 30
Slots, 418
Sorting data, 332
SportsStore
    additional packages, 90
    administration, 166
    authentication, 166
    category selection, 112
    creating the project, 89
    data loading, 155
    data store, 96
    deployment, 189
        build process, 194
        configuration changes, 190
        Docker, 197
        dynamic imports, 192
    formatting data, 103
    form validation, 143
    global filter, 131
    JSON Web Token, 166
    pagination, 104
    route guard, 172
    searching, 161
    shopping cart, 120
    URL routing, 121
    web service, 92, 115
style element, 259

■ T

Template elements, 218, 259
Templates, 218
    data bindings, 210, 263
    defining as strings, 208
    global objects and functions, 265
    script element, 259
    style element, 259
    template element, 259
Tools
    Bootstrap CSS framework, 11
    Code Editor, 5
    Git, 5
    Node.js, 3
    @vue/cli package, 4
    Vue Devtools, 6

Vue.js development tools, 4
    starting, 8
Transitions
    events, 680
    transition classes, 668
    transition element, 666
        attributes, 671
        mode attribute, 673
    transition-group element, 678
    using animation library, 670

■ U

URL routing, 567
    aliases for routes, 582
    catch-all routes, 581
    children property, 619
    configuration, 567
    dynamic segments, 587
    history API, 579
    mode property, 579
    modules, 630
    named routes, 594
    navigation in code, 573
    navigation methods, 573
    nested routes, 617
    props, 654
    push method, 573
    regular expressions, 591
    $route object, 583
    route guards, 632
        redirection, 634
    router-link element, 575
        active routes, 612
        configuration, 606
        exact attribute, 614
        nested routes, 617
    $router object, 573, 583
    router-view element, 570
    setting up, 569
    URL style, 579

■ V

@vue/cli package, 4, 222
vue create command, 222
Vue.delete method, 393
Vue Devtools browser extension, 247
Vue.nextTick method, 440
Vue objects
    creating, 208
    data property function, 215
    el property, 208
    template property, 208

Vue.set method, 323
Vuex, installing, 506

■ W, X, Y, Z

Watchers, 441
Web services
    Axios, 481

cross-origin requests, 488
errors, 500
Fetch API, 487
HTTP methods and operations, 486
HTTP service objects, 494
making requests, 490, 496
response data, 492
responses, 491

Printed in the United States
By Bookmasters